Project Management for Information, Technology, Business, and Certification

Gopal K. Kapur
Center for Project Management

PEARSON
Prentice
Hall

Upper Saddle River, New Jersey
Columbus, Ohio

Library of Congress Cataloging-in-Publication Data

Kapur, Gopal K.
  Project management for information, technology, business, and
certification / Gopal K. Kapur.
    p. cm.
  Includes bibliographical references and index.
  ISBN 0-13-112335-1
  1. Project management. 2. Information technology—Management. I. Title.

  HD69.P75K36 2005
  658.4'04—dc22

                                                    2004009839

Assistant Vice President and Publisher: Charles E. Stewart, Jr.
Assistant Editor: Mayda Bosco
Production Editor: Alexandrina Benedicto Wolf
Design Coordinator: Diane Ernsberger
Cover Designer: Mark Shumaker
Cover art: Digital Vision
Production Manager: Matt Ottenweller
Marketing Manager: Ben Leonard

This book was set in Times Roman by *The GTS Companies*/York, PA Campus. It was printed and bound by Courier Kendallville, Inc. The cover was printed by The Lehigh Press, Inc.

Several names of companies, products, software packages, procedures, and other materials are used within this book. This, in no way, implies ownership by the author or the publisher. All copyrighted and trademarked materials remain the property of their respective owners.

Pearson Education Ltd.   Pearson Education Australia Pty. Limited
Pearson Education Singapore Pte. Ltd.   Pearson Education North Asia Ltd.
Pearson Education Canada, Ltd.   Pearson Educación de Mexico, S.A. de C.V.
Pearson Education—Japan   Pearson Education Malaysia Pte. Ltd.

10 9 8 7 6 5 4 3
ISBN 0-13-112335-1

To my wife Indra,
The love of my life.

PREFACE

This book focuses on the Project Process Architecture (PPA), a project management methodology specifically designed for IT/Business projects. The PPA was first developed to enable the Center for Project Management's (the Center's) clients to move through projects at an accelerated pace, without sacrificing the key steps necessary to produce high-quality products and services. The model has since evolved to its present stage through extensive use by IT/Business professionals in industries that include banking, publications, manufacturing, finance, insurance, health care, education, apparel, communications, and a number of leading public organizations. The current version of the PPA consists of six project stages (Idea, Pre-Launch, Launch, Execute, Implement, and Operation), which in turn contain a total of thirty-three steps. The individual steps guide a project manager through the what, when, and how of the work necessary to take a project from its fledgling idea to successful deployment in an efficient and effective manner.

■ STRUCTURE OF THIS BOOK

Each chapter starts with a list of objectives followed by an in-depth discussion of each of the chapter objectives. The discussion is supported by a proven and practical treatment of the subject matter and a number of quotations and references are provided to collaborate the key points in each chapter. At the end of each chapter, a comprehensive list of questions and discussion points is included to jog your memory and to assess the degree of your comprehension of the concepts and techniques outlined in the chapter. To make the best use of the questions and discussion points, we suggest that you create a file (preferably electronic) to record your responses. Maintain this file as you continue your journey through the book. You may find that, occasionally, you will choose to go back and update your responses as you develop more in-depth knowledge of the subject matter. We also advise that you get together with one or more of your fellow project managers and start a discussion group to jointly explore the subject matter and help each other through group discussion and mutual knowledge contribution.

Chapter 1: Introduction

The chapter starts with a discussion of why project management is necessary to transform ideas into products or processes in an effective and efficient manner. It compares and contrasts project work with day-to-day operations and outlines the key differences between the two. Next, the chapter deals with the important subject of extreme project failures, far too common in IT/Business projects, and the Seven Deadly Sins that lead to such failures. The content includes a detailed discussion of how the principles, practices, and tools for managing IT/Business projects are different from those needed to manage engineering (construction) projects. The chapter also introduces the Project Process Architecture (PPA), a project management methodology designed by the Center for Project Management (the Center), that *retains* the applicable principles and practices of classic engineering project management, and *adds* the principles and practices needed to manage IT/Business projects successfully. The chapter maps the PPA to the Project Management Institute's (PMI's) Project Management Book of Knowledge (PMBOK), to CompTIA's IT Project+ certification, and to Software Engineering Institute's (SEI's) Capability Maturity Model Integration (CMMI). Finally, the need for professionalism and discipline throughout the organization is emphasized, along with the introduction of a mocking post for those who wish to sidestep the project management discipline put forth in this book.

Chapter 2: Fundamentals

This chapter introduces the reader to the fundamentals of project management and starts with a detailed description of the roles and responsibilities of the various project management players. It goes on to describe the key elements of a project, the steps to create a comprehensive work breakdown structure (WBS), and the process to convert the WBS into a task network that shows the logical sequencing of various tasks. Next, the chapter focuses on the steps to compute the project's estimated duration by identifying the critical path through the network using the forward and backward pass methods. The chapter includes an exercise to create a WBS and a task network needed to build a tree house. The exercise serves as a good learning platform for the importance of building a comprehensive WBS and an accurate task network. The chapter finishes with a discussion of the steps to compress the critical path of a project.

Chapter 3: Idea Stage

This chapter focuses on the first stage of the PPA, the stage where newly evolving ideas are assessed for their viability. The important concept of filtering half-baked ideas is explored through an explanation of the wheel of half-baked ideas. The ideas that are deemed of value move on and evolve into well-structured Project Requests; the rest are abandoned or set aside for further consideration. The key focus of this stage is to make sure that only those project proposals that align with a stated organizational strategy, provide value to the business, and do not overlap or duplicate other existing projects are approved.

Chapter 4: The Pre-Launch Stage

This chapter details the thirteen steps in the Launch stage of the PPA, starting with the development of a comprehensive Project Description and ending with the creation of a Project Charter—a proposal to the sponsor for seeking project approval. The steps to tailor the PPA to fit the needs of the project are outlined, and steps to compute a size (high level) estimate for the project, using the phase-based and deliverables-based estimating methods, are explained. The steps to account for sponsor, management, and project management effort are elucidated, along with the steps to incorporate a variety of project reserves. The important step to define the priority of a given project proposal against other proposals is outlined. The chapter ends with a detailed discussion of the key components of a Project Charter and the steps to assemble and submit the Charter for sponsor review and approval.

Chapter 5: Launch Stage: Planning

The longest chapter in the book, Chapter 5, deals with the planning portion of the Launch stage of the PPA. In the section on the important step of Project Staging, the importance and the method of properly launching a project is explained. Project managers often overlook this step; the result is a haphazard start that often culminates in miscommunications and challenged outcomes. The importance of designing a suitable project organization structure for the project is discussed, followed by a discussion of developing a comprehensive project task plan. Once the task plan is ready, the project manager is asked to pay special attention to the steps needed to prepare the key stakeholders for the changes brought about by the project as well as the steps to manage changes to the project scope. Next, we discuss the ways and means of staffing and structuring the project team, the development of a comprehensive project notebook, and the steps to assess the soundness of the project plan.

Chapter 6: Launch Stage: Developing Detailed Estimates

This chapter covers the last two steps of the Launch stage: developing a detailed task-based effort, cost, and duration estimate for the proposed project, then obtaining budget approval from the project sponsor. The task-based estimating method presented in this chapter was developed at the Center for use by a number of our clients. Most project management books simply direct the reader to develop "accurate" estimates without providing sufficient guidance on the detailed steps needed to come up with viable results. The estimating methodology covered in this chapter deals with all the aspects that lead to accurate estimates: skill level, work interruptions, multiple project assignment, and productivity environment. The often-overlooked estimates for sponsor and management effort are discussed, as well as the need for incorporating rework and scope growth reserves. Detailed discussion is included on the important subject of reducing the computed estimates to map to the constraints of the project. We address the reality that there will be "push backs" from project managers who state, "Why bother with all of the work needed to come up with realistic estimates when management is going to cut them by half or more regardless?" We strongly believe that such actions often take place because the project managers have not gone through the necessary steps to develop accurate estimates and they have little to show as proof when management questions their estimates.

Chapter 7: Execute Stage: Schedule, Track, and Control the Project

This chapter covers the Execute stage of the PPA. Between 60 and 70 percent of the project team's time will be spent in this area because of the extent of the work to be accomplished: a project schedule is developed, the team begins to work to produce project deliverables, and the project manager oversees the team's progress to the planned end of the project. The chapter starts with the processes needed to develop a viable project schedule by loading the detailed estimates (developed in Chapter 6) into a calendar that incorporates both the team's and organization's non-work days. Schedule and budget compression, both inevitable realities of a project manager's life, are discussed, as are the steps to manage any changes to the project scope. The chapter includes detailed discussions on the process and steps to monitor, manage, and control project progress. The chapter contains a comprehensive discussion regarding the use of vital signs, as opposed to percentage complete, to monitor the team's progress and the use of the look ahead window as a periscope to what lies ahead. We introduce the concept of the earned value management system (EVMS) as well as a variety of analytical tools as additions to the project manager's tool belt. The chapter includes an extremely important, but rarely discussed, process of identifying and dealing with troubled projects. The chapter concludes with a few words for wise project managers, a summary of action items that have served us in good stead.

Chapter 8: Implement Stage

This chapter deals with the process necessary for a smooth transition from the project development stages (Chapters 3 through 7) to the Implement stage of the PPA. If not done well, the hard work put forth to finish the project can easily dissipate into a series of missteps as most of the development team begins to look for new assignments while the customers and the operations group are still struggling to put the project into production. The chapter details the steps to diligently and properly prepare the customers and the operations group to take over the project from the development team, as well as the orderly shutting down of the project development team. The chapter ends with the important step of collecting and recording the lessons learned (by the team) by reviewing the process used to develop the project. Finally, the chapter reminds the project manager of the importance of celebrating the project's completion.

Chapter 9: Operation Stage

This chapter presents introductory material regarding the ongoing operation of the project. In the strictest definition, the project is completed at the end of Chapter 8, when the end product of the project is handed over to the customer and the operations group. However, we believe it is extremely important for project managers to understand the fundamentals of ongoing operation, the process that actually begins to produce the value promised by the project. This chapter focuses on three important steps: the steps to begin to collect and report the value-to-business metrics, collection and analysis of operations metrics, and the very important step of initiating current system retirement.

Chapter 10: Project Portfolio Management

This chapter outlines a process developed by the Center to help its clients manage the portfolio of their projects. Although this process is the responsibility of either the project office (if one exists) or a management steering group, it is important that project managers are aware of the methods and procedures that can help organizations define, develop, and manage a robust project portfolio. The chapter focuses on a "dashboard view" of the portfolio management process without going into the detailed discussion of day-to-day portfolio management. The chapter includes a comprehensive set of Frequently-Asked Questions (FAQs) and their answers regarding portfolio management.

Appendix 1: Procurement Planning

We believe it is important for all project managers to understand the process necessary for procuring outside services, a growing part of IT/Business project management. This appendix introduces the reader to the various steps and processes for procurement management: Request for information (RFI), Request for quote (RFQ), Request for proposal (RFP), Statement of work (SOW), and Service level agreement (SLA).

Appendix 2: Financial Analysis

This appendix introduces the very important, although often overlooked, subject of financial analysis and justification of projects. The appendix covers the steps to compute a project's financial value (i.e., return), using the four most popular assessment methods: Net present value (NPV), Internal rate of return (IRR), Return on investment (ROI), and Payback period.

Glossary

The book includes a comprehensive glossary of terms related to IT/Business project management principles and practices, an integral part of any project manager's knowledge. We have tried to provide the most descriptive and accurate definition of the various terms. Occasionally, you may find a slight difference in the definition of a term from other sources. Although not every term defined in the glossary is discussed in detail in the text of this book, these terms are included to augment your project management knowledge. We recommend that you take the time to read and familiarize yourself with its content, especially before taking any certification examination.

■ PROJECT MANAGEMENT CERTIFICATION

Within the project management profession, two not-for-profit organizations offer certification for project managers: Project Management Institute (PMI®) and Computing Technology Industry Association (CompTIA®).

PMI Certification

PMI, a global association, serves as the world's largest project management association. It provides two levels of certification:

• Certified Associates in Project Management (CAPM™)
• Project Management Professional (PMP®)

The CAPM certification is intended for practitioners new to the profession. The exam is designed to ascertain the level of knowledge an individual possesses regarding the principles, practices, and procedures of managing projects to success. The PMP certification is intended for practitioners who have in-depth experience in the field. The exam is designed not only to ascertain the level of knowledge an individual possesses regarding the principles, practices, and procedures of managing projects to success, it also poses a number of "what would you do" scenarios to assess the level of experience and competence. Additionally, people with the PMP credential must demonstrate an ongoing commitment to the profession by satisfying PMI's Continuing Certification Requirements

Program. Both the CAPM and PMP exams are based on the Project Management Body of Knowledge (PMBOK®), a collection of project management materials developed and provided by PMI. This book covers all nine areas of the PMBOK as outlined below:

1. Project Integration Management is covered in Chapters 5, 6, 7, and 8.
2. Project Scope Management is covered in Chapters 3, 4, 5, 6, 7, 8, and 9.
3. Project Time Management is covered in Chapters 5, 6, 7, and 8.
4. Project Cost Management is covered in Chapters 4, 5, 6, 7, and Appendix 2.
5. Project Quality Management is covered in Chapters 4, 5, 7, and 8.
6. Project Human Resource Management is covered in Chapter 5.
7. Project Communications Management is covered in Chapters 5, 7, and 8.
8. Project Risk Management is covered in Chapters 4, 5, 6, 7, and 8.
9. Project Procurement Management is covered in Appendix 1.

The Center for Project Management is an official PMI® Global Registered Education Provider.

CompTIA® Certification

CompTIA®, a global association, serves the IT industry as the world's largest developer of vendor-neutral industry-defined IT certification exams and certifications. CompTIA's IT Project+™ certification is a credential acknowledging competency and professionalism in project management, including the necessary business knowledge, interpersonal skills, and project management processes required to successfully manage IT projects. The certification examination covers four domains, and each domain has a number of objectives. This book covers the four domains as outlined below:

1. IT Project Initiation and Scope Definition are covered in Chapters 1, 3, 4, 5, 6, and Appendix 1.
2. IT Project Planning is covered in Chapters 1, 2, 4, 5, 6, 7, and 8.
3. IT Project Execution, Control and Coordination covered in Chapters 3, 4, 5, 6, 7, 8, 9, and Appendix 1.
4. IT Project Closure, Acceptance Testing and Support are covered in Chapters 8, 9, and Appendix 1.

The Center's project management training curriculum has received the CompTIA® Approved Quality Curriculum Certification (CAQC), which is designed to ensure that preparatory curriculum appropriately prepares learners for the IT Project+™ certification.

■ STUDENT RESOURCE CD

The Student Resource CD packaged with the text contains practice questions designed to:

1. Assess your comprehension of the subject matter covered in each chapter, and
2. Help you prepare for the PMI's CAPM™, PMP®, and CompTIA's IT Project+™ certification examinations.

The practice questions will not only prepare you for the certification examinations, but will also make you think about the subject matter in a much broader and deeper manner. In some questions where the answers provided may not lead to the final solution of the problem, simply select the *best* of the provided answers. The *order* of questions and the order of the suggested answers for a given question are *immaterial* to the purpose of the practice examination; don't try to read any meaning in the order of these items.

As you answer the questions, keep in mind that there are always certain nuances and interpretations that can influence your response. We have done our best to state questions and their responses clearly, but don't be alarmed if you select the wrong response. We suggest that you reread the question, carefully reexamine the possible choices, and refresh your understanding of the subject by reviewing the associated text in the related chapter and you should arrive at the same conclusion as we have.

Before answering the questions on the CD, review the questions and discussion points that appear at the end of each chapter of the book. Additionally, take time to review the comprehensive glossary. This will help clarify your thoughts by reinforcing the definitions and explanations for the various important key subject areas.

■ ACKNOWLEDGMENTS

I have had an exceptional group of people assisting me in producing the final work. My heartfelt thanks to my colleagues Donna Koehnen, John Dohm, Robert Shea Bonhag, C. Wayne Peal, and David Lorenzen, who helped shape many of the thoughts presented in this book. Max D. Hopper, Wayne K. Schmidt, Michael J. Stratton, John Tillquist, Cindy Kepner, Joe Cleetus, Larry Young, Tamara Anderson, Jeff Babcock, and Avon D'Cunha spent many hours reviewing the draft and provided valuable guidance to improve the content, structure, and flow of the material. Diligent reviewers checked the mathematical computations, and any mistakes are mine.

My special thanks to George Glaser, a thought leader in project management and a longtime associate and friend, who influenced many of the principles and practices presented in this book. My deepest gratitude to my wife, Indra, who, as always, read the first draft and, with her infinite patience and pervasive knowledge of the language, made the ambiguous clear. Her guidance consistently makes what I write better. My heartfelt thanks to our son, Raj Kapur, without whose persistence and encouragement this book would still be a word processor file. A very big thank you to Teresa Morgan, who edited the text with a skill and dedication to grammar usage that helped improve my message. Her knowledge of the word processing program and understanding of manuscript development worked wonders.

I am grateful to my longtime friend, Massoud Khalilzadeh, who more than two decades ago elucidated to me the need for professional project management skills for IT and business professionals. The professional and helpful staff at Prentice Hall have been exceptional, starting with Charles Stewart for his steadfast support of this book; Maria Rego and Alex Wolf, who were most helpful in their guidance through the many steps, from the draft copy to the final version of the text; and project manager Kelly Ricci and copy editor Tricia Rawnsley, who remained steadfast to the end.

Finally, my most heartfelt thanks and gratitude to this great country, the United States of America—my adopted home—and its most generous people, who have given me the opportunity to learn, grow, and partake of its great bounty.

Gopal K. Kapur
gkapur@center4pm.com
www.center4pm.com

■ ABOUT THE AUTHOR

Gopal K. Kapur, founder and president of the Center for Project Management®, consults, writes, and educates in both the private and public sectors as a noted authority on project management. He has been developing innovative strategies for providing project management solutions to companies of all sizes and disciplines. Kapur's unique rapport with all corporate players, from the CEO to the end user, has equipped him with the insight necessary to provide practical solutions to a wide variety of project management problems. Many Fortune 500 companies have adopted Kapur's highly successful project management methodology titled Project Process Architecture™ (PPA). The PPA provides a practical strategy for managing projects to success.

Mr. Kapur has written two computer-programming textbooks and his articles and features have appeared in management and technology publications worldwide. His white papers and research are utilized by leading consulting bodies such as the Gartner Group, Forrester Group, and The Corporate Executive Board. He has been recorded for the CIO Radio and seven segments of Gartner Group's audio magazine, *Talking Technology*. He has lectured at COMDEX, the Commonwealth Club of California, the National Press Club, PMI national conferences, University of California (Berkeley and Riverside), The Brookings Institution in Washington, DC, and the Kennedy School of Government at Harvard University.

Contents

1 INTRODUCTION

OBJECTIVES

In this chapter, you will learn about the following project management elements:

- Reasons for project management
- Definition of *project*
- Project *v.* operations
- Roles of schedule, scope, budget, and quality
- Definition of *project management*
- Differences between a project and a process
- The state of project management
- Extreme project failures
- The "seven deadly sins" of project management
- Reasons why project management investments may never pay off
- The success equation
- Project management methodology
- Project Process Architecture (PPA)
- Stage gate reviews
- Mapping PPA to PMBOK
- Mapping PPA to CompTIA IT Project+
- Understand SEI's Capability Maturity Model
- Product development methodology
- Celebrating project success
- The mocking post

The chapter starts with a discussion of why project management is necessary to transform ideas into products or processes in an effective and efficient manner. It compares and contrasts project work with day-to-day operations and outlines the key differences between the two. Next, the chapter deals with the important subject of extreme project failures, which are far too common in IT/Business projects, and the problems that lead to such failures. The content includes a detailed discussion of how the principles, practices, and tools for managing IT/Business projects are different from those needed to manage engineering (construction) projects. The chapter also introduces the Project Process Architecture (PPA), a project management methodology designed by the Center for Project Management (the Center), which *retains* the applicable principles and practices of classic engineering project management, and *adds* the principles and practices needed to manage IT/Business projects successfully. The chapter maps the PPA to the PMBOK of PMI, to IT Project+ certification of CompTIA, and to the Capability Maturity Model Integration (CMMI®) of SEI. Finally, the need for professionalism and discipline throughout the organization is emphasized, along with the introduction of a mocking post for those who wish to sidestep the project management discipline put forth in this book.[1]

■ WHY PROJECT MANAGEMENT?

For any organization to develop and maintain a competitive edge, it must be able to flawlessly transform ideas into profitable products and services in a cost effective and timely manner. Within an organization, ideas compete for corporate dollars, management's attention, and the staff's talent, time, and energy. The impact of new ideas is felt at all levels, across all functions, and throughout the supplier, customer, and consumer chain. Lawrence A. Bossidy, Chairman and Chief Executive Officer (CEO) of Honeywell International, Inc., states:

> *It turns out that by themselves, ideas are basically worthless. You need to turn them into reality. In other words, whether you are in the new economy or the old, you need to execute. Most senior managers, including CIOs, don't execute well. . . . Many people regard execution as detailed work that's beneath the dignity of a true business leader. . . . That's wrong.*
>
> Paul Brown, "Just Do It," *CIO Insight* (July 17, 2002,
> http://www.cioinsight.com/article2/0.3959.2124.00.asp).

Mr. Bossidy's view is well corroborated by the following statement:

> *In the end, a vision without the ability to execute is probably a hallucination.*
> Stephen M. Case, *The Mind of the CEO,* Basic Books/Perseus
> Publishing (2001).

Interestingly, two synonyms for the word "execute" are "perform" and "accomplish," which are defined as follows:

> **Perform:** To begin and carry through to completion.
> **Accomplish:** To reach the end of, to complete.

Now consider any number of business development ideas.

- A training program for new employees
- A marketing drive for a new product
- Reducing the office staff by 20 percent because of falling sales and reduced market share
- Establishing a customer service department for a new line of electronic merchandise
- Switching corporate strategy from revenue growth to efficiency of operations
- Creating a website for a new line of business

The organizations that can start, execute, and complete ideas in an effective, efficient, and timely manner are sure to add more revenue to their bottom line than those companies who fumble through, end up spending more money than necessary, and miss the window of opportunity.

---

[1]Project Process Architecture (PPA), the Center for Project Management, PMBOK, PMI, IT Project+, CompTIA, and the Capability Maturity Model Integration (CMMI®) are all registered trademarks, and all rights are reserved by the owners.

The most efficient vehicle for transforming ideas into successful products and services in a cost effective and timely manner is *disciplined* project management. While there are many definitions of the word "discipline" in the dictionary, the two that best convey the meaning of the word, as it relates to project management are:

1. A branch of knowledge or teaching
2. Training expected to produce a specific character or pattern of behavior; especially training that produces mental improvement

The discipline of project management, when practiced correctly, does not mean regimentation, which by its very definition means a rigid order.

■ WHAT IS A PROJECT?

A project is a temporary endeavor to create a unique product or process. The Center thinks of IT/Business projects in a much broader sense. These projects should include the following elements:

1. *A business solution:* It is imperative that the work undertaken in the name of a given project satisfies (solves) a set of well defined business needs and/or problems. Too often, we see projects in progress that are technical solutions in search of a problem. Most such endeavors fail, often after huge investments. The first test of a viable project is to make sure it meets well defined business needs. If it does, it will result in an effective business solution. The key concept is that it must address a well defined business need. Make sure that the business need is clearly defined before proposing solutions.
2. *An investment:* It is important to make sure that the project team clearly understands the relationship between *investing* the money to finish a project and the *return on investment* (ROI) that the project produces for the organization's bottom line. The latter should be larger than the former; otherwise, it would be better to invest the money in another project or vehicle (such as a financial investment instrument).
3. *Appropriate level of ownership:* Before a project ever gets started, everyone involved should know who owns the project. In project management vocabulary, the "owner" is the project sponsor—an appropriate level of business manager who is responsible for seeing the project through to completion, as well as promoting the achievement of promised project benefits. The owner must be an individual, not an "office" or a committee.
4. *A change in the status quo:* The outcome of any given project is a new, different, modified, improved product or process. This is the primary difference between a project and ongoing operations. In the case of the latter, people repeat what has been defined and prescribed. A project produces an altered outcome.
5. *A specific duration:* Projects are temporary. Successful projects finish in a specific time period. Finishing on time is vital because the expected ROI from a project begins only when the project ends and the product or process is put into action.
6. *An undertaking with a specific set of interrelated deliverables, tasks, and milestones to be completed by specific resources (business and technology personnel):* This means that the project team will need to plan out a course of action (project plan) that will take them to the end of the project in an orderly manner.
7. *An entity that operates within a changing environment:* There is the catch. At the start of a given project, the project team promises to deliver a certain end product, by a certain time, and at a certain cost. However, because the work to complete the project is in the future, certain assumptions have to be made. Even under the best of circumstances, a number of assumptions may not hold true; hence the need to change the "promises" made by the project team. This requires flexibility on the part of the project's customer and the project team.
8. *Projects are disruptive:* This is especially true for the project's customers. In any given project, the project's customers will be called upon to spend time and energy to define their requirements, review the design (prototypes), be involved in testing, and eventually spend time to learn the new product or process. All of this effort takes the customers away from their primary job responsibilities—the day-to-day activities they typically engage in to achieve their

job performance goals. Also, during the project's development life cycle, the customer team members' managers continue to expect "as usual" performance from their staff. This expectation invariably results in added time burdens for customer team members, which is not a great motivation to be on the project team.

A thorough review of these points clearly shows that projects are not "business as usual." They promise a certain set of benefits, require a certain set of investments, and carry a certain set of uncertainties inherent in the risk of doing anything new or different.

■ PROJECT *vs.* OPERATIONS

How do projects differ from operations (the day-to-day departmental work)? The key difference is that the end product of a project involves *change*. However, the success of daily work is based on a repeatable set of activities that consistently reproduce predefined results. Within an operation, widely accepted and repeatable processes are set up and carried out to deliver predictable results, at predicable costs, within a predictable schedule. The trait of an efficient operations group is the predictability with which it is able to complete its routine work. Routine work may include the following:

• Fielding customer inquiries at a call center
• Biweekly distribution of paychecks by the payroll department
• Daily pickup by the shipping company driver
• Fulfillment of food orders at a fast food restaurant

The hallmark of efficiency is the establishment of processes and procedures that help the people do their work in an almost rote manner so that the outcome is the same each time. Taken to the extreme, reliance on procedures can result in a bureaucratic organization, where policies and processes are so deeply imbedded that employees are discouraged from taking initiative. They are apt to quote a specific policy they must follow instead of focusing on producing results quickly and effectively. People with such a bureaucratic mentality make reluctant project team members because projects, by nature, change what is currently being done and replace it with a new and different outcome.

Another key trait of routine operations is the fact that the workgroups are supposed to have continuity. The payroll, marketing, shipping, information technology (IT), and finance departments are never expected to close. Projects, have a specific finish date, at which time the end product is put into operations and the team is disbanded.

What are the implications of introducing a new project in the midst of daily business operations? Imagine a restaurant that is open only for dinner service and has had a specific menu for several years. Daily operations of the restaurant include buying supplies, taking reservations, cooking, serving, cleaning, and financial accounting. These activities would not be considered project work. These are well defined, repeatable, day-to-day operations. Now consider some "new" ideas:

• The restaurant owner wants to start lunch service.
• The chef wants to change the dinner menu four times a year to reflect seasonal and regional foods, and wants to emphasize organically grown produce.
• Employees have requested that the restaurant offer employer-contributed medical insurance and retirement benefits.

Obviously, each of these ideas means considerable change in the current way of doing business and each qualifies as a *project*. Similarly, consider the implications for other types of business enhancements:

• The VP of sales for a soft drink company would like to have a new advertising campaign.
• The marketing department sees the need to launch two new products.

Once a given idea is chosen as a viable project, the necessary work that must be done to bring it to closure is project work. The follow-up work needed to maintain the changes is considered operational activities. It is important to point out that, in the case of IT and business projects (unlike engineering), a certain mix of project and operations activities is customary. For example, consider a number of undertakings that are a mix of these two types of activities:

1. *An orchestra tour of ten cities:* A tour involves activities such as shipping and travel arrangements, music selection, instrument repairs and tuning, insurance, venue selection, ticket sales and refunds, promotions, union contracts, auditions (for local talent), rehearsals, accounting, and performances. We would treat the start of the tour (first few performances) as a project, but then the tour would take the shape of an operation. If the venues were all in different countries, we would consider each appearance a project because there would be relatively few repeatable tasks, more uncertainties, more risks, and changing team members (local staff for most of the support work).

2. *Surgical procedure—heart surgery:* For a hospital that specializes in such procedures, most of the surgeries will fall into the operations category. In some special circumstances, if the patient is a prominent public figure, the surgery would take on the shape of a project due to privacy requirements, press relations, and security needs.

3. *Surgical procedure—separation of twins joined at the head:* This is not a routine operation; hence, it would be more of a project. The hospital needs to organize a specialized team of surgeons, physicians, nurses, public relations people, insurance providers, legal consultants, and related specialists.

4. *Upgrading an operating system:* Because many IT organizations do these types of upgrades every few months, we would consider the upgrade a combination of project and operations activities. In fact, the success of the upgrade is highly dependent on how well versed the upgrade team is in the principles, practices, and tools of project management. Most computer operations personnel shun project management, and as a result, many upgrades are chaotic, take too long, and cause too many residual problems.

5. *Deploying robust computer security:* For most IT departments, we would consider this a project because few IT departments have any history of such work. In fact, a majority of security personnel are highly technical people who have highly technical skills. Combine this with the fact that few, if any, have project management training, and the result is a dismal success rate for security projects. The security profession is beginning to pay more attention to the need for project management skills, but given a choice of technical training or project management training, most go for the former. This is a key reason why security projects have performed so poorly and will continue to do so until IT management and security professionals begin to address the importance of project management education, training, and practices.

6. *An inventory of corporate computer assets:* This is a project. If the work were outsourced to a company that specializes in this type of work, then it would be both project and operations work.

From the examples, it should be clear that project management education and training should not to be limited to people charged with doing projects. The fundamental project management practices and principles—planning, estimating, risk assessment, scheduling, work tracking, and issue management—easily cross over and apply to operational activities as well. In fact, people who are well versed in the principles and practices of good project management invariably perform much better in day-to-day work activities than those who are not as well versed in the discipline of project management. The contrast will become more obvious as we delve into the details of project management practices.

■ IT'S NOT A "THREE LEGGED STOOL"

An important, and often misunderstood concept in the project management profession is the theory of "triple constraint." Followers of this concept believe that each project is constrained by three key components:

1. *Scope:* What the project will produce—the collection of various project deliverables and features.
2. *Schedule:* The length of time needed to complete the project.
3. *Cost:* The total cost of completing the project.

This is a "three legged stool," a decidedly unstable structure. A key component is missing: the quality of the end product. With conventional project thinking, quality is wrapped inside the scope. We believe that imbedding quality in scope is a major mistake, and the proof is the massive number of poor quality products and processes—many software products, customer support systems, automated telephone response systems, and consumer products (including many pharmaceuticals). Our definition of a successful project is as follows (the order of the four attributes does not imply any rank order):[2]

$$\text{Project} = \text{Schedule} + \text{Scope} + \text{Budget} + \text{Quality}$$

This means that the project sponsor, the customer, and the team must agree on the relative importance of each of the four components, define the resulting equilibrium, and then manage it throughout the project development life cycle. We will discuss this subject in detail in Chapter 4.

■ WHEN DOES WORK TURN INTO A PROJECT?

Another frequently asked question is, "Must I treat all of my work as a project?" The underlying message in this question is, "I find project management to be too restrictive and I should be allowed to do my work as I please, when I please, and to the quality I please." How is that working for you?[3] Most of the people asking the question are either trying to skirt the discipline and rigor inherent in good project management or have been victims of bureaucratic project management—situations where paperwork is more important that the outcome. A project is a set of interrelated deliverables, tasks, and milestones. If the work at hand involves only a few tasks and results in a couple of deliverables and milestones, then it probably is not a project. Anything bigger in scope should be considered a project—perhaps a very small project—that requires minimal project management activities. As an overall guide, any work requiring more than 200 hours of effort should be considered a project.[4] At 35 productive hours per week, it would take a full-time employee about six weeks to complete the work, assuming no major interruptions. If the work was divided among two or more people, it could be finished earlier. However, someone would need to partition the work among the team members, monitor work progress, and coordinate work closure—all project management activities. In summary:

- Any work that is estimated to take 200 hours or more should be considered a project—a very small project—requiring the application of the fundamental principles and practices of disciplined project management. The threshold value, 200 hours, is not a hard and fast rule. If your organization has a formal project office, consult with them and see if they have a recommended number. If not, check with your manager to see if any such recommendations already exist in the company. If no such guidance exists, it would be a good idea to meet with your fellow project managers, discuss the subject, and start at a specific point.
- If a new assignment is first estimated to take less than 200 hours, but as the work continues you find that the net effort has breached the recommended threshold, it becomes a project. In these cases, our recommendations are twofold. First, look back and determine the reasons for low estimates. The work at hand then needs to be brought under disciplined project management practices. This means taking a short break and completing the project management steps that you would have followed in the first place if the original estimates were correct. Some people may object to this, using the excuse that any retrofits will delay the promised completion date. Try using that excuse with a police officer who caught you driving over the speed limit in a school zone and then notices you forgot to secure the children properly in the back seat.

■ WHAT IS PROJECT MANAGEMENT?

Some synonyms for the word "management" are *organization, direction, supervision, guidance, care, command, control,* and *administration.* From these various meanings, it is easy to conclude that project management involves the execution of a list of activities necessary to turn an idea into

---

[2]In the context of this equation, the terms "budget" and "cost" are interchangeable.

[3]Used with apologies to Dr. Phil McGraw.

[4]We know organizations that use a smaller threshold.

a product or process. Project management involves five key activities:

1. *Defining:* This involves the development of a succinct project charter that clearly defines the project objectives and success criteria.
2. *Planning:* Developing a comprehensive plan of project phases, deliverables, tasks, milestones, and resources needed to take the project from the idea stage to its operation, when the end product is delivered to the customer.
3. *Estimating and scheduling:* The project manager and the team must develop realistic and accurate estimates and schedules, because management and customers make their Go/No Go decisions based on the proposed project's expected cost and delivery time more than anything else.
4. *Directing and leading:* A project's success depends primarily on the quality of leadership and guidance of the sponsor and the project manager's skill in helping the team complete its assigned work in an effective and efficient manner.
5. *Monitoring and controlling:* Work by various team members needs to be monitored to assure that the work progresses as planned. If and when there are variances from the norm, corrective actions have to be considered, replanning may be necessary, and project objectives, scope, resources, and quality may need to be renegotiated.

In addition to these five key areas, effective project management requires the following:

6. *Communications:* The project manager must keep all of the stakeholders informed of the project's progress and any unexpected or unplanned variances in the project's scope, schedule, cost, or quality. The ability to communicate clearly, appropriately, and comfortably is key. Project managers need to understand that they will often be the bearers of bad news, and they must become adapt at dealing with overly critical customers.
7. *Closure:* As defined earlier, all projects have a specific ending point, at which time the end product or process is turned over to the customer. It is important that the project manager plans, and then executes, a well defined closure of the project.

The preceding seven points can easily be summarized as follows: Project management is the art and science of effectively and efficiently converting an idea into a viable product or process.

■ PROJECT MANAGEMENT IS NOT A TOOL

Now that is not a statement many "technical" people, or the purveyors of project management tools, like to hear. People love quick fixes, and many believe that all they need to manage a project is some "flavor of the month" software package. In a survey conducted at a national project management conference by the Center, 85 percent of 127 respondents had more than one project management software package on their workstation. Despite such a proliferation of tools, most projects are still delivered over budget, behind schedule, and are of poor quality. It is ironic that the profession still has not learned the obvious: tools act only as catalysts. During the last two decades, there have been numerous instances where management decided to train people in the use of project management software, without first training them in project management principles and practices. This decision results in disaster—a colossal waste of money and time. However, the practice is still quite common because many managers still believe that project management is a tactical problem that can be easily solved by software. For organizations that have well formulated, disciplined, and forthright project management practices, tools act as a facilitator to success. For organizations mired in chaotic processes, technology only accelerates their path to disaster (see *Extreme Project Failures* in this chapter).

■ THE STATE OF PROJECT MANAGEMENT

The dark side of the corporate information revolution is coming into view. Companies across the country are seeing their cutting-edge computer systems fail to live up to expectations—or fail altogether. . . . The waste is staggering. . . . 42% of corporate information technology projects were abandoned before completion. U.S. companies spend

> *about $250 billion annually on computer technology. . . . Senior executives are starting to say 'no' to vast technology overhauls. . . . Roughly 50% of all technology projects fail to meet chief executives' expectations. . . . More CEOs are firing their chief information officers, or CIOs.*
>
> Bernard Wysocki Jr., "Companies Let Down by Computers Opt to 'De-Engineer' After Clashes," *The Wall Street Journal,* (April 30, 1998, p. A1).

More recently, problems have taken a turn for the worse:

> *. . . almost three quarters of all software development in the Internet era suffered from one or more of the following: total failure, cost overruns, time overruns, or a rollout with fewer features or functions than promised.*
>
> Scott Berinato, "The Secret To Software Success," *CIO Magazine* (July 1, 2001, http://www.cio.com/archive/070101/secret.html).

According to the Gartner Group, the project management software market is expected to reach $1.3 billion in 2004. Add to this the expenditures for project management education, and the investment is even more staggering. Despite these investments, the performance of IT project success has been nothing short of dismal. U.S. companies continue to lose millions of their project investment dollars.[5] As a result, some companies have gone into receivership. The record of public organizations is no better:

> *About 85% of all public sector IT projects are deemed to be failures . . . That does not mean they are total disasters, but they usually take longer to implement, cost more, and deliver less than was planned.*
>
> Todd Ramsey, *The Economist* (June 24, 2000, http://www.mcnees.org/ mainpages/misc/security/sec_subpages/GovnetEconJun24.html).

If this high level of project failure is allowed to continue, the short-term problems caused by missed deadlines and high costs would pale in the face of the following long-term losses:

- Failure to implement strategic business ventures
- Dramatically reduced market position
- Missed opportunities
- Loss of credibility
- Damage to staff morale and effectiveness
- Wasted talent

■ EXTREME PROJECT FAILURES

In "Companies Don't Learn From Previous IT Snafus," published in *Computerworld,* October 30, 2000, author Kim Nash discusses the fate of ten major U.S. companies that lost millions of dollars because of failed projects. Two of the companies eventually filed for bankruptcy: FoxMeyer Corp, a $5 billion drug distributor; and Tri Valley Growers, a 100-year old California-based agriculture co-operative. According to company lawsuits, software projects were key contributors to their demise. Staying the course will ensure the death of many more mission-critical projects, and even more companies.

---

[5]". . . First Security said its revenue and income projections for the first quarter will be down 8% and 25%, respectively, in part because of a system upgrade that appears to have caused more problems than it solved." Dehlayne Lehman, "Software Snafu Could Put Bank Merger in Jeopardy," Computerworld.com (March 13, 2000, http://www.computerworld.com/ news/2000/story/0,11280,41804,00.html). ". . . two railroads merged, botched the integration of their computer systems and, seven months later, are still losing millions of dollars worth of business." Kim S. Nash, "Merged Railroads Still Plagued by IT Snafus," Computerworld.com (January 17, 2000, http://www.computerworld.com/news/2000/story/0,11280,40721,00.html). "Thomas & Betts Corp., a $2.5 billion electrical parts manufacturer, is blaming problems with a new Internet-based order management system for a 50 percent nosedive in fourth-quarter profits—plus another $42 million in losses caused by order and shipping disruptions." Julia King, "Parts Maker Pins Profits Dip on IT," Computerworld.com (February 21, 2000, http://www.computerworld.com/news/2000/story/0,11280,41403,00.html).

Since the early 1990s, the Center has been studying the key reasons for the high rate of failure of IT/Business projects. The findings are as follows:

1. Far too many half baked ideas slip through and mutate into projects. Most of these projects do not have any clear business objectives and eventually fail.
2. Due to inadequate due diligence, project complexity and risks are discovered late into the project life cycle, which leads to a large number of challenged projects.
3. Too many customers wait too long to contact the project management group and then dictate schedules that have no basis in reality.
4. The "estimate-to-please" behavior of an excessive number of technology managers results in the approval of wrong projects. The first estimates that many customers hear come from the managers of project managers, who find themselves in situations where they (managers) feel they must respond to the customer with a favorable answer.
5. Many viable ideas, once launched as projects, eventually fail because of poor sponsorship—the business executives believe that their responsibility is over once they approve the budget. Others have the mistaken belief that it is the job of IT management to oversee projects, because projects are technical entities that need to be managed by technical managers.
6. Business unit personnel take their cues from their managers and often remark that there is no need to spend serious time working with project teams.
7. Complete disregard for important business cycles—new systems implemented during high "transaction" periods result in a significant drop in income-producing activities.
8. Too few qualified project managers—far too many project managers lack the skills to manage high-complexity projects. Our research shows that less than 15 percent of organizations have a comprehensive project manager education, training, and mentoring program in place.
9. All or nothing scope treatment—most projects start out too big and continue to grow; many eventually collapse under their own weight.
10. A majority of the organizations studied do not have a well-designed IT/Business project management process in place.
11. Too many project managers have the belief that state-of-the-art project management software will solve their problems. Most project managers have access to two or more project management tools; only a few have been formally trained in the use of the tools in a predictive manner. Often, the training is limited to the steps of entering data and printing a variety of reports. Few are taught the use of the reports to help manage the project.
12. Many projects failed because of the lack of a well-designed "project health" review process—a project gets ill, the illness festers, and the project withers away. In medicine, this would constitute malpractice.
13. Surprisingly few organizations have put into place a robust project portfolio management process to effectively and efficiently manage the projects underway at any given time.

■ THE SEVEN DEADLY SINS OF PROJECT MANAGEMENT

A more focused study took place when seven[6] chief information officers (CIOs) contacted the Center for Project Management to help them pinpoint the key reasons why a number of their mission-critical projects were chronically over budget and behind schedule. The investigation involved an assessment of forty-nine different projects managed by twenty-three project managers. Our research revealed that the vast majority of failed projects founder because those responsible continue to commit the same seven mistakes over and over. We termed these "The Seven Deadly Sins of Project Management."[7]

1. Mistaking half baked ideas for projects
2. Dictated deadlines

---

[6]None of these were dot-com companies. In their case, project failures were the results of unbridled optimism, sheer stupidity, and universal absence of project management discipline.

[7]The findings of this research were recorded as a part of the Gartner Group's Talking Technology series, February 1997, under the title "The Seven Deadly Sins of Project Management." The Center has continued this study and five additional segments have been recorded.

FIGURE 1.1
Filtering half baked ideas.

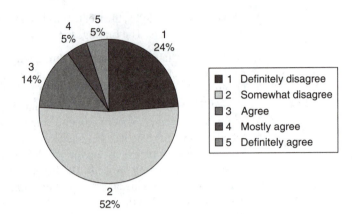

3. Ineffective sponsorship
4. Underskilled project managers
5. Not monitoring project vital signs
6. Failing to deploy a sound project management methodology
7. Not formulating a comprehensive project portfolio

Mistaking Half Baked Ideas for Projects

Traditionally, senior management is charged with conceiving and executing visions that will drive the organization toward profitability and industry leadership. Hence, there is immense pressure on managers and executives to deliver new and innovative ideas that can be turned into products and services, which deliver profit and competitive advantage. However, studies conducted by the Center show that, while there is no dearth of great visions emanating from executive offices, these visions are often intertwined with a large number of half baked, and at times, hare-brained ideas. Many of these can be attributed to the lack of clear and coherent communication between management (proponents of most projects) and project teams. The data in Figure 1.1 shows that 76 percent of the organizations surveyed did not have filters in place to separate half baked ideas from viable projects.

Dictated Deadlines

Most IT/Business projects fall badly behind schedule. A primary reason for this perpetual problem is management's practice of specifying artificially tight deadlines. Some of the reasons for these deadlines are:

- Lack of confidence that the teams are able to develop realistic estimates
- Management's desire to challenge the team to work harder
- Wild goose chases induced by poorly informed customers

Ironically, many project managers who have the skills to develop realistic estimates and schedules know that their numbers will invariably cause management to cancel the proposed project, so they estimate-to-please. These project managers have learned that the only way to get their projects launched is to promise low cost and early delivery—no matter how unrealistic this may be. In the recent past, estimate-to-please behavior has become more prevalent because project teams are routinely threatened with outsourcing. Project managers agree to the client's time dictates because there is more risk in providing realistic estimates than in allowing the project to run hopelessly over budget and late. The executive body is the key in this scenario. They must be convinced that creating an environment in which project managers are tempted to estimate-to-please will only engender constant disappointment as projects come in late, over budget, lacking in functionality, of poor quality, or complete failures.

> *Last September the $125 million Mars Climate Orbiter burned up in the Martian atmosphere because engineers failed to convert pounds to metric weight in their calculations. . . . scientists and engineers simply didn't have enough time or money to test the*

FIGURE 1.2
Project deadlines.

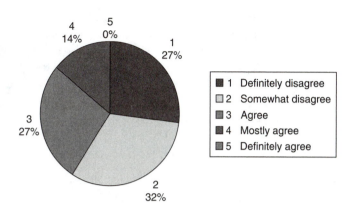

equipment properly, and senior managers failed to watch over the projects carefully. . . .
'I pushed too hard,' he [administrator Daniel Goldin] said, 'and . . . stretched the sys-
tem too thin.'

Andrew Murr, "Final Answer: It Crashed," *Newsweek* (April 10, 2000, p. 46).

The data in Figure 1.2 shows that the deadlines for most projects are neither realistic nor achievable.

Ineffective Sponsorship

The sponsor is the single most influential ingredient in a project's recipe for success. Without a competent sponsor, the project will implode. Despite this, few project managers surveyed by the Center believed that their projects had effective sponsorship. The fact is, IT/Business projects have such a dismal reputation for coming in late, over budget, or being abandoned altogether that there is a general inclination in the upper echelons of corporate executives *not* to become project sponsors. Invariably, they relegate that important responsibility to available IT managers, another sure cause of failed and challenged projects. Being a project sponsor is not a spectator sport; it involves time, effort, and commitment. The responsibilities of a sponsor include:[8]

- Understand the complexity of the project.
- Empower the project manager and the team.
- Provide guidance and direction for key business strategies.
- Ensure timely availability of resources.
- Review milestone-based project progress.
- Ensure project benefits are realized.

A review of the list shows that effective sponsorship requires specific skills and commitment. The project manager must be confident that the sponsor has the time, energy, and the requisite buy-in of the proposed project to fulfill his or her responsibilities. Immediate access to the sponsor by the project manager, and quick decision-making by sponsors, are key elements of successful project management. Our experience shows that, in those instances where the sponsors fail to invest their "skin" in the game, the game is lost. Project managers often complain that they are nothing more than "virtual sponsors." Figure 1.3 depicts that the majority of respondents believe that sponsors from business units do not clearly understand their roles and responsibilities. Too many projects suffer from inadequate sponsorship.

Two additional important points regarding project sponsors are:

1. Sponsors often escape the consequences of failed projects but do reap the rewards of successful ones; whereas project managers and teams always receive the blame for failed projects but seldomly reap the rewards commensurate with their achievements.
2. A strong-headed manager, who lacks the appropriate skills for effective sponsorship, can run a project train right off the cliff.

---

[8]For a more comprehensive list, see *Sponsor's Roles and Responsibilities*, Chapter 5.

FIGURE 1.3
Project sponsorship.

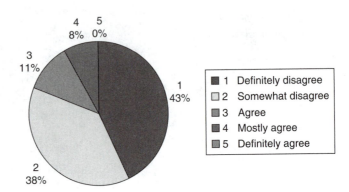

Underskilled Project Managers

Another travesty in project management is the launch of projects that have significantly underskilled project managers. A study of forty-seven high-complexity projects demonstrated that the overall *required* skill level of project managers was an estimated 3.2 (on a scale of 1 to 4, 4 being the highest), their average *actual* skill level was 2.5—a considerable gap. Figure 1.4 shows the data from this study.

The Center's research, Figure 1.5, also shows that only 14 percent of organizations have a well defined, well executed skills development program in place to provide education, training and mentoring to their project managers.

No wonder overwhelmed project managers resort to powerful software packages that they are oftentimes ill equipped to use! This is the equivalent of mounting afterburners on a mule.

Not Monitoring the Vital Signs

Doctors, mechanics, pilots, and engineers do it—just about everyone, in almost every profession, monitors vital signs to track the "health" of their projects. Not so in IT/Business projects. This responsibility lies not only with the project manager, but also with the sponsor. Together, project managers and sponsors must draw up the list of vital signs to be monitored, determine the thresholds that vital signs are to be measured against, and clearly define escalation procedures.

At the Center, we have identified a set of project vital signs (see *Vital Signs,* Chapter 7), along with their acceptable variances and the appropriate reporting procedures. A partial list of vital signs to consider:

1. Strategic fit
2. Customer buy in

FIGURE 1.4
Project manager skill levels.

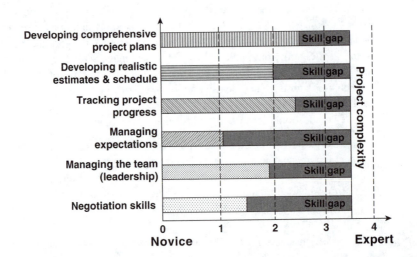

FIGURE 1.5
Project manager skill
development program.

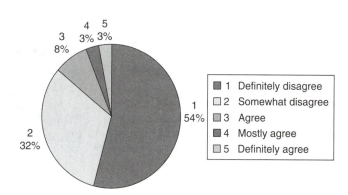

3. Technology viability
4. Status of critical path
5. Actual cost *v.* estimated cost
6. Unresolved issues

Monitoring the variance thresholds of vital signs highlights any project's "health problems" in a timely manner. Unfortunately, the survey data in Figure 1.6 shows that only 32 percent of organizations have instituted a well defined process to monitor project vital signs.

Failing to Deploy a Sound Project Management Methodology

Any methodology is a collection of practices, procedures, and guidelines designed to help someone achieve desired goals in an effective and efficient manner. A primary goal of a well designed project management methodology, not to be confused with a software life cycle methodology, is to provide a common standard across an organization to ensure that projects of varying sizes and complexity, when attempted by different teams, are conducted in a consistent and disciplined manner and result in quality products delivered on time and within budget. To be useful, a methodology must be scalable—easy to tailor to fit the size and complexity of the project at hand. To us, a methodology is akin to a master recipe for a project—a collection of steps designed to help the project manager and the team "cook up" a viable solution to a business problem or need. Figure 1.7 shows that only 35 percent of the surveyed organizations have a well designed project management methodology in place. Absence of a robust and easy to use methodology means that different teams, and at times different people on the same team, act on their whims and scurry about to figure out their next steps.

Not Formulating a Comprehensive Project Portfolio

Project portfolio management is the process by which projects are initiated, approved, managed, and implemented throughout the enterprise. Unfortunately, project portfolio management does not exist

FIGURE 1.6
Monitoring project vital signs.

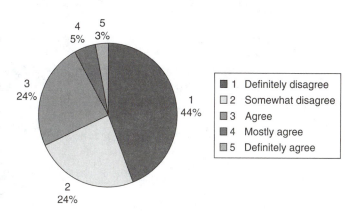

FIGURE 1.7
Project management
methodology survey.

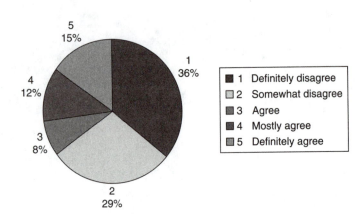

in most organizations, which results in the duplication of effort, unnecessary delay of mission-critical projects, and internal conflict. For example, two CEOs we know asked their CIOs the following questions:

1. How many project requests were in the pipeline?
2. How many approved project proposals were waiting to be launched as projects?
3. How many projects were being executed?
4. What is the status of various projects in execution?
5. What is the capacity of the IT department? Can the IT department undertake more projects?

Neither CIO was able to provide definitive answers to the questions. Even after a week's worth of extensive inquiries, neither CIO had high-confidence answers to most of the questions. Obviously, neither organization was practicing project portfolio management. Project portfolio management does not have a long history in the IT/Business project management profession. Even today, a large number of CIOs and CEOs do not have an accurate picture of all the project work in progress at any given time in their organizations. The best manifestation of a project portfolio, in most organizations, is a hastily-put-together list of the most visible projects underway. The Center introduced a project portfolio management process to two of its clients in the mid-1990s (see Chapter 10 for a detailed discussion). Figure 1.8 shows that only 20 percent of organizations represented had a well designed project portfolio management system. The implications are staggering—a majority of CIOs and CEOs do not have a definite idea about the total number of projects underway at any given point.

Sin Index

At this point, take a little time to assess the sin index—the degree to which mistakes are being made in your organization. Figure 1.9 depicts the Seven Deadly Sins of project management. For each item in Figure 1.9, keeping in mind your organization's performance, check the appropriate box in the right-hand column. A 1 means there are no problems related to the specific item and a 5 indicates the problem is very pervasive. This assessment may be best done by discussing the subject matter with three or four of your colleagues and then coming up with your values.

FIGURE 1.8
Project portfolio
management.

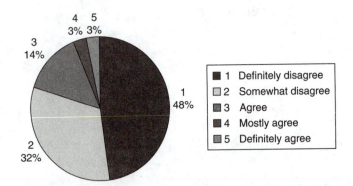

	5 Rarely (Less than 10 percent)	4 Sometimes (10–20 percent)	3 Often (20–59 percent)	2 Most often (60–79 percent)	1 Routinely (More than 80 percent)
1. Mistaking "half-baked" ideas for projects My organization diligently filters out "half-baked" ideas before they are pursued as projects.	❏	❏	❏	❏	❏
2. Dictated deadlines Sponsors in my organization define realistic and achievable deadlines.	❏	❏	❏	❏	❏
3. Ineffective sponsorship Sponsors in my organization commit their political capital, personal time, and resources to their projects.	❏	❏	❏	❏	❏
4. Unskilled project managers Project managers in my organization have the skills necessary to do their jobs.	❏	❏	❏	❏	❏
5. Not monitoring the project vital signs My organization monitors a set of well defined vital signs of its projects.	❏	❏	❏	❏	❏
6. Failing to deploy a robust project management methodology My organization uses a robust process to manage its projects.	❏	❏	❏	❏	❏
7. Not formulating a comprehensive project portfolio My organization maintains a comprehensive portfolio of projects.	❏	❏	❏	❏	❏

FIGURE 1.9
Seven deadly sins survey.

Once you have checked the appropriate boxes for the seven questions, add up the represented numeric values and divide the sum by 7. Your organization's sin index is a number between 1 and 5. Based on the averaged value, our sin index interpretations are as follows:

Sin index = 1   Project nirvana

Sin index = 2   Cloud nine

Sin index = 3　　Can be saved
Sin index = 4　　Project purgatory
Sin index = 5　　Project hell

Project Nirvana　　Congratulations! Your organization is operating at a high level of project management maturity. Completing projects successfully is a standard practice because the necessary fundamentals are in place. Your answers reveal that your organization is a cut above most organizations.

Cloud Nine　　Your organization is highly mature because a well-designed project management process is in place. However, your answers reveal that some people are not doing the right thing. Certain sponsors, customers, project managers, and team members occasionally take the path of least resistance and sidestep the proven methods to success. Be warned that continued missteps by these people will certainly weigh the organization down and may result in many challenged and failed projects. Your mission: identify the unenlightened and guide them on the path to project nirvana.

Can be Saved　　Your organization is skating on thin ice and soon it is likely to fall through to project purgatory. Your responses illustrate that project teams experience sporadic success. Your organization faces several challenges: inadequate project management process, management's lack of support for project management discipline, insufficient education and training of the troops, and too many nonbelievers. It is time to come out of the darkness. Your organization needs a swift kick.

Project Purgatory　　The fire is hot; the good news is that you are still in the frying pan. When it comes to competent project management, your organization doesn't have a clue. In your current environment, practically every idea becomes a project. Your project managers are experts in the art of "estimating-to-please." Many project managers routinely don the "Velcro suit" and customers launch scope balls[9] at will. Project managers and team members receive insufficient project management training and a robust project management process is nowhere to be seen. Management's solution is to acquire site licenses for project management software. When a project is successful, it is due to heroic performances by a few individuals, or just "dumb" luck. In short, your organization needs help. Fast.

Project Hell　　Please do the profession, the stockholders, and the general public a favor. Stop all project work immediately. We know your organization has more technology than it can ever use. Management has bought into ERP, CRM, ASP, B2B, A2A, palm tops, wireless, and any type of "berry" or "tooth" product available. The upside: your vendors are very happy. We are sure many sponsors routinely pronounce mottoes such as: "failure is not an option," "just do it," "e-projects don't need project management," or "no project cancellations on my watch." Does your corporate mission statement proclaim family values? The truth: many team members have not spent valuable time with their families in weeks. Family picture screen savers don't count. Bottom line: Your organization's only hope is to tie up some of the sponsors to the mocking post and let the fun begin.

■ WHY YOUR PROJECT MANAGEMENT INVESTMENT MAY NEVER PAY OFF

Why has the massive investment in IT/Business project management not been able to turn the tide of project failures? A key reason is that the bulk of IT/Business project management education, practices, and tools have been a replication of the principles and practices developed by the engineering profession—especially construction engineers. While many of the principles and practices of classic construction engineering apply to the management of IT/Business projects, it is important to understand that these projects are inherently *different*. We in IT/Business do not build bridges, dams,

---

[9]Our euphemism for the scope increase (new functionality) customers insist on adding to an ongoing project. Velcro is a registered trademark of Velcro, USA, Inc., all rights reserved.

highways, refineries, high rises, or housing developments. Most construction projects start from scratch and are often referred to as greenfield projects. IT/Business projects, on the other hand, most often involve significant changes to ongoing business processes. IT/Business project work is more like overhauling the transmission of a semi, fully loaded with chickens as it shoots down the interstate at 70 mph.

Based on extensive analysis of scores of IT/Business projects, and a number of construction engineering projects, the Center strongly believes that there are distinct *differences* between the two professions. These key differences can be grouped into five categories:

1. The nature of the project
2. Plans and procedures
3. The human element
4. Doing the work
5. Completing the job

These five primary categories of differences are further broken down into thirty-one subcategories, as shown in Figure 1.10.

Differentiating attribute	Engineering projects	IT/business projects
Nature of projects		
1. Green field projects	Conventional and common	Seldom
2. Clearly defined end	Conventional and common	Seldom
3. Customer expectations	Realistic and stable	Unrealistic and changing
4. Rate of change in skills	Steady	Extremely fast
5. Change process	Controlled, documented	Uncontrolled, ad hoc
6. Build-to-last	Long life	Short life
Plans and procedures		
7. Linear and bounded project phases	Conventional and common	Seldom
8. Build to specifications *v.* requirements	Build to specifications	Build to requirements
9. Standardized terminology and symbols	Conventional and common	Seldom
10. Well defined deliverables	Conventional and common	Few and not possible
11. Estimates	Based on history	Best guesses
12. Schedules	Easy to create and stable	Difficult and unstable
The human element		
13. Project sponsor	Low involvement acceptable	High involvement necessary
14. Customer involvement (build phase)	Not involved	Heavy involvement necessary
15. Bounded skills and bounded time	Conventional and common	Not possible
16. Knowledge work *v.* muscle work	Mostly muscle	Mostly knowledge
17. Impact of staff turnover	Low to medium impact	High impact
Doing the work		
18. Fabrication *v.* creating from scratch	Mostly build by fabrication	Mostly build from scratch
19. Robustness of materials	Guarantee for robustness	No guarantees for software
20. Legal baselines	Conventional and common	Not the case
21. Accounting for effort	Conventional and common	Not uniform, difficult
22. Cost of project management	Conventional and common	Customers object
23. Earned value and percent complete	Applicable metrics	Not applicable in its classic form
24. Legal (contractual) obligations	Conventional and rigorous	Poorly defined
25. Completion bond	A requirement	Not available
26. Go back charges	Conventional and common	Never to seldom
27. Project management tools	Well suited	Not well suited to the needs
28. Inspections	Conventional and common	Seldom
29. Testing	Minimal testing	Extensive testing
Completing the job		
30. Documentation for end-users/customers	Minimal	Extensive
31. Customer training	Minimal to no training	Extensive and in depth

FIGURE 1.10
Engineering projects *v.* IT/Business projects.

Before we begin to discuss the thirty-one differences between the two primary project management approaches, let us describe the underlying purpose of this research and its findings:

- Identify and analyze the key differences between classic construction engineering project management and IT/Business project management practices.
- Initiate a serious discussion regarding the specific and different needs of the IT/Business project professionals.
- Show that IT/Business project managers require additional processes, skills, techniques, tools, and training specifically designed to meet their unique project management needs.

The following discussion is not meant to negate the many engineering project management principles and practices fundamental to the success of any type of project. The objective is to show that IT/Business project management professionals need to think outside the conventional project management box.

The Nature of the Project

It is quite difficult, if not impossible, to define the end-state of an IT/Business project. The primary reason is that such projects deal with developing solutions for business problems. Those problems are often nebulous and continue to change with time. A business executive might tell the project team, "We need to create a Web presence for e-commerce by the end of this quarter, the competitors are killing us." A few days later, the project is in full swing. This would never be the case with an engineering project. For example, if a senior executive says to the building engineer, "We have just hired a lot of employees, we need to construct a new 20,000 sq. ft., three-story building." Under no circumstances will the engineering group start construction the week after. Many construction engineers would say, "IT/Business project managers need to follow the practices of the engineering group and not start the Web project." Things are not that simple. The points below outline the key differences between classic engineering projects and the projects faced by IT/Business professionals. Each point will then be explained in detail.

- Greenfield projects
- Clearly defined end-state
- Customer expectations
- Rate of change in skills
- Change process
- Build-to-last

Greenfield Projects   Most engineering projects—high rises, highways, shopping malls, housing developments, dams—start as greenfield projects. They take place on uninhabited land on which the builder has to do minimal work to prepare the site for construction. Most of the preparation work involves clearing the land of any shrubs, trees, and abandoned structures. When engineers are faced with replacement of old structures, they simply implode them. In just a few short minutes, the entire structure is gone. There are even companies that specialize in building implosions. We wish such services were available to IT/Business project managers. Imploding the old systems could have solved the Y2K problem. A majority of engineering projects involve new construction, while most IT/Business projects consist of the following three key actions:

1. Automate a number of existing processes
2. Change many of the existing processes
3. Add a number of new processes

Most large IT/Business projects, such as Enterprise Resource Planning (ERP) and Customer Relationship Management (CRM) implementations, deal with extensive changes to existing business processes ingrained deeply in the work habits of the project's customers—the individuals who will eventually use the new systems. IT/Business teams must make sure that while they are developing their projects, they do not disrupt the day-to-day operation of their customers. Then, at the time of project implementation, project teams must make sure that customers make a smooth transition from the old to the new ways of doing the work.

During the construction phase of an engineering project, workers are able to isolate themselves from their customers with great ease. For example, consider the following engineering projects:

- *Road resurfacing:* The construction crew posts signs warning motorists of the upcoming project and directs them either to find alternate routes of travel or suffer extensive delays, dust, and noise. They also post signs to reduce traffic flow and speed, and warn motorists that any traffic violation within the construction zone will result in the doubling of fines. Imagine an IT/Business project team informing the payroll department that due to the overhaul of the payroll system, the payroll department should either find alternate methods of issuing paychecks or expect long delays! And if they misbehave, they will face fines.
- *Renovation:* The construction crew posts signs to block access to portions of the building under renovation. The building contractor blocks off large sections of the existing parking facilities and some of the access roads. People are left to their own devices to find alternate parking facilities, thereby increasing travel time. Also, fewer and narrower access roads result in heavy traffic congestion, adding extensive time to most travelers' itineraries. The only consolation is the sign proclaiming that all the inconveniences will enable the owner to better serve the public in the future. I wonder how many IT/Business project teams could get away with similar actions!

Consider the project of remodeling a kitchen: replace countertops with granite, resurface the cabinets, replace the sink, upgrade the oven, and install new lighting. Before the construction team begins its work, the homeowner (the customer) must remove countertop appliances, empty drawers and make alternative arrangements for cooking so as not to interfere with the construction crew. Once the work starts, the homeowner has to tolerate the dust, noise and inconvenience that the work generates. IT/Business project teams are afforded no such leeway or consideration. They are forced to do their work amid the equivalent of a fully equipped and operational kitchen, and cannot interfere with the customer's cooking, dining, and dishwashing routines.

Consider a project designed to improve an existing system—upgrade human interface screens (the GUI), add a few new functions, and improve the speed of transaction processing. The customer expects the project team to reorganize data files, do backups, and keep the current system fully functional and stable while making the necessary changes to the system. Seldom can an existing system be disengaged from providing its service to the end users until the new system is fully functional.

Clearly Defined End-State The end-state of any construction engineering project should be clearly defined through well-documented drawings and specifications *before* any construction work begins.[10] Customers get to see and approve the architect's renderings, to-scale architectural models, and detailed engineering drawings of the final product *before* any construction can begin. These help the customer visualize and fine-tune the end product and establishes accountability—architectural drawings and detailed design documents are recorded with appropriate government entities and serve as legal documentation. In IT/Business projects, the converse is true. The end-state of most projects is often not clearly defined, even after the project is completed. A key reason for this ambiguity is that most IT/Business projects automate live business processes that continue to change and evolve as the project progresses. Occasionally, project teams develop prototypes, but customers invariably misunderstand the process and want to use the prototype as the production system. Imagine a customer wanting to move into an architect's to-scale model of an intended high rise.

Customer Expectations Many business customers have developed the mistaken impression that a typical IT/Business project does not require much work and should be completed quickly—within a few days to a few weeks. The blame for this misplaced expectation does not lie entirely with the customers. Pick up any IT magazine and you would see promises of fully operational, complex systems that seemingly require little more than the connection of a telephone line into a jack—the miracle of vendor-supplied packages. One does not see these misleading advertisements

---

[10]An exception to this is certain scientific engineering projects where the architecture, design, and construction evolve as the project progresses; a life cycle quite similar to spiral life cycles of large complex IT/Business projects. Such engineering projects are constructed under negotiated contracts. Historically, few of these projects are completed to originally proposed timelines and many end up costing far more than the originally proposed budget.

or expectation-setting headlines in construction engineering publications. A typical 3,000 sq. ft. house on level ground in California, still takes ninety to 120 days to build, even though the construction industry has been building these houses for decades. A customer seldom expects, or demands, that the house be built in thirty days or less. However, IT/Business project managers routinely suffer from such demands.

Rate of Change in Skills   IT changes so rapidly that some of it may be obsolete as it is being installed. In projects that last more than six months, multiple upgrades of the infrastructure hardware and software (e.g., operating systems, databases and network communications) may be required. This constant state of flux requires the team to invest significant time and resources to simply keep the infrastructure in sync with the latest vendor releases. Also, IT/Business clients continually demand the latest and the greatest technology, but the learning curve to master a new technology can be between three and six months, at best. However, new and highly complex technology is being released at much shorter intervals, and this results in a constant struggle by IT professionals just to keep up with the basics. Engineering project managers seldom face this problem to the same degree.[11]

Change Process   Most IT/Business projects are driven by a number of unpredictable and unstable business drivers. For example:

Management style(s)	Changing priorities
Reorganization	Supporting technology
Key competitors	Interdepartmental politics
Conflicting priorities	Changing customer perception, processes, and needs

In a recent Web project, toward the end of the fifth month of a six-month schedule, the marketing department decided that the colors used on twenty-seven different screens did not *exactly* match the colors of the newly designed corporate logo, and directed the IT team to replace three colors with the new corporate colors. Additionally, the marketing group informed the IT team members that they *must* add four new transaction-processing capabilities because a print advertisement for the product already touted the said new functionality. Their rationale for this premature advertisement was that it was the only way to keep the potential customers interested and keep the competitors at bay. The project manager informed the advertising department of the difficulty in changing the color schemes on the fly, as there were no "find-and-replace" commands for colors. Also, the addition of new functionality would mean restructuring the database and modifying interfaces with at least three other systems: financial, order processing, and warehousing. The marketing department managers were adamant and did not relent, and the project sponsor backed them up. The project manager had no option but to acquiesce to the demands of the customer—they had to make the changes with no increase in project budget or schedule. Consider a similar situation in the case of a fully-booked hotel in which a senior manager directs the building contractor to redo the hotel marquee, repaint the walls of the guest rooms, add new amenities, and make certain improvements without affecting room occupancy. Business projects remain in a constant state of flux. Given changing business problems, the project team has no alternative but to make the necessary changes to the project; the proverbial scope creep.

In the case of engineering projects, any changes to specifications (once baselined) are covered by clear contractual procedures, and specific well defined approval steps are necessary to change the baselined specifications. Many changes may even need approval by regulatory bodies, such as city or county building departments. In engineering projects, the builder typically has the upper hand when it comes to making changes. It is clearly understood by all that changes to the

---

[11]During a meeting with a project manager who is responsible for a $135 million construction project (an office building that took over two years to complete), discussions lead to the question, "How many training seminars have you and your engineers attended during the past two years to keep up with the engineering technology?" Of the seven engineers on his team, one had attended a three-day session on prestressed concrete, and he himself had attended an orientation session on new types of facing materials that replicate marble. Now consider an IT/Business project of similar magnitude and ask, "How much training would the different team members need and how much of the technology will face obsolescence during the project development life cycle?"

baselined specifications result in increased cost and often in increased time. The customer has relatively little negotiating power, especially regarding the cost of making the requested changes. Even some restaurants strongly discourage any changes to their menu. For example, the following notice appears on a menu of a highly popular restaurant in Rancho Mirage, California:

> *We take no responsibility for any changes requested in the preparation of our food. There is a charge for changes and substitutions to the menu.*

Simply stated: In most other professions, in most cases, the customer expects to pay for changes.

Build to Last   The infrastructure—foundation, electrical, plumbing—of engineering structures is designed to last a long time. Homeowners rarely expect to upgrade or replace the infrastructure of their residences within the first decade. Even appliances—refrigerators, dishwashers, and clothes washers—are expected to last ten years or longer. Homeowners don't expect the infrastructure vendors, such as plumbing and electrical vendors, to issue *mandatory* upgrades to their infrastructure components. The converse is the case with IT/Business projects. Both hardware and software have short lifespans, and with the advent of web-based projects, lifespans are getting shorter. Additionally, IT/Business project teams are often at the mercy of vendors who rush their products to market and then follow up with an incessant number of upgrades and patches. Often, this means changes to products that are already in production and development, and customers may not be willing to pay for the cost of keeping up-to-date. Therefore, technology infrastructure must be designed to accommodate frequent changes to hardware and software in an efficient and effective manner.

Plans and Procedures

This is perhaps the area of greatest difference between classic engineering and IT/Business projects. The degree of discipline, procedures, standards, tools, and jurisprudence that drive engineering projects is far more mature than those available now, and in the foreseeable future, to IT/Business professionals. IT/Business project teams need to learn how to adapt classic construction engineering procedures and develop new methods and techniques to help them manage their projects effectively and efficiently. The points below outline the key differences in the area of plans and procedures practiced by the two professions.

- Linear and bounded project phases
- Build to specifications *v.* requirements
- Standardized terminology and symbols
- Well defined deliverables
- Estimates
- Schedules

Linear and Bounded Project Phases   The various phases of a construction project are linear and the boundaries are well defined. For example, in the case of a high rise, the various life cycle phases—architecture, design, specifications, and build—are sequential and well bounded. The construction team lays the complete foundation, erects the total superstructure, and builds all of the floors. It is neither cost effective nor safe to build the first few floors, rent them out, and then continue building the rest of the structure. In the case of IT/Business projects, various phases are not only overlapping,[12] they are often spiral—requirements, design, prototype, first build, deployment, and assessment followed by the next cycle(s) of requirements, design, prototype, build, deployment, integration, and assessment.

---

[12]In the case of most IT/Business projects, the conventional engineering waterfall method where requirements, design, and build are sequential does not work well. In most IT/Business projects, the various life cycle phases need to be overlapped. For example, after a certain point in requirements, the team can begin to design the product while continuing the requirements work. Similarly, after a certain point in the design phase, the team begins to code modules/objects, tests them and deploys a small component of the project. This is followed by more design, coding, testing and deployment.

Build to Specifications v. Requirements   In Webster's Dictionary, the term "specification" is defined as: "A particular and detailed account or description of a thing; specifically, a statement of particulars, describing the dimensions, details, or particularities of any work about to be undertaken." The word "requirement" is defined as: "Something required, something obligatory or demanded."[13] In the case of engineering projects, there are specific and well defined steps to *translate* customer requirements into clearly articulated and documented specifications. For example:

- An architect converts a customer's requirements into architectural drawings, and the customer reviews and approves the architectural drawings.
- The architectural drawings are then converted into detailed engineering drawings, which by law must be reviewed and approved by a duly licensed engineer. This is the earliest point at which reliable bids can be solicited.
- The engineering drawings are then used to produce a work breakdown structure (WBS), comprehensive task plans, and a bill of materials (BOM) by using a standardized set of symbols and vocabulary.

The output from the previous steps becomes the specifications for construction. The construction team then builds the structure using the detailed specifications as its guide. In contrast, the customers of IT/Business projects state their requirements in a cursory fashion and expect the project teams to do their best to devise solutions to meet needs that usually are poorly articulated and often undocumented.

The defining step in the previous list is the second bullet, where detailed engineering drawings are developed. In the case of IT/Business projects, this step has eluded the profession and will continue to do so until IT/Business professionals have a reliable method of documenting detailed requirements. Until that time, IT/Business project teams will continue to face the daunting task of constructing their solutions, primarily from customer requirements—a much more difficult endeavor than that faced by engineering professionals.

Standardized Terminology and Symbols   With engineering projects, the majority of specifications are depicted through standard terminology and symbols and minimal narrative text. Different construction companies do not create new or different symbols and terms to distinguish themselves from others. In a recent project for a house, the landscape map created by the contractor was a to-scale drawing showing the drainage, drip watering, electrical wiring, trees, and shrubs using *standard* symbols, *standard* botanical names, and minimal descriptive text. Conversely, software related vendors strive to be different by inventing new nonstandard terminology, aggravating the difficulties that IT/Business project managers already face.[14] To add to the confusion, most of the business customers' requirements are stated in narrative English, a highly imprecise method to state specifications clearly. Within IT, only database professionals have developed a number of standardized symbols to depict database specifications.

Well Defined Deliverables   In any engineering project, most deliverables—the construction team's end product—are specifically defined. For example: Shaft wall cavity, 1″ steel C-H studs with two layers of 5/8″ gypsum board 1 side, 2-hour fire rating. Subdrainage metal piping, perforated, asphalt coated, 6″ diameter, 18 gallons; 28″ light bar (SL742) at master bath on right wall corner, installed vertically with top of light bar 72″ from the floor (see drawing KAP20B). IT/Business deliverables can rarely be defined to the same degree of specificity and often remain open to different interpretations. This is not the fault of project teams; it is the nature of most business deliverables. One CIO phrased the dilemma aptly:

> *Engineering deliverables meet the test of the physical human senses—sight, feel, hear, and smell, while most IT/Business deliverables meet the test of human emotions, opinions, and philosophy.*

---

[13]Websters Twentieth Century Dictionary, (unabridged Second Edition, Simon and Schuster), s.v. "specification" and "requirement."

[14]Refer to phase names, phase boundaries, and deliverables and task names in system development life cycle methodologies from top vendors and you would discover a plethora of nonstandard, and often quizzical terminology.

The end product of any engineering project is very physical—a bridge, a road, a dam, a building. The end result has a *presence*. One can see it, touch it, and observe it; this is not the case with IT/Business projects. At the end of a typical software project, all the customer sees is a diskette, a CD, or a few printed pages. Often, it is difficult for a business customer to comprehend why such a "small" software project was so difficult, took so long, and cost so much.

Estimates   One of the key questions on the minds of most business customers is, "Why can't our project managers develop estimates as accurately as engineers?" It is a good question, and we believe there is a good answer. In the case of construction engineering, the estimating process follows specific steps:

• Architectural design
• Engineering design
• Detailed specifications
• Estimates

In most engineering departments, there are specialists whose responsibility it is to convert engineering drawings and specifications into a detailed BOM that is used to produce detailed cost estimates. Similarly, effort estimates are derived from comprehensive WBSs, detailed work packages, and extensive historical data. In engineering, extensive historical databases of highly accurate and easily useable effort and cost values are broadly available to project managers. No such historical data are easily available to IT/Business project managers. Also, IT/Business project managers are often faced with providing estimates *well before* the architecture of the proposed project has been finalized. In fact, many customers demand highly accurate estimates during the annual budget cycle, when only single-line project descriptions have been formulated. Essentially, this early in the project life cycle, most projects are still half baked ideas. Another often overlooked fact is that the technology, materials, and skills needed to build most engineering projects change relatively little between the time the estimates are approved and the time the project is completed. The skills of engineers do not become obsolete at the same rapid pace as those of software designers and programmers. Most IT/Business projects that last more than a few months will invariably face one or more of the following:

• The underlying software is sure to go through considerable changes. Just look back six months and see how many software upgrades took place and what new and wonderful software is being touted in various trade magazines.
• Pick up any three IT publications, or visit any technology show, and see what powerful new hardware is available since the design of your current project was finalized.
• Do a quick skills assessment of your department's IT professionals and see if their skills are in concert with the complexity of projects currently under way, and those planned to start within the next six to nine months.

The skills and processes needed to develop estimates for IT/Business projects are considerably more intricate than those needed to estimate engineering projects. Additionally, for engineering projects, the customer can specify a *desired* budget and a *preferred* date for project completion but is seldom able to *dictate* the budget or the schedule for the project. Any disagreements between the builder and the customer are subject to open negotiations. The converse is the case in IT/Business projects. The customers often dictate the budget and the schedule, and the team has little ability to push back.

> *But false scheduling to match the patron's desired date is much more common in our discipline than elsewhere in engineering.*
>
> F. P. Brooks, *The Mythical Man-Month,* Anniversary ed.
> (Reading, MA: Addison-Wesley, 1995).

Schedules   In the case of engineering projects, schedules are developed using the following steps:

1. The project is broken into discrete phases, well defined deliverables, and specific tasks—a WBS.

2. The project manager develops effort and duration estimates for various tasks using organizational and professional historical databases that are publicly available.
3. The project manager creates a task network.
4. Duration estimates are plotted onto organizational and team calendars to create a project schedule.

In the case of IT/Business projects, the nature of most deliverables and tasks is such that they cannot be described with the same accuracy and detail as engineering deliverables. Furthermore, calendars are not as stable and predictable for teams working on IT/Business projects as they are for engineering construction teams. Both the IT and business people are typically assigned to multiple projects, and most business team members still have their routine "day jobs." The next time you are meeting with an IT/Business team, notice how many carry cell phones and pagers and how frequently they are interrupted. The end result is that estimates and schedules cannot be as precise and accurate as construction engineering estimates and schedules can. Therefore, estimates and schedules for IT/Business projects must be expressed using certain range values, such as 110 to 118 work days or as January 15 to January 27. The range is necessary to communicate an appropriate degree of uncertainty. Unfortunately, even if one was able to convince managers and customers[15] to agree to range-based estimates and schedules, project management software tools still produce only single number (date specific) schedules. That is what management and customers see, and that is what they expect. As you have guessed, an *exact* estimate is an oxymoron.

Predictions are hard, especially about the future.
Yogi Berra.

The Human Element

The human element—sponsor, project manager, team members—of IT/Business projects stands distinctly apart from those of classic engineering projects. In the case of the latter, roles and responsibilities are well defined and distinct, work assignments are well bounded and clearly stated, and most individual team members do not impact the outcome of the project significantly. IT/Business projects, on the other hand, are very sensitive to the individuals working on the project. A discussion of each point that follows elucidates the differences.

• Project sponsor
• Customer involvement
• Bounded skills and bounded time
• Knowledge work *v.* muscle work
• Impact of staff turnover

Project Sponsor   In engineering projects, the sponsor works with the architect group to provide the vision and overall needs, and negotiates budgets and schedules. Once contracts are approved and signed, the sponsor's role diminishes considerably. This is in concert with the definition of a sponsor in the Project Management Institute's (PMI's) Project Management Body of Knowledge (PMBOK). "Sponsor—the individual or group within the performing organization who provides the financial resources, in cash or kind, for the project." Once the contracts are signed, other than occasional ceremonial visits to the construction site, the sponsor does not have hands-on involvement with the project.[16] In the case of IT/Business projects, that is absolutely not the case. Also, the IT/Business project sponsor must be highly involved during *all* project phases to make sure that the project proceeds down the right path at the right speed. Unfortunately, this is *not* the norm for most IT/Business projects. Business executives need to learn about the appropriate roles and responsibilities of project sponsors to ensure that individual sponsors perform their responsibilities aptly and in a timely fashion. Most business executives do not really know how to be effective sponsors—it does not come with their job title.

---

[15]All of Center customers use range values for estimates and most use them for schedules as well.

[16]Except in the case of certain scientific projects for which the end-state has not been well defined.

Customer Involvement   In engineering projects, customer management is typically very involved during the architecture phase, somewhat involved during the design phase, and seldom involved during the construction phase. In fact, engineers do their best to keep their customers away from the job site. A typical construction site is fenced and boarded up. Construction workers cut small holes into walls for the customers to observe, from a safe distance, the work in progress. On the few occasions when customer representatives are allowed onto the job site, they have to wear protective helmets, goggles, and safety shoes. Imagine an IT/Business project development area all boarded up, with only observation holes for the customers to watch the project team at work. In engineering projects, customers are *not* asked to be a part of the construction team. In IT/Business projects, the customer involvement needs to stay high during all phases of the project—requirements, prototyping, testing, deployment, and current system retirement. Most customers do not have the time, interest, or skills to live up to their responsibilities, and project managers have little power to influence customer behavior.

Bounded Skills and Bounded Time   In the case of engineering projects, the skills of various team members are well bounded and specific, e.g., structural engineer, design engineer, electrical engineer, steel fabricator, pipe fitter, crane operator, dry wall installer, mason, plumber, painter, electrician. Few members of the labor force are engaged in new construction, maintenance, and customer support activities simultaneously. This enables the project manager to break the project into discrete work packages assigned to people with well defined specific skills. This is not the case with IT/Business projects, for which most of the team members are assigned to more than one project at a time. Project team members not only end up doing multiple tasks—analysis, design, coding, and testing—these same individuals often spend considerable *unscheduled* time on maintenance and support activities as well. This makes the task of resource management very difficult. IT/Business project managers have to learn the skills necessary to continually juggle resource assignments, ascertain the impact on the project's critical path, and try to minimize the resulting ill will and burnout of their team members.

In the case of IT/Business projects, another problem is the vast differences in the skill and productivity levels of various team members. Frederick Brooks quoted a study in his book, *The Mythical Man-Month,* that states:

> *These studies revealed large individual differences between high and low performers, often by an order of magnitude.*
>
> Brooks, 1995.

This is simply not the case in engineering projects. The productivity differences between different plumbers, electricians, drywall installers, painters, or crane operators on the same project is seldom more than a few percentage points. However, IT/Business project managers must deal with team members who have great fluctuations in their productivity numbers. This makes the jobs of resource assignment, critical path management, and resource leveling very difficult.

Knowledge Work v. Muscle Work   In the case of engineering projects, knowledge workers develop the architectural drawings, engineering drawings, and specifications; the construction work is done by a *different group* of workers. This separation of responsibilities forces the architects and engineers to transfer their knowledge—the project specifications—to paper in a detailed manner using standard symbols, vocabulary, and terminology. During construction, only a small number of knowledge workers are present at the site for any last-minute specification clarifications and design interpretations. This separation of responsibilities does not exist in IT/Business, where the same group of individuals (or one individual) does the architecture, design, and construction work. This has resulted in the highly pervasive practice of incomplete documentation. Massive amounts of knowledge about the project remain in the minds of individual team members.

Impact of Staff Turnover   In engineering, the impact of resource turnover is relatively minor, especially turnover among craftspeople. The reason is that resource interchangeability within the same type of work is very high. For example, during construction of a building, if a number of masons, electricians, or painters left the project, new workers can usually pick up the partially completed work and get up to speed in a relatively short time. The key reasons are standardized documentation, standardized materials, standardized skills, and standardized tools. This is almost never the case in IT/Business projects. If an analyst, designer, programmer, or a customer representative leaves in the middle of a deliverable, the replacement person often wishes to start from "scratch," resulting in extensive loss of the to-date effort. This is one reason why partially compete IT/Business deliverables have little "earned value."

Doing the Work

The style, techniques, and tools for doing the work, assessing its progress, and taking corrective actions for IT/Business projects differ vastly from the work done on classic engineering projects. In the case of engineering projects, most construction involves assembling from precut and prefabricated parts. Practically all of the construction materials have been pretested and carry explicit warranties. Most construction work is done by well classified (union) labor, the work effort is meticulously recorded, and contractors have to be licensed and bonded. The project owner (customer) expects to pay for most, if not all, of the changes and for the cost of project management. A discussion of the following items will elaborate this point further.

- Fabrication *v.* creating from scratch
- Robustness of materials
- Legal baselines
- Accounting for effort
- Cost of project management
- Earned value and percent complete
- Contractual (legal) obligations
- Completion bond
- Go-back charges
- Project management tools
- Inspections
- Testing

Fabricating v. Creating from Scratch   In most engineering projects, the construction process primarily consists of fabricating the end product from predesigned, preassembled, and pretested components. The Eiffel Tower, one of the most successful engineering projects, was constructed from precisely preassembled components. Similarly, in the construction of a house, the doors, windows, cabinets, knobs, furnaces, air-conditioning units, appliances, toilets, and water heaters are all delivered to the site. The construction team primarily assembles and erects the final structure from the supplied parts. On the other hand, most software is still written from scratch, resulting in a much more complex building process. In IT, code reuse has been discussed for more than a decade, but the actual practice is still miniscule primarily because business rules, rather than remaining static, continue to change.

Robustness of Materials   Engineering projects are seldom, if ever, built from materials that have not been thoroughly tested against well-defined industry (and often legal) standards. Most construction materials carry specific performance warranties. With software, this is rarely the case. There are practically no performance standards for the software supplied by vendors.[17] Practically every software product has a prominently displayed disclaimer stating that "THE PROGRAM(S) IS PROVIDED 'AS IS,' WITHOUT WARRANTY . . ." In fact, laws are being enacted which will make the shrink-wrapped software licenses legally binding.[18] Now imagine a construction project for which the steel, cement, wiring, nuts, bolts, rivets, electrical fuses, and other construction materials carry similar

---

[17]"Microsoft is shipping a product with tens of thousands of defects the company knows about but hasn't corrected—and that some of those will probably cause customers problems." From a memo by Marc Lucovsky, a Microsoft manager on the Windows 2000 development team. *Computerworld,* February 21, 2000, p. 82. This practice is not limited to Microsoft; practically all vendor software is shipped with a number of defects.

[18]Virginia's general assembly became the first state legislature in the U.S. to pass the Uniform Computer Information Transactions Act (UCITA), the law that makes shrink-wrapped software licenses legally binding. *Computerworld,* February 21, 2000, p. 82.

disclaimers. Interestingly, in many mission-critical IT/Business projects, the use of alpha and beta software—early versions not available for public sale—from vendors is the norm. We wonder if a commercial airline would fly alpha airplanes as part of its regular service. Also, imagine seeing the sign, "Alpha Bridge Ahead," or a notice in a restaurant that exclaims, "All dishes cooked from alpha recipes."

Legal Baselines   The jurisprudence that governs engineering projects requires that engineering drawings, specifications, budgets, and schedules be baselined. Such baselines become the basis for future changes and/or dispute resolutions. No such practices exist in the software profession. The project requirements, budgets, and schedules of most IT/Business projects stay in flux throughout the project life cycle. This instability renders the project manager's job very difficult, and requires the project manager to constantly and diligently walk the tightrope of changing customer needs.

Accounting for Effort   In the case of construction engineering projects, specific practices and disciplines exist for recording the effort expended by various team members of a project (one of the main reasons is that the majority of construction work is done by union members who are paid by the actual hours of work done). Engineering companies develop extensive time-capture systems—manual or automated—to record the labor time spent on a project. This practice ensures accurate and up-to-date actual effort and cost data that is the basis for progress monitoring, labor payments, and customer billing. Additionally, the actual effort data can be compared to original estimates to compute earned value and percent completion. This is not the case with IT/Business teams. Most of the team members are classified as exempt workers, are not paid overtime compensation, and do not record their overtime hours. In fact, many companies do not want project team members to record their overtime hours. The time spent by end-users/customers is seldom recorded, and the same is the case with management's time.

> *. . . the normal workday for any individual contributor on the team was 12–14 hours, six to seven days per week. . . . individual contributors typically spend significantly more waking hours with their project team members than they do with their own family members. . . . but the labor cost savings to the project . . . amounted to more than $12 million (250,000 hours of "free labor") . . .*
> Lee R. Lambert, "Leading the Charge," *PM Network* (September, 2002).

Imagine a construction engineering project sponsor and manager asking the unionized labor to "contribute" $12 million worth of free labor to a project! However, this gratis use of resources is a common practice for projects undertaken by in-house IT/Business teams. As a result, attempts to compute such metrics as earned value and ROI to ascertain the progress and value of IT/Business projects can be futile. IT/Business project managers need to use a different set of metrics—vital signs[19]—to ascertain the progress of their projects.

Cost of Project Management   In the case of engineering projects, customers expect to pay the contractor for the cost of project management. In the case of software projects, customers often do not want to pay for the project management effort. They consider project management an overhead expense and would prefer to eliminate it. We wonder what the same people think of the value of an orchestra leader, an executive chef, a *maitre d'hôtel*, or a construction site supervisor—people who all serve as project managers. The same customers' dim view of the value of IT/Business project managers results in a multitude of problems: project managers are forced to perform technical work to justify their existence and team members do not look to project managers for leadership. As a result, project managers receive little or no respect.

Earned Value   In some projects, earned value is used to measure project progress. The quantities used in earned value calculations are:

- *Planned value (PV):* The sum of the approved cost estimates for work scheduled, at the project status date.

---
[19]See *Project Vital Signs,* Chapter 7.

- *Actual cost (AC):* Total costs for work actually performed, at the project status date.
- *Earned value (EV):* The sum of the approved cost estimates for the work actually performed, at the project status date.
- *Budget at completion (BAC):* The approved cost estimate for the total project.

Typical computations by project managers are:

$$\text{Cost variance} = \text{EV} - \text{AC}$$
$$\text{Schedule variance} = \text{EV} - \text{PV}$$
$$\text{Cost performance index (CPI)} = \text{EV/AC}$$
$$\text{Schedule performance index (SPI)} = \text{EV/PV}$$
$$\text{Estimate at completion (EAC)} = \text{BAC/CPI}$$

The earned value variances, indices, and estimates provide a useful look at project progress, but they have limitations. The indices (CPI and SPI) provide an indicator of whether the project is behind cost, ahead of cost, behind schedule, or ahead of schedule. The estimate at completion is a straight-line projection of how much the project will cost when complete, based on the current spending rate. The project schedule cannot be forecast reliably using the earned value approach alone. The critical path method (CPM) is still the best approach for schedule estimation.

The earned value approach has value as an indicator of project health and as a rudimentary tool in forecasting project cost. It is not the right tool for schedule estimation and it does not provide the details needed to track and control the project to completion.

Percent Complete Another metric commonly used by engineering project managers is the assessment of percent complete. For example, if a tile layer has tiled seventy square feet of a 100 sq. ft. job, we can safely assume that 70 percent of the work has been completed. Partially complete IT/Business deliverables cannot be measured in the same manner. For example, if a programmer is assigned to code a module that is estimated to be 100 lines of code, and he or she has written 70 lines of code, does it mean the work is 70 percent complete? In the same vein, translate the following statement: Debugging is 80 percent complete. Presumably, the programmer expected to find ten bugs, has found eight, and assumes there are only two bugs to go. That is rarely the case. Consider the following statement: ROI analysis of the proposed project is 50 percent complete."

What does it mean? Nothing. In IT/Business projects, rate of progress is not as linear as it is in engineering projects. Partially complete IT/Business deliverables *do not* "earn" any value. Therefore, the *conventional* computations of earned value are very suspect.

Legal (Contractual) Obligations An important milestone in any engineering project is a formal contract between the builder and the owner. A contract clearly defines the scope, budget, schedule, risks, and fiduciary responsibilities of both parties. It is customary for construction project contracts to include a liquidation damages clause that makes the contractor financially responsible to the owner in case of contractor-created delays. Of course, many contracts also include bonus incentives for early completion. In fact, most engineering education programs include a course in contract law. IT/Business education programs typically do not include contract law.

Completion Bond Construction contractors are routinely required to furnish completion bonds as a part of the contracts. In case of nonperformance by a contractor, the owner has the ability to sue the contractor, and the money from the completion bond can then be used to compensate the owner. No such bonds are required of IT/Business vendors or consultants (analysts, designers, coders). In fact, there is no licensing requirement to become an IT/Business contractor. In the case of nonperformance by an IT/Business contractor, few legal avenues are available to the project manager, except in extreme cases where management files lawsuits against vendors. In most cases however, the vendors simply walk away, especially the vendors who supply personnel, because professional nonperformance is almost impossible to prove. Recently, there has been some discussion in the software industry regarding bonding of external development teams. However, all-inclusive bonding of software vendors and contractors is years away.

Go Back Charges   In engineering projects, when the customer requests a change *after* certain predefined milestones have been reached, *go back* charges incur. For example, a construction contractor will invariably levy a go back charge to a customer who requests an additional electrical outlet after electricians have finished the wiring process. Imagine an IT/Business team that is routinely able to bill the business customer go back charges. In the case of engineering projects, there are instances when customer-requested changes cannot be made, even though the customer is willing to pay extra and is ready to accept delayed completion. For instance, adding additional floors to a building after the superstructure has been constructed is simply not practical. In IT/Business projects, customers do not bat an eye before asking the project team to add functionality—even as late as product deployment.

Project Management Tools   This has been the cruelest of all jokes played on IT/Business project managers. Project management consists of five key elements:

1. Planning
2. Estimating
3. Scheduling
4. Tracking
5. Controlling

Until recently, most of the software tools available to IT/Business project managers focused on scheduling. Some of the tools are beginning to add planning and tracking capabilities; however, most are still quite deficient in the areas of estimating and controlling. The problem is that management spends heavily to purchase project management tools and then expects project managers to improve their productivity, which is what the brochures promise. A comprehensive project management software tool should perform the following types of functions:

- *Efficient planning:* This requires access to a comprehensive database of deliverables, tasks, and dependency logic to help the project manager create comprehensive plans.
- *Realistic estimating:* This continues to be the weakest link in most project management software packages and is a big reason why estimates for IT/Business projects continue to be so erroneous. A package should have the ability to compute and adjust estimates based on resource skill levels, work interruptions, number of concurrently assigned projects, and the productivity environment. It should have the ability to use and create a historical database of estimating data. The package should have the ability to incorporate contingency plans and use range values when computing estimates for a project. However, most software packages produce exact (single number) estimates.
- *Viable scheduling:* One of the most important, but consistently missing functions in the majority of software packages, is the ability to create contingency-based schedules. A project manager should be able to include all of the high probability and high impact contingencies in the schedule, and should have the ability to present her sponsor with a number of different schedules, each based on a specific set of contingencies (from none to all).
- *Effective progress tracking:* Project managers need to track the progress of their projects through a set of vital signs and not the percent complete computations so commonly used by construction engineers.

Until recently, most project management software tools were a one-for-one replication of the ways that construction engineers manage their projects. In the recent past, some software package companies have begun changing their processes and algorithms to meet the needs of IT/Business projects. However, the distance between what the brochures promise and what the packages are able to do is still hopelessly wide.

Inspections   In engineering projects, inspections by internal and external inspectors are routine. For IT/Business projects, inspections are a novelty, are seldomly conducted, and are not taken seriously by most project teams. In fact, many IT/Business team members openly oppose inspections and threaten to quit if forced to submit to them in any form. Many do not even welcome walkthroughs of their work in progress. Imagine a construction team that opposes inspections and threatens to quit if their work is examined.

Testing In engineering projects, the actual construction process involves minimal testing—most of the materials and components have been pretested at the point of manufacturing and are warranted. Most of the testing done on-site is actually an inspection—building inspectors primarily make sure that the work is done according to the building code.[20] In IT/Business projects, up to 40 percent of a team's effort can go toward testing because most software development is done from scratch and the acquired vendor software is seldom warranted. This means that IT/Business teams need to learn the specific principles and discipline of robust software testing and then plan, estimate, and schedule extensive testing steps for their projects. Construction engineering teams do not have to spend valuable time on this activity.[21]

> *In examining conventionally scheduled projects, I have found that few allowed one-half of the potential schedule for testing, but that most did indeed spend half of the actual schedule for that purpose.*
>
> Brooks, 1995.

Completing the Job

For IT/Business projects, the word "complete" could be a misnomer. How does one know when a website project or a customer relationship management system is finished? The definition of a complete IT/Business project usually resides somewhere in the customer's subconscious, and is apt to change and evolve regularly. Another issue for IT/Business projects is customer readiness. A perennial question asked of most project teams is, "Is the client ready to use the end-product of the project?" Engineers rarely worry about whether drivers know how to use a new freeway. The project team is not expected to stick around and help drivers navigate. Therefore, two additional burdens that impact project teams are:

1. Documentation for end users/customers
2. Customer training

Documentation for End Users/Customers In construction projects, engineers do not have to spend much effort, time, and energy creating documentation for their end-users/customers. For example, when one purchases a new house, the builder does not give the owner a multitude of thick binders, books, or CDs containing documentation. Only a few booklets prepared by the various appliance manufacturers are left on the counter. The same is true in the case of a new bridge or road; the very nature of these projects dictates that little end-user/customer documentation is needed or produced. Now consider a very small product with embedded software—a cellular phone. A typical cellular phone comes with a 100+ pages of instructions. Most business customers have a hard time comprehending the fact that software projects require extensive documentation that must be produced by highly trained people, must be distributed to a large number of customers, and that it takes a lot of time and money to keep it up-to-date.

Customer Training Construction engineering project teams rarely have responsibility for training their customers in the use of the product they deliver. They have little need to develop skills, tools, techniques, or plans for customer training. For example, when a buyer purchases a house, does the building contractor or real estate agent schedule the owner for training sessions on how to live in the new house? The converse is the case for IT/Business project teams. The need to provide education, training, and ongoing support to customers requires project teams to develop special skills, techniques, tools, and plans. Not only does this add extensive extra time and costs to the project, the skills needed to educate and train a diverse set of customers—executives, managers, line workers,

---

[20]In certain high risk projects, the contractor (or the owner) might set up an on-site test lab to test statistical samples of various materials—steel bars, prestressed concrete beams, pipes, and welding joints.

[21]PMI's PMBOK, the standard source for engineering project managers, does not currently contain any discussion on the subject of testing. Additionally, the index of the publication does not refer to the word "testing" in any form. This is strong proof that engineers spend little time in test activities. Their work revolves more around quality assurance, which gets full attention in the PMBOK. We are certain that, with the passage of time, this and other IT/Business-oriented subject matter will begin to appear in PMBOK. The case is the same for *Documentation for End-Users/Customers* and *Customer Training*.

and field labor—are not easy to develop and require continuous updating. In engineering projects, it is absolutely the customer's responsibility to get ready for the transfer of ownership at the close of escrow. With IT/Business projects, the project team is charged with the task of making sure the customer is ready to receive the end-product, and the team must stick around for weeks to help the customer learn and operate the system. In a typical large IT/Business system, such as ERP or CRM, the startup and ongoing customer training costs can *equal* or *exceed* the cost of the software package.

The long list of differences reflect the reality that managing IT/Business projects successfully requires a vastly *different* set of practices, skills, techniques, and tools than what is practiced by the construction engineering project management profession. In the absence of this realization, IT/Business teams will continue to manage their projects as if they were building bridges, dams, highways, and homes.

> *. . . as long as software engineers act like bridge builders, they are doomed to fail.*
> Scott Berinato, "The Secret to Software Success," *CIO Magazine,*
> (July 1, 2001, http://www.cio.com/archive/070101/secret/html).

Many people who practice engineering project management might question the differences described above and may suggest that the two professions are not that different. Of course, some of the basics of classic engineering project management do apply to IT/Business projects, such as WBS, task networks, and critical path computations. In fact, some people in the engineering profession even suggested that IT/Business project managers should replicate certain engineering project management practices—clearly define the end-state of projects before starting any work, translate customer requirements into detailed specifications, freeze specifications and designs, write legal contracts with internal customers, bill customers for go back charges—to list a few. Those all demonstrate good intentions, but that is not how IT/Business projects get done. The hallmark of a successful IT/Business project team is nimbleness, flexibility, and the ability to quickly adjust to the changing business environment and technology advances. It is important that IT/Business professionals work diligently to appropriately *evolve, change,* and *adapt* the construction engineering-based project management practices, tools, and techniques to the unique needs of IT/Business projects. Though certain basic fundamentals of engineering project management principles and practices *do apply* to IT/Business projects, success will come only to those who are able to understand the key differences between the two professions and then *evolve* their project management principles, practices, techniques, and tools accordingly. Without such a transition, the failure rate of IT/Business projects will stay high, and the massive investment in project management education, training, and tools will *not* pay off. We at the Center have worked diligently over the past decade to study the similarities and differences between the classic engineering and IT/Business project management. We have subsequently developed a project management process specifically aimed at IT/Business-oriented projects—it *retains* the applicable principles and practices of the classic engineering project management and *adds* the principles and practices needed to manage IT/Business projects successfully.

■ THE SUCCESS EQUATION

During one of the periodic meetings of the Center's consultants, someone raised a question, "Is it possible to write an equation for success . . . can it be broken into a set of components which, when practiced together, will result in success of any given endeavor?" An interesting and challenging assignment indeed. After a number of discussions, we put together the following formula for achieving success:

$$
\begin{aligned}
\text{Success} = (((\text{Process} \\
+ \text{Skills} \\
+ \text{Techniques} \\
+ \text{Tools}) \\
*\text{Accountability}) \\
*\text{Discipline})
\end{aligned}
$$

As you can see, the equation consists of a total of six components; notice that the last two are multipliers and have a bigger impact than the first four.

Success: A favorable or satisfactory outcome or result. In the case of project management, success is defined as completing a project on time, within budget, and to the client's satisfaction. Some of the synonyms for success are: achievement, prestige, fame, and prosperity.

Process: A particular method of doing something, generally involving a number of steps or operations, moving forward. In the context of the success equation, *"process"* means a series of actions that result in a predictable outcome.

The implication is that the actions have been tried and tested and have consistently resulted in a desired outcome. An example of a process would be a proven recipe for cooking a dish. Another example of a process would be the requisite steps to assess one's career path opportunities and to apply for the best possible job. In fact, Richard N. Bolles has created a time tested and highly successful process for job hunting and career change in his best selling book, *What Color is Your Parachute?*, published by Ten Speed Press. The Nolo Press, a California-based company, has also published a number of processes that people can use to prepare for subjects such as writing a will, starting a small business, buying or selling a house, managing debt, adopting a child, and dealing with traffic tickets. It should be obvious that if one is to undertake any one of the projects, having access to a well defined and proven process will significantly augment successful completion of the project. Teams responsible for IT/Business projects must follow a well defined and robust project management process specifically designed for IT/Business projects.

Skills: Proficiency, facility, or dexterity that is acquired or developed through training or experience.

To be successful in any endeavor, one must develop certain skills. A project manager needs to be skilled in areas such as assessing and managing project risk, assessing project complexity, coaching, mentoring, filtering half baked ideas, identifying project stakeholders, leading the team, leveraging the good will of project champions, managing expectations, planning, estimating, scheduling, and tracking project progress. This is only a partial list. These skills can be sorted into two categories: hard skills and soft skills; a successful project manager needs to develop both types of skills.

Techniques: Skillfulness in the command of fundamentals deriving from practice and familiarity; the degree of expertness.

To us, the word implies the expression of personal excellence in a given skill. For example: the ability to chop fast without looking at the item being chopped or cutting one's finger; the ability to flip or toss the contents of a frying pan with a twist of the wrist; or the ability of a speaker to put the audience at ease and develop quick rapport through the use of appropriate humor. We all know of colleagues who are highly successful in selling their ideas and can build consensus quickly, even when faced with a disparate group of people. Successful techniques are a result of practicing one's skills with a desire for excellence, and eventually they set people apart from their less capable colleagues.

Tools: A device used to perform or facilitate manual or mechanical work; a labor saving device.

Notice that, in the equation for success, tools are assigned the fourth position—the last item in the additive list. The placement indicates that tools are only helpful after there is a robust process in place; the team members have the requisite skills, and have developed certain high performance techniques for completing their work. As discussed earlier, tools act as catalysts to a process. They can make the process go faster, make it easier to complete, and help attain greater speed and precision. Giving tools to people who lack the fundamental skills is a waste of the investment in the tools. Also, equipping uneducated people with technology actually results in monetary losses. Our advice to people overly enamored with tools is: If you're going in the wrong direction, hopefully you are going slow.

Accountability: This is the first of two *multipliers*—it amplifies the computed value of the equation. It means able to be trusted or depended upon; ability to act without guidance or superior authority; reliable.

To a project manager, accountability means that the team members understand their responsibilities and will work toward achieving the project objectives. Accountability also means that the team members will be forthright in reporting their work status, and when problems occur, they will not resort to finger pointing. This important point is well supported in the following advice:

> *Finger-pointing might be the single greatest cause of sabotaged IT projects. Sutula says that despite due diligence and the most fastidious planning, something unexpected will happen to every major IT undertaking. 'You can't let that destroy teamwork,' Sutula says. 'You have to create an atmosphere where people rapidly admit mistakes, take responsibility, and then you allocate the resources necessary to fix the problem.'*
>
> Gary Sutula, Senior Vice President and CIO of R. R. Donnelley & Sons Co.,
> quoted by Derek Slater. "Faster, Cheaper, and Under Control," *CIO Magazine*
> (August 1, 2000, p.111).

Discipline: Perhaps the most important component of the success equation, defined as: training that develops self-control, character, orderliness and efficiency. Some synonyms for discipline are: train, educate, instruct.

To us, discipline also means order, predictability, and the absence of chaos—team members will attend to their responsibilities in a proactive manner and they can rely on each other for timely completion of assignments. In the context of this equation, *discipline* does not mean regimentation.

As a project manager, a prudent approach is to get together with your team at the start of a project and discuss the different components of the success equation. This session should provide you with a sense of the opportunities and challenges that you and the team will face while working to complete the project. For a project that lasts more than a few months, we recommend that you revisit the success equation at three to four month intervals and make sure that there are not too many obstacles to success.

■ PROJECT PROCESS ARCHITECTURE (PPA)

The success equation reinforces the conviction that having a well defined process is a foundation for success for any endeavor. With this thought as a guiding principle, the Center developed a robust project management process, called the Project Process Architecture (PPA). The objective of the PPA (see Figure 1.11) is to enable project managers to move through the project life cycle at an accelerated pace, without sacrificing the key steps necessary to produce high quality products. The model has evolved to its present stage through extensive use by clients in industries including information technology, banking, manufacturing, engineering, finance, health care, apparel, communications, and insurance.

Figure 1.11 illustrates that the PPA consists of six stages and thirty-three steps. The PPA is designed to be scaleable. The project manager, consults with the project team to choose the appropriate number of steps to fit the size, complexity, and importance of each individual project. Additionally, the effort and time spent on any given step is in proportion with the complexity and size of the project. This scaling process ensures that the degree of effort in a project stays in proportion to its complexity and risk, while the fundamental discipline of the PPA is maintained and followed. The six stages of the PPA are:

1. Idea stage
2. Prelaunch stage
3. Launch stage
4. Execute stage
5. Implement stage
6. Operation stage

FIGURE 1.11
PPA.

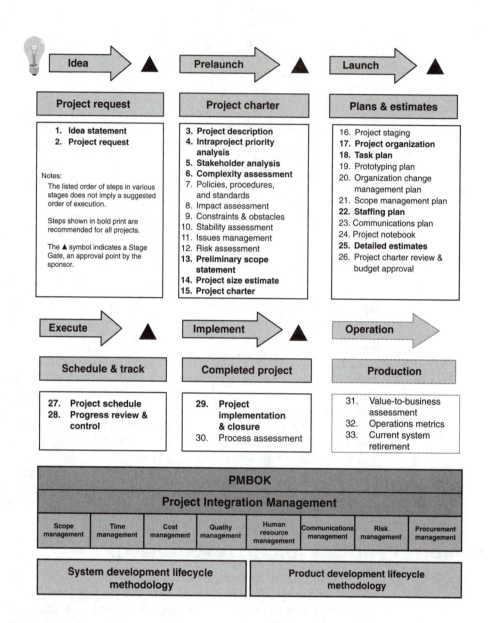

The Idea Stage

This stage consists of two steps, focuses on assessing project ideas for their integrity, and results in a well thought out project request.

Prelaunch Stage

This stage consists of *up to* thirteen steps and focuses on analyzing the project request to help determine whether it should be pursued in terms of its scope, risk, and expected cost. The hallmark of the prelaunch stage is *due diligence*. The end product is a proposed project charter for review and approval by the project sponsor.

Launch Stage

This stage consists of *up to* eleven steps and focuses on developing a comprehensive plan and a detailed estimate for the proposal project. During this stage, the tactics to complete the project are laid out, the project organization is designed, and communication plans are created. Detailed estimates are compared to the high level estimates created in the prelaunch stage and final decisions are made on the project scope and budget.

Execute Stage

Although this stage has only two steps (see Figure 1.11), between 60 and 70 percent of the project team's time is spent in this stage because of the extent of the work to be accomplished: a project schedule is developed, the team begins to work to produce project deliverables, and the project manager oversees the team's progress to the planned end of the project.

Implement Stage

This stage has two steps. The project team begins to transfer the developed product to its customers and to the operations group, and begins to close the project down. An optional step is to assess the steps, procedures, and techniques used to develop the end product. This assessment helps the team focus on any areas of weakness that need to be improved to ensure a more effective and efficient project management process. If the project is successful (or if it is not), all involved will know at this stage: "the proof is in the pudding."

Operation Stage

This stage has three steps. At this point, the project's end product goes into full operation as the development team turns over the reigns of the project to the operations department. The operations group, in concert with the project customer group, begins to gather metrics to assess the accomplishment of the value-to-business and operational performance. The former helps evaluate the degree to which the deployed project is meeting its value-to-business objectives and the latter helps the operations group fine tune the system's performance.

■ STAGE GATE REVIEWS

A stage gate follows each stage of the PPA, as shown in Figure 1.11. At each stage gate, there is a Go/No Go decision. The decision could be Go (proceed to the next stage), or No Go (team to revisit the work done, improve the appropriate area, and seek approval again, or the project may be suspended or canceled). At each stage gate, the sponsor diligently reviews the materials submitted by the project manager. The sponsor and the project manager look ahead and ascertain whether the path to the next stage is clear of obstacles and whether the necessary project infrastructure is in place. This is akin to the process used by the FAA and commercial airline pilots to allow an airplane to take off. The pilot not only has to make sure that all is well with the airplane, but also that it is safe to fly through to the planned destination. During a stage gate review, the sponsor may ask the project manager for further explanations regarding certain components of the already completed work, or may even seek a second opinion from a subject matter expert (SME), perhaps someone from the project office (if one exists). Each stage gate review is a three-step process:

1. The sponsor makes a decision to open the stage gate and lets the team proceed to the next stage. Or,
2. The sponsor directs the project manager and the team to rework certain deficient areas to bring them up to the needed level of quality, and when satisfied with the rework, allows the team to proceed to the next stage. Or,
3. The sponsor decides to initiate the project suspension or cancellation process:

   • After the idea stage, a decision may be made *not* to go ahead with the project request because it does not live up to the necessary approval criteria, such as strategy alignment and value-to-business criteria.
   • After the prelaunch stage, a project charter could be rejected because of high risks and low value-to-business.
   • After the launch stage, the project may be rejected for any number of reasons, such as no appropriate sponsors, an underskilled and inexperienced project manager and/or team, a lack of

appropriate customer buyin, a change in organization strategy, or higher than expected cost estimates.

- During the execute stage, if a project breaches its shutdown conditions, it will become a candidate for review and a Go/No Go decision will be made.
- During the implement stage, if a project breaches its shutdown conditions, it will become a candidate for review and a Go/No Go decision will be made.

This process of progressively assessing a project for its ability to continue may be new to many sponsors, stakeholders, customers, project managers, and teams, but must be put in place to avoid letting massive numbers of troubled projects continue ad nauseam. In too many cases, once an idea is announced, it immediately becomes a project and the first point at which a Go/No Go decision is looked at may be quite late in the project life cycle. This is a key reason for too many half baked ideas continuing as projects for too long. If disciplined and progressive stage gate reviews become part of the routine, the number of challenged and failed projects will decrease considerably, saving IT/Business departments millions of dollars each year.

Tailoring the PPA

The PPA is designed to be scaled to fit the size and complexity of a given project. Complex projects will require more of the steps, as well as more rigor, while simpler projects will do well with fewer steps and less rigor. As you begin to work on the steps in the prelaunch stage in Chapter 4, and have completed the step to assess the project complexity (step 6), you will have the first clue about the extent of tailoring appropriate for the project at hand. The more complex the project, the more steps you will need to include in your plan. For example, if a given project is of low complexity, then most of the optional steps can be omitted. In Figure 1.11, you can see that in each stage, certain steps (shown in bold print) are recommended for all projects; others are optional. This allows the project manager to incorporate only those steps that specifically add value to the project. Additional scaling is accomplished by managing the amount of effort devoted to complete any given step. In the case of smaller and less complex projects, the effort to complete a given step is scaled down to match the project's needs. Keep in mind that none of the thirty-three steps shown in Figure 1.11 are for administrative purposes; each step serves a specific purpose toward successful management of a project. Figure 1.12 shows suggestions for how to tailor the list of steps to use in a given project. Keep in mind that this is not a *rule*. It is a *suggestion* based on experience with a large number of projects. You should err on the side of including a step, rather than dropping steps because you think that will save you time. In Figure 1.12, notice that the number of steps in the two right-hand columns is similar (the letter "R" in the four columns of Figure 1.12 stands for *recommended step*). The main difference is that for zone I projects[22] one would spend extra time in each step because of the inherent complexity of these projects. You should use the suggested list for a few of your projects, and then use your experience to develop a list tailored for your project needs.

In certain situations, an organization will need to add specific steps to the PPA to meet the needs of its project management process. For example, a pharmaceutical firm may need to add steps prescribed by the Food and Drug Administration (FDA), or a financial investment company may need to add steps to comply with the rules and regulations specified by the U.S. Securities and Exchange Commission (SEC). In such cases, we suggest that management convene a group of subject matter experts and have them jointly define the extra steps that need to be added to the PPA.

In the absence of a uniform project management methodology like the PPA, different project management groups within the same organization invariably end up using different processes, vocabulary, tools, and templates. It is not uncommon that the same customer, working with different project managers, may have to deal with completely disparate project management methodologies. The PPA is designed to introduce a uniform project management methodology and vocabulary to the entire organization to help bring transparency to the project management process. The result is more efficient communications and more successful projects.

---

[22]Project complexity zones are discussed in Chapter 4, see *Project Complexity Assessment.*

PPA step	Zone IV	Low zone II & Low zone III	High zone II & High zone III	Zone I
	Simple projects	Average projects	Complex projects	Very complex projects
1. Idea statement	R	R	R	R
2. Project request	R	R	R	R
3. Project description	R	R	R	R
4. Intra-project priority analysis	R	R	R	R
5. Stakeholder analysis	R	R	R	R
6. Complexity assessment	R	R	R	R
7. Policies, procedures, and standards			R	R
8. Impact assessment		R	R	R
9. Constraints and obstacles		R	R	R
10. Stability assessment			R	R
11. Issues management		R	R	R
12. Risk assessment			R	R
13. Preliminary scope statement	R	R	R	R
14. Project size estimate	R	R	R	R
15. Project charter	R	R	R	R
16. Project staging			R	R
17. Project organization	R	R	R	R
18. Task plan	R	R	R	R
19. Prototyping plan			R	R
20. Organization change management plan			R	R
21. Scope management plan		R	R	R
22. Staffing plan	R	R	R	R
23. Communications plan			R	R
24. Project notebook			R	R
25. Detailed estimates	R	R	R	R
26. Project charter review and budget approval			R	R
27. Project schedule	R	R	R	R
28. Progress review and control	R	R	R	R
29. Project implementation and closure	R	R	R	R
30. Process assessment				R
31. Value-to-business assessment		R	R	R
32. Operations metrics				R
33. Current system retirement		R	R	R

FIGURE 1.12
PPA tailoring recommendations.

■ MAPPING THE PPA TO PMBOK

The PMBOK is a collection of project management material provided by the PMI, a nonprofit, international project management organization. The PMBOK consists of nine knowledge areas:

1. Project integration management
2. Project scope management
3. Project time management
4. Project cost management
5. Project quality management
6. Project human resource management
7. Project communications management
8. Project risk management
9. Project procurement management

The first area, project integration management, is the overarching function that impacts, and is impacted by, the other eight knowledge areas. The next four are often referred to as the *core knowledge areas* because they lead to the achievement of specific project objectives. The last four are referred to as *facilitating functions* as these are the means through which project objectives are achieved. Figure 1.11 depicts the six stages of the PPA and its relationship to the PMBOK. As you can see, the PPA is a specifically designed project management *methodology* for IT/Business projects. The work accomplished in the various steps of the project management methodology needs to be supported by a comprehensive *knowledge base*. The PMBOK is an example of such a knowledge base.

The purpose of any body of knowledge is to provide a standard reference for the key principles and practices of the associated profession. The typical organization of a body of knowledge document revolves around *what* needs to be done, with minimal attention given to *why* and *when*. For example, the following is a much-used organization structure for cookbooks:

- Appetizers
- Soups
- Eggs
- Fish and shellfish
- Poultry
- Meat
- Vegetables
- Salads
- Desserts

Others may use a different structure:

- Breakfast
- Desserts
- Dinner
- Hors d'oeuvres
- Lunch
- Sauces
- Soups

Few cookbooks actually teach the reader the step-by-step *process* of planning family dinners: deciding what to cook, the likes and dislikes of various family members, analyzing the nutritional needs of the family and the nutritional contents of the meals, and the sequence in which various dishes need to be prepared. They do not address the reality that one does not always prepare the appetizers first and the desserts last. Similarly, an auto mechanic's manual does not teach a mechanic the principles, practices, and techniques for operating a successful repair shop. In fact, any body of knowledge, by its design, expects the reader to be well informed about the fundamental practices, skills, and techniques of the profession, which explains why most knowledge base documents are organized in cohesive segments (often alphabetically). For example, project scope management is discussed in one chapter of the PMBOK. However, in the life cycle of a given project, the subject of scope needs to be addressed a number of different times—initial scope definition, preliminary scope definition, scope approval, scope planning, scope development, scope change control, and scope verification. Hence, the subject of scope is addressed in Chapters 3, 4, 5, 6, 7, 8, and 9 of this book. The table in Figure 1.13 outlines the mapping of the various segments of the PMBOK to the PPA.

This difference in the structure of a knowledge base is not a *weakness* of the PMBOK, it is a *difference* between it and the PPA, a thirty-three-step process that delineates the order in which projects need to be taken from the idea stage to the operations stage in an effective and efficient manner. The materials presented in this book will provide you with practical knowledge for implementing successful project management principles and practices, knowledge that you can begin to use immediately.

If your organization subscribes to PMBOK, you should become familiar with this body of knowledge and keep a copy of the *Guide to the PMBOK* on hand as a reference as you progress through this book. Many organizations have their own customized project management knowledge base; if that is the situation in your organization, you should take the time to become familiar with the customized knowledge base.

PMBOK knowledge area segments	PMBOK component processes	PPA coverage
Project integration management	• Project plan development • Project plan execution • Integrated change control	Covered in Chapters 5, 6, 7, and 8.
Project scope management	• Initiation • Scope planning • Scope definition • Scope verification • Scope change control	Covered in Chapters 3, 4, 5, 6, 7, 8, and 9.
Project time management	• Activity definition • Activity sequencing • Activity duration estimating • Schedule development • Schedule control	Covered in Chapters 5, 6, 7, and 8.
Project cost management	• Resource planning • Cost estimating • Cost budgeting • Cost control	Covered in Chapters 4, 5, 6, and 7.
Project quality management	• Quality planning • Quality assurance • Quality control	Covered in Chapters 4, 5, 7, and 8.
Project human resource management	• Organizational planning • Staff acquisition • Team development	Covered in Chapter 5.
Project communications management	• Communications planning • Information distribution • Performance reporting • Administrative closure	Covered in Chapters 5, 7, and 8.
Project risk management	• Risk management planning • Risk identification • Qualitative risk analysis • Quantitative risk analysis • Risk response planning • Risk monitoring and control	Covered in Chapters 4, 5, 6, 7, and 8.
Project procurement management	• Procurement planning • Solicitation planning • Solicitation • Source selection • Contract administration • Contract closeout	Covered in Appendix 1.

PMBOK Process Groups

PMBOK organizes the project management activities into five distinct process groups. Brief descriptions of these process groups, as well as their relationships to the structure of the PPA, follow.

1. *Initiating processes:* A project starts and management makes the necessary commitments to the project. Within the PPA, project initiation encompasses two stages: The Idea and Prelaunch stages. The Idea stage focuses on assessing the variety of visions or ideas put forth by various sources for viability, with the express purpose of filtering out any half baked ideas. In the prelaunch stage, viable ideas are further scrubbed through due diligence and the end result is a comprehensive project charter.

2. *Planning processes:* This process group entails the development and maintenance of detailed plans to complete the project. This includes the plans to define the scope, to do the work to produce various deliverables, to compute estimates of effort and cost, to develop schedules, and to manage any changes to the project scope. Within the PPA, these activities are primarily conducted during the Launch stage.

3. *Executing processes:* This process group encompasses the coordination of various resources (people, facilities, and technology) to actually work the plans and to produce the planned project deliverables. Within the PPA, this work is primarily accomplished in the Execute stage.

4. *Controlling processes:* This process group includes the steps to ensure that the project is progressing smoothly. The project manager oversees the team and monitors the progress against the project plans. In the case of any variances, the project manager institutes appropriate recovery procedures. Within the PPA, this work is accomplished in the Execute stage.

5. *Closing processes:* This process group incorporates the steps for the formal acceptance of the project by the customer group and for an orderly close of the project: archiving the necessary documents, documenting lessons learned (process assessment), and dissolving the project team. Within the PPA, this work is accomplished in the Implement stage.

It is interesting to point out that PMBOK does not include the processes related to operations. The reason for the omission is that the project is technically over—the team has delivered the end product to the customer and now moves on to other projects or activities. However, in the case of IT/Business projects, the core project team must stay behind until the operations group has successfully put the project into operations. This overlap may last anywhere from a few days to a few weeks. That is why the Operation stage lies within the PPA structure, even though a different group is ultimately responsible for the day-to-day operations of the project. This text covers all nine areas of the PMBOK in varying degrees of detail. The Center is an official PMI Global Registered Education Provider.

■ MAPPING THE PPA TO COMPTIA IT PROJECT+

The Computing Technology Industry Association (CompTIA), a global, nonprofit association, serves the IT industry as the world's largest developer of vendor-neutral, industry-defined IT certification exams and certifications. IT Project+ certification is an industry-recognized credential that acknowledges competency and professionalism in project management, including the necessary business knowledge, interpersonal skills, and project management processes required to successfully manage IT/Business projects.

The IT Project+ certification examination covers four domains, which each have a number of objectives. Figures 1.14, 1.15, 1.16, and 1.17 list the four domains, their respective objectives, and the chapters in the book where the objectives are covered. Because some of the objectives have quite lengthy descriptions, we have listed their ID numbers only. For a detailed list of objectives, refer to the *CompTIA IT Project+ Certification Preparation Guide,* a supplement to this book. Information regarding IT Project+ certification is also available on the Web: http://www.comptia.org/certification/itproject/default.asp.

FIGURE 1.14
CompTIA Domain 1.0
objectives.

Domain 1.0: IT project initiation and scope definition	Book chapters
Objective 1.1	1, 3, 4, Appendix 1
Objective 1.2	3, 4
Objective 1.3	4, 5
Objective 1.4	4, 5
Objective 1.5	3, 4
Objective 1.6	3, 4
Objective 1.7	4
Objective 1.8	4, 5
Objective 1.9	4, 5, Appendix 1
Objective 1.10	4
Objective 1.11	4, 5, 6
Objective 1.12	5, 6
Objective 1.13	1, 3, 4
Objective 1.14	4, 5
Objective 1.15	5

FIGURE 1.15
CompTIA Domain 2.0
objectives.

Domain 2.0 IT project planning	Book chapters
Objective 2.1	1, 5
Objective 2.2	5
Objective 2.3	4, 6
Objective 2.4	5
Objective 2.5	5, 7
Objective 2.6	4, 5
Objective 2.7	4, 5
Objective 2.8	4, 5
Objective 2.9	2, 5
Objective 2.10	2, 5
Objective 2.11	5
Objective 2.12	2, 5
Objective 2.13	2, 5
Objective 2.14	6
Objective 2.15	6, 7
Objective 2.16	2, 4, 6
Objective 2.17	5, 6, 7
Objective 2.18	6, 7
Objective 2.19	5
Objective 2.20	6, 7
Objective 2.21	6
Objective 2.22	5
Objective 2.23	5
Objective 2.24	4, 5, 6, 7
Objective 2.25	5
Objective 2.26	5
Objective 2.27	5, 6
Objective 2.28	4, 6, 7
Objective 2.29	5
Objective 2.30	3, 4, 7
Objective 2.31	5, 7
Objective 2.32	3, 4, 6, 7, 8

The Center's project management training curriculum has received the CompTIA Approved Quality Curriculum (CAQC) certification. CAQC is a strenuous quality standard established by CompTIA to insure that preparatory curriculum appropriately prepares learners for the IT Project+ certification. This book encompasses the Center's CAQC approved curriculum and is designed to prepare the reader for the IT Project+ certification.

■ MAPPING THE PPA TO SEI'S CMMI[23]

The Center's PPA and the Software Engineering Institute's (SEI's) CMMI[24] have a highly complimentary relationship. The CMMI was developed by the SEI at the Carnegie Mellon University as part of an Air Force funded project. The primary objective of the research work was to define a framework to assess the capabilities of software contractors bidding for work for the Department of Defense (DoD). Early in their assessment of a number of software organizations, the researchers discovered that organizations that had formal, well defined processes produced much

---

[23]The Capability Maturity Model for Software® has recently been incorporated in a broader, integrated framework, the Capability Maturity Model Integration® (CMMI®). The CMMI® also includes systems engineering; integrated product and process development; and supplier sourcing. The conclusions reached in this section are equally valid with regard to the CMMIR framework.

[24]Capability Maturity Model Integration and CMMI® are registered trademarks of the Software Engineering Institute, all rights reserved.

FIGURE 1.16
CompTIA Domain 3.0
objectives.

Domain 3.0 IT project execution, control, and coordination	Book chapters
Objective 3.1	7
Objective 3.2	7
Objective 3.3	7
Objective 3.4	7
Objective 3.5	7
Objective 3.6	7
Objective 3.7	7, Appendix 1
Objective 3.8	5, 7
Objective 3.9	7
Objective 3.10	7
Objective 3.11	7
Objective 3.12	7
Objective 3.13	7
Objective 3.14	7
Objective 3.15	7
Objective 3.16	5, 7
Objective 3.17	5, 7
Objective 3.18	8, 9
Objective 3.19	4, 5, 6, 7
Objective 3.20	5, 7
Objective 3.21	4, 5
Objective 3.22	7
Objective 3.23	7
Objective 3.24	7
Objective 3.25	7
Objective 3.26	7
Objective 3.27	8
Objective 3.28	7
Objective 3.29	7
Objective 3.30	7
Objective 3.31	7
Objective 3.32	4, 7
Objective 3.33	4, 7
Objective 3.34	7
Objective 3.35	4, 7
Objective 3.36	4, 7
Objective 3.37	7
Objective 3.38	7
Objective 3.39	3, 4, 5, 7
Objective 3.40	4, 5

better software than those that had ad hoc processes. The end result of the study was a well defined and well bounded maturity improvement process grouped into five distinct levels:

1. *Initial:* The software organization performs its work in an ad hoc and often chaotic fashion, where most people follow their own processes and have no uniform guidance from the organization.
2. *Repeatable:* The software organization at this level has rigorous project management processes and practices, in place, and the software professionals perform their work in accordance with

FIGURE 1.17
CompTIA Domain 4.0
objectives.

Domain 4.0 project closure, acceptance, and support	Book chapters
Objective 4.1	8
Objective 4.2	8, 9
Objective 4.3	8
Objective 4.4	8
Objective 4.5	8
Objective 4.6	8, Appendix 1

the stated practices. The organization is able to track the cost, schedule, and functionality of its projects.

3. *Defined:* At this level, the principles and best practices of software development and management are fully documented, understood, and practiced by software professionals, who have strong support from management.

4. *Managed:* At this stage, the principles, practices, and processes of software development and management are integrated fully into the day-to-day work practices of software developers. Additionally, quality targets are established for both software processes and products, and quality data is collected consistently and uniformly.

5. *Optimized:* Software organizations at this level are able to devote their efforts to continuous process improvement.

To be able to mature to any one of the levels (past level 1), software practitioners need to change their ad hoc work practices to well defined, formal processes that consistently produce high quality software efficiently. Each of the five levels of CMM has a specific set of key process areas (KPAs) associated with them. The KPAs for level 2 are:

- Requirements management
- Project planning
- Project tracking
- Quality assurance
- Configuration management
- Subcontractor management

A deeper analysis of CMM project planning and project tracking KPAs shows that they include the following key words:

- Plan to perform the work
- Constraints and goals
- Estimates
- Schedule
- Software risks
- Negotiations
- Resource constraints and capabilities
- Progress tracking
- Schedule tracking
- Adjustments of plan
- Dependencies between groups
- Milestone completions
- Tracking critical resources
- Measurement data

PPA incorporates each of these key activities and prepares project managers to perform their work in a consistent manner, based on well documented processes. PPA includes detailed templates that aid the professionals in completing their project management activities. Additionally, the CMM requires a specific set of practices to ensure institutionalization of KPAs. These key practices are:

- Commitment to perform
- Ability to perform
- Measurement and analysis
- Verifying implementation

Commitment to perform: The executive management of the organization clearly and completely comprehends the KPAs, and has specifically set forth a policy statement outlining its commitment to well defined and consistently followed project management practices.

Ability to perform: Project teams have the ability to practice the project management practices put forth by the KPAs.

Measurement and analysis: Project teams use well defined quantitative measures to assess the status of project planning and tracking activities. PPA incorporates specific steps for the project manager to measure and analyze the project status specific vital signs are used to assess the "health" of any project.

Verifying implementation: Routine reviews by peers, quality assurance groups, and managers are conducted to ensure that appropriate activities for each KPA are being followed. The PPA includes specifically designed instruments to help fulfill these requirements. Examples are stage gate reviews at the end of each PPA stage, forty questions the sponsor should ask a project manager, and the postimplementation assessment review list.

From the information presented it is reasonable to conclude that CMM Level 2 (repeatable) requires that the software development group first institute, and then routinely practice, rigorous project management processes to plan and execute their work. PPA is designed to help IT organizations attain Level 2 through Level 5 maturity in an efficient and effective manner.

■ PRODUCT DEVELOPMENT METHODOLOGY

The various steps of the PPA, as listed in Figure 1.11, relate to the work needed to *manage* any given project. Similarly, a project manager must also be familiar with the steps needed to develop the *end product* of the project, which can be a software package such as human resources system, inventory management system or physical products such as consumer goods. The master collection of steps needed to develop the product is typically referred to as the product development method. Within the IT profession, the two most commonly used terms to refer to product development methodologies are:

- System Development Methodology (SDM)
- System Development Life Cycle (SDLC)

In the case of IT, the product life cycle might consist several phases. Keep in mind that the nomenclature of the phases and the number of phases will vary based on the methodology in use, some common phases include:

- Requirements definition
- Logical design
- Physical design
- Coding and unit testing
- System testing
- Acceptance testing
- Implementation

Each phase consists of a number of deliverables and tasks that progressively build the end product. During the past two decades, as the tools and techniques for creating software have evolved, so have the product development methodologies. The following is a list of the most commonly known IT methodologies:[25]

- Agile
- Joint Application Design (JAD)
- Object Oriented
- Rapid Application Development (RAD)
- Rational Unified Process (RUP)

With the passage of time, as new methods, procedures, techniques, and tools evolve, so will new development methodologies. Product development life cycles are not unique to the IT profession; most other professions also use product development methodologies. For example:

- The collection of steps for an audit group to audit company financials
- The collection of steps used by a CPA to file state and federal taxes for its clients
- The collection of steps used by a pharmaceutical firm to file for FDA approval
- The collection of steps used by a financial company to process loan applications

---

[25]Agile™ is a product of Agile Software Corporation; JAD was developed by Chunk Morris of IBM Raleigh and Tony Crawford of IBM Toronto in the late 1970's; and RUP® (Rational Unified Process®) is a product of IBM® Corporation.

- The collection of steps used by an insurance company to issue life insurance policies
- The collection of steps used by a manufacturing company to produce consumer goods

Within the project management process, the project management methodology (the PPA) sits at a *higher* level as it specifies the steps needed to manage a given *project*. A product development methodology sits one level *below*, and specifies the steps needed to develop a given *product*. Within the PPA, the first reference to a product development methodology is in step 18 (task plan) of the launch stage. The reason for this "late" appearance is that the task plan developed as a result of completing step 18 consists of the specific steps needed to develop the end product of the project. If your organization maintains a comprehensive methodology (for developing IT systems and/or other products), obtain the latest copy and begin to spend some time to become familiar with it contents. This knowledge will be very helpful as you and your team begin to build the task plan for your project in Chapter 5.

Confusion may be caused by product development methodologies, especially IT methodologies, because these methodologies incorporate just a *few* project management steps. This abbreviated approach is often adopted to justify the cost of the methodology, as a site license for a vendor-supplied methodology can cost upwards of $100,000. The results are often less than satisfactory. What actually happens is that the teams using the product development methodology assume (or are made to believe) that it *fully encompasses* both the product development and project development steps. However, in real life, such methodologies lack project management steps. To further complicate matters, many large organizations may be using more than one product development methodology, each supplied by a different vendor and each containing a different number of project development steps that have differing nomenclature. The result is confusion among the team members.

The two methodologies—project management and product development—need to be kept *separate*. This way, as new product development methodologies emerge, and the existing methodologies evolve, they do not impact the project management methodology. In addition, separation will allow the enterprise to have a uniform project development methodology while allowing various groups to have their own product development methodologies.

As mentioned earlier, the market hosts a plethora of system development life cycle methodologies, e.g., Agile, JAD, Object Oriented, RAD, and RUP. None of these methodologies will be discussed in this book. However, as a project manager, you and your team must become familiar with the life cycle methodology to be used for developing the detailed task list for your project. You should contact the appropriate group in your organization, responsible for maintaining the methodology, and ask them to educate and train your team in its use.

As you proceed through this book, the following question is sure to come to your mind: "What impact will the use of the PPA have on the time needed to complete a project?" The answer can be summarized as follows:

1. For the first project in which a team begins to use the appropriately tailored steps of the PPA, the typical impact is about a 15 to 20 percent increase in the effort to complete the project work—deliverables and tasks. This increase in effort does not result in an equal increase in the project duration because not every task lies on the critical path. The increase in the project duration hovers around 10 percent.
2. For a project assigned to a group of people who understand the PPA process well and have used it in at least one project, the learning curve for the use of the PPA flattens out, resulting in no measurable increase in effort or duration. However, there is a marked and measurable increase in both the quality of the team's work products and the quality of communications—with the key project stakeholders and within the team.
3. For projects undertaken by a team well versed in the use of the PPA, there is typically a reduction of 10 to 15 percent in the total project effort, usually resulting in about a 10 percent reduction in project duration (schedule).

■ CELEBRATING PROJECT SUCCESS

It is always interesting to watch the gusto with which the entertainment industry celebrates itself with numerous awards for almost every facet of their industry. Why do we rarely hear about project teams holding award ceremonies to celebrate project success?

Within the corporate culture, most celebrations are held by sales and marketing groups, with occasional celebrations by the manufacturing wing—typically at the launch of a new product. Sales groups reward themselves by organizing outings, often at well-appointed resort hotels, where a good time is had by all. People get energized and they are ready to face the next tough situation with vigor. Given the fact that successful IT/Business projects are so rare, one would assume each would be celebrated. We believe the main reason for the this lack of celebration is that most project teams (composed primarily of technical people) do not feel the need for public recognition. To them, the work is the reward, which is very shortsighted. It is extremely important that project managers begin celebrating project successes with an eye for public recognition. We all agree, that everyone loves a winner, so plan a few victory celebrations to provide tangible proof of the project's importance and value to the team and key stakeholders. We suggest the following:

- Project managers must work with their sponsors to define a project celebration budget as a part of the project's budget, and then develop a project celebration plan. Astute project managers create a "goody bag," from which they can dispense rewards to project team members at appropriate times.
- High fives among the team members when someone has gone the extra step or overcome difficult obstacles.
- Key milestone celebrations after successful stage gate reviews. It is always a good idea to involve the key stakeholders. These include both individual and team recognitions and rewards. There are dozens of ways of doing this without having to spend too much money or time.
- A well orchestrated celebration at the successful completion of the project—the sponsor and the project manager need to work with the key customers to have *them* organize such events. Most events should include the team's family members so that they also know that their support is appreciated.

Such rewards and appreciation gestures should come not only from project managers; sponsors and customers must also take the initiative to express their thanks and appreciations.

■ IT'S THE OTHER LEG, STUPID[26]

At this point, we need to take a brief look at the important subject of the general work culture and work environment of your organization, and see if there are any major problems that need to be addressed. We will use a hospital as our model, where "unprofessional" attitudes and behaviors of the staff lead to major problems for a patient.

Imagine the scenario of a patient in the operating room being prepared for surgery. In this scenario, the patient tries to tell the attendant who wheeled her to the operating room, and then the surgeon, that she doesn't need any surgery. Both ignore her. Next, the patient is administered anesthesia and the surgeon inserts a tube, that extends to her heart, into the patient's leg. The surgeon then reads a chart to refresh his thoughts and stops. He whispers something to the anesthetist. She reads the chart and mumbles something under her breath (remember, physicians are taught not to say oops loudly, especially in the presence of their patients and when the recorders are on). They quickly discover that they have the wrong person on the table. This patient was lucky, because many times these discoveries are made in the postoperative recovery rooms (by the patients' relatives). How could this have happened? Everybody is highly trained and hospitals have rigorous procedures (one would hope).

Some Facts

The scenario above is our read of an actual case reported in the *Annals of Internal Medicine*.[27] Consider some disturbing facts:

- The patient was actually scheduled for discharge from the hospital that day. The staff on duty, who were responsible for the patient's well being, did not question the move of the patient to the operating room.

---

[26]The title is taken from stories about surgeons mistakenly amputating the patient's healthy leg because of reading the X-ray incorrectly, wrong orientation of the patient in the operating room, nurses mistakenly preparing the wrong limb, and everybody completely ignoring the protests of the patients. We could also cite instances where the operation is performed on the wrong patient.

[27]Chassin, Mark R., MD and Elise C. Becher, MD. The Wrong Patient. *The Annals of Internal Medicine* 136:11. June, 2000.

- A key staff member failed to recognize the significance of the patient's objection to undergoing the procedure.
- A key piece of information, an executed consent form, was missing from the patient's file, as the staff did not deem it necessary because they considered the procedure routine.
- Three different nurses and the attending physician failed to verify the patient's identity.

The authors of the article provide an in-depth assessment of the series of mistakes, a total of seventeen, that led to the problem. They then follow up with insightful suggestions on remedying such problems. Here are a few extracts from their article:

> *. . . truly involving the patient in the decision making process is not a top priority*
>
> *. . . discrete errors occurred in at least 17 different places*
>
> *The most important latent conditions in this case included failures of communications, teamwork, and identity verification.*
>
> *Physicians failed to communicate with nurses, attendings failed to communicate with residents and fellows, staff from one unit failed to communicate with those from others, and no one listened carefully to the patient*
>
> *A low "culture of expectations" developed, in which participants came to expect a norm of faulty and incomplete exchange of information.*
>
> *The culture of low expectations led each of them to conclude that these red flags signified not unusual, worrisome harbingers but rather mundane repetitions of the poor communication to which they had become inured.*

The Problem

Simply stated, they didn't really care. It happens when people become so absorbed in their own beliefs that they begin to see the customer with a certain disdain and as a source of irritation. Have you ever come across analysts, designers, coders, technical writers, and customer support representatives who find ways to belittle the customers for the inquiries that they (the professionals) deem to be very simple? Another pervasive problem is the belief of so many professionals that they are simply too experienced and too senior to have to bother with proven procedures. Many of them begin to take seriously such inane pronouncements as "just do it" and "extreme project management" in the false hope for high productivity and speedy project completion—the Ephedra of project management. There is also the culture in many organizations of not questioning the senior people, because how could they be wrong? In Chapter 5, we will discuss the intelligent disobedience trait taught to guide dogs to protect their owners from making life threatening mistakes. We suggest that you review that material and discuss it with your sponsor, the key stakeholders, and then your team. It could save the organization a great deal of pain. You could use the following questions to assess your organization's work environment:

1. Is there a pervasive culture of staff members deferring to their seniors—functional managers, sponsors, and executives—for the fear of being labeled as naysayers?
2. Do project team members, especially from technology departments, look down upon their business customers? These superior beings are known to assume that customers never know what they want, or don't understand the power of technology.
3. Do sponsors, functional managers, and customers have the habit of devaluing processes in the face of tight deadlines?
4. Do issues stay unresolved beyond their must resolve by dates?
5. Is active listening and aggressive communications de rigueur in your organization?

By now, it should be obvious what a "Yes" answer to any one of the first four and a "No" answer to the last question means that the project has a high risk for failure. It is vital that you, as the project manager, take some time to assess the overall environment of the project you are about to lead. It would greatly help the cause of good project management to discuss these subjects with your functional manager, the sponsor, and the team as a part of the Project Staging step (Chapter 5) and then occasionally during the project life cycle.

■ ORGANIZATIONAL DISCIPLINE AND INDIVIDUAL SKILLS

Before this chapter ends, we must discuss the importance of organizational discipline *v.* individual project management skills, as they apply to project success. Any organization that expects to manage its projects successfully over an extended period of time must use certain disciplines that encourage and support formal project management. Establishing these disciplines often requires changes in corporate culture, and can only be accomplished when there is sustained commitment from high level management to do so. Processes such as those used to approve new projects or review those in progress are often the mechanisms by which disciplines are maintained. Individual project management skills, in contrast with project management disciplines, can be developed relatively easily through classroom education, on-the-job training, and mentoring. Of course, the level and longevity of skills achieved depends on individual aptitude and the quality of training, but most importantly, it depends on the continuing use of the learned skills and the desire for continuous improvement. Where there are no incentives to use the materials learned, skills and individual motivations erode quickly. Although every organization is unique in its requirements for project management, certain disciplines and skills are fundamental to its ability to complete projects successfully. The characteristics of these two important attributes are summarized in the following lists.

Organizational Discipline

Organizational discipline includes the following:

- The organization will have an enterprise-wide, well designed project management methodology in place, that is strongly supported by management and uniformly followed by project teams.
- All projects have appropriate level, highly committed sponsors.
- Project managers are assigned to projects based on a match between project complexity and the project manager's skills—not mere availability.
- Functional managers understand and respect project managers' authority to manage project resources—people, time, money, and materials.
- Roles and responsibilities for the direction and management of projects are clearly defined and well understood by all involved parties.
- Project managers are expected to develop comprehensive plans and viable schedules and to keep them up-to-date. The specific techniques to be used on any given project are expected to be consistent with its nature, size, and complexity.
- The process of assigning individuals to projects is rational, and the resulting assignments are reasonably stable.
- Project status is systematically, consistently, and forthrightly reported.
- Common terminology is in use for communicating within teams, between projects, with other units of the organization, and with external parties.
- Project costs and schedule data of an appropriate granularity and accuracy is routinely available to project sponsors on a timely basis.

Individual Project Management Skills

Individual project management skills include the following:

- Realistically assess project size, complexity, and risk.
- Plan, estimate, schedule, and track projects.
- Organize, staff, and manage project teams.
- Communicate aggressively and forthrightly with superiors, peers, subordinates, and customers.
- Resolve conflicts related to project scope, staffing, and status.
- Build strong customer relationships.

Of course, the perennial question is: which comes first, the discipline or the skills?[28] Having the disciplines in place before embarking on the development of individual skills creates more opportunities to apply newly acquired skills in planning and managing projects as well as the day-to-day work. In

---

[28]This reminds us of the question, "Which came first, the polka or the accordion?" Note: One of the reviewers stated that copious amounts of beer came first.

situations where disciplines are not in place, individuals become frustrated and revert to their old "this is the best we can do" habits. The bottom line can be summarized as follows: While project managers and team members may acquire basic project management skills with relative ease, their collective ability to manage projects effectively will depend largely on their employer's success in establishing enterprise-wide project management disciplines.

Though individual readers of this book may not have the ability to direct organizational management to own up to their responsibilities for engendering the necessary project management discipline, you and your colleagues should work hard to make management, especially your project sponsors, aware of the need for organizational discipline and the role it so clearly plays in the successful management of projects.

■ THE MOCKING POST

Project managers often say: "I don't really have enough authority to make people do what is necessary. It is the sponsors, functional managers, stakeholders, and vendors who sidestep well defined processes and mess things up. Can you suggest an apt punishment for these people?" Some of you may have similar concerns as well. We have given considerable thought to this pervasive dilemma and have a suggestion—a mocking post.

A mocking post is a befitting solution to unprofessional behavior and is lots of fun at lunchtime, especially during "Bring your kids to work" day. A few caveats:

1. The mocking post should use Velcro straps instead of buckles and yokes (more modern and humane).[29]
2. Instead of rotten fruit, have the project charter document available where people can tear out a few of the pages, wad them into balls, and throw them at the "mockee."
3. Have a list of examples available for those who need help coming up with good mocks.
4. The best mocker, selected by the mockee, gets a prize (immunity from being mocked for a future offence—once only).
5. No pictures allowed, unless someone chooses to use a hidden camera.

Keep in mind that the mocking post is not solely for sponsors who misbehave. In fact, vendors, consultants, project managers, and project team members can all be strapped to the post, depending on their professional misbehavior.

■ SUMMARY

The following is a list of the key subject areas covered in this chapter. Review the list and assess your level of comprehension of each topic. The best approach is to take a separate sheet of paper and write a short narrative to explain your knowledge of the topic and then go back and compare your summaries with the material covered in the chapter. Another approach is to find a colleague who is also interested in these topics and discuss your understanding of the topics with him or her, and then jointly review the chapter materials to assess your degree of understanding.

- Reasons for project management;
- Definition of *project*;
- Project *v.* operations;
- Roles of schedule, scope, budget, and quality;
- Definition of *project management*;
- Differences between a project and a process;
- The state of project management;
- Extreme project failures;
- The "seven deadly sins" of project management;
- Reasons why your project management investment may never pay off;
- The success equation;
- Project management methodology;

---

[29]We believe this will also preclude any interventions by ACLU and Corporate Amnesty International (CAI).

- Project Process Architecture (PPA);
- Stage gate reviews;
- Mapping PPA to PMBOK;
- Mapping PPA to CompTIA IT Project+;
- Understand SEI's Capability Maturity Model;
- Product development methodology;
- Celebrating project success; and
- The mocking post.

■ QUESTIONS AND DISCUSSION POINTS*

Given below are a number of questions and discussion points to jog your memory and to assess the degree of your comprehension of the concepts and techniques outlined in all chapters (the order of the questions does not always reflect the order of the materials in the chapters). To make the best use of the questions and discussion points, we suggest that you create a file (preferably electronic) to record your responses and maintain this file as you continue your journey through the book. You may find that occasionally you will choose to go back and update your responses as you develop more in-depth knowledge of the subject matter. We also advise that you get together with one or more of your fellow project managers and start a discussion group to jointly explore the subject matter and help each other through group discussion and mutual knowledge contribution.

1. What is a project?
2. What are the four key components of a project?
3. Keeping your business environment in mind, list three projects.
4. Keeping your personal environment in mind, list three projects.
5. How does a project differ from day-to-day work (operations)?
6. Keeping your business environment in mind, list three examples of operations.
7. What is the definition of *knowledge base*? Give an example of a knowledge base.
8. What is the definition of *process*? Give an example of a process.
9. How does a knowledge base differ from a process?
10. Briefly describe the six stages of the PPA.
11. For each stage of the PPA, how many steps can you recall? (Don't be concerned about the order.)
12. What is a stage gate, and how many stage gates are there in the PPA?
13. What are the benefits of using stage gates?
14. Does your organization currently have a project management methodology in place?
15. Does your organization currently have a system and/or product development methodology in place?

If yes, comment on its quality, usefulness, and its actual use by project teams.
16. Does the system and/or product development methodology incorporate project management methodology components? If your answer is yes, is that of any concern to you?
17. What is *PMBOK*?
18. How many process groups does PMBOK encompass? Briefly describe each process group. Hint: Five.
19. How would you correlate the six stages of PPA with the process groups of PMBOK?
20. How many knowledge areas does the PMBOK cover? Briefly describe each knowledge area. Hint: Nine.
21. What is *CMM*? Describe it briefly.
22. How does the PPA relate to CMM?
23. What is the primary reason for not using the classic triple constraint in this book?
24. List and briefly describe the seven deadly sins of project management.
25. Think of three recently completed and/or currently in progress projects, and working with a colleague, develop the sin index for these projects.
26. Review the discussion regarding the differences between classic engineering (construction) projects and IT/Business projects in this chapter and identify three items that you agree with. Why?
27. Review the discussion regarding the differences between classic engineering (construction) projects and IT/Business projects in this chapter and identify up to three items that you disagree with. Why?
28. Can you recall the six components of the success equation? Describe each briefly.
29. Why is it important to celebrate project success? Have you participated in any such celebrations? As a project manager, would you plan any? How would you justify it to your sponsor?
30. What is the key message from the discussion under the heading *It's the Other Leg, Stupid*?
31. Can you recall any of the quotations used in this chapter? If so, why this quotation?

---

*Question and Discussion Points presented here and also in the Preface apply to all chapters in the book.

2 FUNDAMENTALS

OBJECTIVES

In this chapter, you will learn about the following project management elements:

- Project management roles and responsibilities
- Key project elements
- Work breakdown structure (WBS)
- Task network
- Task dependency relationships
- Critical path calculations
- Network constraints
- Version 0 network
- Lags and leads
- Float and slack
- Critical path compression
- Resource leveling

This chapter introduces the fundamentals of project management. It starts with a detailed description of the roles and responsibilities of the various project management players. It goes on to describe the key elements of a project, the steps necessary to create a comprehensive WBS, and the process needed to convert the work breakdown structure (WBS) into a task network showing the logical sequencing of various tasks. Next, the chapter focuses on the steps needed to compute the project's estimated duration, by identifying the critical path through the network, using the forward and backward pass method. The chapter includes an exercise to create a WBS and a task network needed to build a tree house. Although this is a simple project, experience shows that participants in the Center's project management training seminars often overlook important tasks. The exercise serves as a good learning platform for the importance of building a comprehensive WBS and an accurate task network. The chapter finishes with a discussion of the steps needed to compress the critical path of a project (ways to reduce its expected duration).

■ PROJECT MANAGEMENT: ROLES AND RESPONSIBILITIES

Within any project, there are a number of people who play different roles that carry specific responsibilities. The word "role" implies that they hold a certain position, and the word "responsibility" means that they will be assigned certain tasks (duties). The key players in a project, along with a brief description of their roles, are:

- Project sponsor
- Project manager
- Program manager
- Stakeholders
- Customers and end users
- Functional managers
- Team members
- Subject matter experts (SMEs)
- Vendors
- Contractors and consultants

Project Sponsor

Because project is a speculative undertaking that will consume valuable resources (people, facilities, funds), it needs a leader—someone to guide and direct the team. The sponsor is an individual, who has the right level of authority and personal commitment, and who will make sure that the team is able to complete the project efficiently and effectively. The sponsor may be the person who originated the project idea, who provides the most funds for the project, or the person whose department will absorb the greatest impact of the project. The sponsor must have sufficient authority and skills to maneuver the project through the organization's political "tar pits." Far too often, sponsorship falls to managers who supply the majority of the people or funds for the project team. Assignment by default is not a preferred model for selecting the project sponsor. We will discuss sponsorship in greater detail in Chapter 5 (see *Project Organization*).

Project Manager

Some synonyms for the word "manage" are: direct, supervise, control, deal with, survive, cope, and run. Ultimately, a project manager is an individual who is responsible to see that the project is completed on time, within budget, and with appropriate functionality and quality—without causing detriment to the organization, team, or customers. Therefore, a project manager must have the necessary skills, authority, and organizational support to fulfill each of these roles. The essential responsibilities of a project manager include planning, organizing, estimating, scheduling, tracking, negotiating, leading, communicating, and expectations management. We will discuss the roles and responsibilities of a project manager in greater detail in Chapter 5 (see *Project Organization*).

Program Manager

The program, in the context of project management, means a group of related projects that each must be completed in a specific order (business people often use the term "initiative" to describe a program). A program manager is an individual who has the responsibility to coordinate and oversee the implementation of the group of projects. For example, the vice president (VP) of sales may be considering a new initiative to revamp the sales department. Within the IT profession, computer programmers have their own definition of the word "program." It is a logical arrangement of computer language instructions used to automate a function. Because of these two highly diverse meanings, be careful how you use the term.

Stakeholders

The dictionary definition of the word is: One who has a share or an interest, as in an enterprise. The origin of the word "stakeholder" in the American vocabulary can be traced to the frontier days when Western land was made available to those who were willing to work and live on it. A stake became a section of land marked off by stakes and claimed by the farmer, the stakeholder. Within a project, stakeholders are those individuals or organizations who have a key interest in the project's outcome because it is going to impact, or be impacted by, their day-to-day operations. Various stakeholders may be internal or external to the organization executing the project; the impacts may be positive, negative, or a combination of the two. We will discuss the roles and responsibilities of stakeholders in greater detail in Chapter 4 (see *Stakeholder Analysis*).

Customers and End Users

Customers and end users include the group (or groups) of people who either asked for the project or will be directly impacted by the outcome of the project. They will use the end product created by the project. Until about a decade ago, the IT profession used the word "end user" to describe people who will be the recipients of the end product of a project. People in the payroll department are the end users of a new payroll system and the sales people are the end users of a new sales information system. In the meantime, most other professions (engineering, manufacturing, sales, and marketing) used the word "customer" to refer to the recipients of the end products of their projects. The term "end user" then fell out of favor, as it came to imply nondescript entities, and IT professionals began to replace it with the word "customer" (the word "user" came to have negative connotations). However, many IT groups still use the two terms, sometimes with a different meaning. For example, in the case of a Web-based commerce system, the corporate group that requests the system are referred to as "customers" and the people that will use the system to conduct business are referred to as "end users." All of this really becomes confusing when the IT customers refer to the end users as the customers (in the true sense of the word). Some organizations, in an attempt to reduce confusion, use the terms "internal customer" and "external customer" (for end users). Our advice to project managers is to clearly define these terms at the start of a project and then be consistent in their use in all communications across the project.

Functional Managers

In the modern IT/Business environment, team members of a given project often come from different departments. In some cases, they come from completely different organizations (contractors, vendors, and business partners). The different team members will have their primary allegiances to their own managers. Their managers hold the strings to their own resources and can reassign them to other projects or work, often to the surprise and dismay of the project manager. Therefore, developing productive and highly professional relationships with functional managers becomes a key responsibility of project managers.

Team Members

Team members include all individuals who will perform the work necessary to develop the deliverables that are needed to complete the project. We will discuss the roles and responsibilities of team members in greater detail in Chapter 5 (see *Project Organization*).

Subject Matter Experts (SMEs)

SMEs are people who have extensive knowledge and excellent skills in specific subject areas, such as database management, security, contract negotiations, facilities, budgeting, and legal. In the context of this book, an SME is a person whom the project team may call upon for advice and guidance, but who is not responsible for completing any deliverables. If a given person is assigned one or more deliverables, the person is considered a team member and has a specific reporting relationship with the project manager.

Vendors

Typically, vendors include the suppliers of hardware, software, and equipment to the project and/or the parent organization.

Contractors and Consultants

This category includes the suppliers of human resources to the project and/or the parent organization. An important point to keep in mind is that, in a given project, an individual or a group may play multiple roles.

■ KEY PROJECT ELEMENTS

The foundation of any given project is a comprehensive plan, also known as the project task plan, which consists of the following key elements:

Phases	Milestones
Deliverables	Resources
Tasks	Issues
Lags	Task Network

The question most project managers and team members pose is: what is the best way to delineate a project into its key elements? Most people grew up using a list to outline the work that needs to be done. However, lists have certain inherent problems:

- The physical order of the list often implies the logical order—the order in which the items on the list will be executed. That is one reason why people begin to erase and reorder a list as they create it.
- When a list begins to span the length of one physical page, another layer of complexity is added because one needs to flip back and forth to see the total list.
- During the list creation, when one begins to discover missed items, one needs to either cram those items into the appropriate places or redo the list.
- It is almost impossible to depict dependencies among different items on the list, other than by drawing arrows or making some notations.

A word processor may reduce the effort necessary for reordering the list, but the fundamental problems still remain. The problems with lists lead to the conclusion that lists are fine when the project consists of a few steps (such as a daily work plan) but in a typical project, that includes dozens of tasks and numerous people responsible for them, lists become cumbersome.

A better approach is to use the WBS technique, which combines the process of progressively delineating the components of a project—phases, deliverables, tasks, milestones—and employing a hierarchical approach without implying any order of execution for the various components. The latter characteristic is perhaps the most useful part of the WBS process. Before continuing with the discussion of the steps needed to develop a comprehensive WBS for a project, let us define a few important terms.

WBS Definitions

Phase   Phases are distinct stages of product development. Projects are typically broken into a set of phases to group together similar activities, such as the requirements, design, build, test, and implement phases. (The phase names are usually based on the system/product development methodology in use in the organization). Phases often end with major checkpoints, such as when management approval is sought prior to starting work on the next phase. Phase names can be verbs and/or nouns. In the case of IT/Business projects, various phases are not usually executed sequentially; more often they overlap. A phase that lasts longer than three months implies that either the project is too big or that there are not enough resources to finish the work in a timely fashion (both situations should be avoided).

Deliverable A deliverable is the result or end product of completing a task or set of tasks and is a measure of *accomplishment*. Deliverables progressively build the body/substance of the project. Deliverables must be tangible and must be well defined to avoid ambiguity. You should use a *noun* to identify (name) a deliverable. A few examples of deliverables are:

- Access control lists
- Audit & control requirements
- Consumer communication plans
- Consumer market analyses
- Focus group test reports
- ISO 9000 compliance reports
- Laptops for sales groups
- Marketing strategies
- Package design
- Preproduction packages
- Product display packages
- Prototypes
- Public relations plans
- Raw materials lists
- Retail strategy plans
- Sales analysis reports
- Security procedures
- Test data
- Test plans

Although multiple people may do the work to complete a deliverable, only one person should be the *owner* of a deliverable. A deliverable may be received by one or more people (some of our clients use the term "thrower" for the owner and "catcher" for the recipients). We recommend that, on the average, a deliverable should take twenty days or less. Deliverables with longer duration should either be divided into smaller deliverables or should have specific milestones inserted at about the 20-day period to assess timely progress. In any given project, the deliverables can be broken into two key categories:

Product deliverables: Deliverables that are components of the end product of the project. Customers will receive and use these deliverables when the project becomes operational.

Process deliverables: Deliverables that are developed as a part of the process to complete the project (project charter, risk analysis, complexity assessment, scope statement, organizational change management plan, scope management plan, test data, project status reports, vital signs variance report).

Typically, product deliverables are given more importance than the process deliverables because the latter are often perceived as being bureaucratic. This view is short sighted, because if the *necessary* process deliverables are done away with, the net quality of the process is compromised and the result is often a poor quality end product. Below are a few helpful guidelines regarding deliverables:

- A deliverable is named using a noun
- A deliverable has only one owner
- A deliverable may have one or more receivers
- Once "thrown," any changes to a deliverable must be communicated in written form to the receiver(s)
- A deliverable should have clearly defined completion criteria
- Development time for a deliverable should be twenty days or less

Task A task is a piece of work assigned to an individual to be completed in a specified period of time, leading to the achievement of a milestone and/or completion of a deliverable. You should use a *verb* to identify (name) a task. A few examples of tasks are:

- Define audit and control requirements
- Design sales analysis report

- Develop prototypes
- Distribute public relations plan
- Gather audit and control requirements
- Interview customers
- Obtain access control list approval
- Order laptops
- Prepare access control list
- Prepare consumer communication plan
- Prepare customer list
- Prepare package design
- Review access control list
- Write customer interviews summary
- Write focus group test report
- Write marketing strategy

Make sure that each task can be assigned to an individual, takes no longer than forty hours of effort, and has no longer than ten days of duration. To control the number of tasks in a WBS, we suggest a lower limit of four effort hours for a task. Within the project management profession, the conventional wisdom suggests a limit of eighty effort hours. People often ask us about our rationale for the forty-hour limit. Our answer is simple: people have not learned from history, folklore, and science.

The number forty is practically ingrained in our collective subconscious. Does this mean that the upper limit for all tasks is *exactly* forty hours? Of course not. Our advice is that if a task's estimated effort exceeds forty hours, you should try to divide it into smaller tasks. Given below are a few helpful guidelines regarding tasks:

- A task is named using a verb
- A task has only one owner
- A task should lead to the achievement of a milestone and/or completion of a deliverable
- A task that takes longer than forty hours of effort is a candidate for further breakdown into smaller tasks

Subtask Subtasks are further decompositions of large tasks. Because we use forty hours as the upper limit for task effort and four hours as the lower limit, we seldom use subtasks to decompose tasks into smaller tasks.

Activity Within the project management profession, a certain level of confusion exists regarding the use of the word "activity." Some consider activities to be a subset of tasks, while others place tasks a level below activities. To us, "task" and "activity" are synonymous.

Event An event is a point in time and has no duration attached to it. An event can be the point in time such as the following: task started, task completed, or hardware upgraded.

Milestone A milestone is an event that indicates *significant progress* or achievement in a project. A milestone can indicate the start or completion of a key task, progress through an extended task (long duration), or completion of a deliverable or a phase (and even the project). Our recommendation is that milestones be named using a *past tense,* such as access control list approved, audit & control requirements completed, sales analysis report approved, or vendor list finalized. We recommend that, at a minimum, a project should average one milestone every ten days or less. In any project, milestones can be grouped or leveled to accommodate the status reporting needs of the specific individual. For example:

- Milestones used by individual team members: high frequency (typically weekly)
- Milestones used by the project manager: medium frequency (typically biweekly)
- Milestones used by the sponsor: low frequency (typically monthly)

As discussed in the previous chapter, it is important that the project manager and the team take the time to celebrate major milestones. This energizes the team and improves the overall team disposition.

For picking the milestones, there is only one relevant rule. Milestones must be concrete, specific, measurable events, defined with knife-edge sharpness.

Brooks, F. P., 1995.

I look at victory as milestones on a very long highway.

Joan Benoit Samuelson.

Issue An unanswered question or a difference of opinion is identified as an issue (e.g., are vendor employees to be included in the Access Control List?). To us, issues are akin to potholes in a road—too many will make the project journey rough, slow down the team, and force workarounds. Consider our maxim: If, at any given time in a project, the number of unresolved issues is greater than the number of deliverables to be completed, the project is in jeopardy. Resolve some issues.

Resource In the context of the discussion of a WBS, the word "resource" refers to an individual team member, preferably by name and at times by job title. In the context of a project, hardware, software, facilities, equipment, and funds are also referred to as resources.

Lag In a task network diagram, a given task can start as soon as its predecessor task is finished. At times, it may be necessary to delay the start of the task. In that case, a lag (a specific period of time) can be specified. Some examples of lag are:

- Wait time for sponsor's review and approval of the project charter
- Wait time for the approval of the purchase order
- Wait time between making an offer to a new employee and the person's response
- Wait time for receiving hardware after order placement

Lags can have definite impact on a project's completion time, so be careful to review your project schedule to ensure that any key lags have not been overlooked. Lag will be discussed in more detail later in this chapter (see *Task Dependencies or Relationships*).

Work Product At times "work product" is used as a synonym for "deliverable." We prefer the term "deliverable."

Work Package The term "work package" is used frequently in the engineering profession, especially construction engineering. The PMBOK defines the term "work package" as: "A deliverable at the lowest level of the work breakdown structure. A work package may be divided into activities." We have come across many different definitions of the term "work package." Permit us to present two additional definitions:

- A deliverable or product at the lowest level of WBS. . . . each work package in a WBS should represent roughly eighty hours of effort.
- It describes in detail the tasks to be done in completing the work for an activity.

These different definitions can be confusing, therefore, a new one will not be presented. The following are examples of the use of work packages by project managers in different situations.

- In most engineering (construction) projects, the construction work can be divided into well defined categories, such as concrete, plumbing, electrical, dry wall, painting, and masonry. Typically, each of these jobs is bid to a different contractor, and each has its own supervisor. To manage such work, the project manager takes the master schedule, extracts the deliverables and tasks for a particular group (along with their start and completion dates), groups them into separate *work packages,* and assigns each package to appropriate supervisors (also referred to as work package managers). Each work package manager is then responsible for timely completion of the assigned work by her team. This process is a good example of the delegation of supervision responsibility when teams consist of a large number of people. The same approach can be used in the case of IT/Business projects that have a large number of team members.

- In another common use of a work package, a project manager extracts (from the master schedule) a group of deliverables and tasks to be completed by each team member in an upcoming period of time, and assembles a number of discrete work packages. This approach works well in the case of dispersed/remote teams, and when team members don't have sufficient face-to-face time with their project managers.
- Finally, when an individual is assigned to more than one project, keeping track of work to be done for different projects can be difficult. In such instances, each project manager can create a distinct work package for the team member who can then track his work more easily.

■ WORK BREAKDOWN STRUCTURE (WBS)

Now that you're familiar with the basic elements of a project, let us look at the best method for delineating these elements for a given project. The process and the end product are known as the WBS. The WBS is a method for successive partitioning of a project into the smaller components (elements)—phases, deliverables, and tasks—needed to complete the project. The basic idea is to progressively break the project into small enough components (tasks), where each can be assigned to one person and can be completed in a reasonably small amount of time. Figure 2.1 depicts the key components of a WBS.

Creating a WBS

At the Center, we prefer to use flip charts and sticky notes[1] for creating and depicting the WBS of a project. Only after a comprehensive WBS has been created will it be entered into the project management software. The use of sticky notes to develop a WBS is more efficient and productive than

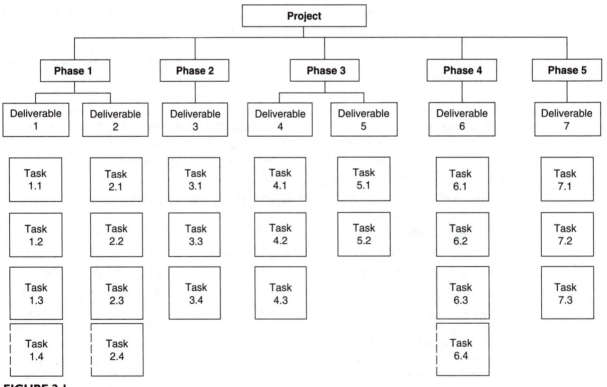

FIGURE 2.1
Example of a WBS.

---

[1]Feel free to use any type of sticky notes you prefer. Just make sure that they will stick to a variety of surfaces—white boards, tabletops, and paper.

FIGURE 2.2
Phase-level WBS.

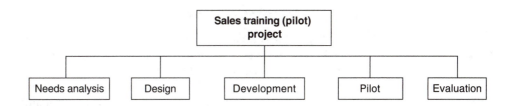

the use of project management software. In the course of the following discussion, you will see that the use of sticky notes has several advantages: it allows all members of the team to participate fully; it allows the team to move the various project elements around easily; it allows for quick disposal of unneeded elements; and it facilitates making changes such as renaming phases, deliverables, and tasks. Also, it allows a large group of people, to hover around the work in progress and view it jointly. With project management software, all of these actions are cumbersome and difficult.

Phase-Level Decomposition

The first step is to define the phases of your project. For this discussion, we will use the example of a sales training (pilot) project, for which the product development life cycle (after the project charter has been approved) consists of the following five phases:

1. Needs analysis
2. Design
3. Development
4. Pilot
5. Evaluation

As shown in Figure 2.2, this is the first level of the WBS for the project. Once the phase names have been decided, obtain as many flip charts as there are project phases and write the individual phase name toward the top of each flip chart.

Deliverable-Level Decomposition

The second step is to select a phase that you are most familiar with. Using the 3" × 5" sticky notes, develop a list of deliverables that must be produced to complete the selected phase. Discussions among the team members will generate the most comprehensive list. A point of caution: at this point in planning, do not concern yourself with the *order* in which the various deliverables will be executed. Remember to use a noun to describe each deliverable. Figure 2.3 depicts the deliverables-level WBS for our model project—the sales training project.

While this process is underway, the project manager should monitor the group conversation and should not allow the team to go in tangential directions. For example, the team might be tempted to revisit the wisdom of attempting the project in the first place. Though an important question to consider, it should have been asked and answered long before the team started to develop the WBS for the project. Also, a number of issues (unanswered questions and differences of opinions) are certain to arise during the session. The best approach is to make a note of the issue and move on with deliverable decomposition. Assign a team member the responsibility to capture each issue and write a brief description on a 1" × 3" sticky note.

FIGURE 2.3
Deliverables-level WBS.

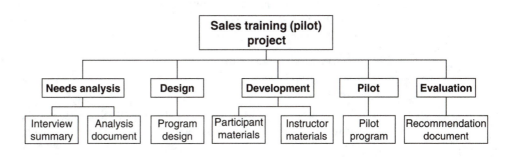

Task-Level Decomposition

The next step is to break each deliverable into the tasks needed to complete it. To identify tasks, the 3" × 3" sticky notes work best. Be sure to use a verb to describe each task. As a task is defined, write it on a sticky note and place it under the associated deliverable. Continue this process until the team cannot think of any more tasks for the deliverable in question. Now, move to the next deliverable and decompose it into its associated tasks. Continue the process until all of the deliverables have been decomposed. Figure 2.4 is an example of a task level WBS. During this process, make sure that the team does not spend too much time discussing the sequence in which various tasks of a given deliverable will be executed (you will see the reason shortly). Another important dimension to this process is the issues that will arise during discussion. One team member should be designated to focus clear attention to the ongoing discussions, disagreements, and unanswered questions; record them as issues; and then post them for all to see.

The next step is to tag each deliverable with a numeric identification. A very important point to mention here is that these are simply *identification* numbers of various deliverables and the numbers *do not* imply the order of development of these deliverables. Now you can tag tasks with individual identification numbers. Define the "parent" and "child" relationships between each deliverable and its tasks. Figure 2.5 depicts the same WBS as in Figure 2.4, but here each deliverable and task has an identification showing its relationship to a specific deliverable—parent/child relationship. As before, the various task IDs do not imply the execution order of the tasks. Later, when we convert this WBS into a task network, a higher numbered task may actually precede a lower numbered task. This can be confusing to some people, especially those who are very committed to using lists. Keep in mind that in a WBS and a task network, task IDs are simply identification tags, nothing more.

At this point, we need to acknowledge that personal preferences exist in the timing of numbering individual tasks to the level shown in Figure 2.5. As we mentioned earlier, the result of the numbering scheme shown above is that, when you create a task network for this WBS, a task with a higher ID number may actually precede a task with a lower ID. For those who may find this unsettling, the solution to the problem is *not* to specify the decimal numbers in the IDs of various tasks at this stage of the WBS, as shown in Figure 2.6.

Here, all of the tasks for a given deliverable have the same ID as the deliverable. The individual IDs for various tasks are then assigned *after* the WBS is converted into a task network. This way, tasks in the network have a sequential numbering order. The problem is that this may not hold true for long because of the following types of events:

- Soon after the numbering has been completed and the task network has been entered into the project management software, one may discover that the task sequencing was incorrect and some of the tasks need to be moved around. To keep the various task IDs in sequential order, one will need to renumber all of the related tasks.
- While reviewing a task network, or later when actually doing the work to complete a set of tasks, one may discover that new tasks need to be added to the task network or some of the existing tasks need to be discarded. This will also require renumbering the related tasks.

If one is totally committed to matching the task IDs with their order of execution, each of the two events in the list will mean spending a lot of time with the software package just to keep the task IDs in sequence of their execution—not a good investment of time. The point at which you number the various tasks is up to you, but *do not* associate a task ID with its order of execution, and make sure that anyone who reads a WBS, or a task network, understands the reason for assigning IDs to tasks: purely for the purpose of identification.

Once a task-level breakdown has been completed, a wide range of information can be noted for each task within the WBS. For example, the following information can be noted:

- the person responsible for the task
- estimated effort (hours) and duration (days)
- lag values, where appropriate

Some project managers wait until after the WBS has been converted into a network to generate and record the three items in the preceding list. It is purely a matter of personal preference.

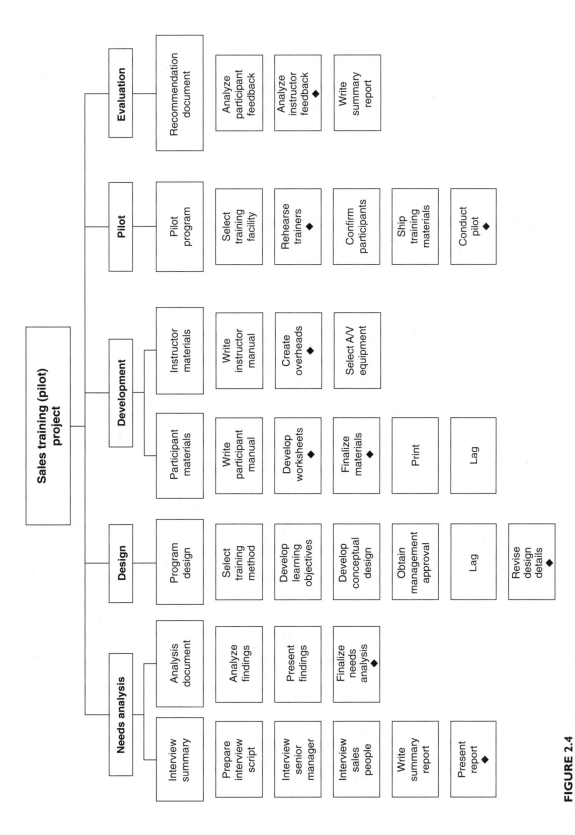

FIGURE 2.4

Task-level WBS. ◆ Symbols indicate milestones.

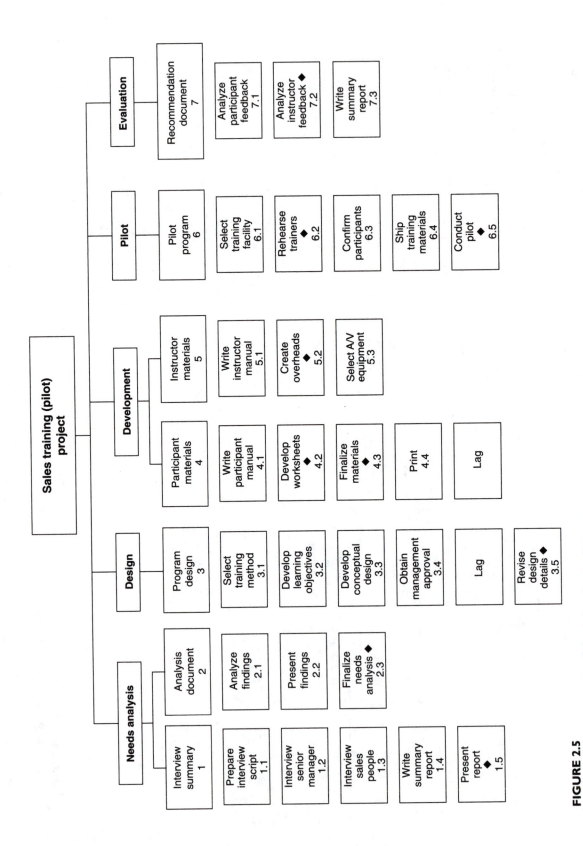

FIGURE 2.5
Task-level WBS with task IDs. ◆ Symbols indicate milestones.

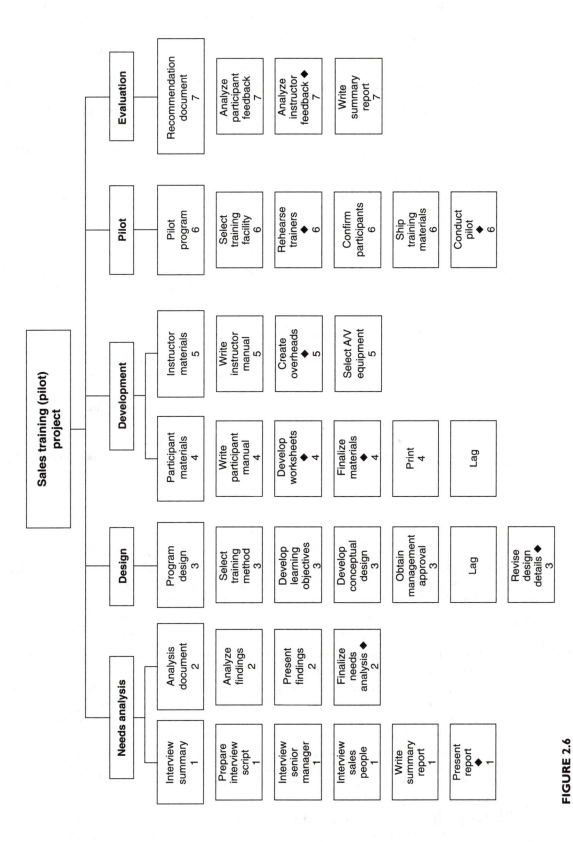

FIGURE 2.6
Task-level WBS with partial task IDs. ◆ Symbols indicate milestones.

While developing a WBS, phases do not need to be fully detailed in the order of their execution. This is an extremely important characteristic of the WBS process because it allows the team to focus on the parts that are better understood and then fill in the details of other components as more information becomes available. As a WBS is being developed, discussion among team members results in further clarification and WBS components are addressed in more detail.

Order of WBS Decomposition

Among the questions frequently asked by project managers and team members new to the process of developing a WBS are:

- Should I start at the highest level and then progressively break the WBS into subsequent levels of detail? This is known as the top down approach.
- Is it OK to start from the lowest level of detail (tasks)? When sufficient tasks have been defined, can I group them into deliverables and then into phases? This is known as the bottom up approach.

The answer to both questions is "yes." There are no specific rules and regulations regarding the order in which one goes about developing the various components of a WBS. Our advice is to use the approach you are most comfortable with and don't force others to follow your approach to the letter. Consider the creation of a WBS a brain storming session, the intended result being a comprehensive WBS for the work at hand.

Level of WBS Decomposition

Another interesting question often raised by project teams is, "When does one know that a given deliverable has been broken into the right number of tasks?" This is indeed a difficult question to answer directly, but the following discussion should help.

Think about the instructions on a typical shampoo bottle: wet hair, apply shampoo, lather, rinse thoroughly, and repeat.

Now, after the last step when one returns to the first step, does one have to wet her hair again? Of course not; it is already wet. Also, when should you stop shampooing? The directions on a typical shampoo bottle provide no specific guidance. Let us consider the following options:

- Until the shampoo is gone?
- Until the water is gone?
- Until the hair is gone?

Of course, it is none of the above; you should stop when the hair is clean. The shampoo bottle manufacturer *assumed* that the person using the shampoo will have a certain degree of knowledge of the purpose and process of using the product. The same is the case with creating a WBS. While developing a WBS, keep in mind the knowledge and skills of the team members who will be assigned to the project. Any WBS should be evaluated using the following set of questions. A "yes" answer to these questions means that the WBS has been decomposed to the appropriate level of detail.

1. **Will the team members assigned to the project be able to understand what the task is and what they need to do to complete it?**
   This explanation begs the question: "What is the skill level of the project team?" Therefore, it would behoove the project manager to jot down the assumed team skill level(s) before starting the WBS process. A quick test would be to select about 10 percent of the lowest level of tasks from the WBS and have those team members who did not participate in the creation of the WBS assess the clarity of the task definitions. If it passes this test, the WBS is at the right level. A quick note: if the team members assigned to the project are at a lower level than assumed for creating the WBS, selected portions of the WBS may need to be decomposed further to match the needs of the project team.

2. **Is it possible to develop accurate and viable estimates from the WBS?**
   One of the key reasons to develop a WBS is to help the team create realistic task effort, cost, and duration estimates. The larger the task, the more inaccurate the estimate. Our metric for this

test is that the resulting effort estimates for most of the tasks should be less than forty hours each. For tasks that are estimated as more than forty hours of effort, we suggest further decomposition. In fact, for projects that have fixed bids, it may be necessary to decompose most tasks into smaller than forty-hour chunks in order to assure accurate estimates.

3. **Will the project manager be able to monitor task completions effectively?**
   For any project to be successful, the project manager must be able to monitor its status accurately and in a timely manner. Typically, project managers hold weekly project status meetings; therefore, the expectation is that most tasks should be able to be completed in a week's time. We suggest a limit of ten days for task duration because tasks that take longer can be difficult to monitor, especially when team members are not able to complete their assignments in the allocated time periods.

Another area of the project that requires attention is the number of new tasks discovered when the team begins to execute the plan. If the effort estimates for the newly discovered tasks are greater than 10 percent of the original effort estimate, the original WBS was not created at the right level of detail. A few new tasks are sure to be discovered after the work starts, but when this number breaches the 10 percent mark, it suggests either hasty original planning or the start of big scope creep. Make sure that the tasks in the WBS are clearly articulated and that each task can be assigned to an individual and takes no more than forty hours and ten days to complete.

To summarize the discussion on WBS, focus on the following important points:

- A WBS is not a plan. It is a list of ingredients for the project.
- When creating a WBS, do not spend time trying to put tasks in their order of execution. This is a waste of time, which will become apparent when you read *Developing a Task Network* later in this chapter.
- Without a detailed WBS, the probability of missing crucial details during planning, estimating, and scheduling is high. This results in tasks actually being discovered as the work progresses, resulting in last minute scrambling to finish the newly discovered work.

Postimplementation assessment of a large number of projects has shown that the discovery of new tasks during project execution is a major cause for cost and time overruns. Therefore, take extra care to ensure that a comprehensive WBS is prepared *before* any estimates are developed.

WBS Exercise

At this point, you may find it useful to practice developing a plan for a small project, such as building a tree house. The tree house is to be built in one of the five trees closest to your house. The trees are located in a park-like area in your neighborhood. The requirements for this project are:

- The tree house is 20 sq. ft. in size
- Only one room
- Approximately 6 ft high—one story
- No electric or plumbing lines
- You will need to form a neighborhood team to help you build the tree house
- You will have access to all of the tools for the project
- You will need to buy/acquire the building materials

Your assignment is to first create a WBS for building the tree house, and later we will discuss the process of creating a task network for the project.

WBS for the Tree House

Involve some of your colleagues, if you wish, to help you develop the WBS. Use flip charts and appropriately sized sticky notes, as discussed earlier in this chapter. Because it is a small project, you do not have to break the project into phases. At this point, do not convert the WBS into a task network; that process is covered in a later exercise. Limit your time to less than one hour. After you finish, save the WBS for later use.

■ TASK NETWORK

A piece of information that is inherently missing from a WBS is the specific logical order in which various tasks should be executed. To establish a viable sequence, you need to create a task network that depicts the logical execution order of tasks. A task network is to a WBS what a recipe is to a list of ingredients: a depiction of the various tasks of a project in their logical execution order. A network depicts the logical sequence and concurrence of various deliverables, tasks, and milestones in a project. The network is built by analyzing the order in which various tasks can be executed. Initially, the network is drawn without regard to any constraints, which are accounted for during subsequent revisions. Some of the other commonly used terms for task network are "PERT chart," "PERT network," "precedence chart," or "precedence diagram," and "task flowchart." Figure 2.7 depicts a network of eight tasks.

FIGURE 2.7

Task network example.

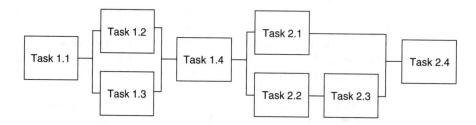

Occasionally, you may come across people who dislike some of this terminology and prefer to search for new terms. In a meeting with a client a few years back, a project manager objected to the use of the word "network" in association with such mundane things as tasks. He proclaimed that networks exist between humans trying to get to know each other in social situations. This individual also found the word PERT too "mechanical and old" and wanted to know whether there was a more modern term, perhaps something the Japanese may have come up with. Just then there was an earthquake and we all exited the building. "Mother Nature" came to our rescue.

The two most common methods for constructing a task network are:

1. Activity-on-arrow method
2. Activity-on-node method

Activity-On-Arrow (AOA) Network

Figure 2.8 depicts a network using the activity-on-arrow (AOA) method. In this network, tasks are shown as connecting lines or arrows between events, which are shown as small circles. The length of the line has no particular significance. Typically, each task's ID and/or description are written above the line, and the task effort and/or duration is written below the line. This method requires the use of dummies (dashed lines) to indicate additional dependencies across tasks. Because of the need to use dummies, as well as the advent of computer software (most of which had trouble drawing AOA networks), these networks are seldom used in the profession and are not discussed in any more detail in this book.

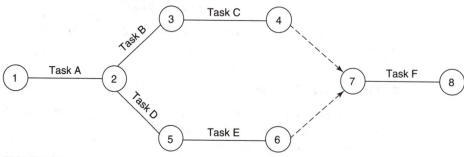

FIGURE 2.8

An AOA network.

Activity-On-Node (AON) Network

Figure 2.9 depicts a network using the activity-on-node (AON) method. In this method, each task is represented *inside* a box (node) and lines are used to show dependency relationships among various tasks. Typically, each box contains the ID and/or the name of the task, task effort, task duration, and the individual responsible for the task.

According to the network in Figure 2.9:

1. The first step is to obtain budget approval.
2. "Order hardware" and "Assemble candidate list" *can* begin as soon as "Obtain budget approval" is completed.
3. Hardware installation cannot begin until after hardware ordering is finished.
4. Candidate interviews cannot begin until after "Assemble candidate list" is finished.
5. "Conduct training" cannot be started until after *both* "Install hardware" and "Interview candidates" have been completed.

This form of relationship (or dependency) between tasks is the most common and is known as a finish-to-start (FS) relationship. Within a given project, not all tasks may have the simple FS relationship depicted in Figure 2.9. For example:

- A successor task may need to begin some time *after the finish* of its predecessor task. After ordering hardware, one would need to wait a certain number of days before it arrives and can be installed. Once the task "Order hardware" has been completed, it may be necessary to wait a specific number of days before the task "Install hardware" can be executed.
- In other situations, it may be necessary to start a successor task *before* the predecessor task has finished. The task, "Assemble candidate list" may take many days and it may not be necessary to *finish* assembling the list before *starting* the "Interview candidates" task.

Task Dependencies or Relationships

To accommodate this need for different relationships, four types of dependencies are used in task network charts:

- Finish-to-start (FS)
- Start-to-start (SS)
- Finish-to-finish (FF)
- Start-to-finish (SF)

With each dependency, you can also specify a specific lag value (the amount of time delay associated with the dependency). Figure 2.10 illustrates the same tasks as shown in Figure 2.9, but with FS and SS relationships and associated lag values for some of the tasks.

Finish-to-Start (FS) Relationship   In case of the FS dependency, the successor task can, but does not have to, start as soon as the predecessor task has been finished. Another way to state this

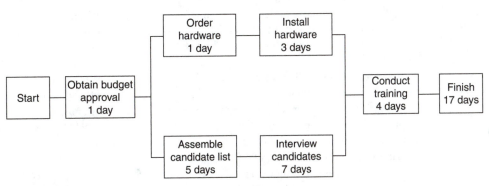

FIGURE 2.9
An AON network.

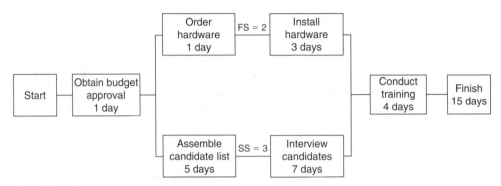

FIGURE 2.10

Task dependencies and lag values.

dependency is that the predecessor task must finish before the successor task can begin. This is the most commonly used dependency relationship in task networks, and the *absence* of any specific dependency notation *implies* the FS relationship. However, if the successor task's start must wait a given period of time after the predecessor task has finished, an equivalent lag value is assigned to the FS dependency (the start of the successor task is delayed by the amount of the specified lag). An example of this type of dependency and lag is ordering a part, waiting for it to arrive (the lag), and installing the part. The lag *begins* when the order is sent and *ends* when the part arrives and installation begins. Therefore, according to Figure 2.10, "Order hardware" can begin as soon as "Obtain budget approval" is finished. However, the estimator knows that there is a two-day wait for the delivery of the hardware by the vendor and that the start of the "Install hardware" task has to be delayed until after the finish of "Order hardware." This lag value is depicted in Figure 2.10 as a FS lag of two days between these two tasks.

Start-to-Start (SS) Dependency The SS dependency means that a successor task can begin once the work on its immediate predecessor has begun. The SS dependency is typically specified when the start of the successor task is to be delayed a specific amount of time after the start of the predecessor task. For example, according to Figure 2.10, the "Assemble candidate list" task is estimated to take five days. It may not be necessary to *finish* assembling the list before *starting* the "Interview candidates" task. Therefore, the project manager has specified a SS lag of three days between these two tasks (the "Interview candidates" task can begin three days after the start of the "Assemble candidates list" task). The assumption is that after three days there will be a sufficient number of candidates on the list to start the interview process. Another example of this type of lag is the construction and finishing of walls in a building. You might choose to give the crew putting up the wallboard a one- or two-day head start before you bring in the finishing crew.

Finish-to-Finish (FF) Dependency In the case of this dependency, the successor task is scheduled for completion a specific number of days following the predecessor task. As an example, if work on one part of a larger piece of hardware must be finished three days after completion of another, so that the next project tasks can move ahead, you can define a FF relationship between the tasks, along with lag of three days. This dependency is seldom used in IT/Business projects and is not described further in this book.

Start-to-Finish (SF) Dependency In this type of dependency, the successor task is scheduled to be completed a specific number of days following the start of the predecessor task. As an example of this type of dependency, you may need to have a specific part in hand five days after the start of a major repair on a piece of equipment to remain on schedule. To specify this situation, you will need to define an SF relationship between the tasks, with a lag of five days. The SF dependency relationship is used rarely in IT/Business projects and is not described any further in this book.

It is important to note here that different project management software packages might interpret the algorithms behind SS, FF and SF relationships (especially the last two) differently and produce unexpected results. Also, if you use any of the dependencies and associated lag values in a software package, remember to record the reason you chose the specific dependency and the lag value—either in a comments field in the software or other project documentation. A few weeks or months later, when the tasks are actually being executed and there is a review of the project schedule, you may need to explain the reason behind the selected dependencies and lags. Now that we have discussed the various task dependencies and the use of associated lag variables, we can focus our attention on converting (arranging) the WBS components into a task network based on the logical execution order of the various tasks. In a task network, when no specific dependency is specified, the default is a FS dependency without any lag. The dependent task can begin as soon as the precedence task is finished.

Developing a Task Network

The purpose of a network is to depict the logical order in which various tasks of a given project can be executed. To make the process easy, tape two or three blank flip chart pages horizontally on a wall (or on a table) to allow adequate blank space to construct a network. As a first step in creating a task network, focus on the WBS for the first phase of the project and decide which task can be done first (if more than one task can be done first and simultaneously, select all such tasks). Place the sticky note representing that task in the left-hand/middle area of the flipchart. Now decide on the task or tasks that can be done next, and place these tasks on the flipchart to the right of the previously affixed sticky note.

In our approach to creating a network chart, when we have moved all of the tasks of a given deliverable from the WBS to the network, we take the represented deliverable sticky note, turn it sideways, and stick it *above the last task* that completed the specific deliverable. Figure 2.11 depicts the network created from the WBS shown in Figure 2.5. The resulting network produced by this method shows you the progressive work that needs to be done to complete various deliverables (depicted as shaded boxes). Continue this process until all of the tasks and deliverables in the WBS have been moved to their proper place in the task network.

As a next step, we take each issue sticky note and stick it to the *latest tasks* (moving from left to right) by which the specific issue must be resolved. The next step is to take a pencil and draw lines depicting the flow of the tasks within the chart. At this point, you can enter any lag values by specifying both the type of dependency and the duration of the lag (if known). In Figure 2.11, deliverables are shown in shaded boxes, the project manager has not yet specified the amount of various lags, and the network you draw may have tasks in a different order. As long as the logical order of tasks is correct, this type of variance is natural.

When you enter the task network into a project management software package, you will not be able to depict the deliverables as shown in Figure 2.11. Also, the network chart printed by your project management software package may not look as orderly as the one produced using the sticky notes.

While creating the first network, assume that there are no constraints (that any and all resources needed to execute the various tasks will be available as needed and there are no other limitations). This creates what is known as a nonconstrained network or potential network: the Version 0 network. You will probably need to convert it into a new network to reflect the actual constraints on the project. This is called a constrained network (we will discuss this later in this chapter in the *Network Constraints* section).

At times, there may be considerable discussion among team members regarding the order and placement (sequential or parallel) of certain tasks. This is natural and should be encouraged (however, do not let it go on unnecessarily). While creating the task network, the team may think of a few new deliverables and/or tasks (deliverables and tasks that were not in the WBS). This is not only natural, but it is also encouraging because it indicates that the team is paying attention to the deliverables and tasks needed to complete the work. If the team thinks of too many new deliverables and tasks while creating the task network, it means that they hurried through the WBS, which is unfortunate. A rough metric we use is that if the number of newly discovered tasks exceeds 10 percent of the tasks in the WBS, the team did not spend enough thought on completing the WBS. The team may wish to discard some of the deliverables and/or tasks that were in the WBS. This is fine, as they may have put unneeded deliverables and/or tasks in the WBS. However, before

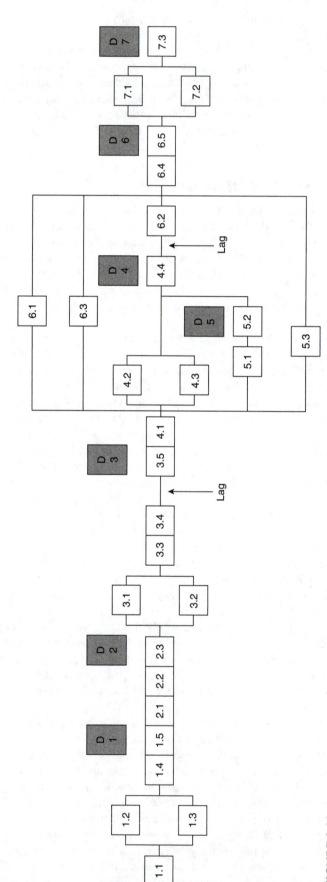

FIGURE 2.11
Task network.

they simply discard these items, see if they fit into a different project phase. If so, save them for later use.

The same steps can be used to create WBS and network charts for the remaining phases of the project. Keep in mind that the various phases, although planned separately, may overlap.

The following is a technique that we find very useful when developing the WBS for a large project. Each subteam (marketing, facilities, sales, human resources, and IT) should use a different colored set of sticky notes to record their own deliverables, tasks, and issues. When the WBS is converted into a task network, different teams can see how their deliverables and tasks are distributed throughout the project plan. The visual representation of the project deliverables, tasks, and issues in the resulting task network gives the subteams a clear graphical view of their interdependencies.

> *Laying out the network, identifying the dependencies, and estimating the lags all force a great deal of very specific planning very early in the project.*
> Brooks, F. P., 1995.

■ CRITICAL PATH CALCULATION

Once the task network has been created, the estimated duration values for various tasks have been computed, and the appropriate lag values have been specified, you can compute the estimated project duration. Begin the estimating process by identifying the critical path through the network using the critical path method (CPM). By definition, the critical path through a network is the collection of tasks that represent the longest path through the project—the earliest the project can be completed. In order to delineate the critical path through a project, one needs to take the following steps:

1. Keeping in view the various task dependencies, identify all of the possible paths through the project task network.
2. Compute the net time to complete the tasks of each path.
3. Identify the longest time.

The *longest* time is the critical path. Because a given project can be made up of a number of linked tasks with sequential, parallel, and other more complicated dependencies and lags, even a small project can have many paths through it. A critical path computation using the steps outlined above would be quite complicated and time consuming. A better way to compute the critical path is to use a set of well defined computations called the forward path and backward path method.

Forward Path and Backward Path Computation

The forward path is used to determine the earliest possible start and finish times of each task in the network, and the backward path determines the latest start and finish of each task. The key terms used in this method are: early start (ES), early finish (EF), late start (LS), and late finish (LF). The typical convention for annotating a task with start and finish times is shown in Figure 2.12.

Early Start (ES)   The earliest starting time for a task is dependent upon completion of the task(s) preceding it. Thus, the ES of a task is simply the soonest it can be started (the moment its predecessors are complete).

Early Finish (EF)   The EF of a task is defined using the following formula:

$$(EF = (ES + task\ duration) - one\ time\ unit)$$

FIGURE 2.12
Task with start and finish annotations.

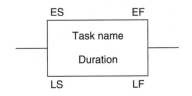

FIGURE 2.13

EF and ES computations.

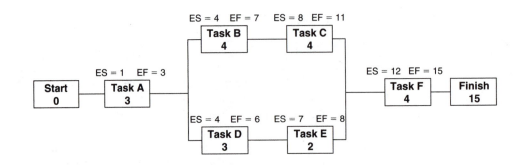

FIGURE 2.13

EF and ES computations.

Figure 2.13 depicts the ES and EF times of the various tasks computed using the forward path method. Individual task computations are as follows:

- The ES of task A is 1, its duration is 3, and its EF is 3
- The ES of task B is 4, its duration is 4, and its EF is 7
- The ES of task C is 8, its duration is 4, and its EF is 11
- The ES of task D is 4, its duration is 3, and its EF is 6
- The ES of task E is 7, its duration is 2, and its EF is 8

Task F introduces a slight complication. Task F has two predecessors: Task C and Task E. Now, how do we decide on the ES of Task F? Remember we mentioned earlier that, for a task to be executed, all of its predecessors must be completed. Therefore, the earliest Task F can start is the later of the two finishes of Task C and Task E. As Task C has a later finish (11 days), the ES of Task F is 12. Now we can continue with the computations.

- The ES of Task F is 12, its duration is 4, and its EF is 15

Working through the example, we see that the forward path computations give the earliest possible start and finish times for each task in the network. The next step is to compute the late finish and late start times for each task. To do this, we start from the end of the network and work backwards, from right to left.

Late Finish (LF) LF time is defined as the latest time a task can finish without impacting the project's completion time. The LF of the last task is the *same* as its EF (computed using the forward path computation previously described). For all other tasks, LF is computed as the minimum of the LS of the dependent (following) tasks minus one time unit.

Late Start (LS) To compute the LS of any other task, use the following formula:

$$(LS = (LF - \text{task duration}) + \text{one time unit})$$

Figure 2.14 depicts the LF and LS computations for the various tasks. Individual task computations are as follows:

- The LF of Task F is 15, its duration is 4, and its LS is 12
- The LF of Task C is 11, its duration is 4, and its LS is 8
- The LF of Task B is 7, its duration is 4, and its LS is 4

FIGURE 2.14

LF and LS computations.

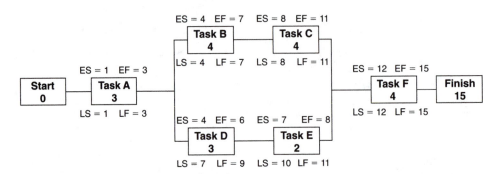

- The LF of Task E is 11, its duration is 2, and its LS is 10
- The LF of Task D is 9, its duration is 3, and its LS is 7

Again, there is a small complication. Task A has two successors: Task B and Task D. How does one decide on the LF of Task A? The start of both Task B and Task D depends on the finish of Task A. Therefore, the lesser of the two LSs minus one unit of time is the LF of Task A. As such, the LF of Task A is 3. Now we can continue with the computations as follows:

- The LF of Task A is 3, its duration is 3, and its LS is 1

Determining the Critical Path

The critical path through a network is composed of a grouping of those tasks that have no slack (if any one of them is delayed, the entire project will be delayed). No slack means no time to spare. Therefore, to identify the critical path, one needs to identify the tasks that have no time to spare. In project management terminology, the two terms that define this spare time are "float" or "slack." Most engineers prefer the term "float," whereas IT/Business people tend to like the term "slack." Soon you will see that the vocabulary around this subject can get quite confusing. One needs to be very careful when discussing the topic with people who are not familiar with the subject matter. The project management literature describes many types of floats, two of the commonly used terms are:

1. Activity float, free float, or free slack
2. Path float or total slack

Activity Float, Free Float, or Free Slack. This applies to individual tasks in a network. This float (slack) refers to the total time (days) the completion of a task can be delayed without impacting the ES of any *successor* tasks. We will use Figure 2.15 to discuss this slack. To compute the slack of any given task, use the following equation:

$$\text{Slack} = (\text{LF} - \text{EF})$$

We can compute the slack of different tasks as follows:

- Task J, slack = (7 − 4) = 3
- Task K, slack = (7 − 2) = 5

FIGURE 2.15
Task network.

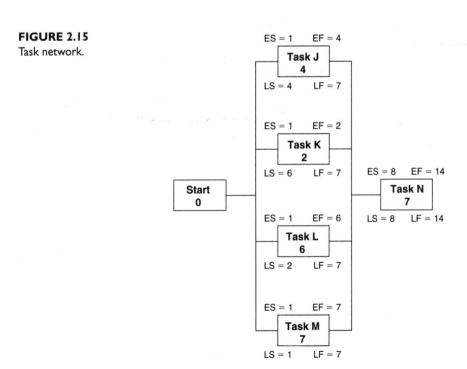

FIGURE 2.16
Display of free slack.

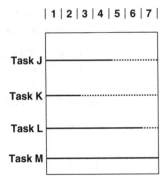

- Task L, slack = $(7 - 6) = 1$
- Task M, slack = $(7 - 7) = 0$

From these calculations, we see that Task M has no slack. Therefore, any delay in completing Task M will certainly delay the start of Task N, which will delay the completion of the project unless one could make up that delay in the execution of Task N. Figure 2.16 illustrates the slack graphically by using a Gantt chart (the dotted lines depict the slack).

Looking at the slack values of Task J, Task K, and Task L, we can tell that the start or finish of these tasks can be delayed by three, five, and one day (respectively) without impacting the start of Task N. This allows the project manager some leeway in the actual start of these tasks, thereby making adjustments for resource availability. However, this can be a double-edged sword, because both the project managers and team members can get lazy and can delay the start of such tasks to their LS date, thereby losing all available free slack. For example, if the starts of Tasks J, K, and L were delayed by three, five, and one day (respectively), all tasks would be on the critical path and the delay of anyone's completion will impact the start of Task N, resulting in a delayed start of Task N. This example emphasizes the need for the project manager to ensure that tasks start on time, thereby greatly improving the odds that they will finish on time. From Figure 2.16, we also see that if the same team member could do Tasks J and K, these two tasks could be assigned to that person without any delay in the start of Task N, thereby reducing the need for one team member at this point.

Now let us look at Figure 2.17 (this is a duplicate of Figure 2.14, with critical path tasks identified in shaded boxes). Task D and Task E both have a free slack of three days each. If the finish of Task D is delayed for more than three days, Task E has lost its slack.

Path Float or Total Slack This denotes the amount of time (days) by which the completion of a task on the path in question can be delayed without impacting the critical path of the project. The total slack on the path with Tasks D and E in Figure 2.17 is three days, because any more delay in completing the tasks on this path will impact the critical path of the project (the start of Task F).

Take a look at Figure 2.18. Notice a new dependency between Task D and Task C. Note that Task D now has a late finish of 7 as compared to 9 in Figure 2.17 (this is due to the new dependency between Task D and C). Now we see that Task D has a free slack of one day because any more delay in its completion will impact the start of Task C. Task E still has a free slack of three days.

FIGURE 2.17
Task network with critical path identified.

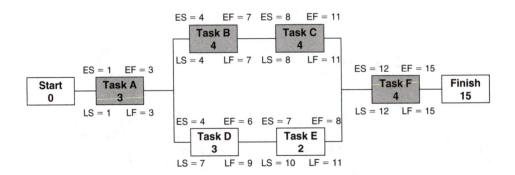

FIGURE 2.18
Task network with new dependency.

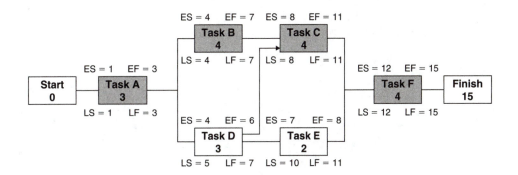

Back to computing the critical path: what we need to do is to identify those tasks that have no slack—their ESs and LSs, as well as EFs and LFs have *identical* values. In Figures 2.17 and 2.18, we see that Tasks A, B, C, and F fulfill these conditions and make up the critical path—15 days—the earliest time to complete the project. Another way to state this is that these tasks have zero slack (no time to spare). Hence, they comprise the critical path through the network. It is customary to identify the critical path tasks by shading the task boxes. Most software packages show the lines connecting the various critical path tasks in bold and/or red. The idea is to highlight the critical path through the network.

Multiple Critical Paths   In any given task network, there can be times when multiple paths compute to the same amount of time duration (there are *multiple* critical paths). This simply means that a larger number of tasks have no slack/float and if any one of these tasks is delayed (takes longer than planned), the project will be delayed.

Near-Critical Path   On occasion, a group of tasks on a given path through the project has little float. This means that although this path's duration does not compute exactly the same as the critical path, it is very close to it. We consider any path whose duration is within 20 percent of the critical path to be a near-critical path. The implication here is that if the tasks on a given near-critical path take longer than estimated, it could then become the critical path.

Critical Task   The use of the word "critical" can create confusion, because it can be construed to mean "important" or "necessary." Recently a number of business unit employees were asked: "What does the statement 'critical tasks' mean to you?" They answered: "a must do list," "tasks that are very important to a process or a procedure," "tasks that are essential or vital," or "mandatory tasks."

Obviously, that is *not* what the term implies when used in reference to the tasks on the critical path of a project. Make sure your audience is clear on the message you are trying to communicate. If you had presented the same people with a list of the tasks on the critical path, then asked them which of those could be deleted (in order to reduce project duration), you are giving two opposite messages. One is that the tasks are *mandatory,* but at the same time you want them to suggest which of the tasks could be *deleted.* Always be careful of the message you are conveying; techno talk can lead to misunderstandings and confusion. Within the lingo of the CPM, the word "critical" has only *time (project duration)* implications. In fact, the Center suggests two important checks of any task network:

1. Once a WBS for a project has been converted into a task network, have selected team members review the network to see whether all necessary tasks have been included. Some project managers call it the "missing task review."
2. After computing the critical path through a project, review the critical path and any near-critical path(s) to see whether all the tasks are really needed. Removing unnecessary tasks from the critical path will directly reduce the estimated project duration.

Network Constraints

The need for first creating a task network that is based on the assumption that all the required resources will be available as needed—the task sequencing is based purely on the order in which various tasks can be executed—has already been discussed. In the case of any project with more than a

FIGURE 2.19
Task network.

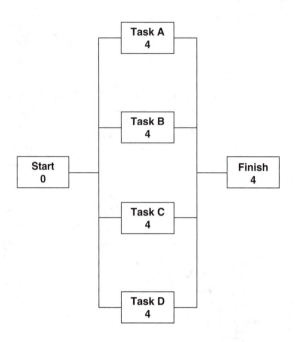

few tasks, the network typically has multiple parallel lines of tasks, indicating that more than one resource (usually many) will be needed to complete the project in the estimated duration—the critical path of the project is *not* constrained by the number of available resources. In real life, the number of resources available may be *fewer* than assumed, and there may be other types of constraints on the project. Invariably the end result is a new, and often longer, critical path of the project. In fact, management may want you to carry out a "what if" analysis using a variety of resource combinations. Typical constraints to keep in mind are resource constraints, cross-project constraints, and date constraints.

Resource Constraints   These involve both the number of resources available to the project manager and the timing of their availability. For example, in the case of the task network depicted in Figure 2.19, because the four tasks do not have interdependencies, four team members can be assigned with a completion time of four days. However, if only two people are available to do these tasks, they will take eight days to complete the four tasks. With one person, the duration will extend to sixteen days.

Now assume that anyone on the team can be assigned to Tasks A, B, and C, but only Chris has the knowledge and skill to work on Task D and he won't be available for ten more days. This means that if the three team members were to start work on Task A, B, and C, today, the start of Task D will need to be delayed for six days after they finish their tasks because that is when Chris will be able to start work on Task D. Figure 2.20 shows the impact of this constraint. The project manager has used

FIGURE 2.20
Resource constrained task
network.

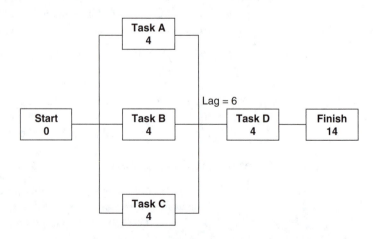

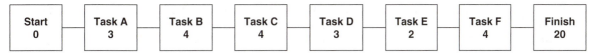

FIGURE 2.21
Resource constrained task network with one resource.

a FS = 6 dependency to show the resource constraint. The critical path now has become 14 days. Of course, the project manager could decide to wait ten days before the start of these four tasks.

Now, let us go back and look at the network shown in Figure 2.17. The resource needs are going to be as follows:

- One person for Task A.
- After the finish of Task A, there are two parallel lines of tasks. That means we will need two team members to execute the tasks in these two paths simultaneously.
- One person for Task F.

Now, let us assume that only *one person* is available for this project. Figure 2.21 depicts a redrawn task network of Figure 2.17, using only one resource. As you can see, the network is now a series of tasks (with no parallel tasks) because only one task can be executed at any given time. The critical path through the new network is now twenty days, five days longer than if two resources were available. An interesting point to keep in mind regarding the tasks in Figure 2.21 is that because Tasks B and C are independent of Tasks D and E, their execution sequence could be reversed. In fact, a number of other combinations are also possible (Tasks B, D, C, E or Tasks B, D, E, C, and a few others). The one caveat about these tasks is that Task C cannot start until Task B is finished and Task E cannot start until after Task D is finished. Additionally, Task F cannot begin until both Task C and Task E are finished.

Cross-Project Constraints   This is the case where output from another project are input to your project. For example, consider the situation where a deliverable within your project is being designed and developed in another project. In that case, your project's progress is dependent on the other project. There will be a point in your project's schedule where any delay in completion of the said deliverable will delay your project (will negatively impact your project's critical path). This is a new constraint, and you will need to monitor it closely.

Date Constraints   Consider a report that must be filed with a regulatory agency by a given date. Now consider a case in which, when you schedule your project, you discover that the report will not be ready for seven days after the required filing date. Of course you will need to adjust the work to make sure that the report is finished and filed by the due date. Another example of a date constraint is that when a competitor makes a bold move and announces the release of a competitive product before the scheduled completion of your project. At this point, management decides to move the completion of your project back to beat the competitor's release time. Now, you have a new date constraint on your project and may need to compress the remaining project schedule to meet the new date constraint.

Extra Resources

Up to now we have discussed resource constraints. Let us assume that management offers *extra* resources in order to get the project finished earlier. We will use the network example in Figure 2.17 and consider the following scenarios:

- Assign two resources all the way through; would that help complete the project in less than fifteen days? What do you think? The answer is, only if the additional person would help finish Tasks A and F in less time.
- Another scenario involves assigning additional team members to Tasks D and E. This is not going to be of any help because these two tasks are not on the critical path. Therefore, reducing

their duration by assigning more people is really a waste. However, if the additional team member(s) can help reduce the combined duration to Tasks B and C to five days (same as the combined duration of Tasks D and E), that will reduce the project critical path by three days. Any further reduction in the duration of Tasks B and C will require a proportionate reduction in Tasks D and E, because now all four tasks are on the critical path.

Why Version 0 Network?

This is a frequently asked question and needs explanation. Take a look at the tasks in Figure 2.21. Can you tell which dependencies are due to the logical order of tasks and which are due to resource constraints? Given the offer of more than one team member, how will you know which tasks could be made parallel? That is one reason that the task network, unconstrained by available resources (what we call Version 0) should be saved. You can then use it to complete your "what if" analysis.

As you can see, constraints can have a marked impact on the critical path. Therefore, it is important that you investigate and identify all applicable constraints to your project. You will need to use these constraints as you develop the resource constrained task network for your project. Keep in mind that the constraints might change as a project progresses. For example, you may have developed the project schedule assuming five team members, but two months into the project there is a budget cut and two of the team members are laid off. You will then need to reschedule the project due to the resource constraint.

To summarize, the CPM uses network analysis steps to compute the estimated duration of various paths through a network of tasks. It helps identify the longest path through the network, called the critical path, which represents the estimated project duration. The tasks on the critical path do not have any slack. Any delay in a critical path task will delay the project completion time unless the delay is made up later in any of the remaining critical path tasks. In order to reduce the project duration, focus on the critical path tasks, because any reduction in their estimated duration will represent equal reduction in the project's duration.

Now is a good time to retrieve the WBS you created earlier for the tree house exercise and convert it into a task network chart. As you develop the network, assume that you will have all of the resources you need (develop a nonconstrained task network). A few points to keep in mind: As you create the network, if you discover new project elements (deliverables, tasks, milestones, or issues) either use a different color of sticky notes than you used to create the original WBS, or use a different color of ink. The idea is to distinguish between the original WBS elements and any newly discovered elements.

If you come to an impasse at any point, do not spend too much time trying to solve the problem; note it as an issue and continue. You will be able to examine a suggested WBS and task network for the tree house shortly. Let us summarize the key points of creating a WBS and a task network:

- A WBS maps out the elements of a project.
- Phases define the project in manageable units.
- Deliverables need to be listed in a clear and concise manner.
- Tasks need to be defined to produce each deliverable.
- Lags need to be incorporated into the project plan.
- Milestones must be established that highlight the significant points of progress during the life of the project.
- A network diagram maps out the sequence of project events.
- Responsibilities should be clearly defined.
- Issues must be identified and recorded.

As we finish the discussion on the techniques to develop a WBS and then a task network, we are pleased to bring to your attention the sage words of a famous author who truly understood the value of what WBS and task networks try to convey:

The secret of getting ahead is getting started. The secret of getting started is breaking your complex overwhelming tasks into small manageable tasks, and then starting on the first one.

Mark Twain.

■ TREE HOUSE: SUGGESTED WBS AND TASK NETWORK

The deliverables and tasks for the project are presented in the two following lists. There are no phases because of the small size of the project. Keep in mind that the listed order of the deliverables and tasks does not imply the order of their execution. This is an example of first creating the list of deliverables and tasks and then the WBS.

Deliverables

- Project manager
- Team
- The tree
- Tools
- Materials
- Tree house design
- Insurance
- Permits
- The tree house
- Kids' orientation

Task List

The small diamonds next to selected tasks below designate milestones.

1. Assign a project manager ◆
2. Analyze requirements (talk to kids)
3. Survey trees (strength and suitability)
4. Check homeowner association's regulations
5. Check insurance needs and cost
6. Select the tree ◆
7. Draw the tree house plans ◆
8. Obtain home owner association's permit ◆
9. Obtain insurance ◆
10. Determine tools
11. Determine building materials
12. Determine team's building skills
13. Obtain tools
14. Obtain building materials
15. Recruit team ◆
16. Clean work area
17. Build access ladder
18. Modify the tree to build a tree house floor ◆
19. Build the tree house floor
20. Build walls
21. Install windows and door
22. Install carpeting (artificial turf)
23. Build the roof ◆
24. Establish kids' behavior rules
25. Orient/educate the kids and their friends ◆
26. Clean up around the tree
27. Celebrate ◆

You may have a few less (or a few more) tasks in your plan. As discussed earlier, there is no hard and fast rule for WBS decomposition. The next step is to develop a WBS and then a task network. Figure 2.22 depicts a suggested WBS for the tree house exercise (because of the lack of space, only the task numbers are shown). Notice the nonsequential numbering of tasks. The reason is that

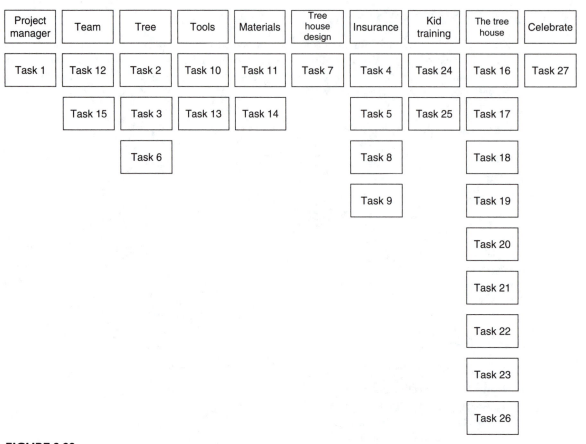

FIGURE 2.22
WBS—tree house.

the team had first numbered the list of the tasks (as shown above), and then created the WBS. In real life, the primary information in each box in Figure 2.22 will be the various task names. Remember, the numbers are just identification tags.

Issues

- Who will continue to pay for the insurance?
- What is the budget?
- Who will contribute funds and how much?
- Who gets to use the tree house? All the neighborhood kids?
- Who will settle disputes?

These are interesting issues, because the group needs to decide on the amount of money to spend on the tree house materials. The next issue deals with the money itself. Who contributes how much? Discussions about money are often quite lively.

Task Network

Figure 2.23 depicts a task network developed using the tasks in the WBS shown in Figure 2.22. In Figure 2.23, only the task IDs are shown because of space limitations.

Your task network does not have to exactly mimic the network shown in Figure 2.23 because you may have a slightly different number of tasks and may decide to do a few tasks in a different order. Just make sure the order of tasks is logically correct. A question sure to arise at this point is, "Do we really need to develop this level of detail to just build a neighborhood tree house for the kids?" We will answer this question with another: "Have you ever known a neighbor who, while working

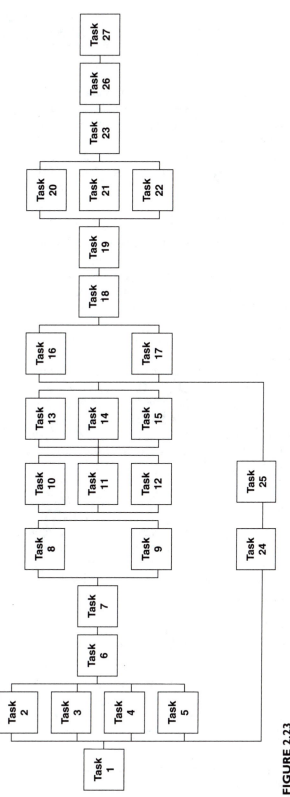

FIGURE 2.23
Task network—tree house.

FIGURE 2.24
Task with FS relationship.

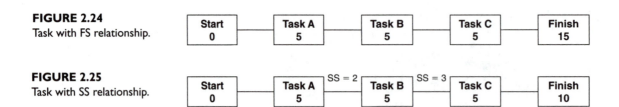

FIGURE 2.25
Task with SS relationship.

on a home improvement project, drove to a hardware store three or more times in a day for progressive acquisition of parts?" That is exactly what happens when people don't plan. The WBS and the task network shown should not take a person with some experience in carpentry longer than two hours. We do not believe that is an excessive amount of time for planning the job. Additionally, the group discussion regarding the need to obtain the homeowner association's permission and the need for insurance may show that the project is not feasible. It is better to find that out now rather than after finishing the project.

Critical Path Compression

The FS relationship of tasks is a prime contributor to the length of the critical path of a project. When there is a need to compress the critical path, the project manager and the team should specifically review all of the tasks on the critical path with the FS relationship and see how many could be converted to a SS relationship with an appropriate amount of lag. For example, consider the three tasks depicted in Figure 2.24; each is five days long and because of the FS relationship, the critical path computes to fifteen days.

Now, let us change the dependency relationship to SS with a lag of two days and three days, as shown in Figure 2.25.

With this relationship, Task B can start two days after the start of Task A and Task C can start three days after the start of Task B. The Gantt chart in Figure 2.26 illustrates these three tasks with the SS relationship. Notice that the critical path now is ten days instead of fifteen days, as shown in Figure 2.24, where each task has the FS relationship.

However, there is a catch. With the SS relationship shown in Figure 2.26, two team members will be needed from day three and day six. We will further discuss the steps to compress the critical path in Chapters 6 and 7.

Lead Time

Earlier in the chapter, the concept of lag, which is a way to indicate a delayed start of a successor task, was discussed. Another concept necessary to discuss is lead time. While lag specifies a delay between two tasks, lead is the acceleration of time between two dependent tasks. For example, Figure 2.27 specifies a lead time of three days for Task B and two days for Task C. This means that Task B can begin three days before the finish of Task A and Task C can begin two days before the finish of Task B.

Based on the project management software package you are using, there can be a number of ways to specify lag, lead, and task dependencies. Make sure you and the team clearly understand the

FIGURE 2.26
Task Gantt chart.

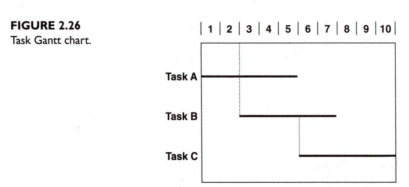

FIGURE 2.27

Lead time annotation.

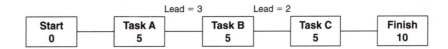

different methods, as it is quite easy to make a mistake and get unreliable results. We suggest that you talk the matter over with your organization's project management software expert(s) and then decide on a *uniform* method; it will simplify everyone's life.

Resource Leveling

After you have scheduled your project, you will often find that the resource (team member) utilization may fluctuate over the course of the project. The need may grow from a few team members to a sizeable group, continue with the larger number for a few days or weeks, plummet back down to a few people, and then climb again. This fluctuation is primarily due to the number of parallel paths in your project's task network. This phenomenon is more prevalent in large engineering (construction) projects, where the team size can easily approach hundreds of people. Large fluctuations in the number of team members over a short period of time can result in numerous coordination problems. For example, if the number of workers fluctuates from thirty, to fifty, to eighty, then down to sixty, and finally back to thirty within a period of three months, the problems of parking, personal facilities, payroll, and general coordination may far outweigh the benefits of a reduced schedule. In such circumstances, the project manager tries to reschedule, that is, *delay* tasks that have sufficient *free slack* to smooth out the resource utilization. Fortunately, IT/Business projects seldom face the types of extreme resource fluctuations experienced by engineering (construction) teams. Nonetheless, it is important for a project manager to be aware of the need for resource leveling and its specific implications on the project. Let us take a look at a simple example of a task network in Figure 2.28.

Our first look tells us that the network could use four team members for the first set of four parallel tasks, three for the next set, and two for the last set. The estimated duration for this set of tasks is twenty days (Tasks A, E, and H). Even though the resource fluctuations are not that large, the example will help explain the resource leveling process. The Gantt chart in Figure 2.29 shows the first attempt to schedule this set of tasks, and we see that the number of team members reflects the number of parallel tasks at any given point: 4, 3, and 2 people. We also see free slack with Tasks B, C, D, G, and I.

FIGURE 2.28

Task network.

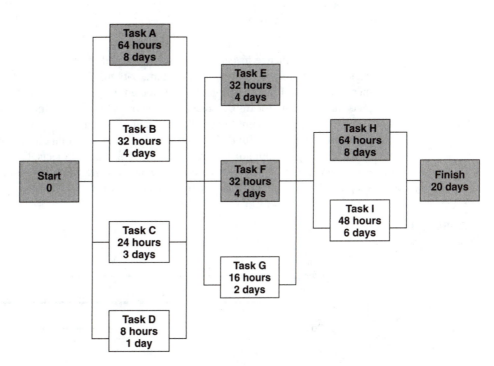

FIGURE 2.29
Resource assignment.

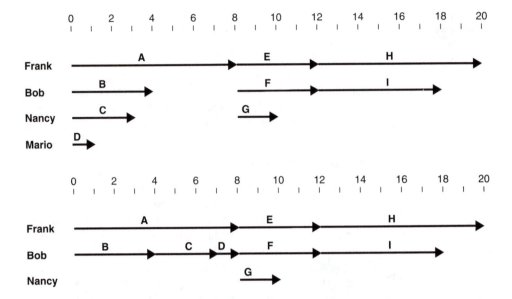

FIGURE 2.29
Resource assignment.

FIGURE 2.30
Leveled resources.

Figure 2.30 depicts a schedule in which the project manager took advantage of these free slacks and leveled resource use by rescheduling task assignments. Because Tasks A, B, C, and D do not have any dependencies, the project manager assigned Tasks C and D to Bob, taking advantage of the four day slack following Task B. Of course, the assumption is that Bob has the skills to finish Tasks C and D within the planned time.

In Figure 2.30, we see that the resource need has fallen to two (for the first eight days), then three (next two days), and then two (after day ten). The critical path still is twenty days, as in Figure 2.28. In the purest form of resource leveling, a project schedule is *not* allowed to increase. However, there are instances where the process of resource leveling will result in a longer critical path, and you will need to decide between the leveled resources or the critical path delay. If there were an urgent need to reduce the resources to only two people, an option would be to have Bob work overtime and finish Task G *while* working on Task F, as shown in Figure 2.31.

Now we have the following situation:

- Resources needed: two
- Critical path: twenty days
- Bob is working overtime

A new challenge has arisen: an over-allocated resource. Most project management software packages will produce a resource histogram that will show the allocation information for any team member, which allows you to quickly see the amount of over (or under) allocation. Figure 2.32 depicts the histogram for Bob. Notice that he is overallocated for four days.

The important point to consider is whether Bob has the requisite knowledge and skills to be assigned to Task G. Assume that Bob can do this task and that he can do it in the estimated time. While this is quite common in construction (engineering) projects, IT and business people are not so easily replaceable. Therefore, be careful when you start leveling resources, because you need to keep much more in mind than just the number of people.

FIGURE 2.31
Leveled resources.

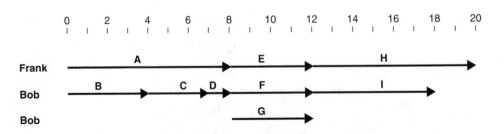

FIGURE 2.32
Resource allocation histogram.

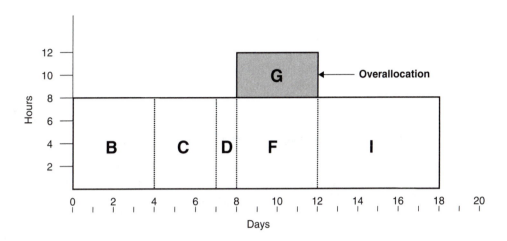

Resource Leveling Software

Project management practitioners have developed a number of different algorithms to compute the optimum number of resources for a given task network.[2] However, the problem is that different software packages seem to interpret the leveling algorithms quite differently and end up producing markedly different results, given the same input. A recent assessment of six different project management software packages by one of the Center's clients produced strikingly dissimilar results. In fact, at times, the same software produced widely different results with only minor adjustments to the input data. Here is some good advice from a tool expert:

> *Be careful when using the resource-leveling feature provided by any project scheduling software. Some products will actually re-assign tasks to different available individuals. For carpenters, painters and sheet rockers this may work very well, but for IT/Business team members this can produce unfeasible work assignments.*
>
> Wayne K. Schmidt, President, The Sirocco Group, Ltd.

If you do decide to use the resource-leveling capability, you should be prepared to visually inspect each task to ensure that the software has assigned the appropriate resource to them. Make a backup copy of the schedule and keep it in a safe place before beginning the leveling process, because if you don't like the results, you may have no way to return to the preleveled schedule.

■ SUMMARY

The following is a list of the key subject areas covered in this chapter. We invite you to review the list and assess your level of comprehension of each topic. The best approach is to take a separate sheet of paper and write a short narrative to explain your knowledge of the topic and then go back and compare your summaries with the material covered in the chapter. Another approach is to find a colleague who is also interested in these topics and discuss your understanding of the topics with him, and then jointly review the chapter materials to assess your degree of understanding.

- Project management roles and responsibilities;
- Key project elements;
- Work breakdown structure (WBS);
- Task network;
- Task dependency relationships;
- Critical path calculations;
- Network constraints;

---

[2]For an in-depth discussion of the subject, refer to J. Moder, C. Phillips, and E. Davis, *Project Management with CPM, PERT and Precedence Diagramming*, 3rd ed. (New York: Van Nostrand Reinhold Company, 1983).

- Version 0 network;
- Lags and leads;
- Float and slack;
- Critical path compression; and
- Resource leveling.

■ QUESTIONS AND DISCUSSION POINTS

1. List and briefly describe the roles and responsibilities of the key players in a project.
2. List and briefly describe each of the key project elements.
3. What are the key components of a WBS?
4. What is the WBS process?
5. Why develop a WBS for a project?
6. List the key guidelines for a deliverable.
7. List the key guidelines for a task.
8. List the key guidelines for a milestone.
9. List the key guidelines for an issue.
10. What is the intended message of the shampoo bottle discussion?
11. How can you tell when a WBS is well defined (adequately complete)?
12. What is the key difference between a WBS and a plan?
13. How many task dependency relationships can you recall? Describe each.
14. What is a critical path, and why should the project manager pay attention to it?
15. Which of the task dependency relationships contributes most to the length (duration) of the critical path?
16. Under what situation may extra resources not help compress the critical path of a project?
17. Why be concerned about any near critical path(s)?
18. Can you recall any of the constraints that can impact the critical path of a project?
19. What is the Version 0 task network, and what is its importance?
20. What is the key purpose of resource leveling? Think of a situation in a project where resource leveling would be advantageous.
21. What can a resource histogram tell a project manager?
22. Can you recall any of the quotations used in this chapter? If so, why this quotation?

3 IDEA STAGE

OBJECTIVES

In this chapter, you will learn about the following project management elements:

- Idea stage of the PPA
- The Wheel of Half Baked Ideas
- Filtering half baked ideas
- Developing the project idea
- Value-to-business
- Critical success factors
- Developing a well structured project request
- Stakeholder analysis
- Organizational change
- Stage gate review

This chapter focuses on the first stage of the PPA, the stage where newly evolving ideas are assessed for their viability. The important concept of filtering half baked ideas is explored by making use of the Wheel of Half Baked Ideas. The ideas that are deemed valuable move on and evolve into a well structured project request; the rest are abandoned or set aside for further consideration. The key focus of this stage is to make sure that only those project proposals that align with a stated organizational strategy, provide value to the business, and do not overlap or duplicate other existing projects are approved.

Organizations thrive by transforming viable ideas into processes and products in an effective and efficient manner: the definition of successful project management. However, successful projects remain an enigma to the IT/Business world:

> *Only 10 percent of the respondents indicated that their organizations' most important initiative of the past two years had been completed both on time and on budget . . .*
> Anne Field, "Project Management," *CIO Insight* (September 1, 2001, http://www.cioinsight.com/article2/0,3959,2333,0.asp).

The end result of poor performance is not only wasted investments and lost opportunities; failure of mission critical projects can actually jeopardize the existence of an organization. Consider the examples[1] of FoxMeyer Corp. and Tri Valley Growers. In the case of FoxMeyer Corp., a $5 billion drug distributor, a failed ERP project was a critical factor in its bankruptcy filing. Perhaps the saddest example is that of Tri Valley Growers, a 100-year old California company, which also filed for bankruptcy due to a failed IT/Business project. Ironically, as a part of their justification, practically every project has one thing in common: the promise of the proverbial competitive advantage. For both of these companies, their *competitors* gained the competitive advantage.

> *Hundreds of careful studies show that most new companies, products, and services are flops—even during the best of times.*
> Robert I. Sutton, "The Creativity Dilemma", *CIO Insight* (October 1, 2001, http://www.cioinsight.com/article2/0,3959,7345,00asp).

This is a sobering statistic. Focusing on the reference to products and services, one of the key contributors to the high failure rate is the undisciplined manner in which ideas for projects are generated and treated. Far too many projects start as a result of cursory remarks by senior executives. These impromptu suggestions often occur in an informal setting, such as discussions following a negative article about the company or a favorable article about a competitor or after reading an article about some state-of-the-art technology that is guaranteed to build the competitive edge (information often "planted" by the vendor's PR firm). The higher up in the company the person is, the chances of due diligence in exploring the brainchild are significantly reduced. Consider recent quotes from publications that target corporate executives:

> *CEOs have irrational expectations for what [software] can do, and CIOs don't have the gumption to tell them the truth . . .*
> Scott Berinato, "The Secret to Software Success," *CIO Magazine*, (July 1, 2001, http://www.cio.com/archive/070101/secret.html).

> *Problem is, in the past, there were plenty of veteran managers and staffers around who could talk . . . out of going too far out on a limb. . . . staffers often end up playing guessing games in which they debate what they think the CEO wants.*
> Louise Lee, "Gap: Missing That Ol'Mickey Magic, *BusinessWeek* (October 29, 2001, http://www.businessweek.com/magazine/content/01_44/63755100.html).

Unbridled expectations of executives, feckless behavior of functional managers, and begrudging compliance by project managers are the leading causes of the high rate of IT/Business project failures. In too many organizations, functional managers and project managers do not feel empowered to question the ideas of senior executives, no matter how half baked. In many cases,

---

[1]Kim S. Nash, "Top 10 Corporate Information Technology Failures," *Computerworld* (October 30, 2000, http://www.computerworld.com/networkingtopics/networking/management/story/0,10801,53014,00,html).

this can be a career limiting activity. This problem is further complicated because the quality of communications among business executives and project managers often leaves much to be desired. For example:

> *According to a nationwide survey, executives believe that 14 percent of each 40-hour workweek is wasted due to poor communication between staff and managers—amounting to a stunning seven weeks a year . . . Managers should invest the necessary time to ensure that project goals and instructions are free of ambiguity and foster an environment that encourages the open exchange of ideas.*
>
> "Do You Hear What I Hear?" *Business Leader Online*
> (www.businessleader.com/bl/nov98/73.html).

This means that for about six hours per week, managers and staff function in a confused state of mind. The two groups exchange babble. Neither party gives a signal that distinguishes between serious discussion and babbling. How many half baked ideas slip through as projects? We believe that quite a few do. Most such projects either are abandoned late in their life cycle or are not used. Our experience shows that low-value "pet" projects of overbearing managers can consume up to 30 percent of the corporate project budget.

The problem is further complicated by the fact that many project managers, especially IT project managers, rarely refuse a request—no matter how ill conceived it might be. The primary reason for such behavior is the misinterpretation of the phrase "committed to customer service." Many misconstrue it to mean, "Say 'yes' to anything the customer wants because saying 'no' would be interpreted as not being customer friendly." Unfortunately, many IT managers support this behavior because it is the politically expedient thing to do. In organizations that have no mature project management discipline, immediate "punishment" occurs for saying 'no' to a customer, but few (if any) repercussions ensue for the eventual late delivery or poor quality of the end product.

Many projects are deliberately *underestimated* (cost, resources, time) to please the sponsor and the customers and to obtain project approval. Combine this with the optimism present at the start of any given project, when most people are so excited about the idea that the natural tendency is to think only about the benefits to be achieved with little (or no) discussion of the difficulties of the proposed project. Those who dare to draw attention to the difficulties are labeled as naysayers. The result is two dimensional: overstate the "value to business" and understate the "cost to business" and the idea is sure to be approved as a project. In most organizations, idea generation occurs during annual budget development—typically the busiest time of the year—which results in less than adequate quality time to assess new project ideas.

The problem is further complicated because many project managers (who are usually technologists promoted to project management positions, and who lack education or training in the practices and principles of project management) do not further query the visionary. This lack of open and meaningful discussion often stems from the project managers' fears that any questioning may be perceived as being ignorant or arrogant. Most project managers rationalize: "Isn't the visionary, usually a senior executive, always right?" The higher the executive's rank, more validity is awarded to the idea.

Not all of the blame for "half baked" ideas becoming projects lies entirely with overly-aggressive business executives. Many project management professionals are more driven by the lure of new technology that will be acquired to complete the proposed project than by the business reasons for the project. They are often aided in this misguided choice by technology vendors and system integrators, who make huge profits by selling the leading edge technology and providing extensive consulting services. It is a win-win situation for everyone except the customer. The whole scheme can be summarized by saying: "We have a neat trick; who do we play it on?"

■ THE WHEEL OF HALF-BAKED IDEAS

A few years back, a CEO asked the Center to look into the reasons for an unusually high number of ill-conceived projects underway in the IT department and the inordinately long time between the start and end of most projects. He also pointed out that, while everyone appeared to be very busy, the number of projects actually completed and deployed was quite small.

We started the assignment by interviewing the CIO and her direct reports. Within two days, we discovered that they had a list of 198 recorded project requests and between thirty and forty project ideas—items being discussed, but not yet on anyone's to do list. Our discussions with the heads of six business units showed us that each of them had at least ten more "important" project ideas but had not discussed these with the CIO or her direct reports because the project wait list was already very long. Some of the business unit managers raised the issue of hiring outside consulting companies to backfill the IT department. Then, we focused on the ten IT project managers and learned that they were jointly managing between twenty and twenty-three projects (most of them were also responsible for support and maintenance of a number of recently deployed projects). Follow up discussions with the CIO and her direct reports revealed that they were surprised by the high number of projects in progress (they believed that only fifteen to seventeen projects were under way). We were fascinated by the ranges used by both groups, but discovered that they truly did not know the exact number of projects in progress because not all projects had specific official starts. In our discussions with the CIO, we also learned that the maximum number of projects the IT department could undertake at any given time was fifteen, because of the number of resources (project managers and team members) available for project work. The technology department was overstressed and mental fatigue was beginning to set in—project teams were making obvious mistakes, some of which resulted in financial and PR problems for the company.

After analyzing the initial data gathered from our interviews, we asked the CIO and her direct reports the following questions:

- What is the process for requesting new projects?
- Who authorizes the project managers to start new projects?
- If the maximum project capacity is fifteen projects, why were project managers managing as many as twenty-three projects?
- Why was the project wait list allowed to grow to 198?
- What leads to the creation of new projects?

Then, we asked the same questions of the project managers and the heads of the various business units. From our assessment and analysis of their responses, we prepared a presentation for the CEO. The phrase "Wheel of Half Baked Ideas" originated from our presentation. Figure 3.1 depicts our interpretation of the processes and practices that result from projects that are "half baked" ideas.

What we discovered was that a business executive would think of an idea or a solution (sometimes to some undefined problem) and call a meeting with a manager from IT. They would discuss the idea briefly. Then, the manager would contact an IT project manager with the message: "The boss needs this done, needs it done soon" followed by, "When can you have it done?" The project manager, believing that there is no other option, round-up a few team members and assigns yet another emergency project. The team members begrudgingly start to work on the new project so that the managers can report some progress to the appropriate executive. Most of the time, none of this resulted in any real progress. In fact, even more projects would fall behind schedule. The process, as depicted in Figure 3.1, can be illustrated in this way:

1. The executive (a big wheel—a gear with lots of torque) moves a few notches in one direction and the team below immediately goes through dozens of revolutions. Lots of action and noise, but likely to achieve little real progress because they lacked proper direction.
2. A few days go by and the big wheel either thinks of another new idea, or sends a message for the team to look into alternatives for the previous idea. The big gear moves in the reverse direction by a few notches.
3. The hapless project manager then redirects the team and they revolve in the reverse direction; their counter revolutions are fast and furious. Invariably, this results in negative progress in the previously promised project schedules and they are forced to work overtime to make up the lost time. This senseless churning produces lots of project documentation, long issue lists, innumerable meetings, and lots of progress reports—but little real progress.
4. One project manager mentioned that at this point, a laser jet printer used by a team would display the message: "Toner Low." To her surprise, she discovered that some managers interpreted the lack of toner as an unquestionable sign of progress. To them, it meant that the team was hard at work.

FIGURE 3.1
The Wheel of Half Baked
Ideas.

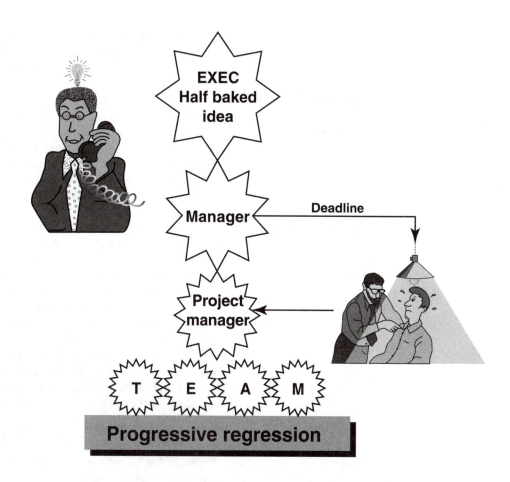

The result was that the teams made little progress. Progress is defined as the act of moving forward toward a goal. They did not have a goal and they were not moving—they were simply spinning. We gave this phenomenon the name "Progressive Regression," which can be defined as screwing yourself into the ground as you stand still.

Having spoken casually in a private meeting about new ideas, the executive or senior manager will likely be oblivious to the ensuing project development work. One of the most fascinating examples of this corporate ignorance involves a CIO and his two direct reports, who more than once learned about new projects listening to the radio on the way to work. One time the CEO announced new offerings and services without ever having discussed these with the CIO. In the other two cases, the head of marketing made similar surprise broadcasts. All three new products required extensive work by the IT department.

We used the diagram in Figure 3.1 in our presentation to the CEO. Though he was not happy with it, the CEO did see how the haphazard process for creating new projects was resulting in undue pressure on the project management group. He did acknowledge that something needed to be done to improve the process of starting new projects in the business units and in the project management group.

Genesis of a Project—A Dangerous Scenario

Mid-level IT Manager to a Project Manager:	The senior VP of sales just called me because he has a great idea for a new project that will get our company into many new markets and he wants me to be the sponsor. I need you to put a team together and start on this project ASAP.
	(The manager will now be referred to as the sponsor.)
Project Manager:	Which specific strategy is the idea aligned with? Have they defined the value-to-business using any specific metrics? Why isn't the VP of sales sponsoring the project?

Sponsor:	The VP of sales knows what he is talking about. I want you to interview some of the direct reports to the VP to define the value-to-business. The VP is a very busy person and doesn't have the time for sponsorship.
Project Manager:	You know we have a steering committee that approves all new projects; will you be making the presentation to the committee?
Sponsor:	No, I will be on a two-week vacation (climbing the second highest peak on Mt. Kilimanjaro). You will need to make the presentation and get funding approval from the committee. It is important that you convey the value of the project to the committee emphatically, because the VP of sales is relying on us to get the job done.
Project Manager:	Aren't we taking unnecessary risk and putting our necks on the line? This is not an IT project—the customer should be responsible for the justification and approval.
Sponsor:	Your thinking is not going to get us anywhere. The VP of sales needs a big success, we need a big success, and it will certainly move you a couple of notches up the line of promotion if this project is a success. I wanted to give you the first option on this project, but if you don't think you are up to it, I have a couple of other people in mind, especially that outsourcing group. I talked with their onsite representative, and he agreed that it was a great idea and told me that they are ready to take on the job. I need your decision soon because of my tight time schedule.

You might think that we simply conjured up this scenario to make a point. Wrong. Remember the statistics regarding the high rate of failed and challenged IT/Business projects? Scenarios similar to the one given are key contributors to that dismal state of affairs. Where do you think the project will end up? It will fail, and it will take the project manager and the team with it.

I am the director of business development. Our president has the habit of walking throughout our facility, periodically peeking into our offices. One day he came in to my office very excited and exclaimed, "I have a plan. We're going to double our business revenues in two years!"

I replied, "That's great, what's the plan?"

He looked at me with a combination of sadness and confusion, then turned and walked away muttering, "You just don't get it."

> Dilbert Newsletter 46.0 © 2003, United Feature Syndicate, lnc. (February, 2003, http://www.dilbert.com/comics/dilbert/anrc/html/newsletter46.html).

Ask yourself, "Does your organization have a well defined process to separate (filter) real visions from half baked ideas?" To be successful, project managers must develop the skills to separate the truly sound projects from half baked ideas. Then they must focus their team's energies to bring such projects to success in a cost efficient and effective manner.

An ingenious man has many projects, but, if governed by sound sense, will be slow in forming them into designs.

> Webster's Revised Unabridged Dictionary (MICRA, lnc., 1996, 1998, http://dictionary.reference.com/search?q=project).

Another problem area revolves around project ideas that originate among the lower levels of the organization—day-to-day employees. These ideas usually deal with improvements of existing services and products and occasionally with introducing new products and services. It is hard to believe that few organizations implement a well thought out process to capture such project ideas and give them the needed attention in a timely manner. Your organization must make it a priority to implement such a process.

FIGURE 3.2
The Idea stage.

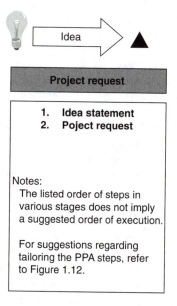

The Idea stage of the PPA, shown in Figure 3.2, outlines two steps to help both the originators of project ideas and project managers to separate viable project ideas from half baked ideas effectively and efficiently. The end result is a comprehensive project request. The Idea stage is the *beginning* of the due diligence needed to ascertain the soundness of new ideas.

■ IDEA STATEMENT—PPA STEP I

The genesis of a successful project is a clearly articulated statement of the project idea by the customer. To guide the customer in formulating the project idea, we suggest inclusion of the following key items:

- Idea ID
- Requestor name
- Date of request
- Situation analysis
- Purpose of the project? What will it do?
- Who will use it?
- Where will it be used?
- Key search words
- Strategy alignment
- Value-to-business
- Critical success factors
- Customer's deadline
- Project impact
- Consequences of doing nothing
- Security requirements
- Window of opportunity

At this point, let us spotlight a number of key items in the list above.

Situation Analysis

This is the foundation for all other items needed to complete a comprehensive project request. The person making the request needs to look back and describe recent history, the current situation, and how we got there. The purpose here is to provide a historical perspective, for both the person who will eventually write the project charter as well as the sponsor who will be called upon to approve the new project. A good approach is to focus on the current problem (or need), describe what is wrong or missing, and explain why it needs to be fixed.

Purpose of the Project

This is perhaps the most cogent component of the information needed to justify the idea. The best approach to describe the purpose of the proposed idea is for the requestor to paint a picture of the end state of the project and describe why that is better than where the organization is now. To present the idea effectively, focus on the intent of the proposed idea. This is the first validation of the idea. If the individual is not able to describe the future and state the improvements and associated benefits, the idea is not that viable and has a slim chance of survival.

Focus on the Business Problem

The person who requests the new project must concentrate on the problem at hand and actively avoid proposing a specific solution. The latter misstep can lead to significant trouble because it begins to limit the thought process and directs it into a preconceived approach to solving the problem, which may not be the prudent way to proceed. An even bigger problem is created if the person suggesting the solution is high up in the organization, has a forceful personality, and the proposed solution really is not the best choice. The project manager is then stuck in a no-win situation, the Catch-22 of project management.

Who Will Use It?

The person who had the idea must think through the scope of the impact of the resulting solution. Will the ensuing project impact just a few, or will it impact a large number of disparate groups? At times, even senior executives can have a myopic view of the world around them and not realize the extent of the impact of a new idea. Overlooking such information can result in an idea being rejected. For example, a project is designed to improve the defect rate of a process that is in use by thousands of people across the organization. Forgetting to include this information and highlight it as a potential benefit may actually result in rejection of the proposal, especially if ROI is an important part of the project approval process.

Key Search Words

Later in this chapter, you will see that an important step is to ascertain the presence of any duplicate/overlapping ideas/projects. The best approach to facilitate this search is to create a specific documentation item, "key search words," and then to imbed key words to facilitate the search for duplicate/overlapping ideas. During the life cycle of an active project, the project manager should take specific care to keep this documentation item updated to reflect changes to the project scope (additions, changes, and/or removal of functionality).

Strategy Alignment

A well run organization will implement several strategies to guide the organization to its optimal performance. For example:

- Greater market share
- Greater operational efficiencies
- Greater volume
- Higher customer retention
- Improved customer service
- Improved financial reporting
- Improved productivity
- Improved profit margin
- Increased brand awareness

- Increased customer collaboration
- Increased profits
- Reduced cost

An important consideration for any new idea (project) is to ensure that it supports a specific strategy (or strategies); otherwise, it would not be considered a wise investment.

> *One of the biggest things we do in demonstrating value to the CEO and the board is showing that everything we do reflects the company's business strategy," says Rick Omartian, chief financial officer for Guardian's IT department.*
> Thomas Hoffman, "How Will You Prove IT Value?" *Computerworld* (January 6, 2003, http://www.computerworld.com/managementtopics/ management/story/0,10801,77166,00.html).

To achieve the best results, the customer proposing the idea needs to clearly answer the question: "Which specific corporate strategy is the project linked to?" For example: The proposed project is linked to the market share and operational efficiency strategies. Often, discussions on this important subject are limited to private conversations among corporate executives, with minimal communication of vital information to the project manager. In fact, many organizations lack the essential discipline necessary to ensure that only those project ideas that contribute to corporate strategy are considered. It is not uncommon for business unit managers to push pet projects down the line. Most of these projects either fail to deliver value or are outright failures.

> *Things handed down from on high by fiat tend not to ever work.*
> David Pearson, "To Hell and Back," *CIO Magazine* (December 1, 1998, http://www.cio.com/archive/120198/turk.html).

Value-To-Business

The questions to ask are: what value does this project bring to the organization? What is the business need of the project? One of the essential decisions that must be made regarding any project idea is whether the project is worth doing. The customer, prior to investing scarce project management resources, must make this decision upfront. A comprehensive value-to-business assessment states the degree to which the proposed project will contribute to achieving a specific strategy. This means the business customer must clearly state the *specific* tangible benefits that the proposed project will bring to the organization. Some examples of value-to-business are:

- Additional revenues
- Competitive advantage
- Cost savings
- Customer service
- Efficiency of operations
- Higher ROI
- Increase in capacity
- Mandate (describe the mandating authority)
- Market share
- Reduced head count
- Revenue generation

These benefits must be *quantifiable* so that they can be measured against the investment the organization will make in the proposed idea. For example:

- Reduce head count in the call center by 42 people (7 managers, 32 call center operators, and 3 support staff) resulting in a saving of $2,500,000.

While reading project proposals over the years, we routinely came across statements of project benefits (value-to-business) that on the first reading sounded really good. Then came the project implementation stage, and all of the sudden, management was faced with a number of unpleasant questions. For example:

- Do the promised savings of $2,500,000 include any severance pay or other appropriate settlement costs for the people to be laid off because of the head count reduction?
- Will the human resources and legal departments approve the layoff, and will the finance department approve any financial settlement options?
- Will the company be able to absorb the 42 employees into other departments?
- Will the company absorb some employees and lay others off?
- Keeping the most viable option(s) in mind, what are the actual cost savings to the company?
- Is the project still viable?

You may be surprised how often the people proposing new projects overlook these questions. The results of such oversights can range from low employee morale to damaged corporate reputation and lawsuits. Therefore, any proposed benefits need to be thought through completely. Only then can actual values be attached to the arguments used for project justification.

The trouble with people is not that they don't know but that they know so much that ain't so.
Josh Billings.

At times, the value-to-business statement may be based on certain legal or policy mandates imposed by regulatory agencies. For example:

- The proposed project is designed to bring the corporate accounting practices in line with the Sarbanes-Oxley[2] act.
- The proposed project is designed to prove compliance with the latest residential rates ruling by the Public Utilities Commission (PUC).
- The proposed project is designed to satisfy an OSHA labor safety ruling.

In the case of legally mandated projects, it may be helpful to state the consequences (financial penalties, legal exposure, lost opportunities) of not proceeding with the proposed project. It is imperative that each project has a comprehensive justification, developed by the business customers and based on generally accepted risk and reward computations used by the organization to justify capital acquisition projects. For example:

- Internal rate of return (IRR)
- Net present value (NPV)
- Payback period
- Return on investment (ROI)

Most technical project teams, IT or otherwise, typically do not understand the customers' day-to-day business operations and processes well enough to accurately compute the value-to-business of the proposed project. In fact, most technical teams—IT, engineering, manufacturing—may even be deficient in the knowledge and skill needed to accurately compute the proposed project's value-to-business. Therefore, it is imperative that knowledgeable business people be called upon to *define* and *justify* the value-to-business computations. If necessary, a subject matter expert from the finance department may be asked to validate the computations. *Never* let a vendor do the work to develop justification for a proposed project.

Believing that "if we don't do it, it won't get done," IT sometimes justifies the project value for the project sponsor. In assuming the role of the customer, however, the IT group is threatening the potential success of the initiative. Better to let an initiative fall by the wayside than to start a project without the necessary business commitment and leadership.
Susan H. Cramm, "The Business Knows Best," *CIO Magazine* (November 1, 2002, http://www.cio.com/archive/110102/hs_agenda_html).

The simplest way to look at the value-to-business is to envision the degree to which a given project will contribute to the stated corporate strategies. The data collected here, combined with the project's complexity to be computed in the prelaunch stage, will help the project sponsor decide on

---

[2]This law, passed by the U.S. Congress in July 2002, created new SEC rules forcing top corporate executives to sign off, for the first time, on the integrity of their internal financial controls.

the merit of the proposed project. To make this process equitable and uniform, the business unit should capture the current business value metrics so that an accurate comparison can be made between the before and after numbers. Once a project is in production, the appropriate business unit must capture the project benefits data to compare the actual project performance with the value proposition used to justify the project. This two-pronged approach has two possible benefits:

- It will help minimize the start of low-value projects
- It will help management decide on the ongoing value of projects in production and the future investments in these projects

Critical Success Factors

A small number of well defined indicators (accomplishments) will help determine the success of the proposed project. Wherever possible, each indicator needs to be accompanied by a quantified measurement. These factors can be grouped into two major categories:

1. *Product related:* The functionality, features, quality, usability, security, customer acceptance, schedule, budget performance, and operational efficiency.
2. *Process related:* Customer-team communications, customer preparation for product deployment, organizational change management, sponsor effectiveness, team disposition, and the quality of the project development process.

Examples of critical success factors for a project to improve the performance of a call center are shown in Figure 3.3.

Over the years, we at the Center have discussed the benefits of specifically defining and monitoring the opposite of critical success factors. We call these the "unmitigated failure factors." Some examples are:

- Estimate-to-please
- Heavy trust in bleeding edge technology
- High degree of unmanaged change
- Lack of a committed sponsor with the authority to guide the project to success
- Lack of continuous customer involvement
- Lack of explicit buy-in by key stakeholders
- Under-resourced and underskilled teams
- Underskilled and overburdened project managers
- Unfettered scope creep
- Unrealistic expectations

Customer's Deadline

Dictated deadlines are the bane of most project managers. Customers often dictate deadlines for their project before anyone has had time to develop even a conceptual design to solve the problem at hand. Too many project managers acquiesce to these deadlines, and then miss them. Therefore, if a customer specifies a deadline this early, it is important to ask the customer some questions:

- What are the reasons for this deadline?
- Is it competitive pressure, financial limitations, legal requirement, executive mandate, or by arbitrary order?

FIGURE 3.3

Examples of critical success factors.

Critical success factors	Metrics
Reduced turnover of new recruits	10 percent within first year of employment
Decrease in ramp up time of new recruits	Independent within 60 days of employment
Increase overall skill level of the staff	1st review score of 3.5 or more (4 pt. scale)
System up time	99 percent
Accuracy of data	98 percent
Technical assistance calls	Less than 3 in 100 uses

- What are the implications of not meeting this deadline?
- In case the deadline cannot be met, what tradeoffs are possible?

Often, too much emphasis is placed on project deadlines and little, if any, on the quality of the end product. Management often dictates artificially tight deadlines for a variety of reasons—lack of trust in the team to come up with a realistic schedule, desire to challenge the team to work harder, and pressure to pursue wild goose chases by ill-informed customers and managers.

> *Don't start a project with a deadline in mind. Figure out the project requirements, then determine how long it will take to accomplish them.*
>
> Ben Worthen, "Nestlé's ERP Odyssey,"
> *CIO Magazine* (May 15, 2002, p. 64).

Our advice to project managers is to document the desired deadline, the reasons behind it, and any customer suggested tradeoffs (if it becomes difficult to meet the deadline). If the deadline seems to be unreasonable, make a note and inform the customer of your concerns. Just make sure that you do not imply to the customer, by any of your pronouncements or lack thereof, that you will be able to meet the deadline. There are good reasons for this caution:

- The first notion of the estimated duration of the proposed project will emerge at the end of the next stage, prelaunch, when a size estimate is developed for the proposed solution. At this point in the idea stage, your estimate to complete will have a high error range so coming up with an estimated completion date will be close to impossible.
- The point at which you and the team will have a better opinion of the possible finish date is at the end of the launch stage, when you will develop task-based estimates and the critical path (the expected duration) of the project.
- The project's estimated completion date will be computed when you take the task-based duration estimates and plot them into the team's calendar. The act of developing a schedule is the first step in the Execute stage.
- Considerable changes may take place in the project scope, budget, and/or quality components because of the work done in the remaining part of this stage and the prelaunch stage.
- The proposal may even be rejected at the end of this or the next stage as a nonviable project.

At this point in the process, the project manager/team is still a long way from discussing a realistic deadline for completion of the project. Of course, the client may have a desired deadline in mind and may be very adamant about it. These preferences should be duly acknowledged and noted, but not agreed to.

Project Impact

Identify any existing systems, projects, and processes that will be impacted by the proposed project. Of special interest is the degree of change that the proposed idea will bring to the current way of doing things. It is amazing how often the person proposing a new project overlooks the extent of the impact of a new process or product on existing systems, processes, and projects. This oversight is a key reason for the customer to underestimate the true extent of the work that will be needed to integrate the new project into any current products and/or systems.

Consequences of Doing Nothing

Many customers resist considering this option. The reason for the reluctance is that it forces them to look deeper into the need for the proposed project and find specific and viable arguments for justifying their request. The question, "What are the consequences of dong nothing?" though a little off putting, is worth discussing because it requires the customer to state the value of the proposed project in a succinct manner. Conversations with a number of project managers revealed that many did not wish to raise this question out of the fear of not having a project to work on. Our experience shows that a large number of projects that eventually fail or are challenged would not have been approved if this question was asked in earnest and was given due thought by business customers. This tendency for project managers and teams to go without "pushing back" is a major cause of many failures, some quite spectacular.

> *We could have told you it was a piece of junk.*
>> Xerox employee to David Kearns, then CEO, Xerox, on the disastrous 1979 launch of a new copier. *Executive Book of Quotations* (New York: Oxford University Press, 1994, p. 63).

Of course, there is the other side of the coin, where inaction could mean a major hit on the organization, such as noncompliance with a regulatory policy. Therefore, this specific question is good for rejecting, as well as justifying, a new idea.

> *It is a great evil, as well as a misfortune, to be able to utter a prompt and decided "No."*
>> C. Simmons, *The New Dictionary of Thought, A Cyclopedia of Quotations,* (United States: Standard Book Company, 1957, p. 300).

Security Requirements

Certain projects, especially projects related to development of products and services that need to be protected from competitive market knowledge and those being undertaken by certain governmental agencies, require controlled information dispersal. Some projects may even need to be assigned code names. If the proposed idea falls under such needs, consult the organization's policies and proceed accordingly. Additionally, the person proposing the idea must think through the security needs when the project goes into the Operation stage.

Figure 3.4 shows our suggested template for an idea statement. It can take the originator of the idea two to four hours to supply all of the needed information (it may take longer the first few times someone uses the template). Just to be clear, this represents the time needed by the originator to sit down, concentrate, and complete the idea statement template. It does not include the time the same person may spend researching background information, having discussions with colleagues and subject matter experts, and surfing the Internet for information to bolster the proposal.

Window of Opportunity

The successful deployment of some projects can be highly dependent on a specific time window. For example:

- A student registration project at a university must be fully operational prior to the start of a semester/quarter registration.
- A project centered on product shipping for card and candy companies like prior to Mother's Day and Valentine Day, and for car companies prior to the release date of next year's models.
- Release of a new technology product by a computer manufacturer just prior to a major industry conference, e.g., COMDEX and CeBIT.

These projects are highly sensitive to specific, and usually short, windows of opportunity. If not fully operational by the right target date, the next opportunity may be months away, or there may be no next opportunity, resulting in major financial and public relations losses to the organization. Therefore, it is imperative to clearly state any window of opportunity constraints of the proposed project.

Some customers, who are accustomed to doing nothing more than sending cryptic messages to get new projects started, might object to and complain about the extent of information needed to propose a new project. The most popular objections are: "This degree of bureaucracy doesn't work for creative people like us"; "you don't need all this information;" "we will cross that bridge when we come to it;" and the most alarming of all—"just trust me." If you buy the arguments and start working on such half baked ideas, you are not ready to be a successful project manager and you

Idea statement
Idea ID:
Requestor name:
Date of request:
Situation analysis: Provide a brief historical perspective; then focusing on the current problem or need, describe what is wrong or missing and why it needs to be fixed. Concentrate on the problem at hand; avoid proposing a specific solution.
Purpose of the project: Describe the end state of the project and explain why that is better than where the organization is now.
Who will use it? How many people or groups will the proposed project impact? A few groups or a large number of disparate groups?
Where will it be used? What is the deployment scope of the proposed project? Is it local, national, or international?
Key search words: List any key words that will help people search the ideas database to ascertain whether duplicate and/or overlapping ideas/projects currently exist.
Strategy alignment: Specify the particular strategy or strategies the proposed project is aligned to.
Value-to-business: State the specific tangible benefits that the proposed project will bring to the organization.
Critical success factors: What are the indicators (accomplishments) that will help determine the success of the proposed project? Each indicator must be accompanied by a quantified measurement.
Customer's deadline: If there is a deadline, describe the reason for the deadline and the implications of not meeting the deadline. If the deadline cannot be met, are any tradeoffs possible in scope, cost, and quality?
Project impact: Identify any existing systems, projects, and processes that will be impacted by the proposed project. What degree of change will the proposed idea bring to the current way of doing things?
Consequences of doing nothing: Describe the impact on the organization if the idea is scuttled. (This point can help scuttle a "half-baked" idea and justify a good one.)
Security requirements: Describe the overall security needs of the proposed project—the nature of its sensitivity to unauthorized exposure.
Window of opportunity: State any window of opportunity constraints of the proposed project.

FIGURE 3.4
Idea statement template.

certainly would benefit from attending a course on negotiations. An example of the havoc caused by half baked ideas:

> . . . almost three-quarters of all software development in the Internet era suffered from one or more of the following: total failure, cost overruns, time overruns, or a rollout with fewer features or functions than promised.
>
> Scott Berinato, "The Secret to Software Success," *CIO Magazine*, (July 1, 2001, http://www.cio.com/archive/070101/secret.html).

Keep in mind that all of the elements of the idea statement are the domain of the person requesting the new project, because it is primarily a statement of the problem and the expected benefits. People who do not clearly understand the concept may object to the work needed to prepare an idea statement. They may prefer to send an inexplicable message to their staff: because profits are down, we must quickly acquire greater market share for our services. The wheel of half baked ideas will soon begin to spin.

Our discussions with a large number of project managers has shown us that new ideas are often born during dialogues among business executives, managers and selected subject matter experts. However, because most of the thinking regarding these notions is still tentative, not much is documented and little is communicated to the project managers and teams eventually responsible for transforming these undefined ideas into projects. We strongly believe that a well documented idea statement not only helps the business customer develop a clearer definition of the problem and the expected benefits, it also communicates the underlying reasons and appropriate background information to the project manager and the project team. The information for an idea statement should *not* be created/completed by the group responsible for developing the solution.

> *Never ask the barber if you need a haircut.*
> Warren Buffet.

The customer may not be capable of completing the required information for one of two key reasons:

1. The customer does not have the skill. In such cases, the project management group should offer to educate and train the customer and should be ready to provide assistance, but should not take on the responsibility.
2. The customer does not have the time. It is still their responsibility. When they have the time, and can clearly articulate their idea, then the project management group can proceed with the next step: developing a project request.

If, for whatever reasons, you succumb to the customer's pressure and take on the responsibility to complete the idea statement, revisit Figure 3.1; your name will soon appear on the PM gear so get ready to spin—or would you prefer the mocking post?

■ PROJECT REQUEST—PPA STEP 2

Once an idea statement has been reviewed and recorded in the appropriate database, the next step is to develop a project request. Typically, *not* every idea statement would qualify to be advanced to the project request step; the individual or the group responsible for managing the idea statement database makes this decision. For more discussion on this subject, refer to Chapter 10, *Portfolio Management*. The development of a project request requires additional examination of the idea statement. The purpose of this step is to provide enough information to the requesting customer and to the decision makers to facilitate an informed and intelligent evaluation of the proposed project. The responsibility to prepare a project request is usually assigned to a project manager, or same level individual, who then works with the individual who initiated the idea and appropriate business unit and technology subject matter experts. The additional items of information that are typically needed to complete the project request are:

Key stakeholders	Funding source
Key assumptions	Ownership
Organizational change	Project duplication/overlap
Spending limit	

Key Stakeholders

It is necessary to identify and document the key stakeholders—those individuals or organizations that have a *vested interest* in the project's outcome because it is going to impact their well being,

FIGURE 3.5
Project stakeholders.

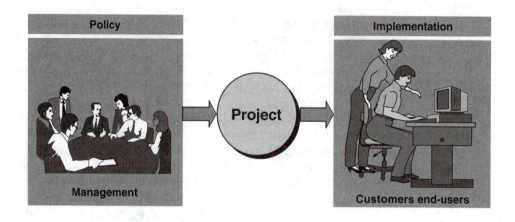

authority, status, and/or day-to-day operations. We put project stakeholders into two key groups (see Figure 3.5).

1. Policy-level stakeholders
2. Implementation-level stakeholders

Policy-Level Stakeholders   Individuals/groups who make the prime decisions and set the policies that will shape the project. Imagine that the project is a puppet that has strings attached to it. Policy-level stakeholders are the individuals or groups (internal or external) who have control of the strings and make the puppet move; these people will shape the project. It is essential to identify all of the policy-level stakeholders as well as their interests in the project.

Implementation-Level Stakeholders   These are the individuals and groups (internal or external) that will be impacted by the outcome of the project—their day-to-day work life will be *changed* and *reshaped* by the project. A particular stakeholder may appear on both lists. In the case of an executive information system, managers define their information needs and are also the recipients of the information produced by the system. Depending on the nature and scope of a project, the number of policy-level stakeholders can vary from a few to many, and the number of implementation-level stakeholders can vary from many to hundreds. Because the list of stakeholders must be comprehensive, practice vigilance when developing your list. Possible stakeholders to include on your list are:

Accounting	Manufacturing
Board of directors	Marketing
Civil/citizen groups	Public relations
Construction	Purchasing
Distribution	Real estate
Employees	Regulatory agencies
Engineering	Research and development
Finance	Safety
Financial organizations (external)	Sales
Human resources	Security
Investment community	Shipping
IT	Trademark and patent management
Labor unions	Vendors
Legal	Warehousing

When developing the stakeholders' list for a given project, keep the phrase "vested interest" in mind. Focus on the organizations and/or people who will have a measurable impact on the project and/or who will be measurably impacted by the project. At this early stage, the objective is to identify the various stakeholders; the steps to conduct a detailed stakeholder assessment are discussed in Chapter 4 (*Stakeholder Analysis*).

Key Assumptions

Assumption: Something taken for granted or accepted as true without proof; a supposition, i.e., an opinion or belief without sufficient evidence.

All projects start with certain assumptions—promises by a variety of people, such as managers, vendors, and other project managers—about events or conditions that will come true in the future at an appropriate time. Assumptions, though necessary for any project, can result in problems if they don't hold true. Therefore, it behooves a project manager to review each assumption and give it a test of reality—what is the probability that it will come true at the appropriate time? For example, consider the following three assumptions:

1. The security group will have the new password management system in operation by March 15.
2. The sales manager will assign three senior full-time sales people starting November 12 for a period of two months to help define the requirements of the new system.
3. The vendor will install a fully tested system (hardware and software) by February 15.

An important step for the project manager at this point is to try to validate these assumptions. In the case of the first assumption, discuss the item with the project manager or the individual responsible for developing the security system, and discuss the probability of the timely completion of the system. If their project is already in progress, ask to review their schedule and any outstanding issues that might negatively impact their project. The inquiry must be conducted in a professional manner, without implying any distrust of their commitments. Similarly, to verify the second assumption, we would suggest that the project manager personally meet, or contact, the appropriate functional manager of the sales people and discuss the importance of their promised availability. The project manager should also take the initiative to contact the people directly and inquire about their availability. Make sure that the same people have not been promised to other projects. An important consideration is timing: Does the two-month period starting on November 12 fall in the midst of the busy sales cycle? If so, it is realistic to assume that the sales people will be available to participate in the requirements definition sessions. Instead, you must expect that they will be busy making those all-important sales, because they have quotas to meet and their bonuses depend on their ability to close sales.

In response to the assumption related to the vendor, the project manager should investigate the history of the vendor's ability to meet commitments. Information to obtain would include:

- Who from the vendor's side made this promise?
- Is the person authorized to do so?
- Is there a clearly documented record of the promise in the project file?
- Is there a specific penalty for noncompliance?

At times, long lists of assumptions put the project proposal on shaky ground. However, on closer inspection, we invariably find that issues have been recorded as assumptions. The project manager and the team need to learn to differentiate between an issue and an assumption; the former is defined as an unanswered question or a difference of opinion and the latter is a supposition of a future event. For example, consider the following statements:

- Will the customer laptops have Version 7 of the operating system (OS) installed by June 21?
- Will the real estate group have an approved lease for the proposed office space by May 15?
- Will two senior designers be available full time, starting the first week of July?
- Do we have a sufficient number of licenses for the vendor software package?
- All team members will be trained and certified by vendor *x* by the end of August.
- Two expert-level designers will be hired and assigned, full-time, to the project by the first week of July.

The last two statements are assumptions; the rest are issues and should not appear in the assumptions list. All assumptions must be tested throughout the project life cycle to determine whether they remain valid and/or relevant.

Organizational Change

The project request should include a high-level statement regarding the degree and nature of the organizational change—cultural, political, or technical—as a result of the deployment of the proposed project. Because change is an extremely sensitive area, the person proposing the project needs to carefully ascertain the degree and magnitude of the change that the proposed project will produce.

Spending Limit

The customer might have a specific limit on funds available for the proposed work. Knowing that limit can be advantageous for the person who will complete the project request document and the project charter. However, customers are not always comfortable divulging any numbers this early in the project, believing that providing this information will limit their options. This is a question of mutual trust and the quality of the work environment, and should be addressed and resolved.

Funding Source

Which department(s) will cover the budget for the project, and who has the authority for funding approval?

Ownership

The department that will take ownership of the end product or process once the project is completed. We know of projects in progress, for which the project manager is not able to identify the group that will take ownership of the project at its completion. These are "orphan projects."

> *Worse still, no one owned the project. IS thought the business users owned it, the business users thought IS owned it, and the CEO thought the vendor owned it. There was an unwritten project plan with five or six major milestones, but not a single one of those had been met and no one on the project team could say when they might be met.*
> D. Pearson, "To Hell and Back," *CIO Magazine,* (December 1, 1998, http://www.cio.com/archive/120198/turk.html).

> *A company wide survey showed that 128 different projects were already in progress, many of which had no business owner . . .*
> Jay Gardner, quoted in Julia King, "Identify, Kill Non-essential Projects, CIO Recommends," *Computerworld* (March 3, 2003, http://www.computerworld.com/managementtopics/ management/story/0,10801,78940,00.html).

Project Duplication/Overlap

It is necessary to document the amount of duplication (or overlap) with any project(s) that might be on a wait list, in development mode, or already operational. In most organizations that do not have a well-maintained project database, the likelihood of duplicate and overlapping projects is very high. For example:

> *In Europe, there were 11 different J&J companies working on 20 new technology applications, five of them for bar-coding alone.*
> JoAnn Heisen, "Thinking Out Loud," *CIO Insight,* (December 1, 2001, http://www.cioinsight.com/article2/0,1397,134845,00.asp).

These are not isolated examples. In the case of the client referred to in the discussion of the Wheel of Half Baked Ideas, of the 198 projects on the waiting list, twenty-five were absolute duplicates, twenty-one had major overlaps, and twenty-seven had considerable overlaps. In some cases, the requesting customers had actually forgotten that they had already requested certain projects/work, or new people had come into the department and did not know what had already been requested. Of course, the problem was perpetuated because the project management group did not have a process in place to check for duplicate/overlap project requests. Because of the amount and variety of information required, the person responsible for completing the project request needs a thorough knowledge of the customer's business as well as access to the organization's project database of project ideas, project requests, project charters, projects in progress, and operational projects.

An important component of the project request development step is to make sure that the individual who is responsible for completing the task reviews the lessons learned database (developed as a part of PPA Step 30, the implement stage) and draws out any applicable dos and don'ts from the historical record. If such a database is not available, the individual should then attempt to discuss the proposed project with fellow project managers and appropriate business functional managers who have had experience with similar projects.

What should you *not* incorporate in the project request? Two important guidelines to follow are:

1. Do not delve into a solution for the problem; that will come later in the Prelaunch and Launch stages. At this point, focus on stating the business problem the best you can.
2. Do not include any estimate in the project request. First of all, it is too early to develop *any* estimate. Secondly, your customer will definitely remember the numbers you submit and they will come back to haunt you (both the numbers and the customers).

Why must there be so much work to formulate the idea statement and project request? Review the statistics regarding failed and challenged projects: over 60 percent of projects either fail or do not deliver the promised functionality and quality. Most projects ultimately cost far more than the original estimates indicate and are delivered long after the promised delivery date. A key contributor to these dismal statistics is the practice of launching half baked, ideas into full-fledged projects without the necessary due diligence.

We recommend using the template depicted in Figure 3.6 to complete a project request. For a medium size project (from 6 to 9 months in duration), a project manager or similar level person will take from 6 to 8 hours of effort to complete the necessary information. It may take longer the first few times someone uses the template. This estimate *does not* include the time the person may spend tracking people, researching obscure background information, having discussions with elusive subject matter experts, and searching the corporate project database for duplicate/overlapping projects.

■ THE FILTERING PROCESS

All of the discussion related to documenting the idea statement and the project request underscores our effort to filter out unviable project ideas as early as possible, thereby improving the probabilities of project success. The various questions and the key information items highlighted are the filters that help the decision makers focus on the most viable ideas. The diagram in Figure 3.7 depicts this process.

This process may seem too rigorous to some, but without such due diligence, the results are all too predictable:

- "Bad" projects push out "good" projects and compete for management time.
- Resources are wasted on ill-advised projects.
- Teams work on projects that are redundant, incompatible, and in conflict with each other.
- There is a poor ROI.

■ STAGE GATE NO. I

The purpose of this stage gate is to ensure that sufficient due diligence has been practiced to help filter out half baked and unreasonable ideas, and to verify that ideas that seem practical have been duly processed to create a comprehensive and viable project request. Figure 3.8 depicts an example of list of attributes for the stage gate review of the Idea stage.

The project manager and the core team meet to assess the degree to which each of the attributes has been accomplished. To make the assessment useful, we suggest that the team members, under the facilitation of the project manager, collectively review their work and decide on the quality of each related item in the assessment. In the column titled "Confidence level," the value of 1

Project request

Key stakeholder:
Identify the policy-level stakeholders—those who will shape the project.

Identify the implementation-level stakeholders—those who will be shaped by the project.

Key assumptions: Describe the assumptions (an opinion or belief *without* sufficient evidence) being made/stated at this point.

Organizational change: Provide a high-level statement regarding the degree and nature of the organizational cultural, political, and technical change the proposed project will bring to the key stakeholders.

Spending limit: Has a limit been set on the budget/expenditure for this proposed idea? If so, what is the reason for the limit?

Funding source: Who has the authority to approve the budget? (Who holds the purse strings?)

Ownership: Which organization will take responsibility for the ongoing ownership of the end product of this proposed project?

Project Duplication/Overlap: Is there any duplication of, or overlap with, any other project (waiting to start, in development, or operational)?

FIGURE 3.6

A project request template.

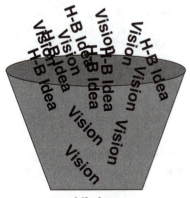

FIGURE 3.7

The filtering process.

Stage gate no. 1: attributes	Confidence level					Action plan
1. Strategy alignment	1	2	3	4	5	
2. Value-to-business	1	2	3	4	5	
3. Critical success factors	1	2	3	4	5	
4. Project impact	1	2	3	4	5	
5. Stakeholder assessment	1	2	3	4	5	
6. Key assumptions	1	2	3	4	5	
7. Organizational change	1	2	3	4	5	
8. Spending limit	1	2	3	4	5	
9. Ownership	1	2	3	4	5	
10. Project duplication/overlap	1	2	3	4	5	

FIGURE 3.8

Stage Gate No. I—Idea stage.

implies low quality or incomplete work and the value of 5 implies high quality and comprehensive work. For example, a value of 5 for item 10 implies that the project manager is very sure there are no duplicate or overlapping projects.

Any item in the assessment rated lower than 3 means poor quality or incomplete work and, if not corrected, will cause problems during future project stages. A better approach to ensure that the stage gate review progresses smoothly is to check the quality of the work for any given item as it is completed—rather than waiting to do the assessment at this late point in the Idea stage. Adhering to that practice would make the final review meeting short and sweet.

Once the team has completed the assessment, the project manager meets with the sponsor to review the status of the completed work. At the end of the review session, the sponsor decides whether to open stage gate no. 1 to let the team proceed to the Prelaunch stage, or to have the team go back and rework the proposal to improve any of the low quality or incomplete work products. Occasionally, the sponsor may open the stage gate even if certain items are not up to par. This *conditional* approval implies that the team will remedy the situation to the sponsor's satisfaction in the near future. For example, the sponsor may find that the ownership (item 9) is not very well defined, but believes that the matter can be resolved during the early part of the next stage. In another example, the spending limit (item 8) might appear disproportionately low and the requesting person/unit needs to rethink the matter. If conditional approval is given, the condition itself is recorded as an issue and a must resolve date is specified. The project manager takes the responsibility to track the issue and report its resolution to the sponsor in a timely manner. If the stage gate review does not pass the sponsor's acceptance test, the final option is to move the project to the suspend portfolio or the canceled project portfolio (refer to Chapter 10).

If a sponsor has not been assigned to the proposed project, the stage gate review becomes the responsibility of the individual or group responsible, or designated manager for managing the project portfolio. The responsibility must not fall into the lap of the CIO or any other technology manager.

■ SUMMARY

While there is no dearth of great visions emanating from executive offices, these visions are sometimes accompanied by half baked ideas. In far too many IT organizations, an inordinately large number of these ideas slip through and mutate into full-fledged projects. Although most of the projects resulting from these ideas eventually fail, the truth is that many organizations lack the essential discipline necessary to focus on and identify ideas (projects) that will add serious value to the organization. The end result of the steps outlined in this chapter is a well defined project request that, if approved, moves to the Prelaunch stage, and if rejected, becomes a candidate for either the suspended or canceled portfolio.

Given below is a list of the key subject areas covered in this chapter. We invite you to review the list and assess your level of comprehension of each topic. The best approach is to take a separate sheet of paper and write a short narrative to explain your knowledge of the topic and then go back and compare your summaries with the material covered in the chapter. Another approach is to find a colleague who is also interested in these topics and discuss your understanding of the topics with her, and then jointly review the chapter materials to assess your degree of understanding.

- Idea stage of the PPA;
- The Wheel of Half Baked Ideas;
- Filtering half baked ideas;
- Developing the project idea;
- Value-to-business;
- Critical success factors;
- Developing a well structured project request;
- Stakeholder analysis;
- Organizational change; and
- Stage gate review;

■ QUESTIONS AND DISCUSSION POINTS

1. What is the key purpose of having the Idea stage within the PPA?

2. How many steps does the Idea stage contain? Can you name each step? (Don't worry about the order.)

3. Who has the primary responsibility for completing the various steps of the Idea stage? Why?

4. What process group of PMBOK does the idea stage relate to?

5. What message does the Wheel of Half Baked Ideas convey to you?

6. Why include key search words as a part of the Idea statement?

7. Why place so much importance on projects being aligned to a specific organization strategy?

8. Who (IT or business) is more suited to define the value-to-business? Why? Can you recall Warren Buffet's quote that refers to this situation?

9. If a customer specifies a must-meet deadline in the idea stage, what key questions should you ask him?

10. Why do you believe we have differentiated between the Idea statement and the project request?

11. Why worry about the "ownership" of the project this early in the project life cycle?

12. What is the purpose of the stage gate at the end of the idea stage?

13. Can you recall any of the quotations used in this chapter? If so, why this quotation?

4 THE PRE-LAUNCH STAGE

OBJECTIVES

In this chapter, you will learn about the following project management elements:

- Pre-Launch stage of the PPA
- Project description
- Stakeholder analysis
- Intra-project priorities
- Complexity assessment
- Value to business *v*. project complexity
- Policies, standards, and procedures
- Impact assessment
- Constraints and obstacles
- Stability assessment
- Issue management
- Risk assessment
- Developing project scope statement
- Scope chunking
- Developing size estimates
- Use of range values in estimates
- Rework and scope growth
- Project outlook assessment
- Assemble the Project Charter
- The signing ceremony
- Stage gate review

This chapter details the thirteen steps in the Launch stage of the PPA, starting with the development of a comprehensive Project Description and ending with the creation of a Project Charter, a proposal given to the sponsor to request project approval. The steps necessary to tailor the PPA to fit the needs of the project are outlined, and the steps needed to compute a size (high level) estimate for the project are explained using the phase-based and deliverables-based estimating methods. The steps necessary to account for the sponsor, management, and project management efforts are explained along with the steps needed to incorporate a variety of project reserves. The important step of defining the priority of a given project proposal as compared to other proposals is outlined. The chapter ends with a detailed discussion of the key components of a Project Charter and the steps to assemble and submit it for sponsor review and approval.

■ THE PRE-LAUNCH STAGE

As we saw during the Idea Stage, customers elucidate ideas that they believe will add value to the organization. Project manager level individuals then work with the customers to produce comprehensive Project Requests. Selected Project Requests, those that pass through the stage gate review, become candidates for the Pre-Launch stage. Now that the least viable ideas have been filtered out, the project manager, working closely with the sponsor,[1] needs to conduct rigorous due diligence to further assess the viability of the proposed project. The purpose of the Pre-Launch stage is to systematically analyze the Project Request to help determine whether it should be pursued. Please note that a reasonable outcome of a carefully conducted Pre-Launch might be the decision to not proceed with the project. The primary reason for assessing projects to determine viability is that people in a typical organization have more visions, ideas, and projects than can be worked on due to their finite resources—dollars, people, skills, and technology. Therefore, organizations must establish a rigorous filtering process to trap any nonviable project proposals and deter the business units, as well as IT, from investing scarce corporate resources unwisely.

We expect an astute investment banker to examine the books of a startup, a homebuyer to have a potential property inspected and appraised, or a prospective customer to take a previously owned vehicle to a trusted mechanic for a thorough checkup. In the same way, the project manager will need to investigate any proposed projects before moving to the Launch stage. The outcome of the Pre-Launch stage is a comprehensive Project Charter, which is used to obtain final approval for the project and to begin detailed planning. Figure 4.1 depicts the steps that compose the Pre-Launch stage. Keeping in mind that the hallmark of the Pre-Launch stage is due diligence, the focus as we proceed through the various steps is a question: "Are we doing the right thing?" The key deliverables of this stage are a project description, a stakeholder assessment, complexity and risk assessments, a scope statement, and a size estimate, which all lead to the assembly of a comprehensive Project Charter.

In Figure 4.1, we see that the Pre-Launch stage consists of a total of thirteen steps. The project manager chooses the appropriate steps to fit the size, complexity, and importance of the project at hand. Additionally, the effort and time spent on any given step is in proportion to the complexity and size of the project. The two inevitable questions by project managers at this point are:

1. How does one decide which steps to select for a given project?
2. Is there a specific sequence in which the various steps of the Pre-Launch stage need to be executed?

We will answer the first question after we complete step 6 (Complexity Assessment) later in the chapter. Once the complexity has been assessed, the project manager can make a decision regarding the tailoring and scaling of the PPA steps. For an answer to the second question, we will wait until the end of the chapter.

---

[1]At this early stage, if a sponsor has not been identified, it is the "proposed" sponsor or a similar level manager who guides the project manager.

FIGURE 4.1
The Pre-Launch Stage

Project Charter
3. **Project Description**
4. **Intra-Project Priority Analysis**
5. **Stakeholder Analysis**
6. **Complexity Assessment**
7. Policies, Procedures, & Standards
8. Impact Assessment
9. Constraints & Obstacles
10. Stability Assessment
11. Issues Management
12. Risk Assessment
13. **Preliminary Scope Statement**
14. **Project Size Estimate**
15. **Project Charter**

Responsibility

Typically, the responsibility for completing the various steps of the Pre-Launch stage falls upon a project manager who has comprehensive knowledge of the business area as well as the infrastructure in which the project's end product will be deployed. For example, if the project has to do with manufacturing, human resources, or shipping, the person assigned to develop the Project Charter should have ample knowledge of the appropriate area. If a given project crosses functional lines, such as a project involving automation of job applicant resume submission via the Internet, then the person should be familiar with the human resource department's processes for resume acceptance as well as Internet technology. Another example is a proposed project that is designed to reorganize a warehouse to improve order fulfillment efficiency and quality. In this case, the person assigned to develop the Project Charter must have comprehensive knowledge of warehouse management. Of course, the next question might be: "What if the person does not have the requisite knowledge?" The probability of getting a comprehensive and accurate Project Charter has just decreased. If an individual who has the requisite knowledge and experience is not available, and a Charter still *must* be developed, then we suggest the following steps:

- Provide access to appropriate SMEs.
- Have the person visit the appropriate customer department(s) and start learning as much as possible in the available time.
- Establish interim milestones, at which point an experienced person can review the work in progress and provide necessary guidance.
- Do not assume that the Project Charter will be comprehensive and accurate.

Our views fly in the face of those in the profession who proclaim that a "good" project manager can manage any type of project successfully. To comprehend the naïveté, of this belief, imagine a project manager who does not speak French, has no knowledge of cooking, has never worked in a food service related job, and is asked to organize a French cooking contest. Twenty chefs, over a four-day period, will prepare and serve a seven course French dinner, with appropriate wine pairings, to a panel of seven judges. *Bon Appétit!*

Before starting the work to complete the Project Charter, the person responsible needs to ensure that the following people are easily accessible:

- The originator of the idea for the proposed project
- The person who prepared the Project Request
- SMEs from appropriate business and technology groups

Under the ideal project management environment, the Pre-Launch would be the responsibility of the group requesting the project. However, because in most cases customer groups do not have sufficient project management knowledge and experience, the responsibility for doing the requisite work is delegated to a project manager outside of the group. In such instances, we strongly recommend that the *justification* of the proposed project remain the responsibility of the group proposing the project. We do not believe the responsibility to "justify" the project belongs to a project manager. The responsibility of the project manager is to do his or her best to compose the Project Charter. We further believe that the customer who requested the project has the responsibility to obtain Project Charter approval from the appropriate authority. The project manager can and should assist the customer with preparation of the Charter presentation. At times, we have heard people espouse the noble suggestion that the project sponsor should create the Project Charter. This is a nice idea, but we have yet to see it happen.

■ PROJECT DESCRIPTION—PPA STEP 3

The project description is key to developing and communicating your understanding of the purpose and benefit of the proposed project. The inputs to this step are the Idea Statement and Project Request information completed in the Idea stage. The additional key components of a comprehensive Project Description are:

Nature of the project	Conceptual build
Project objectives	Runaway trigger
Business cycles	Shutdown condition
Side effects	Current system retirement
Validated assumptions	

Specific topics to be addressed and questions to be answered will depend upon the nature and complexity of the project. Figure 4.2 depicts a suggested template for documenting the key components of the Project Description.

The Nature of the Project

What factors, if any, distinguish this project from similar projects undertaken by the requesting organization previously or currently? The focus should be on the degree of novelty of the proposed project. The key areas to explore are:

- Is there an unusually high degree of risk?
- Is there a significant penalty for failure?
- Does the project include new technology?
- Does the project include a new process?

Project Objectives

Four synonyms for the word "objective" are: "aim", "reason", "purpose", and "intent". Keeping this in mind, develop a clear and comprehensive statement of what the project will accomplish. The best way to ensure that individual objectives are well constructed is to make sure that each objective has a specific measure attached to it. For example, increase sales in the western division (objective) by 18 percent (measure), or reduce operational expenses (objective) by $50,000 per month (measure). You might think that defining specific and measurable objectives is not that difficult to do. Well, think again. Commonly, IT/Business projects do not meet customer needs because objectives are too often defined inadequately. The list of objectives, taken from real life project charters, prove the point. The comments in italics are ours and are designed to illustrate the nonspecific nature of these objectives.

FIGURE 4.2
Project Description Template

The nature of the project

- What are you introducing? What factors distinguish this project from similar projects undertaken previously (or currently)? Does the project entail significantly new processes and/or technology? What is the penalty (exposure) of failure?

Project objectives

- What are you trying to accomplish? What is the value of doing so?

Validated assumptions

- Review and verify the assumptions stated as a part of the Project Request (during the Idea stage.

ID	Date	Assumption	Source	LOC	Negative impact	Owner	Final disposition	Comments

Conceptual build

- What key components need to be built to complete the project? What will it accomplish? Who will use it? What are the key deliverables? Where will it be used?

Runaway triggers

- Under what conditions will the project be considered in "runaway" mode?

Shutdown conditions

- Under what conditions should the project be shut down?

- Achieve successful system performance (*what defines "success"?*)
- Avoid cost (*by how much?*)
- Cause minimal disruptions (*what defines "minimal"?*)
- Expanded customer base (*by how much?*)
- Expanded product line (*by how much?*)
- Faster turnaround (*by how much?*)
- Fewer defects (*by how many?*)
- Greater market share (*by how much?*)
- Higher ROI (*by how much?*)
- Immediate response times (*what constitutes "immediate"?*)
- Improved customer service (*in what specific manner?*)
- Improved employee morale (*what does this mean?*)
- Increased profit per customer (*by how much?*)
- Increased revenue (*by how much?*)
- Reduced cost per transaction (*by how much?*)
- Reduce employee turnover (*by how much?*)
- Reduced risk (*which risks and by how much?*)
- Take advantage of client-server architecture (*what does "advantage" mean?*)
- Keep competitive[2]

---

[2]This is an objective in the lease of the Cincinnati Bengals. Because the team has not had a winning season in the last 12 years, the County Commissioner wants a review of the lease with the team. See "NFL Losers Never Win . . .", *Newsweek*, December 9, 2002. This is the latest, and perhaps the best example of a poorly defined objective. A quick look at the synonyms for the word "competitive" shows: "bloodthirsty", "aggressive", "ready" for action, "cheap", and "live". What did the leaseholder have in mind?

All of the objectives in the list are taken from real contracts between organizations and their systems integration vendors. Each of these contracts was under dispute, and the customers had filed lawsuits against their vendors. We were fascinated by the objective, "Improved employee morale," which immediately raises a few questions:

- How is "morale" defined?
- Is there a current baseline of employee morale?
- How will the improvement be measured?

Unfortunately, project objectives are often a hodgepodge of mumbo jumbo. The best way to make objectives specific is to attach a specific *measure*, an indicator of success, to each objective. For example:

- Decrease system response time from the current 9 seconds to 2 seconds (at the maximum, 5 seconds)
- Bring the system uptime to 99.5 percent
- Improve data accuracy to 98 percent or more
- Train 80 percent of call center operators by August 15
- Certify 65 percent of call center operators by October 15
- Improve customer service by 8 points
- Reduce cost per transaction by $.78
- Improve productivity by 150 percent

An effective method to assess the clarity of an objective is to put it through the SMART[3] filter:

S: Specific
M: Measurable
A: Achievable
R: Relevant to the strategy
T: Time bound

Let us focus on A: Achievable. Assume that the current data accuracy was at 50 percent and the objective states an accuracy rate of 98 percent. That objective requires almost 100 percent improvement. Is this really possible, given the reasons behind the current error rate? Consider the last objective: Improve productivity by 150 percent. We believe this is the result of someone reading an advertisement, or an article in an airplane. This is the classic management by magazine (MBM) syndrome. Often, we see objectives that are quite laudable but not achievable. Setting aggressive objectives is fine, but those objectives also need to be realistic. Therefore, the SMART filter is reliable for objectives.

We do acknowledge that not every objective can be easily stated in a specific and measurable manner. For example:

- Cause minimal disruptions
- Take advantage of client-server architecture

These objectives need to be analyzed in more detail and the customer may need some help in articulating these in a manner that they can be quantified.

> *Management by objectives works if you know the objectives. Ninety percent of the time you don't.*
> Peter Drucker (http://www.brainyquote.com/quote/quotes/p/peter/dru129829.html).

Business Cycles   Most business operations are driven by predictable cyclic events which, if disturbed, invariably result in significant interruption, marked drop in income, unhappy customers, disgruntled employees, and bad publicity. Here are a few examples of important business cycles:

- Month-end, quarter-end, and year-end for payroll processing companies
- Months of April and August for tax services companies

---

[3]Doran, George T. 1981. There's a S.M.A.R.T. Way to Write Management Goals and Objectives. *Management Review* (November).

- Halloween, Easter, Valentine's Day, and Mother's Day for companies specializing in gifts of flowers, sweets, and greeting cards
- Months of November and December for companies specializing in holiday goods and services

It is the fundamental tenet of well-thought-out project implementation and an immutable project management principle that states: "Never implement a major change [most projects do this] in the midst of an important business cycle." Unfortunately, too many sponsors and project managers seem to overlook this advice or believe that no harm will befall their business processes if they implement a new project during these important business cycles. That attitude is no surprise to Mr. Murphy as is evident from the example below:

> *... suffered a glitch in a $112 million new enterprise system built to automate and track every step of the company's candy-selling business. Just days before Halloween the problem was still unresolved, and business took a scary turn . . . . The lost orders, missed shipments, and disgruntled customers that resulted from the company's systems woes were well publicized in both the trade and business press.*
> Polly Schneider, "Another Trip to Hell," *CIO Magazine* (February 15, http://www.cio.com/archive/021500/hell.html).

Project implementations might fall smack in the middle of key business cycles for any number of reasons, but we have encountered the following reasons multiple times:

- The development team was so focused on getting the project done that they overlooked asking the end-users about the busy business cycles.
- The original estimates and schedules were mostly wishful thinking and bore little resemblance to reality regarding the time and resources needed to complete the project as promised (far ahead of an important business cycle). Once it was into the Execute stage, the schedule continued to slip and ran into the business cycle, but nobody had the foresight and courage to delay implementation for fear that any additional delays would be counted against the team's performance.
- The original schedule was good and did not conflict with any key business cycles, but unmanaged scope creep (growth) slipped the schedule into a key business cycle.
- The development team held the belief that the end-users will have no choice but to make the system work, even during busy business cycles.

As you develop the project description, specifically ask a number of front line people about important business cycles (there may be more than one such cycle in a given year) and carefully assess the impact that the new project could have on the business. Make sure to document the information clearly so that it is available for easy access when you develop the project schedule, especially the implementation and operations schedule for the project. A number of project managers have begun to include key business cycle information as a vital sign to be monitored routinely once the project goes into the Execute stage.

Side Effects "Side effects" is a term commonly used in the medical profession, especially in the medical field. Side effects: a peripheral or secondary effect, usually undesirable, of a drug or therapy.[4]

Pharmaceutical companies and health professionals are required, by law, to inform and educate their customers of any such effects. Without going into the detailed analysis of the reasons and benefits of this precaution, it should be obvious that the customer needs to clearly understand the implications of any proposed actions and then make an informed decision. In terms of IT/Business projects, the benefits of thinking through the side effects of an action is well demonstrated by the following example (an actual event).

1. The CEO of an organization that employs about 2,000 people instructed the CIO to work with the various division heads to plan for a 15 percent reduction in head count across the organization. The need for the reduction in force was caused by lower sales and increasing expenses. The company had five divisions; three of them were in Europe. When we learned about this project, our first question was: "Why was the CIO asked to take on this project when it has nothing to with technology?"

---

[4]Source: http://dictionary.reference.com/search?q=side%20effect.

Not surprisingly, we were never able to get a satisfactory answer. The CIO approached the five division heads regarding the project, and some of them thought this was a scheme hatched by the CIO to get into the good graces of the CEO. Once the CIO convinced them that this really was a directive from the CEO, they begrudgingly assigned representatives to the project.

2. The team, over a nine week period, working with various executives and managers from the five divisions, developed a list of candidates for possible termination. The reasons that it took so long to get to this point were:

   - Because the five divisions were in five different locations, the team had difficulty compiling the list of employees, along with the needed details regarding their tenure, salary levels, and other pertinent information.
   - The various executives and managers used this reduction process to get rid of their low-performing employees and people they did not like personally (regardless of performance levels or the company's need for their skills).
   - Some of the people on the proposed termination list were personal friends of the division representatives on the team and the information leaked out (in fact was specifically communicated to these select few). This resulted in quite a ruckus and some of the lists had to be revised. The group eventually developed a list of 315 employees as candidates for termination (just slightly higher than the 15 percent requested by the CEO). Most of the division heads developed progressively greater dislike for the CIO because he was the obvious sponsor of the project (by default).

3. During this time, the CIO had only two 15-minute face-to-face meetings with the CEO, due to their cross-country locations and heavy travel schedules.

4. Finally, the list was turned over to a senior manager in the human resources department, who then worked with a senior representative from the legal department and a financial analyst from the budget group. To everybody's chagrin, the group summarized their findings as follows:

   - About 60 of the 315 employees on the list could not be terminated because of legal restrictions—rules of different countries. The project team was asked to come up with a list of 60 different employees to replace the ones already on the list.
   - The cost of terminating another seventy employees on the list was disproportionately higher than the savings their termination would produce, again due to severance policies of the company and certain employee contracts.
   - Because of the 15 percent cut to one of the small, but highly profitable divisions, employee termination would actually result in a 70 percent reduction in the division's sales and a deep cut in the company's bottom line. When the division head learned about this impact on the division, he went ballistic.

The group built a spreadsheet showing that the net savings from terminating the proposed 315 employees would fall short of the true objective the CEO had set in the first place—a 20 percent reduction in the operational cost of the company (someone was finally able to extricate this information from the CEO).

Let us think about this project in medical terms. The group has been directed to perform surgery on the body of the organization and remove 15 percent of the mass. Some simple questions to consider are:

1. Are all body parts created equal—from the brain to the toes?
2. What is the cost of this surgery?
3. Would postoperative recovery cost the organization any money?
4. What are the risks to the organization for this size of disruption?

The project was eventually dropped, and because the CEO still needed the reduction in the operational cost, he directed the five division heads to submit a plan to reduce their budgets by 20 percent each. They were told that this did not have to be done solely by reducing head count; they were free to look into any operational areas of their respective divisions. This directive resulted in the start of a new project to resolve same problem. At this point, the CIO left the company, in large part because of the outrageous mess caused by the original project. The process is best illustrated by the following list:

- Enthusiasm
- Disappointment

- Panic
- Search for the guilty
- Punishment of the innocent
- Promotion of nonparticipants
- New project is announced
- Back to enthusiasm

Another unpleasant side effect of this failed project was that about thirty-five senior, highly productive employees left the company; some of them joined the company's competitors. This situation provides a clear example of what can happen when the side effects of a proposed solution are completely ignored. We strongly advise that serious attention be given to this subject, starting with the Project Description and continuing through the work required during the Launch Stage. The Project Charter should clearly outline the appropriate assessments and recommendations regarding possible side effects. Then, as the project continues through the Execute Stage, the project manager must pay specific attention to the emergence of any undesirable side effects and take appropriate corrective actions. For those of you who have more interest in the subject of systems side effects, we recommend the book: *Systemantics—The Underground Text of System Lore.*[5] The excerpt below describes a classic example of an unexpected side effect:

> *The Aswan Dam, built at enormous expense to improve the lot of the Egyptian peasant, has caused the Nile to deposit its fertilizing sediment in Lake Nasser, where it is unavailable. Egyptian fields must now be artificially fertilized. Gigantic fertilizer plants have been built to meet the new need. The plants require enormous amounts of electricity. The dam must operate at capacity merely to supply the increased need for electricity which was created by the building of the dam.*
>
> J. Gall, 1986, p. 21.

Validated Assumptions

In the Idea Stage, certain assumptions were defined as a part of the Project Request. At this point, the person responsible for developing the Project Description must perform due diligence and try to validate the various assumptions. This activity involves contacting the appropriate groups and discussing the assumptions and the possible negative impacts on the project if the assumptions do not hold true. Wherever appropriate, we would advise you to communicate this information in writing and save a copy for your Project Notebook. Figure 4.2 depicts a chart for recording and tracking project assumptions. The various fields in the chart are described below:

ID: A progressive numeric number.

Date: The date on which the assumption was recorded.

Assumption: Statement of the assumption.

Source: The individual (or organization) who stated or created the assumption.

LOC (level of confidence): The level of confidence (low, medium, high) that the project manager has that the assumption will come true as stated. Document any research done to support your findings.

Negative impact: The impact on the project (schedule, scope, budget, and quality) if the assumption does not come true as stated.

Owner: Indicates the individual who is responsible for tracking the assumption and reporting on it. Some project managers use the word "tracker" as the heading for this item.

Final disposition: This column will be completed at a later point in the project. Did the assumption come true as stated or were there any variances?

Comments: Any remarks or explanations made or noted by the owner and/or the project manager.

---

[5]J. Gall, *Systemantics: The Underground Text of System Lore, How Systems Really Work and How they Fail.* Ann Arbor, MI: The General Systemantics Press, 1986.

A word of advice: If, during the Execute stage, the number of outstanding assumptions becomes greater than the number of deliverables yet to be completed, the project is entering the problem zone—too many potholes on the road to success.

Conceptual Build

The purpose of the conceptual build is to construct a high-level solution to the customer's problem. This includes a list of project phases, high-level deliverables and features, key milestones, and the technology infrastructure needed to solve the problem and achieve the customer's objectives. A good way to get started describing the conceptual build of the proposed project is to answer the following questions:

1. What will it accomplish?
2. What functionality will be built?
3. Who will use it?
4. Where will it be used?

Part of this description may include information regarding any alternatives considered for solving the problem at hand. Only a summary description of each possible alternative, including its benefits and drawbacks, and the key reasons for its rejection is needed at this point in the project. Details regarding different alternatives can be included in the appendix to the Project Charter. The discussion of alternatives becomes much more important if different approaches to solve the problem have been discussed or if certain stakeholders have differing views of the problem and its solution. Figure 4.3 shows an example of a conceptual build of a project.

Runaway Triggers

By now, you are aware that too many IT/Business projects fail; however, most IT/Business professionals and business customers are not fully aware of the massive financial losses caused by the failed projects. The Center's research shows that in midsize and large organizations, the average

FIGURE 4.3
An Example of a Conceptual
Build

What is the product?

- A web-based system for new hires for training enrollment

What will it do?

- Automate the enrollment process
- Track completion
- Provide management reports

Who will use it?

- Newly hired IT staff
- Human resources department
- Training department
- Functional managers
- Project managers

What are the key deliverables?

- Database of course offerings
- Database of facilities
- Enrollment notices
- Attendance and completion records
- User interface
- Reports

Where will it be used?

- Employee desktop

financial loss of a failed IT/Business project is close to $4 million, and many projects cost tens of millions of dollars. One of the questions that begs to be asked is: "Did the project manager, working with the sponsor, define a dollar and/or schedule threshold above which the project would be considered in a 'runaway condition' and would automatically come under management scrutiny?" Examples of runaway conditions, sometimes referred to as *jeopardy points,* might be

1. If actual cost to date is running 20 percent over planned cost to date for more than 30 days.
2. If the actual schedule is behind the planned schedule by more than 15 percent for a period of more than 30 days.
3. If the scope growth to date has exceeded the planned scope reserve.

These types of performance variances indicate that the project is in trouble and that management must make a specific Go/No Go decision. Keeping all of this in mind, it is important that the customer be asked to define the runaway triggers at the start of a proposed project.

Shutdown Conditions

This situation represents the next threshold, after the runaway triggers, at which a project becomes a candidate for shutdown. The project manager *and* the customer will have to convince the sponsor why the project should not be scuttled. The rationale is that when a project is beyond a certain point of budget and/or schedule overrun, the probability that the project will ever be completed is quite low. The obvious question is, "Why don't the sponsors put a halt to these projects before pumping millions of dollars into what are obviously troubled projects?" Discussions with a number of project managers points to a common cause—an attitude displayed by too many sponsors and born of such empty pronouncements as:

• Failure is not an option
• Just do it
• No project cancellations on my watch

As a result, organizations are left with a long list of projects that are canceled *after* millions of dollars are poured into the proverbial project "black hole." Our research shows that few organizations have a well-defined process in place to identify and shut down troubled projects (see Figure 4.4).

In an article titled *Companies Don't Learn From Previous IT Snafus*[6] Kim Nash lists ten major project failures that cost the respective companies millions of dollars. Two of the ten companies eventually filed for bankruptcies, largely due to the failure of their IT/Business projects. For equally large disasters in the public sector, we offer the following example:

FIGURE 4.4
Shutdown Conditions—a
Survey

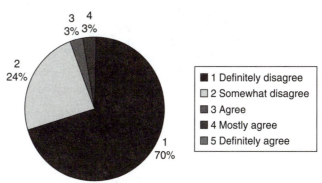

Project sponsors consistently define, and communicate to project managers, the shutdown conditions for their projects.

- 1 Definitely disagree
- 2 Somewhat disagree
- 3 Agree
- 4 Mostly agree
- 5 Definitely agree

---

[6]Kim S. Nash "Companies Don't Learn from Previous IT Snafus," *Computerworld* (October 30, 2000).

Veterans have received little benefit from a $40 million computer system that processes benefit payments by the Veterans Affairs Department, according to a congressional audit. The VA has been developing the VETSNET system since 1996. [The] VA uses the system to make benefit payments to only nine of the 3 million people who receive benefits . . . . [The] VA intends to transfer the nine recipients on the new system back to the old system by the end of November, until the system is fully developed by December 2004 . . . .
                              "System Upgrade Delivers Little to Veterans," *Federal Times*
                                                                    (November 11, 2002): p.3.

In the example, the project started in 1996. By late 2002, six long years and $40 million later, management finally figured out that the project was in dismal straits. Incredibly, after spending $40 million, only *nine* people were being served by the new project. Obviously, the sponsor(s) have been comatose at the wheel far too long while the money pipeline was flowing unabated. The bizarre part of the story is that they actually believed that the project would be fully operational by the end of 2004. In another example, a $30 million dollar contract bulged to $90 million; the sponsor actually allowed an extra $60 million to be paid while absolutely nothing of significant value had been delivered. Can you see why we propose the reintroduction of the mocking post?

This contract did not have any shutdown conditions defined. We suggest that a 40 percent overrun of the budget or schedule should be established as a point of no hope for any project. The sponsor must decide what the point of no return is for a specific project. Once the defined threshold is breached, the sponsor, key stakeholders, and the project manager must meet to discuss and decide the future of the project. For a detailed and well-defined process to assess the fate of a troubled project, see ProjectHALT™ in Chapter 7.[7]

Current System Retirement

In any project where the end product is a major enhancement and/or replacement of the current system, the completion of the new project will inevitably result in the existence of two systems: the current (now old) system and the new system. Many project managers overlook the fact that the current (old system) must be retired in a planned and orderly manner for the new system to be successful. In the case of IT/Business projects, the question of current system retirement needs to be raised during this early stage to get a feel for the customer's comfort level regarding retiring the current system—the extent of their emotional attachment. You shouldn't be surprised that many customers are not going to give up the current system easily or soon.

End-user resistance is often the biggest challenge IT teams face when doing a major migration. . . . Experienced technology managers said what's deadly is forgetting that end users might like their old systems and almost certainly are comfortable with them.
              Sharon Gaudin, "System Migration? Don't Forget to Consider Users," Stewart
                 Deck and Jaikumar Vijayan, contributors. *Computerworld* (October 26, 1998,
                         http://www.computerworld.com/news/1998/story/0,11280,33136,00.html).

Even though it is quite early in the project life cycle, it is important for the customer to begin to think about the retirement of the current system (if the proposed project will replace a system/product currently in place). Keep in mind that such retirement will require specific resources—people, time, and budget. Additionally, there is the question of people's emotional attachment to what they already have. We suggest that you raise the question with the customer at this point to start their thinking process.

I'm on a project now where the customer wanted 12 months of parallel processing before they would agree to retire the current system. (This is unnecessarily long but what it did point out was the degree of emotional attachment the customer has to the current system.)
                                                                   Comments by a project manager.

Knowing the level of a customer's emotional attachment to the current system will help the team plan a retirement process that will provide a reasonable comfort level for the customer, while not taking an inordinately long time or consuming excessive resources. Keep in mind the need for

---

[7]ProjectHALT is a registered trademark of the Center for Project Management. All rights reserved.

additional budget to keep the current system in parallel operation while the old system is being retired. This estimate must be included in the cost estimates for the new project, but often is ignored.

Despite a general acknowledgment that the various items discussed previously are the foundation for developing a succinct project description, the pressure on project managers to conform to the dictates of their customers often discourages them from asking these important questions. This reluctance may exist because the customer is too high in the hierarchy and does not wish to have his or her ideas questioned by a "lowly" project manager. At times, added pressure is placed on project managers by their own managers, who insist that the customer needs the product by a specific date, thus insinuating that the project must be launched without further delay. In such environments, most communications from the customer to the project manager are in the form of a dictate rather than a two-way professional discussion.

During a recent seminar for senior-level project managers, some of the participants showed certain trepidation regarding the prospect of questioning their customers. When further queried, a number of the participants responded with the following points:

• Customers will be irritated, they don't like to be questioned.
• Our managers do not allow us to speak to the customers.
• Asking questions of the customers is often seen as "us not being knowledgeable."
• Most sponsors are too busy to spend any time with us.
• Most sponsors believe that it is our job to figure out all these things.
• We just cannot bring up the issue of canceling a project, many of our customers believe that is a set-up for failure.

In most of these cases, project managers are then left to their own devices and are forced to *conjure* project descriptions. Without this critical input, the majority of these projects will fail to meet customer expectations.

We have demonstrated that it requires time and energy to develop a comprehensive Project Description. Remember, the Project Description creates the foundation of the project. If it is not thorough and accurate, the result will be an inferior product and a waste of scarce resources.

> *Too often, business units approve projects and then confusion sets in when the IT staff is asked to deliver on something that's unclear. At Cardinal Health, all of that is resolved before approval.*
> Stacy Collett, "How Will You Connect With Customers?" *Computerworld* (January 6, 2003, http://www.computerworld.com/managementtopics/ management/itspending/story/0,10801,76951,00.html).

We strongly believe that it is the responsibility of the sponsor to make sure that the project manager develops a comprehensive project description. Unfortunately, most sponsors do not even consider this course of action. Project managers are simply left to their own devices. This statement is corroborated by the data in Figure 4.5, which shows that an overwhelming number of sponsors do not spend sufficient time with project managers to help them with due diligence. If the project managers

FIGURE 4.5
Project Description—a Survey

Sponsors spend sufficient time with project managers in developing succinct project descriptions.

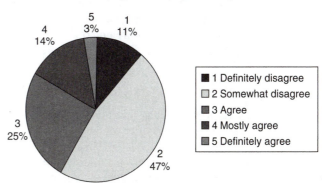

fail, they are often accused of acting unprofessionally. We strongly believe that the sponsor and the project manager should jointly write the project description or the seeds of failure will be sown.

■ INTRA-PROJECT PRIORITY ANALYSIS—PPA STEP 4

In Chapter 1, we defined the key components of a successful project as:

$$\text{Project} = \text{Schedule} + \text{Scope} + \text{Budget} + \text{Quality}$$

At this point, the customer needs to define the *relative* priorities of these four components. Toward the start of a project, when excitement is high, a typical customer's view of a project can be summarized as follows:

Schedule: Is yesterday too soon?
Scope: I want everything and the kitchen sink.
Budget: I don't have that much in my budget.
Quality: It just has to be the best.

Who can blame them? Just read the advertisements about the wonders of technology in various magazines. Then, read the glowing articles and testimonials, written by corporate executives of the competitive advantages of the newly acquired technology—many of those testimonials are written and planted by product vendors. When faced with unrealistic combinations of scope, schedule, budget, and quality, project teams are often urged to "give it the old college try!" In the absence of well-defined (and realistic) customer expectations, no matter what the project manager delivers, the customer will not be satisfied with the outcome. Let us look at a few examples of prioritizations. When booking a cruise, a customer could specify the following priorities to the travel agent:

- Schedule is the most important because the cruise starts two days after the customer's wedding and the wedding date has already been set.
- Quality is rated 2nd because it is a honeymoon cruise. The customer is not willing to compromise on the quality rating of the cruise line. The couple wants a midship cabin on an upper deck, with a balcony. They may be open to negotiate the level of the deck but the balcony is a must.
- Scope is rated 3rd because, to meet the schedule and the quality rankings, the passenger is willing to accept a route that would not otherwise be the first choice.
- Budget ranks 4th because, although the passenger is reluctant to spend money needlessly, getting the best price is not a key driver for this cruise because they did not contact the travel agent with sufficient lead time.

For another cruise, the same passenger could have the following priorities:

- Budget is of the highest priority—the passenger has a limit and is not willing to go above that amount.
- Quality is rated 2nd because, to save money, the passenger is willing to drop down a couple of notches on the quality rating of the cruise line. He will also compromise on the view and the cabin location (still wants an outside cabin).
- Scope is rated 3rd because, to meet the budget and the quality rankings, the passenger is willing to accept a route that would not otherwise be the first choice.
- Schedule is not that important, because the passenger will be available to take the cruise on short notice.

Now consider a passenger who gives the travel agent the following priorities:

- Schedule is extremely important—the customer actually has a specific date in mind. It so happens that the date of travel falls during a prime cruise period.
- The passenger has a limited budget and will travel only if a major discount is made available.
- The passenger insists on a midship, higher deck cabin with a spacious balcony.
- The passenger will travel only with the highest rated cruise line.

As you can see, the priorities are not rank ordered; in fact each component is rated as 1—a truly painful condition. This type of situation is not uncommon in IT/Business projects and results in mixed messages to the project manager and the team. The result is all around confusion.

Definition of Quality

Let us focus on the quality component of the project equation for a moment. During our discussions with a number of project managers, we discovered that many have great difficulty defining the "quality" of the end product. They also find the concept of assigning quality a ranking other than 1st unacceptable. A common concern, voiced by many project managers, is: "It is not easy to discuss the subject of assigning quality a low ranking with the customer as that would be seen as compromising the quality of the end product." To prepare for such discussions with the customer, and to make that sure everyone on the team has the same point of view, let us look at the definition of quality of a software product. The following (alphabetically sorted) list contains software quality attributes compiled from a number of our IT/Business clients:

- Amount of training required
- Difficulty of misuse
- Ease of adaptability
- Ease of configuration
- Ease of maintenance
- Efficiency of hardware utilization
- Efficiency of human resources utilization
- Functionality
- Mean time to repair
- Quality of graphical user interface (GUI)
- Quality of system documentation
- Quality of user documentation
- Reliability (mean time to failure)
- Reusability
- Safety
- Security
- Usability

Because the list of quality attributes is quite long, you will need to discuss with your key customers, as well as the quality assurance group, which of these may need to be "compromised" due to limited time, budget, and/or resources. It is also possible that certain additional attributes may be added due to the specific needs of a given project. We strongly advise you to work with your quality assurance group to define a master list of quality attributes for the types of projects your organization undertakes most frequently. Once a master list has been created, individual project managers can develop project-specific lists.

Perception of Quality   Quality is in the eye of the beholder—our take on the old adage. The problem with the quality attribute is that different stakeholders may have different views on the quality component of the final product. For example, let us consider just a few of the attributes from the bulleted list:

Amount of Training Required: The development group may state that, due to the limited time and resources, they are not able to design intuitive user interfaces and don't have the time to develop detailed documentation. The customer then must undergo extensive training to use the system, and therefore gives a low quality rating to the product. The development group states that, given the time and the budget, they can certainly produce the quality desired by the customer, but the sponsor is unwilling to release additional funds or extend the completion date. What should the project manager do?

Difficulty of Misuse: This is also known as robustness of design. For example, while inputting data from a keyboard, if the possible response is alphabetic, all of the numeric keys are disabled. Similarly, if the only response is a Y or a N (for yes or no), then only these two keys are active. Customers may give such a design a high quality rating, but the designers and developers may object because it requires extra work. Who is right?

Ease of Maintenance: Customers who use software, hardware, and all types of products applaud those that are easy to maintain, add to, or change. However, that requires thoughtful and intelligent design, which means more experienced designers and developers. The development group may not want to underwrite the added expense. Who makes the call?

Functionality: This, perhaps, is the foundation of the definition of the term quality. This means that the end product contains all of the customer specified deliverables and features (to be more specific, the end product maps to the latest baselined scope statement for the project). This mapping is also referred to as conformance to requirements.

Reliability: This implies a very low defect rate. Such design and development requires extra up front investment, resulting in low failure rates and low maintenance costs. What if the developing group is able to bill (charge) customers for postdelivery repairs and support services, thereby assuring substantial income for the parent organization? What should the team do?

Reusability: This design approach will reduce the overall long range cost of future development to the organization, but the reusable components will require extra time to design, develop, test, and document. The sponsor in charge of the original product may not want to bear the burden. Who decides?

Security: Most people want it, but many do not wish to be inconvenienced by robust security protocols. Who is going to convince the vast number of customers (users) of the need for, and the value of, the security procedures?

Usability: This means the quality of human-to-machine interface (sometimes called the user experience), the aesthetics (look, feel, sound), and the consistency of design.

At the start of most projects, the stated priorities often conflict—such as a tight schedule in the face of vaguely defined scope, a low budget, and unrealistic quality expectations. Also, different stakeholders may have differing priorities and interests. The existence of such conflicts makes it essential that priorities be well defined and clearly understood by both the customer and the project team.

As emphasized earlier (the cruise example), the *ideal* situation is when the customer agrees to *rank order* the four attributes (schedule, scope, budget, and quality). Four additional examples follow, each for a different project, and each with a different priority ranking.

Intra-Project Priorities—Example 1

Figure 4.6 shows a situation where the customer has rank ordered the intra-project priority of the proposed project. Let us analyze the meanings and implications of this ranking:

- The customer has placed the utmost priority on the project schedule; there is absolutely *no compromise* in the delivery date of the project. The project is driven by a tight deadline that, if breached, will result in major problems for the customer.
- With quality ranked 2nd, the customer is stating that *if* the schedule cannot be met, she would be willing to trade a *few* agreed upon quality components for an earlier completion date.
- With scope ranked 3rd, the customer will agree to *more compromise* on the number of deliverables and features in the final product.
- With budget ranked 4th, the customer is offering the *most compromise* on the budget set aside for the project.

FIGURE 4.6
Intra-Project Priorities

Attributes	Ranking example			
	1st	2nd	3rd	4th
Schedule	✓			
Scope			✓	
Budget				✓
Quality		✓		

FIGURE 4.7
Intra-Project Priorities

		Ranking example			
		1st	2nd	3rd	4th
Attributes	Schedule		✓		
	Scope			✓	
	Budget				✓
	Quality	✓			

Intra-Project Priorities—Example 2

In the project represented by Figure 4.7, the customer rank ordered the four attributes, but in a *different* order. Let us now analyze this priority ranking:

- Quality is ranked 1st, meaning that there can be no compromise of the quality of the finished product. This project involves an airline company's need to upgrade onboard hardware and software for the navigation equipment.
- Schedule was ranked 2nd because the regulatory agency's directive had two sets of dates: an early *recommended* date and a later *must finish* date. In this case, the customer was ready to delay the project completion for thirty days beyond the earlier recommended date in order not to compromise the quality of the end product.
- Scope was ranked 3rd because management decided that if all of the airplanes could not be upgraded by the scheduled date, they would be willing to reduce the number of scheduled flights until the remaining planes were appropriately upgraded. Of the 1,000 airplanes, the customer was ready to accept 800 upgraded airplanes (the remaining 200 to stay out of service until upgraded at a later date).
- Budget was ranked 4th, because management understood that, in order to meet the first three priorities, extra budget would be necessary. The customer was willing to increase the budget by up to 20 percent.

Ranking the budget 4th often riles management, especially the finance group. At face value, many people assume this means an open cash drawer for the project team. That is not the case at all. The budget being ranked 4th simply means that the customer is willing to spend certain extra money to ensure that the team is able to meet the stringent schedule and quality directives. In fact, it is not prudent to mind pennies for a project like this. However, keep in mind that the allowed variances are not a green light for nonperformance.

Intra-Project Priorities—Example 3

In the project represented in Figure 4.8, the four attributes are *not* rank ordered. This project relates to the passenger food service for a commercial airline. In this case, *both* schedule and budget are ranked 1st, scope is ranked 2nd, and quality is ranked 3rd. Management's reasons for the stated rankings were as follows:

- Schedule was ranked 1st because the food must be on the airplane at specific times.
- Budget was also ranked 1st because, as a part of cost cutting, management wanted to spend very little budget on food and they were not willing to make any allowances.

FIGURE 4.8
Intra-Project Priorities—Not
Rank Ordered

		Ranking example			
		1st	2nd	3rd	4th
Attributes	Schedule	✓			
	Scope		✓		
	Budget	✓			
	Quality			✓	

- Scope was ranked 2nd as the trend in the industry is to cut down on the quantity of each serving and offer no choices. Someone in the management team suggested that this attribute should be ranked 4th.
- Quality was ranked 3rd because the low budget per serving meant reduced quality. The overall feeling was that only the safety of the food, not the appearance, amount, or taste, mattered.

The customer's priority ranking implies that schedule and budget cannot be negotiated. There is some compromise available on the scope; the major restriction is that it cannot be any higher than specified. Quality is ranked lowest. These requirements gave the project team little space to maneuver, but did set specific objectives. The project manager was eventually able to convince the sponsor of the need to *rank order* the priorities and they jointly ordered the project priorities as 1) schedule, 2) budget, 3) quality, and 4) scope.

Over the years, our consultants and client project managers have engaged in repeated discussions regarding whether nonrank ordered priorities should be allowed (the priorities shown in Figure 4.8). Although the preference is that the priorities for a project be rank ordered, the customer sometimes *insists* on nonrank ordered priorities. In such cases, our advice to the project manager is to further explain to the customer the problem of having two or more priorities ranked the same. If the customer does not relent, the project manager should do whatever is possible to accommodate the customer, just as a travel agent would to placate a customer with similar demands. A prudent approach is to inform the customer of the associated risks clearly and *in writing*.

Intra-Project Priorities—Example 4

Now consider the project ranking depicted in Figure 4.9, where all attributes are ranked as 1st. Unfortunately, many customers tend to see their projects this way. They must have it by the dictated deadline, to the highest possible quality, it must include all of the asked-for scope, and it must not cost too much. Our response to project managers faced with this dilemma is, "It will build character." We do not recommend this type of priority ranking because these expectations cannot be met without stressing the end product and the team to the extreme.[8]

FIGURE 4.9
Intra-Project Priorities—Not
Rank Ordered

		Ranking example			
		1st	2nd	3rd	4th
Attributes	Schedule	✓			
	Scope	✓			
	Budget	✓			
	Quality	✓			

Each project has its own urgencies and must be looked at individually. The best approach is to *rank order* the four attributes so that no two attributes have the same ranking (importance). If this is not possible because of certain circumstances, make sure the customer clearly understands the risk the project is carrying, as well as the consequences if the team is not able to mitigate those risks. Keeping the risks in mind, work diligently, keep good records, eat well, exercise, and read Dilbert.[9] You will need your health and your sense of humor. Once the customer has stated the priorities, we recommend the following steps:

- For the attribute(s) ranked 1st, define the consequences of failing to meet the stated priority and clearly communicate the same to the project team.
- For the attribute(s) ranked 2nd, 3rd, or 4th, define which parts of the attribute the customer would be willing to negotiate.

It is important to know who has the final say in defining the relative priorities of the four project components. Is it the customer who requested the project? Is it the sponsor? Should we be

---

[8]If you are not ever able to persuade your customers to rank order the intra-project priorities, you will certainly benefit from attending a course on effective negotiations.

[9]Dilbert is a registered trademark of United Media. All rights reserved.

FIGURE 4.10

Multiple Stakeholder Intra-Project Priorities

Priority attribute	Sponsor	Customer	End user	Team	Final
Schedule	1	3	2	3	
Scope	4	1	3	2	
Budget	3	4	4	4	
Quality	2	2	1	1	

concerned about the priorities of the end-users? What about the input from the team? The answers to these questions become critical when the relative rankings by the various groups do not converge, which often is the case.

When key stakeholders' priorities differ, the project team can find it very difficult to decide on a course of action. One of the responsibilities of the project manager is to facilitate the alignment of the project priorities among various stakeholders. The best way to proceed is for the project manager, working with the sponsor, to ascertain which stakeholders must be consulted about the project at hand. Once a decision has been reached, the next step is to specifically document selected stakeholders' priorities. Figure 4.10 depicts a matrix of the priorities of four key stakeholders for a given project.

In Figure 4.10, we see that the project manager selected the following four key stakeholders:

1. *Sponsor*—always included.
2. *Customer*—always included. In the case of projects that include a diverse group of customers, such as a project that will be deployed in multiple geographic locations, each customer group may need to be represented in a separate column.
3. *End user*—in this case, the project has a second level of implementation-level stakeholders, and they are grouped under this heading. For example, the customers could be the tellers in a bank and the end users would be the bank's business customers. Another example would be where checkout clerks in a supermarket are the project's customers and the public is the end-user.
4. *Team*—this project manager has decided to include the team because of their strong impact on how the project is carried out. Teams do not always show up in Intra-Project Priority assessments and the decision is primarily up to the project manager. Our advice is to include the team as a key stakeholder only in the case of high complexity projects.

Figure 4.10 clearly shows that the priorities of the four different groups do not converge. The next step for the project manager is to use appropriate information to influence the key stakeholders towards a collective common view of the Intra-Project Priorities. The objective here is to establish priorities that best serve the needs of the project as a whole rather than the needs of any one group. This convergence is facilitated by assessing and comparing the consequences to the business if the highest priority of each key stakeholder is not met. Once consequences have been examined and tradeoffs have been developed, a governing set of priorities for the project should emerge. In the case of nonconvergence, the project manager may need assistance from the sponsor to help different stakeholders come to a common understanding of the Intra-Project Priorities. Figure 4.11 shows the final decision on the ranking of the priorities.

A question frequently asked by many project managers at this point is, "What if the various stakeholders cannot agree on a common ranking of the priorities?" The answer is one of two options:

1. The project manager and the sponsor work together to assess who is the most influential stakeholder and then see whether that stakeholder's priorities should prevail. If that is the case, then the project manager and the sponsor will need to work with other stakeholders to build consensus.

FIGURE 4.11

Intra-Project Priorities—Final

Priority attribute	Sponsor	Customer	End-user	Team	Final
Schedule	1	3	2	3	1
Scope	4	1	3	2	3
Budget	3	4	4	4	4
Quality	2	2	1	1	2

2. If the previous step is not practical, or does not produce consensus, then the sponsor decides on the priority rankings because the project sponsor is responsible for project success and needs to manage the priorities.

The final step is to communicate the Intra-Project Priorities to the various stakeholders. The project manager must also keep the defined priorities in mind when deciding on the project scope, creating the project task plan, developing the project schedule, and managing the activities in the Execute and Implement stages.

■ A CHANGE IN INTRA-PROJECT PRIORITIES

Remember that the stated priorities can shift during the project development cycle. For example, assume that the priorities of a project designed to bring a new product to the market had been defined as follows:

Functionality: 1
Quality: 2
Budget: 3
Schedule: 4

Considering these priorities, one would assume that the sponsor wanted a high quality, functionally rich product. To achieve this goal, the customer was open to a higher development cost and also had not conveyed any urgency of the timing of the product introduction into the market. Then in the middle of the development cycle, the marketing department discovered that a competitor was working aggressively to bring a similar product to the market and planned a highly orchestrated product introduction event at an upcoming industry convention. The sponsor agreed with the marketing department's concern, wanted to change the ranking on the schedule to 1st priority, and wanted a proposal from the project manager. What were the options? Look at an alternative:

Option 1

Schedule: 1
Quality: 2
Functionality: 3
Budget: 4

The schedule was the 1st priority and the project manager kept quality as the 2nd priority, which changes the functionality to the 3rd priority. This meant that the customer was willing to work with the project manager to *reduce* the product functionality—fewer deliverables and features. The budget was the 4th priority, which does not mean that the customer does not care about the development cost. What it means is, that because the schedule has been tightened, higher cost resources may need to be used to meet the new objectives. If the customer chooses not to reduce the functionality by as much as suggested by the project manager, the following priorities could be considered:

Option 2

Schedule: 1
Functionality: 2
Quality: 3
Budget: 4

This ranking of priorities implies that the team can deliver more functionality than proposed in option 1, but the quality of the end product will be further compromised. Now, many people might proclaim, "There is no way the quality can be compromised, it has to be the best." We would invite these people to read *Consumer Reports*' review of products and see whether different products in a given class are all of the same high quality (even by the same manufacturer). Of course not. In no way are we implying that the product's quality be compromised to the extent that the customers do not buy/accept it or that it does harm to the end-users. The rational thing to do is to visit the list of quality attributes of the product and decide which of these could be compromised, to what extent, and still meet the market acceptance. If the decision is made to go with this option, it would behoove the organization to improve the quality in a later version of the product.

Option 3

> Schedule: 1
> Budget: 2
> Functionality: 3
> Quality: 4

Whoa, we can hear your protests now——"no way; the customer will not accept such a product." Interestingly, this does not seem to bother most software vendors, especially some of the largest. In fact, this type of thinking—we need it all, we need it soon, and quality be damned—has resulted in the dismal quality of many software products.

> *Software bugs are costing the U.S. economy an estimated $59.5 billion each year, with more than half of the cost borne by end users . . .*
> Patrick Thibodeau, "Study: Buggy Software Costs Users, Vendors Nearly
> $60B Annually," *Computerworld* (June 25, 2002).

A primary reason for this grim state of software quality is the fact that, until recently, the software project management profession did not have the quality attribute in the project equation. Most of the automobile industry in the U.S. behaved in a similar manner until the early 1990s.

Worst Case Scenario

When defining the relative rankings of the four components of the Intra-Project Priority, it is a good idea to raise the question of the worst case scenario for each of these items. For example:

> *Scope:* The minimal scope that must be delivered to the customer.
> *Budget:* The maximum amount of money the customer is willing to spend on the project.
> *Schedule:* The date the project must be finished and implemented.
> *Quality:* The level of quality below which the product will be unacceptable to the customer.

These conditions, collectively, can be summed up as the performance baseline for the project. If the stated thresholds of any of these items are breached, the project is in jeopardy.

There will be situations when there is pressure to change the "weight" of one or more of the components. When this is the case, ask the sponsor what tradeoffs she is willing to accept. For example, the list below suggests a tradeoff for each of the four components:

> *Add scope:* Lengthen schedule, reduce quality, increase budget.
> *Reduce schedule:* Reduce scope, reduce quality, increase budget.
> *Reduce budget:* Reduce scope, reduce quality, lengthen schedule.
> *Improve quality:* Reduce scope, increase budget, lengthen schedule.

If the sponsor will not agree to any of the tradeoffs, the risk of not completing the project successfully has just increased.

In summary, each project attribute (schedule, scope, budget, and quality) must be managed. The sponsor and the key stakeholders must play an active role in helping establish their relative priorities for the project. Sponsors must learn to define equilibrium among the four project attributes: schedule, scope, budget, and quality. Priorities may change during a project's life cycle, so revisit priority assessment every two to three months. A word of caution to project sponsors: "If the priorities have to be changed, forthrightly describe to the team the reasons for the proposed change, the downside of not making the change, and then work with the project manager and the team to develop the plan to meet the new priorities." We strongly believe that most well managed teams will do their best to meet the customer's needs.

Many in the project management profession still use the notion of triple constraint—scope, schedule, and budget. When this is the case, quality is a subset of the scope. However, more and more authors and project management practitioners are beginning to use the four-attribute decomposition. If your colleagues, and your managers, insist on using the triple constraints, our advice is that you try to educate them on the benefits of parsing quality into a separate attribute. However, we don't advise engaging in any arguments. If they persist in the use of triple constraints, and it would benefit the overall environment to go that way, go with the flow.

■ STAKEHOLDER ANALYSIS—PPA STEP 5

In Chapter 3 (refer to Figure 3.5), we grouped project stakeholders into two primary categories:

1. Policy level stakeholders: those who shape the project
2. Implementation level stakeholders: those who will be shaped by the project

Additionally, stakeholders can be internal or external to the organization that is undertaking the project. For example, internal stakeholders might include organizations or individuals not working directly on the project, but whose operations, costs, and risks could be impacted by the project. External stakeholders are those individuals or groups outside of the organization who will be impacted by the implementation of the project, or those who control policy that impacts the project. Such groups might include business partners, vendors, unions, regulatory agencies, or the public at large.

At this point in the project, the project manager must analyze the attitude and behavior of various stakeholders toward the project. Stakeholder behavior can be classified into the following categories:

Champion: An individual who sees the merits of the proposed project and is willing to use his political capital to remove obstacles from the path of successful project completion.

Neutral: An individual who presently does not perceive any particular stake or interest in the project. She could be converted to champion status if shown how successful project completion could benefit her.

Nemesis: An individual who does not see any merit to the project and may very well use his political capital to place obstacles in the path of successful project completion. Not all nemeses are bad people. It could be that their current perception is such that the proposed project makes no sense to them or they don't like the manner in which the project is being handled.

If people resist your overtures, it doesn't necessarily mean they are against your program. They may be uninformed or unaware of the potential benefits. Don't assume people are against you just because they fail to leap on the bandwagon immediately. Create a communication plan that provides stakeholders with appropriate information.
Paul C. Dinsmore, "Five Ways Not to Pitch Project Management in Your Organization," *PM Network* (February, 2003): p. 60.

Comatose: People who are known to have a stake in the project but have such minimal interest, or are so distracted by other events, that they pay no attention to the proposed project.

Invisible or Ignored: People who are somewhat removed from the project at this early stage and are either outside the peripheral vision of the project team or are being purposely ignored by the project team. This category typically includes such groups as human resources, legal, purchasing, testing and systems integration, and operations.

Stakeholder Assessment

It is imperative that project managers identify the key players in the project and judiciously assess their views of the project, especially any turf issues—it is extremely important to focus on the politics of the proposed project.

Too many project managers, especially newly promoted, technology-minded individuals, take pride in proclaiming, "I don't like corporate politics and pay no attention to it." These people tend to ignore this important component of successful project management—understanding the organization's politics and then maneuvering around it in a professional manner.

FIGURE 4.12
Policy Level Stakeholders

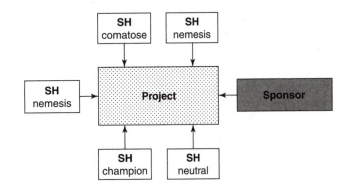

Policy Level Stakeholders

The most important stakeholder is the project sponsor—an appropriate level executive or manager who has accepted the responsibility for guiding the project to its successful completion. Another way to describe a sponsor is the individual who controls most of the strings of the project—the person who can make it dance. Figure 4.12 depicts a policy level stakeholder diagram, with a number of stakeholders, and their views toward the project.

In Figure 4.12, we see that the project has a number of champions (those who wish the project well and are committed to making it a success). The project might also have several neutral individuals who are on the sidelines and do not see much intrinsic value in the proposed project (some of the neutrals may even be comatose and will need to be awakened by the project manager and/or the sponsor). Be wary of a project that no one wants to champion. For people to "just agree" with the benefits of the proposed project is not enough. Policy level stakeholders must have a vested interest in the successful completion of the project. They have much to gain from its implementation and much to lose if the project is not deployed successfully.

Finally, a project will likely have nemeses (people who are against the project for real or perceived reasons). It behooves a project manager to be aware of these nemeses and not ignore them in the hope that they will go away. In some cases, if not properly managed, project nemeses may actually take active steps to derail the project. Even though two project nemeses are identified here, you must decide whether it is politically correct to publicly document this term. Discuss this subject with your sponsor as well as your functional manager, and then act accordingly.

Implementation Level Stakeholders

Our focus now turns to the implementation level stakeholders—those individuals and groups whose lives will be shaped by the project. Figure 4.13 depicts an implementation level stakeholder diagram, with a number of stakeholders and their views towards the project.

For each implementation level stakeholder group, the project manager must analyze the following points:

1. The degree of alignment between policy level stakeholders' objectives and implementation level stakeholders' expectations

FIGURE 4.13
Implementation Level
Stakeholders

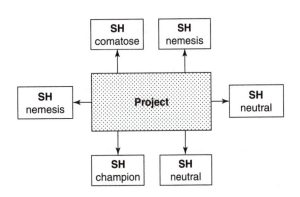

2. The degree of change—functional, technical, and political—the project will bring to the implementation level stakeholders
3. Stakeholders' perceptions of win or lose
4. The degree of readiness to absorb the change
5. The degree of influence across the organization
6. Hot buttons, perceived priorities, and turf issues

Degree of Alignment   Until this point in the project, we have focused on the objectives and needs of the person (or the group) requesting the project, which invariably means the desires and needs of management (because a vast majority of projects are initiated by people at these levels). Now we must pay attention to the people who will be the recipients of the end product of the proposed project. In the case of most projects that fail, or are not well accepted by customers and end users, the most glaring mistake is that their needs have been overlooked—the project has been thrust upon them. For example:

> *The business units couldn't decide among themselves what they wanted, the CEO had a grandiose vision of a dynamic system that would never happen in the allotted time frame, and the hotel managers who had to implement the program wanted nothing to do with the whole mess.*
>
> Polly Schneider, 2000.

Degree of Change   The impact of change is perhaps the most overlooked area of any new project. By definition, projects mean changes—abandonment of the known and familiar to acceptance of new and unfamiliar (and often unpredictable). In the heat of excitement over the possibility of new ideas producing great new benefits for the organization, many overlook the extent of the unlearning and relearning required by implementation level stakeholders. Most of the time, the relearning must be done without any appreciable reduction in workload. Such an oversight is the primary reason for poor implementation of a large number of projects (especially massive, life-changing software projects).

> *No major software implementation is really about the software. It's about change management. . . . We were really naive in the respect that these changes had to be managed. . . . Nobody wanted to learn the new way of doing things. Morale tumbled. Turnover among the employees who forecast demand for Nestlé products reached 77 percent; the planners simply were loath or unable to abandon their familiar spreadsheets . . .*
>
> Jeri Dunn, in Ben Worthen, "Take Home Lessons from Nestlé's ERP,"
> *CIO Magazine* (May 15, 2002).

Perception of Win or Lose   In the ideal world, all projects will result in a win/win situation for the policy level and implementation level stakeholders. Real life, unfortunately, is not ideal. In many projects, the implementation level stakeholders have to learn new processes, new procedures, new technology, and are then assessed on new performance measurements. Many projects, especially driven by efficiency objectives, result in layoffs, job transfers, reduced budgets, and reduced authority. Therefore, it is essential that the project manager responsible for developing the Project Charter clearly understands the net impact of the project on various implementation level stakeholders and carefully documents any no win situations. This insight will certainly help develop a considered and equitable Organization Change Management Plan (see Chapter 5).

> *Change is not made without inconvenience, even from worse to better.*
> Richard Hooker (http://www.bartleby.com/66/28828.html).

Degree of Readiness   The implementation level stakeholder assessment gives the project manager the first glimpse into the degree of change the proposed project will bring, and the degree to which the implementation level stakeholders are ready and willing to accept the changes. This information will be used as an input to risk assessment as well as for developing a comprehensive Organization Change Management Plan.

You are challenging their principles, their beliefs and the way they have done things for many, many years. . . . All the divisional functions—manufacturing, purchasing, accounting, and sales—would have to give up their old approaches and accept the new pan-Nestlé way.

Ben Worthern, 2002.

Because of what is required of them, it is easy to conclude that policy level and implementation level stakeholders can have an extensive impact on the success or failure of any given project. Therefore, in addition to the items already discussed, the following items need to be assessed for both the policy level and implementation level stakeholders:

Degree of Influence   It is important to assess the degree and type of influence each key stakeholder wields. As we described earlier, a stakeholder can be a champion, comatose, neutral, and at times, outright destructive. The influence could span just a few people or an entire division. Knowing this information, and then developing appropriate plans to leverage or appropriately manage the stakeholder, can spell the difference between successful and challenged projects (or even failure).

Hot Buttons   It is important to ascertain what specific actions, events, processes, and types of projects elicit a strong reaction—positive or negative—from the key stakeholders. Having this information will help you anticipate the response the proposed project will elicit.

Perceived Priority   Most stakeholders are sure to be faced with a myriad of operational issues, day-to-day activities, and new projects. The project manager must determine the amount of interest the stakeholder will have in the proposed project. Will it get the right place on the person's list of priorities? If not, what will be the impact on the proposed project?

Turf Issues   As it applies to business, "turf" means the range of a person's authority or influence. A question to keep in mind: "Will the proposed project in any way reduce or dramatically change the range of any particular stakeholder's influence?" If so, how will the individual react to that change? Knowing this information will help the project manager understand the risks involved with the proposed project.

Finally, building collaborative and synergetic relationships with key stakeholders should be the prime goal of every project manager. Even when your efforts do not specifically lead to converting any nemeses into champions, or at best into neutral parties, the time and effort you invest in the process will be seen as professional behavior by others and will produce positive results in the long run. Figure 4.14 depicts a list of items designed to help you identify, define, and document the primary stakeholders' interests and support levels and their impact on the project's key attributes: schedule, scope, budget, and quality.

Once you have identified and analyzed the information gathered in Figure 4.14, the next step is to focus on the stakeholders in greater detail to begin to define the education and training needs of various stakeholders, as this will help you prepare the stakeholders for successful project development and deployment. Figure 4.15 displays the items of information designed to help you define any education and training needs of various stakeholders.

Once completed, the data compiled in Figures 4.14 and 4.15 will provide both the project manager and the proposed sponsor with good insight into the project's acceptance (or rejection) by the various implementation level stakeholders. It is imperative that project managers develop a plan, with help and guidance from their sponsors, to leverage the champions, involve the uninterested, neutralize the nemeses, and wake up the comatose. Poor management of project stakeholders has caused countless projects to languish and fail.

Examples

Following are three examples of situations where the project managers overlooked the interests and the resulting impacts of key stakeholders. The first problem involves an external policy level stakeholder, the second example is of a large group of implementation level stakeholders, and the third problem relates to external policy level stakeholders (labor unions). All three cases resulted in major problems.

FIGURE 4.14
Stakeholder Analysis

Name:

Title:

Functional/Business Area:

Degree of alignment:
• How well does the project meet the needs of the stakeholder?

Key concerns/turf issues:
• What are the stakeholder's concerns regarding the proposed project? Are there any turf issue problems? Will the proposed project negatively impact this stakeholder's span of control, power, influence, or budget?

Degree of change:
• Describe the degree of technical, political, and cultural change the stakeholder will experience from the deployment of the proposed project.

Win/lose perception:
• How does the stakeholder perceive the project?

Hot buttons:
• What project objectives are most important to this stakeholder?

Perceived priority:
• When it comes to the stakeholder's day-to-day work and any other projects in progress, what priority does the stakeholder place on the proposed project?

Readiness:
• How ready is the stakeholder to successfully deploy the project?

Type/level of support:
• What type of support/attitude does the stakeholder demonstrate: champion, nemesis, neutral, or comatose?

Impact on project:
• Considering the collected information, what impact will the stakeholder have on the project schedule, scope, budget, and quality?

Leverage/management plan:
• What plans are in place to leverage the championship behavior? If the stakeholder is a nemesis, neutral, or in a comatose state, what plans are in place to manage the situation?

FIGURE 4.15
Stakeholder Education/
Training Needs Assessment

Implementation stakeholder	Training required	Type of training required	When	Provider	Action required
	❑ Yes ❑ No				
	❑ Yes ❑ No				
	❑ Yes ❑ No				
	❑ Yes ❑ No				
	❑ Yes ❑ No				
	❑ Yes ❑ No				
	❑ Yes ❑ No				

■ EXAMPLE 1

A project manager at a manufacturing company was assigned to a project that was designed to develop a training program for about 1,000 employees. Two key deliverables of the project were a student training manual and an instructor's guide. The training would be provided by a number of the company's employees who would be trained by a vendor (we call them WeTrain group). During his research, the project manager discovered that close to 60 percent of the training manual content was already being taught in a series of seminars by a *different* vendor (we call them ProductExperts). The project manager, without any discussion with ProductExperts, directed his team to use a large chunk of their materials (copyrighted intellectual property) to expedite the completion of the training manual and the instructor's guide. Later, it was discovered that a few team members did raise the question of obtaining intellectual property use permission from ProductExperts. The project manager told the team members that ProductExperts would be thrilled that the company was using their materials and would be most thankful for recognition of their work. After the instructor's guide was completed and submitted to the sponsor for review, the sponsor happened to ship a copy of the guide to ProductExperts. The project manager did not really understand the extent of the problem caused by *unauthorized* use of intellectual property of third parties. With the proliferation of the Internet, too many people don't give a second thought to downloading and using cartoons, research materials, music, software, and pictures without permissions and appropriate credits. Fortunately for the project manager, the instructor's guide had not yet been sent to WeTrain (they were competitors of ProductExperts). The project was canceled because there was no budget to obtain an intellectual property use license from ProductExperts. ■

■ EXAMPLE 2

A major consumer goods company had outsourced the enhancement and upgrade of a sales management system to an out-of-town vendor. One of the requirements of the contract was that the upgraded system was to be installed over a weekend or a holiday so it did not disrupt the day-to-day sales operations. This was especially important because the upgrade was to take place during one of the busiest sales cycles for the company. This was their first mistake, but it got worse. The outsourcing of the project caused a major rift between the company's internal IT staff and the vendor. The two groups were not on good terms and the vendor project manager exploited the situation by "bad-mouthing" the IT staff to company management. During the six-month project, only minimal communications existed between the two groups. Unfortunately, the project sponsor, who was the corporate VP of sales, was not at all interested in details; he was only concerned with the budget and the delivery date. The vendor opted to install the upgraded system during the Thanksgiving holiday, which always falls on a Thursday. Many people leave their offices for the holiday weekend by the early afternoon on Wednesday. This gave the vendor almost four days to complete the implementation. By Sunday afternoon, the vendor team had installed the new system and the project manager was pleased with the outcome. Then came Monday morning. The sales people began to boot up their computer systems from their offices, homes, hotel rooms, automobiles, and from airplanes. All found completely new screens—new colors, new formats, new interfaces, and new vocabulary. Many thought that they had dialed a wrong number and somehow connected to either a different system or perhaps a different company. Disconnecting and reconnecting did not produce different results; they still saw the same new screens. Many called the help desk. Nobody from the vendor's team had informed the help desk group of the new system upgrade. The help desk group belonged to a third party vendor; their offices were located in a city four states away (in a different time zone). The help group saw the old screens on their system and had no idea what the people on the other end of the telephone were talking about. Some help desk people even inquired whether the person was calling the right number for support. In the meantime, most of the vendor team, having worked the long weekend, had taken a few days off and were not readily available. Remember that this was one of the busiest sales seasons for the company. The sales people did not know how to navigate the new system and the help desk was useless. As a result, the IT department had to reinstall the old system until a later date when the vendor could train the help desk support staff and also provide training to selected salespeople. Many in the IT department, nemeses of the project because of their poor relations with the vendor, sported "I told you so grins" over this debacle. The company threatened a lawsuit and the vendor made major financial adjustments.　■

■ EXAMPLE 3

To aid in the fund-raising drive, a not-for-profit organization was planning a major event at a public arena owned by the city government. They approached the president of a pizza chain headquartered in the city and asked if one of their outlets could set up a booth where they would make fresh pizzas and involve the attendees in pizza tossing and pizza making contests. The company would receive major exposure and the mayor would personally thank the company president during the awards ceremony. With the promise of primetime TV and radio station coverage of the event, the president considered this to be a worthwhile project. He assigned the project to a newly promoted project manager who was thrilled to have the opportunity. The project manager contacted the owner of a franchised restaurant near the charity event venue, discussed the project with the owner, and developed an estimate of out of pocket expenses for the materials and people time. The project manager and the outlet owner (who was also pleased with the promise of press exposure and photo opportunities) presented their budget, which included four major items: supplies, people time, promotional materials, and truck rental for moving the ovens and preparation equipment to and from the event site. The president, in order to reduce the out of pocket expenses, offered the use of the corporate print center for the promotional materials as well as two trucks and warehouse employees to transport the equipment. Everything was set, the mayor was informed, and promotional materials were printed. On the day of the event, two trucks loaded with portable ovens, premade pizza dough, a variety of utensils, and equipment arrived at the site. Problems immediately began to unfold. The project manager had overlooked the need for obtaining a permit from the fire commissioner, and the venue manager wanted to see appropriate liability insurance coverage before allowing the group to move their equipment to the event hall. At this time, the labor union supervisor showed up and informed the project manager that only union employees were allowed to move anything from the curb to inside the event hall, and that only union plumbers and electricians were authorized to provide appropriate electrical and plumbing connections. The estimated labor cost shocked the project manager. Ultimately, the pizza making show did go on, though a little late. The pizza franchise owner was very unhappy because he got stuck with part of the bill from the union; the corporate legal counsel was upset because he got pulled out of a social function to make last minute arrangements for liability insurance; and the CEO was dismayed that the project was handled so poorly. The project manager got a bad mark for botching up the project.　■

Who is at fault? None of the projects had an involved sponsor. In each case, a senior level manager expressed a need and the next step was a project manager fully engaged in the execution of the project—the inevitable large leap from the idea to execution. Project managers are told to hit the ground running. What actually happens is that they simply hit the ground.

Stakeholders' interest analysis and expectations management does not end with this step of the PPA. Stakeholder management continues through all project stages. Here are a number of key points regarding project stakeholders and their contributions during the different stages of the project life cycle:

1. *Pre-Launch:* Help develop a realistic, business-oriented, and comprehensive Project Charter.
2. *Launch:* Help structure an effective project organization, develop a comprehensive task plan, staff the project team, and obtain final project budget approvals.
3. *Execute:* Help ensure timely resource availability, remove obstacles, support the project manager through championship behavior, and adopt a supportive role. Act as a mentor to the project manager.
4. *Implement:* Help with project deployment to respective business units, prepare frontline project customers for timely and smooth transition to the new project, and help ensure that planned project benefits are realized.

■ COMPLEXITY ASSESSMENT—PPA STEP 6

Projects vary widely in their complexity, depending not only on their objectives but also on the environment in which they will be executed. To illustrate the point, consider the three structures illustrated in Figure 4.16. Each wall is the same size: 400 sq. ft.

Will the construction of each wall take the same amount of time? Will each require the same type of materials? Will each cost the same? Will each take the same degree of skill to build? Does each carry the same risk? Let us analyze all three:

- *Wall 1:* This wall can be built without having to elevate either the masons or the masonry. No scaffolding would be required (a typical mason's height is more than the height of the wall). Obviously, this wall will cost the least amount per square foot and carries the least amount of risk.
- *Wall 2:* Building this wall will certainly require scaffolding, because both the masons and masonry will have to be elevated to finish the top portion of the wall. This wall will take longer to construct, cost more per square foot, and will carry more risk than Wall 1.
- *Wall 3:* This wall is a complex undertaking. The design, foundation, materials, and scaffolding must be given serious thought. The masons must not be afraid of heights. A crane or an elevator might be needed to raise the masonry and masons to the high end of the structure. Additional items to consider are zoning regulations, insurance, rights-of-way, staging areas, risk to nearby structures, and perhaps an environmental impact assessment.

A review of these illustrations makes it obvious that *complex* projects require many more tasks than *simpler* projects. The cost of Wall 3 (a more complex structure) is going to *far exceed* the cost of the least complex project (Wall 1). Additionally, the construction of Wall 3 will require workers with higher skills and will carry a higher degree of risk. This point is habitually overlooked when considering IT/Business project complexity and estimates. It is extremely important that the project manager clearly communicate to the customer the complexity of the project at hand and its impact on the effort, cost, resource, and duration estimates.

Project Complexity Assessment

In many projects, complexities and complications are discovered only as work progresses, causing missed deadlines, budget overruns, and thwarted management expectations. If a project's complexity is not assessed at the start, the later discovery of complexity results in a last minute patchwork of quick-fix solutions—a key cause of scope creep and poor product quality. Invariably, the project team becomes overwhelmed by problems and loses control of the project. By ascertaining the complexity of a project at its early stage, most eventualities can be preempted and surprises can be kept to a minimum. Additionally, knowing the complexity of any project can be of considerable assistance when faced with project planning, estimating, and staffing decisions.

For the purpose of assessing the complexity of a project, imagine that the project has two dimensions that each consist of a series of attributes. The two most common dimensions of project complexity are business complexity and technical complexity.

Each dimension can be characterized by a set of attributes that can vary in number depending on the project. Typical business attributes include size, geography, and financial exposure. Typical technical attributes include level of technology integration, security needs, stability of hardware/

FIGURE 4.16
Three Walls

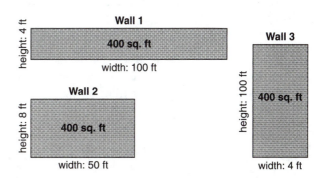

FIGURE 4.17
Project Complexity Chart

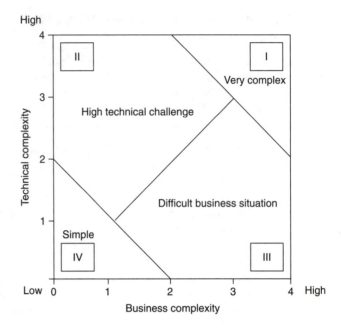

software, and team experience. Technology does not necessarily mean IT; it could be any technology used to build the proposed system and/or product. The complexity introduced by each of the individual attributes can be scored on a scale ranging from low to high, and the composite score developed for each of the two dimensions. The two composite scores, when plotted in a two-dimensional chart, depict the project's relative business and technical complexities, as shown in Figure 4.17.

In Figure 4.17, we see that the two-dimensional space in the complexity diagram is divided into four primary zones:

1. Zone I: Projects in this space are highly complex—very high business and technical complexity
2. Zone II: This space of the diagram depicts high technical complexity projects
3. Zone III: This space of the diagram depicts high business complexity projects
4. Zone IV: Projects in this space are of low complexity—simple or routine projects

From Figure 4.17, it should be obvious that projects get more complex as they move from the lower left hand side to the upper right hand side.

Business Environment

Every organization, and each specific project, will be driven by its own business complexity attributes. The following is a list of typical business complexity attributes:

Business rules	Geography
Competitors	Market knowledge
Cross-functional interactions	Regulatory restrictions
Current business processes	Time scale
Customer/end user buy-in	Visibility
Financial exposure	

When assessing the complexity of a given project, you will need to create a *tailored* attribute list to reflect the needs of the given project. A complexity continuum needs to be defined for each attribute. For example, considering the first five attributes listed in Figure 4.18, the continuum values could be defined as follows:

1. Business rules
   a. *Static:* The business rules that impact the project at hand are static and will stay that way during the development life cycle of the project.

Low complexity	Business attribute	High complexity	Rating
0 1	2 3	4	
Static	Business rules	Changing	3
Static	Current business systems	Changing	4
Low	Financial exposure	High	4
Familiar	Markets	Unfamiliar	3
Local	Geography	Global	3
Few and routine	Interaction with other departments	Many and new	3
Few and straightforward	Issues	Multiple and contentious	4
Clear	Objectives	Vague	4
Established	Policies	Nonexistent	3
Minimal	Politics	High	4
Experienced	Team	Inexperienced	3
Loose	Time scale	Tight	4
Low	Visibility	High	4
		Total	**46**
		Complexity	**3.5**

FIGURE 4.18
Business Complexity Assessment

    b. *Changing:* The business rules that impact the project at hand have changed and might change even further during the development life cycle of the project.

2. Current business systems

    a. *Static:* No known changes are planned for the various business systems with which the proposed project will interface (e.g., manufacturing, payroll, and shipping).

    b. *Changing:* Significant changes are planned for the various business systems with which the proposed project will interface (e.g., manufacturing, payroll, and shipping).

3. Financial exposure

    a. *Low:* In case the project is not successful, the direct and indirect financial losses to the organization will be minimal (or within acceptable range).

    b. *High:* In case the project is not successful, the direct and indirect financial losses to the organization will be high—beyond the acceptable risk range.

4. Markets

    a. *Familiar:* The organization sponsoring the project is highly familiar with the market(s) into which the proposed project's end products will be introduced. The people in the sponsoring group have experience in this market.

    b. *Unfamiliar:* The organization sponsoring the project is not familiar with the market(s) into which the proposed project's end products will be introduced. They have no knowledge of the market intricacies and have little or no experience with similar product introductions.

5. Geography
   a. *Local:* The area in which the project will be managed and implemented is limited to local offices and markets.
   b. *Global:* The area in which the project will be managed and implemented spans a vast number of geographic locations, perhaps internationally.

Assume that the markets are unfamiliar and the geography is global. The complexity level and the project risk have just risen dramatically. If this were the case, the solution to the problem would include steps such as:

1. Revisit the stakeholder assessment to make sure that key global stakeholders have not been left out of the assessment and that comprehensive plans will be made to identify and leverage project champions and minimize any nemesis behavior.
2. Break the project into manageable smaller chunks to minimize introducing extensive changes in one fell swoop.
3. Extensive prototyping of key deliverables to obtain predeployment acceptance.
4. Active and pervasive involvement by the sponsor for continuous marketing of the project to key stakeholders.

Figure 4.18 depicts a chart designed to assess the business complexity. The *Business attribute* column lists a number of attributes applicable to the project at hand. The columns to its left and right list the characteristics associated with the low and high end of the complexity continuum, where the value of 0 implies no complexity and the value of 4 means high complexity. While creating the specific list for a project, include *only* those attributes that apply to the project in a *significant* manner.

Low complexity		Technical attribute		High complexity	Rating
0	1	2	3	4	
Local		Communications		Global	4
Established		Delivery mechanism		New	4
Local		Geography		System wide	4
Proven		Hardware		New	3.5
Standalone		Level Of integration		Tightly integrated	4
Established		License compliance		Not established	3.5
Proven/stable		Networks (L/W)		New	3
In place		New technology architecture		Not in place	3.5
9–5, Monday–Friday		Operations		24-hour, 7-day	4
Light		Security		Tight	4
Proven		Software		New	3.5
Established and in use		Standards and methods		None	3
Experienced		Team		Inexperienced	3
High		Tolerance to fault		Low	3.5
Low		Transaction volume		High	4
				Total	54.5
				Complexity	3.6

FIGURE 4.19
Technical Complexity Assessment

Careful selection will ensure that none of the attributes will have a complexity rating of 0. Record a value indicating the level of complexity of each applicable attribute in the *rating* column.

The steps to compute a project's business complexity are as follows:

1. Assess each applicable attribute on a scale of 0 to 4, where 0 means no complexity and 4 indicates a highly complex situation. You should use increments of 0.5 to depict the complexity of a given attribute (0.5, 1, 1.5, 2.0 . . .). Although we have observed the use of 0.25 increments in some cases, we believe that is being too precise. It is difficult to do when assessing the value of individual attributes.
2. Add all of the assessed values.
3. Divide the total assessed value by the number of *nonzero* attributes.

In Figure 4.18, the total number of attributes is 13 and their total assessed value is 46. Therefore, the net business complexity is computed as:

$$46 \div 13 = 3.5$$

Technical Environment

Figure 4.19 depicts a list of technical environment attributes and their assessed values for a sample project. When assessing the complexity of a specific project, you will need to create a tailored attribute list to reflect the needs of that project. When developing this list, include only those attributes that apply to the project in a *significant* manner.

The steps needed to compute a project's technical complexity are the same as those needed to compute business complexity. In Figure 4.19, the total number of attributes is 15 and their total assessed value is 54.5. Therefore, the net technical complexity is computed as:

$$54.5 \div 15 = 3.6$$

The number of attributes in the two categories (business and technical) *does not* have to be the same. For example, you might choose to specify eleven business complexity attributes and only ten (or fewer) for the technical complexity (or vice versa).

Complexity Zones

Now the project can be plotted in the complexity diagram shown in Figure 4.20. In this chart, the ▲ symbol represents the project we just assessed using the values in Figures 4.18 and 4.19. The placement of the proposed project in *Zone I* indicates that this is a highly complex project because practically all of the business and technology attributes are rated towards the higher end of the complexity rating.

FIGURE 4.20
Project Complexity Chart

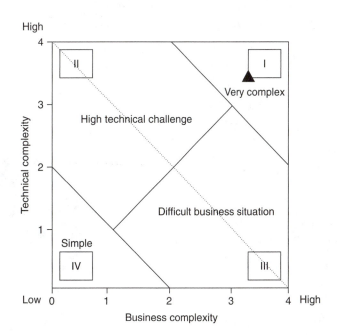

A note of caution—*do not* be concerned with the *precision* of a project's placement within the complexity diagram. The purpose is to ascertain the key complexity contributors and the zone in which the project falls—not the precise placement of a project within the complexity chart.

Understanding the project's complexity helps when assembling the right sponsors, a project manager, and the team, as well as getting the first glimpse of the risks inherent in the project. Despite the importance of understanding and managing complexity, the data in Figure 4.21 shows that project complexity is not generally well understood.

Three frequently asked questions, along with our responses, regarding the complexity assessment are:

1. **Question:** Should each attribute carry the same weight, or would it be better to assign relative weights to various attributes?
   Response: Of course, assigning each attribute a relative weight and then assessing each attribute's degree of complexity would certainly result in a more accurate complexity assessment. However, our experience assessing a large number of projects has shown us that the resulting complexity values are not *significantly* different. Complexity assessment is not a precise tool; it involves a certain degree of subjectivity.

2. **Question:** Why divide the total assessed complexity value by the number of *nonzero* attributes?
   Response: We have found that many project managers tend to include a large number of insignificant complexity attributes, which they rate as 0. They then divide the sum of the values by the number of attributes. Because many of the attributes carry a 0 rating, the net complexity computes to a low figure, implying that this is a low complexity project. The results are misleading. We suggest the following approach: Be careful when creating the complexity attributes and include only those that have values higher than 0. At times, project managers want to include attributes that currently have an extremely low complexity rating (zero), but may become more complex later in the project's life cycle. In these cases, do not count them in the total number of attributes used to compute the net complexity value. If any of the attributes rated as 0 become more complex at a later date, use the new value to recalculate the complexity.

3. **Question:** My business complexity included a total of six attributes; one was assessed at 4 and all others at 1 each. This resulted in the total complexity value of 9 and a complexity of $9 \div 6 = 1.5$. This indicates a relatively low business complexity, but the high complexity attribute (rated as 4) cannot be ignored.
   Response: That is the right conclusion. To make sure that any individual attribute that has a high complexity rating is not overlooked, each attribute that has a high complexity rating will become an input to risk assessment (discussed later in this chapter). The same approach applies to technical complexity assessment.

Finally, a few quick reminders regarding complexity assessment:

- A complexity analysis is useful to project managers in project staffing decisions, where individual skills must be carefully matched to project complexity.

FIGURE 4.21
Project Complexity—a
Survey

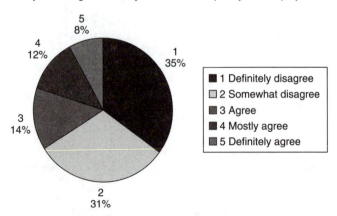

Project managers routinely assess the complexity of their projects.

- Do not concern yourself with the precision of a project's placement within the complexity diagram. The purpose is to ascertain the key complexity contributors and the zone in which the project resides.
- Any attribute, business or technical, that is given a rating higher than 3 should be treated as a potential risk to the project. Carefully consider how to manage these high complexity attributes to reduce the risk potential. We recommend the development of a risk management plan for each attribute rated higher than 3.
- The complexity assessment process is dynamic and a project's complexity should be reviewed and updated any time key changes take place (such as major changes in scope, resources, technology, and/or corporate strategy). Some project managers routinely visit the project complexity every month; this practice helps them keep a clear view of any complexity shifts.

■ VALUE-TO-BUSINESS *v.* COMPLEXITY

As a part of the Idea Statement (see Chapter 3), the customer documented the value-to-business of the proposed project. Now that the project manager has assessed the complexity of the proposed project, the next step is to work with the customer and plot the proposed project on the grid shown in Figure 4.22.

In Figure 4.22, we see that the diagram is composed of four quadrangles. They are described in the following sections.

High Value and Low Complexity: Sure Bets

Located in the lower right-hand side of the diagram, this quadrangle represents the optimum project value—these are low complexity projects that are expected to provide high value to the organization. Such projects are often referred to as sure bet projects because they have low risk and promise high returns. These projects do not require new, unproven technology. They represent new ideas and new ways of doing business that can be delivered using existing or well-proven technology. For these projects, we suggest that the project manager organize a brainstorming session comprised of key stakeholders, business area SMEs, and the core team to further assess the possibilities of increasing the value-to-business and reducing the net complexity. Successful organizations educate their employees to understand the value of such projects and provide due recognition and rewards to those who are able to identify suitable situations and help launch them as projects.

High Complexity and High Value: Challenging

Located in the upper right-hand side of the diagram, this quadrangle represents what is known as challenging projects—though they are of high value, these projects carry high risk and greater chances of failed or challenged projects. Research and development projects, for example, would fall in this area. These are "bet the company" projects—major upfront investment of money, time, and skills with great promises of attractive ROI. Our experience shows that many of these projects are underestimated and overpromised. Justification for these projects is often based on the elusive competitive advantage or the simple desire to "keep up with the corporate Joneses." The latter

FIGURE 4.22
Value *v.* Complexity

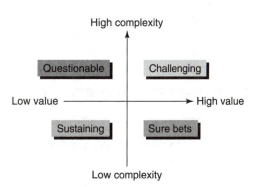

follows a well-worn path to a major hit on the bottom line, and in many cases, corporate bankruptcies. These projects require extra due diligence. Project justification should include hard proof of promised returns. If the benefits are soft, don't spend hard money on the project.

Most of these projects include massive expenditures of new hardware and software; many are actually suggested by vendors and system integrators. One way to reduce risks on such projects is to propose risk sharing to the vendor; you will be surprised how quickly their proposals become more realistic. Again, these are high-risk projects, but if managed with due diligence and chunked into manageable sized progressive releases, they can provide a high return to the organization.

A mark of astute sponsors and project managers is their willingness to work hard and dig deep inside these projects to determine how the complexity could be reduced, hopefully to the point where the projects shift into the lower right-hand quadrangle of the diagram in Figure 4.22. Whenever overly complex projects can be simplified through diligent analysis, the contribution to the organization's bottom line can be huge.

High Complexity and Low Value: Questionable

Located in the upper left-hand side of the diagram, this quadrangle represents projects that have poor business value and carry high risk. The obvious question is, "Why would anyone launch projects of this type?" Interestingly, up to 40 percent of projects in progress in many organizations fall into this area. These organizations clearly do not have a robust project idea filtering process in place. Projects get started because of personal preferences and pressures from people with big money, big authority, big push, and big egos. A convincing parallel to such projects is the reality that in any given neighborhood in any given city, home attics and garages are full of expensive items people bought (exercise equipment, copper cooking utensils, tools, recreational gear, kayaks) because it seemed like a great idea. What causes people to make such useless investments? Poor due diligence, impulse buying, and an "I'll worry about it later" mentality are among the likely reasons. The same mindset exists at the start of high complexity and low value projects.

Low Complexity and Low Value: Sustaining

Located in the lower left-hand side of the diagram, this quadrangle represents projects with reasonable complexity and minimal value added. These are often termed "sustain the business" projects. Any business needs to undertake projects to efficiently and effectively run the business. However, directing most of the organization's project budget to these types of projects would mean slow and continuous loss of business leadership and competitive advantage. It is important that the project manager work with the customer to ascertain the value-to-business v. project complexity, because this information will play a key role in the sponsor's decision regarding the future of the project.

A final note regarding complexity, don't try to take on a project whose complexity outstrips the teams' capabilities unless it is a prototype and the organization, you, and the team plan to learn from it.

■ TAILORING THE PPA

In Chapter 1 we introduced the topic of tailoring the list of steps needed for a given project. As mentioned there, the number of steps selected, and the amount of time spent on a given project, is directly proportionate to the project's complexity. Now that the complexity has been assessed, we can refer to the recommendations shown in Figure 1.12. The highly complex projects of zone I require the most number of steps. Remember, the amount of time spent on a given step will be proportionate to the complexity of the project.

■ POLICIES, PROCEDURES, AND STANDARDS—PPA STEP 7

Let us define these terms as related to the needs of project management:

Policy: A course of action prescribed to comply with legal requirements (regulations). Three key entities to keep in mind are corporate policies, regulatory agencies' (government) policies, and labor union policies.

Procedure: A set of established methods for conducting the affairs of the business; a series of prescribed steps taken to accomplish a goal.

Standard: A practice that is widely recognized or employed, especially because of its proven value; a practice to ensure uniform outcome.

Following is a list of policies, standards, and procedures that may impact a given project. It is the responsibility of the project manager to review this list, and then create a list of specific items that apply to the proposed project. (This list, like all other lists in the book, is not designed to be complete. You may need to add additional items that are specific to your project.)

ADA	Infrastructure	Public interest groups
Audit (internal)	Insurance	Regulatory agencies
Audit (external)	Intellectual property	Reuse
Contracts	Interface design	Security
Database	ISO	Six Sigma
Disaster recovery	Labor unions	Testing
Documentation	Organizational policies and procedures	Travel
GUI	OSHA	Warranties and guarantees
Icons	Procurement	

Policies, procedures, and standards can significantly impact project resources, schedule, and cost. As a part of the work to produce the Project Charter, the project manager must determine the specific items that apply to the project at hand. This list will then be used as input to risk assessment as well as the steps to plan, estimate, and schedule the project. The template in Figure 4.23 is designed to assist you in documenting the specific policies, standards, and procedures that apply to your project and the impact they can have on project schedule and budget.

In Figure 4.23, the first column lists a number of policies, procedures, and standards. The second column identifies the source of the item—the group that defined (or owns) the particular policy, procedure, or standard. The third column indicates whether the particular item applies to the project under consideration (remember, templates contain master lists, which means that not every item in the template applies to every project). If a particular item is not applicable, skip the rest of the items in that row. A *no* answer in the fourth column should be a matter of concern to the project manager, because that implies the particular policy, procedure, or standard either has not been defined or is ill defined. Often, the responsibility for defining the details of such items falls on the project team—extra work for which the project's customer may not want to pay. The fifth and sixth columns are used to record the expected impact of complying with the particular item on the project's schedule and/or budget. The last column is used to record any recommended action to assist with proper compliance.

Let us look at the first five items in Figure 4.23. Our discussions with the project manager yielded the following information:

1. Master contract: A master contract must be negotiated with a new vendor. The project manager, from experience, knows that negotiations leading to a signed contract can take from four to eight weeks. This information will be very helpful when the schedule for the project is developed.
2. Regulatory agency approval: In this case, a local and a state agency were policy-level stakeholders and certain regulatory compliances would be required. The project manager identified the need for a SME to help the team develop the right protocol to achieve timely compliance.
3. Union contract: One of the project objectives is to reduce the personnel head count (a number of these positions are held by unionized employees). The project manager indicated that the procedures for the head count reduction have not been defined and is seeking clarification on the subject.
4. Travel restrictions: During some of the discussions with the software development group, the project manager learned that the company might outsource software development work to three different countries, one of which was under the government's restricted travel advisory. The project manager considered this a red flag and brought it to the attention of the sponsor.
5. International standards: According to the implementation level stakeholder diagram for the project, three of the deployment locations were in Europe, which generated a discussion of the need to meet ISO standards. The project manager needed further clarification regarding this compliance.

FIGURE 4.23
Policies, Procedures, and
Standards

Policies & procedures	Source	Applicable Yes/No		Defined Yes/No		Schedule impact	Budget impact	Action required
Master contract		❑	❑	❑	❑			
Regulatory agency approval		❑	❑	❑	❑			
Union contract		❑	❑	❑	❑			
Travel restrictions		❑	❑	❑	❑			
International standards		❑	❑	❑	❑			
Internal policies and procedures		❑	❑	❑	❑			
Disaster recovery		❑	❑	❑	❑			
OSHA		❑	❑	❑	❑			
Security		❑	❑	❑	❑			
Six Sigma		❑	❑	❑	❑			
		❑	❑	❑	❑			
		❑	❑	❑	❑			
		❑	❑	❑	❑			

It is important to keep in mind that policies and procedures of local, national, and international regulatory agencies, as well as industry regulations such as ISO, can have a significant impact on some projects. Make sure that you carefully research the effect of all regulations on the project's budget, schedule, and quality requirements.

Our experience regarding the execution of this step shows that far too many project managers either overlook or purposely circumvent this step. The primary reason for this decision is that the work involved is considered part of the administrative or bureaucratic process. The more technical the project manager, the higher the desire to skirt this step. Common outcomes of executing this step are the disagreements and rancor that build up among key project stakeholders, resulting from the requirement to comply with certain policies, procedures, and standards. At times, the reason for the oversight is simply wishful thinking—if I ignore it, it will go away. Wrong. The purpose of the Pre-Launch stage is due diligence. The project manager has the responsibility to discover the elements that can impact the project's probability of success and present the findings to the customer for appropriate consideration. The customer may eventually assume the risk of not complying with certain policies, procedures, and standards, or she may restructure the project to reduce the level of risk.

■ IMPACT ASSESSMENT—PPA STEP 8

Earlier in this chapter we discussed the Stakeholder Analysis, which focused on identifying the people and organizations that shape the project, and will be shaped by the project. Now we will do a similar analysis based on systems and projects. The objective of the Impact Assessment is to identify any systems, processes, or projects that will impact, or be impacted by, the proposed project. For example:

- A new software system may increase the number of calls (transactions) to the call center.
- Deployment of a new software package may require all PCs to be upgraded to the latest version of the operating system.
- Introduction of a new product into the market may render certain current products obsolete, and they must be retired (existing warehouse stock may need to be liquidated).
- The implementation of a project may impact the redesign of the database structure used by another project currently under development.

The following subsections suggest common factors that can have an impact on a project (these items are in addition to the information collected in the Idea stage; see *Project Impact* in Chapter 3). Keep in mind that, during this stage, the idea is not to define the exact extent of the impact for each item; the purpose is to identify the events and situations that will impact the proposed project:

Data Quality

This focuses on the quality of data to be input to this project. It is surprising how many people do not realize that data from disparate current systems may not share the same wavelength. The one-time cost of preparing the existing data, especially if it resides in legacy systems, may approach 40 percent of the total planned project budget, thereby becoming the "black hole" of the project. Make sure data quality problems are understood and solved long before implementation begins. Trying to clean up the data during the Implementation stage is an exercise in futility and is almost always unsuccessful. It reminds us of the saying, "Punishing the data until it confesses." Many mission-critical IT/Business projects have come to a dead halt due to data quality problems and have subsequently taken the organization down the path of financial ruin. Poor quality data will require that additional deliverables, in the form of software programs and procedural steps, be included in the project plan. Because this is overlooked until late into a project, the team is forced to scurry to clean up the "bad" data by writing last minute software programs (most of which are also of poor quality); and the vicious cycle begins.

Volume

An assessment of the system's ability to effectively and efficiently handle the transaction volume generated by the deployment of the project is essential. Countless examples abound of instances where accounts receivable, shipping, and billing systems were not able to process the volumes of transactions generated by the deployment of a successful project. Some of the companies involved suffered extensive financial losses. The worst scenario is created when the project team has to deal with a high volume of bad data at the last minute.

Frequency

The objective here is to assess the likelihood of episodes of high transaction volume. In many cases, a system is able to handle the transaction volume but not extremely high spikes in transaction volume.

Media Compatibility

This deals with the ability to read data from, and write data to, other systems. Ignoring this important item can create major problems because of the variety of disparate hardware and software systems. Most new projects mean new and updated technology for the development team. However, many of the implementation-level stakeholders may not have the same "new and improved" technology infrastructure that you will soon have. You will encounter people who work with outdated technology, even as outdated as rotary telephones (you'd be surprised). Would the new system be able to communicate with them, or would you require them to become compatible? Who is going to cover the expenses of their technology upgrade (hardware, software, data porting, and training)?

Security

The degree of protection needed from unauthorized access. Security is often an afterthought for many project managers, producing the commensurate results: high risk and unstable systems.

Timeliness

The ability to provide data to, or receive data from, other systems in a timely manner. A common manifestation of negative behavior by nemeses is their tardiness in supplying data due from them. The problem is further aggravated when the proposed project is heavily dependent on receiving data from these nemeses.

Infrastructure

Stability and quality are the primary concerns when assessing the impact to infrastructure. It is important to ascertain the degree of stability of the infrastructure for this and other related projects. Unplanned hardware and software upgrades and obsolescence are not only expensive, but will add extra cost and time to the entire project. Similarly, the reliability of the infrastructure can also have significant impact on time and cost of the proposed project.

Cross-Project Dependencies

The objective here is to identify the various projects this project is dependent upon, such as certain deliverables to be completed by other projects are key inputs to this project. In the same vein, it is important to identify the projects that are dependent on your project.

We have found that far too many project managers overlook many of the situations and events that might impact their projects. Inevitably, most discoveries are made late in the Execute stage, the project team must rush to patch things up, and the end results are less than desirable. Figure 4.24 depicts a template designed to help project managers perform an Impact Assessment in a timely manner. The information will become input for the risk assessment step and will also help the project manager develop a comprehensive scope statement.

Remember that the purpose of the action required component of the template in Figure 4.24 is not to develop a solution to solve the problems uncovered through this assessment. At this point in the project life cycle, the Pre-Launch stage, the focus is to discover the vagaries that may impact the successful completion of the project and also uncover the scope of the work to be done to complete the project successfully. If the proposed project is approved, then the findings from this assessment, along with recommended actions, will become input to the task plan to be developed in the Launch stage.

■ CONSTRAINTS AND OBSTACLES—PPA STEP 9

Some of the synonyms for these two words are: hindrance, restriction, difficulty, barrier, and limit. Constraints and obstacles are the barriers that can drive up the time and cost, limit the functionality, and drive down the quality of the end product. The purpose of this step is to identify things that may stand in the way of the project's progress. As always, the most effective approach is to start with a master list like the one that follows:

- Audit and control requirements
- Budget shortfall
- Competitive markets
- Customer sophistication
- Deadlines
- Environmental considerations
- Human resources: skills, availability, turnover

- Infrastructure maturity
- Legislation
- Litigation
- Nemesis stakeholders
- Other projects
- Paradigm shift: concepts, values, and practices
- Public/community relations
- Regulatory requirements
- Resource availability: people, technology, facilities
- Security
- Sponsorship
- Structure of installed systems
- Supplier/vendor capability and capacity
- System architecture
- Technology viability

Like all lists in the book, this is a comprehensive, but not universal, list. You should develop a list of potential constraints and obstacles that are common in your work environment and use that list to determine if any of those constraint factors apply to the proposed project. The key challenge is the

FIGURE 4.24

An Impact Assessment

Name of the system/project: **Owner:**

Type of interaction:

- The interaction will be: ❏ Automated   ❏ Manual

Describe the nature of the impact:

- Data quality:
  _____

- Volume of transactions:
  _____

- Frequency of transactions:
  _____

- Media of transactions (any compatibility issues?):
  _____

- Security requirements and issues:
  _____

- Timeliness of data availability:
  _____

- Infrastructure:
  _____

- Cross-project dependencies:
  _____

Action required:

  _____

  _____

  _____

difficulty of deciding which specific constraints and obstacles to consider. Of course, worrying about every little item is counterproductive. The productive approach is to:

1. Prepare a comprehensive master list of constraints and obstacles that impact projects in general.
2. Working with appropriate SMEs create a list of items that apply to the proposed project.
3. Use a numerical scale to rate the probability (likelihood) of occurrence of each item in the selected list.
4. Use a numerical scale to rate the expected impact of each item in the selected list.
5. Compute the risk level of each item. The level of the risk is a number derived by multiplying the probability value by the value of the impact.
6. Decide on threshold levels to define low, medium, and high risk items.
7. Focus on the high risk constraints and obstacles.

In Figure 4.25, we used a scale of one to five for both probability and impact. A rating of 1 for probability indicates a low probability that the constraint or obstacle will materialize, and a rating of 5 indicates a high probability that the constraint or obstacle will occur. Similarly, a rating of 1 for impact indicates a mild impact while a rating of 5 indicates a severe impact. By multiplying the two values, the risk level of a given constraint or obstacle can range from a low of 1 to a high of 25.

At the Center, we use the following threshold levels to assess the risk of a given constraint or obstacle:

Risk value 1–9	Low level risk
Risk value 10–15	Medium level risk
Risk Value > 15	High level risk

Let us analyze the data in Figure 4.25:

Audit and Control Requirements

The probability level of 4 indicates that, from what is currently known, the new audit requirements are still under extensive discussions among the project sponsor, finance, and audit departments. The project manager does not believe there will be an agreement in a timely manner. This item is a high probability constraint. The potential impact rating of 4 indicates that, if resolution is not achieved in a timely manner, by the start of the task plan step in the Launch stage, the project will be in high jeopardy. The net risk level of this attribute is $4 \times 4 = 16$, a high level of risk.

Budget

In her discussions with the sponsor, key customers, and the finance department, the project manager had a certain degree of concern about timely budget approval for the proposed project (there were some discussions of overall budget cuts for projects). The sponsor had assured her that, if approved, the proposed project would not face budget problems. However, because this was still a concern to her, she chose to use it as a constraint item. The probability value of 2 reflects the assurance given to her by the sponsor; however, the potential impact rating of 5 suggests that if the budget is not approved in a timely manner, the project could not be delivered with the functionality and by the

FIGURE 4.25
Constraints and Obstacles

Constraints and obstacles	Probability (1–5)	*	Potential impact (1–5)	=	Risk level (1–25)
Audit and control requirements	4	*	4	=	16
Budget	2	*	5	=	10
Technology infrastructure	4	*	5	=	20
Vendor capability	1	*	4	=	4
Vendor capacity	4	*	5	=	20

deadline requested by the customer. Though the net risk level of 10 indicates a medium level of risk, this item needs to be tracked diligently because if the probability of budget rejection rises sharply, the net risk will also soar. The net risk level of this attribute is $2 \times 5 = 10$, a medium level of risk toward the lower end of the spectrum.

Technology Infrastructure

The probability rating of 4 indicates that the technology (hardware and software) to be used for this project is unstable and unproven. The potential impact of 5 indicates that the net impact of unstable technology is going to be extremely high because this project is highly dependent on technology. The net risk level of this attribute is $4 \times 5 = 20$, a high level of risk.

Vendor Capability

The vendor responsible for supplying the human resources for the project has a good record with the organization, hence the low probability rating of 1 for this constraint. However, the potential impact of nonperformance by the vendor will certainly have drastic impact on the project progress, therefore the high value of 4. The net risk level of this attribute is $1 \times 4 = 4$, a low level of risk.

Vendor Capacity

This is an interesting and rather important item to consider. From the assessment, we see that the project manager has assigned a value of 4 to the probability of this constraint—a high probability that the vendor will not be able to support the needs of the project exists because the project manager's research shows that the vendor is currently overcommitted. Because the majority of the development team on this project would be vendor-supplied professionals, the potential impact is assigned a high value of 5. The net risk level of this attribute is $4 \times 5 = 20$, a high level of risk.

Of course, you may need to alter the threshold levels up or down to fit your organization's risk tolerance. When using this approach, we highly recommend that you rate the probability *prior* to rating the impact. Our experience has shown us that when events are rated as having a high impact potential, the probability is almost always overstated.

■ STABILITY ASSESSMENT—PPA STEP 10

The last four steps, Complexity Assessment; Policies, Procedures, and Standards; Impact Assessment; and Constraints and Obstacles; focused on defining *what* might cause a risk to the project. The purpose of step 10 is to define the *timing* of the risk. Consider the example of a transcontinental airline flight. During the winter months, the weather is a key risk item. Each pilot must know where, during the flight, the airplane might encounter adverse weather conditions and to what degree. Based on the reported weather conditions, the pilot may decide on one of the following options:

- Forecast is for clear skies, no adverse weather; proceed as planned.
- Mostly good weather, occasional turbulence; inform the crew, make an announcement to the passengers, and proceed as planned.
- Persistent bad weather but still within safe flying conditions; inform the crew and caution the passengers regarding seat belt use, ask them to stay seated, and proceed as planned. Because of the turbulent weather conditions, the cabin crew will need to plan the timing of food service to minimize mishaps and accidents.
- Mostly bad weather, not deemed safe for flying but with a forecast of improvement in the conditions; inform the crew and the passengers about the bad weather conditions and delay the departure until improved weather is forecast.
- Mostly bad weather, not deemed safe for flying, and no forecast for better conditions; inform the crew and the passengers about the bad weather conditions and cancel the flight.

At this point in the Pre-Launch, the project manager must assess the "weather conditions" of the project by opening a look-ahead window to the end of the project development life cycle. The sponsor will then need to make certain decisions about "flying" the project. Risks in a given project, at this point in the project life cycle, can emanate from any of the following areas:

- **Project Description:** Any poorly defined objective must be considered a risk because it cannot be met to anyone's satisfaction. Similarly, assumptions that do not hold true and *most* dictated deadlines are also sources of project risk.
- **Intra-Project Priority Assessment:** The item that is ranked as a number 1 priority is certainly a source of risk; at times the item ranked 2nd can also result in considerable risk.
- **Stakeholder Analysis:** Any nemesis stakeholder is a definite source of risk. At times, comatose and neutral stakeholders can also pose problems.
- **Complexity Assessment:** Any business or technical attribute rated higher than 3 represents a certain risk.
- **Policies, Procedures, and Standards:** Any of the policies, procedures, and standards that would adversely impact the intra-project priority ranked 1st is a source of risk.
- **Impact Assessment:** All items in the impact assessment list that could have an adverse affect on the project must be considered.
- **Constraints and Obstacles:** Any constraint or obstacle that is assessed at a threshold of greater than 15 would be considered a risk.

Once the various sources of project risk have been identified, the next step is to analyze the probable *timing* of each risk and the impact the risk would have on the project. Figure 4.26 depicts an example of a number of risks, and discusses their time of occurrence and their impact on the project. The five columns below the column titled *Stability Assessment* represent the look-ahead window to the end of the project development life cycle (i.e., from Pre-Launch, the current stage to operation).

In the example in Figure 4.26, the project manager communicated the following information to the sponsor:

1. Audit and control requirements will cause the highest problem at the beginning of the project. The project manager expects these to be resolved by the end of the launch stage.
2. The nemesis stakeholders will be a concern through the execute stage, but if their issues are not satisfactorily resolved, they will become a problem during the implement and operation stages as well.

FIGURE 4.26
Stability Assessment

Risk drivers	Probability (1–5)	*	Potential impact (1–5)	=	Risk level (1–25)	Stability Assessment Project life cycle	Impact
Audit and control requirements	4	*	4	=	16		
Nemesis stakehoder	4	*	4	=	16		
Technology infrastructure	4	*	5	=	20		
Vendor capacity	4	*	4	=	20		
Politics	4	*	4	=	16		
Security	4	*	5	=	20		

3. The risk of problems occurring as a result of the technology infrastructure will be high throughout the project. This is due to the incompatible technology at one of the major end-user sites.
4. Vendor capacity could cause major problems during the implement and operation stages because the vendor has shown major reluctance in providing written assurance of fully tested hardware and software delivery. Due to recent good press on their technology, they have a huge backlog of orders.
5. Politics, a reflection of the nemesis stakeholders, will continue to be a problem unless management is able to resolve the outstanding "turf" problems.
6. Security will be a big problem toward the end of the project life cycle. The key implementation level stakeholders have shown a great dislike to the current security protocols, and the proposed project will require even more stringent security procedures.

The next step is to define the impact of the identified risks on the schedule, scope, budget, and/or quality of the proposed project. Understanding how a risk will impact any of these project components will enable the project manager to negotiate for the additional resources (money, time, people, tools) necessary to manage the risk. For example, if the project is schedule driven and a risk exists that would cause the duration to be extended, the sponsor will be more open to adjusting one of the other project dimensions (scope, budget, or quality) so as not to jeopardize the completion date. Any given risk can impact one, two, three, or all four of the project dimensions.

■ ISSUES MANAGEMENT—PPA STEP 11

In Chapter 2, we defined an issue as an unanswered question or a difference of opinion. We also stated that issues are akin to the potholes on a road—the more issues there are, the more difficult it becomes to navigate the project. Accordingly, issues must be managed conscientiously and in a timely manner. Once an issue has been analyzed and recorded, it is important to assign a specific person as owner of the issue resolution. The owner's responsibility is to facilitate, rather than dictate, the resolution process. Best results occur when the nonagreeing people jointly determine the issue resolution. The project manager's negotiating skills are vital components of issue resolution. If issue resolution hits an impasse and begins to impact project progress, we recommend the use of the root cause analysis approach.[10] This approach helps to get to the crux of the problem and facilitates consensus. Issues that remain unresolved past their latest time for resolution become risk drivers and must be escalated to the appropriate decision maker. While it may be difficult to bring controversial issues to the attention of senior management, hiding problems is not going to make them go away. It is important that project managers learn to document important issues and their impact on schedule, functionality, budget, quality, and any of the critical success factors and then work diligently for their timely resolution. Further, as work on a project continues and as issues are resolved, it is equally important to document and *broadly* communicate the resolution to appropriate stakeholders and team members. This practice not only keeps those affected by the resolution informed, it also discourages "second thoughts" that might develop later in the project. Figure 4.27 depicts a template that is designed to document issues.

Issue description	Impact	Who raised it	Date raised	Who can best resolve it	When resolution is needed	Owner	Action taken to date	Current status

FIGURE 4.27
Issues Log

---

[10]See *Analytical Tools*, Chapter 7.

Issue Description: A succinct definition of the issue.

Impact: The impact on the project if the issue is not resolved satisfactorily.

Who Raised it: The name of the person who raised the issue.

Date Raised: The date the issue was raised.

Who Can Best Resolve it: The individual(s) who have the knowledge and/or authority to resolve the issue.

When Resolution is Needed: The latest point in time by which the issue must be resolved. Each issue should have a "must resolve" date/point.

Owner: The person who has the responsibility to get the issue resolved by its resolution date.

Action Taken to Date: Lists any effort made, to date, to resolve the issue.

Current Status: Resolved or unresolved. The project manager must anticipate that issues arise throughout the project life cycle and need to be managed judiciously. Any issue that stays unresolved past its "must resolve" point should be seen as a pothole in the path of the project. Too many will make the journey difficult. The optimum approach is to diligently track unresolved issues past their resolution point.

■ RISK ASSESSMENT—PPA STEP 12

Risk is exposure to perils that can adversely impact the project. From the discussion thus far regarding risk, it is clear that most medium- to high-complexity projects carry some degree of risk—a strong possibility that emergencies will arise and that team members will be distracted from their planned path of action. These distractions invariably require last minute actions that add extra effort, cost, and duration to the project and drive down the quality of the end product. Such ad hoc responses often leave much to be desired in efficiency and effectiveness and they convey an impression of "loss of control" on the part of the project manager. The solution lies in foresight and planning. Therefore, let us think through the types of responses one could have to a given risk:

Ignore the Risk

Fundamentally, to ignore a risk means to pay no attention to the risk. This approach works well for most low-level risk items. Statistically speaking, most low-level risk events will not happen; or if they do, the net impact on the project is usually negligible. Most project teams, under the guidance of perceptive project managers, are able to handle these types of risk events without many distractions. Developing any type of mitigation or contingency plans for such risks will certainly bog the team down. However, ignoring medium- and high-level risks is a risky business in itself. A risk that you choose to ignore may later evolve to a point where ignoring it is sure to result in high risk to the project. Therefore, it is important to put into place a process that helps you and the team monitor any risk that breaches the "ignore this risk" threshold.

Avoid the Risk

Fundamentally, to avoid a risk means to stay clear of, pass up, or sidestep the risk item. For example, if the technology under consideration does not meet project requirements, avoid the risk by not choosing the specific technology; investigate alternatives instead (change the plan). Similarly, if the capabilities of a vendor under consideration pose a risk to the project, do not use that vendor; research other vendors. However, if the lack of customers' readiness to adopt and use the new system represents a risk, avoiding the customer or the situation is not the most prudent decision. Doing so compounds the risk. A decision to avoid a risk does not mean *ignoring* the risk. These actions are completely different.

Transfer the Risk

To transfer a risk means to shift or reassign the risk to some other party, such as a customer, end-user, contractor, or insurance. Some examples of risk transfer are as follows:

• *Purchasing a cruise ticket.* A typical cruise ticket, once purchased, can be canceled without penalty only up to a certain date specified by the cruise operator. If the ticket is not canceled properly, but the customer is not able to travel, regardless of the reason, the cruise owner can charge the entire amount. One way to transfer the risk is to buy insurance. Though it adds to the cost of the trip (the insurance premium), it protects the customer from losing the ticket purchase price in the case of any problems covered by the insurance contract.

- *Construction:* In the case of engineering construction, it is possible to purchase a surety bond that is designed to provide funds in case the contractor is not able to finish the work. Again, it adds to the cost of the project but protects the customer in the event of contractor nonperformance.

In fact, any type of insurance is a form of risk transfer to the insurance carrier. It is important to do sufficient due diligence to make sure that the insurance carrier is in sound financial condition.

Within most IT/Business projects, risk transfer is not as easy to accomplish as it is in retail and engineering industries. Lack of insurance coverage, as well as the overall jurisprudence covering hardware, software, and business relations (for example, consulting services), preclude a straightforward transfer of risk. It is therefore very important for project managers to consult with appropriate legal experts to make sure the contracts with vendors and consultants provide adequate risk protection. Also, in the case of projects for which people working for the organization do most of the work (in-house development), insurance is seldom an option.

Transferring a risk to a third party does not automatically absolve the project manager of all responsibilities. If one of the customer groups for your project is in a distant location, and has accepted the responsibility to develop and deploy their own program to train the end users of the product, simply documenting such agreements may not be the sensible risk transfer action. We would suggest that you ask the responsible customer to submit the following information to you in a timely manner:

1. The name of the individual (preferably at a management level) responsible for end user training.
2. The name of the project manager, or equivalent individual, responsible for creating and executing the training plan.
3. A task-level plan and schedule for the training program.

With this type of planning and documentation, the project manager has clearly established that the risk, specifically any of its adverse impacts, is no longer the responsibility of the project team. Make sure that you document and communicate this decision to the appropriate stakeholder(s) and the sponsor.

Accept the Risk

To accept a risk means to recognize, acknowledge, and understand that the risk item is the responsibility of the project team and must be managed. Once a given risk has been accepted, the next step is to devise ways to manage the risk (outline the step to monitor the risk and to limit, or restrict, its adverse affects). Mitigating the risk requires proactively planning a set of actions before the risk happens. Three different approaches to deal with accepted risks follow.

Prevention Plan   A prevention plan consists of a set of steps to take to inhibit or thwart the risk. For example, for the risk related to a vendor's ability to deliver the ordered hardware by August 1, the action might be to move the delivery date in the contract to an earlier date. This adjustment may add to the cost of the project (extra payments to the vendor because of earlier delivery). Similarly, in the case where a project's life cycle spans into the next fiscal year, and the continued availability of funds is a risk item, getting the entire project budget approved in this budget cycle and having the funds *moved* to the project's account would constitute preventive action. Prevention planning entails taking *anticipatory* counteraction against the risk.

Mitigation Plan   In situations where risk prevention is not an option, but the risk still must be managed, a mitigation plan defines a set of tasks and actions that, if taken, will help alleviate (lessen) the risk. For example, consider the case of the risk that the vendor will not deliver the hardware by August 1. If the prevention plan of having the hardware delivered by July 1 is not workable, then the mitigation plan might include obtaining written commitments from senior level vendor management. As a further mitigating measure, the project manager could negotiate contract language that would mean strong penalties for late delivery of the hardware. Once a risk is mitigated, it does not mean the problem is permanently solved. The risk may return. Therefore, it behooves the project manager to monitor the risk until it is fully resolved.

Contingency Plan   In instances where the prevention and mitigation plans do not provide sufficient reduction in the risk level of an item, a contingency plan is needed. This plan consists of a set of tasks that will be undertaken if and when the risk materializes–it is plan B.

> *. . . if contingency plans are built in to your project plan, that's the plan everyone has signed off on in the beginning. They've bought into plan B–and now your contingency plan is politically correct."*
> Frank Hayes, "Frankly Speaking," *Computerworld* (September 27, 1999): p. 106.

Let us look at three different risk examples using the four risk management precepts: ignore the risk, avoid the risk, transfer the risk, and accept the risk.

■ EXAMPLE 1

POOR DATA QUALITY

- *Ignore the risk:* Ignoring this risk is not an option because poor quality data will consistently produce poor quality information, hardly the objective of any project.

- *Avoid the risk:* This response means not using the data in question. Using data that is more reliable is an option, if such data is available. Also, if the data were to be collected in the future, appropriate audit and verification filters could be put into place to avoid, in other words not accept, any poor quality data. Finally, a decision could be made not to proceed with the project due to the poor quality of data. However, if none of these options are viable, the poor quality data must be accepted and dealt with through mitigation and contingency actions.

- *Transfer the risk:* This choice means that the customer would be advised that they will receive bad data, and they will assume the responsibility to clean it up. We neither consider this option wise nor advisable.

- *Accept the risk:* Acceptance is the prudent response and the project team will need to develop a mitigation and/or contingency plan to deal with the poor quality data. Our preference would be a mitigation plan—a set of actions to be taken to alleviate the problem (clean up the data) combined with a contingency plan.   ■

■ EXAMPLE 2

THE TEAM IS STATIONED IN DIFFERENT COUNTRIES THAT USE DIFFERENT LANGUAGES, ARE LOCATED IN DIFFERENT TIME ZONES, AND COME IN CONTACT WITH DIFFERENT CULTURES

- *Ignore the risk:* This is not an option because poor communications among such diverse team members will certainly lead to misunderstandings, mistakes, and poor relations; which will eventually put the project at high risk.

- *Avoid the risk:* In this case, the risk can be avoided through one of two possible actions. One option is to move the entire team to one central location, and make sure that all of the team members are well versed in the language and culture of the country of location. This change solves the problem of different time zones, but the cost to the project will rise significantly and the logistics to move the various team members to the central location will likely pose new risks. Another option is to establish a central team (this means no cross functional or international participation). Unfortunately, this team will be far removed from the ultimate project customers and end users, which might transform project acceptance into a new risk.

- *Transfer the risk:* This is not a viable option unless all team members could be taught a common language very quickly. Even so, although the language problem might be solved, the problem of managing meetings due to different time zones, different holiday schedules, and different work ethics and etiquettes (and don't forget politics) would still exist.

• *Accept the risk:* Accepting the risk is the sensible response. The project team will need to develop a mitigation and/or contingency plan to deal with the communications problems. The plan would include developing a team orientation and training program to ensure awareness of the diversity needs, and establishing a well-designed process of written and oral communications. ■

■ EXAMPLE 3

THERE IS A RESOURCE SHORTAGE AS A RESULT OF BOTH BUDGET CUTS AND STAFF TURNOVER

• *Ignore the risk:* This is not a viable option unless there is no concern about the functionality and quality of the end product.

• *Avoid the risk:* This would be possible if the project functionality and quality attributes could be restructured to meet the skills of the team—hardly a way to meet customer needs. Another way to avoid the risk is not to attempt the project—no skills, no project.

• *Transfer the risk:* One way to accomplish this would be to outsource the project. However, this may not be an option because of budget cuts.

• *Accept the risk:* If this option is chosen, management has a few things to do. First, see what skills are available, within the organization, that can be transferred to this project's team in a timely manner. This approach would involve the transfer of resources and certain skill development programs. The latter may not be possible because of the budget cuts. Another task is to restructure the project to match the team's skill. This option seldom works well because the customer is unwilling to compromise and people who have the skills to do it are scarce. Eventually, the only sensible option is not to undertake the project until people with the *critical* skills become available. ■

Probability *v.* Impact

In the discussion regarding prevention, mitigation, and contingency planning, the resulting action is to lessen the risk as much as possible and to plan for an appropriate set of actions if and when the risk happens. At this point, let us revisit the two components of a risk:

1. The probability (likelihood) of occurrence of a risk event
2. The degree (magnitude) of impact if the risk ever should occur

When laying out a plan to lessen or react to a risk, we suggest that you *first* focus your energies toward controlling the likelihood of its occurrence and *then* work on minimizing the magnitude of the impact. The reason for this priority is that, even though we have used a scale of 1 to 5 for both the probability and impact attributes of a risk, the probability carries a higher weight.

At times, there is a tendency on the part of some project managers to limit their risk assessment and management activities to the risks they believe they can control. When questioned, a common response from such project managers is, "If I can't control it, then why worry?" This view is very short-sighted because there are numerous risks that one cannot control but must be managed nevertheless. For example:

• Financial well being of a vendor
• Change in the organization's strategy
• Hackers' attacks
• Electrical current surges and outages

Risk Management Plan

Figure 4.28 depicts a chart the Center uses to document risk management plans. We suggest this level of documentation for all high-level and selected medium-level risk items.

FIGURE 4.28
Risk Management Template

Description				
Level				
Cause/trigger				
Impact	❏ Schedule ❏ Scope ❏ Budget ❏ Quality ❏ Visibility	❏ Schedule ❏ Scope ❏ Budget ❏ Quality ❏ Visibility	❏ Schedule ❏ Scope ❏ Budget ❏ Quality ❏ Visibility	❏ Schedule ❏ Scope ❏ Budget ❏ Quality ❏ Visibility
Objectives affected				
Stakeholders affected				
Prevention plan				
Mitigation plan				
Contingency plan				
Owner				

Let us briefly review each item in this chart:

Description: A brief description of the risk.

Level: The level of the probability and impact of the risk. The values can range from a low of 1 to a high of 25.

Cause/trigger: A brief explanation of the reason/cause of the risk and the event that will trigger (materialize) the risk.

Impact: Which different project attributes will the risk impact? Also note the *additional* attribute: visibility (some of our clients use the term "exposure"). By "visibility," we mean the extent of exposure of any adverse outcome of the risk, in other words, how conspicuous will the results be. For example, will visibility be limited to:

• The project team?
• Project team and stakeholders?
• Project team, stakeholders, and key customers?
• Project team, stakeholders, key customers, and executive group?
• Project team, stakeholders, key customers, executive group, and local press?
• Project team, stakeholders, key customers, executive group, local press, and regional press?
• Project team, stakeholders, key customers, executive group, local press, regional press, and national press?
• Project team, stakeholders, key customers, executive group, local press, regional press, and Mike Wallace from *60 Minutes*?

The implications of the varying degrees of exposure are quite obvious. The project manager of any high-complexity project should discuss the subject of visibility (exposure) for each high-level risk item with the sponsor and plan accordingly.

Objectives Affected: The key project objectives that will be adversely impacted if this risk materializes.

Stakeholders Affected: The key project stakeholders who will be adversely impacted if this risk materializes.

Prevention Plan: The set of steps to take now to inhibit or thwart the risk—your anticipatory counteraction.

Mitigation Plan: If the prevention plan does not result in a sufficient degree of comfort regarding the risk, then a mitigation plan is considered necessary. This plan consists of a set of tasks and actions, which, if taken soon will help alleviate or lessen the risk.

Contingency Plan: If the mitigation plan does not result in sufficient degree of comfort regarding the risk, then a contingency plan is considered necessary. This plan consists of a set of tasks and actions that will be undertaken if and when the risk event materializes. Simply stated: if things go wrong, this is what you plan to do about it—your "plan B."

Owner: The person responsible for monitoring the risk and putting the appropriate plan in action.

The secret to any successful investment is to be able to ascertain the probable risk of the venture *v.* the potential return. Whereas today's corporate culture often refers to risk as the root of opportunity, risk is too often mismanaged and projects fail to deliver the benefits initially promised to customers. To manage risk effectively, the project manager must ask some difficult questions up front. However, when project managers convey to their sponsors the level of risk involved, they may be met with the retort: *"You need to be more aggressive."* Or the familiar: *"We will cross that bridge when we come to it."* Then there are the sponsors who specifically forbid project managers from incorporating any contingencies in their project plans, estimates, and schedules.[11] For fear of being perceived as a wimp or a harbinger of doom and gloom, project managers often minimize the risk involved and assume the head in the sand posture. For many project managers this can be a painful process. As we discussed earlier, when the sponsors are high-ranking officials in the organization, the project managers may feel uncomfortable asking them to justify their visions. Far too many project managers have come to believe that to say "no" to a high-powered executive would result in losing the assignment or even the job. On the other hand, project managers who support even the craziest risk-laden ideas, despite their convictions that such projects have no true worth, are often regarded as team players and may even be rewarded with accolades and job promotions. Therefore, it is imperative that project sponsors provide the project managers with the opportunity to conduct a *forthright* risk assessment.

Finally, risk assessment and management is not a one-time step. It starts in the Pre-Launch and continues *throughout* the project life cycle. New risks are sure to arise as the project progresses. Also, some of the expected risks might not materialize. The project manager and the team will need to diligently monitor the environment and make adjustments to fit the needs of the project.

■ PRELIMINARY SCOPE STATEMENT—PPA STEP 13

The project scope defines the sum total of deliverables and features (the total functionality to be delivered to the project customer at the completion of the proposed project). Toward the end of the Pre-Launch stage, although we know a lot more about the project than what we knew at the end of the Idea stage, it is not possible to clearly define the final scope because detailed customer requirements are not yet defined. However, as a part of the Project Charter to be submitted to management, we need to provide a reasonable idea of the "size" of the proposed project so that a decision can be made whether or not to move forward with the project. Hence, the title *Preliminary Scope Statement* for this step of the Pre-Launch stage; the key word is "preliminary." The idea is to communicate clearly to the customer and any key stakeholders that the proposed scope will need to be revisited and *reapproved* later in the project life cycle (*Project Charter Review and Approval*, Chapter 5).

Before we discuss the steps to construct the scope statement, let us define a few terms:

Function: Describes the purpose or utility of an object.

Deliverable: Any tangible item that is built to provide (deliver) a function.

Feature: Characteristic, trait, or attribute of a deliverable (the elements that enhance the ease of use, or add utility above and beyond the essential functionality, of a deliverable).

---

[11]At a recent national project management conference, during a session on risk management, a project manager in the audience made the following remark, "Our management does not allow any contingencies in our project plans. They have the belief that having contingencies means either the project manager is not able to overcome the risks involved or is too risk averse."

Figure 4.29 illustrates a few examples of these three elements.

It is important that everyone involved with the project—sponsor, customers, key stakeholders, and the team—clearly understand the distinction between a deliverable and its features. A deliverable adds to the functionality of a product, whereas features enhance the ease of use or add to the utility of a deliverable. This distinction becomes rather important when a project manager needs logical means to negotiate the scope of a project due to limitations such as time, money, resources, or skills.

FIGURE 4.29
Function, Deliverable, Feature—Examples

Function	Deliverable	Feature
Illumination	Electric lightbulb Lantern Candle	Fluorescent, incandescent Kerosene, pressurized gas Dripless, long lasting, scented
Transportation	Automobile Motorcycle Rickshaw Bullock cart	Gas, diesel, electrical, all wheel drive, front-wheel drive, air, power steering, ABS brakes Auto start, kick start Auto, bicycle, manual One bullock or two
Baking/roasting appliance	Built-in oven	Gas, electric, convection, commercial grade, rotisserie, self-cleaning
E-commerce	Website	Animated graphics, streaming audio/video, hyperlink, secure credit transaction, site links
Traveler accommodation	Hotel room	Standard, suite, smoking, nonsmoking, view, ADA conforming
Internet access	Modem	Telephone, DSL, T1 line, wireless

Customer Expectations

The fundamental nature of a relationship between a supplier (the project manager) and a customer is that customers expect everything they talked about, and then some, to be included in the project scope. When the completed system is first delivered, many customers may actually accuse you of leaving out certain functions and features that you or someone on the team had agreed to include in the project scope. After a fact-finding expedition, one is sure to uncover the following types of facts:

1. They believe they asked for the items in question but can't really remember when.
2. They will remind you of the times when they asked for the items in question and you nodded your head in agreement and made note of their request. You will discover that your head movement did *not* mean, "Yes, I hear you, and I will make a note of your request," as you *intended*. They read your head movement as an *explicit agreement* to incorporate the requested items.
3. They will remind you of hallway and elevator discussions they had with you after certain meetings, during which they told you of the items in question.
4. They will remind you of the e-mails they sent to various team members regarding these items. Because they did not hear back, they assumed these items were now in the scope of delivery.

You have two types of contracts with your customer. An explicit contract that includes all that is documented and an implicit contract that includes all they wished for but was never really promised. Unless project managers learn to clearly document the explicit contract with their customers, the curse of eternal scope creep will be upon them. We have found the use of Figure 4.30 very helpful when documenting and communicating the proposed project scope to customers.

Current Scope   The current scope is a statement of your understanding of the functions, deliverables, and features that are planned for inclusion in the project.

Future Opportunities   The future opportunities section of the preliminary scope statement is critical. It requires careful deliberation of what future development could, or should, occur for the

FIGURE 4.30
Preliminary Scope
Statement—Suggested
Format

Current scope	Future opportunities	Out of scope	Scope issues
Function	Function	Function	Function
Function	Reason	Reason	Function
Deliverable	Deliverable	Deliverable	Deliverable
Deliverable	Reason	Reason	Feature
Deliverable	Deliverable	Feature	Feature
Deliverable	Reason	Reason	
Deliverable	Deliverable		
Deliverable	Reason		
Feature	Feature		
Feature	Reason		
Feature			

end product of this project. Notice that each item listed in this column is accompanied by a reason for its exclusion from current scope list. The reasons vary:

- Tight deadline
- Shortage of funds
- Lack of resources
- Lack of skills
- Deficit in technology

It is always important to provide this type of explanation to the customer who requested the project so there is no misunderstanding of the reason for exclusion. The customers may be so committed to some of the items in the future opportunities list that they will then demand their inclusion in the current scope. In such a case, the customer should take on the primary responsibility for removing the stated hurdles; otherwise, you will end up spending your scarce time on "wild goose chases."

Outside of Scope   This column lists items that are outside the scope of the project. It is our strong belief, based on extensive experience, that unless outside of scope elements are clearly described, many customers will revert to the implicit contract we mentioned previously. As a result, anything they ever thought about, or even made cursory remarks about, will be expected in the end product. Woe to the project manager who says, "But I never said this would be included." To the customer, if you did not explicitly say no, in writing, it was an implied promise of delivery. By making a clear statement of what is outside the scope of the project to the customer, you can more effectively manage their expectations. As with the future opportunities list, always provide the reason(s) for any exclusion.

At times, project managers are reluctant to show the scope items listed in the *future opportunities* and *outside of scope* columns in the belief that the customers will be upset. Yes, many customers will be upset, but they will get over it as you explain to them the reasons behind the exclusions. However, if you do not communicate to them what you know now, and instead they begin to learn about what is missing from the delivered product close to the point of implementation, they will be livid. They may even accuse you of misleading them on purpose. The best approach is to hone your negotiation skills, take a deep breath, and confess. In the short and long run, it is the most professional thing to do.

Scope Issues   In this column, list the items that are still undecided. A look at this list will tell you the degree of disagreements among the various decision makers. Although we are not able to provide a specific metric here, a long list of items in this column is a harbinger of troubles to come— disagreements, arguments, and dissatisfaction. Consequently, it will be very difficult to satisfy the stakeholders' needs.

Scope Decision Drivers

The proverbial question is, "How to decide what goes in which column of Figure 4.30?" We suggest that you use your best negotiating skills to convince the key stakeholders to respect the pithy maxim regarding scope: "less is more" (we prefer "least is best"). Not all functions, deliverables, and features are created equal. Many will have very little value and some will have no value at all. However, each is certain to have its own stalwart champion. The astute project manager is able to work with the key stakeholders to focus on the high-value items.

> *The problem was keeping the team to the 80/20 rule . . . noting that certain team members wanted to script responses for the rarest types of customer issues. 'I had to keep pointing out the goals of the project. We didn't need a Ferrari.'*
> Jann Davis in Julia King, "Back to Basics," *Computerworld*
> (April 22, 2002): p. 36.

A method that has worked well involves classifying each function, deliverable, and feature into one of the following categories:

1. Must have
2. Should have
3. Nice to have
4. Fluff

Once the classification is completed, the task of focusing on the high-value items is rather simple. First, get rid of all of the fluff. Next, ask the *customer* to justify the *nice to have* items. Some may be accepted, many will be discarded, and the rest will be saved for consideration in a future version of the product. Now decide whether any of the *should have* items can be discarded or moved to the future opportunities column. Keep in mind that most processes and software products, especially the latter, have an excess of functions and features that nobody uses but were obviously requested by someone of influence. The problem becomes acute when the product is being proposed by a large number of disparate groups, and each wishes to incorporate some of their items into the final product. When you ask them why, the answer is often nothing more than: "because." Although satisfying everyone's whims clearly is not the right way to design a product, dealing with these wish lists is one reality of project planning. Another important item to keep in mind, at this point of scope definition, is the distinction between function and form. By definition, function relates to the purpose, substance, and utility of the product whereas form relates to its appearance and shape. A common mistake in developing IT/Business products/processes/services is to invest heavily in the form at the expense of the functionality. As you are working through the selection of various scope items, be sure to keep the function of the product foremost in consideration. Enhance form only to the extent the project priorities allow. Don't let "perfection of form" delay the project. Deliver it fit to use and then fine tune it as customer experience dictates.

Developing the Preliminary Scope Statement

The first step, when defining the preliminary project scope, is to review the conceptual build developed as a part of the Project Description earlier in the chapter and, working with the key customer, define the various functions, deliverables, and features that will be built to meet the project objectives and the conceptual build.

Scope Chunking

An impressive number of sound studies have shown, beyond any doubt, that the larger the project, the greater the chance of it being compromised (delivered beyond schedule, over budget, and of poor quality) or ending in outright failure. We divide projects into four categories:

3 to 6 months	Small
6 to 9 months	Medium
9 to 12 months	Large
>12 months	Mega

We have also found that most project managers, due to a consistent lack of education and training in developing accurate estimates, grossly underestimate their projects. Another key reason for such underestimating is the desire to please the customer. At the Center, we have a saying: "Projects are bigger than they appear." This perception is well corroborated by the following:

90 percent of the surveyed companies said they often underestimate their project's size and complexity.

http://www.costxpert.com/resource_center/sdtimes.html

Every example and quotation related to challenged and failed projects presented in this book has to do with large and mega projects. Therefore, it behooves any project manager to work hard to keep most projects in the medium or small range. Potential failure is not the only high risk that large projects face. Large projects are often challenged with:

- Dramatic changes (increases) in scope
- Changes in organizational strategy
- Changes in business requirements; internal and external
- Changes in the economic, political, and competitive environment
- Changes in technology, including obsolescence
- Reduced team effectiveness due to fatigue, reassignments, and turnover
- Loss of interest by customer

Another major problem with projects of long duration is that customers often cannot wait for the product and begin to develop ad-hoc solutions, often without the knowledge of the project team. Most of these solutions are developed using poor processes and dismal quality control steps. Eventually, these customers become so invested in the ad-hoc solutions that they demand their integration into the project's end product. Much of this is not discovered until the system integration and deployment phases of the project, resulting in last minute patchwork. You are doomed if you do and doomed if you don't.

Any large system is going to be operating most of the time in failure mode.
John Gall, *Systemantics* (Ann Arbor, MI: The General Systematics
Press, 1986): p. 77.

An additional area of concern with large and mega projects is that the ROI, the benefits to be gained as a result of the deployment of the project, is delayed by a long period of time—financially speaking, a poor choice. Figure 4.31 depicts a project that was estimated to take 18 months to develop, a mega project indeed. As you can see, the investment on this project will begin to pay off only after 18 long months. Keep in mind that a project of this size also potentially faces a number of high risks (refer to the previous bulleted items).

Consider the chunked project plan for the same project, as depicted in Figure 4.32. The mega project has been divided into five smaller projects:

1. Product and infrastructure architecture and design: 3 months
2. Release 1: electronic catalog and ordering: 4 months
3. Release 2: accounts receivable and point of sale: 4 months

FIGURE 4.31
Mega Project—ROI

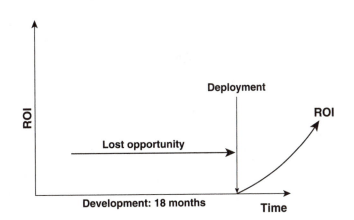

FIGURE 4.32
Chunked Project Structure

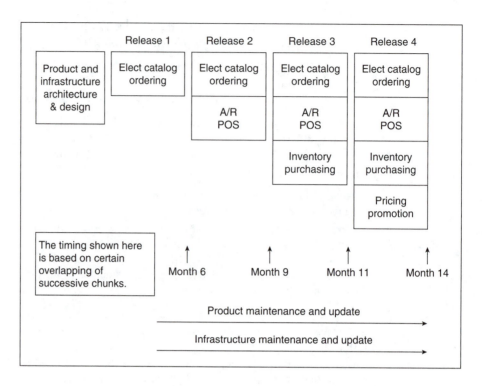

4. Release 3: inventory and purchasing: 3 months
5. Release 4: pricing and promotion: 3 months

Three key benefits resulted from this approach:

1. During the discussions to parse the mega project into smaller chunks, the project manager and key customers worked hard to assess the *must have, should have, nice to have,* and *fluff* deliverables and features, and were able to reduce the project scope by about 15 percent.
2. Although the five projects in Figure 4.32 are shown as linear for the sake of simplicity of diagramming, each had a certain overlap. This reduced the total development and deployment time to 14 months.
3. The ROI, as depicted in Figure 4.33, of the *electronic catalog* and *ordering* chunk began after the 6th month, on the *accounts receivables (A/R) and point of sale (POS)* chunk after the 9th month, on the inventory and purchasing chunk after the 11th month, and on the pricing and promotion chunk the 14th month.

FIGURE 4.33
Chunked Project—ROI

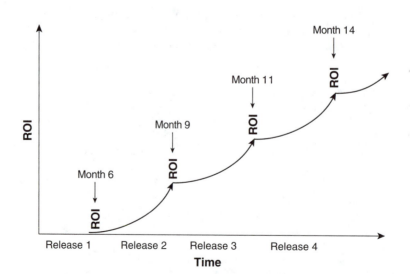

Figure 4.33 shows that, when a mega project is parsed into a number of smaller chunks, the ROI begins quite early—in this case the 6th month. Chunking reduces the size of the promised functionality from "big bang" to a manageable subset of the most useful deliverables and features delivered in progressive rollouts. Chunking reduces the amount of change by breaking the "big change" into a series of smaller changes over a longer period of time, resulting in reduced stress to the customer. Additionally, whenever a project is parsed into progressive chunks, early successful deployment provides the momentum for the total project. It also provides the opportunity to test customer acceptance. When selecting the first chunk, focus on highest priority customer needs.

Recently, a project manager from one of our client organizations sent us the following advice he had received from a web-based project management consulting service:

> *If the project is going to take 50,000 effort hours or 500,000 hours, it may take a number of weeks or months to get the project charter documented and approved. In these cases, a distinct project will be established to develop a common understanding of what will be accomplished. The final deliverable of this project would be the project charter.*

He had heard us espouse endlessly on the need for chunking larger projects into smaller projects that had a maximum duration of nine months and wanted to know why he could not use the web-based firm's approach to deal with large projects. Let's look at the advice:

1. They are actually talking about projects that can take 500,000 hours. Doing a quick size estimate, we figure this much effort will translate into a 5- to 6-year project—a mega project indeed. Just imagine investing money into an IT/Business project for 6 years before any ROI begins. Any IT/Business project over 18 months has the potential to run into serious trouble and here they are talking about a project that will run three times longer. Even if 500,000 hours is an exaggerated estimate, or just a figure of speech, we still believe that projects designed on such an exaggerated scale will experience major problems.
2. They suggest making the project definition a project in itself. We will agree that any part of a project needs to be completed using sound project management practices, but to make the start of a project into a "project" because of the massive size of the final project is simply inane.

The Rule of 777 We know that in real estate, the key to success is location. In IT/Business project management, the path to success is break it down. Therefore, our rule of 777:

1. Break all IT/Business projects into maximum of 7-month chunks.
2. Keep the team to less than seven core team members, as many full-time as possible.
3. Keep the budget under $700,000 (the dollar figure is a guide and does not include any capital costs and may vary due to salary fluctuations).

With the natural scope growth, the inevitable rework, and a few unexpected risks, this is sure to grow into a 9-month project that has about a $1 million budget, which to us is the maximum size of any IT/Business project. Any bigger project will certainly face problems and become a candidate for the challenged or failed statistic. It is imperative that sponsors and clients play a strong role in developing a project chunking strategy.

> *The team must be quite small, with five to seven members at most. The members have to be trained together and must work together for quite some time before they fully function as a team.*
>
> Peter F. Drucker, *Managing in a Time of Great Change*,
> New York: Truman Talley Books/Dutton, 1995.

For projects that cannot be chunked into the recommended size, we offer the following advice:

1. Make sure that the sponsor is at the appropriate hierarchical level to ensure the requisite level of authority and that she is fully committed to the success of the project.
2. Assemble a highly skilled full-time team.
3. Identify the best of SMEs to provide you and the team with guidance.

4. Make sure the vendors and contractors involved have impeccable performance history, and that they have made a personal commitment.
5. Do your best to ensure continued buy-in by the key stakeholders and customers.

After you have done that, make sure that you keep your resume updated. If the project is a success, you can certainly ask for a big raise or find a new employer who will give you one. If the project is a failure, they are sure to fire you and you *will* need your resume.

Technology Obsolescence—Moore's Law

A major problem faced by projects that fall in zone I and high zone II of the complexity chart is technology obsolescence. Ever since the first proclamation, by Gordon E. Moore in 1965, that chip capacity will double every 24 months, Moore's Law has held true. In many cases, the time has been reduced to 18 months. As a result of such spectacular developments in computer technology, obsolescence is a fact of life. The important question is: how many project managers specifically address the effort, time, and cost of such obsolescence for high complexity projects? Very few. Most react to new technology as they face it. Keep in mind that the problem is not limited just to the cost of technology upgrades; one must also consider the time and cost of people's skill upgrades. The cost of the latter can easily surpass that of the former. It is important for the project manager to incorporate the effort, time, and cost of technology obsolescence into the project plan and inform and *educate* the sponsor, key stakeholders, and customers about this important subject.

> *If I could redo the project plan, I would go back and figure out how to do it in chunks, in smaller pieces versus the mass distribution as we ultimately did it.*
> Edward Cone, "Detroit Financial System Sputters after Overhaul,"
> *Baseline* (August 6, 2002).

■ PROJECT SIZE ESTIMATE—PPA STEP 14

As a part of the project charter, the project manager will need to include an estimate of the proposed project's duration, resources, and cost. Your dilemma as the project manager, at this early stage, is reconciling the degree of accuracy desired by the customer with project reality. The customer would like an estimate that will be close to the actual cost and time to complete the project. However, unless the proposed project is less than four months in duration, you do not have sufficient information to create accurate estimates. The best that can be done at this early stage of a project is to create a *high-level* estimate, known as the *size* estimate and also known as the *rough order of magnitude* and top-down estimate.

Range Values

Size estimates can typically have an error range of up to +35 percent. Therefore, size estimates are stated as ranges. For example:

- 100 to 120 days (+20 percent range)
- 80 to 108 days (+35 percent range)
- 150 to 185 days (+23 percent range)

Unlike most project management professionals, we do not use the customary ± range to express estimates, we use only the + value. Here is why: Suppose a project manager was to state the estimated duration of a project as 100 ± 20 days. What do you believe the project manager was *hoping* to convey to the customer? Certainly, the project manager was hoping to convey: $100 + 20 = 120$ days. The customer reads the same estimate and expects the project might be finished in as short a time as 80 days ($100 - 20 = 80$ days). How far apart are the two interpretations? 40 days. The project manager's and the customer's expectations differ by a huge margin.

Another frequently asked question is: Why not simply use the higher of the two estimated values? In this case, 120 days. For the answer, we will need to look at the definition of the word "estimate": an estimate is an *approximate* number. However, an estimate of 120 days (a single point estimate) does not convey approximation; it conveys precision. Any single point estimate elevates an estimate to a commitment, which can, too easily, result in disappointment and frustration for both the customer and the project manager.

Regarding the use of the minus range when giving an estimate, consider this provocative question: "How often have projects finished ahead of the promised dates?" The answer is: "rarely." Then, why create the expectation that the project might be finished early? The most likely result will be frustration and disappointment for all. Therefore, we strongly advise against single point estimates and recommend that only a plus range value be used. Our motto: "The road to project hell is paved with exact estimates."

A final note: some of your colleagues, managers, instructors, and even authors of project management articles and books may consider range values unacceptable. We have come across written statements to that effect. The underlying belief is that range values encourage nonperformance (actuals map to the higher cost and time estimate values). We strongly believe that such a belief is shortsighted and misplaced. Our advice to you is to don your negotiator's hat and do your best to educate the individual about the reason for, and the benefits of, *realistic* range values. However, if a question regarding the use of range values appears in a quiz by your instructor or in a certification exam, and you know the expected answer is "range values are not desirable," grit your teeth, and answer the question as expected. No need to lower your score.

Size estimates are typically developed using models based on historical data. The various size estimating methods can be grouped into the following four primary categories:

1. Phase-based model (also known as an effort/cost distribution model)
2. Deliverables-based model
3. Function point model
4. Parametric model

These models, with the exception of the deliverables-based model, are statistical templates used to generate effort, duration, resource, and cost *size estimates* at a point when little is known about the project. The use of more than one method to verify the size estimate for a given project is not uncommon. In this book, we will limit our discussion to phase-based and deliverables-based size estimating models.

Phase-Based Size Estimate

Our experience shows us that phase-based models are best suited for developing size estimates for the following types of projects:

1. Projects based on a well-defined, and consistently used, life cycle methodology
2. Medium to large projects (6–12 months in duration). Projects that have a greater than 12-month expected duration should be chunked into smaller projects.

For projects less than 6 months duration, we would advise the use of deliverables-based estimating (discussed later in this chapter), as it produces more accurate size estimates.

We have found that phase-based models are not particularly suitable for developing size estimates for emerging technology projects because of a lack of historical data. Also, it is not possible to accurately calibrate (adjust) these models for evolving technology projects.

Creating a Size Estimate Using a Phase-Based Model

The foundation for creating an accurate size estimate is the comprehensiveness of the work completed to this point in the Pre-Launch stage. It is very important to note that a simple project description is not sufficient to develop an accurate size estimate. The steps necessary to create a size estimate using a phase-based model are listed in the following subsections.

Create or Select a Phase-Based Model   Create or select a phase-based model that is similar to your project. The source of the model can be:

- Your own experience
- Experience of other teams in your organization that are currently working on similar projects
- History of similar projects previously completed within your organization
- Industry data

Figure 4.34 shows an example of a phase-based model for a project.

FIGURE 4.34
Phase-Based Model

Phase	Percent of total
Requirements	25
Logical design	15
Physical design	15
Code & unit test	15
System testing	20
Implement	10

Calibrate the Phase-Based Model   The next step is to determine whether the selected model needs to be calibrated/adjusted to fit the specific needs of the project you are estimating. An adjustment would be necessary if the project does not fully map to the structure of the selected model. A model is calibrated by adjusting (expanding or reducing) the percentages of appropriate phases of the model in concert with the specifics of the project you are estimating. For example, Figure 4.35 shows that the project manager decided to *increase* the percentage of the physical design phase by 5 percent. The reasons vary. One reason could be that the team is not well versed in the concepts to be used in designing the proposed system. Similarly, the code & unit testing phase has been *increased* by 7 percent perhaps because of the need to do more rigorous unit testing. Notice that the remaining phases of the model are *not* reduced to make the total to 100 percent. The total of the effort percentages of a calibrated model could actually be more or less than 100 percent. If the project you are estimating is less complex than the model, the total of the calibrated model should be less than 100 percent. In all cases, document your reasons for adjusting the percentages.

Select and Estimate the Base Phase   The next step is to compute a base estimate that is as accurate as possible. The base estimate is defined as the number of *effort hours* needed to complete the

FIGURE 4.35
Calibrated Phase-Based
Model

Phase	Percent of total	Calibration
Requirements	25	
Logical design	15	
Physical design	15	+5%
Code & unit test	15	+7%
System testing	20	
Implement	10	

base phase (minimally 15 percent, preferably 20 percent, and ideally 30 percent of the total project). The base estimate can be developed using either the deliverables-based or task-based estimating methods discussed later. In Figure 4.35, we see that the requirements phase is 25 percent of the model and will suffice as the base phase. It is not necessary that the base phase be composed of the earlier phase(s) of the project. Any project phase(s) can serve as the base phase, as long as it comprises a minimum of 15 percent of the total project life cycle. Let us *assume* that we have a base phase with a base estimate of 500 effort hours.

Extrapolate Effort Estimates for Various Phases   The next step is to extrapolate the effort estimates for the remaining phases of the project. The extrapolated estimated effort for each remaining phase can be computed as follows:

1. Compute the total extrapolated effort for the project:

$$\text{Base Phase Estimate} \div \text{Base Phase Percent Value}$$
$$500 \div 0.25 = 2,000 \text{ hr}$$

2. Compute the estimated effort for each remaining phase:

$$\text{Total Effort} \times \text{Phase Percent Value}$$

For example, the estimated effort for the logical design phase (15 percent of the project) would be:

$$2000 \times 0.15 = 300 \text{ hr}$$

Figure 4.36 shows the extrapolated values for various phases of the project. Keep in mind that we *adjusted* (*increased*) the estimated effort of the design phase by 5 percent and of the code & unit test phase by 7 percent because of the calibration depicted in Figure 4.35. The calibration results in a total extrapolated estimated effort of 2,240 hr.

FIGURE 4.36
Phase-Based Model—
Estimated Effort

Phase	Percent of total	Effort hours
Requirements	25	500
Logical design	15	300
Physical design	15 + 5	300 + 100
Code & unit test	15 + 7	300 + 140
System testing	20	400
Implement	10	200
	Total:	2,240 hr

Compute the Estimated Work Months for Each Phase   The following is an algorithm used for converting the estimated effort hours of each phase into estimated work months. For each phase of the project, convert the estimated effort hours to estimated work months (WM) by dividing the estimated effort hours of the phase by the *average productive hours* of one full-time equivalent (FTE) resource for that phase. The value used for the productive hours/month (PHM) will vary, depending on the productivity environment of the project. The productive hours/month value is typically computed by multiplying the average productive hours/day and the average workdays/month. Many of the Center's clients use 6.5 productive hours per day and 17.5 productive days per month. In this case, average productive hours for a full-time resource would be:

$$6.5 \text{ hours/day} \times 17.5 \text{ d/mo} = 114 \text{ hr/mo}$$

FIGURE 4.37
Phase-Based Model—
Estimated WM

Phase	Percent of total	Effort hours	Productive hr/mo	WM
Requirements	25	500	114	4.38
Logical design	15	300	114	2.63
Physical design	15 + 5	400	114	3.50
Code & unit test	15 + 7	440	114	3.85
System testing	20	400	114	3.50
Implement	10	200	114	1.75

Total: 2,240 hr

Make sure the numbers you use represent the realistic productive hours per month, not what someone would like the numbers to be. We often see project managers use high numbers, thereby implying a high productivity environment. This will result in estimates that look good but prove unreliable. The estimated WM value for various project phases (when only one full-time resource is considered) is shown in Figure 4.37.

In this example, the project manager used a rate of 114 productive hours for *all* project phases. While this might have been the case for the model project, we strongly recommend that you carefully ascertain the productive hours per month value for your specific project. In projects lasting over three months, the productive hour value might fluctuate considerably. For example, the period between mid-November to mid-January is usually a time of fewer productive hours in North America due to social, seasonal, and year-end activities. The month of August is considered a time of reduced productivity in Europe, while in Brazil, especially Rio de Janeiro, the month of February has low productivity when Carnival takes front stage.

Compute Optimal Full-Time Equivalent Resources   To arrive at an accurate number of resources (team members) that can be assigned to a project, you first need to develop a comprehensive WBS, and then create an accurate task dependency network for each phase of the project. When developing size estimates, however, it is not possible to create a detailed WBS and an accurate task dependency network chart because the needed details are not known. What you need to figure out at this early point is a reasonable *approximation* of the total number of resources that could be absorbed by the project. This estimate is called the Optimal Full-Time Equivalent (OFTE) team size. A simple, but reliable, heuristics-based formula to compute the number of OFTE resources that can be absorbed by any given project phase is as follows:

$$\text{OFTE} = \left(\sqrt[2]{\text{WM}} \right) + 1$$

The burning question at this point in estimating is: "What is the basis for the formula to compute the OFTE for a given project phase?" The answer is best illustrated using the set of tasks depicted in Figure 4.38.

Figure 4.38 shows a set of fifteen *parallel* tasks. All of them can be executed at the same time, and each task is estimated to require one day of effort by an FTE. Figure 4.39 illustrates the impact of assigning a varying number of resources to this set of tasks.

An interesting factor to analyze in this chart is the impact on estimated duration as each additional resource is assigned to this set of tasks. From the data in Figure 4.39, you can see that:

- One resource will take fifteen days to finish all fifteen tasks
- With two resources, the total duration drops to eight days (a reduction of seven days)
- With three resources, the total duration drops to five days (a further reduction of three days)
- With four resources, the total duration drops to four days (additional reduction of one day)
- With five resources, the total duration drops to three days (another reduction of one day).

FIGURE 4.38
Set of Parallel Tasks

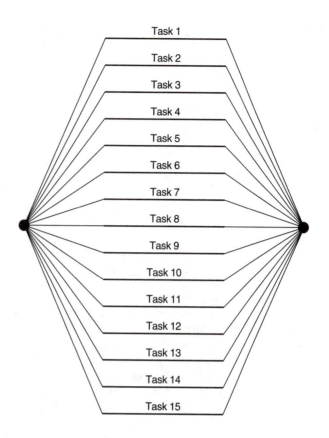

FIGURE 4.38
Set of Parallel Tasks

- The duration *does not further diminish* until we assign eight resources. With eight resources, the duration drops to two days.
- The duration *stays at two days* until fifteen resources are assigned, at which point the duration drops to one day.

From the resource loading explanation just given and illustrated in Figure 4.39, we can conclude that the *best fit* is the assignment of four or five resources, which will result in a duration of four or three days, respectively. The resource loading heuristics just outlined are the foundation for computing the number of OFTE resources that can be productively absorbed on a project. We at the Center, along with a sizeable number of our clients, have used this formula for over 10 years and

FIGURE 4.39
Resource Loading

Number of resources	Duration days
1	15
2	8
3	5
4	4
5	3
6	3
7	3
8	2
9	2
10	2
11	2
12	2
13	2
14	2
15	1

FIGURE 4.40
Phase-Based Estimate—
OFTE

Phase	Percent of total	Effort hours	Productive hr/mo	WM*	OFTE
Requirements	25	500	114	4.38	3.0
Logical design	15	300	114	2.63	2.5
Physical design	15 + 5	400	114	3.50	3.0
Code & unit test	15 + 7	440	114	3.85	3.0
System testing	20	400	114	3.50	3.0
Implement	10	200	114	1.75	2.0

* The values in this column represent the time taken by one FTE resource.

have found it to be quite dependable. Figure 4.40 depicts the computed OFTE resources for each of the project phases. Remember, OFTE = $(\sqrt[2]{WM}) + 1$; the OFTE values have been rounded.

Our experience shows that the formula *does not* always work well under two conditions:

1. Projects expected to last longer than 12 months that include a large number of parallel tasks. For many such projects, the number of resources computed by the formula is consistently smaller than the number of resources that can actually be assigned to the project. We do not see this as a problem, because we consider any project estimated to last over 12 months to be a risky undertaking—in fact, a quest. Our solution is to break these mega projects into smaller projects,[12] resulting in reduced risk and improved estimates.

2. When the value of the estimated effort for a phase falls below one WM, $(\sqrt[2]{WM}) + 1$ produces messy numbers. In such cases, the OFTE is computed as 1.

Determine the Probable Full-Time Equivalent Resources Before executing this step, an important question to consider is: Will the number of resources, as computed by the formula for OFTE, actually be available for the project? We have often discovered that qualified resources are in short supply, and the number of resources computed, as the OFTE, may *not* be readily available. If this is even remotely possible, we suggest that you establish realistic assumptions for resource availability. We call this estimate the probable full-time equivalent (PFTE) team members for the project. The number of PFTE can be *equal to or less than* the computed OFTE. It is important that you not succumb to the pressure of using a PFTE value higher than the computed OFTE. Doing so will reduce the duration of the project, at least on paper, but the higher number of team members can seldom be absorbed by the project due to the lack of sufficient parallel tasks. Figure 4.41 shows the computed OFTE, along with the PFTE, for each project phase. Notice that, for certain phases, the PFTE number is *smaller* than the computed OFTE because of resource availability.

At times, we encounter some serious challenges to the algorithm for computing the OFTE and PFTE values. For example, the PFTE value of 3 for the Requirements phase in Figure 4.41 implies

FIGURE 4.41
Phase-Based Estimate—PFTE

Phase	Percent of total	Effort hours	Productive hr/mo	WM	OFTE	PFTE
Requirements	25	500	114	4.38	3.0	3
Logical design	15	300	114	2.63	2.5	2
Physical design	15 + 5	400	114	3.50	3.0	2
Code & unit test	15 + 7	440	114	3.85	3.0	3
System testing	20	400	114	3.50	3.0	3
Implement	10	200	114	1.75	2.0	2

---

[12]Breaking a mega project into smaller individual projects does not mean that the smaller projects need to be executed in a linear fashion. One or more projects could be underway at the same time.

that all three resources will work at a constant pace. This is possible only if the task network for this phase contains three parallel paths, which is not likely. Additionally, it further implies that the three resources will work at the same level of productivity, which is not always the case. If the skills of various team members vary widely, appropriate adjustments will be necessary. These variables demonstrate exactly why we suggest the use of range values for all estimates. We also strongly advise that size estimates should not be converted into schedules.

Compute the Estimated Duration for Each Phase   To compute the estimated duration for a phase, divide the estimated WM by the number of PFTE. We use the PFTE values for this computation and not the OFTE values. Figure 4.42 depicts the estimated duration values (rounded) for each project phase.

FIGURE 4.42
Phase-Based Estimates—
Estimated Phase Durations

Phase	Percent of total	Effort hours	Productive hr/mo	WM	OFTE	PFTE	Est. duration (WM)
Requirements	25	500	114	4.38	3.0	3	1.5
Logical design	15	300	114	2.63	2.5	2	1.3
Physical design	15 + 5	400	114	3.50	3.0	2	1.75
Code & unit test	15 + 7	440	114	3.85	3.0	3	1.3
System testing	20	400	114	3.50	3.0	3	1.2
Implement	10	200	114	1.75	2.0	2	1.0

Total: 2,240 hr

We *do not* recommend using range values for *intermediate* estimate calculations. For example, in the case of the estimate shown in Figure 4.42, there are no range values for individual phase estimates. The range values are used only for the *final* estimate. Using range values for each phase is not only tedious, it conveys too many uncertainties to management and customers.

Estimate Project Duration—WM   The rightmost column in Figure 4.42 depicts the estimated duration, in months, for each phase. Do not total up this column to compute the estimated project duration because phases may overlap. To estimate the duration of the project, develop a phase-based Gantt chart that depicts the order of execution and appropriate overlaps of various project phases. Figure 4.43 shows a phase-based Gantt chart for this project. The estimated project duration is 6 to 8 work months (using the +35 percent range)

How do you know which overlaps to use? You must use your best judgment based on your knowledge of the project (consultation with team members and SMEs can be very helpful). Your

FIGURE 4.43
Estimated Project Duration

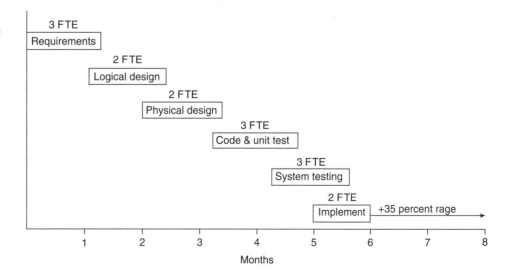

judgment could contain errors, but most errors are addressed by using the appropriate range value for the *final* size estimate communicated to the customer.

Estimate Sponsor, Management, and Customer Time

Sponsor Effort: Figure 4.44 depicts the recommended values for the sponsor's time. It is important that the project manager clearly and specifically convey (to the sponsor) the time demands created by the project. Too often, this communication does not happen and the sponsor does not actually set aside the time needed to "oversee" the project. Our recommendation is that the project manager and sponsor jointly define the role and responsibility of the sponsor, and then use the values depicted in Figure 4.44 as a guide to decide on the time commitments for a given project.

FIGURE 4.44
Recommended Sponsor
Effort

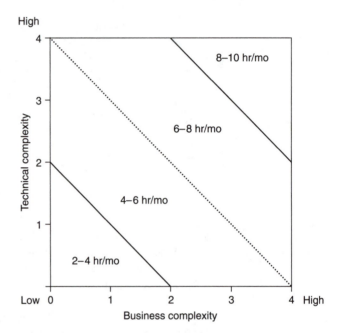

Management and Customer Effort: Figure 4.45 shows the Center's recommendations for functional managers' and customers' time commitments. Our recommendation is that the project manager and sponsor jointly define the extent of participation of functional managers and customers, and then use the values depicted in Figure 4.45 as a guide to decide on the time commitments for a given project.

- *Projects in zone I:* Typically, functional managers will need to spend between 15 to 20 percent of the estimated development effort. Additionally, customers will need to set aside approximately 25 to 40 percent of the estimated development effort to participate in a variety of tasks during the project life cycle.

- *Projects in zone II:* Functional managers will be needed for 10 to 15 percent of the estimated development effort. In addition, customers will need to set aside between 10 and 15 percent of the estimated development effort to participate in a variety of tasks during the project life cycle. Zone II projects are more technology sensitive than those in zone III and do not require extensive customer time.

- *Projects in zone III:* Functional managers' time for these projects amounts to approximately 10 to 15 percent of the estimated development effort. Customer time commitment is between 20 and 25 percent of the estimated development effort. The reason for the extra time is that such projects deal heavily with new and difficult business issues and will require more time from the customers.

- *Projects in zone IV:* Functional managers' time for these projects amounts to approximately 5 percent of the estimated development effort. Customer time commitment is between 10 and 15 percent of the estimated development effort.

The recommended estimated time values are derived from data collected from a number of projects from different customers and should be used as *guidelines*, not as hard and fast rules. You

FIGURE 4.45
Recommended Management
and Customer Effort

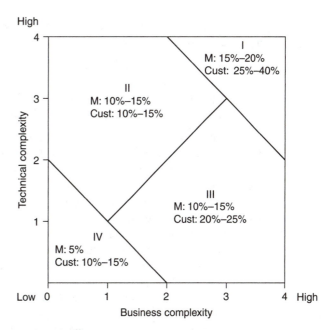

M: management time
Cust: customers' time

will need to track a number of your projects, compare the recommended figures with your experience, and adjust the values accordingly.

We will continue with the estimating process for the project in this example. The project manager gave his project a medium-complexity rating and specified 6 hours per month of sponsor time: 10% for management time, and 20% for customer time. Carrying forward the estimated 6 to 8 months of duration and 2,240 effort hours of development, the estimated values are:

Sponsor effort: 36 hr
Functional managers' effort: $2,240 \times 0.10 = 224$ hr
Customer effort: $2,240 \times 0.25 = 560$ hr

$$\text{Development Effort Estimate: } (2240 + 36 + 224 + 560) = 3,060 \text{ hr}$$

Estimate Project Manager's Effort   At times we hear people, usually customers, use the word "overhead" when they refer to the cost and time taken up by project managers. When asked to elucidate their views, a common response is: "project managers don't actually do any "real" work—design, build, and test.[13] Our typical follow up question is, "Does Zubin Mehta[14] play any instruments while he conducts an orchestra? Did he sing when he directed the famous Three Tenor opera recital?" The answer is "no." Is Zubin Mehta, or any symphony conductor, considered overhead? Is the executive chef in a large restaurant overhead, or is he/she providing value to the business? The answer is obvious: any large restaurant needs an executive chef. Project managers provide similar and essential *value added* services to any project. The project manager's effort to manage a given project can vary because of a number of different factors. For example:

Political environment	Team location
Project complexity	Team size
Project manager's skills	Team/customer synergy

Our experience, from data collected over the past 10 years, shows that the time needed to manage a team can vary from a low of 8 percent to a high of 20 percent of the estimated project

---

[13]Ironically, many project managers, especially newly promoted ones, wish to do just this type of work, which causes the project (team) to suffer.

[14]Zubin Mehta is an internationally acclaimed conductor. He served as director of the Montreal Symphony (1961–1967), The Los Angeles Philharmonic Orchestra (1962–1978) The New York Philharmonic (1978–1991), and the Israel Philharmonic (1977).

development effort.[15] The development effort means the effort by the team, sponsor, functional managers, and customers. We suggest using the following percentages:

Zone IV projects: 8 percent of the total development effort
Low zone II and low zone III projects: 12 percent of the total development effort
High zone II and high zone III projects: 15 percent of the total development effort
Zone I projects: 20 percent of the total development effort

Another way of stating the percent figure is that each FTE team member will need anywhere from 8 percent to 20 percent of a full-time project manager's time. For the first set of projects in the list, a full-time project manager can manage approximately twelve FTE team members. Similarly, for the second set of projects, it would be nine FTE team members. For the third set, it would be about seven FTE team members. For zone I projects, it would be about five FTE team members. The team for most zone I projects is going to consist of greater than five FTEs; in these cases, the project manager will need to delegate certain responsibilities to senior team members (project managers in training) and to the project office, if one exists. We also recommend that project managers responsible for managing zone I projects hire or make use of an administrative assistant (see *Administrative Support*, Chapter 5). The skill of aggressive delegation with the right set of controls is essential for a project manager to assure the time needed to perform his necessary duties. In cases where the team is small enough not to require full-time management, the project manager can handle more than one project or can even be a part-time member of the team.

The next step is to compute the estimated effort needed to manage this project. In the example, the project manager computed the project management effort as follows:

$$PM\ Effort = 3{,}060 \times 0.15 = 459\ hr$$

Therefore, the total estimated effort is $3{,}060 + 459 = 3{,}519$ hr.

Impact of Phase Overlaps on Resource Loading: Notice the overlaps between different phases in the Gantt chart in Figure 4.43. In the example, when the work on the logical design phase begins, two *additional* resources will be able to start the work *while* the three resources are busy completing the work on the requirements phase. Similarly, when the work on the physical design phase begins, two *additional* resources will be needed to work on the logical design. We often find that project managers have overlooked the need for additional resources created by the overlaps among multiple phases. Figure 4.46 shows a resource histogram for the project estimated in Figure 4.43.

There may never be more than three people available to work on the project at any given time. In that case, the Gantt chart for the project (as shown in Figure 4.43) will need to be redrawn to reflect the resource limitation, much to the chagrin of everyone involved (especially the customer who was shown the Gantt chart in Figure 4.43 by an eager project manager). We have found the use of a histogram to plot the resource utilization to be quite helpful, as it clearly documents the resource load. Also, be wary of over allocation of the project manager. This problem develops when two or more phases overlap and more than eight resources are assigned to work simultaneously. In such cases, some of the project management responsibilities will need to be delegated to another person on the team.

Compute Estimated Cost The project manager assumes a billing rate of $95 per hour for core team members and $115 per hour for the project manager. The estimate *does not* include the cost of sponsor, management, and customer effort (department policy). The cost estimates are:

$$(2240 \times 95) + (459 \times 115) = 212{,}800 + 52{,}785 = \$265{,}585$$

When computing the total *labor cost estimate*, the estimator used a range value of 25 percent.

$$\$265{,}585 \times 0.25 = \$66{,}396$$

The customer was given an estimate of $265,585 to $331,981.

---

[15]Any project requiring greater than 20 percent project management effort is running in crisis mode and would be practically impossible to estimate with any accuracy.

FIGURE 4.46
Project Resource Histogram

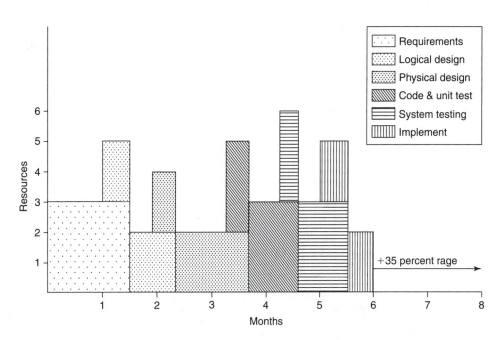

Here is an interesting example of the use of a phase-based size estimate where the project manager used the estimate as a foundation for adjusting the scope of the proposed project. To develop the phase-based size estimate for a project, the project manager used historical data from similar projects and defined the following phase-level model for the project at hand:

Requirements: 20 percent
Design: 30 percent
Construction and test: 35 percent
Implementation: 15 percent

The project manager chose the requirements phase (20 percent) as the base phase, decomposed the phase into a set of deliverables, and then created a deliverables-based estimate of 2,060 hr. He then extrapolated the total effort of the project as follows:

Requirements phase effort = 2,060 hr
Core team effort = 2,060 ÷ 0.20 = 10,300 hr

The project manager computed the additional effort estimate values as follows:

Sponsor effort: 80 hr
Functional managers' effort: $10,300 \times 0.10 = 1,030$ hr
Customer effort: $10,300 \times 0.15 = 1,545$ hr
Project development effort:

$$(10,300 + 80 + 1,030 + 1,545) = 12,955 \text{ hr}$$

Project manager effort = $(12,955) \times 0.15 = 1,943$ hr
Estimated cost: (core team effort + PM effort) × billing rate

$$(10,300 + 1,943) = 12,243 \times 125 = \$1,530,375$$

In the cost computations, the project manager did not account for the sponsor or functional managers' time (organization's policy). $125/hr is the averaged burdened billing rate for team members, including the project manager.

From earlier discussions with the customer, the project manager knew that the estimated cost of $1,530,375 was far above the customer's budget for the project, and considerably above the budget for the current budget cycle. As a result, the project manager and a senior customer manager worked together to "chunk" the project into two smaller projects. While doing the chunking, the customer dropped enough functionality, which represented approximately 2,000 hours of effort, to bring the two smaller projects within the customer's budget. This is a good example of using a size estimate to conduct a quick analysis of the overall effort, cost, and duration of a project, and then using this information for decision making.

Level of Accuracy The level of accuracy of the size estimates developed using a phase-based model depends on:

- Understanding the model's assumptions
- The similarity of the model's structure to the project at hand
- The calibration of the model to project-specific variances
- The completeness and accuracy of the information used to develop the base phase estimate
- The experience of the person using the model. An individual must work through the complete estimating process three to four times before she can begin to develop accurate size estimates.

■ DELIVERABLES-BASED SIZE ESTIMATE MODEL

Phase-based models are typically used to develop size estimates for projects expected to be longer than six months in duration. For projects shorter than an expected duration of six months, deliverables-based size estimates produce better results. The steps to compute deliverables-based size estimates are:

1. Break the project into phases.
2. Break each phase into deliverables.
3. Describe each deliverable.
4. Estimate individual deliverables.
5. Develop a project Gantt chart.
6. Estimate project cost.

Figure 4.47 shows a template we use at the Center to define deliverables in a comprehensive manner prior to developing deliverable-based estimates.

Deliverable Name: The name of the deliverable. For the sake of clear communications and for developing accurate estimates, we advise that different people in the same organization learn to use common (standard) names for their deliverables. Use a noun to name a deliverable.

Owner: The specific person responsible for making sure the deliverable is completed (built) to its specifications. A few words to the wise:

- Only one person should be the "owner" of any given deliverable. More than one person might work to finish a specific deliverable, but the primary responsibility should lie with only one person.
- The responsibility for completing a deliverable may lie with a member of the core team, a member of a cross-functional department, or a third party (such as a vendor). It is a sign of trouble when the responsibility for a deliverable spans the groups listed above (a jointly held deliverable). Developing estimates for deliverables that are the responsibility of the core team would be easiest; others will require extra effort, care, and supervision.

Description: A brief, but clear, description of the deliverable. The objective is to make sure that everyone, including the estimator, gets the same picture of the deliverable. Our advice:

- If a deliverable is the responsibility of the core team, a brief description will suffice.
- For deliverables where the development responsibility lies with a member of a cross-functional team, we recommend two to three lines of description.
- For any deliverable to be developed by a third party, we suggest a brief paragraph of comprehensive description or an actual example. This level of detail will provide a clear picture of the deliverable and will help develop estimates that are more accurate. In extreme cases, a prototype may be necessary.

Completion Criteria: Succinct criteria that ensures that the developers of the deliverable clearly understand what constitutes completion of the deliverable. For example: Review and approval of the document by Bob Smith, Vice President of Product Design. Detailed definitions help you better conceptualize the amount of work needed to complete the deliverable, which results in estimates that are more accurate.

FIGURE 4.47
Deliverable Definition
Template

Deliverable name: _____

Owner: _____

Description: _____

_____

_____

Completion criteria: _____

_____

_____

Required resource(s): _____

_____

_____

Probable resource(s): _____

_____

_____

Estimated effort: _____ hr

Estimated duration: _____ d

Lag (if any): _____ d

Estimated cost: $ _____

Required Resources: The type of resources and skills needed to complete the deliverable. For example, a senior analyst with executive interviewing skills; a senior course developer; and a mid-level programmer with object-oriented design, C++, and XML experience.

Probable Resources: Name of the person who will be assigned to complete this deliverable. If it is not possible to provide the name of the individual, then a job title is acceptable.

• The skill levels of the resource (novice, competent, proficient . . .)

• The percentage of the resource's work time that is being allocated to this deliverable

Estimated Effort Hours: The hours of work required by the resource(s) defined in the previous step to complete the deliverable.

Estimated Duration: The number of work days required to complete the deliverable.

Estimated cost: The total number of estimated dollars. Cost is computed by multiplying the total estimated effort for the deliverable by resource billing rates.

Lag: Certain deliverables can have delay (time) associated with them. For example, it might take 4 hours of effort to order computer equipment, but it might be 10 days (*lag*) before the equipment is received from the vendor. Dependencies between two or more deliverables can also result in lag.

Figures 4.48 and 4.49 show examples of two deliverables defined and estimated using the template described previously.

We do not recommend using range values for *individual* deliverable estimates. The range values are used only for the *final* duration and cost figures. Using range values for each deliverable is not only tedious, it conveys too many uncertainties to management and customers.

FIGURE 4.48
Deliverable Estimate—
Example 1

Deliverable name:	Updated corporate vacation policy
Owner:	HR manager
Description:	A document that details the vacation policy rules and regulations.
Completion criteria:	Approved by legal. Approved by HR. Reviewed by three employees.
Required resources:	One mid-level HR analyst, one mid-level technical writer, legal (HR attorney), HR manager, three employees
Probable resources:	Same
Estimated effort:	30 hr mid-level HR analyst 10 hr mid-level technical writer 6 hr legal (attorney) 4 hr manager 6 hr employee review (56 hr)
Estimated duration:	9 days
Lag:	0 days
Estimated cost:	Not computed as yet

FIGURE 4.49
Deliverable Estimate—
Example 2

Deliverable:	Customer requirements for GUI
Owner:	Business analyst
Description:	A document that details the specifications needed by the customer for the graphic user interface.
Completion criteria:	Ready for customer review
Required resources:	One mid-level business analyst and one mid-level technical writer
Probable resources:	Same
Estimated effort:	24 hr mid-level technical writer 10 hr mid-level business analyst (34 hr)
Estimated duration:	6 days
Lag:	5 days
Estimated cost:	Not computed as yet

To calculate the project cost, add up the estimated cost of each deliverable, the project manager's cost, and any additional cost items (hardware, software, facilities, supplies, consulting services, and travel). If applicable, you may add the cost of sponsor, management, and customer time.

Deliverables-Based Estimate—Example 1

A technical documentation specialist supplied this estimating example. He used the deliverables-based size estimating method to develop estimates for his portion of the project. His responsibility in the project involved developing three different technical manuals: a user manual, an administration manual, and a new hires guide. The resource assumptions for the project were as follows:

- He would be working full time on this portion of the project.
- He would have a senior-level documentation specialist available to work on the project half-time. This person's responsibilities included writing, background research, and proofreading.

His first step to develop the estimate was to develop a list of deliverables for the project:

- Deliverable descriptions
- Approved deliverable descriptions
- Reformatted user manual
- Reformatted administrative manual
- Updated user manual (draft)
  - 20 screen shots
  - 10 graphics
  - 11 reports
- Updated administrative manual (draft)
- Updated new hires guide (draft)
- Final user manual
- Final administrative manual
- Final new hires guide
- Print/production

At this point, he met with the project manager and a customer representative and reviewed the list of planned deliverables. During the review, the customer representative expressed the need for having the user and administrative manuals available in HTML for online downloading by end users. This, added two more deliverables. The project manager approved the added requirements. As a next step, the developer created a deliverables-based estimate shown in Figure 4.50. He assumed 6.5 hours of productive time per day for himself and 3.5 hours for the documentation specialist, with occasional overtime for both.

The final estimates were as follows:

- **Development work:** 93 to 103 days (he used a 10 percent range because he was confident that the end products were well-defined). An extremely important point: the only reason the estimated duration is a sum of individual duration values is because one person is doing the development work on the project (the person assisting the primary individual will not be completing any deliverables on his own).
- **Project manager's time:** $657 \times 0.08 = 53$ hr. The developer felt that 8 percent of the total development effort was a reasonable number to use because of the low complexity of the work.
- **Customer's time:** $657 \times 0.10 = 66$ hr. This is the time needed to review some of the deliverables with the customers and for occasional discussions for clarifications of requirements.
- The developer did not include any time for the sponsor or functional managers because of the nature of the deliverables.

In our discussion with the person who supplied this example, he made a number of important observations:

- The first two steps in Figure 4.50 refer to the work needed to describe the various planned deliverables in detail, using the template in Figure 4.47. He remarked that these two steps were new to him because, in the past, he would simply develop a list of deliverables and start working on them.

FIGURE 4.50
Deliverables-Based Estimate

Deliverable	Estimated effort (hours)	Estimated duration (days)
Deliverables descriptions	12	3
Approved deliverables descriptions	4	1
Reformatted user manual	45	7
Reformatted administrative manual	50	7
Updated user manual (draft) • 20 screen shots • 10 graphics • 11 reports	110	11
Updated administrative manual (draft)	115	12
Updated new hires guide (draft)	36	6
Final users manual	45	7
Final administrative manual	50	8
Final new hires guide	50	8
User manual (HTML)	60	10
Administrative manual (HTML)	60	10
Print/production	20	3
Total	657	93

- Prior to developing estimates using the deliverables-based method, the estimates would have reflected much higher levels, perhaps four or five deliverables instead of the thirteen deliverables (Figure 4.50). At that high granularity, the probability of the resulting estimates being accurate would have been low, but that is how estimates were developed for quite some time. The deliverables-based approach also provided a better view of the total work involved.

When the developer communicated the estimates to the project manager, the project manager was a bit surprised by the amount of effort and time (duration) required to complete the work. The project manager was expecting much lower estimates. In fact, he had figured about 75 workdays compared to the estimated 93 workdays as shown in Figure 4.50. As a result of this gap, the developer's discussions with the project manager revolved around the following points:

1. Which of the thirteen planned deliverables was not needed and could be removed from the list? The project manager could not think of any.
2. Next, they discussed the estimated effort and duration of each of the thirteen deliverables. After a quick look at the various numbers, the project manager realized that both the effort and duration values were reasonable, in some cases even a bit conservative (on the low side), and agreed to the submitted estimates.

One might wonder why this person spent the time to develop a deliverables-based estimate using detailed deliverable descriptions for a small project. The reason is that the individual had just learned the deliverables-based estimating approach, and wanted to try it on the small phase of a project to get his "feet wet." He was pleased with the fact that the two additional deliverables were discovered before any estimates were developed. The use of the deliverables description template provided the developer with the right amount of support information needed to negotiate his estimates with the project manager.

Deliverables-Based Estimate—Example 2

This example comes from a project manager who was responsible for deploying a major upgrade to a manufacturing package at eight different manufacturing plants in the U.S. The upgrade was to be attempted in three phases:

1. Install the upgrade at the local manufacturing plant. Use the lessons learned from the first upgrade to fine tune the subsequent upgrades.

FIGURE 4.51
Package Installation—
Deliverable-Based Size
Estimate

Deliverable/task	Estimated days
D1. Management orientation	5
D2. Staff orientation	5
D3. Configured factory hardware	5
D4. Configured training hardware	5
D5. Basic computer training	10
D6. Configured office hardware	5
D7. Configured database	5
D8. Configured process flow	5
D9. Approved process flow	10
D10. Operator training – batch 1	5
D11. Security training	5
D12. Operator training – batch 2	10
D13. Follow-up training	5
D14. Partial parallel run	5
D15. System adjustments	10
D16. System documentation	20
D17. Security test	10
D18. Full parallel run	10

2. Install the next three plant upgrades concurrently.
3. Install upgrades at the remaining four plants concurrently.

Figure 4.51 lists the deliverables and their duration estimates; Figure 4.52 depicts the Gantt chart for the project.

The project team consisted of a project manager, three senior team members from the central office, four local (plant) team members at each location, and a central coordinator in the head office (all assigned full-time to this project). For this estimate, the project manager focused more on the number of days for any given deliverable rather than the effort hours, because each plant site upgrade had to be completed within ten weeks of its start. Figure 4.52 depicts the Gantt chart for one plant upgrade. Because of the 10-week window, the project manager planned for an 8-week

FIGURE 4.52
Package Installation—
Grantt Chart

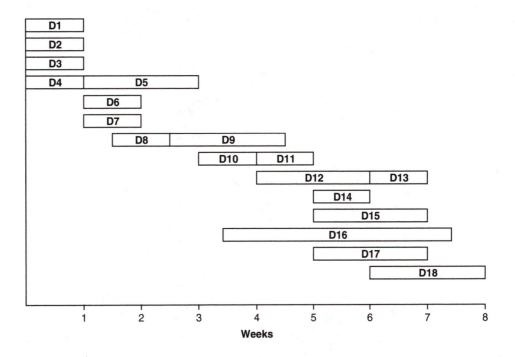

installation, which allowed the team a two-week reserve for any last minute problems. The estimate assumed a consistent need for overtime (about 15 percent) because of the tight installation window.

The installation of the package at the first plant took 12 weeks due to the difficulties in acquiring the needed training space, which in turn delayed the installation of the necessary computer hardware. The upgrade at the next three plants took 11 weeks each, and the third phase (last four plants) took 9 weeks each. For the third phase, the project manager added two additional team members and rented portable trailers for hosting the various training sessions.

Historical Deliverables Database

At the Center, we have been advising our customers to keep a history of their deliverables-based estimates for future use by different project managers. Many have taken heed and have developed good historical data. Figure 4.53 shows a sample *partial list* of deliverables extracted from information supplied by some of our customers (the list is sorted alphabetically for ease of reference). In the database, each deliverable has been further defined using the template shown in Figure 4.47.

Our analysis of dozens of size estimates, developed by a variety of teams, tells us that overlooked deliverables are a major reason for underestimating. Therefore, it is important to have a colleague review the list of your deliverables before developing the size estimates for your project. Having access to a master list of deliverables similar to the one in Figure 4.53 would certainly help create a comprehensive list of deliverables for a project. In light of this concept, consider the following three questions:

1. Could a list similar to the one in Figure 4.53 (along with historical size estimates) be useful to other project managers in your department?
2. Would it help to develop accurate size estimates?
3. Does a similar list of deliverables currently exist in your department?

If your answers to the three questions are all "Yes," congratulations! If your answers are "Yes," "Yes," and "No," you should have a good talk with your colleagues and your manager and devise a plan to begin building a database of deliverables.

FIGURE 4.53
Sample List of Deliverables

Deliverables list
Application-specific data model
Approved project charter
Approved vendor list
Audit and control features list
Business case
Cost/benefit analysis report
Data conversion plan
Data dictionary
Development strategy
Disaster recovery plan
Feasibility study
Issues list
Logical data model
Phase-end review report
Physical data model
Progress tracking procedures
Project notebook
Project start-up document
Regulatory-fit analysis
Request for information (RFI)
Request for proposal (RFP)
Risk analysis report
Seminar overheads
Test data
Test plan
Training manual (instructor)
Training manual (students)
Usability test plan
Usability test results

Use of Deliverables-Based Size Estimates

Our experience shows that deliverables-based estimating is best suited for developing size estimates for the following types of projects:

- Medium size projects (4–6 months in duration). For projects lasting longer than 6 months, it would be difficult to predict what specific deliverables will need to be built 6 months hence. Therefore, for large projects, you might use the deliverables-based size estimate for the first 6-month span of the project, followed by size estimates developed using a phase-based model for the remaining project phases. For projects lasting less than 4 months, we suggest the task-based estimating technique.
- Major enhancements
- Emerging technology projects

Level of Accuracy

The level of accuracy of the size estimates developed using deliverables depends on:

1. The comprehensiveness of the list of deliverables for each project phase. Missing just a few deliverables can result in gross errors.
2. The accuracy of the assumptions regarding the resources' skills and availability.
3. Accounting for all applicable lag values.
4. The experience of the person developing the estimates. It is only after a person has developed estimates for three or four projects that he can begin to develop accurate size estimates. The size estimates for the first few tries may have several inaccuracies.

Following are a few words to the wise regarding deliverables-based size estimates:

- Make it a practice to formally review the planned list of deliverables and their ownership before finalizing your estimates.
- Do not forget any lag values due to peer group reviews, management reviews, and long approval cycles when developing the deliverables-based Gantt chart.
- Each project is subject to the vagaries of the development environment, personal work habits, management style, and a host of other related productivity issues. Make sure that your size estimate reflects the development environment accurately.
- It is always a good idea to present your estimates to a group of your peers for review and feedback before submitting them to your sponsor, manager, or customer.

Rework and Scope Growth Reserves

Before we close the subject of developing size estimates, we need to discuss two important points: the need for rework and scope growth.

Need for Rework   High complexity projects, and those that exceed 4 months of design and build time, invariably require certain rework while the project is still underway. The key reasons for rework are technology upgrades, design redefinition, latent defects, and steep learning curves. The typical work progression and associated rework can be depicted as shown in Figure 4.54.[16]

FIGURE 4.54
Project Rework Scenario

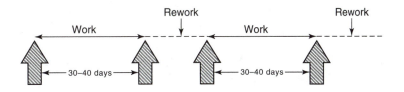

---

[16]The 30- to 40-day interval shown in the chart is not meant to imply that rework will be needed at such intervals. In real life, the frequency will vary.

FIGURE 4.55
Project Complexity and
Rework Reserves

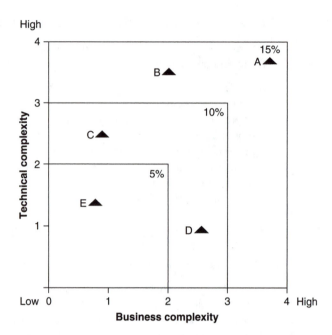

Toward the start of the project, the team does its best to do all of the right things—right architecture, right specifications, right design, and right build. However, if they have limited experience, their best can often leave much to be desired. As time passes and experience develops, the team learns what they should have known all along. Consequently, some members of the team will realize that the work they did during the past 30 to 40 days needs improvement. At this point, they have two options:

1. Rework the already finished work
2. Skip it and deal with it later

Often, the team members are forced to take the latter path because time is running out—the original estimates communicated to the customer *did not* account for this predicament. Our recommendation for rework reserves is depicted in Figure 4.55 As you can see, rework reserves of up to 15 percent are recommended for high complexity projects.[17] Figure 4.55 shows four different projects with varying complexity. Our advice is as follows:

1. Project A: If the estimated duration for this project was 100 days, add 14 days as reserve for rework.
2. Project B: If the estimated duration for this project was 100 days, add 12 days as reserve for rework.
3. Project C and Project D: If the estimated duration for these projects was 100 days each, add 8 days as reserve for rework to each estimate.
4. Project E: If the estimated duration for this project was 100 days, add 3 days as reserve for rework.

If your manager and/or your customer objects to such reserves for rework, and you cannot convince them of your point of view, at least you know the extent of overtime the team will have to work in order to deliver the project according to your estimates. Not to worry, the team will get it all back in "comp" time (sure they will).

Scope Growth   It would be accurate to state that complexity and uncertainty go hand in hand. In the case of a highly complex project (zone I), the team will face many uncertainties, resulting in

---

[17]Rework reserve and scope growth values are derived from data collected by the Center from a variety of customers. The Center's data is well corroborated by similar research in the industry.

discovery of new deliverables and tasks during the later stages of the project—the dreaded scope growth. The primary reason for scope growth in such projects is the lack of a clear understanding of the customer's business combined with a *highly unstable* development environment. Even rigorous prototyping, to define the customer's requirements and comprehensive change management procedures, *does not* preclude scope growth. Keep in mind that, as scope is added to a project, you must be concerned not only with the effort, time, and cost to incorporate the additional deliverables and features, but also with the impact the scope growth could have on the technology infrastructure. There comes a point in scope growth where any additional scope will require upgrade of the infrastructure—database, hardware, software, and telecommunications (see *Scope Growth—The Limit*, Chapter 5). Unfortunately, many project managers ignore this side effect of scope growth. A professional way to deal with the inevitable scope growth is to incorporate appropriate cost and time reserves into the project estimates and schedules. This way, when late discoveries are made, the estimates and schedules carry the appropriate effort, cost, and time reserves to allow the project team to respond in an orderly fashion. Figure 4.56 illustrates the amount of scope growth that is possible *after* the project charter has been approved. We will further discuss the process of incorporating rework and scope growth reserves into project estimates and schedules in Chapters 6 and 7.

FIGURE 4.56
Project Complexity and
Scope Growth

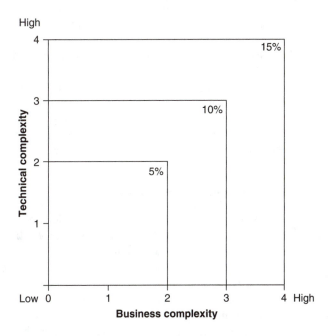

Throughout the many years of our consulting work, we continually come across managers and sponsors who show reluctance to accept the use of rework and scope growth risk reserves. Invariably, they cite the adage, "Work will expand to fill the available time." Their fear is that, if the project managers and teams are allowed these reserves, they will end up using the time and budget even if there is no real need. We believe this is a legitimate concern that must be addressed. At the same time, we do not agree with the desire of many managers and sponsors not to allow their teams any reserves based on their fear of teams mismanaging the reserves. To prove our point, we will digress for a moment to the field of financial management. A basic piece of advice given by any financial advisor to a client is to set aside a certain amount of funds for quick access in the case of emergencies. Now let us consider an individual who sets aside certain liquid assets (cash) and then spends it on nonessential purchases—vacations, expensive jewelry, and hobbies. In fact, this individual then goes into debt by spending more than the cash on hand. We can safely state that, in this case, the expenses have risen to match and exceed the savings. Now, is it the *principle* of saving that is at fault, or is it the poor *discipline* on the part the individual? It is the latter. Therefore, it is not the reserves that are the problem; it is the lack of discipline and cognizance that reserves are to be used for designated needs that creates the problem. Therefore, which of the following two items would you recommend?

1. Provide the individual with counseling, and even turn over the finances to an expert who monitors the individual's financial transactions until the person has learned sufficient discipline and is able to manage her finances.
2. Tell the person not to bother with the savings because he will misuse them regardless.

No sane person would choose the latter. Now, let us get back to the question of reserves in the case of a project. Our advice to sponsors is to make sure that the project manager and the team are appropriately educated in managing the "finances" of the project—they don't squander the reserves for nonessential deliverables and tasks. Make sure that they clearly understand that the reserves *belong* to the customer and if any are not used, they need to be *returned* to the customer. As a result, if the time (duration) reserves are not used, the project should be completed and delivered at an early date. If effort (dollar) reserves are not used, the unused funds must be credited back to the customer.

Throughout the years of consulting with a large number of project managers, we consistently advise them to develop as much reserves (time and budget) as possible during the early part of the project by implementing efficient and effective project management practices. The reason for being proactive is that there will be surprises down the line and the reserves established earlier will act as a cushion for later inevitable problems. Unfortunately, building reserves has actually caused some project managers significant problems because, when their managers and sponsors learn about the reserves, their first reaction is, "the project manager overestimated, (padded the estimates), and that is where the reserves came from." The next edict from these managers to their project managers is to add more scope and/or cut the project schedule and the budget. So much for hard work and efficiency. As a result, many project managers have learned not to develop reserves, or to hide them deep in their project schedules. Ironically, these project managers are being forced to be duplicitous (not a sign of a healthy project management environment). Our advice to sponsors and managers is not to throw away the practices of good project management just because you have not taken the time to educate your project managers and teams regarding the management of reserves set aside for future "tough" times.

Management Reserve

Within the project management profession, the two reserves already discussed, combined with contingency reserves for potential risks that are difficult to predict, are collectively known as management reserves. We have chosen to break this overriding category into three different components so that they can be planned, estimated, scheduled, and managed separately. Our experience shows that this provides the project manager with greater control over the different types of reserves.

Now that you have developed the size estimates for the proposed project, you need to compare the estimated values to the customer specified spending limits, if any (see *Spending Limits*, Chapter 3). If the size estimates are considerably higher than the customer's spending limit, you need to revisit the client and discuss the situation. Often, the customer's first reaction is, "Your estimates are too high. There is no way that it can cost that much!" We are confident that you have developed realistic estimates and can back them up. Your next action should be to direct the customer to the constraints and obstacles and the scope statement of the project. Make it clear to the customer that, in order to reduce the estimates, certain constraints and obstacles must be removed and scope may need to be cut back. The combination of these irrefutable facts and your negotiation skills will get you over this hump.

Cost of Ownership (Life Cycle Costing)

When developing estimates for a proposed project, you must keep the following three items in view:

1. Cost of the project's (end product) development
2. Cost of the project's end product maintenance and support
3. Cost of the current system's retirement, if applicable

Often, estimates include only the first of the three items (occasionally, estimates incorporate the second item). The resulting estimate will not convey the total cost of the project to the customer, who may then be surprised when other costs come into play. For example, consider a project to *replace* 100 laptop computers. In this case, the total cost of ownership of the project should include the following estimates:

1. The cost of acquiring the 100 laptops (this means the cost of the hardware, associated software, and the cost of the team's time)
2. The cost of porting current laptop resident files to the new hardware (especially the cost of the support team's time)
3. The cost of maintenance, repairs, and support of the acquired hardware and software over a specified period of time
4. The cost of retiring the current laptops. Keep in mind that the laptops can't just be tossed into the garbage dump. The hardware may need to be turned over to a disposal firm who may charge a fee for their services. (In which case they reimburse your organization for the hardware. The amount reimbursed will be deducted from the sum of the previous three estimates.)

The same logic will apply to most projects in an organization. Therefore, it is important that you find out (from the project office, if one exists) the underlying practices and policies for computing estimates for a proposed project. Throughout our many years of consulting, we have seen different people in the same organization use quite different combinations of values when computing such estimates. This disparity results in major problems when proposed projects are evaluated for their relative financial merit because one is no longer comparing apples to apples.

■ FIXED PRICE QUOTES

If you work for a commercial organization that develops software projects for its customers, your organization may be asked to submit fixed price quotes. Let us define the term before we discuss the steps to prepare a fixed price quote.

> *Quote:* The dollars at which the proposed project is promised (sold) to a customer. In the case of a fixed price quote, if it costs your company more money to complete the project than the quoted price, the customer is not obligated to reimburse the difference. At the same time, if the actual cost to complete the project is less than the quoted price, the difference is the added profit margin for your company. Keeping in mind the historical performance of IT/Business projects, the chances of the latter happening are highly unlikely, if not impossible. This means that, if not handled correctly, most of the fixed price contracts will result in lost revenue to the organization.

Therefore, it is imperative that estimates for fixed price projects be highly accurate. The key components of an accurate estimate are:

- A comprehensive WBS that encompasses the necessary product, processes, and administrative deliverables
- Realistic resource profile assumptions
- Accurate and pragmatic task network
- Appropriate rework, scope growth, and risk reserves based on project complexity
- Profit margin

Once the project team has developed the estimate, management can create the quote for the customer. Keep in mind that the terms quoted to the customer can be the same as, or higher or lower than, the estimated values. Why? Because the quote to the customer is a strategic, at times even a political, decision. Managers in professions such as automobile dealerships, real estate, manufacturing, consumer goods, and commercial software routinely practice this approach. They are all known to quote terms at, below, or above the estimated values. The decision to quote a project at a price lower than the estimate can be due to any number of situations:

- Maintain competitive position in the market.
- Use a project as a showcase to achieve market leadership and then reap greater profits from future business.

- Expect to make higher profits from the expected scope creep during the project build phase.
- Use the project to get a foot in the door of the customer's business and expect to obtain additional business with higher profit margins.

Visit any supermarket and you will find many items on sale, some of them priced at, or below, cost. These are typically known as "loss leaders." Supermarket management knows that, once customers are in the store, many will buy items that have high profit margins, thereby making up for any losses incurred on the items for sale. Hotels in Las Vegas routinely do this by offering very low room rates. It is not unusual for four-star hotels to offer rooms at $69 per night; they hope to make up the difference in their casinos and upscale restaurants (some of which have a profit margin of 25 percent or higher). If too many projects are quoted at numbers lower than what it really costs to complete them, the business will go broke.

Another commonly asked question is: "Are all IT/Business projects fit for fixed price quotes?" The answer is "No." To discuss this topic, we need to refer to the complexity chart depicted in Figure 4.20. Here are our recommendations:

- *Zone IV projects:* These projects are highly suited to fixed price quotes because of the low probability of unexpected rework, scope growth, and risks.
- *Low zone II and low zone III projects:* For these projects, we suggest that the development life cycle be broken into specific system development life cycle phases (listed below)[18] and we recommend fixed price quotes for the design, development, and implementation phases:
  - Project charter
  - Business requirements
  - System requirements
  - Design
  - Development
  - Implementation
- *High zone II and high zone III projects:* Keeping the same system development life cycle phases in mind, we recommend fixed price quotes for the development and implementation phases.
- *Zone I projects:* Not suited for fixed price quotes due to highly unstable technology and business environments.

When delving into fixed price quotes for IT/Business projects, it is important to keep the following points in mind:

- Make a highly disciplined, repeatable project management process operational (such as the PPA explained in this book).
- Include key representatives from the sales organization in the scope of your company's project management education and training program, so that they clearly understand the principles, practices, and techniques used to develop viable estimates. Without this, they are prone to quote low estimates to clients (just to sign up their business) and your team will then be stuck with completing the project within the quoted fixed price (usually through extensive unpaid overtime).
- Avoid "fairy tale assumptions."
- Ensure that a highly disciplined scope management process is in place.

■ PROJECT PRIORITY

Typically, at any given time, there are many more potential projects than can be undertaken by the organization because of resource and budgetary limitations. The problem becomes acute when a number of proposed projects align well with the stated organization strategy, but the organization does not have the resources to execute all of the projects. What are the criteria for project approval? The answer begins with a well-defined process that helps management make good decisions.

---

[18]The life cycle phase demarcation and nomenclature are for example only; these may be different in your organization.

Although the responsibility for project prioritization lies with the organization's management, it is important that project managers understand the underlying principles and practices for such prioritization. This knowledge will be of great value when your customers face the problem of more projects than they have the capacity to execute.

> *They were attempting to do many more projects than they had the capacity to do. Bad projects squeezed out good projects. There was no visibility of what was being done throughout the organization.*
>
> Ron Kifer, in Todd Datz, "Portfolio Management: How to Do It Right,"
> *CIO Magazine* (May 1, 2003).

While countless methods for project prioritization exist, we have found the following process to be very effective and easy to adapt to specific organizational needs. Our process consists of the following steps:

1. Define a uniform criteria to assess project priority
2. Define criteria weight points
3. Score each project
4. Prioritize projects

Uniform Criteria to Assess Project Priority

Uniform criteria refer to the specific metrics to be used to assess the priority of each project vying for approval. Some examples of priority criteria are as follows:

- *Cost:* The estimated cost for the proposed project (typically, this is the total cost of ownership over a given period of time)
- *Customer service:* Projects to improve customer service and customer retention, such as a call center, and Customer Relationship Management (CRM)
- *Duration:* The estimated time (months) to implement the project
- *Innovation:* Project creates new business opportunities, probability of significant future business such as ERP, and knowledge management
- *Operational necessity:* Project to ensure uninterrupted business operations, (the Y2K remediation, improved computer security)
- *Prerequisite:* A project that needs to be done before another high priority project can be started
- *Regulatory (statute):* Legislative mandate, projects to meet regulatory requirements (national, international, and local). For example, the Sarbanes-Oxley Act of 2002 (passed by the U.S. Congress to protect investors by improving the accuracy and reliability of corporate disclosures), the Health Insurance Portability and Accountability Act (HIPPA), and California law SB 1386 that requires companies to disclose information security breaches
- *Risk exposure:* The degree of business and technical risk associated with the project
- *Financial analysis:* Expected, well-documented return on the investment into the project. This may include NPV, IRR, ROI, and/or payback period (see Appendix 2).
- *Technology infrastructure:* Project designed to maintain and improve network performance, Internet connectivity, and other "utility" type service improvements. This may include projects forced upon the organization as a result of hardware and/or software vendor required upgrades (loss of support and maintenance by a vendor).

We advise our clients to limit the list of assessment criteria to a maximum of ten items; a longer list of items makes the assessment process unwieldy.

Define Criteria Weight Points

The next step is to assign weight points to the various items in the selected list. The idea is to take a standard total value, usually 100, and spread it among the various assessment items. The weight points could be evenly distributed or could have a bias toward certain items. Figure 4.57 depicts the weight points used by one of the Center's clients.

FIGURE 4.57
Project Priority Assessment
Scorecard

Project priority criteria	Weight points	Project points
Cost	10	
Customer service	15	
Duration	10	
Innovation	10	
Operations necessity	10	
Prerequisite	5	
Regulatory (statute)	15	
Risk exposure	10	
Financial analysis	10	
Technology infrastructure	5	
Total	**100**	

Score Each Project

For each proposed project, the appropriate management group (with advice and assistance from IT) scores the project for its relative value by entering a numeric value in the rightmost column (*project points*) of Figure 4.58. The criteria for assigning project points to a given project are:

- *Cost:* A value between 1 and 10. The lower the cost, the higher the value. Responsibility: business unit and IT
- *Customer service:* A value between 1 and 15; the bigger the improvement, the higher the value. Responsibility: business unit
- *Duration:* A value between 1 and 10; the shorter the duration, the higher the value. Responsibility: IT and business unit
- *Innovation:* A value between 1 and 10; the greater the innovation, the higher the value. Responsibility: business unit
- *Operational necessity:* A value between 1 and 10; the greater the necessity, the higher the value. Responsibility: business unit
- *Prerequisite:* A value between 1 and 5; the greater the need, the higher the value. Responsibility: IT and business unit
- *Regulatory (statue):* A value between 1 and 15; the greater the penalty (exposure) for noncompliance, the higher the value. If there is no regulatory mandate, then the value is 0. Responsibility: business unit
- *Risk exposure:* A value between 1 and 10; the lower the risk, the higher the value. Responsibility: IT and business unit

FIGURE 4.58
Project Priority Assessment
Scorecard

Project priority criteria	Weight points	Project points
Cost	10	10
Customer service	15	8
Duration	10	5
Innovation	10	5
Operations necessity	10	8
Prerequisite	5	0
Regulatory (statute)	15	0
Risk exposure	10	7
Financial analysis	10	7
Technology infrastructure	5	0
Total	**100**	**50**

- *Financial analysis:* A value between 1 and 10; the greater the financial return, the higher the value. Responsibility: business unit
- *Technology infrastructure:* A value between 1 and 5; the greater the necessity, the higher the value. Responsibility: IT

The value for any given project point item must be within the range of the corresponding weight point for that item. A summation of the various values in the project points column of Figure 4.58 will reflect the relative priority of the project. The primary responsibility for input to the assessment lies with the business unit(s) proposing the project, while IT plays a secondary role with responsibility for more "technical" information.

> *I believe that all of this is the responsibility of those managing the business. It must be the user managers who determine what systems they need to get the job done.*
> Paul Ingevaldson, Senior VP, Ace Hardware, "It's Not Your IT Portfolio—
> It's Theirs," *CIO Magazine* (November 15, 2002).

Prioritize Projects

Once the priority assessment steps have been completed for projects competing for approval, management can use the information to establish their relative priority. Figure 4.59 shows the assessment of five projects. If the organization had the capacity to undertake only three projects, the projects to consider would be Project C, Project E, and Project D.

FIGURE 4.59
Project Priority Assessment
(Multiple Projects)

Project ID	Priority value
Project A	50
Project B	60
Project C	90
Project D	78
Project E	80

The priority assessment criteria carry a number of important caveats:

- Deciding on the number of criteria items and their specific weight points will require extensive discussion among key project sponsors before an agreement is reached.
- You should pilot the agreed upon criteria list using a number of projects to test the algorithm for its stated purpose—helping management decide on the relative priority of a group of projects.
- Once a final agreement is reached, it is not a good idea to change either the list of items or their weight points midstream. If needed, changes should be considered at the start of the next budget cycle (when most projects are proposed and approved).

Keep in mind, the purpose of this assessment is *not* for project justification; it is to define the *relative priority* among a group of projects. Although one size does not fit all when it comes to project prioritization, we have found the process outlined above very workable and easy to tailor to fit individual organizational needs.

■ SPECIAL RECOMMENDATIONS

Over the many years of consulting with a large number of IT/Business project managers, we have found that zone I projects possess certain characteristics that require special attention from senior management. We have used a side heading titled special recommendations to spotlight the underlying problems and to summarize possible solutions and alternatives. Following is an example of such a recommendation.

- A large number of internal and external business, support, and regulatory agencies are involved, some of them have divergent or conflicting, interests. Complicating the matter is the fact that not all of these entities report to the project sponsor. The conceptual build of the project shows that long-standing relationships and well-established business practices will be significantly altered, resulting in dramatically changed organizational structures, duties, and responsibilities. Individual compensation mechanisms and procedures will also need revisiting and revision. Ongoing operations must be maintained, despite the fact that the business infrastructure will be undergoing considerable changes. An analogy that comes to mind is operating on all of the vital organs simultaneously—risks should be obvious and must be managed. The short-term operating results will inevitably take a hit, as management's attention and marketing and sales activities are diverted by the energy required to proceed with the proposed project. Not only will the profitability be impacted negatively, but the personnel turnover is likely to increase as individuals, many high performers, sort out the personal impact of changes they observe but do not fully comprehend. The problem of turnover may be further exacerbated if the proposed project is seen as being challenged by our key employees. In light of the obvious complexity and the inherent risks of the proposed project, it is imperative that senior management takes the following actions:
  1. Name a fully committed and accountable sponsor who has ultimate responsibility for the success of the project. To be successful, the sponsor will need strong visible support throughout the organization. Although not a full-time assignment, the sponsor would be assuming a significant responsibility—one that would consume a majority of the person's time and energy over the project duration.
  2. Assign a full-time project manager who has a strong functional background, good grounding in the technology to be used to develop and deliver the project, substantial political clout, and a broad range of personal skills. The project manager must be both empowered and permitted to literally manage the project.

As you can see, the person making the recommendation has targeted the key areas that can have considerable impact on the success or failure of the project.

Build or Buy (Procurement)

As a part of your Project Charter completion work, you may be asked to investigate the build or buy options (whether the project should be carried out in-house or be contracted with an outside organization). If the latter is an option worth considering, you will need to delve into the steps to identify, assess, and select one or more qualified vendor/contractors to undertake the project. This means that you and your team will not be executing most of the steps outlined in the Launch and Execute stages of the PPA (Chapters 5, 6, and 7) because that work will be carried out by the selected vendor/contractor. For an introduction to the vendor/contractor selection process, refer to Appendix 1, *Procurement Planning*. In the case of a buy decision, you still need to be appropriately skilled in the various steps, skills, techniques, tools, and processes described in Chapters 5, 6, and 7, because you will need to oversee the work of one or more outside parties. It will be your responsibility to make sure that the selected vendor/contractor performs to the right level of project management discipline. If not, your project will likely contribute to the high statistics of challenged and failed projects.

■ PROJECT CHARTER—PPA STEP 15

A Project Charter is the principal item of project documentation that is presented to an appropriate level decision maker, often the proposed project sponsor, for review and approval. The length and formality of the document should correspond to the importance of the venture and its inherent cost and risks. It must contain enough information to enable the decision makers to make an intelligent and informed decision. Many organizations have their own formats and templates for Project Charters, and it is a good idea to find out if such a template exists. Even then, many sponsors have their personal preferences regarding the manner in which the information is organized within a proposed Charter. The person responsible for compiling the Charter should discuss the contents and the organization of the document with the individual who will be the final signatory to the Charter. This way, any last-minute scrambling to reorganize the final document can be avoided. A comprehensive, alphabetically sorted list of side headings of a Project Charter follows. The list is quite long and you will need to select appropriate items to fit the needs of your organization's policies and procedures. In addition, while developing a table of contents for your Project Charter, you will need to organize the selected items in a logical (not alphabetic) order. You should work with your fellow project managers and the appropriate departmental manager(s) to develop a standard template to be used by all project managers.

Project Charter Components

Alternatives	Nature of the project
Areas of impact	Objectives
Assumptions	Ownership
Authorizations	Project complexity
Background and current situation	Project description
Business requirements (customer needs)	Project duplication/overlap
Charter authorizations	Project priority
Charter ID	Proposed project manager
Competitive analysis	Proposed name for the project
Conceptual build (key deliverables)	Proposed sponsor
Consequences of doing nothing	Regulatory agency policies and procedures
Constraints and obstacles	Risk assessment
Critical success factors	Runaway triggers
Customer acceptance criteria	Scope statement: current scope, future
Executive summary	opportunities, and out of scope
Expiration date	Security requirements
Financial justification	Shutdown conditions
Funding source	Side effects
Glossary	Size estimates: cost, duration, and resources
Impact assessment	Special recommendations
Industry policies and procedures	Spending limit
Intraproject priorities	Stakeholders: Policy-level, Implementation-
Issues	level
Key deadline(s)	Strategy alignment
Key words	Tactical fit with other projects
Lessons from history of previous projects	Value-to-business
Market window	Window of opportunity
Measure of success	

We would like to draw your attention to three items from the list:

Expiration Date   This is the date after which the current Project Charter will expire—it will need to be formally reviewed to make sure that critical changes have not taken place to impact the essence of the Project Charter. Most of the Center's clients use a number between 30 and 45 days from the date of the approval of the Charter. The following scenario provides a compelling rationale for the use of an expiration date: Over the years, we have seen Project Charters approved and then, because of the lack of the needed resources (people, dollars, and/or technology), the Charter is simply filed away. Sometime later, someone in the organization sends a message and, a team picks up the Charter and begins to work on it. After even more time, the project manager contacts the customer to resolve some issue and the customer's response is, "We don't need that anymore, things have changed." Or, "Because we did not hear from anyone in the project group, we hired our own resources and they are working on it." Or, "The person who requested it is not here anymore, so we don't really know much about the project you are talking about." Each of these responses would mean that whatever work the team put into the project is now a total loss.

After a number of the Center's clients instituted the use of the expiration date, they became aware of the large number of effort hours spent on Charters that would run out of time. At one client site, the total number of expired Charters reached 44. At an average of 135 hours per Charter, this meant a lost investment of over $700,000 (they used a burdened hourly rate of $120 for their resources responsible for Charter development work). We believed the loss figure was underestimated, as it did not include the time spent by customers, SMEs, and managers. With their time accounted for, the investment loss was over $1 million.

Glossary   With all the confusing acronyms around, it is important to have quick access to their meanings. A comprehensive glossary is especially important because, in the case of a cross-functional project, the same acronym can have different meaning. For example the commonly used acronym "CRM" means "customer relationship management" to IT professionals, while for someone in the crew-scheduling department of an airline it stands for "crew resource management." Additionally, as much as one wishes to stay away from colloquialisms, certain terms become a common part of a group's vocabulary but may be confusing to team members across wide geographic locations, especially overseas. If such terms are used, make sure that they are fully explained in the glossary. The glossary is a part of the Charter that should be available online for quick and easy access.

Key Words   An important question at the start of any project is, "Are there any duplicate or overlapping projects already in place or in progress?" Often, this question is difficult to answer without having a central repository of project information—a comprehensive and up-to-date project portfolio. Even when such a portfolio becomes available, searching for duplicate and overlapping projects can be a challenge without embedding specific search keys. Therefore, we strongly recommend the use of a separate field within the Project Charter document, where specific search-oriented words can be recorded to help discover duplicate and overlapping projects.

We have discussed, in detail, the contents of a charter. Now let us discuss a couple of items that should *not* be included in a Project Charter. The following items are culled from a number of Charters we have had the opportunity to review:

Items that Should Not be Included in a Project Charter

Project ID   We believe that a unique Project ID should be assigned to each project *after* the Project Charter has been approved *and* the project is moved to the Launch stage. One of the first actions by the project manager in the Launch stage would be to obtain a unique project ID. Assigning a project ID to a Project Charter would imply that the Charter has already been approved, which is not the case. An *officially unique* name will be assigned to the proposed project as part of the first few activities in the Launch stage.

Summary Project Schedule   We see this quite often and find it troublesome. To develop a viable schedule, one needs a task-level WBS, a task network based on specific resource assumptions, and the work calendars of the proposed team. Any schedule developed at this early point in the project life cycle, summary or not, can reflect little more than wishful thinking. Inclusion of a schedule also implies that the project has been approved and is ready to be started. This cannot be the case because the key reason for a Charter is to obtain specific approval to start the proposed project. However, the customer's desired delivery date or the specified deadline, if one exists, can be included at this point.

Charter Assembly

By now, you have completed all of the requisite steps of the Pre-Launch stage for the proposed project and are finally ready to assemble the Project Charter for submittal to the sponsor for review and approval. However, before you do that, we recommend that you assess the quality of the work performed to complete the Pre-Launch stage. The best approach for this assessment is to start with the template depicted in Figure 4.60.

FIGURE 4.60
Pre-Launch Stage—Project Outlook Assessment

Prelaunch step	Applicable		Level of confidence					Action plan
3. Project description	Yes	No	1	2	3	4	5	
4. Intraproject priority analysis	Yes	No	1	2	3	4	5	
5. Stakeholder analysis	Yes	No	1	2	3	4	5	
6. Complexity assessment	Yes	No	1	2	3	4	5	
7. Policies, procedures, and standards	Yes	No	1	2	3	4	5	
8. Impact assessment	Yes	No	1	2	3	4	5	
9. Constraints and obstacles	Yes	No	1	2	3	4	5	
10. Stability assessment	Yes	No	1	2	3	4	5	
11. Issues management	Yes	No	1	2	3	4	5	
12. Risk assessment	Yes	No	1	2	3	4	5	
13. Preliminary scope statement	Yes	No	1	2	3	4	5	
14. Project size estimate	Yes	No	1	2	3	4	5	

In the first column is a list of all of the steps of the Pre-Launch stage. As you may not have selected all of the steps, indicate your selection by circling "Yes" or "No" for each selected step. Another approach is to simply list only those steps that you selected for the project at hand and delete the second column from the chart. The next step is to assess the quality of work done to complete each of the selected steps, using the scale values between 1 and 5 (where 1 designates poor quality work and 5 indicates a high quality of work). For this assessment to have any value, one needs to be forthright in one's responses. A good way to arrive at accurate values is to ask one or two of your key team members, who were involved in doing the work with you, to independently develop their assessment. Then, you can compare the different assessed values and arrive at a consensus. If you did all of the work alone, ask an experienced colleague to review your work and provide her assessment to you. This type of independent review can be quite helpful. If any of the individual items is rated below 3.0, we suggest a review of the work done to complete that item to see what needs to be done to improve the quality rating to 3.0 or above (you can design a similar outlook assessment for any other stage). Once you are satisfied with the quality of the work on all items, you are now ready to assemble your Project Charter.

Do not lock yourself in your office and single-handedly compose the Project Charter. It is extremely important that you invite the appropriate business unit representative(s) to work with you to complete the Charter. If they are hesitant to get involved (don't have the time, have other important things to do, trust you fully in doing the right things), you should view their behavior as a definite early warning that their interest level in the proposed project is low. To us, this indifference is a clear signal not to proceed with the project because their current behavior is a harbinger of a challenged and failed project.

Look over your shoulder now and then to be sure somebody's following you.

Gilmer's Motto for Political Leadership,
http://membres.lycos.fr/TheWalrus/g.html.

Charter Approval

Getting the Charter approved can take from hours to days, largely depending on the extent of controversy surrounding the project's objectives, risks, and scope. In the simplest of cases, the sponsor is also the final authority on the charter, so approval is relatively straightforward. For large projects (and particularly for large cross-functional projects) the sponsor may be required to seek approval from a higher authority—perhaps even the general manager and executive committee. Good communications between the sponsor and the project manager are the key to speedy approval. This suggests that the two individuals reach a clear understanding on all matters of substance: most importantly, the project objectives and scope and the roles each of them expect to play in managing the project.

As we mentioned toward the start of this chapter, even though a project manager eventually ends up with the responsibility to compose the Project Charter, we strongly believe that the Charter is still *owned* by the business customer who proposed the project. Therefore, the final responsibility for obtaining Charter approval lies with the customer. This leads us to two important questions:

1. Will every Project Charter be approved?
2. Does disapproval mean a failure on the part of the group responsible for developing the Project Charter?

The answers are "No" and "No." The very purpose of the Pre-Launch stage is to conduct up front due diligence to assess the viability of a proposed project. Discovering information that shows that the proposed project is not worthy of investing organizational resources is a mark of success. One of the positive outcomes of a comprehensive Pre-Launch is discovering the weaknesses in the proposed project and then restructuring the proposal to make it attractive.

Our experience with a number of our clients shows that *at least* 20 percent of the proposed projects were crossed off the "to do" list when the practice of forthright due diligence was consistently supported by management. In some organizations, this number approaches 30 percent. As a result, these organizations are undertaking fewer questionable projects and bringing more projects to successful completion.

The Signing Ceremony

We strongly believe that a Project Charter should actually be viewed as a *contract*. The signatories are the proposed sponsor and the key stakeholders. To us, these signatures mean the following:

- A sponsor has been assigned and he has accepted and approved the proposed project.
- The key stakeholders understand and agree with the Charter and are committing to provide the necessary resources and support to the project team.

Once the Charter is approved, it then serves as the basis for the project plan and it must be kept updated throughout the project life cycle. Once the Charter is signed, the project manager should make a copy and file it away as Version 0 (if using an electronic media, make Version 0 a read-only file). As the work on the project progresses and any changes need to be made to the charter, do not change the Version 0 document. This way, at any given time, one can compare the Version 0 charter with the latest edition. We further suggest that the project manager save the pen(s) used to sign the Charter and distribute them at the award ceremony to be held to celebrate the successful completion of the project.

The Moment of Truth

Inevitably, a proposed project of a difficult nature will arise. It may result in massive layoffs, a reduction of services and benefits to selected rank and file, or it may clash with your personal (social, religious, cultural) beliefs. The question is, "Will you have the ability to lead the team to successful project completion with the requisite leadership, and at the same time be at peace with yourself?" If the answer is "No," you will have some difficult decisions to make.

■ PRE-LAUNCH STAGE BENEFITS

Before we discuss the benefits of all the work needed to complete the Pre-Launch of a project, let us look into the state of IT/Business project management. Consider the following two quotations:

> *The dark side of the corporate information revolution is coming into view. Companies across the country are seeing their cutting-edge computer systems fail to live up to expectations—or fail altogether. . . . The waste is staggering. . . . 42% of corporate information-technology projects were abandoned before completion.*
> Bernard Wysocki Jr., "Pulling the Plug," *The Wall Street Journal* (April 30, 1998: p. A1).

> *Between 1996 and 2000, companies invested $1.7 trillion in technology—nearly double the amount spent in the previous five years, according to the U.S. Bureau of Economic Analysis.*
> Peter Burrows, "The Era of Efficiency." *Business Week* (June 18, 2001).

This combination of colossal failures and huge investments has its roots in the dismal project management discipline practiced by far too many IT/Business organizations. As we pointed out earlier, many projects follow the following life cycle:

1. Have vision
2. Conjure a deadline
3. State cursory requirements
4. Throw requirements over the wall
5. Project manager with velcro suit passing by
6. Project manager acquires hardware and software
7. Project team spends time and money
8. Deliver dysfunctional and poor quality products
9. Have more visions

Is this too disparaging? Not if one looks at the extraordinarily high rate of challenged and failed projects. Therefore, we strongly advise the disciplined due diligence of the Pre-Launch stage to filter out any half-baked ideas that may have escaped the filtering system of the Idea stage. Additionally, the various steps in this stage further help the project manager to analyze the vagaries that are inherent in any new idea. Collectively, the various steps in the Pre-Launch stage accomplish the following important objectices:

* Alleviate management fears and apprehensions
* Allow management to decide, up-front, whether a project is viable before effort is extended
* Clarify customers' goals and objectives
* Define accountability
* Help illuminate political factors
* Identify constraints and obstacles
* Identify risks
* Improve probability of success by involving key stakeholders up front
* Increase sponsor involvement
* Minimize indecision by key departments by providing clear and concise goals and objectives
* Reduce wasted and duplicated effort
* Test sponsor's support

■ STAGE GATE NO. 2

At this point, the sponsor must decide whether to allow the Project Charter to move to the Launch stage. Figure 4.61 depicts a template typically used to help make the Go/No Go decision.

Strategy Alignment: The value of 5 means that the project is still fully aligned with the stated organizational strategy.
Value-to-Business: The value of 5 means that the sponsor and key stakeholders still see a high value to this project.

FIGURE 4.61
Stage Gate No. 2—
Pre-Launch Stage

Stage gate no. 2: attributes	Confidence level					Action plan
1. Strategy alignment	1	2	3	4	5	
2. Value-to-business	1	2	3	4	5	
3. Ownership	1	2	3	4	5	
4. Project charter	1	2	3	4	5	
5. Sponsor	1	2	3	4	5	
6. Project manager	1	2	3	4	5	
7. Project team	1	2	3	4	5	
8. Customer buy-in	1	2	3	4	5	
9. Project duplication/overlap	1	2	3	4	5	

Ownership: The value of 5 means that a specific department, group, or individual has been identified. The owner is fully prepared to take ownership of the project once it goes into the Operation stage.

Project Charter: The value of 5 implies that the project charter was comprehensive and fully accepted by the sponsor and the key stakeholders.

Sponsor: The value of 5 means that an appropriately placed, committed sponsor is in place to lead the project.

Project Manager: The value of 5 means that an appropriately skilled project manager is ready to start with the next project stage.

Project Team: The value of 5 means that the project manager will be able to assemble a skilled team for this project without any hitches.

Customer Buy-In: The value of 5 means that there is still a high customer buy-in of the proposed project.

Project Duplication/Overlap: The value of 5 means that there are no duplicate or overlapping projects in progress or in production.

We will reiterate the stage gate review process here.

1. The project manager and the core team meet to assess the degree to which each of the attributes has been accomplished. To make the assessment useful, we suggest that the team members, under the facilitation of the project manager, collectively review their work products and decide on the quality of each item. In Figure 4.60, in the *confidence level* column, the value of 1 implies low quality or incomplete work, and the value of 5 implies high quality and comprehensive work.

2. In any such assessment, differences of opinions on the value of some of the items in the list are likely to occur. The project manager should encourage well-focused discussions of any such item and make a note of key points raised by different team members. Any item with a value lower than 3 means low quality or incomplete work that, if not corrected, will result in problems during the future project stages. A better approach to ensure that the stage gate review passes muster is to check the quality of the work for any given item as it is completed, rather than waiting to do the assessment at this late point. If an ongoing assessment process had been followed, the team meeting at this point would be short and sweet.

3. Once the team has finished the assessment, the project manager meets with the sponsor to review the assessment. At the end of this review session, the sponsor decides whether to open stage gate no. 2 to let the team proceed to the Launch stage, or have the team improve any of the low quality or incomplete work products. Occasionally, the sponsor may open the stage gate even if certain items are not up to par. This *conditional* approval implies that the team will remedy the situation to the sponsor's satisfaction in the near future. For example, the sponsor may find that there could be a problem assembling a skilled team because two current projects have been delayed and some of the team members for the proposed project were going to be transferred from those projects. However, the sponsor feels that the problem could be resolved by delaying the start of the proposed project. If a conditional approval is given, the condition itself is recorded as an issue and a must resolve date is specified. It becomes the project manager's responsibility to track the issue and report its resolution to the sponsor in a timely manner.

4. Another possibility is to move the project to the suspend portfolio or the canceled project portfolio (refer to Chapter 10).

■ ORDER OF PPA STEPS

At this point, let us address the question raised at the start of the chapter: Is there a specific sequence in which the various steps of the Pre-Launch stage need to be executed?

Figure 4.62 depicts our recommendation.

Begin with step 3 and you can then start working on steps 4 through 6: Intra-Project Priority Analysis, Stakeholder Analysis, and Complexity Assessment. It is not necessary to *completely* finish one step before starting the next step. You will discover that the process of completing the various steps is iterative—no one step may be completely finished as you start on a new step, and you may revisit

FIGURE 4.62
Suggested Execution Order
of Pre-Launch Stage Steps

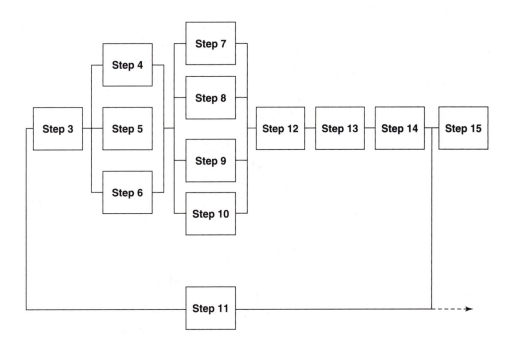

some of the steps more than once. The underlying theme of this stage is research, which is not a purely linear activity. You may find yourself stuck in a given step, waiting to hear from different people, when it becomes necessary to begin another step. Typically, Complexity Assessment (step 6) is a good indicator of the level of detail and depth one needs to go through for the remaining steps—the higher the complexity, the more detail and depth will be required. Once step 6 is complete, you can start on steps 7 through 10 (notice that in Figure 4.62, these four steps are shown in parallel to each other):

Step 7: Policies, Procedures, and Standards
Step 8: Impact Assessment
Step 9: Constraints and Obstacles
Step 10: Stability Assessment

At this point the remaining four steps, 12 through 15 can be executed:

Step 12: Risk Assessment
Step 13: Preliminary Scope Statement
Step 14: Project Size Estimate
Step 15: Project Charter

Notice that these four steps have a finish-to-start relationship. Step 11, will stay active throughout the stage. Also, notice the dotted line extending to the right. This is to denote that issues will continue to arise throughout the project life cycle and will need to be managed continuously.

As we discussed in Chapter 1, the PPA can be scaled to fit the size and complexity of a given project. Complex projects will require more of the steps as well as more rigor, while simpler projects will do well with fewer steps and less rigor. Please refer to Figure 1.12 for the steps recommended for simple, average, complex, and very complex projects.

■ SUMMARY

A disciplined Pre-Launch helps to describe the proposed project clearly and succinctly, lays out the conceptual build, identifies the key stakeholders, assesses the complexity of the proposed venture, defines the magnitude of its impact on the organization, ascertains associated risks, and describes the scope of the proposed work.

A well-executed Pre-Launch results in the preparation of a comprehensive Project Charter—a proposal to management for their Go/No Go decision. Having painted such an attractive picture of the Pre-Launch stage, one would assume that most project managers would follow the process most of the time. In fact, one would assume that corporate management would *insist* on the use of the process universally. Unfortunately, that is not the case. Far too often, the reaction we get from many corporate executives and their project managers can be summarized as follows:

> *It will take too much time to write a comprehensive Project Charter. We don't have the skills, it seems too bureaucratic, I was just told to get the project done fast and I don't have any time for formalities. My customer is not ready to wait for a Project Charter; they already know what they want. We are using this new and improved product development methodology that tells us to take risks, trust the customer, be creative, and just do it.*

These responses remind us of the Wheel of Half-Baked Ideas, and the start of the proverbial progressive regression. However, all is not lost. More and more, we come across sponsors who are beginning to see the value of the due diligence and the importance of developing a comprehensive Project Charter. Recently, in a seminar conducted by one of the Center's consultants, on the second day, a senior business executive exclaimed that he had seen the light. On the third day, he announced that his team was preparing a Charter for his big and sensitive project, even though they were beyond the Pre-Launch part of their project.

Following is a list of the key subject areas covered in this chapter. We invite you to review the list and assess your level of comprehension of each topic. The best approach is to take a separate sheet of paper and write a short narrative to explain your knowledge of the topic and then go back and compare your summaries with the material covered in the chapter. Another approach is to find a colleague who is also interested in these topics and discuss your understanding of the topics with her and then jointly review the chapter materials to assess your degree of understanding.

- Pre-Launch stage of the PPA
- Project description
- Stakeholder analysis
- Intraproject priorities
- Complexity assessment
- Value to business *v.* project complexity
- Policies, procedures, and standards
- Impact assessment
- Constraints and obstacles
- Stability assessment
- Issue management
- Risk assessment
- Developing project scope statement
- Scope chunking
- Developing size estimates
- Use of range values in estimates
- Rework and scope growth
- Project outlook assessment
- Assemble the Project Charter
- The signing ceremony
- Stage gate review

■ QUESTIONS AND DISCUSSION POINTS

1. What is the key purpose of the Pre-Launch stage of the PPA?

2. How many steps does the Pre-Launch stage contain, and can you name each step (don't worry about the order)?

3. Who has the primary responsibility for completing the various steps of the Pre-Launch stage?

4. What process group of PMBOK does the Pre-Launch stage relate to?

5. When defining project objectives, what are the key considerations?

6. What does the acronym "SMART" stand for, and why is the concept important?

7. What is the purpose of discussing and defining the side effects of a proposed project?

8. What is so important about focusing on assumptions this early in the project life cycle? If any of the key assumptions change during the life cycle of a project, what actions should the project manager take?

9. What is the value of discussing the project's runaway triggers and shutdown conditions? Who should elucidate these items?

10. Name the four Intra-Project Priorities. Why is it important to rank order the various priorities?

11. If a sponsor and/or key customer wishes to have more than one of the priorities ranked at the same level, what problems could it cause? How would you handle such a situation?

12. Once prioritized, can Intra-Project Priority rankings be changed?

13. How do policy level stakeholders differ from implementation-level stakeholders?

14. When assessing the implementation level stakeholders, what are the key areas of focus?

15. What are the different categories of stakeholder behaviors (responses) toward a project?

16. In this chapter, we presented three scenarios where the stakeholder interests were overlooked. Can you relate to any of the examples? Can you think of any similar situations? What were their outcomes?

17. What are the two key drivers of project complexity?

18. What is the importance and value of assessing a proposed project's complexity?

19. Do you know of any situations where complexity was not appropriately assessed? What were the outcomes?

20. Why is it important to relate a project's complexity to its value to business?

21. What important information does the Stability Assessment (PPA step 10) produce? How can this information be used to improve the success of the project?

22. Why is it important to track issues in a project?

23. What is risk? What is a risk trigger?

24. What are the various responses to risk discussed in this chapter? Give a brief example of each type of risk response, using examples of both business and personal risk situations.

25. Once you accept a risk, what type of plan is used to manage it?

26. What is a contingency plan? What type of risk warrants a contingency plan?

27. Why develop a scope statement? What are the characteristics of a good scope statement? Why document the "out of scope" items?

28. What does scope "chunking" mean? What are its benefits?

29. What is a size estimate?

30. What are some methods (models) used to compute the size estimate of a project?

31. Briefly describe the key steps in developing a size estimate using the phase-based model.

32. What does "calibrate the historical phase-based model" mean? What role does model calibration play in computing size estimates?

33. What role does the computation of OFTE resources play in computing the phase-based size estimates?

34. What is the meaning of PFTE resources?

35. Why should the value of PFTE always be equal to or less than the OFTE? What if more people than indicated by the OFTE are easily available?

36. When computing the estimates for a proposed project, other than the team's effort (cost) estimates, what other types of estimates need to be included? Why?

37. What is the difference between cost to develop and cost to own?

38. What would be the purpose of using phase overlaps when computing estimated duration of a project?

39. What impact can phase overlaps have on the number of resources needed for a project?

40. What is a deliverables-based size estimate? How is it different from the phase-based model? Why use a deliverables-based size estimate instead of the phasebased model?

41. Why consider rework and scope growth reserves when developing size estimates?

42. What are some of the reasons for specifying range values to estimates?

43. What is the final key document produced toward the end of the Pre-Launch stage?

44. Why specify an expiration date for a Project Charter?

45. What role does the project sponsor play when the Project Charter is being developed?

46. Who should sign the Project Charter? Why?

47. What is the purpose of the stage gate at the end of the Pre-Launch stage?

48. Can you recall any of the quotations used in this chapter? If so, why this quotation?

5 LAUNCH STAGE: PLANNING

OBJECTIVES

In this chapter, you will learn about the following project management elements:

- Launch stage of the PPA
- Project kickoff (staging) meeting
- Project organization models
- Team size
- Project task plan
- Prototyping plan
- Organization change management plan
- Scope management plan
- The Velcro suit
- Change control board
- Staffing plan
- Sponsor's roles and responsibilities
- Intelligent disobedience
- The Forty questions
- The Kiviat chart
- Roles and responsibilities of the project manager's supervisor
- Roles and responsibilities of functional managers
- Project manager's roles and responsibilities
- Project manager's skills and competencies
- Dumb mistakes and good traits
- Team selection and teamwork
- Cross-functional teams
- Conflict management and team motivation
- Active listening
- Communications Plan
- Project Notebook
- Characteristics of a sound project plan

Chapter 5 deals with the planning portion of the Launch stage of the PPA. It starts with the very important step, Project Staging, which explains the importance and the methodology behind launching a project properly. Project managers often overlook this step, resulting in a haphazard start and often culminating in miscommunications and challenged outcomes. The importance of designing a suitable project organization structure for the project is discussed, followed by a discussion of developing a comprehensive project task plan. Once the task plan is ready, the project manager is asked to pay special attention to the steps needed to prepare key stakeholders for the changes brought on by the project as well as the steps to manage the changes to the project scope. Next we discuss the ways and means of staffing and structuring the project team, the development of a comprehensive Project Notebook, and the steps needed to assess the soundness of the project plan.

■ LAUNCH STAGE—AN OVERVIEW

Let us take stock of what has transpired up to this point. Someone in the organization had an idea that, if properly implemented, would either solve an important problem or add value to the organization. During the Idea Stage the proposed idea was analyzed, investigated, evaluated, and then turned into a Project Request. The finished request was further evaluated through the Idea stage's stage gate review and an appropriately authorized person decided that it was viable and should be moved to the Pre-Launch stage. During Pre-Launch, the proposed project went through a series of assessments and the result was a Project Charter—a proposal to management to seek their approval for going forward. Arriving at the Launch stage means that the Project Charter was deemed worthy of further investigation—the development of a detailed plan and estimate. At the end of the Launch stage, management will be presented with the updated Project Charter and a detailed estimate. If the charter and the estimate meet management expectations, and the proposed project is deemed viable, the project will proceed to the Execute stage and work to complete the project will begin. The focus of the Pre-Launch stage was on *whether or not* to do the project. The focus of the Launch stage will be on *how* to do the project. Launch stage activity centers on the following key components of a project:

- Project Staging
- Developing a comprehensive plan
- Designing a team organization
- Starting the Project Notebook
- Developing Detailed Estimates
- Updating the Project Charter
- Obtaining management approval

Figure 5.1 depicts the steps that compose the Launch stage.

As you can see, the Launch stage consists of a total of eleven possible steps. The project manager chooses the appropriate steps to fit the size, complexity, and importance of the project at hand. Additionally, the effort and time spent on any given step must be adjusted in proportion to the complexity and size of the project. For our suggestions regarding the selection of steps, please refer to Figure 1.12. Regarding the question about the specific order in which the various steps need to be undertaken, let us wait until the end of Chapter 6 (once we have discussed all of the Launch stage steps).

■ LAUNCH STAGE RESPONSIBILITY

The responsibility for completing the various steps of the Launch stage falls upon the project manager and a small number of core team members. We will discuss the team structure and staffing later in this chapter.

■ PROJECT STAGING—PPA STEP 16

Two words that best explain the purpose of this step are "gathering" and "assembly." In this step, the project manager gathers or assembles the infrastructure of the project, getting things ready to start the project. The activities in this step can be compared to the advance work done before an important person comes into town—a politician, a celebrity, or an author on tour. The work is usually handled

FIGURE 5.1
Launch Stage

Plans & estimates
16. Project staging
17. Project organization
18. Task plan
19. Prototyping plan
20. Organization change management plan
21. Scope management plan
22. Staffing plan
23. Communications plan
24. Project notebook
25. Detailed estimates
26. Project charter review & budget approval

by a small number of experienced people who have the wherewithal to get things done on their own. Their responsibility is to "scope the landscape" and prepare for a smooth start. Another example of staging a project is the work done at a construction site before the construction actually begins—move in a trailer as a temporary office, figure out the parking area for delivery trucks and the crew, and just walk the terrain to get familiar with the site. Although competent preparation is an extremely important step, it is not often discussed adequately in project management literature. As a result, too many projects tend to have an erratic start, the team loses precious time, and the project appears to be out of control right from the beginning. We recommend a more orchestrated project start. The degree of work done will depend both on the size of the proposed project and how much experience the project manager has with the organization's polices, procedures, and guidelines. It depends on the connections the project manager has with the people who can help the project manager get things done quickly. Therefore, our advice is to go out and build connections—show up in the offices of the right people, introduce yourself, and get to know them long before you need their help.

Let us discuss the role of the sponsor in this step. In fact, the staging step can be a test of the sponsor's interest and commitment as well as how effectively the sponsor might relate to the project, once it starts. However, before we discuss that matter, let us first focus on you, the project manager. "The powers that be" had strong confidence in your abilities to bring this important project to success, which is why you were selected for the position. Congratulations. We hope you were not chosen by one of those selection processes one sees in some military movies where the sergeant lines up new recruits and announces, "I have a very important assignment and would like a volunteer. If you would like to volunteer, please take one step forward." Suddenly, one recruit finds that he has volunteered because everyone else took a step backward. Potential project managers, in any organization, who indulge in such a haphazard recruitment process must have good peripheral vision.

Now that you are the project manager, the first thing to do is search out the approved copy of the Project Charter and verify that the expiration date is in the future. Your next step should be an in-depth review of the charter (if you are not the one who did most of the work during the project's Pre-Launch). Your review should focus on the following items:

1. The strategy to which the project is aligned
2. The degree to which the project is expected to contribute to achieving the specific strategy
3. The key business problem the project will solve and/or the key opportunity it will create
4. Critical success factors
5. Background and current situation
6. Project description
7. Key stakeholders (make a note of the champions, any nemesis, and the comatose)

8. Intra-project priorities (pay special attention to the priorities ranked 1st and 2nd)
9. Complexity assessment (pay special attention to any attributes that are rated at a value of 3 or above)
10. Assumptions (do a quick review to see if they seem realistic to you)
11. Risk assessment
12. Scope statement (do a quick review to see if the planned scope will help meet the project objectives)
13. Size estimates

A thorough review will give you a clear picture of the reasons for the project, its objectives, and the overall environment in which the project will be developed. If anything is unclear, or if you have specific questions or issues, make detailed notes. Next, we would advise you to contact the person(s) who requested the project and the key stakeholders and arrange to visit each of them to introduce yourself. Discuss the project, its objectives, the strategy that it is aligned with, and the critical success factors. Use this opportunity to raise any questions or obtain clarification on items relating to the project. Our advice is to keep these meetings on a positive note and leave discussion of any issues and disagreements for a later time; do not focus on the negative.

Use this time to look at yourself as well (use a logical mirror) and determine how well prepared you are to manage this project. The following is a short list of a project manager's roles and responsibilities. Using this list as a guide, conduct an objective self-assessment of your skills (for a more comprehensive list see Figure 5.28).

Achieve project objectives	Business knowledge
Coaching and mentoring	Communications
Conflict resolution	Estimating
Expectations management	Facilitation
Hire/fire team members	Leadership
Negotiations	Planning
Procurement	Risk management
Scheduling	Scope management
Team member appraisals	Technology assessment
Tracking project progress	Vendor management

The skills you need are dependent on the needs of the project; not all projects require the highest degree of skill in each area. This type of assessment will help you identify the areas where you can benefit from any help—general advice, specific consulting, mentoring, education, and training—and then work with your immediate manager to develop a plan of action.

To be ignorant of one's ignorance is the malady of the ignorant.
A. B. Alcott (http://www.thebroadroom.net/fun/wit_wisdom.html).
American Educator, 1799–1888.

Next, find out if your organization has a project office to help project managers. If so, make an appointment. During your visit, familiarize the person with your project and inquire about the services that the project office can provide to help you manage the project more professionally. To prepare for your meeting, make a list of key questions. For example:

1. Are there any templates, tools, advisory, consulting, educational, and training services that will help you be more efficient and effective as a project manager?
2. Is there a specific system/product development methodology that must be followed?
3. What type of training and assistance is available for the team?
4. What is the process for obtaining a unique Project ID and an official name for your project?
5. What are the policies and procedures regarding security and safety—the need for badges and any access restrictions (both electronic and physical)?

Other important matters to investigate are the availability of office accommodations, hardware, software, telecommunications equipment, furniture, meeting rooms, and supplies (including flip charts and sticky notes).

Your initial investigation should also include the availability of any historical information from similar projects. The project office and/or other project managers, your functional manager, and key stakeholders are the primary sources of information. Additionally, we would advise research through your corporate library as well as the Internet. If you find any useful materials, obtain copies, make notes, and file the information for easy reference.

Now you are ready for a visit with the sponsor: the moment you have been waiting for. It is an accepted fact, overwhelmingly corroborated by research by the Standish Group, Gartner Group, and Meta Group, that a primary reason for project failure is the absence of a committed sponsor. Combine this observation with the inordinately high number of challenged and failed projects, and it is obvious that sponsorship has been, and continues to be, an ongoing problem. Therefore, it is imperative that every project has an appropriate level sponsor. The first place to look for the sponsor's name is the Project Charter. As a part of the stage gate review for the Pre-Launch stage, one of the key requirements is the name of the proposed sponsor.

Unfortunately, if a sponsor has not yet been assigned, the fundamental process of the Pre-Launch is already in *jeopardy*. If, by chance, a proposed sponsor is not specified, you will need to work with your functional manager to make sure an appropriate sponsor is assigned to the project. We will now assume that a sponsor exists and you have arranged a meeting. The purpose of the meeting with the sponsor is to engage in a summary review of the charter, with special focus on the items of concern to you. We strongly advise that this interaction and communication take place, even if the sponsor has recently reviewed and approved the charter. Besides setting a firm expectation for the sponsor's commitment to the project, it is also an opportune time to discuss the sponsor's preferences regarding management approaches, communication style, and project organization structure. Finally, determine the sponsor's personal critical success factors for the project. During this interview process, it is also important to meet with your functional manager to discover what role he/she plans to play throughout the project and what is expected of you regarding project status reporting and issue escalation procedures. To manage expectations, you have to first find out what they are. At this point, you should be ready to arrange the project kickoff meeting.

The Project Kickoff Meeting

The purpose of the project kickoff meeting is to formally announce the start of the project to the policy- and implementation-level stakeholders, key customers, and the core team. Another important objective of the meeting is to give the sponsor the opportunity to officially introduce the project manager to the key stakeholders and to formally and publicly designate the project manager as the person charged with the responsibility for successful completion of the project. The nature of most project teams is such that project managers do not have hierarchical authority over the team because few, if any, of the team members truly work for the project manager. Project managers get their authority from the authority delegated to them by their sponsors and certain other functional managers.

Because a kickoff meeting typically involves the attendance of a number of middle- and senior-level managers, key stakeholders, key customers, functional managers, and a number of core team members, we suggest that the sponsor distribute the meeting announcement under his name. The project manager may need to follow up personally with any number of invitees to be certain that they all attend the meeting. We suggest a two-part meeting:

1. The first and the primary meeting is the entire group: the sponsor, project manager, key stakeholders, key customers, and the core team. The sponsor will chair the meeting, which is typically designed to last one hour or less. Plan a short break at the end of the meeting and take the time to thank all of the stakeholders and customers for their participation.
2. The second part of the meeting involves the sponsor, project manager, and the core team. This meeting is also scheduled to last one hour or less.

The sponsor must open the meeting and introduce the project and the project manager to the group. The focus is on the importance of the project and its contribution to the organization. The best approach is for the sponsor to paint a picture of the end state of the project and help everyone understand why that product is better than the current situation. This information is a part of the Idea Statement (see *Idea Stage*, Chapter 3). If the sponsor is unable to achieve this objective, we must assume that she is not communicating effectively. If the project has been approved without a clear picture of the end state and the specific benefits it will bring to the organization and the key people, we doubt that the project has a realistic chance of success. The sponsor must also stress the importance of disciplined project management principles and practices and the need for everyone's cooperation with the project manager and the project team. We recommend the following steps to a successful project kickoff meeting:

1. Strive to make the experience enjoyable. Do not dwell on the negative.

2. Work with the sponsor to plan the meeting and decide on the overall agenda. Keep the meeting to less than one hour.

3. Make sure each invitee receives a copy of the Project Charter before the meeting. Call each key stakeholder personally to see if any clarifications or explanations on any part of the charter are needed.

4. Make sure that each team member invited to the meeting has read the charter and is familiar with its key components—strategy alignment, objectives, critical success factors, risks, and the scope statement. Anyone who comes unprepared to the meeting is a candidate for a one-on-one discussion.

5. Arrive at the meeting site earlier than anyone else; make sure the room is appropriately arranged and welcome people as they arrive. Make sure the various team members do not form their own group and sit together. They should all spread out and sit next to customers. Ask them—in fact warn them—not to engage in "techno talk."

6. If appropriate, ask the participants to suggest an acronym for the project. Break people into small teams, and offer a prize for the winning group, to be selected by the sponsor or by majority vote (remember the "goodies" budget we talked about in Chapter 1). Make sure the acronym does not spell an objectionable or ominous word. For example, we recall a project named SCARS. Unfortunately, the project was not successful and it left nothing but scars. Another project we recently learned about, named DRMS (dreams), later turned into a nightmare. Also, if your project crosses national boundaries, have local representatives review the proposed project name/acronym for propriety. Above all, do not spend too much time trying to be creative and cute.

  • Entertain questions and comments by the participants that need to be addressed by the sponsor and/or the project manager. Have sufficient flipcharts available to record the questions, comments, and any issues raised by the participants.

  • The sponsor should close the meeting by thanking participants for their time, participation, and contributions. A number of project managers we know have developed a "ceremony" where they have the participants sign a special page included in the Project Charter. The page heading typically contains the following items:

    • Project name
    • Project objectives/purpose
    • The rest of the page is left blank so that the participants can sign their names. The purpose of this declaration is to convey support of the project—they are signing on for the duration. This reinforces the participants' sense of ownership and their understanding of the need for their support of the work that lies ahead for the team.

  • At the conclusion of this ceremony, take a short break.

  • The project manager opens the next meeting. After about 15 to 20 minutes, the sponsor usually leaves and officially turns the meeting over to the project manager. The focus is to review the key items from the previous meeting and respond to any questions put forth by the people in attendance.

Now, it is your turn to take charge. This is your first meeting. It will set the tone of your leadership style. First impressions carry a strong impact, so arm yourself by being well prepared. The key elements of this meeting are:

• Importance of the project, its links to strategy, key objectives, and critical success factors
• Review of information from the previous meeting
• The principles, practices, and guidelines by which the project will be run
• Your expectations of the team—the role of the team in project success
• Your role as the project manager

A very useful exercise during this session is to have various team members work together to develop two distinct lists of their experiences (use two flipcharts):

1. Lessons from previous projects that they would like to bring to this project (title the page "Embrace")
2. Lessons from previous projects that they would like to avoid in this project (title this page "Avoid")

While discussing these items, make sure the participants do not resort to finger pointing and placing blame; focus on practices, not people.

Creating these lists is a useful activity for you to facilitate; this exercise will give you control of the process; allow you to get to know different people's likes, dislikes, and ways of thinking; and provide an opportunity for you to practice your facilitation skills. The result of this session should be the foundation of the best practices list for the project. At this point, retain the list of negative experiences. If, in the future, you notice a team member practicing any of the items on the "Avoid" list, take the opportunity to discuss the behavior with the person (privately) and use your management skills to channel the person in the right direction. In addition to the two lists, find out if your organization already has a best practices list, and make sure to incorporate the appropriate project management related items into the list for your team. For example:

1. Team members are fully responsible for completing their assignments on time, within budget, and to the defined quality.
2. Team members are responsible for informing the project manager about any variations in project vital signs, beyond the agreed upon thresholds, in a timely manner.
3. Team members are responsible for reporting problems and any potential delays promptly and forthrightly, and presenting plans for avoiding or recovering from them.
4. Team members are responsible for contributing actively to the project's success.

Developing and reviewing the best practices list is not a one-time effort; the team should use the list at the start of each project stage. A number of project managers post the list in project meeting rooms to remind people of the "Embrace" list. Some project managers even post the "Avoid" list.

As you plan and conduct the two meetings, keep in mind that the extent of effort and energy should be in concert with the project's value, complexity, size, and visibility. The attendance and participation in these meetings are good indicators of things to come.

By the finish of the kickoff meeting, you should have obtained (or decided upon) the following information:

Project identification (ID)	Project name
Project acronym (optional)	Project sponsor
Project manager	Key stakeholders
Core team members	Key reference materials
System and/or product life cycle(s)	List of best practices
Look-ahead window (What next?)	

Why the Staging Session?

Far too many project managers are assigned to the position but are not privy to the discussions and decisions leading to project approval. Because the discipline of developing a comprehensive Project Charter is not very wide spread, many project managers receive only cursory orientation to the project and are then told to move full speed ahead. Their managers assign them to the project management position without much documented information regarding important areas such as strategy alignment, key objectives, critical success factors, and the rationale behind the proposed deadline and budget. The principal reason for this lack of preparation is that nobody has taken the time to record any of this information in an orderly manner. When asked if they have tried to contact the key customers, many project managers answer: "We are not supposed to do that." They further state, "All we can do is tell our managers what information we need and they then talk to people and provide us with answers." In this type of environment, project managers are then held accountable for outcomes over which they have no control. No wonder that the project success rate in such organizations remains at a very low level.

Helpful Tools and Tactics

Over the years, project managers have developed a number of interesting tools and tactics to help with the overall management of their projects. These include:

Project Website   We recommend project websites only for zone I projects because of the underlying cost, time, and energy needed to establish and maintain the information. If you decide to establish a website, find out if there is a corporate standard structure and format. If so, follow it; do not take the time to customize it or make it unique for your project. The effort is not worth the time and it will irritate the viewers because of nonstandard formats and navigation protocols. As a project manager, do not take on the responsibility for updating the content and monitoring the website on a day-to-day basis; delegate the responsibility to a team member. You will need to spend time on roles and responsibilities that are more important.

Team Name, Slogan, and Logo   We would consider creating these items only for zone I projects. Again, don't spend too much time on this activity. It sounds nice, but it can be too time consuming and it can detract from the purpose of the project.

Monthly Newsletter   Newsletters are a good idea, but creating and maintaining them can be very time- and cost-intensive. For zone I projects and projects that cover large geographic areas, a newsletter can be of great help in communications. Where a project website exists, a newsletter represents duplicate effort and should not be developed.

Periodic (Monthly) Lunch Sessions   Lunch is always a great idea. Develop a fun/information agenda, but be careful to manage the time and cost. Refrain from alcoholic drinks, even if team members wish to pay for them out of their own pockets. Keep in mind that the focus is the camaraderie, not the food. Invite your customers.

Family Outings   Family activity is another excellent choice. Make it more fun than work. Be sure to select family-oriented and kid-safe venues.

Individual and Group Recognition Programs   Recognition is essential for morale, with a strong emphasis on group, rather than individual, recognition. Combine this with the periodic (monthly) lunch sessions.

Project Completion Celebration   This is a very good idea. Don't put the team to work; outsource it. See if your team, group, or company can provide a "professional" photographer. Take lots of pictures, and make sure people receive copies. Remember the pens you saved from the Project Charter signing ceremony at the end of the Pre-Launch stage or during the kickoff meeting? Use them as party favors.

As you consider this list of items, be wise. In your zeal to compensate for all the previous projects that did not include these types of activities, you might be tempted to go overboard. These are process deliverables that must be handled in moderation and with tact.

Before we close the discussion on Project Staging, we have one more notable meeting to address. This meeting involves the sponsors, various functional managers, and the project manager. The project sponsor should call and manage this strategy meeting. The key items to discuss and decide upon are:

- The roles, responsibilities, and accountabilities of the functional managers
- The functional managers' responsibilities to provide timely availability of resources for the project.
- The project manager's degree of authority over the resources assigned to the project by the functional managers. Establish the degree of input the project manager will be asked to provide regarding a resource's performance on the team.
- The process of issue escalation from the project manager, to functional managers, and to the sponsor.

The sponsor should play a role in the performance assessment of various functional managers. The functional managers' bosses should seek input from the sponsor regarding functional managers' performance of their roles and responsibilities on the project. The sponsor, in turn, should base her assessment of functional managers on specific input from the project manager. This type of accountability will contribute significantly to smooth project execution.

Experts to the Rescue

For projects that fall into zone I, and high zone II and III, we recommend that you seriously consider the process of inviting respected authors and speakers to occasionally address the project executive team, project team, and key stakeholders. A quick review of books and magazines related to the business of your project, key technology areas, and the subject of effective project management will produce a substantial list of names. By reviewing their writings, you can develop a short list of individuals whose experience could help the project stay on course. Discuss the subject with your sponsor, the core team, and key stakeholders to see if such meetings can add value to the success of the project and to individual knowledge and experience within the overall project team. If you decide to move forward with the plan, contact the human resources department and/or the communications department and seek help to formalize your plans.

■ PROJECT ORGANIZATION—PPA STEP 17

Many project managers do not take the step to design a specific team organization structure for their projects. Instead, they accept the existing team structure and try to make it work. This approach leads to less than desirable results—inadequate control by the project manager, poor reporting structure, a lack of accountability on the part of the team members, interference by functional managers, and a chaotic project environment.

A few years back, at the start of a consulting assignment, we asked the client project manager, Derek, to draw the project organization structure of his recently started project. During our early interviews with the project manager, he conveyed his frustrations with the poor quality of the project organization structure and his lack of authority to manage the project team. After some discussion and reflection, he drew the chart shown in Figure 5.2.

This was intriguing to say the least, especially the following three elements:

1. The line toward the bottom of the inverted pyramid with the *ground level* annotation
2. PM placement was below the team's placement
3. The acronym, "SOE"

Assuming that the PM misunderstood the acronym "SME," we inquired about "SOE." Derek assured us that he knew exactly what SME meant and that the acronym "SOE" stood for "Scum of the Earth." He said, "That is how they treat me." Unfortunately, this is more prevalent than one would like to think. Most failed and challenged projects suffer from similar ailments.

Our advice to project managers is to work hard to design an organization structure that is tailored to fit the project at hand, and then work diligently to put it into practice. The extent to which

FIGURE 5.2
Dysfunctional Project
Organization Structure

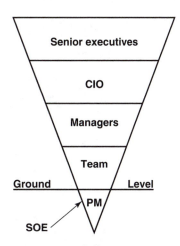

the designed structure cannot be made practical represents the degree of added risk to the project. If the resulting risk is considerable, the next prudent step is to invoke the risk management process discussed in Chapter 4.

Before we start our discussion of the various forms of project organizations, we must discuss the subject of organizational hierarchy. Any team organization implies a certain level of hierarchy; some people have more authority than others do, and the people who have authority will determine what needs to be done and how it needs to be done. Hierarchy also means that certain people will be privy to more information than others and are assigned greater responsibility, as well as the authority to make decisions. Many people resent the fundamental nature of a hierarchy and may object to it in explicit and implicit ways. The latter behavior manifests itself when these people outwardly agree to the hierarchical authority and then fail to follow through with their work assignments in the manner and time communicated to them by the person in authority. Other people equate an organizational hierarchy to a bureaucracy. Bureaucracy for its own sake—having to follow a multitude of procedural steps just because they have been prescribed—is not recommended. All teams can benefit from a well-defined decision-making hierarchy. However, the hierarchy should contain as few levels as possible, thereby spreading the decision-making responsibility down through the ranks.

> *We need hierarchy. To talk of the death of hierarchy is nonsense. In a crisis there has to be somebody who makes the final decision. If a ship goes down, the captain does not call a meeting. He gives an order—or everybody else perishes. . . . But then the same person also will have to act as a team leader . . . and in other situations will have to act as a team member and partner. These are three different functions to be discharged by the same person as the situation demands it. And so far I know very few people who have learned which role they play, and how to play it, and under what conditions. Equally rare are the people who realize that it is their job to make it clear to their associates what role they are playing in a different and given situation.*
>
> Patricia Panchak (interview with Peter Drucker), *Industry Week* (September 21, 1998).

Project Organization Models

Let us now discuss the different types of organization structures and their relative advantages and disadvantages. We will discuss five primary types of organizations.

Functional Organization   Examples of functional organizations in a company are sales, marketing, human resources, distribution, manufacturing, IT, and research & development. A functional project team is best suited to a project where all of the work falls *entirely* within a functional group— *none* of the stakeholders are *outside* the group. Figure 5.3 depicts the structure of such teams.

In the case of such projects, the project manager's assignment is given to one of the functional managers (the level of the manager is based on the level of complexity of the project) and the

FIGURE 5.3
Functional Organization
Structure

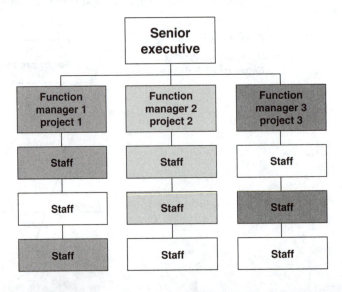

various team members are selected from within the functional organization (function). Figure 5.3 shows three projects, each being managed by a functional manager with a team comprised of staff from within the function. The key benefit of this structure is that all reporting is vertical, eliminating the inherent problems of cross-functional turf issues and assignment problems. The team members can be assigned part-time or full-time. With only a part-time assignment, they could handle one or more projects in addition to their day-to-day responsibilities. The more divided they are between assignments, the greater the possibility of conflicts arising from availability, work focus, and cross-project loyalties. With this organization, even though various team members report to a project manager, their own managers retain control over their career paths and promotions.

In the modern corporate environment, few projects reside totally within a given function; hence, this type of team organization rarely applies. For example, if the VP of sales wishes to revamp an existing compensation policy, there is a high probability that the human resources group will need to be involved to ensure compliance with corporate policies. Similarly, if the human resources department initiates a project to revise the policies and procedures for employee performance evaluations, they will need advice from the legal department to ensure compliance with any regulatory policies. Unfortunately, what really happens is that because these projects are first seen as purely functional, project management responsibility is assigned to a functional manager (who often has no experience in the principles and practices of project management) and the work starts immediately. A few weeks into the project, the project manager discovers the need for cross-functional roles, contacts the appropriate groups, and expects them to fit the project work into their schedules because the project is vitally important and is already falling behind schedule. The Wheel of Half-Baked Ideas begins to spin and failure looms on the project horizon (along with some very bad feelings).

Matrix Organization   Figure 5.4 illustrates the matrix organization structure. In this case, the project team is comprised of team members from a number of different functions. Team members may be assigned full- or part-time to the project team, and each reports to two bosses: his own function manager and a project manager. A team member who is assigned to two different projects that each have a different project manager may report to three different people: two project managers and a function manager. This scenario applies to some of the staff of *function manager 2* (refer to the last box below *function manager* in Figure 5.4; they are assigned to both projects). The reason for the multiple reporting requirements is that the resource is assigned temporarily to the project, for a given period of time, and will return to the function when the project is finished.

In a matrix organization, team members' career paths and performance assessments stay under the control of their function managers (vertically). This particular attribute of a matrix team results in the situation where the project manager has no real authority over various team members because they are not accountable to the project manager. A matrix organization structure can vary from a weak matrix, where the project manager has a low level of authority over team members; to

FIGURE 5.4
Matrix Organization
Structure

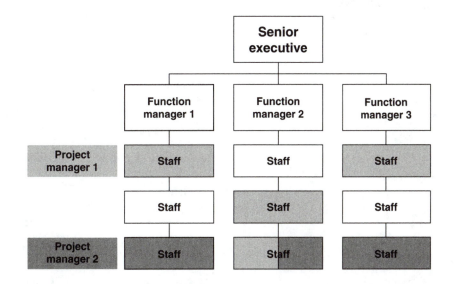

a strong matrix, where the function managers have agreed to give the project manager substantial authority over team members.

The fundamental problem with the matrix organization is that the team members have dual/multiple reporting responsibilities. The problem is further complicated when function managers decide to flex their authority over team members (bypassing the project manager), thereby causing a split in team members' loyalties. The situation further degenerates when the project managers and the function managers get into turf wars and the function managers flex their muscle by yanking their resources from the project. With all of its inherent problems, the weak matrix organization is still the structure most commonly used to manage IT/Business projects and is a major factor in the large proportion of challenged and failed projects. This is one reason why matrix organizations require high quality communications and relationships between project managers and function managers. Good negotiation skills on the part of project managers can greatly alleviate some of the inherent problems of matrix teams. In matrix projects, team members can be easily switched between projects. The key benefit of a matrix organization is that it facilitates efficient resource utilization. However, because IT/Business project teams members are not that easy to interchange, the matrix organization does not provide any such benefits.

Project Organization   From the point of view of a project manager, project organization (also referred to as projectized organization) is the best structure because it gives maximum authority to the project manager. The entire team is fully dedicated to the project at hand and reports directly to the project manager. This structure is depicted in Figure 5.5. The entire team is devoted to only one project at any given time. Various people on the team are either hired for the project and/or *transferred* from their current departmental duties and are assigned to the project full-time; they *do not* have any responsibilities for their day-to-day jobs during the project life cycle (in real life, this is easier said than done).

In the case of the structure depicted in Figure 5.5, the project manager has total authority over the team members, which includes the power to hire, assign, reassign, and fire people (from the project). At the completion of the project, people hired solely for the project are released (let go) and the others, who were transferred from within the organization, go back to their own departments or groups. Two key drawbacks of this organization include inefficient resource utilization and a negative impact on career growth. In the first case, certain people who are internal transfers and are not otherwise needed full-time, are still assigned full-time to the project. In the case of long duration projects, the senior level team members' career path development can suffer because project budgets seldom include funds for general skills development. Construction companies use this structure to resource engineering and labor pools and they often rely heavily on external contractors to supply the people as needed.

FIGURE 5.5
Project Organization
Structure

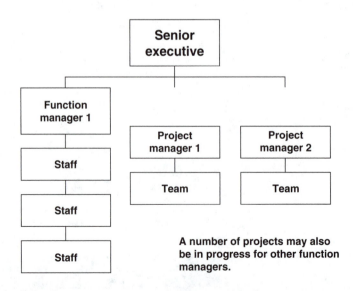

Self-Managed Organization   In self-managed teams, the work is assigned and accomplished through consensus. No one has any real authority over the team—everyone is at about at the same level—and the project manager's role can shift to different team members. This fluid structure does not absolve various team members from individual accountability. The key requirement of this structure is that all of the team members must be highly trained, be well experienced, have a clear understanding of what needs to be done, and have the flexibility to change/adjust to the situation quickly. Dependence on the self-managed organization structure carries several important stipulations:

- Projects last a short time.
- Facilities and equipment are in place and maintained to the requisite quality.
- Team members have the requisite skills and authority to make on-the-spot decisions.
- SMEs are readily available.
- Budget is invariably the last priority, and as such, project costs can be extremely high.
- Efficient use of resources, though a concern, is not always possible.

Surgical teams most often adopt this model; other examples are fire fighting teams and SWAT teams. It is important to point out that the self-managed aspect of these teams does not always extend to every team member.

One inherent problem with self-managed teams is that, because the members are so highly trained and are held in high esteem, some of them can develop a "we know best" attitude. This arrogance often results in condescending behavior toward customers and results in deplorable situations. Examples abound of surgeons performing the wrong surgery on the wrong patients, even when the patients objected (see *It's the Other Leg, Stupid* in Chapter 1) and law enforcement agencies raiding the wrong houses (and grossly mistreating the residents) without later owning up to their mistakes. The latest example of poor oversight at the highest levels is that of corporate boards and senior executives of some of the biggest companies in the country.

Task Force Organization   A typical task force is a group of SMEs that represent a variety of different functions (internal and external) brought together to investigate a given subject area and produce recommendations. Task forces are quite common in the public sector, and less common in the private sector.

The members of a typical task force continue to perform their current management duties in addition to the work needed on the task force. Task force team members typically select one or more of their direct reports to handle most of the work, which is primarily research. The primary contribution of the task force members is their collective influence, access to appropriate resources, and decision-making authority.

Project Types and Project Organization

Having discussed the various types of commonly used project organizations, the question arises, "How does a project manager decide which type is most suitable for a given project?" To answer that, we will revisit the complexity chart, shown in Figure 5.6.

From our experience with a large number of projects executed by a variety of clients, we recommend the following:

- *Zone I projects:* The best approach is to use the Project Organization structure. This structure is recommended because projects in this zone of the complexity chart require an organization that has minimal levels of reporting hierarchy, quick access to key stakeholders and decision makers by the project manager, team members fully committed to a specific project (with minimal distractions from any other work), and a project manager who has a high degree of authority over the team. Obviously, the cost of having full-time team members is going to be high; however, so is the cost of failure of such projects.
- *High zone II and high zone III projects:* The first recommendation is to determine whether the project organization structure is viable, particularly from the resource availability and cost perspectives. If not, then a strong matrix organization structure is recommended. A strong matrix

FIGURE 5.6
Project Complexity Chart

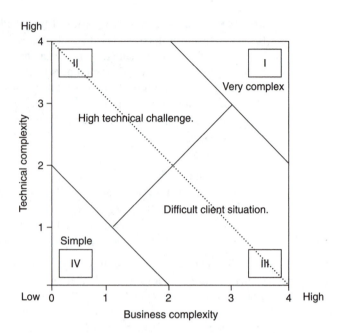

structure ensures that the project manager has sufficient authority over the resources to assure timely completion of project work and that the functional managers have agreed not to usurp the project manager's authority. In addition, many of the core team members are full time, thus providing a focused team.

- *Low zone II and low zone III projects:* These projects, by definition, are far less complex and do not require the same level of resources as the previous two project types. For these projects, a medium to strong level of matrix organization is appropriate.
- *Zone IV projects:* Most of these projects are relatively small and simple, and most lie within a specific function and have minimal outside interfaces. For these projects, the functional organization works well.

Sound judgment presumes that none of these structures are absolute. Any real-life project team is a hybrid structure based on the established organizational practices and the needs of a given project. The important points to keep in mind are:

- Project teams are formed specifically to manage a given type of project. Project team structures are not intended to replicate the corporate command and control structure. For example, a project manager can be junior to a team member, but the team member is still accountable to the project manager for timely completion of all assigned tasks/deliverables. This type of reporting structure can be tricky, but it nevertheless needs to be acknowledged and managed.
- The more full-time the project team members are assigned to a given project, the more efficient and effective the team will be. Multiple project assignments, especially combined with ongoing responsibility for day-to-day work, can lead to major inefficiencies and a lack of focus, which can result in errors and omissions.
- Project managers must have authority over the team members—they should be able to hold team members accountable for their assigned work. If functional managers begin to undermine a project manager's authority, team discipline will erode and the project will suffer.
- The project managers should recognize the natural division of loyalties of cross-functional resources, and work diligently both with the appropriate team members, as well as their respective managers, to minimize any conflicts.
- Because of the very nature of IT/Business projects, it is important for project managers to realize that they will need to focus more on influencing and negotiation skills than on their hierarchical authority.
- Project managers must learn to read the politics (power structure) of their work environment and recognize the centers of authority within the framework of their projects.

Gaining this insight, understanding the implications for their environment, and then learning to chart a safe and efficient course are the hallmarks of successful project management. Over the years we have come across a sizeable number of project managers, usually recently promoted senior technical people, who take a certain pride in exclaiming, "I don't like politics." Not so ironically, most of them do not make successful project managers.

Let us look at a definition of the word "politics" as it pertains to a given project.

Politics: maneuvering within the context of the project to gain control or power.

Given the cross-functional nature of most projects—with different managers and executives having competing interests combined with the uncertain nature of the final outcome—it should not be a surprise that some people will try to gain a position of advantage. The problem is exacerbated when a project is forced upon a group without any real demonstration of resulting benefits. In such mandated projects, concerns of key stakeholders are often overlooked and the ultimate outcome for the project manager is loss of power, control, and job security.

Project managers need to understand that most projects have a certain amount of "body politics." Success comes from understanding the underlying reasons, helping plan solutions that minimize the resulting problems, and a compassionate view toward the people who have a contrarian view. Our advice: do not get mired in the politics, or do anything to further complicate the problem, and work diligently to rise above the fray. For those who are new to the job or new to an environment, we advise you to consult with appropriate function managers, other senior-level project managers, and the sponsor to determine the organization structure most suitable for the project.

The Center's Project Organization Model

We have consistently used the model shown in Figure 5.7 for designing project teams because it works very well. We suggest that you start with this model, use it for at least two projects, and then modify it to meet the needs of your organization and the specific project needs.

Project Sponsor   In Chapter 2, we defined the sponsor as an individual who has the right level of authority and personal commitment, and will make sure that the team is able to complete the project efficiently and effectively. A project should have *only one* sponsor. One area of concern is what happens when a project crosses multiple function lines. In that case, should each department supply a sponsor to the project? This implies that certain projects could have more than one sponsor, which would be the ultimate project nightmare. Any given project should have *only one* sponsor, because if there are multiple sponsors, the project manager will receive direction from multiple executives. In the case of conflicting directives, who should the project manager follow?

Executive Steering   Projects in zone I and selected projects in zones II and III of the complexity chart may benefit from the formation of an oversight group composed of senior managers from the various cross-functional groups impacted by the project. The justification for such a group is that the sponsor alone may not have the sufficient decision making authority, especially related to

FIGURE 5.7
Recommended Project
Organization Model

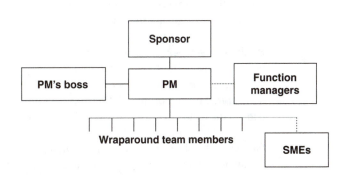

FIGURE 5.8
Recommended Project
Organization Model

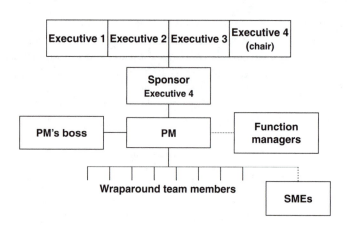

the changes that the project will bring to various cross-functional groups. Under these circumstances, we suggest the project organization depicted in Figure 5.8.

The organization includes a steering group composed of a number of executives from cross-functional departments. We *do not* refer to them as "sponsors" or "executive sponsors" because, for any given project, there is only *one* sponsor. The most workable process to decide which steering group member will be assigned the role of the sponsor is for the group to answer the question, "Who will chair the group?" The person designated as the chairperson is assigned the role of the sponsor (the person who has ultimate authority over the project). Here are a few stipulations for the steering group:

1. Any and all directives from the steering group to the project manager must be communicated *only* through the sponsor.
2. Members of the steering group will *not* direct team members to do anything on the project. The main reason is that, when this happens, the respective team member will have difficulty saying "no" to the executive, which will usurp the project manager's authority over the team—a sure path to major problems down the line.
3. When there are disagreements among the steering group members, they will resolve their conflicts within the group and any directions to the project manager will flow through the sponsor. Once the group has come to a specific decision, it is extremely important that they present a unified front regarding the project. If that is not the case, various team members, as well as implementation-level stakeholders, are sure to take their cues from their respective steering group executives and mimic the dissenting behavior. This will, invariably result in challenged, if not failed, projects.
4. The steering group, the sponsor, and the project manager must define the type and frequency of project status information that the project manager will supply to the steering group.

The steering group should keep in mind that there will be times when heads of various functions will not be driven by the same objectives and performance goals or will not have the same view of the proposed benefits. In any given project involving multiple business departments, someone is going to come up with the short end of the stick. The sponsor must be cognizant of these divergent needs and views. Such projects not only need a politically astute sponsor, but it is imperative that a well-focused executive steering group oversee the project strategically. Sustained commitment over a long period of time, in the face of corporate politics and changing business needs, is imperative. The sponsor must be at a level where she has the authority and wherewithal to bring consensus and maintain it.

Project Manager　　A project should have only *one* project manager who reports directly to the project sponsor. The sponsor and project manager must meet routinely, at least on a semimonthly basis, to review the project progress and status. The project manager also reports to his own boss, and has a dotted line reporting relationship with function managers (managers of the various team members on the team). For some projects, the project manager's boss might also be the sponsor.

By placing the appropriate function managers in the official project organization structure, they can be held responsible for supplying the agreed-upon resources to the project and are accountable for their time and performance on the project.

Remember that the project organization is a temporary entity put together for the duration of the project. Whatever political challenges the organization structure introduces, at the end of the project, the organization will be dissolved and people will return to their parent organizations—they are simply on loan to the project.

Team   We use the term "wraparound team" to mean that team members represent all of the composite areas of the project and the organizations that will be impacted by the deployment of the project. This means that the project team is represented by all of the appropriate groups, rather than just the people responsible for the design and development of the end product. To build a wraparound team, consider the following groups:

Business	External consultants
Finance	IT (development, implementation, and operations)
Legal	Procurement
Quality	Risk
Security	Vendor (if applicable)

Most of the team members are on the project for the duration, but many may come in as needed.

Vendors/Consultants/Suppliers   A frequently asked question (FAQ) regarding these entities is, "Are they members of the project team?" To answer the question, let us look at the definition of a team member

> *Team Member:* anyone who is responsible for producing a deliverable is considered a team member.

Therefore, if a vendor/consultant/supplier is responsible for a deliverable, then an appropriately skilled and authorized person from that group should be depicted on the project organization chart (it does not matter that the individual is only on the team for a short period of time). Keep in mind that many of these people's deliverables may fall on the critical or near-critical path of the project, and without being held to the full responsibility of a team member, they may take their job lightly. A key piece of advice we give to project managers, and especially to sponsors, is that the representatives of these entities should clearly understand and respect the authority of the project manager. They must not be allowed to usurp the project manager's authority.

End Users/Customers   These are the people who will eventually use the process or the product produced by the project. A large number of them will be involved in various group meetings, discussion sessions, prototype reviews, and test activities. Of course it is neither convenient nor necessary to depict each on the project team diagram. The best approach is to show selected representative members from each group on the project team diagram (sales, marketing, security, facilities, human resources, training, legal, and purchasing).

Project Politics   A perennial problem facing many project managers relates to the need for developing and maintaining good working relationships between the project team and the various client organizations. Most project managers are warned to watch out for the "we *v.* them" syndrome. The root cause of this problem is the manner in which a team is structured—most teams are comprised of the IT (technical) people and have minimal representation from the client groups, resulting in the familiar project politics. A considerable number of the team members must come from client organizations, and they must be given responsibilities throughout the project life cycle. This practice puts the client organizations' skin squarely in the game. When this is done consistently, the problems of client involvement, buy-in, and political turf issues are resolved in a more professional manner.

> *When it comes to project execution, CIOs who follow the 'IT knows best' approach assign IT managers to head up all projects and trained systems analysts to drive the requirements definitions. While it's true that business managers are typically too busy managing the process to build strong expertise in project management or analysis,*

adopting these roles misaligns authority and accountability. It is IT's job to use its expertise and influence to coach the business on how to set up projects for success by helping line managers strike a good balance among scope, approach, staffing and oversight.
Susan H. Cramm. "Leadership Agenda," *The Business Knows Best.*

Team Size

In Chapter 2, while discussing the "chunking" process, we suggested that the maximum size of the core team be seven people (with as many full-time as possible). One reason for keeping the team small is the disproportionate growth of interactions as new team members are added. The formula[1] for computing the number of interactions (communications lines or channels) among a team is as follows (where *n* denotes the number of team members):

$$\text{Number of interactions} = (n^2 - n) \div 2$$

Consider the following values:

- 2 team members: interactions $= (4 - 2) \div 2 = 1$
- 3 team members: interactions $= (9 - 3) \div 2 = 3$
- 4 team members: interactions $= (16 - 4) \div 2 = 6$
- 5 team members: interactions $= (25 - 5) \div 2 = 10$
- 6 team members: interactions $= (36 - 6) \div 2 = 15$
- 7 team members: interactions $= (49 - 7) \div 2 = 21$

As the number of team members rises, the number of possible interactions escalates disproportionately. This problem is not as critical for most engineering (construction) teams because their work is typically laid out through detailed blue prints, standardized specifications, universal symbols, consistent interfaces, and repeatable deliverables. A group of electricians, plumbers, carpenters, and painters working in one part of a large structure don't need to closely interact with similar groups working in other parts of the structure. One seldom sees the entire construction crew, often numbering in the hundreds, come together in weekly meetings to report project progress and discuss individual issues. However, that is not the case for IT/Business projects, for which the work (deliverables and tasks) is highly intertwined, and a single individual may need to communicate with a large number of colleagues on a routine basis. Therefore, the larger the team, the greater the number of possible interactions and the greater the possibility of missed connections. One way many IT/Business teams deal with the problem of missed communications is to put everyone on the e-mail distribution list, thereby adding fuel to the fire—now people pay no attention to the large number of e-mails they receive, which increases the probability of missing important communications. This phenomenon of increased communication interactions is a key reason for trying to get as many full-time people as possible. For example, eight half-time employees instead of four full-time team members will result in 28 *v.* 6 possible interactions, a vast difference. In addition to the increased number of interactions, the larger group of part-time team members also has more needs and distractions such as family and technology issues. Two methods to keep the team within manageable size are:

1. Project chunking
2. Full-time team members

Multiple Sponsors and Multiple Project Managers

We will reiterate our strong belief: a project, no matter what size, should have one (and only one) sponsor. The situation of multiple sponsors for the same project is akin to having multiple conductors for a large symphony. It simply does not work. For large projects, a steering committee of

---

[1]Frederick P. Brooks, Jr. *The Mythical Man-Month.* Anniversary Edition. Reading, Massachusetts: Addison Wesley, 1995, p. 78.

senior managers who have decision-making authority for their respective departments is needed. This steering group then needs to elect/appoint a chairperson. This chairperson serves as the *one and only* sponsor. All of the directives to, and reporting from, the project manager are to the sponsor. Any one of the steering group members can request any information about the project from the project manager, but they are not to give directives to the project manager and/or to any of the team members.

Only one project manager should be appointed to the project. Problems arise when the business unit proposing the project and the IT department both assign a project manager. This practice arises primarily from the belief that the other side's project manager is not fully qualified. The irony of this solution is that then there are two underqualified project managers. Our suggestion is to treat the situation similarly to that of an airplane cockpit where there is a captain and a copilot or a first officer. Both are responsible for their well-defined duties, but the captain makes the final decisions. Therefore, in the case of two "project mangers," one should serve as the project manager and the other as coproject manager, who *reports directly to* the project manager.

■ TASK PLAN—PPA STEP 18

A task plan represents the *how to* tactics of completing the project. Outside of the classic engineering discipline, there has been, and continues to be, a certain aversion to developing detailed task plans. Some find the process too time consuming, others avoid planning because they know the plan might change, and others are unaware of the effective and efficient steps used to create a comprehensive task plan. The incorrigible few will state, "We have done something like this before and don't need a plan." The last statement causes one to consider the case of an airline pilot who routinely flies the San Francisco-New York-San Francisco route. Should the pilot spend any time plotting the flight plan? After all:

- The pilot flies this route with regular frequency.
- She knows the location of New York. It does not move. San Francisco does experience a bit of movement (earthquakes), which is immaterial to a plane in flight.
- She knows how to get there. Simply point the airplane toward the East Coast and take off. About five and half hours later, depending on head or tailwinds, New York should appear over the horizon.

Would you fly with this pilot? She is a licensed professional with extensive experience, the equipment is first class, and the weather is ideal (a useful assumption). Regardless of her skill or competence, does the FAA allow a pilot to fly without first filing a fight plan? No. Similarly, should a sponsor allow a project manager to start work on a project without first ensuring that a comprehensive plan has been developed? No. Develop a comprehensive plan before the team starts any development work.

Before we discuss the steps to create a task plan for a given project, we will describe a few stipulations regarding our definition of a plan:

1. A task plan consists of the work breakdown structure (phases, deliverables, tasks, milestones) *and* a task network.
2. A task plan does not include any estimates of any type. Estimates are developed after a plan, or at least the WBS, has been created.
3. A task plan does not include any time lines, or schedules of any type. Schedules are developed after the appropriate authorities have approved the estimates.

We often come across situations where items such as Gantt charts, budgets, and schedules are included as a part of the plan. We believe that the preparation of these materials, this early in the project, is a mistake because it sets the wrong expectations with management and customers—they expect to receive all of this information at a point in the project where specific resources (team members) and their availability have yet to be finalized. In fact, the start signal has not been given— the sponsor needs to see the detailed estimates and then decide whether the project should continue as is, be rescoped, or perhaps be abandoned.

To develop a comprehensive plan efficiently and effectively, we recommend the following steps:

1. Formulate a work group that consists of the core team members, key customers, and appropriate SMEs.
2. Obtain a work room with sufficient wall space to hang flip charts. There should also be several tables on which to spread supplies and materials.
3. Obtain sufficient quantities of sticky notes. Some project teams use a specific color of notes for the work to be done by a specific group. For example, yellow notes for the sales group, purple for human resources, orange for IT, green for finance, and red for the security group. The use of different colors is simply to visually delineate the work of different groups.
4. Set up a work session to last between four and six hours. Anything less does not allow adequate time to build up steam and lay out enough of the plan. More than six hours can get tiresome—people lose focus, need to attend to other routine responsibilities (e-mail, voice mail), get irritated, and tune out.
5. Make sure all of the participants have thoroughly reviewed the Project Charter. Also, have a copy of the charter available during the work session(s) for quick reference.

Regarding the last item, review of the Project Charter, make sure that team members clearly understand the importance of keeping the key information contained in the charter in clear view as they develop the task plan. For example:

1. The attribute ranked first in the Intra-Project Priority Analysis must be satisfied.
2. The information gathered through Stakeholder Analysis will impact the steps needed for a well-thought-out organizational change management plan.
3. The team may need to include steps to define and develop policies and procedures that impact the project but have not been fully deployed.
4. The impact assessment step may have uncovered a number of new deliverables that must be completed as part of the project.
5. The constraints and obstacles documented in the charter must be kept in view as the team develops the task plan.
6. The stability assessment needs to be reviewed to make sure that uncertainties are addressed adequately.
7. All high risk items that warrant contingency plans should be noted.

Teams often overlook much of this information only to face problems during the Execute stage when they can only be reactive (try workarounds and quick solutions).

Task Plan Source

Let us focus, for a moment, on the question: "What is the source of a task plan?" Typically, a task plan can have one or more of the following three sources:

Innovative Guess   This approach is acceptable when a well-documented knowledge base is not available and the team has very little experience related to the project at hand (they have some general experience but nothing specific). Under these circumstances, the task plan they develop will have many holes—especially missing deliverables and tasks.

Memory and Experience   This approach is acceptable when a well-documented knowledge base is not available, but a number of team members have worked on similar projects in the recent past. In such circumstances, the project manager and the team will need to rely on their collective memory to create the task plan for the project. If the collective experience of the team developing the project task plan is insufficient, it is highly advisable to seek help from others who have the requisite experience. When team members develop a project task plan based on memory and experience, the probability that the plan will not include certain deliverables and tasks increases because it is difficult to remember too many details at once. The completeness of the project task plan is in direct proportion to the degree of experience and the team's ability to recall pertinent details.

Knowledge Base   This is the ideal source of a task plan. The organization has a collection of historical data regarding the deliverables, tasks, policies, and procedures typically needed to complete a given type of project. The team can then use the knowledge base as a point of reference as it starts developing a task plan for the project at hand. With the use of a knowledge base, team members don't have to start from scratch. Instead, they are able to select phases, deliverables, and tasks directly from the knowledge base. The simplest form of such a knowledge base is a collection of previously developed project plans by different project teams in the organization. Some organizations do take the time to collect a myriad of previously developed project plans, merge them into a master list, purge all of the duplicate and redundant deliverables and tasks, and add deliverables and tasks that might be missing from the list. As we pointed out in Chapter 1, within the IT profession, the resulting database is referred to as the System Development Methodology (SDM), sometimes referred to as System Development Life Cycle (SDLC). Similarly, within the manufacturing profession, the resulting database is often referred to as the Product Development Methodology (PDM).

A methodology may be developed in-house or purchased as a package from a vendor and adapted for the local environment—terminology, project types, development methods, policies, and procedures. Any methodology, developed in-house or purchased, must be continually updated to meet changing needs—new methods, techniques, technologies, policies, and experiences. In addition to the list of deliverables and tasks, methodologies can also include recommended templates, techniques, and guidelines for creating different types of project plans. The project team, under the guidance of the project manager, chooses which deliverables, tasks, tools, and techniques need to be included for the project at hand.

Because it contains a comprehensive master list of deliverables and tasks, the use of a methodology can help reduce the time needed to develop a new task plan and can minimize the number of omissions (overlooked deliverables and tasks). Some of the primary benefits of a methodology are:

- Provides a guide for project teams for developing their project plans
- Offers a source of baseline task effort estimates (historical estimating data)
- Supports enforcement of organizational system and/or product development policies and procedures
- Facilitates sharing of information among developers

No methodology can ever be so complete that all of the deliverables and tasks needed in a given project will reside in its master list. The team will need to add a few project-specific deliverables and tasks to their project task plan. If any of these newly added deliverables and tasks seem like good candidates for the master list, the project manager should communicate the appropriate information to the group responsible for maintaining the methodology.

Having listed all of the benefits of a knowledge base, one would think that most project teams would be waiting, with bated breath, to have access to life cycle methodologies. Unfortunately, the history of their use has been less than illustrious. Some of the reasons for the lack of interest are:

- Because they are master lists, some get extremely lengthy—hundreds upon hundreds of tasks.
- To make them seem worth the price they charge, many vendors include detailed "how to" instructions for each task, resulting in many hundreds of pages of documentation.
- Many of the methodology vendors also choose to add a sprinkling of project management deliverables and tasks in their methodology to convey the feeling that the methodology encompasses everything the team needs to know. Further confusion results because what the methodology includes about project management is often buried deep inside the task list.
- To make their methodologies appear original and proprietary, vendors use new and obscure terminology and vocabulary for phases, deliverables, tasks, and even position titles.
- Many methodologies are extremely difficult to tailor down to match the complexity and size of individual projects.
- At times, management purchases a methodology to placate internal and external auditors but does not support the methodology's use by the teams. A common proof of such behavior is the minimal training provided to teams regarding the use of the methodology. Combine this attitude with the fact that absolutely no education or training is provided to project customers, thereby implying that all tasks in a methodology (and hence the project plans) belong to the IT team members.

- When project schedules are tight, management allows—even encourages—team members to bypass the methodology.
- Finally, the techniques, technology, tools, and methods of developing software remain in constant flux and new methodologies constantly emerge.

We hope that your organization is not mired in any of the various problems listed. Well defined and well organized methodologies are a great help to project teams. We strongly support the use of an automated master list of deliverables and tasks, sans the ubiquitous detailed descriptions, from which team members can select the deliverables and tasks most suited to their project. Then, they can construct a complete plan by adding items not present in the master list. Our advice to you is to find out if a knowledge base is available, learn about it, and see how its use can help you and your team develop a comprehensive task plan in an efficient and effective manner. If your organization does not have such a knowledge base, and you and your colleagues are interested in developing one, you can take the steps listed in the following section to build a comprehensive knowledge base rather quickly. You will need support from your management group as the process requires your time and energy and because the resulting knowledge base will need to be maintained.

Developing a Master Task List

To develop a master task list, you must do the following:

1. Form a working group (a task force) of senior project managers, with varied project experience, interested in developing a knowledge base. Do not include any nemesis types or those who have the tendency to nitpick.
2. Because this is a team of volunteers, have the team select a project manager and a facilitator. Also, recruit a documentation specialist, if possible.
3. Have the various team members review their project files and retrieve any project plans that they believe contain deliverables and tasks that could populate the knowledge base. Each team member should work independently to prepare a list of deliverable and tasks. At this point, sort each list alphabetically for easy reference.
4. Organize a group meeting where each team member brings a prospective list. The purpose of this meeting is for the group to review the various lists and then create a new master list by purging duplicate items, merging the nonduplicate items, and adding any new items that may emerge during the discussion. A number of our client project managers have named this the "purge, merge, and emerge exercise." This process may take two or three meetings. At the end of the process, your group will have a master list of deliverables and tasks that can be of great help in planning future projects.
5. To keep the knowledge base updated, the group will need to meet about every three to four months to review and revise the master list.

As you develop the master list of deliverables and tasks for your SDM, make sure that it does not incorporate any project management steps. The reasons for this recommendation are:

1. Most organizations have multiple system/product development methodologies, usually supplied by multiple sources—different in-house groups and/or vendors.
2. System/product development methodologies have a higher rate of change and evolution because of the changing methods, technologies, and tools used to develop products.
3. Organizations tend to change the vendors used for system/product development and the new vendors bring in their own methodologies.
4. Because every vendor-supplied methodology is protected under copyright laws, a change in the vendor might result in the host organization's inability to use components of the vendor's project management methodology, specifically any templates.
5. The suppliers of system/product development methodologies are seldom experts in the project management principles and practices, and most of their project management content is less than adequate.
6. Merging the various system/product development methodologies with project management methodology results in a huge list of deliverables and tasks, which is a major turnoff to anyone asked to use the resulting methodology.

In summary, when the project management methodology is intertwined with system/product development methodologies, changes in the latter automatically mean changes in the former, a pointless and extremely costly process.

Now, let us get back to the steps required to develop a task plan for the project. Keeping in mind our fondness for flip charts and sticky notes, we will assume that you have the appropriate amount of supplies for the work at hand. We hope that each participant of the planning session has taken the time to thoroughly review the project charter and the agenda for the session. We advise an agenda similar to the following outline:

- The date and location of the session
- The start and end times of the session
- The end product of the planning session. For example, is it the WBS only? Or, does it include the WBS and a task network?
- Roles
  - Time keeper
  - Minutes and notes
  - Issues log
  - Facilitator
  - Contributors
- Opening and orientation: 15 minutes
- Phase names and descriptions: 30 minutes
- WBS for phase 1
  - Develop a deliverables list: 30 minutes
  - Develop a task list: 45 minutes
- Break: 15 minutes
- WBS for phase 2
  - Develop a deliverables list: 30 minutes
  - Develop a task list: 45 minutes
- Break: 15 minutes
- WBS for phase 3
  - Develop a deliverables list: 30 minutes
  - Develop a task list: 45 minutes
- Task network: 45 minutes
- Closure: 15 minutes

The suggested time slots are approximate and can be adjusted as needed. The project manager should plan to participate in the session to provide guidance and assistance to the team. The role of the timekeeper is very important because the planning session needs to be managed with great attention to the time spent on the different activities. The timelines cover a 6-hour session (times are approximate). Because this is a planning session, we advise the use of the brainstorming approach. Make sure to record all issues, but do not get bogged down in resolving them during the planning session. In addition, keep in mind that the steps are iterative and not necessarily sequential. Two or more cycles may be needed before a comprehensive task plan will emerge. The agenda shows only three phases; however, additional sessions may be needed to complete the definition of the rest of the project.

A discussion of the detailed work that needs to be done to develop the WBS and task plan for the project follows. The material covered here is a summary of the step-by-step process outlined in Chapter 2. The team needs to move quickly and be highly focused. One member of the team needs to record all issues, make sure that discussions not related to the work at hand are kept to an absolute minimum, and mind the clock.

Phases

Using your system/product development methodology as a reference, break the project into phases and write a brief narrative of what specific functionality will be achieved by the end of each phase. Clearly state the assumptions, constraints, and key risk items associated with each phase. Use a flip

FIGURE 5.9

Task-Level WBS Example

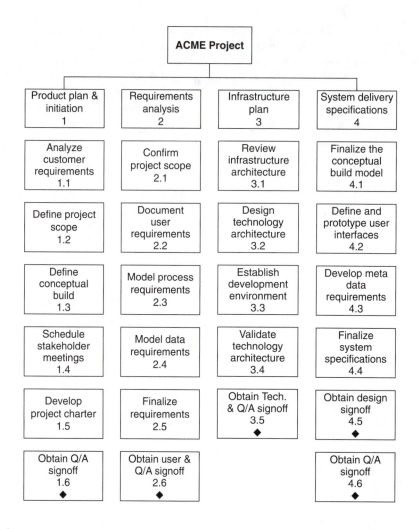

chart for each phase and hang the flip charts on the wall. From Figure 5.9, we see that the project has the following four phases:

1. Product plan & initiation
2. Requirements analysis
3. Infrastructure plan
4. System delivery specifications

Deliverables

Pick a phase and begin to list the deliverables to be produced in that phase. Use a 3" × 5" sticky note to record the name of each deliverable (a noun such as "employee vacation policy"). Place all of the deliverables for a given phase on the appropriate flip chart. Do not concern yourselves with the order in which the various deliverables need to be executed; doing so will only slow the team down. At this point, you may wish to tag each deliverable with an ID. We simply use progressive numbers (1, 2, 3, 4, and so on). Once the team has listed all the deliverables, they can move to the next step—developing a detailed description for each deliverable. The description should include a description, completion criteria, an owner.

Figure 5.10 shows that the project has the following four deliverables:

1. Approved project charter (APC)
2. Approved requirements (REQ)
3. Approved technology architecture (TA)
4. Approved system specifications (SS)

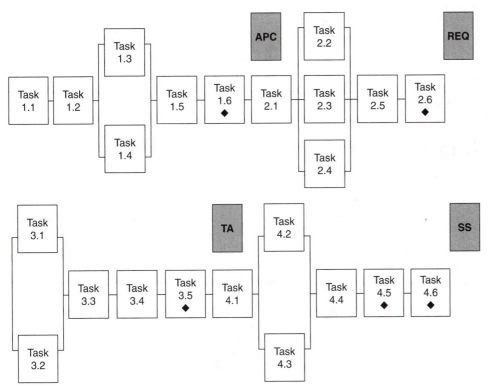

FIGURE 5.10
Task Network Example

Description   The description should be a brief, one or two line, description of the deliverable. Example: A document that delineates the exempt employee vacation policy rules and regulations.

Completion Criteria   Completion criteria are used to ascertain the completion of the deliverable. Examples are: approved by legal, approved by human resources, reviewed by three employees for clarity and comprehensiveness.

Owner   The owner is the one individual responsible for the completion of the deliverable. Although a given deliverable has only one owner, multiple people may work to complete it. Example of a deliverable owner: senior analyst from the HR department. If a name of the individual responsible is known, specify the name.

   The process to define deliverables should be a group effort, guided and facilitated by the project manager. Plan to take 10 to 15 minutes for each deliverable description. The project manager should be present in the session the majority of the time. Encourage the team members to complete their deliverable descriptions in a timely manner. Remind them not to dwell on issues; just record them and move on.

Tasks

The next step is to define the tasks needed to complete each deliverable. Depending on the number of people in the session, it may be advantageous to form subgroups of two members each and assign each subgroup a number of deliverables. Each deliverable will require one or more tasks; we suggest the use of 3" × 3" sticky notes to record task names. Do not concern yourselves with the order in which the various tasks of a given deliverable need to be executed. If there are any differences of opinions or unanswered questions, write them down as issues and move on. At this point, you may wish to give each task a unique ID. We simply use progressive numbers (1.1, 1.2, 1.3, 1.4, and so on). Figure 5.9 depicts an example of a WBS. Once the team cannot suggest any more tasks, they can move to the next phase or to the step of developing the task network.

Milestones

Figure 5.9 depicts that the WBS includes five milestones at tasks 1.6, 2.6, 3.5, 4.5, and 4.6.

Issues

Issues are any differences of opinions or unanswered questions. During the various steps described previously, if there are any issues, simply record them on 1" × 3" sticky notes and move on.

Task Network

A task network depicts the logical order of the various tasks in the project. Typically, you will need to develop two networks:

1. The first, which we refer to as Version 0, is developed without considering any constraints. You assume that any resource needed to complete a given task will be readily available and that there are no other constraints.
2. In real life, it is rare that all things needed are readily available. In such cases, you will need to develop a network to reflect the applicable constraints. Keep in mind that the various tasks are still in their logical order of execution but reflect the constraints on the project.

   To create a task network, review the various tasks in the WBS and decide on the first task or tasks that can be started. The first task is the task (or tasks) that does not have predecessors. Place the appropriate sticky note(s) toward the left edge (center) of a flip chart positioned horizontally. If more than one task can start at the same time, place them vertically one above another. Now review the remaining tasks in the WBS and decide on the next task(s) that can be executed. Peel off the appropriate sticky note(s) and place them to the right of the already-posted tasks. Repeat this process until all tasks are posted. During the posting process, when you run out of tasks for a given deliverable, signaling that it is now complete, remove the sticky note with the name of the deliverable and place it vertically above the last of its associated tasks. You should now have posted a row of deliverables toward the top of the task network; their order of placement will indicate their order of completion. The team can then take the following actions:

1. Take each issue sticky note and decide the latest point at which that issue must be decided. Now place the specific issue sticky note on the task corresponding to that point.
2. Decide on the milestones—points of considerable progress in the project—and mark the associated deliverables and/or tasks with the milestone symbol (a small diamond). Each milestone must be described in a past tense. A list of the various milestones in the order of their appearance on the network, from left to right, should convey the progressive build of the project.

Figure 5.10 depicts the task network for the WBS shown in Figure 5.9.

While developing the task network, the team may discover new deliverables and/or tasks that they had overlooked while creating the WBS. Record the new deliverables and tasks on appropriate sized sticky notes, post them publicly, and continue with network development. Towards the end of the session, the entire group should review the new deliverables, tasks, and issues. Under the guidance of the project manager, they should be incorporated into the project plan, as appropriate.

During the various planning sessions, new issues and uncertainties regarding the project scope and the logical order in which various tasks need to be done will emerge. This is natural and expected. It is the responsibility of the project manager to make sure that the team receives an appropriate level of information and guidance to facilitate their progression though the planning session. The project manager's leadership and guidance play a strong part in the team's ability to develop a comprehensive and accurate plan.

At this point in the training seminars conducted by the Center, the instructor poses the following question to the participants, "Do you believe your project plan is complete?" After a bit of discussion, most people reply, "Yes." At times, participants suspect that it might be a trick question, but after reviewing the plan they just finished developing, they reply in the affirmative. Wrong answer. It is a trick question. The answer should be "No." Why? Let us go back to Chapter 4 and look at the subject of risk assessment and associated contingency plans (Figure 4.28). Whenever a project is susceptible to high probability and high impact risk items, the project manager must develop a contingency plan—a set of tasks to be executed if and when the risk becomes a reality. Over the years, we have observed an unfortunate tendency in regard to contingency planning. Project teams spend time assessing and identifying high probability and high impact risk items. They create a contingency plan, which is typically a *narration* of the actions to be taken in case the risk materializes. However, too often the plan never amounts to more than a paragraph of documentation. Later, during project execution, when a risk does materialize, they scurry to determine what actions need to be taken to react to the risk. They then discover that the action plan was never translated into a set of deliverables, tasks, and milestones and no specific responsibilities have been assigned for any of the work. Often the result is a last minute scramble to find the time, resources, and budget to respond to the risk event. What is needed is a specific list of tasks to be completed if and when a predefined risk materializes. They need a "Plan B."

Risk Management Tasks

Not all risk items will require a contingency plan. For each item that you decide does require a contingency plan, complete the following steps:

1. Review the risk assessment and contingency plan to make sure the group responsible for developing the task plan has a clear understanding of the risk and its impact.
2. Have the group develop a list of deliverables and tasks, using the approach just described, to create a contingency plan for the risk.
3. Have a SME review the contingency plan. This person could be the project manager or someone else who has appropriate knowledge and expertise.
4. Review the deliverables and task list to determine who will be responsible for executing the tasks if the risk materializes. For example, is it the core team, a customer group, or a vendor? For any work to be completed by people outside the core group, it is important to make sure that an appropriately authorized representative reviews and agrees with the action plan. The participation of a representative means that they understand the risk and that you have suitably transferred the risk responsibility. If the group does not take over the responsibility, or your level of confidence in their ability is low, you must accept that you still own the risk. Talk to your functional manager and/or the sponsor to ascertain your next action.

Now comes the question: what is the best way to depict risk-related tasks within the overall project plan? Before we discuss that, let us further separate risks into two different types.

Time Dependent Risk   These risks have a certain predictable time window; such as when a vendor does not deliver the hardware by a certain date. For such risks, we suggest that you incorporate the contingency deliverables and tasks within the primary task plan of the project. If a given risk does not materialize, simply skip over the tasks and continue with work as usual.

Floating Risk   An example of a floating risk is the possibility of a key team member leaving at an inopportune time or a security breach of the corporate website. You may have decided that these are high-risk items, but there are no specific time windows for these risk events. We suggest that you develop an appropriate contingency plan for each risk and have it ready for execution if and when the associated risk materializes.

Figure 5.11 depicts the physical representation of contingency plans for these two types of risks. We believe the process is simple and time efficient, and the resulting plan serves as a guide to the entire project team.

Current System Retirement

The last, but very important component, of a comprehensive task plan is the subject of current system retirement. Three important points to raise and discuss are:

1. How long should the new and current system run in parallel before making the decision to retire the current system?

FIGURE 5.11
Depiction of a Contingency
Plan

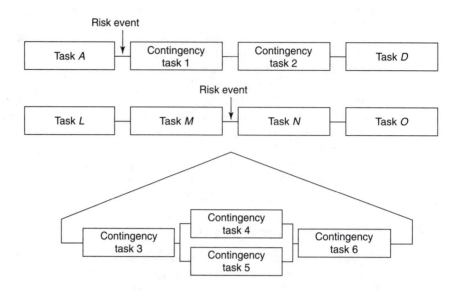

2. What are the criteria that must be met before the current system can be retired?
3. Once these criteria are met, how much time must be allowed before the current system can be shut down?

Some may consider this too early in the project to think about current system retirement. However, many project managers arrive at the Operation stage without having given serious thought to this important subject. In addition, when the customers and the team know that the current system has a finite life span, they begin to think more positively and creatively about the new project.

Project Manager's Responsibility

Over the many years of consulting with a large number of project managers, a question that typically arises at about this point is, "How involved should the project manager be in the planning process?" Additionally, many project managers and team members raise the issue of micromanagement and all of its associated problems. Another concern of many project managers relates to the process of delegating the planning responsibility to the team. Most want to do it but are hesitant because the team may not be sufficiently skilled to develop comprehensive plans. We offer the following suggestions:

- For the first one or two sessions of task planning, the project manager stays with the team and helps plan (WBS and task network) by providing the necessary guidance and direction. The idea is to complete the work in a timely manner and assure accuracy and quality.
- For the next one or two planning sessions, the project manager stays with the team until a deliverables-level WBS has been completed. At that point, the project manager leaves the group. Then the group, under the guidance of a senior team member, continues to develop the task-level WBS. Once the group has completed the task-level WBS, the project manager returns to review and discuss the work. After the review, the project manager leaves again and the team members continue their work to create a task network from the WBS. They then invite the project manager to review and discuss the network and the issues that the project manager can resolve.
- By that point, the team should have developed sufficient skills to develop a WBS and task plans on their own, and the project manager does not have to be heavily involved in the planning process. From then on, the project manager typically stays with the group until they have defined a number of deliverables, then quietly excuses herself from the session and returns to review the completed plan. It is wise to check in once or twice just to see if the team is progressing well.

This process results in a number of benefits for the project manager and the project team, and ultimately leads to more successful projects. Some of the benefits are:

- Team members learn to develop comprehensive plans on their own.
- The project manager has sufficient control and oversight on the planning process.

- The final task plan has a high degree of buy-in by the team because they developed it.
- The estimates and schedule developed using these types of plans will be more realistic and viable.
- A number of issues that would otherwise arise when the team is actually doing the development work are identified at this early stage.
- Team members understand the whole picture and how their personal work fits in, resulting in higher synergy and collaboration within the team.
- Because the team is allowed and encouraged to take the lead in planning out the project, they are put into the position of making decisions and resolving conflicts—excellent training for any team member.

These steps are in contrast to a more common practice where the project manager, bent over a keyboard, uses a project management software package to create the project plan—at times in excruciating detail. This plan is often generated with little or no input from the team, and the most common explanation for developing a plan in isolation is that it is more efficient. In reality, most such project managers have little faith and trust in team members' knowledge and contributions. The result is a set of deliverables and tasks in which the team had little input and, not so surprisingly, little buy-in. The process has certain inherent problems:

- The only person who knows how the task plan came together is the project manager, and that knowledge remains all in his head, not easily accessible by various team members.
- Individual team members will focus only on the portions of the plan they are responsible for, without developing an understanding of the total solution.
- It is a well-known fact that, when people contribute to developing a plan and a solution, they feel more committed to the cause and build a sense of ownership—crucial to the success of any project. Of course, the process of the project manager developing the plan without team input is counterproductive to the cause.

Some people will still do their best to cast doubts on the net benefits of planning. In fact, many are going to use arguments such as: "Our work is so creative that planning is a waste of time." Just recently, one of the Center's consultants attended a Web seminar where the presenter, a purveyor of the latest and greatest software development methodology, was quite emphatic in stating that the focus of the team is to find creative ways to produce function after function, without having to define (in advance) the tasks that will be done to accomplish the function.

Mind you, all of this is based on the claim that programming is such a creative and unpredictable endeavor that planning is neither possible nor beneficial. We would have liked to ask the presenter the following questions:

1. Are all of the team members so well-trained and highly-skilled that they instinctively know what needs to be done to complete the functions assigned to them?
2. In the absence of a comprehensive plan, how do junior team members learn from their senior colleagues?
3. In the absence of a written plan, how do project managers ensure that all of the necessary tasks are actually carried out by appropriately-skilled team members? What about the likelihood of simply forgetting to do certain tasks due to day-to-day work distractions? We wonder whether these people ever make lists when they go shopping for groceries.
4. If a team member leaves to join another project or another organization prior to completing a given function, how does the next person take over?
5. In the absence of task level plans, how do team members develop realistic and accurate effort, resource, cost, and duration estimates? Or, because they are creative artists, are such mundane concerns beneath them?
6. In the absence of comprehensive task plans, how do different team members learn about cross-functional dependencies? Once we asked this question of a project manager who disliked planning and his response was, "They all need to be colocated in the same room, and then they can all talk to each other all day long about everything." This is *not* realistic.

For over two decades, the myth has been perpetuated among many in IT that programming is an art and programmers cannot be held to the discipline of project management—they need to be given the freedom of spontaneous creativity. Their proverbial refrain is, "Having to plan slows us down." To this complaint, we respond: "If you are going in the wrong direction, hopefully you are going slow."

Unfortunately, during the past two decades, far too many in IT have been going in the wrong direction. The result has been an inordinately high number of failed and challenged projects and inferior quality finished products, especially in the area of software.

Plans? We Don't Need No Stinking Plans[2]

During a recent presentation to a group of software developers, one of the "gurus" of the latest productivity approach to developing software products made a point that the best way to achieve high productivity was for the team to define only the functions of the software and none of the associated tasks or plans. According to the proponent of this new approach, the developers can then focus on finding creative ways to produce function after function, without having to define the tasks that need to be done to accomplish the function, and enjoy a nonrestrictive path to creativity. Many designers and programmers in the audience showed enthusiastic approval of the approach because it would allow them *not* to be burdened by the need for developing comprehensive plans. Our guru then pointed out that, if there are no plans, the developers are also free from any checks by the project manager—a direct path to developers' Nirvana.

Now let us assume that the product consists of 101 functions that will be rolled out in four iterations. So far, so good. Further assume that the product is to be built and rolled out as follows:

1. Iteration 1: 25 functions, assigned to five programmers
2. Iteration 2: 20 functions, assigned to four programmers
3. Iteration 3: 24 functions, assigned to four programmers
4. Iteration 4: 32 functions, assigned to five programmers

Someone needs to define the order in which the various functions within a given iteration are to be developed, tested, and integrated. After the first iteration, someone needs to identify the next set of functions and the order of their development, testing, integration, and so on. If no overall plan is developed and documented, how do the developers find out what to do next? Keep in mind that not every developer will have the necessary knowledge and skills to take on the next "to be developed" function, and someone (the project manager) will need to manage the assignments. Now, if no plans are ever developed (in the name of creativity and productivity), what will happen if one or more of the developers leaves midstream? Without a project manager and no plan, how are developers going to estimate the cost and implementation time of each function? Who will know what to do next? Also, in the absence of detailed plans, what about each of the four iterations? It must be obvious that, without those pesky plans, accurate estimating would be almost impossible. Deciding who is assigned to what function would be reduced to a guess, and any turnover in the team will be chaotic.

> *Let's start where conversations about software usually end: Basically, software sucks. In fact, if software were an office building, it would be built by a thousand carpenters, electricians and plumbers. Without architects. Or blueprints. It would look spectacular, but inside, the elevators would fail regularly. Thieves would have unfettered access through open vents at street level. Tenants would need consultants to move in. They would discover that the doors unlock whenever someone brews a pot of coffee. The builders would provide a repair kit and promise that such idiosyncrasies would not exist in the next skyscraper they build (which, by the way, tenants will be forced to move into). . . . The absurdity of this is the point, and it's universal, because the software industry is strangely irrational and antithetical to common sense. It is perhaps the first industry ever in which shoddiness is not anathema—it's simply expected. In many ways, shoddiness is the goal. . . . "Don't worry, be crappy." Guy Kawasaki wrote in 2000 in his book,* Rules for Revolutionaries: The Capitalist Manifesto for Creating and Marketing New Products and Services. *"Revolutionary means you ship and then test,"* he

---

[2]With apologies to John Huston's 1948 movie, "The Treasure of the Sierra Madre," and thanks to the 1974 Mel Brooks' movie, "Blazing Saddles."

> writes. " . . . *The only thing more shocking than the fact that Kawasaki's iconoclasm passes as wisdom is that executives have spent billions of dollars endorsing it."*
> Scott Berinato, "The Big Fix," csoonline.com (October 7, 2002).
> http://www.csoonline.com/read/100702/fix.html.

Our advice to all those who are opposed to developing comprehensive plans is to recognize that the problem is not with the discipline and processes used to develop comprehensive plans, the problem is in their lack of fundamental skills in the art and science of developing plans efficiently and effectively. The process of planning has a number of important benefits:

- The initial brainstorming enables the participants to think collectively about the project from beginning to end, and the result is a more complete and valuable product.
- Good planning processes include referring to the organization's collective knowledge—any system/product life cycle methodology, similar previous projects, and the knowledge of various team members.
- Well-managed and well-run planning sessions help bring disagreements and issues to the forefront during the early part of a project when they can be discussed and resolved in a timely manner.
- Planning sessions are excellent venues for junior, as well as new, team members to learn from the more experienced team members.
- The act of listing the various deliverables, tasks, and milestones provides people not directly involved in building the project with a good view of the extent of effort needed to complete the project. A comprehensive project plan, especially if developed using sticky notes, provides all observers with a solid physical elucidation of the extent of work involved in completing the project.

Whenever we hear the lament that planning takes too much time and is not worth the time spent, we like to respond by presenting the following scenario: Imagine that the design, build, and testing of a typical function (module) by a programmer takes between 20 to 30 days. Typically, this type of work will entail between two and four deliverables, eight to twelve tasks, and up to three milestones. Now, how long would it take a skilled programmer to think through, write down, and organize eight to twelve tasks into a network? We would suggest an effort of close to 60 minutes, with an additional 30 minutes if there are multiple cross-team dependencies. Now, if a programmer objects to spending this relatively small amount of time to plan out work that will last more than a month, then that person must learn about efficient and effective ways to plan rather than chalk it up to the need for being creative.

This habit of belittling the planning process is a key contributor to the perennial scope explosion of most IT/Business projects. We strongly subscribe to the following quotation, which so aptly points to the benefits of the *process* of planning:

> *Planning is everything. Plans are nothing.*
> Dwight D. Eisenhower (http://www.eisenhowerinstitute.
> org/programs/livinghistory/solarium.htm).

Comprehensive Task Plan

The three synonyms that best explain our vision of a comprehensive task plan are: complete, all-inclusive, and across-the-board. The reason for this discussion is that most project task plans we come across are far short of complete and end up causing major problems when project managers continue to discover omitted tasks long after estimates and schedules have been communicated to management and customers. A comprehensive task plan for an IT/Business project would consist of the following components.

Contingency Tasks   Contingency tasks are the tasks to be executed in case expected risks become a reality.

Current System Retirement Tasks   The tasks for retiring the current system need to be a part of the planning process. Unless this is handled skillfully, many customers will continue to use parts of the old system, resulting in duplicate work, added cost, and duplicate and noncompatible data.

The old system is now the new problem.
John Gall, *Systemantics: The Underground Text of System Lore,*
How Systems Really Work and How They Fail (Ann Arbor, Michigan,
The General Systematics Press, 1986, p. 37).

Customer Training Tasks   Customer training tasks are the tasks that need to be executed to train the project customers in the use of the new system, which includes both the new processes and the new technology. In our analysis of scores of challenged and failed projects, we have consistently found customer training to be the most overlooked part of a project plan. This oversight is especially true with projects being developed by vendors and consultants.

> *Training costs quickly ballooned to as much as five times the anticipated amount, . . . There was a gigantic training curve. . . . We did an assessment and the numbers that came back were staggering. We had to train people on what a mouse was and how to use it. This was not 10 or 20 people, there were hundreds. Scheduling that amount of training was hard, and people could only learn so much so fast.*
> Edward C. Cone, "Detroit Financial System Sputters After Overhaul,"
> *Baseline* (August 6, 2002).

This happens more often than one would like to think. One of the main reasons is a total disregard for the implementation-level stakeholder assessment discussed in Chapter 4.

Deployment Tasks   Deployment tasks are tasks related to turning the product over from the development team to the customers and the operations group.

Development Tasks   Development tasks are the tasks related to requirements gathering, design, construction, and testing the project deliverables. Make sure that the tasks necessary for assuring the right level of security and quality are incorporated into the project development tasks.

Infrastructure Upgrade Tasks   These tasks relate to the steps necessary to keep the technology infrastructure up-to-date. In Chapter 4, we discussed the importance of dealing with the problem of technology obsolescence, especially for long duration projects with high technology complexity. The project manager must make sure that appropriate tasks to keep the technology up-to-date are incorporated within the project task plan.

Operations Tasks   Make sure that the necessary tasks for moving the project from the Implementation stage to the Operation stage are included in the project plan. The best method to ensure that this portion of the task plan is comprehensive is to include appropriate representatives from the operations group in the project team.

Organization Change Management Tasks   These are tasks related to the work that needs to be done to prepare the customers for the needed changes in work processes, technology, and culture. These tasks mostly focus on the cultural and behavioral aspects of the changes imposed on the customer by the new project.

Project Closure Tasks   These are tasks related to turning the project over to the appropriate customer and operation groups, transfer of key team members to new projects or their home bases, deactivating access passwords and security badges, returning the equipment, and any similar activities for an orderly project closure.

Quality Management Tasks

> *The National Institute of Standards and Technology (NIST) estimates that software errors cost U.S. users some $59.5 billion each year.*
> (http://www.nist.gov/public_affairs/releases/n02–10.htm)

The word "lacking" aptly describes the quality of most software products. Unfortunately, this adjective applies as much to products developed in-house as it does to commercial software. The primary reasons for this pervasive problem can be summarized as follows:

- Quality is not defined as a specific attribute of project priorities. We addressed this problem by including quality as one of the four intraproject priorities (see Chapter 4).
- Because quality is not defined as a separate project attribute, specific measures to assess the product's quality are absent. We addressed this problem by outlining a specific set of attributes to define software quality (see *Quality Definition* and *Perception of Quality* in Chapter 4).

Because of these two problems, most task plans do not specifically include quality management tasks. Comprehensive quality management includes three key components:

1. *Quality planning:* This involves defining the ranking of quality as it pertains to schedule, scope, and budget; and defining the quality standards (thresholds) for the end product (these were discussed in Chapter 4, see *Intra-Project Priority Analysis*). Now is the time to define the requisite deliverables, tasks, resources, and milestones to ensure that the end product will meet the defined quality standards.

2. *Quality assurance:* This is the process of determining whether the plans (deliverables, tasks, resources, and milestones) to create the quality are appropriate and adequate. It also includes periodic assessment of the project in progress to assure that the finished product will meet quality requirements. This is best done through independent review by SMEs who are not a part of the project core team (they are not the people who are responsible for creating the overall functionality of the end product).

3. *Quality control:* The process of specifically assessing project deliverables (as they are being defined, designed, built, and used) to ensure that they map to the defined quality standards and variance thresholds. Some of the tools to assess product quality include prototyping, testing, statistical sampling (Pareto charts, quality control charts, seven run rule), walk-throughs, inspections, and fishbone diagrams. Quality control steps are typically the domain of the Execute, Implement, and Operation stages of the project.

It is important to point out that, for projects where quality is ranked number one or number two (as a part of its Intra-Project Priority Analysis), the steps become highly important. Without a well-defined and disciplined quality management approach, the end product quality will be at the mercy of individual team member actions, which may not all be synergetic.

To ensure the expected level of quality in the end product, the project manager and the team need to review the quality attributes defined in Chapter 4 and then verify that the task plan includes appropriate tasks to *build* the quality into the product.

Team Education and Training Tasks   These are tasks related to the skills development and skills improvement of team members, including the project manager. It is extremely important that, in the case of IT/Business project teams, the IT team members' skills development program not be limited to technology-based skills.

> *. . . training of IT staff contributes to greater overall customer satisfaction. This emphasizes the importance of investing in IT staff and building an IT skill base with an understanding of the company's business needs and customer requirements.*
> C. K. Prahalad, M. K. Krishnana, and Sunil Mithas, "The Technology/
> Customer Disconnect," optimizemag.com (http://www.
> optimizemag.com/issue/014/customer.htm).

Milestones   Milestones are the points of considerable progress and/or the points at which the project manager plans to measure project progress. Include celebration milestones because too many teams get too busy to take the time to celebrate key milestones.

Keep in mind that the task plan will consist of two subplans:

1. *Product development plan:* deliverables, tasks, and milestones for developing the end product of the project. The primary source for these items will be your organization's system/product development methodology such as Agile, JAD, Object Oriented, RAD, or RUP.

2. *Project management plan:* deliverables, tasks, and milestones for managing the project. The primary source for these items will be your organization's project management methodology such as the PPA.

Sponsor Sign-off

Occasionally, we come across project managers who have been told that a good way to assure a comprehensive plan is to have the sponsor formally review and then sign off on the WBS for a project. In our experience, a formal review of the deliverables-level WBS by the sponsors is a good step, as it not only familiarizes them with the deliverables that need to be developed but also brings the *extent* of the work that the team must do to complete the project to their attention. You should discuss those deliverables in which you have a low level of confidence with your sponsor. There is an important side effect of the formal sponsor review: When the team knows that the sponsor will be reviewing the WBS, they seem to work more diligently to produce a complete WBS. Then comes the step of the formal sign-off of the WBS by the sponsor. We do not believe this to be of any intrinsic value because, if the team discovers new WBS components at a later time, the fact that the sponsor signed off the WBS does not absolve the team of its responsibility. Plan on the formal review but don't insist on the sponsor's sign off.

Comprehensive Task Plan—Summary

This level of detailed planning is mandatory for all complexity zone I projects and highly recommended for projects in high zone II and high zone III. Projects with lesser complexity may not need the degree of detailed planning previously outlined. To ensure that a task plan contains all of the necessary tasks for each of the twelve subsections listed in the previous section, we suggest the following steps:

1. At the start of the task planning session, decide which of the categories need to be included in the task plan.
2. Start with developing the WBS for the development and deployment tasks. After you believe the team has a comprehensive WBS for these areas of the project, have the team focus on each of the other selected areas and have them develop an appropriate WBS for each. The team members may benefit from the presence of a SME as they develop the WBS for each component.
3. While entering the WBS into your project management software, consider tagging each task with a predefined standard code to designate the category to which it belongs (most software packages have the ability to house such codes).

Once the entire WBS has been loaded into the software, print out the project plan as a series of subplans, such as a plan listing only the tasks for Q/A, another plan listing only the tasks for testing, and so on. Each of these plans then can be reviewed with appropriate SMEs to make sure they are comprehensive. We have found this practice to be effective, because it not only results in comprehensive plans, it also involves the appropriate groups in the planning session. As a result, different groups begin to develop an appreciation of their responsibilities and the extent of their commitment. Figure 5.12 depicts the different types of plans (contingency tasks and milestones are not depicted). The placement of individual plans within the diagram is approximate and does not imply exact start and end of tasks for respective plans.

At this point in the project life cycle, you have a comprehensive plan to translate the vision (defined early in the Idea stage) into a product. It may seem like a lot of work to go from the vision to a well-defined task plan. Many people, by this time, would have skipped several of the intermittent steps and already jumped into the Execute stage—started the work to develop a solution. Most of these endeavors fail, but that has not kept a large number of people from trying.

Important Considerations

Planning begins in the Pre-Launch stage and continues through the life of the project. At all stages, both management and the project team must be willing to acknowledge the need to modify plans

FIGURE 5.12
Project Plan Components

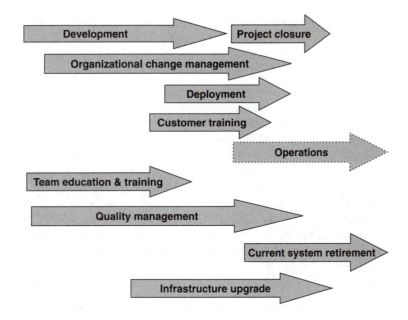

whenever events so dictate. To change a plan may be painful, but the impact of clinging to a plan known by all concerned to be unattainable can be far worse.

> *It is a bad plan that admits of no modifications.*
>
> Publilius Syrus (http://www.sysprog.net/quotmain.html).

A plan is of little value unless and until it has been communicated to, and accepted by, all parties.

■ PROTOTYPING PLAN—PPA STEP 19

A prototype can be defined as a working model of a product or a process, built as a basis for the final version. Some examples of a prototype are:

- A screen design for appearance, color mixture, font types, and placement of key items such as the organization's logo, telephone number, and key messages.
- A report designed for customers to assess the placement of various data items, font style, and general usability assessment.
- Design of a screen or computer interface for the use of keys, tabs, visual comfort, and maneuverability through different links.
- A physical mockup such as a display package for a new product.
- A scaled model of a new product.

In any given IT/Business project, a number of deliverables may need to be prototyped. Our approach to determine the need for prototyping is for the core team and key customers to come together and review the WBS and the task plan developed earlier to identify the deliverables that are good candidates for prototyping. The following checklist is typically used to assess whether a given deliverable is a candidate for prototyping or not:

- Customers' degree of difficulty to state or communicate the design and content of the deliverable
- Design team's degree of difficulty in comprehending the customers' needs regarding the layout and content of the deliverable
- The need to select from a number of possible designs for a given deliverable (different designs being driven by differing needs of key customers and/or varying design approaches by the design team)
- Major changes in human-to-machine interfaces
- Need for early familiarization with a deliverable by the intended customers

- Different groups of customers, as well as development team members, who have different views of the look and feel of certain deliverables
- Need for developing multiple scenarios (pictures) of the deliverable, by the design team, to test out efficiency, robustness, and ease of use

Architects of major building complexes have learned, to their chagrin, that people do not always use the neatly laid out sidewalks; they prefer to walk on the grass and make their own pathways because they are more convenient. The same is the case with end users of software products—people find ways to get around the processes and interfaces prescribed by the new system because of discomfort in using the new design. Prototyping is the best way to flesh out the needs, likes, and dislikes of customers long before the design is finalized. Don't skimp on it. Make sure that both the project team and the customers know how to use prototypes to flesh out requirements, interfaces, and human-to-system interfaces. Creating a prototype may add some extra time to the development work, but it will save you significant grief during project deployment and ongoing operations. The team members developing the prototypes must have excellent listening and observation skills. The project manager should lead these sessions, and make sure that the development team is sensitive to the customers' needs and suggestions. If you don't know what you are doing, don't do it on a large scale, and don't do it in public. Do it on a small scale and do it in a test lab.

> *. . . his technical team designed dropdown boxes that they thought were logical, but a focus group of end users found the feature cumbersome and the wording hard to understand.*
>
> Stacy Collett, "How Will You Connect With Customers?" *Computerworld* (January 6, 2003).

At times, the people who develop the prototypes become very committed to their own ideas and try to belittle their customers' suggestions. Because the design team has their mind set on a certain way to do things, they become inflexible regarding customer needs, and in subtle (or not so subtle) ways, they try to dissuade the customers—the exact antithesis of the purpose of prototyping. Keep in mind the purpose of a prototype: observe, analyze, and improve.

> *We were so committed to [the portal]; we were like a cult. So when someone talked about changing anything for the business, there was a lot of resistance from us. The friction just built.*
>
> Kent Odland in Scott Berinato, "Recipes for Disaster," *CIO Magazine* (July 1, 2001): (http://www.cio.com/archive/070101/secret_sidebar_2.html).

Figure 5.13 depicts the template we use to help the project team document the deliverables that are candidates for prototyping.

Occasionally, we run across situations where the design team builds a set of prototypes and gives them to the customers for their review and approval, and the customers then come to the erroneous conclusion that the system is ready for use. In this too common example, the project team sets the wrong expectations for the customer. The team must make it clear to the customers that prototypes are *early* mockups of final deliverables to be produced *later*. Customers must understand that a typical early prototype may not have the ability to read real data, does not have the robustness necessary for a production system, and may have been created with technology that will not be ported to the final production level deliverable. For example, a report may be prototyped using spreadsheet software, but it will need to be reprogrammed in a different language for the production level software release. Be careful when presenting the customer with scaled models (prototypes) of physical objects. Make sure they understand the scaling *ratios* clearly.

> *A lecturer gave a talk on the tsetse fly and illustrated his remarks by reference to an eighteen-inch model of the fly. Following the lecture, one of those attending said he quite understood that such flies could pose a problem, but the local variety were much smaller . . .*
>
> John Gall, *Systemantics: The Underground Text of System Lore, How Systems Really Work and How They Fail* (Ann Arbor, Michigan: The General Systemantics Press, 1986, p. 102).

FIGURE 5.13
Prototyping Template

Identify prototypes

Deliverables

- Which deliverables are candidates for prototyping?

_____

_____

Objectives

- Which objectives will be met by developing this prototype?

_____

_____

Stakeholders

- Which stakeholders will be impacted by developing this prototype?

_____

_____

Tools & Skills

- What tools and skills will be needed to complete the prototype successfully?

_____

_____

The author goes on to state, "Every picture tells a story—but not the same story." The lesson to be learned is that prototyping is useful, but only when done intelligently and effectively.

■ ORGANIZATION CHANGE MANAGEMENT PLAN—PPA STEP 20

One of the greatest pains to human nature is the pain of a new idea.
Walter Bagehot (http://www.brainyquote.com/quotes/quotes
/w/w/walterbage136261.html).

Any project, by its nature, means new ideas, which means a change to the status quo. Changes to status quo invariably cause resistive behavior in many. Therefore, just because a project has been sold to, and approved by, some highly placed executives, it does not automatically mean that there will be little resistance among the rank and file. The reasons for resistance are many; let us look at a few key causes:

1. The people have developed certain competencies and a level of comfort with the current process; they have invested extensive energy and time in learning and mastering it.
2. The more senior and experienced people consider their current level of expertise as their professional asset. Their level of expertise sets them apart from the more junior and new colleagues. With the deployment of the new system, they will have to give up the old and embrace the new, thereby reducing many of them to novice level. Their future professional performance will be judged on their ability to quickly master the new processes and interfaces.
3. If asked to describe their view of the current system, some of the phrases will certainly be: "familiar," "knowledgeable," "expert," "predictable," and "know how to work around problems." In reference to the new system, most of them are sure to use phrases like: "unfamiliar," "unproven," "start at the bottom," "apprehension," "fearful," and "feelings of inadequacy."

Now let us look at the proposed new system from the development team's point of view. The team is specifically charged to bring about the change, they are paid for instituting the change, and they will be rewarded if they bring about the change quickly and efficiently. Once the new system is deployed, the team members move on to different assignments. They seldom live with the change they bring about, and their job performance is seldom measured by how well they managed the change process. Few project teams realize that the new system will require end users to abandon what they have spent considerable time learning. Management expects end users to come up to speed on the new systems quickly and start producing the benefits used to justify the cost of the new system. Interestingly neither management nor the team is held accountable for the promised benefits; most of the burden falls on the end users. Finally, keep in mind that the project team has been involved in developing the system for a considerable period of time but the deployment takes place over a period of just a few days. For the end users, the change is sudden and quite disruptive. Then the project team wonders, why the end users don't flock to the system and begin to use it right away.

> *It should be borne in mind that that there is nothing more difficult to handle, more doubtful of success, and more dangerous to carry through than initiating changes . . . The innovator makes enemies of all those who prospered under the old order, and only lukewarm support is forthcoming from those who would prosper under the new.*
>
> Niccolo Machiavelli, *The Prince* (Penguin Classics).

This quote is an excellent example of the need for a well managed organizational change management plan to help ease the customers from the old to the new. What are the project manager's options for dealing with this aspect of the project? We suggest a series of actions:

- Learn about the psychology of change
- Perform project stress analysis
- Develop a change management plan
- Be kind to the customers/end users

Psychology of Change

The primary goal is to become a good change agent. To do that, one needs to take a look into the psychology of change and the best ways to bring about changes. Some of the earliest research, especially the Hawthorne Studies,[3] showed a marked positive relationship between workers' productivity and the manner in which the changes were made to their environment. The key findings from these studies can be summarized as follows:

1. Worker performance was improved if they were treated with professional *respect*.
2. Worker performance improvement was in direct proportion to their *involvement* in the discussions leading up to the planned changes.
3. Worker performance improved in proportion to the amount of *attention* bestowed upon them by their immediate supervisors.
4. Sustained worker performance was dependent on the degree of coworker (group) influence and *support*.

From this brief look at the fundamentals of the change process, it should be obvious that the people to be impacted by the change must be brought into the game very early, they must be treated with professional respect, and a support process needs to be established before the changes are actually put into place.

> *An organization's processes are embodied by its personnel. . . . Countless bitter experiences have shown that people do not change simply because an edict is made, but through education, training, persuasion, motivation, and leadership.*
>
> David Carney, *Quotations from Chairman David*, Software Engineering Institute, Carnegie Mellon University.

---

[3]The studies were conducted by Elton Mayo, a Harvard professor, from 1927 to 1932 at the Western Electric Hawthorne Works in Chicago.

Project Stress Analysis

The next step is to look back at the work done during the Pre-Launch stage and focus on the information gathered during policy and implementation level stakeholder assessments, with a special emphasis on the latter. As a quick review, we will list the four key items:

1. The degree of alignment between policy level stakeholders' objectives and implementation level stakeholders' expectations
2. The degree of change—functional, technical, and political—that the project will bring to the implementation level stakeholders
3. The degree of readiness of the implementation level stakeholders to absorb the change
4. Perception of win or lose

An in-depth review of these findings will indicate to the project manager the degree of risk and the amount of work that needs to be done to ensure a smooth transition to the new system.

> *We were going to try to adapt an archaic system to modern-day software. . . . It was like painting over rust. . . . People were resistant to change. They were doing it the old way and the new way at the same time.*
> Edward Cone, "Detroit Financial System Sputters after Overhaul,"
> *Baseline* (August 6, 2002).

For selected high-complexity projects, we advise a more formal and measured stress analysis using five attributes. Each attribute is an approximation, a reading of the situation by the project manager. Involving senior team members and senior customer representatives in the assessment process will certainly improve the quality of the measurement values.

Time Away From Primary Responsibility   This measures the amount of time the customers will need to spend away from their primary job responsibilities in order to meet their project responsibilities.

Time away	Value
<15%	1
15% to 30%	2
31% to 50%	3
51% to 75%	4
>75%	5

Degree of Change   This attribute is used to ascertain the amount of change the proposed project will bring to the customers' work environment—technology, processes, and culture.

Degree of change	Value
Negligible	1
Modest/slight	2
Medium	3
Significant	4
Major	5

Willingness to Absorb the Change   Some synonyms for "willingness" are "motivation," "enthusiasm," and "eagerness," precisely what this attribute is designed to assess. This attribute deals more with the customers' attitude and mind-set.

Willingness	Value
Unwilling	5
Somewhat unwilling	4
Somewhat willing	3
Willing	2
Very willing	1

Ability to Absorb the Change   Some of the synonyms for "ability" are "skill," "talent," and "knack." This attribute has to do with the customers' competence and qualifications.

Ability	Value
Unable	5
Somewhat unable	4
Somewhat able	3
Able	2
Very able	1

Timing of the Change   This attribute assesses the appropriateness of the time at which the customers will be asked to participate in the project—requirements definitions, review of prototypes, deployment of a pilot, and the rollout of the project.

Timing	Value
Very inappropriate	5
Inappropriate	4
Somewhat inappropriate	3
Appropriate	2
Very appropriate	1

It is important for the project manager to work with the key customers to assess the stress caused by the proposed project and to communicate the net stress values to the sponsor. The project stress analysis shown in Figure 5.14 is an example of the impact of a proposed project on its customers.

FIGURE 5.14
Project Stress Analysis

Project stress attributes	Value	Comment
Time away from primary responsibility	4	
Degree of change	3	
Willingness to absorb the change	2	
Ability to absorb the change	2	
Timing of the change	5	Look into this
Total project stress value	16	High stress

Project Stress Interpretations

Total: 1–9	Low stress
Total: 10–15	Medium stress
Total: 16–20	High stress
Total: >21	Extreme stress

The data in Figure 5.14 shows that the timing of the proposed project is not reasonable. If the timing was changed to suit the needs of the customer, and the value of this attribute could be brought down to 2, the total stress value will drop to 13, making it a medium stress project. Figure 5.14 also shows that the customers will need to spend an inordinate amount of time away from their primary job responsibilities. Usually, the project manager can do very little about this situation. However, one possible action is to contact the appropriate functional managers within the business unit to see whether they can reduce the day-to-day job time requirements to compensate for the time needed on the project. This type of project stress analysis provides sufficient advance notice to all concerned parties so that they can attend to any problem areas in a timely manner.

Develop Organization Change Management Plan

Following are four key steps to develop a comprehensive organizational change management plan. The degree of effort will depend upon the degree of stress, expected customer resistance, and the resulting risk to the project.

1. Form a subteam composed of influential customer representatives who have a championship attitude towards the project. Do not rely heavily on the hierarchical organization chart to select

the members of this subteam. Keep in mind that there is often an informal organization, within any formal organization, with its own power center(s). Prudent project managers take the time to learn and understand the intricacies of their customers' informal power structure, and then compose the subteam accordingly.

2. Create an atmosphere of mutual support and professional respect. You should not mandate a specific change management plan to the customer. The idea is for the customer to look at the overall project strategy, objectives, critical success factors, and the proposed solution, and then help develop a plan for a transition that is as painless as possible. It is important not to belittle their concerns and apprehensions. Be careful not to let the team members responsible for development of the project take over the planning session; a senior customer representative should be the lead person. Here we are reminded of the saying, "Imposition invariably fails, people support what they build."

3. Find out whether your organization has any SMEs in the field of organizational change management. If so, contact them and see what help they can give you and your team in developing and executing a comprehensive plan.

4. Planning to bring about the requisite organizational change is not a one-time event; it will need to be repeated a number of times during the project life cycle. Make the organizational change management plan—deliverables, tasks, milestones, resources—an integral part of the project plan. In Chapter 2, we discussed the differences between product and process deliverables. The organizational change management plan primarily consists of process deliverables and, as pointed out earlier, these are often given lower value by management and even by the project team.

Like any other plan for the project, the organizational change management plan must be communicated to the key stakeholders and must be approved by the sponsor. In our analysis of many failed and challenged projects, a key reoccurring problem has been the poor quality of the organizational change management plan. The problem has ranged from poor quality plans to the complete absence of plans. For some obscure reason, far too many project teams overlook this important area. The underlying, unreasonable, belief seems to be that, if they build it, the customers will love it.

> *I said, 'No way. I know how our company acts; I'll just go out and give a speech or two and they'll follow me like crazy, and there will be no problem.' But I was a fool. . . . We tried doing that, and it collapsed. We didn't get training out to people quickly enough or well enough. Change is hard to sell.*
>
> David Goudge quoted in Marcia Stepanek, "Management Matters,"
> *CIO Insight* (December 2002).

Our kudos to Mr. Goudge for being so forthright in discussing the down side of not implementing a change management process. Let us look at an example of an organization that routinely does the right thing and reaps major benefits:

> *Southwest Airlines, for example, regularly sends developers of its customer-facing Web applications to visit call centers so developers can gain a deeper understanding of what customers want and expect from contact with the company. This practice has led to customer-pleasing changes to the Southwest Web site, such as letting customers book hotel reservations quickly and easily on the site.*
>
> C. K. Prahalad, M. K. Krishnana, and Sunil Mithas, "The Technology/
> Customer Disconnect," *Optimize Magazine* (http://www.
> optimizemag.com/sue/014/customer_p3.htm).

Before closing the discussion on this topic, let's summarize the key steps to successful organization change management:

1. Make sure that the project team has a sufficient number of customer representatives as working team members. Far too many teams consist primarily of people who will design and build the product—IT, engineers, and similar technical professionals. Most technology professionals have limited business knowledge and even less business vocabulary; the combination is always a threat to project success.

2. Locate selected senior team members with the key customers. The proximity will help them learn about the customers' day-to-day business at close range, and the more astute members of

the team can also begin to "read" customers' reaction to the proposed system. This information can be very helpful to the team as they progress through the project.

3. Keep key implementation-level stakeholders in the loop. Make sure that they are invested in the project from the very start and stay involved throughout the development and implementation stages.

4. Create an atmosphere where customers are appreciated and rewarded for their efforts in helping to define requirements and review prototypes, volunteering to test the early versions of the system, and for being first in line to use the system. These people deserve extra attention. You should express your thanks to these customers for their time and contributions. Make sure the development team does not brand them as troublemakers, even when they lash back because of their fears and frustrations. Dip into the goody bag and disperse some choice items to these customers.

Change Agent

For projects that lie in zone I of the complexity chart, the use of change agents becomes a necessity. A change agent, usually a person from the professional services group (or corporate communications group), is an individual professionally trained in negotiations, conflict resolution, facilitation, rumor detection, and rumor quashing techniques. We recommend that you discuss the involvement of one or more change agents with your sponsor during the Project Staging step, and have the right person(s) identified before you start with the Execute stage.

> [Jack] Cranmer of the Mayo Clinic subscribes to the same philosophy. For his customer relationship managers, he taps only analysts or IT project managers who are former nurses and lab technicians.
>
> Elana Varon, "Ambassdors of IT," *CIO Magazine* (April 1, 2003), (http://www.cio.com/archive/040103/practices_ambassador.html).

The number of change agents will depend on the complexity of the project, the number of customers, their overall reaction to the project, and the number of deployment sites. Your change agents will serve as SMEs until you get to the midpoint of the Execute stage, and from then on, they will become progressively more involved. By the time the project reaches the Implement stage, the change agents will be spending most of their time on the project. We recommend that at least one change agent stay with the project to the end of the Implement stage.

The key skills, roles, and responsibilities of a change agent are as follows:

- Extensive business knowledge
- Project knowledge and technology awareness
- Change management skills
- Strong communication skills
  - Listening
  - Speaking
  - Writing
- Negotiations, collaboration, and conflict management
- Rumor (office grapevine) management

A change agent should not be seen (by the key stakeholders and customers) as an advocate of the project team trying to push the project through. Rather, she should be seen as an ombudsman for customers. The change agent should be readily available to customers, should possess good "project side" manners, and should be sympathetic to customer concerns. To be successful, the change agent must have the full support of the sponsor and the confidence of the project manager and the team. If, after all of your efforts to the contrary, substantial resistance to change persists, may we suggest the following as prominently posted placards:

> *There is nothing permanent except change.*
>
> Heraclitus.

> *It is not necessary to change. Survival is not mandatory.*
>
> W. Edwards Deming.

■ SCOPE MANAGEMENT PLAN—PPA STEP 21

Creeping scope is the bane of all project managers. Ask any project manager in any profession, and each one will tell you that creeping scope, the ever-present changes to customer requirements, is a perennial problem. Now, consider the following research finding:

> *Projects completed by the largest American companies have only approximately 42% of the originally-proposed features and functions. Smaller companies do much better. A total of 78.4% of their software projects will get deployed with at least 74.2% of their original features and functions.*
>
> The Standish Group, "The Chaos Report" (http://www.
> pm2go.com/sample_research/chaos_1994_1.php).

There seems to be a dichotomy here. On one side, project managers complain about scope creep (additional functionality), and at the same time the findings indicate that projects are routinely deployed with fewer functions than originally agreed upon. Interestingly, both statements are true. What actually happens is that the scope creep eats heavily and disproportionately into the project schedule to the point that, at times, the rate of scope change exceeds the rate of progress. Ultimately, as the team begins to run out of time, they begin to shed scope—bad scope pushes out good scope. Most of this is the result of a poorly defined and poorly administered scope management plan. Before we discuss our suggestions on how to manage the demands of increased scope, let us review a few attributes of project scope:

Scope Growth

In Chapter 4, Figure 4.56, we pointed out that scope changes after the Project Charter has been signed are inevitable. Reasons for changes to project scope include:

1. In the case of IT/Business projects, the preliminary scope statement and estimates are developed very early in the project life cycle—at the end of the Pre-Launch stage. Invariably, the scope is underestimated and it begins to grow as the work on the project continues—the Execute stage.
2. There is a lack of clear understanding of the customer's business, on the part of the project team, which too often is heavily loaded with technical people.
3. As the project moves through the Execute stage, more and more of the neutral and comatose stakeholders begin to wake up and want their requirements incorporated into the project.
4. In the absence of a well-defined scope management plan, most of the future opportunities, and many of the out-of-scope deliverables and features (as defined in Chapter 4, see Figure 4.30), begin to creep into the project scope.
5. The pressure to respond to changing business, customer, competitor, and general economic environments as the project moves through the Execute stage.
6. Rigorous prototyping to define the customer's requirements and comprehensive change management procedures can reduce the amount of the growth, but cannot completely prevent scope growth.
7. Project managers' inability to say no.

The Velcro Suit

Over many years of consulting work with scores of clients, we have come to the conclusion that far too many project managers don virtual Velcro suits, and customers launch scope balls at will. Project managers, typically in their first assignments, are so driven to please their customers that they pick up stray scope balls and attach them to their own suits. Most project managers simply lack the negotiation skills, and at times the authority and the political capital, to push back and say "no" to their customers. In our discussion with many project managers, we have found that they have the strong belief that they cannot say "no" to their customers, even if the added scope continues to put the project in jeopardy. Now combine this phenomenon with a dispersed team, away from the day-to-day control of the project manager, where various team members also continue to agree to most of their customers' needs. All this increases scope. Project scope does not just creep; it overwhelms the project.

Contractors and Consultants

Contractors and consultants are reimbursed for the work they do. It is not in their best interest to minimize scope creep. They may complain about it, but the managing partners love it all the way to the bank. The worst situation is when a company hires a vendor to do the project development and then assigns full project management responsibility to the vendor project manager. Unfortunately, we see this combination often. In most of these cases, the final project budgets are at least 100 percent over the original budgets.

Project Team

Keep in mind that scope changes don't always come from the customers. Often, project managers fail to aggressively manage scope changes originating from the team itself. There are instances where team members think of deliverables and features that they believe the customer should have, even though the customer has not asked for them. We call this phenomenon "underground scope creep." Team originated scope changes are harder to detect and control because they can be done without drawing much attention. We recommend three specific methods to forestall such problems:

1. The project manager should clearly and emphatically communicate to the team the problems resulting from such behavior.
2. Because persistent delays in milestone and deliverables hit rates can be a result of the underground scope creep, the project manager needs to watch milestone and deliverables hit rates closely (discussed in Chapter 7).
3. During project status review meetings, make a specific point of discussing "new tasks and deliverables that were added but were not planned." These items offer a reasonable clue to the probable source of any scope changes.

Uninvolved Sponsor

A sponsor's neglect is a problem that has the potential to ruin the project. We hold the sponsor responsible for any "unmanaged" scope growth. Our experience shows that a sponsor needs to speak routinely with the project manager about the state of the project scope. All project managers should discuss the subject of scope creep with their sponsor and then institute a well-defined scope management plan.

Another important point to keep in mind is that the true cost of scope increase is much higher than the direct cost of the additional work. For example, in Figure 5.15, we see that the project was originally budgeted for $1 million and was supposed to start producing its benefits by August 1—a profit margin of 10 percent on an expected cash flow of $100,000 per day.

FIGURE 5.15
Expected Timing of ROI

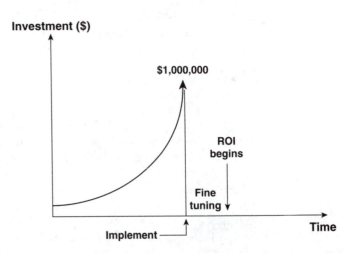

FIGURE 5.16
New Timing of ROI

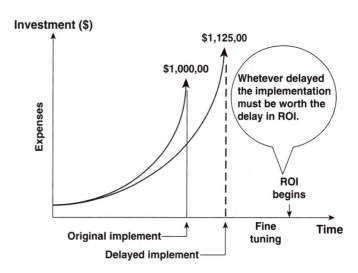

Now assume that, due to increased scope, the project is delayed by forty-five days and the extra work adds $125,000 to the original budget. Figure 5.16 depicts the new timing of the ROI.

So, what is the net cost to the project? It is much more than the added $125,000. Let us look at the numbers:

- Loss of $4,500,000 cash flow
- Loss of the 10 percent profit margin on $4,500,000 of expected business: $450,000

Were the benefits of the added scope worth the loss of the cash flow and the loss of the profit margin? This question must be answered *every time* a change of any type is requested by anyone on a project. Before discussing our recommended approach to managing scope changes, let us look at a few additional important items regarding the impact of scope changes:

- Always review the intra-project priorities defined in the Pre-Launch stage and see how the proposed change will impact the priorities ranked 1st and 2nd.
- Does the work needed to incorporate the change request fall into the future schedule, or will the team have to go back to the work already completed and change any parts thereof? For example, a change request that is made while the team is defining requirements has a markedly different impact than the same change request made when the team is in the midst of building the solution. The latter situation will cause a greater amount of rework. Now assume the worst case. The change request comes just before the team is getting ready to deploy the solution—they now have to revert to a much earlier stage of the project and redo the design and the corresponding solution. This will not only take more time, but is prone to introduction of new errors, which then will have to be discovered and corrected.
- Does the work necessary to accommodate scope increase require newer types of resources (people and/or technology)? If this is the case, the project will be delayed for a longer period of time and any new technology will add new risks.
- There comes a point in the life cycle of any project when any additional scope cannot be safely added onto the existing infrastructure—technology infrastructure, database, bandwidth, and so on. Our experience shows that when the scope growth approaches 30 percent of the original scope defined in the Project Charter, the project infrastructure needs to be redesigned because the weight of the new scope will begin to crack the infrastructure. However, we rarely see this happen. Infrastructure redesign adds both cost and time to the project, and people do not want to start over. What usually happens instead, is that teams simply patch up the infrastructure, and then chaos ensues as the project enters the production (Operations) stage.

Obviously, managing scope creep is a critical project management goal. In support of this important objective, we would like to offer the following well-tested process that provides appropriate discipline and rigor to scope management and at the same time allows for scope additions, when appropriate.

Scope Management Process

The project manager, in consultation with the project sponsor, should identify *one* representative from the customer group who will have the authority to receive change requests from different people in the business community. For each change request submitted, the requestor needs to provide the following information:

- Change description
- Reason for the change
- Benefits of the change (the requestor must state this information in financial terms)
- The impact of not making the change
- Categorize the change into one of the following three categories:
  - *Must have:* A feature necessary for functional viability of the project; For example, an overlooked or new regulatory requirement
  - *Should have:* A feature that will help reduce the work on the part of the customer and/or improve the quality of the end product; for example, a customer might have forgotten to ask for averaging the value of a column of numbers in a report and would like that feature added now
  - *Nice to have:* A feature that enhances the ease of use of the product (this type of change typically deals with the form and not the function of the product); this could be a request to change the font size, move the placement of an object on a screen, or apply a different shade of color
- The designated customer representative should collect various change requests, review each to ensure comprehensiveness, check for duplicate/overlapping change requests, and prioritize the requests using an agreed-upon prioritization method—make sure the customer representative is fully familiar with the Project Charter and understands the intra-project priority rankings
- The project manager and the customer representative must meet routinely (weekly or biweekly) to review the various change requests and decide on those that are candidates for consideration
- The project manager, working with appropriate team members, reviews the various change requests and develops the following information for each item:
  - Estimated effort to complete the change request
  - Estimated cost to complete the change request
  - Any medium to high risks associated with the change request
  - Impact of the estimated effort and risks (if any) on the intra-project priorities ranked as 1st and 2nd
  - Estimated effort to complete the information previously outlined. This is an important metric because the customers should know the amount of time and energy it takes to develop estimates for their change requests. The project manager must make it a habit to report this figure to the customer representative on a monthly basis.
- The project manager should now meet with the customer representative and discuss the information gathered, regarding the various change requests. This will include the benefits of the requested change (computed by the requestor) and the "cost" of making the change (computed by the team). Then, they should jointly decide on which requests can be accepted and should clearly define the net impact of the accepted change requests on the project's estimated cost, schedule, resources, and quality. If the project manager and the customer representative disagree, the issue(s) may need to be escalated to the sponsor for review and a decision. Fundamentally, only those changes where the benefits exceed the cost should be considered. People's whims should not be allowed to drive the project scope.

Some people may object to this process, arguing that it is too time consuming, and that all that is needed is good relations between the developers and customers to jointly solve any resulting problems. We would like to remind these people of a most perceptive observation:

How does a project get to be a year late? . . . One day at a time.

Frederick P. Brooks, Jr., p. 153.

Another important point to discuss is the closure points for different types of change requests. We suggest the following guidelines:

- The "nice to have" changes should be frozen (not incorporated) once the requirements for the project have been approved.
- The "should have" changes should be frozen (not incorporated) once the design phase has been completed.
- The "must have" changes should be frozen (not incorporated) once the testing phase has begun.

Any changes frozen out of the current project life cycle are bundled together and considered for the next phase/version of the project. Figure 5.17 depicts a template for documenting change requests. Notice the last item in the template: change request ID. This is an official sequential number assigned by the project manager to help track the change requests.

Project managers must make sure that no individual customers, no matter how high in the organization, should ever directly contact team members and ask them to make changes to project requirements. They can discuss proposed changes with a team member, but under no circumstances should any such discussion be assumed to mean an acceptance of the change by the team member. The worst scenario is when team members don the Velcro suit. If this infringement is allowed to happen, slowly the discipline of formalized scope management breaks down and the seeds of failure will be sown.

Keep in mind that scope change does not always mean the addition of new functions and features. Scope change also includes changing and/or deleting already completed deliverables. This type of change will always add effort and budget to the project and may not reduce the project schedule. Therefore, clearly and emphatically communicate to the customers and the team that any change to already finished work, even work in progress, means scope change.

Scope Creep—An Example

The following are extracts from correspondence between a project team member, the project manager, and the sponsor regarding problems that occurred when the team member agreed to scope change requests made by the customer. The problem arose when the team member, assigned to a client's project at a remote site, accepted a number of new deliverables from the customer without the project manager's knowledge. As a short background to this problem, the project manager has had difficulty with this customer in earlier projects, where the customer would add scope without wanting to pay for additional work and at the same time would blame the team for delayed delivery. This particular project was a fixed price contract with well-defined original scope. The team member sent an e-mail to the project manager with the following information:

Team Member's E-Mail

- Evaluate customer's Requirements template to identify new content: 4 hours, done.
- Link all templates so that any change to a common item in one place is automatically updated in all locations: eight hours (pure guess), four hours spent already.
- Divide Chapter 2 into two subchapters: four hours, done.
- Additional book edits (add graphics, graphics from slides): 4 hours, not done.
- Research and develop a Requirements template based on the template supplied by our customer's system development methodology vendor—contact the vendor to obtain permission to use vendor's graphic exhibits: eight hours, five hours spent already.

Project Manager's Response

- This adds 28 hours of new effort to the project (this is a low estimate and does not include the time needed for telephone conversations and follow-ups).
- Add to this at least 20 percent project management time, and the total is now 34 hours.
- Add to this the time to be spent by our support staff to do any word processing and edit the changes (a minimum of 6 hours). This means the total increases to forty hours of additional work.

Provide a description of the change:

_____

_____

Specify the change category:

Category	Definition	Rationale
❏ Must have	Necessary for the functional viability of the product	
❏ Should have	Will significantly increase product quality/marketability	
❏ Nice to have	Would enhance the ease of use	

What are the quantifiable benefits this change will provide to the project? (Think in terms of cost savings, added revenue, or competitive advantage.)

_____

_____

Describe the impact(s) that the change will have on the project:

Attribute	Impact	
Schedule	How many days will be added to the schedule?	
Cost	How many dollars will be added to the cost?	
Quality	How will the quality of the product be impacted?	
Resource availability	Will there be adequate resources to make the change? Will there be adequate resources downstream if the change causes a delay in the schedule?	
Risk of new errors	What is the probability that new errors will occur? What is the level of impact of those errors?	

What actions must be taken to manage the risk of making the change?

_____

_____

Approval

Change request submitted by:	
Change request reviewed by:	
Change request approved by:	

Change request ID:

FIGURE 5.17
Change Request Template

- The last item in the list—contacting the vendor to get permission—will cause us major problems because this deals with a third party's intellectual property and we will need to clear it through our corporate legal council (who will pay for these services?). Why is it our responsibility to obtain intellectual property releases from a third party?
- The 40 hours of new work is a 32 percent increase in scope of the original contract of 125 hours and that does not include the attorney's time. As a result, all of our profit margin has been eaten up. In fact, we are now in a loss mode on this project and the end is not in sight.

At this point, the project manager brought the project sponsor into the loop because the scope increase had breached the 10 percent threshold. Given below is the response from the sponsor to the team member.

Sponsor's Response

- The project manager is the only person who can approve any additional work with the client. However, because you agreed to the work request by the client (without even informing the project manager), and in fact have already completed quite a bit of the work, we are not able to go to the client and ask for payment for this work (remember, this is a fixed price contract). Because you are the team member on site with the client, you are our agent and we cannot back out of this additional work without causing problems with the client and the project. Your actions send a clear message to the client that they can get additional work done without going to the project manager. You have completely usurped the project manager's authority.
- As a closure to this problem and in the interest of finishing this project promptly, you and I agreed that, in the future, if the client has ANY NEW requirements, you are to record them, estimate them, and send the information to the project manager for follow up. Please DO NOT MAKE ANY COMMITMENTS to the client, even in any implied manner (do not even nod your head up and down the next time you are in a meeting with them). Make sure that the client clearly understands that your recording their new requests is nothing more than documenting their needs, and that the project manager must review the information and then decide on the next step.
- It is important that you inform the client, in written communication, that they need to contact their methodology vendor for obtaining any intellectual property use permissions. Make it clear to them that we are not authorized to execute any contacts with their vendor.
- For closure, as we discussed, please send me an e-mail message stating that you will not agree to do any additional work with the client without obtaining written approval from the project manager, and please send a copy of the message to the project manager. This will help ensure that we do not lose any more money on this contract.

Team Member's Response Given below is the response from the team member to the sponsor (with a copy to the project manager):

- I will not commit to any additions to our work at the client site.
- Any additions suggested by the client will be transmitted to the project manager along with my estimate of time necessary to complete.

Summary We believe this is a good example of both the problem caused by a breach of an established change management process and the subsequent recovery from the problem. There *was* a happy ending to this episode. According to the project manager, soon after the discourse, the team member held a meeting with the customer and explained the need for a disciplined and orderly change management process. All future change requests and associated estimates were first discussed between the project manager and the customer. Only the changes specifically approved by the project manager were forwarded to the team member. As a result, the project manager was able to bill the customer for all subsequent changes to the project and, according to him, the customer even accepted billings for a number of previously made changes.

Any scope creep in the case of contracted projects is to the great benefit of the contractor and a huge cost to the host organization. Contractors are typically able to make higher margins on scope creep than on equal functionality in the original contract. The key reason for this incongruity is that the host does not have the same negotiation prowess for the scope creep work as for the original work. For one thing, it is not possible to go out for multiple bids on scope creep. When multiple people are allowed to submit scope increases to the contractor, no real control can be exerted over the amount of additional billing the contractor can submit on the project. In fact, most contractors prefer poorly defined scope statements and an ill-defined change management processes because the more confusion there is, the higher the billing is likely to be. Therefore, in the case of a contract, clearly state the specific people who can authorize scope changes and insist that the contractor routinely report on the status of the project scope.

Change Control Board

In the case of projects with more than a few customer groups, the use of a single customer representative to funnel all change requests may not be practical because each customer group may wish to have a say in the decision-making process. In these cases, it may be necessary to establish a change control board that includes a representative from each key customer group. This arrangement will not only act as repository for direct input from different customer groups, it will also transfer the responsibility for managing change requests to the board. Of course, the board needs a leader who will resolve any disagreements and problems among its members. The project manager should make sure that the elected leader is fully aware of the principles and practices of a robust change control process and clearly understands the need to manage project scope.

During the Execute stage, as scope changes are accepted and they begin to impact the baselined schedule, cost, quality, and/or functionality, document the changes and formally report them to the customer representative(s) and the project sponsor. Once the changes *breach* any of the baselined items, hold a formal meeting with the sponsor and discuss the need for revising the affected baselines. For example, if the cumulative changes have eaten up all of the reserve set aside for the schedule, from that point on, no additional changes that will impact the project schedule can be accepted. Similarly, if the cumulative changes have exhausted the budget reserve, any more changes that affect the budget will not be considered. If these decisions are not acceptable to the customers, the sponsor will need to officially announce a new project schedule and/or a new project budget. If the sponsor is not willing to rebaseline the schedule and/or budget, and customers are not willing to curtail any more changes, failure may be imminent.

Scope Growth—The Limit

You should decide the point at which any additional scope will begin to stress the underlying infrastructure design (database, hardware, software, and telecommunications). Will the infrastructure be robust enough to support the demands of additional functionality created by the new scope? There are countless examples of situations where scope growth added so much demand on the processing capabilities of the infrastructure, that at the time of final system implementation, the system came to a halt. Then comes the inevitable last minute scramble to shore up the infrastructure by patching in additional technology, making the problem even worst. Our experience shows that, when scope growth approaches 30 percent of the original scope statement (described in the first approved version of the Project Charter), the infrastructure starts to wobble. It will not be able to deliver the expected performance. At this point, the design team will need to *formally* review the infrastructure to ensure that expected performance is still viable. This rarely happens in a well-planned and organized fashion because too many projects suffer from a lack of rigorous scope control mechanism. Also, infrastructure redesign invariably means additional budget and time for infrastructure upgrades, which result in yet another trip to the sponsor for more money and time. Not wanting to face the sponsor, many project managers take the easy way out with the thought, "We'll cross that bridge when we come to it." Unfortunately, when they do come to it (in the Operation stage), they discover that there is no bridge—just a wide chasm.

> *. . . for urgent projects it's easy to minimize network needs and focus on the application. The oversight can be costly in more ways than one.*
>> Polly Schneider, "Another Trip to Hell," *CIO Magazine* (February 15, 2000).

Our advice to project managers can be summarized as follows:

1. In concert with the technology design SMEs, define the scope growth threshold for infrastructure review (we suggest a 30 percent increase in scope as the trigger point).
2. Convey the importance of infrastructure review to the change control board members.
3. Define a robust scope management process.
4. Rigorously record all scope growth.
5. Diligently monitor scope growth.
6. Make sure to activate the technology viability vital sign (Chapter 7) when the scope growth approaches the infrastructure review threshold.

Project managers who make it a practice to monitor scope growth are able to head off most infrastructure performance problems in a timely manner. It is important to keep in mind that here in the Launch stage we are simply defining the procedures to be followed to manage any changes to the scope once the project moves to the Execute stage.

Configuration Management

Another important component of a Scope Management Plan is configuration management. Any system or product is composed of a set of constituent components that change and evolve as the system or product is being developed. For example, computer hardware and/or software may be updated a number of times during the development life cycle of an IT/Business system. Similarly, the Project Charter and the Project Schedule may undergo a number of revisions as the project progresses. Configuration management is the process of documenting, controlling, and managing any changes to key project components and deliverables throughout the project life cycle. Without a well-defined and rigorously followed configuration management system, various project components can easily get out of control as different people access these to review, change, and update their contents. Duplication, overlaps, and out-of-date hardware, software, and documentation are the primary results of poor configuration management. The overall configuration management of hardware and software in any given organization is not the domain of individual project managers; the responsibility typically rests with a special group within the IT department. Talk with your functional manager, the project office (if one exists), or the operations group to learn about the configuration management standards, procedures, and tools. You and your core team should become fully conversant with the official configuration management processes and tools, and then make sure to educate your entire team (anyone who develops and finalizes a deliverable) accordingly. Far too many project managers learn, too late in the project life cycle, that the team has not followed the requisite configuration management discipline and the instances of duplicate, overlapping, and out-of-date deliverables begin to consume extensive team time—a waste of valuable resources and a sure hit on the product quality.

Project Change Management Plan

From the discussion regarding an Organization Change Management Plan (step 20), and Scope Management Plan (step 21), it should be clear that you are dealing with two different types of changes. The former relates to the changes needed in the general day-to-day work environment of the project's implementation-level stakeholders, and the latter relates to the changes that need to be made to the project scope (requirements). The project change management plan represents the sum of these two change management plans.

■ STAFFING PLAN—PPA STEP 22

Earlier in the chapter, we discussed the various forms of team structures, along with our recommended project organization model (Figures 5.7 and 5.8). Now we will discuss staffing the project organization, i.e., building the team. The following elements influence the step of team design and staffing:

- Project objectives
- Stakeholder Analysis
- Complexity Assessment
- Risk Assessment
- Scope statement
- Task Plan
- Organization Change Management Plan

The purpose of a team's structure is to bring together the right group of people, who will collectively provide the necessary skills to complete the various project deliverables in a timely manner and to the right quality and cost. The secondary requirement of a well-designed team structure is its ability to add to the professional growth and maturity of the various team members. The various elements of a project team are as follows:

- Management team
- Sponsor
- Project manager's supervisor
- Functional managers
- Project manager
- Team members
- SMEs

Management Team

In any organization, different levels of managers and executives have different levels of authority; for example, the authority to approve budgets up to a certain limit, the authority to commit the company to different types of contracts, and the authority to hire/transfer/fire employees. For any given project to be successfully executed, people at the right level need to be involved so that they are available for timely and effective business decisions. Projects that fall within zone I of the complexity chart will require the collective authority of the senior executives of the various cross-functional organizations impacted by the project. Having them as a part of the management team assures their attention, time, and commitment to the project. They will need to meet on a routine basis (monthly, bi-monthly, or quarterly) to review the project status and progress and resolve any issues escalated to their level. For zone I projects, typically the senior executives who report directly to the CEO would compose the management team. For high zone II and high zone III projects, vice president and director-level managers will typically form the management team. Management teams are seldom needed for projects that have less complexity.

Some of the prerequisites of an effective management team are as follows:

- They should represent all of the primary policy- and implementation-level organizations impacting, and impacted by, the project.
- The sponsor of the project should chair the management team.
- The management team expressly agrees not to commandeer the authority of the sponsor or the project manager—they will refrain from giving orders or directions to any team member. Any such communications will be conveyed through the sponsor.
- They will meet at agreed-upon intervals and take into consideration any issues escalated to their level and make timely decisions.
- They will use their personal influence and the power of their office to champion the project.

A project manager does not typically have the authority or wherewithal to formulate a management team or to hold them responsible for their actions. However, for projects that will benefit from such a team, the project manager must work with the sponsor to make sure that an appropriate team is formulated and that the sponsor spends the necessary time and effort to educate (orient) the management team members about their roles and responsibilities toward the project. Some of the other terms for "management team" are: "management review committee," "steering committee," "executive steering group," and "executive steering." Whichever term you elect to use, make sure it is the term used among all project managers.

Sponsor

The project sponsor is perhaps the most important person on the project team. If one were to use the analogy of an arch, the sponsor would be the keystone (the one piece that keeps the arch in balance and structurally feasible). The sponsor, an appropriate level manager with the requisite authority and necessary personal commitment, is the key to the success of any project. Without the guidance, leadership, and authority of a committed sponsor, project success is a shot in the dark—the chances of hitting the target are close to none (about the same as winning the lottery to fund one's pension plan).

FIGURE 5.18
Suggested Project Sponsors

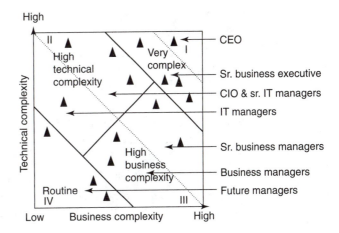

The two key questions at this point are:

1. Who should be the sponsor?
2. What are the primary roles and responsibilities of a sponsor?

In order to decide on the best sponsor for a given project, we refer again to the complexity chart (see Figure 5.18), and depending on the placement of the project within the chart, determine who the ideal candidate is. The primary reason behind this assessment is that a project's complexity highlights the intrinsic structure of the project, and the sponsor should be able to clearly understand and manage the project structure and its complexity. The skill, experience, and authority of the sponsor should be greater than the demands of the project so that it is the sponsor who envelopes the project and not vice versa. Keeping this in mind, we suggest the sponsor selection as depicted in Figure 5.18.

Figure 5.18 shows that, as the complexity level rises, the level of manager needed as a sponsor also rises. Let us look into the various levels of sponsorship (moving from the top right of the complexity chart toward the bottom left of the chart).

1. For projects at the top right of the chart, high zone I, the sponsor must be the CEO, as these are "bet the company" projects (mergers, major acquisitions, and corporate spin-offs). In these projects, the board of directors would serve as the management team. For projects in the lower zone I area, the senior business executives must take on the sponsorship.
2. For projects in the high zone II area (the technologically sensitive area of the chart), the senior technology executives are best equipped for sponsorship. For projects in the lower zone II area, technology managers and supervisors can be the sponsors.
3. For projects in the high zone III area (business-sensitive area of the chart), middle-level business executives and managers are best suited to act as sponsors. For projects in the lower zone II area, junior managers and supervisors can be the sponsors.
4. For projects in zone IV, newly appointed supervisors and managers, as well as selected experienced project managers, can be the sponsors.

The sponsor must be at the appropriate level of authority for prompt decision making. If the sponsor has to continually go to a "higher court" to resolve day-to-day issues, the project will undoubtedly flounder. Our test for the appropriate level of authority of a sponsor is whether she can make 80 percent of the decisions, which include resolving policy issues and cross-functional disagreements, without having to get approvals from colleagues or higher-ups. In our discussions with business executives, a frequently asked question is, "Because I don't really have the time to sponsor this project, can I delegate sponsorship to one of the managers who reports to me?" We always respond with: "If that person will be able to make 80 percent of the necessary decisions, without having to get approvals from you, that person should have been the sponsor in the first place. Going to a higher level is, in fact, a drawback because the higher-ups will seldom have the time and may not have the interest in being the sponsor."

This discussion makes it clear that business executives and managers need to sponsor zone I and zone III projects. Unfortunately, this is not usually the case. Responsibility of almost all of zone III and most of lower zone I projects falls into the laps of technology managers, and sponsorship is spread among the CIO and his direct reports.

> *... DRMS unraveled because it was run by Detroit's technology managers, not the financial users who were to be the system's ultimate beneficiaries.*
> Edward Cone, "Detroit Financial System Sputters after Overhaul," *Baseline*
> (August 6, 2002).

We have known cases of the CIO being the sponsor of dozens of projects at once. We call this "foster sponsorship"—projects that have been abandoned by their business executives and taken over by the CIO. Most of these projects either fail outright or are delivered in a challenged position (over budget, behind schedule, and of poor quality). We prefer the term "delinquent projects."

> *... the lack of a business sponsor was the ultimate oversight.*
> Polly Schneider, "Another Trip to Hell," *CIO Magazine* (February 15, 2000).

> *U.S. suspends medical research aid to Johns Hopkins. Johns Hopkins University, one of the USA's leading research institutions, has been blocked by U.S. health officials from doing federally funded human research following the death last month of a 24-year-old research volunteer in an asthma study. In a letter suspending human research ... investigators for the federal Office of Human Research Protection (OHRP) detailed 24 violations. ... Overall, the letter suggests that the board members were too few, overseeing too many projects, with too little help.*
> *USA Today* (July 20, 2001).

We strongly believe that project sponsorship is an excellent platform for management skills development. As such, the sponsorship role should be made available to individuals being groomed for management positions (including senior project managers). It is crucial to the success of the project to have a sponsor who has the time, will pay attention, and has a vested interest in the successful completion of the project.

Sponsor's Roles and Responsibilities   The sponsor has many roles to play, as is evident from the following list of sponsor roles and responsibilities:

1. Appoint an appropriately skilled project manager
2. Approve project charter, task plan, estimate, budget, and schedule
3. Champion the project, project manager, and project team
4. Commit time and political capital to the project
5. Conduct formal appraisals of the project manager's performance
6. Empower the project manager with the appropriate authority
7. Encourage intelligent disobedience
8. Ensure sustained buy-in at all levels
9. Ensure timely availability of needed resources
10. Follow up to ensure that promised benefits are realized
11. Formally manage project scope
12. Keep informed about project status
13. Keep the team out of political minefields
14. Provide feedback on performance *v.* expectations
15. Provide guidance and direction for key business strategies
16. Resolve major policy issues
17. Shield project teams from unrealistic customer demands
18. Understand project complexity

Although they appear to be self-explanatory, let us discuss these roles in some detail. Far too many sponsors do not take their responsibilities seriously, and many have the belief that all that is needed is cursory oversight. We completely disagree with the cursory oversight view and strongly believe in a highly involved sponsor with full oversight of the project. Project sponsorship is not a spectator sport.

Appoint an Appropriately-Skilled Project Manager: It is the responsibility of the sponsor to make sure that the project manager has the requisite skills to manage the project. One of the first

FIGURE 5.19

Kiviat Chart—Skills
Assessment

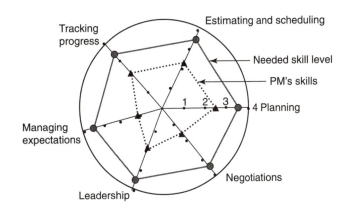

actions a sponsor needs to take at the start of any project is to work with the appropriate manager(s) to decide on the individual who will be appointed as the project manager. In the case of an IT project, the discussions might be with the CIO or the project office (if one exists). Similarly, for a business project, the sponsor will need to contact the business unit manager in charge of project managers. The sponsor and the appropriate manager then jointly identify candidates for the project manager's position. As a part of this selection process, the sponsor should review the overall skills of the primary candidates. One of the simplest and most effective tools for portraying an individual's skills is the Kiviat chart[4] depicted in Figure 5.19.

In Figure 5.19, different spokes of the wheel represent the collection of skills that the project manager must have to successfully manage the project at hand. The small triangle on each spoke represents the level of that particular skill *possessed* by the project manager. The small circle on each spoke represents the level of the skill *needed* to successfully manage the project. The placement of these circle points also reflects the complexity of the project; the higher the complexity is, the higher the level of skill required to manage the project. If a triangle is placed toward the inside of a circle, the gap represents the *deficiency* in that particular skill. When a triangle is placed toward the outside of a circle symbol, the gap is the degree of excess of that skill. Two key questions here are:

1. How should the Kiviat chart be plotted?
2. How should the plotted information be used?

The skills assessment and selection of the project manager must be done jointly by the sponsor and the manager responsible for supplying project managers. For this discussion, let us assume that one of the managers for the IT group and the project sponsor are involved in this step. The ideal scenario is where the IT manager has reviewed the Project Charter, with special attention to the Stakeholder Analysis, Complexity Assessment, and Risk Assessment and has developed a Kiviat chart depicting the level of skills needed for the project (let us assume that the project at hand is of medium-to-high complexity). Additionally, the manager should have also developed a short list of candidates, along with their skill profiles, as depicted in Figure 5.20.

FIGURE 5.20

Candidate Skills List

Skill description	Candidate 1	Candidate 2	Candidate 3
Planning	3.0	3.5	3.5
Estimating	2.5	3.5	3.0
Scheduling	3.0	4.0	4.0
Tracking	3.0	3.5	4.0
Negotiations	2.0	3.0	4.0
Leadership	2.0	3.0	4.0
Expectations management	2.0	2.5	3.5
Technology	3.0	3.5	3.5
Business knowledge	4.0	2.0	2.0
Average skill level	**2.7**	**3.2**	**3.5**

---

[4]The chart is named after its originator, Philip J. Kiviat.

FIGURE 5.21
Kiviat Chart—Candidate 1

During the meeting with the sponsor, the two can review the skills of the various candidates and decide on the best person for the job. Let us analyze the suitability of candidate 1 for the position. Figure 5.21 depicts the complexity *v.* the skill levels of candidate 1.

Once the data has been recorded, the manager and the sponsor need to decide on any education, training, and/or mentoring needs for their prime candidate. Our recommendations regarding the gap (shortage) between what is needed and what the proposed project manager possesses are as follows:

Gap	0.5 to 1.0	On the job training (OJT)
Gap	1.0 to 1.5	OJT + education
Gap	1.5 to 2.0	OJT + education + mentoring
Gap	> 2.0	No primary responsibility

"OJT" means that the person has sufficient skills to be able to undertake that responsibility without any measurable risk to the project, and will be able to quickly learn from experience and gain the needed skill. "Education" means the person needs to undergo *formal* education on the subject. Of course, the education option is not limited only to people who have a gap of 1.0 or greater; many of those with a lesser gap will certainly benefit from formal education programs. Mentoring means that the person needs access to a SME who will advise and guide the project manager in a nonjudgmental manner. The SME does not carry out any performance assessment of the project manager; the person is there solely to help provide the needed expertise to the project manager. People who have a gap of 2.0 or more do not have the skills to be given primary (sole) responsibility. If they are given sole responsibility, the project has a high risk of poor performance. When the given skills fall so short of what is needed, the work related to that skill should be delegated to someone else while the person in need is being educated and trained in the specific area. We know of a number of situations where the sponsor and the functional manager included the selected project manager in this assessment process. We strongly second this approach, because the process goes a long way toward helping the project manager understand the requirements of the position and the specific skill areas where he might need help.

Getting back to candidate 1 the individual has considerable gaps in negotiations, leadership, and expectations management skills and will not make a good fit for the project because of its high complexity. Candidate 2, on the other hand, appears to be better qualified, except in the area of business knowledge (see Figure 5.22). We also see that the expectation management skill shows a gap of 1.0 between the project complexity and the candidate's skill profile and this gap needs to addressed. Because of this degree of gap, it will behoove the manager to reassess the candidate's negotiations skill (it may have been assessed too high).

From the data presented in Figure 5.20, one can conclude that candidate 3 is the most qualified of the three, perhaps too qualified for the project's complexity. This individual may not find the assignment very challenging.

FIGURE 5.22
Kiviat Chart—Candidate 2

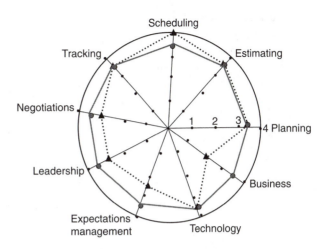

Approve Project Charter, Task Plan, Estimate, Budget, and Schedule: This means that the sponsor has taken the time to review each of these key components of the project and has put her stamp of approval on them. Of course, a one-time evaluation of these items is not sufficient; the sponsor will need to review them at multiple points during the project life cycle. The minimum review milestones are the five stage gates within the PPA—one at the end of each stage. These reviews and approvals not only assure that the right processes are being followed, but give a clear message that the sponsor is interested and involved in the disciplined project management process.

Champion the Project, Project Manager, and Project Team: Every project needs champions, and the foremost champion must be the sponsor. The sponsor needs to send a strong and continuous signal that the project is important, the project manager is his agent, and the team has the sponsor's full support. Imagine a football coach who does not like the upcoming game, has little faith in the quarterback, questions the team's ability to win, and displays general disdain for many players. Occasionally, we encounter sponsors who have little interest in the projects they were sponsoring or other sponsors who actually display nemesis behavior toward their projects. None of these projects were successful, the project managers were traumatized, and the team members worked under great stress.

Commit Time and Political Capital to the Project: The long list of sponsor's roles and responsibilities emphasizes the fact that being a project sponsor is not a spectator sport; it *requires* specific skills, commitment of personal time, energy, and political capital. The project manager must be confident that the sponsor has the time, energy, and the requisite buy-in of the proposed project to fulfill her responsibilities. In the case of business projects that have high IT content, a committed sponsor is hard to find. The reason is that far too many business executives suffer from the mistaken belief that they have neither the need nor the time to get involved. The common refrain from many business executives is, "That's why we hire the IT people." The sponsor must not succumb to these pretexts. The amount of a sponsor's time needed to oversee a project will depend on the complexity of the project. As we have suggested before, our recommendations are:

- Zone I projects: 8 to 10 hours per month
- High zone II and high zone III projects: 6 to 8 hours per month
- Low zone II and low zone III projects: 4 to 6 hours per month
- Zone IV projects: 2 to 4 hours per month

These recommended hours are averaged minimum values; actual time will depend on the specific conditions of a given project, the leadership qualities of the project manager, and the skills of the team. However, take note that these recommended times are on the lower side of the scale and in many instances the sponsor may need to spend even more time. The recommended

FIGURE 5.23
Sponsor's Time
Commitment—Survey Data

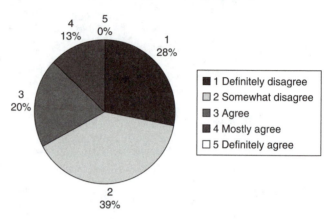

Project Sponsors from Business Units Live Up to Their Time
Commitments (to the Project Team)?

- 1 Definitely disagree
- 2 Somewhat disagree
- 3 Agree
- 4 Mostly agree
- 5 Definitely agree

times can also be used to assess the total number of projects a person should sponsor at any given time. We often see the names of senior executives appear as sponsors on multiple projects, often without their knowledge or consent, because project managers believe that their names will give the projects certain legitimacy. We term this practice "trolling for sponsors." If the sponsor is too busy running the business or too low in the corporate hierarchy to wield the necessary influence, the corresponding project is a prime candidate for failure. The sponsor's neck has to be on the line.

Immediate access to the sponsor by the project manager and a quick response from the sponsors are the key elements of effective sponsorship. We constantly advise our clients that if a sponsor of the requisite authority, time commitment, and interest is not available for a proposed project, it is better to postpone the start of the project. Doing otherwise sends the project down the path of certain failure. The data in Figure 5.23 shows that 28 percent of the sponsors absolutely did not live up to their time commitments. Even worse, 0 percent were fully invested in their projects.

Over the years, countless project managers have expressed their angst over their inability to get committed sponsors for their projects. In the past, the sorrowful renditions of one project manager inspired us to write this sad refrain.

> "My sponsor done left me,
> don't come round no more,
> no more."

To the uninitiated, we point out that this has the makings of a great country western song; just the grammar tells us that. The complete lyrics of the song contain the requisite train, rain, mom, truck, cheating heart, tears, and Shepp, the faithful dog. For those project managers who are vocally challenged, go to your local novelty store, get one of those inflatable sponsors, and pump it up. It may not help you manage your project any more successfully, but people have told us that if you buckle it up in the front passenger's seat, it may help you get into the faster commute lanes—at your own risk.

Conduct Formal Appraisals of the Project Manager's Performance: A typical project manager has two bosses: the functional manager to whom the project manager reports and the project sponsor. This creates an interesting dichotomy, because typically, the project manager's career path is managed by the functional manager, but while assigned to a given project, the project manager does not really do any direct work for that person. Also, a project manager, during any given year, will work for one or more project sponsors, who typically have little involvement with the project manager's career path.

So how does the project manager's functional manager know about the performance of the project manager? Functional managers are supposed to work closely with appropriate sponsors to assess the performance of their project managers. In order to conduct fair and realistic performance assessments, it is imperative that the sponsors clearly understand the principles, practices, tools, and techniques of project management, and then with consultations with appropriate functional managers, complete project manager performance appraisals. We suggest that informal appraisals be done at about 3-month intervals with formal (recorded) appraisals being performed every 6 to 9 months.

Empower the Project Manager with Appropriate Authority: What does that mean? To us, it means that the project manager has an appropriate level of decision-making authority without first having to check with his functional boss or the project sponsor. This authority should be well-defined, documented, and communicated broadly. The degree of authority needs to be in concert with the complexity of the project. The higher the complexity, the greater the degree of authority that is required. The authority would include such areas as spending limits, the ability to hire and fire people from the project, the ability to say "no" to the demands of customers, and the ability to reward team members for their performance or issue warnings for poor performance. If a project manager does not have the requisite authority in concert with his responsibility, the person is, in reality, an administrator—someone who carries out someone else's wishes, commands, and directions. In fact, when project managers are not given the authority and are forced to act as administrators, no one is in charge. In these cases, team members lose focus. They are continuously distracted due to the directives now coming from a multitude of directions (their functional managers, customers, other project managers, and occasionally from the sponsor). The results are confusion and chaos— a sure road to failed and challenged projects. Our strong advice to all sponsors is for them to work with their project managers and clearly lay out their roles and responsibilities as well the accompanying authority. It is important for the sponsor to explicitly ascribe sufficient status and public recognition to the project manager to enable him to perform his duties effectively. This is especially important when the project manager is junior (in hierarchy and pay) to one or more team members. In such situations, assigning a senior mentor to the project manager is highly recommended because the mentor's guidance and support can go a long way toward helping the project manager navigate the turbulent waters of the corporate hierarchy. If, during the course of a project, any of the sponsor's colleagues, functional managers, customers, or vendors try to bypass the project manager's authority, the sponsor should promptly intervene and remind the errant party of the need for respecting the project manager's authority. The best method for a sponsor to empower a project manager is to provide him with the necessary visible support.

For zone I, high zone II, and high zone III projects, it is paramount that various stakeholders, functional managers, key customers, and the project team see the project manager as a person of appropriate authority. Even though we have made a strong point that a project's organization structure is not a replication of a corporate authority structure, in real life, *perceived* status of the project manager still counts. In our experience with two projects that landed toward the very right upper corner of zone I, and had a fairly large number of third party vendors as implementation-level stakeholders, the project managers were actually promoted to two levels above their positions, with appropriate pay increases, new titles, and office locations. They were each assigned personal assistants. The job promotions were widely announced within the respective organizations, as well as to the management of third party implementation-level stakeholders. As a result, all of the cross-functional managers, as well the third party managers clearly understood the value the corporate management placed in the success of the proposed projects.

> *Without diluting the effectiveness of the project manager, the direct involvement of the sponsor strengthens the project manager in dealings with superiors, peers and team members.*
>
> George Glaser, "Projects: Orphans at Birth," *Meridian Report*
> (Winter 1993, Volume 2).

One of the best ways for a sponsor to find out whether a project manager feels empowered is to ask the question, "Will this project manager volunteer to manage another project for me?" Mind you, the project manager answering the question must feel fully comfortable with her answer. It must not be asked under duress.

Encourage Intelligent Disobedience: At this point, we turn to a discussion of the "intelligent disobedience" trait exhibited by guide dogs for the blind. The following scenario illustrates this behavior well: At an intersection, based on traffic sound and a general sense of safety, the blind person initiates the move to cross the street, giving a signal to the dog. However, if there is traffic blocking the crosswalk, the guide dog will disobey the move forward command. The owner learns through training to trust the dog. In the guide dog training lingo, "intelligent disobedience" is the ability of the dog to sense and decide that the path ahead is dangerous, even though the dog's owner wants to proceed.[5] Now consider a different scenario: The dog disobeys the owner's command because it sees traffic blocking the intersection and the dog's owner *punishes* the dog for disobeying the command. You can imagine the consequences. Guide dog owners are trained to trust their guide dogs because the two have to work as a *team* for the protection and safety of the owner.

This message applies to both the sponsor and the project manager. It is important that project managers be empowered to *push back* when they believe that a proposed action will put the organization in harm's way. The sponsors must learn to trust their project managers to do the right thing. Of course, if project managers are not well trained in reading the danger signals, or sponsors do not trust them, accidents are inevitable. In the absence of implicit trust between sponsors and project managers, sponsors place minimal value in what project managers have to say and all project communications become a series of dictates from sponsors to project managers. As a result, project managers feel that their only option is to do as they are told, though they know that the outcome may harm the organization. This begrudging compliance is an unfortunate attitude in any circumstance. In the extreme case, this attitude will lead a project manager to make an egregious error in judgment. Although thoroughly convinced that the directive from the sponsor or the customer will cause irreparable harm to the project, the project manager, nevertheless, proceeds with the work to put the directive into action. Sponsors must develop an awareness of these different attitudes and behaviors, and must work hard to establish an environment of open and forthright communications with due trust and respect for their project managers.

We frequently ask sponsors whether project managers in their organizations are encouraged to practice intelligent disobedience. How do you believe your sponsor would answer this question? How would you?

Ensure Sustained Buy-In at All Levels: This means reviewing the policy-level and implementation-level stakeholder assessments, and making sure that all key people sustain interest in the project and support it. Buy-in, means that the key stakeholders continue to see the value of the project and understand the need for their ongoing support through championship behavior and release of appropriate resources in a timely manner. One technique to ensure sustained buy-in is for the sponsor to pick up the phone and contact key stakeholders to discuss any issues related to the project and to "sell" the project. To those who would comment that this is a lot of work, it is, and that is the job and a key responsibility of the sponsor. If the key stakeholders do not hear positive words from the sponsor about the project, they will lose interest, and the project will suffer.

Ensure Timely Availability of Needed Resources: Some people might argue, "Isn't that the job of the project manager?" The operative words here are *ensure* and *timely*. Earlier, in the project organization section, we made the point that a given project organization is a temporary structure, and that most people on the project team are on loan from their respective departments. In addition, many of the team members have other jobs—their regular day jobs and/or assignments to other projects—and are not assigned solely to the project at hand. These people are easily distracted by their other responsibilities and might not be ready to join the team at the time specified by the project manager. In such cases, the project manager must work with appropriate functional managers to ensure timely availability. However, there will be instances when other priorities become urgent and people are just not available. Of course, these crises will likely compromise the project schedule. Under such circumstances, the project manager, after exhausting his effort, needs to escalate the issue to the sponsor. Then it becomes the sponsor's responsibility to step in and push the functional managers toward making the right resources available at the right time. Again, keep in mind that the authority over resources is shared among the functional managers and the project manager, with the project manager at the lower end of the totem pole. It is important for the sponsor to understand that the project manager will occasionally need the support of the sponsor to get things done as planned.

---

[5]Our thanks to Guide Dogs for the Blind, Inc., A nonprofit, charitable organization, San Rafael, CA, for explaining the "intelligent disobedience" trait of Guide Dogs (www.guidedogs.com).

Follow up to Ensure That Promised Benefits Are Realized: This is an extremely important point of discussion. We strongly believe that, ultimately, the project's objectives are "owned" by the sponsor and it is the sponsor's responsibility to make sure that the stated benefits do actually materialize. In this sense, the sponsor's responsibilities do not end when a given project is deployed; they continue through the Operation stage. You will later see that the Operation stage has a specific step to measure value-to-business, which is where the assessment of project success eventually lies. The project sponsor's performance should be tied to the degree to which the project objectives are actually achieved.

Formally Manage Project Scope: Isn't that the responsibility of the project manager? At this point, we direct the sponsor to the dismal history of scope management—the fact that most projects suffer from excessive scope creep and many die from scope explosion. Under the earlier discussion of the Scope Management Plan, we clearly outlined the problem with scope management.

Therefore, we strongly recommend that the sponsor take on the *oversight* responsibility regarding project scope, especially if a project is schedule and/or cost driven. At every meeting with the project manager, the sponsor should inquire about the state of the scope and make sure that it is under control.

Keep Informed About Project Status: This point reminds us of the story of when someone asked an executive, "Is it true that many sponsors are ignorant about their projects and are quite apathetic?" The response was, "I don't know and I don't care." Unfortunately, there is too much truth to this quip. In our discussions with scores of project managers, we have learned that many sponsors get involved only when things are going sour. This is not a good habit. Project sponsors and project managers need to jointly discuss and decide on the process to be used to assess, validate, and report project status, from the team members to the project manager, from the project manager to his boss, and from the project manager to the sponsor. We suggest the use of well-defined vital signs and look-ahead windows (see Chapter 7). Project managers and sponsors must meet routinely to *formally* review the project status—schedule, cost, scope, quality, risks, and issues. Cursory meetings in the hallways and elevators where the sponsor asks, "How's the project doing?" and the project manager responds, "Oh, we are doing just fine, thank you" are the makings of major bad news later in the project's life cycle.

Keep the Team Out of Political Minefields: This is an important area to focus upon because one of the main things that will sap the team's energy is organizational politics—struggles for position and power among high-level stakeholders. Some of the ways in which different people can manifest the political infighting are:

1. Nemesis stakeholders badmouthing the project, the project manager, and the team
2. Nemesis stakeholders displaying nearly comatose behavior during Project Charter development, requirement definitions, and product design
3. Functional managers usurping the project manager's authority by moving, removing, and reassigning their resources from the team at will
4. Consultants and vendors bypassing the project manager and approaching key stakeholders directly, even the sponsor, and negating the project manager's control and authority

All of these are damaging to any project. Unfortunately, they are far too common in many organizations. They also represent another key reason for the high number of challenged and failed IT/Business projects.

Provide Guidance and Direction for Key Business Strategies: As we discussed in the Idea and Pre-Launch stages, any given project is designed to translate specific organizational strategies into processes and products. One question we like to pose to project managers and team members is, "What specific strategy is the project linked to?" We suggest you, the sponsor, do the same. In our discussions with hundreds of project managers and countless team members, we are still chagrined to learn that a surprising number do not have a clear understanding of the strategy with which the

FIGURE 5.24
Sponsors' Support and
Guidance—Survey Data

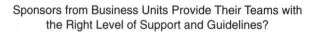
Sponsors from Business Units Provide Their Teams with
the Right Level of Support and Guidelines?

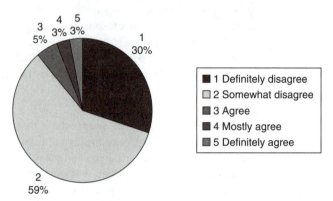

project is aligned. Data in Figure 5.24 clearly shows that too many sponsors are remiss in this important responsibility.

The sponsor must take the time to discuss, with the project team, the manner in which the project at hand will help meet the strategic needs of the organization, and then repeat the discussion periodically.

Provide Feedback on Performance v. Expectations: Do the project manager and the team clearly understand what is expected of them and how they are doing? Even when the first part of the statement is true, the latter may not be. It is imperative that the sponsors take the time to clearly convey to the project manager, at regular intervals, their feedback on the project manager's performance.

Resolve Major Policy Issues: We define "issues" as the "potholes in the road to project success." Therefore, major policy issues can be compared to sink holes. If not properly attended to in a timely manner, they will begin to devour key components of the project—scope, budget, quality, time, and even some team members. Typically, major policy issues are outside the power and authority of the project manager and need sponsor and management attention. It is important that the project manager escalate these types of issues to the appropriate functional managers. If no resolution can be achieved at this level, the next escalation is to the project manager's boss. If no resolution is in sight, the issue is brought to the attention of the sponsor. The sponsor, in turn, may have to convene the management team to resolve certain highly sensitive cross-functional issues. It is important for the sponsor to realize that, when issues at this level go unresolved, the team slows down its work and waits for management decisions. Consequently, no real progress is being made on the project. Any work that is done may need to be redone when the issues are finally resolved; more often, the work may have to be completely discarded. This mix up will negatively affect the team's morale and their trust in the sponsor's leadership.

Shield Project Teams from Unrealistic Customer Demands: We all know that, at times, customers can be unreasonable and unrealistic in their expectations. Often, they wait too long and then want the project team to quickly complete work to meet deadlines they ignored all along. Customers are also subject to external pressures they cannot control—government regulations, competitive positioning, and emerging opportunities, and the classic "silver bullet" syndrome (also known as Management By Magazine[6]). Forcing the team to agree to unattainable deadlines and unrealistic cost figures is clearly not the solution. Unfortunately, many project managers cannot win these fights on their own because they do not have the political chips, and most are not sufficiently skilled, to negotiate with "unreasonable" customers. They need the sponsor's help and support. Whether project teams react with "intelligent disobedience" or with "begrudging compliance" largely depends on the sponsors' cues.

Understand Project Complexity: One would assume that when a sponsor approves the Project Charter, he would have carefully reviewed the project's Complexity Assessment and associated risks. That assumption is based on two premises:

---

[6]This occurs when the customer reads an article on an airplane while 35,000 feet over Kansas and forms a new vision.

1. The project manager has conducted a comprehensive complexity assessment. In our experience with a large number of projects in a large number of organizations, we have seen very little of this work. A well-designed complexity assessment process is not prevalent in the profession, and most project management methodologies pay cursory attention to the subject.
2. The sponsor has carefully reviewed the Project Charter. Unfortunately, it is not in the nature of many sponsors to do this. They are too busy, they expect project managers to take care of it, or they believe in sayings such as, "We will cross that bridge when we come to it." When they come to it, it is often too late to deal with the problem.

Our advice to sponsors is for them to carefully review the Complexity Assessment, discuss the findings with the project manager, and make sure that the project manager has included all complexity elements rated as 4 in the Risk Assessment.

> *One of the most important things I expect my team to learn is that we must educate our business partners on the complexities and challenges of information technology. All too often, IT professionals are guilty of condescendingly telling business partners that they don't need to understand the technical aspects of a project.*
> Robert B. Carter, "Forging Partnerships," *Computerworld*
> (August 26, 2002): p. 39.

Without a strong sponsor, the project will fall apart. Despite this well documented truth, too few projects have the benefit of skilled and committed sponsors. Many sponsors have the mistaken belief that their responsibility to a project is over when the charter is approved and they can then move on to other important endeavors like coming up with more new ideas. The fact is that ideas are a dime a dozen; it is the execution that takes time, money, and energy.

> *Projects are launched which are orphans at birth. No manager can be identified who is willing to take on responsibility for their success.*
> George Glaser, "Projects: Orphans at Birth," *Meridian Report 2*
> (Winter, 1993).

In the case of two major project failures—Sobeys Inc.'s (Canada's second-largest supermarket chain) abandonment of an $89 million project and Nike's scuttling of a troubled $400 million project—sponsorship was most probably relegated to the respective CIOs. When the inevitable failure does happen, the higher-ups of the organization need a sacrifice. Who is a better candidate than the CIO? That is what happened in the case of Sobey's Inc.

> *Sobey's ditches a grocery application and its CIO, Bradley Jardine.*
> "The Secret to Software Success," *CIO Magazine* (July 1, 2001).

When asked about the problematic state of the sponsors' time commitment towards their projects, some sponsors have quipped, "You know, I have an open door policy, the project manager can walk in at any time." We often ask in response: "Yes, but when your office door is open, are you in there?" Too many projects are launched without the stewardship of committed sponsors and then they wander aimlessly through the treacherous waters of corporate politics without direction or propulsion. Inevitably, these projects founder and fail. This is well corroborated by the findings regarding the failure of NASA's Mars Polar Lander mission:

> *An independent panel of scientists attributed the failure to a common cause: . . . senior managers failed to watch over the project carefully.*
> *Newsweek* (April 10, 2000): p. 46.

Occasionally, signs of encouragement appear when one learns about a CIO who refuses to let projects proceed without appropriate business sponsorship:

> *Every time there's a big project, she [Jean Holley, CIO USG Corp] makes sure there's a senior executive sponsor, and if no one will raise his hand, then she's not going to do it.*
> Kathleen Melymuka, "Building a New IT Culture," *Computerworld*
> (October 1, 2001): p. 25.

It is imperative that CIOs, in consultation with the corporate executive group and with the specific approval of the CEO, establish project governance procedures that place the sponsorship of mission critical projects on the shoulders of the appropriate *business* executives. It is important for the project manager's immediate boss to understand that project managers do not always have the political prowess or savvy to insist that their business sponsors own up to their responsibilities. The sponsors (project managers' bosses) and the CIOs can play an important role by working to educate corporate executives on the importance of a sponsor's role in the success of their projects.

Sponsor Self-Assessment

Figure 5.25 depicts the list of sponsor's responsibilities. Sponsors should review the detailed discussion regarding each responsibility and then self assess their level of performance. In the *value* column, a "1" would mean a poor performance and a "5" would a very good performance. Any assessment is only as good as the objectivity of the responses. On occasion, some sponsors have tried to have their project managers do the assessment of their (sponsor's) performance. We have not seen this work very well because most project managers were not sufficiently forthcoming in their responses. The project managers did not feel comfortable giving poor and low assessment values, even when their sponsors assured them of the importance of being candid. However, the experience we have had with a number of sponsors regarding their self-assessments has been very positive because most were exceptionally realistic and actually took steps to improve their roles and responsibilities towards their projects.

Our interpretation of the averaged value of the assessment using the list in Figure 5.25 is as follows:

Value <1	Poor
Value 1.0–1.9	Grim
Value 2.0–2.9	Fair
Value 3.0–4.0	Good

The *action plan* column is used to outline the steps the sponsor plans to take to improve the situation if any of the assessed values is below 3.0. This assessment should first be done soon after the

FIGURE 5.25
Sponsor's Roles and Responsibilities

Sponsor's roles and responsibility	Value	Action plan
1. Appoint an appropriately skilled project manager		
2. Approve project charter, task plan, estimate, budget, and schedule		
3. Champion the project, project manager, and project team		
4. Commit time and political capital to the project		
5. Conduct formal appraisals of the project manager's performance		
6. Empower the project manager with the appropriate authority		
7. Encourage intelligent disobedience		
8. Ensure sustained buy-in at all levels		
9. Ensure timely availability of needed resources		
10. Follow up to ensure that promised benefits are realized		
11. Formally manage project scope		
12. Keep informed about project status		
13. Keep the team out of political minefields		
14. Provide feedback on performance *v.* expectations		
15. Provide guidance and direction for key business strategies		
16. Resolve major policy issues		
17. Shield the project team from unrealistic customer demands		
18. Understand project complexity		
Average		

Project Staging step, then at about the fourth month into the project, and finally as a part of Process Assessment (Step 30 of the Implement stage).

Within the context of the project management discipline in most organizations, it is important that the following question be raised: "Is the experience, responsibility, authority, and stature of the project sponsor in concert with the nature of the project's size, complexity, and politics?"

This lack of insight, and the resulting assignment of wrong sponsors, is a leading cause of the high degree of poorly performing IT/Business projects. We routinely advise our client executives and managers, who take on the sponsorship responsibility, to routinely assess their own performance in a forthright manner because the greatest influence on a project's success or failure is that of the sponsor's skills and performance.

> *The executive in charge of the project was a senior user with no experience leading such a project, which only contributed to the politics. He was far more concerned about spinning the right message to the executive committee than he was about applying good oversight.*
>
> Polly Schneider, "Another Trip to Hell," *CIO Magazine* (February 15, 2000).

The Forty Questions

As a part of our consulting work with a number of client executives who were preparing to assume the responsibilities of a sponsor, we created a list of questions that a sponsor should ask a project manager. The primary reason behind the development of these questions was that the sponsors did not always ask the right questions of their project managers. Therefore, they did not receive the right information from them. As a result, many sponsors were often surprised by the "bad news" they heard about projects they thought were proceeding well. These questions cover the following key components of a project:

Project description	Team
Due diligence	Communications plan
Project sponsor	Estimating
Scope definition	Scheduling and tracking
Task plan	Implementation

Project Description

1. Do you have a succinct Project Description? Have the key customers reviewed the Project Description? What is their reaction to the proposed project? Do they clearly understand the reasons for, and the benefits of, the project? Are they in agreement with the stated objectives? Do the members of the core team clearly understand the Project Description?
2. What specific organization strategy is the project linked to? Who and what are the key drivers of the project?
3. How will we know if the project is successful? What are the specific, quantifiable measures of success? How achievable are they? How are we going to measure these success factors?
4. Will the project adversely impact any other projects currently in progress or those planned for the near future (schedule, budget, staff, technology, and management time)?
5. Do you, the team, and key customers clearly understand the runaway triggers and the shutdown condition(s) for this project? Do you clearly understand the escalation procedures to follow when these conditions occur?

Due Diligence

6. Who are the key stakeholders? What is their reaction to the project—champions, neutral, not interested, nemesis? Are there any turf issues?
7. What is your plan to leverage the champion stakeholders?
8. In the case of any nemeses, what are the reasons for their adversarial behavior? What plans do you have to work with the nemeses? Do you need any special help?

9. Are the intraproject priorities (schedule, scope, cost, and quality) clearly articulated? What do the key customers think of the ranking? Are the items ranked 1st and 2nd achievable (given the current circumstances)?
10. What process was used to derive the project deadline? How realistic is it?
11. Have you assessed the complexity of the project? Have you discussed your findings with the core team and key customers? What plans do you have in place to manage any high complexity attributes?
12. Are there any constraints and obstacles that will hinder your ability to meet the project objectives?
13. Do you regard any of the key assumptions as unrealistic? How will you handle this?
14. What are the top risk items and what contingency plans do you have in place to react to these risks?

Project Sponsor (Self-Assessment Questions)

15. In regard to the project complexity, am I the right sponsor for this project?
16. Do I clearly understand my roles and responsibilities toward the project?
17. Will I have adequate time and interest to fulfill my sponsorship role?

Scope Definition

18. Are the key customers in agreement with the currently defined project scope? Are future releases anticipated? If so, is the design team aware of the scope of the future releases?
19. Is there a well-defined scope change management plan? Have you discussed this plan with key customers and the core team? Do you believe the customers and the core team will follow the plan?

Task Plan

20. What is the source of your task plan? Is it a life cycle database? Experience and memory? Innovative thinking? What is your level of confidence in the comprehensiveness (completeness) of the task plan?
21. Does the task network reflect resource availability constraints in a realistic fashion? If these constraints were eliminated, what would be the result? Have you saved the version 0 plan?
22. Is there comprehensive definition for each deliverable (name, description, completion criteria, owner)?

Team

23. What is the overall composition of the core team: how many IT people and how many business people? How many full-time and how many part-time? Are you comfortable with the team mix? How confident are you of the assumed availability of the team members? Do you believe their other assignments will interfere with the timely completion of their deliverables? If so, have you discussed your concerns with appropriate team members and their managers?
24. In view of the project complexity and risks, do you believe you have an appropriately skilled team? If not, what specific skills are missing?
25. Do you need any support from resources outside the core team?

Communications Plan

26. Have you mapped out the communication structure for the project? How do you intend to keep the key stakeholders informed in a timely fashion? In case of remote (virtual) team members, how do you plan to deal with performance, time zones, cultural, and language issues?
27. Do you have a plan to develop (and maintain) a formalized project notebook for this project?

Estimating

28. What is the estimated size of the project: Less than 6 months? Six to 9 months? Longer than nine months?
29. What specific techniques did you and the team use to develop estimates? Do team members agree with the estimates? How did the key customers react?

30. What range values did you use in your estimates? Have the key customers accepted the use of range values? Are they aware of the estimated expiration date?
31. What is your level of confidence in the current estimates (cost, resources, and time)? What needs to be done to improve your confidence level?

Scheduling and Tracking

32. How far into the future is the current schedule?
33. What considerations have you given to the turnover rate (this includes internal transfers, resignations, and terminations) of the project team?
34. Is the computed project completion date consistent with management's expectations? If not, how will you reconcile the two? What are the implications of not meeting the deadline? If the deadline cannot be met, what are some of the trade-offs? Are the key customers aware of these trade-offs? Have they bought into the trade-offs?
35. Which vital signs will you use to monitor the project? Are the team members (especially cross-functional team members) in agreement with the selection of the vital signs?
36. Do you believe that team members will provide you with accurate vital sign information in a timely fashion? What are your plans to ensure the accuracy and timeliness of the information?
37. Have you planned any milestone-based celebrations? Is there a budget?
38. How skilled are you in the use of the project management software package(s) used to schedule and track this project? Do you need any assistance?

Implementation

39. What is your assessment of the key customers' degree of readiness to deploy (accept) the project? Do you see any major obstacles toward effective and efficient project implementation?
40. What type, and what level, of support are you planning to provide to the key customers during the transition time (from development to deployment)? Have you identified the resources (people, facilities, equipment, and budget) needed to provide the necessary support?

Of all the resources needed for a project to be successful, the project sponsor is, without debate, the most important. Therefore, a proposed project *must not* be moved from the Pre-Launch to the Launch stage *unless* a sponsor, who has the requisite personal commitment and time, is available to oversee the project. Additionally, if at any point in the project life cycle there is a loss of the sponsor, and an equally qualified replacement is not available, the next best step is to either move the project to suspended status or to the canceled project portfolio (see Chapter 10).

We often come across situations where an organization has so many projects in the pipeline that fierce competition develops among various project managers to try to win the right sponsor. We believe this is a case of "putting the cart before the horse." Rather than project managers vying for sponsors, the responsibility belongs to the individual/group who proposed the project in the first place. In organizations where project managers are forced to go out and "troll for sponsors," the project failure rate stays very high.

Project Manager's Supervisor

This supervisory position is an interesting role to analyze. As depicted in the project organization model in Figures 5.7 and 5.8, the project manager reports directly to the sponsor, not through her boss. This temporary chain of command does not mean that the project manager's boss is kept out of the loop of information. When we discuss the use of the vital signs to assess and report project status (Chapter 7), you will see that, before reporting any negative variances to the sponsor, the project manager reports the information to her boss. The project manager's boss is directly involved, is kept in the loop, and works with the project manager to solve any associated problems throughout the project life cycle. The project manager's boss should meet with the sponsor routinely, perhaps monthly, to review the overall team performance (especially the performance of the project manager). The project manager's boss also needs to be an integral part of all key milestones of the project, such as stage gate reviews and Project Staging. Finally, the project manager's boss is primarily responsible for the career path planning of the project manager—education, training, mentoring, performance reviews, job assignments, bonuses, and pay raises.

Functional Managers

These are the managers of the various team members on the project team. Most often, they are from cross-functional departments. The functional managers directly control the career paths of the people they supply to various project teams, and many of their people may have multiple responsibilities: their regular day jobs (sales, operations, manufacturing, marketing) as well as assignment to one or more projects. The ideal situation is when such resources are assigned full-time to one project. However, that is rarely the case, especially for IT/Business projects, which leads to two important questions:

1. What role do the functional managers play in a project?
2. What is their relationship with the project manager?

The functional managers play an extremely important role because they are the holders of the key resources for any given project, and project managers must establish a close working relationship with them. The project manager typically requests the needed resources from appropriate functional managers, who must balance the needs of the day-to-day business, other projects, and the career and personal needs of their people. Business unit managers often fail to comprehend the need for making appropriate business personnel available as dedicated team members because of the long-held belief that any project using technology is an IT project and does not require business personnel. Unfortunately, IT management has unwittingly contributed to this problem by staffing project teams with IT professionals and begrudging participation from business unit personnel. Therefore, project managers should personally contact the appropriate functional managers as early in the project life cycle as possible to discuss the resource needs of the project, along with a number of other important items. Key items for discussion are:

1. The process by which the project manager will inform the functional managers of the need for various resources—people, equipment, facilities, and budgets.
2. The process by which the team members will be assigned, reassigned, and removed from a project. Project managers should have a say in the hiring and firing of people from their projects (this does not mean the person is fired from their job; that decision is made by the functional manager and the human resources department).
3. The process by which the team members will be assessed for their performance. Project managers should play a strong and active role in team members' performance assessments.
4. The process by which team members' salary increases and bonuses will be impacted by the input from the project manager. We believe that functional managers should seek and use project manager's assessments in their own final decisions.
5. The process by which any performance and discipline-related problems regarding team members will be escalated from the project manager to the functional managers. Once the process is agreed upon, the functional managers should communicate the same to their people, so that there are no misunderstandings or ill feelings toward the project manager if any performance-related problems have to be escalated.

A frequent topic of discussion is the reporting relationship between the two: Does the project manager report to the functional manager(s)? An interesting point indeed. When asked, most functional managers would like it to be so. When we ask functional managers to tell us what type of reporting, from project manager to functional managers, would be beneficial, we typically get the following types of responses:

1. Inform them of the needs for resources (people, facilities, budgets, and equipment) in a timely manner—with sufficient lead time.
2. Apprise them of the performance of their resources in a timely manner.
3. Have the authority to assess the performance of the project manager.

We completely agree with the first two points and have discussed them in the prior list of items. The third item needs more elaboration. Our belief is that, if a functional manager is to assess a project manager's performance and report it to the project manager's boss and/or the sponsor, this process should be reciprocal—the project manager will then also have the opportunity to assess the performance of the functional manager and report the assessment to the proper people. A project's success is heavily dependent on the manner in which functional managers carry out their responsibilities. The sponsor and the project manager's boss, with appropriate input from the project manager, should routinely assess functional managers' performance of their responsibilities. Where these performance assessments have been formally done during a project, the project managers expressed the view that the resource procurement went very smoothly and saved them considerable time and grief. Remember the adage, "What gets measured, gets done."

Before we close the discussion regarding the roles of the functional managers, we need to address the problem of functional managers usurping the project manager's authority. The most common manifestation of this behavior is when functional managers bypass the project manager and begin to direct the team members that belong to them. We suggest the following set of actions for the project manager:

1. Approach the individuals who are actually doing the usurping and discuss the negative impact that their behavior is having on the project. Don't be confrontational and don't focus on yourself. Communicate to the perpetrators that their action is placing the team in a difficult position.
2. If this does not solve the problem, escalate the issue to your functional manager. Communicate to your manager the specific facts and the resulting problems. Your manager has the responsibility, and should have the authority, to contact the people causing the problems, discuss the problems, and resolve the problem.
3. If these actions do not yield success, your next action is to have a serious discussion with the sponsor and raise the issue of removing the team members in question from the team. If the problem is not solved, you will lose all control over the team.

Project Manager

> *A manager . . . sets objectives . . . organizes . . . motivates . . . and communicates . . . measures . . . and develops people. Every manager does these things knowingly or not. A manager may do them well, or may do them wretchedly but always does them.*
> Peter Drucker (http://www.stthomas.edu/gradbusiness/syllabi/Courses/MBOP/mbop600_nicolay.htm).

Next to the sponsor, the most important person on the team is the project manager. Some would suggest that the project manager is more important than the sponsor because an astute and experienced project manager can overcome the absence of a sponsor or the presence of a poor sponsor. We would suggest that this could be true for short-term emergency situations for projects in lower zone II, lower zone III, and zone IV of the complexity chart. All other projects are too complex, cross multiple organizational boundaries, have extensive turf (political) issues, and require high-level organizational authority to resolve conflicts. We would define an emergency as a situation where the risk of not doing a project at all is higher than the risk of its failure due to the lack of a sponsor. However, keep in mind that this does not erase the need for an appropriate sponsor. Absence of a sponsor will put both the project and the team in great jeopardy.

Project Manager's Roles and Responsibilities   From what has been said thus far, it is easy to conclude that a project manager's responsibilities closely mimic those of the sponsor, but the scope of the responsibilities and the span of authority are much narrower. That is why we believe that the project manager position is a very good stepping stone for moving into general management of the organization. A comprehensive list of project managers' responsibilities includes:

1. Achieve project objectives
2. Anticipate problems and take corrective action
3. Champion the project and the team
4. Maintain client communications

5. Commit political capital to the project
6. Conduct job transition interviews for core team members at the completion of the project
7. Conduct periodic formal appraisals of team members
8. Develop comprehensive project plans, realistic estimates, and viable schedules
9. Empower the team
10. Ensure smooth and efficient project deployment
11. Ensure sustained buy-in at all levels
12. Keep informed about the project's status
13. Manage project scope
14. Manage the expectations of clients and team members
15. Manage the project team
16. Obtain resources in a timely manner

If you compare this list to the list of roles and responsibilities of the sponsor, you will find many duplications and/or overlaps. Earlier in the chapter, we discussed many of these duties as they related to the sponsor. We will now discuss these items as they relate to the role of a project manager.

Achieve Project Objectives: This is the end game, the very purpose of the project. The project manager needs to achieve objectives on time, to the agreed upon quality, and on budget. A summary list of the various project objectives should be the project manager's "elevator speech" about the project. We advise you to review the Project Charter, make a list of the objectives, post the list prominently in your office and always start each project meeting by reviewing it first. Many project managers find it difficult to state the list of objectives when asked to do so. The real accomplishment is when the core team members are able to recite the list of project objectives. When project objectives are clearly understood and held in sharp focus, all work is aimed at getting the project done effectively and efficiently.

Anticipate Problems and Take Corrective Action: The hallmark of a successful project manager is the ability to know what lies ahead and not be surprised by the obvious. Two well-tested tools to accomplish this include the look-ahead window (Chapter 7) and management by walking around (with your eyes and ears open). If your management style is to sit in your cubicle poring over the schedules developed by your project management software and relying on e-mails every few minutes, you're sure to develop myopic vision and run into obstacles.

> *"A successful project manager has an AWAC flying overhead."*

Champion the Project and the Team: Earlier in the chapter, we discussed the importance of championship behavior by the sponsor. The same holds true for the project manager. On a day-to-day basis, stakeholders, customers, and team members are more in touch with the project manager than the sponsor. As such, the project manager must send a positive message regarding the project. While the sponsor serves as the coach, the project manager is the captain who must show a strong belief in the value of the project and speak well of the team. Project managers who have a gloomy view of the project and a dour outlook toward the team cause huge problems for the project. Occasionally, project managers are assigned to projects they don't find interesting and have team members they are not too thrilled about. As professionals, they must do their best to bring the project to successful completion. Not all assignments are going to be to their liking.

Maintain Client Communications: In discussions with project managers, we typically place this as the first item in the list. In fact, the operative term is "aggressive communications." Communicating aggressively does not mean being violent, hostile, or belligerent, or typing your e-mail message in all capital letters; it actually means being forceful, assertive, and uncompromising. Aggressive communications are those in which the sender anticipates the need for communicating, takes the initiative to send a clear, well structured message, and follows up to ensure that it was received and understood by the addressees. This holds true for all forms of communication: face-to-face, telephone, fax, and e-mail. We remember an often-pronounced maxim by one CEO, "Call your customer before they call you, and call often."

Commit Political Capital to the Project: This means putting one's reputation on the line for the success of the project. The project manager must have a strong belief in the benefits the project is designed to bring to the organization and must be willing to make the best possible effort to bring the project to a successful conclusion.

Conduct Job Transition Interviews for Core Team Members at the Completion of the Project: As the project winds down, core team members need to know that the project manager will do his best to help them make a transition to the next assignment. The first step to ease this transition is to meet with core team members individually to assess their career path aspirations. Next, the project manager must work with appropriate functional managers and the human resources department to help team members with their transition. A good self-assessment question for the project manager is, "Will these team members volunteer to work on my team in a future assignment?"

Conduct Periodic Formal Appraisals of Team Members: For any team to function effectively and efficiently, the team members must know how well they are performing. The widespread approach to team member performance assessment, which occurs towards the end of the project, is rather anticlimactic. The process does nothing to improve the person's performance during the project. If they have any value, such assessments can only help subsequent projects. Why wait so long? The reasons are many: that is the way it has always been done, assessments are too time consuming, team members don't really report to me (nonsense). We strongly advise a quarterly, one-on-one, meeting between the project manager and individual team members to discuss team member performance and any specific needs and expectations of the team members. A typical session takes no more than 30 minutes, but provides a valuable opportunity for team members to receive timely feedback and to communicate their needs and concerns to the project manager.

Develop Comprehensive Project Plans, Realistic Estimates, and Viable Schedules: These are the tactics needed to achieve the project goal—finish the project on time, on budget, and to the agreed upon quality. Often there are strong pressures from managers, customers, and even team members to rush through these important steps in the name of shortsighted efficiency. It is the professional responsibility of any project manager to resist these pressures and insist on developing comprehensive plans, realistic estimates, and viable schedules. The best approach, in the face of any pressure to bypass these important processes, is education of the perpetrators.

Empower the Team: Very much like the project manager's need to be empowered by the sponsor, the team members need a similar ability to do their work without constant interruptions and micromanagement from their functional managers, project manager, and customers. The best way to empower team members is as follows:

- Clearly define and communicate roles and responsibilities.
- Work with functional managers to minimize reassignments.
- Do not allow customers to pressure team members into scope changes.
- Set clear project status and issues reporting protocol using well-defined vital sign variances (see *Vital Signs* in Chapter 7).

In addition, make sure that the power struggle among the various stakeholders does not burden the team. We have often seen this happen when disgruntled stakeholders, especially customers who either feel left out or have major disagreements with project objectives, begin to contact team members directly and pressure them into changing the project direction. It really gets ugly when the customers who disregard this protocol are senior level managers and executives. If such an environment is allowed to develop, the team is sure to land right in the middle of a political minefield, with disastrous results.

Ensure Smooth and Efficient Project Deployment: Within the life cycle of a project, two of the more risky areas are project initiation and project deployment. The latter is fraught with such problems as major changes in the customer's environment, a team suffering from fatigue due to extensive work in the design and development phases of the project, and the team's desire to move on to new assignments. A large number of projects fare poorly during this stage and leave an overall adverse impression with customers. Imagine that you take a trip, during which the airplane arrived early, but the gate agent and the ground crew did not know about the early arrival. So, you beat your luggage to the claim area by 40 minutes and are left standing around, empty-handed. This unfortunate description fits far too many project deployments. It is very important that the project manager pay special attention to the project deployment phase of the project.

Ensure Sustained Buy-In at All Levels: Don your PR hat, put on a big smile, rehearse your "elevator speech" and go out and talk to the key stakeholders, especially the nemesis, neutral, and comatose. Invite any nemesis to join you for coffee or lunch; it will surprise them. Get out of your cubicle and talk to people—keep them informed about the project and spread the good news.

Keep Informed About the Project's Status: It is the job of the project manager to know, at any given time, the status of the project—functionality, schedule, cost, and quality. The two key steps to keeping current on the project are to define a viable set of vital signs to assess the project's status and to make sure the team is monitoring and reporting the vital signs in a forthright and timely manner. A key component of project status assessment is the look-ahead window, which allows the project manager and the team to have a clear view of the near future of the project. Consistent use of the look-ahead window helps the project team anticipate problems and take corrective action in a timely manner (see Chapter 7).

Manage Project Scope: The first step is to take off your Velcro Suit. Then, stand before a mirror and recite the scope mantra, "No, not in this version. We will consider it in the next version." Next, perfect your negotiation skills, find another project manager who excels at negotiations, and seek some guidance. Review the Scope Management Plan developed earlier, make a copy for key stakeholders, and deliver it to them personally. Take the time to discuss the importance of the process with them.

Manage the Expectations of Clients and Team Members: Some of synonyms for "expectations" are: "look forward to", "hope for", and "wishes". In the case of project customers, it could even be defined as wishful thinking. The problems regarding managing expectations arise when there is a considerable gap between what people want to see in the final product *v.* what is actually planned. The problem is further compounded when customers are not informed about the gaps, the reason for the differences, and possible future actions. The underlying reason for this mismatch is that many customers have unreasonable expectations of what technology can do, and many project managers don't have the courage to say "no." This is not limited to project managers; the problem goes all the way up to the department heads.

> *CEOs have irrational expectations for what [software] can do, and CIOs don't have the gumption to tell them the truth . . .*
>
> Scott Berinato, "The Secret to Software Success,"
> *CIO Magazine* (July 1, 2001).

Therefore, make sure that neither you nor the team members, say "yes" to simply please or appease your customers. In too many instances, the mere up and down headshake of a project manager, while listening to a customer, gets interpreted as an agreement to add the scope to the project.

Manage the Project Team: Project team management is the most important role/responsibility of any project manager. The project manager must lead the way, provide guidance, supervise or oversee progress, control situations (take charge) when necessary, coordinate activities, administer policies and procedures, reward effort, and punish transgressions if necessary.

Obtain Resources in a Timely Manner: When it comes to smooth project execution, timely resource deployment is the key. Resources include people, technology, budgets, and facilities. It is important for the project manager, working with core team members, to review the detailed task plan, develop a comprehensive resources list, and then work hard to obtain the appropriate resources.

When designing the project organization structure, (Figure 5.7), make sure that you include all of the appropriate functional managers in the project organization. Additionally, do not overlook the appropriate functional managers from departments such as purchasing, human resources, facilities, finance, and computer security. It is amazing to hear project managers complain about their projects being behind schedule because it takes days, if not weeks, to get project teams set up with their workspace, office equipment, computers, cell phones, pagers, and security passwords.

Soft Skills   The majority of the skills just discussed can be classified as hard skills—skills that are easy to define, easy to observe and assess, and relatively easy to teach and learn. There is another set of equally important skills that are more difficult to define, observe, and assess, and are also rather difficult to teach and learn. These skills, often called "competencies", are related to social, political, and general management aptitudes. They are sometimes referred to as "soft skills." Explanations of some of these soft skills are as follows:

1. Charisma
2. Decisiveness
3. Delegation
4. Integrity
5. Leadership
6. Negotiation
7. Positive outlook

Charisma: Notice that the list does not include the word "power". Most project managers do not have a high degree of authority over their team members. Therefore, they need charisma—personality, charm, and appeal. People who have abrasive and uncompromising personalities seldom make successful project managers. They may be able to bully their way around initially, but not for long and not very successfully. Therefore, project managers must develop charm (good manners) and should not be abrasive in their dealings with customers, stakeholders, and team members. Over the years, we have come across a small number of project managers who take pride in pronouncements such as, "Real project managers don't need charm; I tell it like it is, or I call it like I see it." Most of them were quite unaware of what other people called them. We are not against being assertive. Most people who have charisma are quite assertive.

Decisiveness: Some of antonyms for "decisiveness" are: "wavering", "vacillation", "doubtful", and "timid." How would you like your team members to brand you with these attributes? A key reason people have difficulty making decisions is that once a decision is final, the decision maker becomes responsible for the outcome—and the outcome could be undesirable. This certainly is a risk, but to be a successful project manager, one will need to take many risks. Being indecisive is also a risk. What separates good project managers from mediocre project managers is that the former learn to take calculated risks and then monitor them diligently. Decisiveness is a behavior one can learn to exhibit, but here are a few suggestions to help you until you adapt:

1. Gather as much accurate information as possible. Don't let feelings and emotions sway you in this quest.
2. During the early part of information gathering, rather than ignoring people who have opposing views, listen carefully to any dissent.
3. Play detective and check out the information that your intuition tells you may not be correct. Pay attention to your hunches.
4. Draw your own conclusions, but seek advice from an uninvolved, knowledgeable party (this is where a mentor can really help).

Now that you have done your homework, convene your team, present your preliminary decision, and seek input without showing your approval or disapproval. Note any reactions. At this point, you have more than sufficient information to make a decision. It is always a good idea to monitor the results of your decision. If you discover negative results, stop the work and reassess your options. If you are uncomfortable with proceeding further, it is a good time to escalate the problem one or two levels above you and see what type of help you can obtain from any of the SMEs, functional managers, your own boss, or the sponsor.

Delegation: "Delegating" is easier said than done. Delegation means relinquishing control over certain tasks, deliverables, and milestones to someone else—and trusting them to be successful. Loss of control is a key source of anxiety and discomfort. That is the primary reason that people do not delegate work to others. They would rather do it themselves even when they are already overworked. A few suggestions to help those who find it difficult to relinquish control: Make a list of the tasks you need to complete in the near future, using a 2–4 week window. Highlight the ones that you don't have the time to complete. Next to each of these tasks, write down the name of the best candidate on your team. Decide what type of risk is involved in turning over these tasks to the individual(s) and document the potential risk. The next step is to communicate both the tasks and the perceived risks to the appropriate team members and then ask them what steps you both can take to minimize your sense of risk. Possible steps to reduce risk might be to develop more detail for selected tasks, define them more clearly, and establish progressive, short-interval milestones to review progress. The first few times you employ this method, you will discover that (although the net time to complete the tasks has not decreased by much) you are becoming increasingly more successful in the delegation of work. Resist the temptation to micromanage. Being micromanaged irritates people, slows their progress, and communicates a low confidence in their abilities, all of which are counterproductive to the cause. We are confident that as you practice delegation (starting with small items and then progressing to more important items) you will develop self-confidence in your ability to delegate and your team members will benefit from their greater responsibility and new experiences. Be certain to thank people for their effort and help along the way.

Integrity: An antonym for "integrity" is "dishonesty". It is practically impossible to continue to be dishonest over time *and* be successful—dishonesty will catch up with you eventually. Being dishonest means losing trust. Once you lose the trust of your colleagues, it becomes extremely difficult to lead them effectively. Two words that aptly describe someone with integrity are "honest" and "ethical"—a person who will do the right thing even in the face of adversity. On a recent radio talk show, the host and the guest were discussing the subject of ethics. The host asked the guest, "Is it possible to teach people ethics?" After a considerable pause, the guest replied, "I am not so sure, but I am very sure that they [ethics] can be learned." It is extremely important that you exhibit unquestionable integrity in all your dealings and communications. Doing otherwise leads to taking risky shortcuts that may serve some immediate purpose but will result in a damaged reputation.

Leadership: This perhaps is the most challenging trait to write about because it deals with a subject that is difficult to quantify. The best way to explore the subject is to review the different traits often exhibited by leaders. Here are a few:

Communicator	Courageous
Curious	Energetic
Loyal	Self confidence
Sense of purpose	Synergetic
Teacher	Visionary

Keeping the list in mind, you can probably recall a number of people who possess most of these traits but are *not* ethical and honorable human beings. Examples include corporate chiefs, football coaches, politicians, and even religious leaders. Most of them achieved great success in their careers, but ultimately were purveyors of an excessive amount of grief and outright misery. Therefore, we need to add a few important traits to the list.

Concerned about other's well being	Conscientious
Ethical	Trustworthy
Sense of humor	

With these added traits, the leader becomes a person who is highly concerned about doing the right thing, the common good, and the well being of others. To possess each of these traits in the highest degree is a tall order for anyone. Project managers, in order to develop their leadership skills, must examine their personal behaviors from the perspective of the two lists and then conscientiously strive to be an exemplary leader. It will take time and practice to develop these important competencies. Toward this goal, we respectfully suggest a couple of exercises. The first exercise involves a two-step process:

1. Review the list of competencies and leadership skills and create a tailored list for yourself. Enter this list in the left-hand column of Figure 5.26.
2. Think of three *public* figures you admire and enter their names at the top of the three remaining columns. For each person, assess how well he or she practices, or practiced, the various leadership traits you have selected and then enter the appropriate number in the column below the name. The value of 1 implies a low level of the skill and a value of 4 means extraordinary performance.

FIGURE 5.26
Leadership Competency
Profiles—Public Figures

Competency	Name	Name	Name

As you analyze the skill profiles of the three people you selected, you will probably discover that one does not need to possess every skill to its fullest extent to be successful. In fact, it is almost impossible for any one person to possess every needed skill. That is why a well-rounded team is critical to the success of any project.

For the next exercise, think of three people you know *personally* (people from your work and/or social circle). Then, using Figure 5.27, develop a skills profile for each. Hopefully, you have just defined a list of people who can help you improve your leadership skills. The next step is to exercise your negotiation skills and ask these people to mentor you in the areas of their expertise.

FIGURE 5.27
Leadership Competency
Profiles—People Known
Personally

Competency	Name	Name	Name

Actions are more important than words. Therefore, to be an effective leader, you must actively strive to practice what you preach. As the leader of your project team, you must maintain a positive outlook, be enthusiastic, be willing to learn from your failures, and have a good sense of humor. Few people will be willing to follow a person who is pessimistic, dwells on the negative, and is a perpetual grouch.

What you are will show in what you do.

Thomas A. Edison.

Example is leadership.

Dr. Albert Schweitzer, *Executive's Book of Quotations*,
Oxford University Press, p. 162.

Negotiation:[7] Of all the skills of a project manager, you will need to be especially proficient in the skill of negotiations because by the very definition of the job, a project manager does not have hierarchical power or authority over most of the resources needed to complete a project. In addition, most organizations (due to poor project portfolio management processes), launch too many projects at any given time and stress their resources unnecessarily. The result is that project managers must negotiate with a number of different people who are in charge of the resources needed for the project. For example:

- Negotiate with the sponsor for additional time, funds, people, and resources.
- Negotiate with functional managers for a variety of resources.
- Negotiate with SMEs for their time and advice.
- Negotiate with customers for adjustments in functionality, quality, and schedules.
- Negotiate with team members for their time and commitment, because many may be assigned to multiple projects in addition to their regular job responsibilities.

Much of the literature on negotiations focuses the discussion around terms such as "bargain," "exchange," and "trade between two parties," and there are clear winners and losers at the end. Such writings are full of examples of negotiation successes and failures among attorneys, government heads, buyers and sellers of properties, warring politicians, and CEOs of opposing companies. In most of these examples, each party holds certain items considered valuable by the other party. Situations that require negotiation are not quite the same for project managers. Let us take a look at what items of value project managers typically come to possess and what value functional managers and potential team members would place on them. Some of the items are the Project Charter, the Task Plan, the resources needs list, the project estimate and schedule, and the issues list. What *bargaining* value do you believe these items have? They have none. Therefore, an extremely important caveat of negotiation for project managers is that they own practically nothing to give to the other party. This lack of a real commodity makes the need for negotiation skills even more important because at any given time, in any given organization, the number of resources needed by various project managers far exceeds the number of available resources.

Any negotiation process consists of the following two important components:

1. *Substance:* the matter or material that one is interested in acquiring. For a project manager these would include people, time, budget, facilities, and equipment.
2. *Relationship:* the bond or link that one forms with the other party during and after the negotiation session.

In order to properly frame the negotiation needs of a typical project manager, keep the following facts in mind:

1. Most of the negotiations are with colleagues and contemporaries, regarding a variety of project resources.

---

[7]For additional information, refer to *Negotiating Style Profile,* by Rollin Glaser and Christine Glaser, Organization Design and Development, Inc., 1996.

2. At the end of the project, and sometimes prior to that, most resources are turned back to their respective "owners."
3. Because most of the people involved in negotiations are colleagues, a high probability exists of working with them, as well as having to negotiate with them, in the future.

Keeping these facts in mind, it behooves a project manager not to sacrifice a relationship over the desire to obtain maximum substance. In the language of negotiation, the approach or style a negotiator uses can be classified into one of the following categories:

1. *Aggressive:* The aggressive negotiator takes a hard line towards the substance of the negotiation and places little value on the relationship with the other party. The negotiator establishes a position of power with the intent to obtain the maximum possible from the other party; the modus operandi is pressure and intimidation. The aggressive approach is often used by purchasing agents to obtain highly favorable deals from vendors, especially when the purchasing agent knows that the vendor is vulnerable. Many of them will deny it, but their attitude and communication style gives them away each time. This type of negotiation is not successful in the long range. Most such deals fall apart because the vendor is not able to fulfill promises made under duress. Even though this approach will result in short-range favorable outcomes, we do not recommend it because the benefit is short term, the other party feels mistreated and misused, the other party may think of revenge or getting even, and the other party will begin to interpret the agreement to the tiniest detail, the letter of the law, resulting in nitpicking and finger pointing. There are times when the other party comes to the table with this aggressive and hard line approach. Under such circumstances, we strongly advise the project manager to get help from a professional negotiator such as a SME.

2. *Accommodating:* The accommodating negotiator is very compliant in nature (yielding and considerate). In this case, the person has a disproportionately high need for establishing and maintaining good relations based on harmony and friendship. During a negotiation, if an accommodating negotiator is *asking* for resources, she will most probably ask for too little to start with because of the concern for the other party's needs. In situations in which the negotiator does ask for everything that is needed initially, but the other side shows resistance, the negotiator agrees to whatever the other party is willing to offer. On the other hand, some people view the situation in which an accommodating type of person is on the other side as beneficial, because one can negotiate without limits. That can be the case, but not for long, because soon someone in their area (perhaps their boss), will figure out that they gave away too much and will renege on the agreement. Some drawbacks of the accommodating approach to negotiation are that the benefit is short term, the other side feels manipulated, and that the approach results in one side agreeing to far too much and being unable to deliver (they are willing, but unable).

   Consider the scenario where a project manager might believe that he has hit the jackpot. The three functional managers he negotiated with were all very accommodating, and promised everything that he asked for—four full-time senior team members, all of the office and meeting space needed by the team, and the latest model laptops, pagers, and cell phones for everyone. What are the chances that the same managers are making similar promises to other project managers in need of the same resources in the same time period? How are they going to fulfill their commitments? When they don't, all you can do is complain to someone, pointing your finger at the culprits, but you still won't have the resources needed to get the job done.

3. *Withdrawing:* This type of behavior is exhibited when the other side feels powerless and has a sense of helplessness—they are between a rock and a hard place, feel that they have few options, and agree to whatever the negotiators want. In this case, the person asking for resources has most of the power and is dictating the terms to the other side. In the true sense of the term, this scenario does not represent a negotiation; it is a dictatorship. In reality, project managers are rarely in a position of authority as they negotiate with their colleagues and contemporaries, which is a good thing. Any agreements reached as a result of withdrawing behavior is fraught

with the following problems: there is no concern for a good relationship of any kind, there is a feeling of powerlessness followed by a sense of sacrifice and surrender by the other side, and the other side views themselves as victims, and will try to renegotiate the agreement at a later time.

At times, we see this type of negotiation taking place between sponsors and customers on one side and project managers on the other. The project managers feel powerless, primarily due to their position within the hierarchy, and agree to schedule and budget demands that they know cannot be met. We know that these are empty promises. Most such projects are going to finish beyond the agreed upon schedules and budgets, and many will fail. For any project manager, such a situation is a disaster.

4. *Collaborative:* This attitude results in the ideal negotiation. Collaborative negotiators have a balanced concern for both the substance of the agreement and the relationship, both short- and long-term, on both sides. In this approach to negotiation, both sides try to forge an agreement such that neither side loses more than it can afford. In negotiations lingo, this is called a "win/win situation". Some of the key underpinnings of the collaborative approach are as follows: Both sides are interested in solving the problem; both sides have common interests in the success of the outcome; and both sides are principled and do not resort to tricks.

The collaborative approach consistently results in the best outcome for both sides, but it takes time to create the environment and trust needed for this type of negotiation. Although this approach may not always be possible when dealing with every outside (third party) organization, it should be business as usual for internal negotiations. It is important to keep in mind that concern for relationship needs to be in step with the desire to obtain the maximum substance. It is also important to realize that one should not walk into any negotiation situation without adequate preparation. You must decide on your objectives; research supporting information, especially why the person should be willing to meet your needs; profile the other party—do your best to analyze the other party's negotiation style; define your bottom line—the minimum you will be willing to accept or the maximum you are willing to give up; develop your negotiation strategy—how you are going to approach the negotiations session; and focus on being collaborative.

Over the years, we have found that project managers who prepare well and then follow through are consistently more successful in their negotiation efforts. Here are some of the common traits of a successful negotiator: Successful negotiators have a strong sense of purpose about the project. This comes from understanding the strategy to which the project is linked and the benefits it will bring to the organization. They also have a high degree of support from the sponsor, and good relationships with functional managers. A good starting point is to make sure to meet with them long before you need their resources. Successful negotiators also have good communication skills. Carefully assess your style. Being arrogant and unnecessarily aggressive is not effective. Giving people sufficient advance notice of your needs always helps in the negotiation process.

Even with all of this preparation and your best effort, let us say you are not able to achieve your goals (there is a considerable gap between your needs and what you were able to negotiate). We suggest that you treat the gap as a risk contributor and invoke your risk management process. If you are continually unsuccessful in your negotiations, it's time to seek help—see if your organization has education and training programs on the subject. At least seek a SME as a mentor.

Positive Outlook: Any project manager knows that a good deal can go wrong during a project's life cycle—ranging from small daily distractions to occasional showstoppers. It is extremely important that project managers do not become gloomy, pessimistic, and low spirited. Team members take their cues from their project managers, and if the project manager is persistently depressed, the team is sure to follow or find another path and leave. The "cup is half-empty" view is certain to sap energy from the team, especially in difficult times. Having a positive outlook does not imply that the project manager needs to paste on a false smile and hide problems from the team. It simply means that one needs to maintain a positive outlook and see how problems can be overcome rather than get mired in them.

The Business of the Business Now that you have the responsibility for managing a project, make sure that you do your best to learn as much as possible about the customers' business.

> *. . . it's more important for IT personnel to have a rich understanding of the company's focus . . . It's about infusing technology into a business environment to create better products and more value . . . It's a formula that seems to keep P&G products moving— and its people staying.*
> John Soat and Stephanie Stahl, *Information Week* (February 24, 2003),
> (http://www.informationweek.com/story/IWK20030221S0003).

We suggest the following steps:

1. Make a list of key business people and ask them for their help in learning the ins and outs of the business.
2. See if there are any publications related to the business of the project, and make it a habit to routinely read these publications to keep up-to-date about the latest business developments.
3. See if there are any professional associations, meetings, or conferences that you could attend to learn more about the business.
4. Ask your key business contacts to forward any business-related articles to you.
5. Take the time to routinely visit the customers' work area, talk to different people, ask them how their business works, and learn about their day-to-day operations first hand.

We believe these actions will not only equip you with comprehensive knowledge about the business, it will also show the customers the degree of your commitment to the project. As you can see, the list of skills is extensive, and project managers need to do their best to learn, practice, analyze, and improve their performance in these areas.

> *You must learn from the mistakes of others. You can't possibly live long enough to make them all yourself.*
> Sam Levenson (http://www.creativequotations.com/one/2009.htm).

Figure 5.28 depicts a list of a project manager's skills, responsibilities, and traits. The list can be used for three different purposes:

1. At the start of a project, the list can be used to assess one's degree of expertise to manage a project.
2. In the midst of a project, the list can be used to assess how well one is managing the project.
3. At the end of a project, the list can be used to assess how well one did manage the project.

As you use this list, keep the following three points in mind:

1. Will I need this skill, responsibility, or trait to manage the project efficiently and effectively?
2. Have I done this type of work in the near past and how well did I do it?
3. What is my current level of expertise in this skill?

In Figure 5.28, for the column titled *level needed*, enter a value between 1 and 4, where 4 implies that you need to be highly competent (an expert in the particular skill) and 1 implies that the skills will not be that necessary. Typically, the values in this column are in direct proportion to the complexity of the project at hand. Using the same range of values, the column headed *skill level* is used to document the degree of expertise you currently possess in that particular skill. Because this is a self assessment and will not be made public, it is extremely important that you are very *forthright* in the values you specify for the various skills because you must develop an accurate mapping of your knowledge and experience.

At this point, it would be a good idea to contact your functional manager and/or the project sponsor to ask whether they already have developed a similar map of your skills as part of their research for the project manager selection process. If so, ask for their assessment results and see how their evaluation compares to your self assessment. If there are major gaps, and they perceive you to be less skilled than you think; you should discuss the subject matter with both your manager and then the sponsor. In the areas where they have assessed you at a higher level than your own evaluations, take it as a compliment and work hard to meet their expectations.

FIGURE 5.28
Project Manager's Roles
and Responsibilities

Skills/responsibilities/traits	Level needed	Skill level	Skills gap	Action plan
1. Achieve project objectives				
2. Broad perspective				
3. Business knowledge				
4. Champion the project and the team				
5. Charisma				
6. Coaching and mentoring				
7. Commit political capital to the project				
8. Communications				
9. Conduct job transition interviews for core team members				
10. Conflict resolution				
11. Conduct periodic formal appraisals of team members				
12. Decisiveness				
13. Developing comprehensive project plans				
14. Developing realistic estimates				
15. Developing viable schedules				
16. Empower the team (delegate responsibility and authority)				
17. Ensure smooth and efficient project deployment				
18. Ensure sustained buy-in at all levels				
19. Facilitation				
20. Hire/fire team members				
21. Integrity				
22. Keep informed about the project status				
23. Leadership				
24. Manage project scope				
25. Manage expectations				
26. Manage the project team				
27. Negotiation				
28. Obtain resources in a timely manner				
29. Positive outlook				
30. Procurement				
31. Risk management				
32. Team member appraisals				
33. Technology knowledge				
34. Tolerance for ambiguity and uncertainty				
35. Track project progress				
36. Vendor management				

Skills Gap Assessment: Once you have finalized the various skill values in Figure 5.28, we recommend that you review the skills gap recommendations and develop an action plan to remedy any big gaps.

Gap	0.5 to 1.0	OJT
Gap	1.0 to 1.5	OJT + education
Gap	1.5 to 2.0	OJT + education + mentoring
Gap	> 2.0	No primary responsibility

1. **OJT:** This means that although there is a gap between what you need and what you have, you have sufficient skills and experience in this area to take on the responsibility and will learn through work experience quickly enough. There may be some hiccups here and there, but nothing to worry about.

2. **Education:** This means formalized and well-targeted education on the principles and practices of the skill in question is needed as soon as possible.

3. **Mentoring:** This means that the skills gap is wide enough that you will benefit from the advice, counsel, and guidance of a mentor—an expert-level person who will volunteer to help you, will

be nonjudgmental in her relationship with you, and under whose guidance you will feel comfortable. Said mentor must not be a person to whom the project manager reports or a person who will assess the project manager's job performance.

4. *No primary responsibility:* This means that the gap between what is needed and what you have is large enough to result in major risk to the project (and even you—stress, worry, need for extended time). The best approach to compensate for this degree of gap is to delegate the responsibility to an appropriately skilled team member or an SME, and then work hard to develop your own skill in that area. As a project manager, you may have difficulty with such delegation because doing so can convey to the team that you are not an expert in all areas of the project. However, if you take on the responsibility without the needed skill, they will soon discover that your skills are deficient, which will be an even greater cause for concern. They may also extrapolate your lack of skills in one area to several other areas of the project and lose confidence in your leadership. It is better to admit your limitations and have someone with the appropriate skill level temporarily take on the responsibility while you concentrate on learning the necessary skill through observation, mentoring, education, and training.

> *It is easy to fool yourself. It is possible to fool the people you work for. It is more difficult to fool the people you work with. But it is almost impossible to fool the people who work under you.*
>
> Harry B. Thayer, AT&T archives.

Notice that the list in Figure 5.28 *does not* contain the item, "Become an expert in a project management software product." This is not an oversight; this is by design. In real life, we find that a large number of project managers are just that—experts in some project management software product. To make sure they stay that way, many spend too much of their time fiddling with the software package instead of managing the project. In a survey conducted at a project management conference in early-2004, we found that the respondents (127) had an average of 2.3 of these packages on their computers. It is important to keep in mind that any technology is merely an accelerator of the current state. If, for example, a project has a comprehensive plan, has been accurately estimated, and is properly resourced, the use of project management software will help the project manager run it with greater efficiency and ease. However, if a project was poorly planned, was estimated using the estimate-to-please approach, and was scheduled with lofty resource assumptions, a software package will certainly help move it to its demise quickly (that may actually be a blessing). Therefore, our advice to all project managers is to first develop your general management skills (as listed in Figure 5.28) and, once you feel you have a sufficient level of knowledge and experience, begin to develop your expertise in project management software.

Dumb Mistakes and Good Traits We have often observed project managers who made the same bad mistakes, often repeatedly. However, we have also come across a sizeable number of project managers who seemed to have a handle on the situation and consistently managed their teams with admirable leadership. Listed below are the dumb mistakes too many project managers tend to make; each dumb mistake is followed by an effective trait of successful project managers. We find that when a project manager makes only a *few* of these mistakes, but steps for recovery are *not* put immediately into action, the project risks begin to escalate.

- *Bad:* Mistaking half-baked ideas for viable projects
  Good: Working diligently to filter half-baked ideas—practicing intelligent disobedience
- *Bad:* Overlooking the stakeholders, forgetting the champions, and ignoring the nemesis
  Good: Diligently assess both the policy-level and implementation-level stakeholders, develop a plan to leverage the champions, work hard to awaken the comatose, and attempt to convert nemesis stakeholders into neutral stakeholders or champions.
- *Bad:* Not assessing project complexity
  Good: Underestimated or overlooked project complexity is sure to raise its ugly head at the most inopportune time in the project—an astute project manager works with both the business and technical SME to pragmatically assess the project complexity and then uses the findings to formulate appropriate risk reduction and mitigation plans

- *Bad:* Not developing a comprehensive Project Charter
  Good: A comprehensive Project Charter serves as a proposal for review and consideration by the project sponsor. Once approved, it becomes a business plan for the project team. Successful project managers make sure that they develop comprehensive and high-quality Project Charters, and then diligently and routinely review and update the charter to reflect the latest findings
- *Bad:* Not developing a comprehensive task plan
  Good: Imagine a commercial airline pilot who does not develop and file a flight plan before take-off. It is imperative that project managers develop appropriately detailed project plans for all of their projects. Because a project plan is a process deliverable (rather than a product deliverable), some project managers (as well as managers and customers) develop a belief that the time spent creating a plan (WBS and associated network chart) is a waste. Most such projects end up over budget, behind schedule, and of poor quality
- *Bad:* Not designing a robust project organization
  Good: Too often, project managers do not take the time or invest the effort to design a robust organization for their projects. They tend to take what is given to them and try to do their best under the circumstances. Astute project managers work hard to design appropriate and robust project organizations and fight to have them properly staffed
- *Bad:* Developing unrealistic estimates
  Good: Unfortunately, too few project managers know how to develop realistic and accurate estimates. This skill is least developed among IT/Business project managers because most receive no training in the subject. Hence, many of their estimates are nothing but best guesses. Successful project managers seek out good estimating education and training, work hard to develop the necessary skills, and then practice professional negotiations with their managers and customers
- *Bad:* Developing unviable schedules
  Good: Far too many schedules are based on incomplete and incorrect plans, poor estimates, and untenable assumptions regarding resource availability and skill levels. All these compromises have been made to temporarily please the customer. Knowledgeable project managers clearly understand the implications of such actions and work hard to educate their customers on the need for developing viable schedules. Where necessary, they work with their customers and the team to develop trade-offs for scope, budget, and quality to meet any tight schedules.
- *Bad:* Not monitoring a project's vital signs
  Good: Dumb project managers track the progress of their projects by their gut feelings or by basing their decisions on inaccurate and untimely information begrudgingly given to them by various team members. Then there is the use of the percent complete—a totally dumb idea indeed. Astute project managers practice the art and science of managing project progress through the use of vital signs, well-defined variance thresholds, and jeopardy signals
- *Bad:* Looking back and not ahead
  Good: Imagine an automobile where the windshield is the size of the rear view mirrors and the rear view mirrors approach the size of the windshield. This is how dumb project managers attempt to track and control the progress of their projects. Perceptive project managers spend most of their time looking ahead for the upcoming deliverables, tasks, resource needs, obstacles, and milestones.
- *Bad:* Not following a robust project management process.
  Good: A robust project management process is analogous to a great recipe. Dumb project managers don't have any, they don't follow any, they follow their whims instead and they scurry about to figure out their next steps. Most of their team members follow in their footsteps and do the same. Astute project managers practice a robust project management process to ensure disciplined, focused, and well-planned execution of their projects.

Before we close the discussion regarding the requisite skills of a successful project manager, we need to discuss the important subject of finance and accounting—the language of business. As projects get bigger and more complex, they require bigger investments, and management will want to know about the "economic" value of the investment (especially the expected returns). Keep in mind that management has the option of spending money on the project you are about to start, a number of other projects, or simply investing the money in safe financial instruments that have assured returns.

In their conversations with you regarding the justification of a proposed project, they may wish to discuss one or more of the following items:

Before and after tax profit	Breakeven period
Cost/benefit analysis	Future worth
Internal rate of return	Investment opportunity analysis
Market share and volume	Net present value (NPV)
Payback period	Profit margin
Return on investment (ROI)	

How would you fare during such discussions? If you are not well versed in these concepts, contact someone in the finance department and ask for help. Also, speak with your functional manager and see if the company offers any education and training in these important business topics. Once you come up to speed on these subjects, take some time to begin educating your team. It is important that they understand the business lingo and are able to communicate confidently with various business customers.

> *Four out of 10 executives contend that a lack of financial knowledge among IT staff precludes the use of IT portfolio management in their companies. Eight out of 10 say a lack of staff financial skills makes it difficult to track IT investments' value. Unlike staff in departments such as marketing and operations, most IT staffers aren't trained in finance.*
> Ingmar Leliveld, in "I.T. Staffs Lack Financial Chops For Project Analysis,"
> Eric Chabrow, *Information Week* (March 24, 2003): p. 20.

How Many Projects Can a Project Manager Manage? Perhaps you thought we would never address this question. For an answer, we need to refer to the complexity chart as shown in Figure 5.6. Our recommendations regarding the maximum number of projects a project manager should manage at any one time are as follows:

Zone I project:	One
High zone II and high zone III projects:	Two
Low zone II and low zone III projects:	Three
Zone IV projects:	Four

When sponsors learn about these recommendations, many of them have great difficulty accepting what they consider an extremely low number of projects. Some try to tell us that their project managers must manage a larger number of projects because of the sheer number of projects under way at any given time. The only solution to this dilemma is a well-designed and well-managed project portfolio (see Chapter 10). With the absence of robust organizational discipline, there will always be many more projects to execute than possible, given the number of available project managers. Our years of research and experience with a large number of projects clearly shows that when project managers are given more than the recommended number of projects to manage, both the projects and the project managers suffer, projects fail, and project managers develop severe burnout.

Team Leader

In the case of a project that has a large number of team members, the project manager may not be able to supervise each team member because of the extensive time demands or some of the team members being located off site. In such cases, it is a common practice to appoint one or more team leaders who have the responsibility to manage a group of people on the team. For example, a project manager may decide to have the following reporting structure:

- *Team leader 1:* Four quality assurance team members report to this individual
- *Team leader 2:* Three security analysts and designers report to this individual
- *Team leader 3:* Six offsite programmers report to this individual

In this case, the first and the second team leader will probably be responsible for some development work because each is overseeing a small group. However, the third will more likely be busy full-time, managing six programmers. Think of each team leader as a junior project manager who is being prepared to take on full responsibility for managing projects in the near future.

Administrative Support

From the detailed discussions regarding the roles and responsibilities of the project manager (there are more yet to come: estimating, scheduling, tracking), it should not be a surprise that project managers keep busy, especially the ones who manage high complexity projects. Typical support duties include recording and distribution of meeting minutes, arranging meetings and travel, collecting and recording metrics, updating the data in the project management software, producing reports, and a variety of other support activities. Use of a support staff allows the project managers the time, energy, and focus needed to successfully manage their projects. From our experience with a large number of projects, we suggest the following:

- For zone I projects, we suggest a full-time administrative support person.
- For projects in high zone II and high zone III, two project managers could share an administrative assistant if their offices are close to each other, if they have a good professional relationship, and if they understand the need for equal sharing of the administrative assistant's time
- Though some of the projects in low zone II and low zone III may benefit from the services of an administrative person, it may not be financially justifiable.

From the detailed discussion of project management skills, it should be clear that project managers need four types of skills:

1. General management
2. Project management
3. Business
4. Technology

The degree of these skills needs to be in concert with the complexity of the project and the quality of the environment in which the project will be executed.

For zone I projects, if the project manager is from a technology background but lacks the appropriate business experience, we suggest that the project manager, along with two or three senior team members, establish a small office within the business unit. This arrangement will put the project manager and the core team in the midst of day-to-day business activities. Also, the project manager and senior team members should take turns attending business unit meetings related to the project at hand. This presence will help the project manager and the core team keep in touch with the daily workings of the customer and learn about the customer's business processes, procedures, and policies that are seldom documented but can greatly influence the project.

> *Being on the spot, one can detect trouble at the start and deal with it immediately; if one is absent, it is discerned only when it has grown serious, and it is too late.*
>
> Niccolo Machiavelli, *The Prince*, Penguin Classics.

Team Members

With the right project manager in place, the next step is to start the selection of project team members who possess the necessary quantity and quality of business, technology, and team skills. Team composition is primarily a function of the tasks in the project task plan. Use the task plan developed earlier as a guide for selecting team members. Some of the examples of skill areas that need to be covered for an IT/Business project are analysis, design, development, testing, quality, documentation, business and technology knowledge, operations, database, procurement, training, security, and change management. On a large project, the team composition will change as the project progresses through its life cycle. Ideally, the team should be constituted in a manner that all key stakeholders, especially implementation-level stakeholders, are represented on the team. This structure is certain to facilitate buy-in of the results. At times, having representation from those who are adversaries may create a sticky situation. However, having those people within the camp rather than outside can actually be a benefit to the project. Those who join the team must realize that they are making a commitment to the success of the project and they are expected to place a high priority on the project work, even if they are not assigned full-time. They must also understand and accept their personal responsibilities in supporting the project manager.

Before we delve into a detailed discussion about formulating the project team, we believe it would be educational to review some findings from interviews with a number of project managers regarding their experiences and observations about project teams:

- Staffing requirements must be established and resources authorized far ahead of the start of projects. This way the appropriate administrative work (job postings, interviews, selection, hiring, and transfers) can be performed before the project resources are actually needed.
- Budget approval for resources does not necessarily mean that we can obtain the resources right away. Both technology and people acquisition can have long lead times, ranging from a few weeks to many months.
- Building a team for a project is not just a question of finding the people who have the right skills and knowledge; each member must fit the team well. Highly skilled people may not always combine to produce optimum collective effort. People skills are at least as important as technical skills.
- For more complex projects, not enough focus or emphasis is placed on the responsibilities of the wider team beyond the core team members. Many such projects need significant contributions, usually information and access to undocumented knowledge from several individuals outside the immediate core team.
- The involvement of many sponsors and most of the functional managers was cursory (at best).
- There is no formal business training, or opportunity for business training, for team members from the technology areas—IT, manufacturing, and operations, and especially the new hires. Most of the vendor's people were completely ignorant of the business component of the project. This not only caused problems in requirements gathering, it greatly annoyed a number of the business people.
- There is no formal project management training, or even orientation, for team members supplied by vendors. They don't understand much of the terminology. In fact, the vendors have their own terminology and methodology. This lack of knowledge causes major confusion and irritation.
- There is no formal approach to addressing the problems that occur when people are transferred from their routine business jobs to project teams. The day-to-day project activities are quite different from people's routine jobs, where performance is measured by the "busy work" that keeps them occupied—telephone calls, visits with customers, meetings with managers, problem solving. This busy work is not present to the same extent in project work. Metrics to measure the value of their contributions are different. The result is confusion, especially during the first few weeks of their assignment to a project team. The company needs a short, "How to be an effective team member," training course for all team members, especially those who have never before worked on projects.
- Team members from cross-functional groups such as sales, purchasing, research, merchandizing, and finance are quite unsure of their career development possibilities beyond the project. Many are also unsure how a lengthy assignment to a project team will impact their regular job and career path. For example, as a member of a project team, the salespeople are not selling a product or a service and they wonder how their performance can be measured appropriately. Once the project is over, and the cross-functional team members return to their departments, how will they be reabsorbed? Neither the sponsor nor the project manager seems to have an answer. These concerns need to be addressed and answered before people are transferred to the project team. Unless a satisfactory process is established to handle these issues, there may be difficulties finding the right people who are willing to transfer from their routine jobs to projects.
- The use of SMEs as advisors and internal consultants has not worked well. The reasons for this state of affairs include:
  - Supply *v.* demand. There are not enough SMEs to respond to the number of people seeking their advice. Often, they are not available when needed by project teams.

- Lack of commitment to projects. Because most SMEs are not formally evaluated on their contributions to projects, and often the role is in addition to their regular jobs, they do not seem to have any real commitment to projects. Availability of SMEs is usually on a first come, first served basis. They seem to allocate only a certain (undefined) amount of time for that role.
- SMEs aren't briefed on the project, so they give incorrect or conflicting advice.
- Team members from different cross-functional departments are reassigned, often without prior discussion with the respective project managers. Practically all of the cross-functional managers outrank the project managers, and they do not hesitate to "pull rank." This makes it difficult to recruit new project managers.
- Many sponsors know very little about the project management process. Only a few have had any education on the subject, and most believe that being a sponsor is no different from being a department manager. Many do not regard planning (WBS, task networks) as very important, and they run projects as day-to-day operations—short term planning, meetings every day, and expecting daily progress reports.
- There are few, if any, formal or informal recognition/reward incentives available to project managers to award to team members. Despite all the discussion about the project manager's goodies bag, nothing concrete has been offered. Donuts and muffins occasionally appear for some meetings; they really have little value for motivating the team.

Presenting this long list of items is not meant to suggest that all projects suffer these problems. The list is a compilation from a number of project managers, but it does highlight the problems that can sap the energy from a project team. You should review the list before the start of your project, and then discuss the items of most concern with your manager as well as the sponsor. In addition, a list like this can be used as a master checklist to help avoid repeating the problems that have been experienced by other project managers.

> *Despite a mountain of evidence of unsatisfactory outcomes, projects are often launched which are so poorly staffed and organized that they are highly unlikely to achieve their stated objectives on time and within budget. The people aspects of project management are simply ignored or taken for granted.*
> George Glaser, "Projects: Orphans at Birth," *Meridian Report* 2
> (Winter, 1993).

It is important for the project manager to develop the requisite skills to effectively and efficiently coalesce the wide variety of people who will form the team.

Team Selection   Selection of a solid project team is an extremely important step toward the success of any project. Ideally, the project manager should be the primary person responsible for selecting the team. However, that may not always be the case, as the sponsor or the project manager's boss may already have selected the team. Although it is not highly desirable, this situation can still work with minimal problems. We will discuss this point a little later in this chapter. Let us now focus on the fundamental principles and practices of selecting a strong team:

1. Revisit the detailed task plan developed earlier (see *Task Plan*). The purpose of the review is to ascertain the types of skills needed to complete the variety of tasks outlined in the plan.
2. Review the Complexity Assessment and use the information to define the degrees of the skill and experience needed. The higher the complexity, the higher the necessary skills.
3. Review the Risk Assessment, any issues, and the Organizational Change Management Plan. This information will help you define the degree of management skills—people and political— the team will need to manage the project to success.

With this information at your disposal, the next step is to work with the various functional managers to begin to build a list of candidates for your project team. Make sure to keep both your functional manager and the sponsor in the loop of these discussions. In fact, you may need their help identifying the appropriate candidates for the team; don't hesitate to ask for help where necessary. What you need to make is a thorough shopping list. We have found that project managers who do their homework, and go about this process in a professional manner, consistently end up formulating better skilled teams than their colleagues who approach the job of team recruitment in a haphazard manner. Towards this goal of assembling a high-performance team, we would like to suggest the following four steps:

1. Keeping in view the information you garnered, define the team member needs in terms of professional titles instead of specific names. For example: three financial analysts, two actuaries, two web designers, four programmers, two technical documentation experts, one quality assurance analyst, two security experts, and one administrative assistant.

2. For each position, create a list of key skills needed for the project at hand. As you develop this skills list, keep in mind the technical, business, and team skills. Once the skills list is complete, designate the level of each skill the individual will need to be an effective member of the team. As you do this assessment, try not to think that each position needs to be filled by an expert level person. In fact, team members who are more highly skilled than necessary may eventually be more of a liability than an asset—some of them may get bored and leave, others may want to show off and create dissension in the team, and some may demonstrate their expertise by gold plating the product (adding bells and whistles that nobody really asked for).

3. Using a Kiviat chart, plot the needed points for each skill to create a skills profile for that particular *position*.

4. Repeat this process for each of the other positions identified for the project team. This will provide you with the skills and experience profiles of the various *positions* that you need to fill.

Depending on your experience and the complexity of the project, you may benefit from a formal review of the skill profiles you developed. For such reviews, we would suggest another experienced project manager and/or someone from the project office (if your organization has one). Your own functional manager can also be of help in this area. Once you have developed Kiviat charts for the various team positions, you are ready to recruit the team.

To Clone or Not to Clone   We often come across project managers who have a deep-seated desire to clone themselves. They accomplish their dream by hiring team members in their own image—same background, same experience, same education, same alma mater, same likes and dislikes, same aspirations, and even the same gender. The end result is a group of compliant people, who are not likely to think out of the box or indulge in any real creativity. We urge you to think a bit differently—spread your wings, be creative, and hire team members who have a variety of backgrounds, experiences, and thought processes. The result will be what social scientists call "creative tension." You will have to be on your toes to manage such a team, but if you are successful, the results will astonish you. We are confident that any inconvenience in leading such a team will be outpaced by its creativity and the quality of its output.

Team Recruitment   Simply stated, you need to go fishing. As any fisherman knows, having the right bait is very important. Your bait is the collection of the project strategy, its objectives, the sponsor, yourself, and the perceived value of the project. At this point in the project, you have practically no control over the first three components, but the last two are yours to manage. We suggest that you project a highly professional picture and have your best "elevator speech" ready for prospective team members.

If you have not had experience recruiting team members, we advise you to make an appointment with a recruiter in your organization's human resources department to discuss the principles and practices of an effective and efficient recruiting process. During your meeting, make sure to focus on the fundamentals of effective interviews and the types of questions and areas of discussion to avoid. It is important that you become familiar with any organizational policies and procedures as well as the applicable government policies. Mistakes in these areas can result in serious problems.

The next step is to determine the best possible sources for the various team members. In this book, we will limit our discussion to internal recruiting and leave the process of hiring people from outside the organization to your functional managers and your human resources department. Typically, within the organization, you will have the following venues for possible recruits:

1. *Core team members:* Up to this point in the project, you have probably not been the lone worker; you have had a core team helping you. The members of the core team are excellent sources for possible recruits. They should know the project as thoroughly as you do and can help you identify the candidates with the best match to the project's needs.
2. *Functional managers:* Contact the functional managers who control the resources needed in your project and inform them of your recruitment needs. You should have met most of these people during the project kickoff meeting. Give them your specific requirements and ask for the names of possible candidates. The Kiviat chart is very helpful tool in conveying your needs to them in a well-documented manner.
3. *Grapevine:* Never underestimate the power of the office grapevine (the informal communication channels). Let people know that you are in the process of staffing your project and will appreciate their help with spreading the word.
4. *Job posting:* Most companies have internal job posting procedures. Make use of them, and make sure you do it in a timely manner to convey the message to those seeking internal job reassignments.
5. *Personal contacts:* Certainly, through your work experience, you have a list of people you would like to have on your project. Contact them to let them know of your upcoming recruitment needs.
6. *Project office:* Project offices usually serve as a clearinghouse for internal recruitment. Make sure the project office knows of your needs.
7. *Sponsor:* The sponsor can be a great help in identifying the right candidates for many key positions.
8. *Stakeholders:* Key stakeholders, especially the project champions, can help in the recruitment process.

By this time, you should have a comprehensive list of candidates and be ready to start your recruitment process—one-on-one interviews. If you do not have a good list of candidates, determine which of the following situations apply to your predicament:

1. You have not done a good job of communicating your needs.
2. There are so many projects in progress that there is already a shortage of needed resources.
3. Your project is seen as one of those "this too shall pass" endeavors (a half baked idea that is waiting to fail) and people do not want to risk investing their time, energy, and reputation in a no win situation.
4. Your project is not viewed as a career building or skill building opportunity and people are reluctant to join the team.
5. The project sponsor has a bad reputation, and people who have choices do not want to be on the team.
6. You, as a project manager, do not have a stellar reputation and people are not too keen on joining your team.

Take a good look at this list to decide which items apply to your project. We hope your assessment points to the first item on the list. All others are indicators of systemic organizational problems and their solution is primarily outside the scope of this book.

Recruiting Interviews   Before we begin the discussion on interviews, it is important to focus on the behaviors that, if left unchecked, can result in dissension and discord among team members. The mere presence of any of these traits is not a deal breaker when it comes to building your team. However, we would raise a red flag whenever an individual exhibits any of these traits in a significant manner.

1. *Aggressor:* This type of individual has the need to always be in the lead position and must demonstrate personal proficiencies all the time. Aggressive personalities enjoy provoking others and can be highly self-centered. As a team member, aggressors mostly stay in the storming stage

(explained later in this chapter, see *Teamwork*). These people often make a point solely for the sake of making a point.

2. *Compliant:* The compliant personality is rarely willing to give a dissenting view, has the proclivity to wait for a majority opinion to develop, and then will cast an assenting vote. They are of little use in "bouncing ideas" or in having a discussion to assess alternatives. Additionally, this type of person will rarely take the initiative to point out a problematic decision by others for fear of being wrong.

3. *Defender:* People with this type of personality simply defend any wrong by anybody, even strangers. As a first reaction, they will even defend vendors who have breached their contract or professional obligations. Typically, the defender wants to be liked by everybody and does not like to see people being taken to task (even habitual nonperformers).

4. *Destroyer:* This person is "the bull in the china shop." Around the destroyer, no one and nothing is ever right. They tend to criticize and denigrate other team members, especially behind their backs. Often, this behavior is a mark of deep self-doubt camouflaged by overt offensive behavior. Don't ever allow this personality to review someone else's work, especially not the work of people who have mild manners or who are new to the group.

5. *Jumping jack:* The jumping jack can rarely make a decision and has a short attention span. These personalities will ask everyone on the team for their opinion and then ask again. They also have difficulty focusing on one activity at a time. When attending a meeting, they will try to hop through the agenda rather than follow the order of items. They also tend to interrupt, ask a question, pay little attention to the answer, and then ask another, often unrelated, question.

6. *Look at me:* These people are perennial attention seekers. They are the first to speak, the first to respond, and the first to ask questions. These people always have a better idea than others. They will cut into other people's time and presentation.

7. *No problem:* This is their watchword to everyone for any situation. They will attract scope balls through solid walls, even when the project is far behind the announced schedule. These people strive to please everyone they meet by saying "yes" to anything asked for. As team members, they will agree to all changes, additions, and improvements requested by customers; without consulting the project manager. They may even elect not to inform the project manager of the commitments they have made because, to them, none of this creates any cause for concern.

We do not mean to imply that an individual should never exhibit any of these personality traits. In fact, smart project managers know that in certain situations, one of these traits may be exactly what is needed to deal with the problem at hand. The goal is to staff a team with people who exhibit a variety of positive personality traits that can be used to the project's advantage.

Although this list includes a number of attributes that can lead to dissent and discord, given below are the key characteristics for a productive and synergistic team:

Accountability	Commitment
Desire to learn	Disciplined
Flexibility	Forthright
Intelligent disobedience	Politically astute
Respect for colleagues	Results-oriented
Team player	

Keep in mind that in each interview you conduct, you have two primary interests:

1. No matter how exciting and promising your project, you still have to "sell" it to many of the prospects.
2. Assess whether the person will be a good fit for the team you are trying to build. The fit should encompass both the technical skills and the team skills (the ability to work with others in a synergistic manner).

The key to a successful interview is the preparation made prior to the actual session. Unfortunately, our experience with scores of project managers shows us that many just do not spend the time and energy to do their homework. The best approach is to use the skills definition profiles you built using the Kiviat charts and develop a comprehensive job description for each job classification. The key components of a comprehensive job description are as follows:

1. Key role and responsibilities
2. Estimated tenure—full- or part-time, expected duration of the assignment
3. Business knowledge
4. Technical knowledge
5. Experience
6. Education
7. Any other pertinent information (shift hours, travel requirements, security/access requirements, overtime expectations)
8. Growth potential—professional skills and promotion opportunities (be careful regarding the latter, do not convey more than what is realistic)

Because these job descriptions serve as the foundation for your recruiting effort, make sure that you consult with other project managers, the project office, and your functional manager to help you produce well-targeted job descriptions. In addition, we suggest a session with the sponsor to review the finalized job descriptions. This will serve a number of important purposes:

1. The sponsor will become aware of the extent of skills needed for the proposed project.
2. The sponsor can help the project manager recruit the right people through her relationship with various functional managers.
3. It is a test of the sponsor's interest in the project. If the sponsor does not see any value in this session, the sponsor must go to a "being an effective sponsor" training session.

Once the job descriptions have been finalized, you can begin to build the interview session questionnaire list. Keep in mind that the purpose of the interview is to assess whether the person has the requisite skills, knowledge, experience, and drive to be a productive team member.

The Interview   To help you prepare the right types of questions, let's discuss the variety of questions that can be asked and how they can be used to assess qualifications:

Closed Questions: These questions elicit a "yes" or "no" response and are designed to obtain specific information. For example: "Have you delivered 3 to 5 day classroom sessions on project management to IT and business professionals?" When a person responds to such questions with a long sentence, there are three possible explanations:

- You did not pose your question well
- The person did not understand the question clearly
- The answer to the question may convey some degree of deficiency in the person and he is trying to distract you from the real answer.

Open-Ended Questions: In the case of these questions, the interviewer is trying to elicit deeper explanations and usually follows up with additional conversation to learn more information. For example: How would you respond to a class participant who exclaims: "This type of project management does not apply to my project?" Answers to open-ended questions can provide you with information regarding the person's behavior and insight into work habits. Another open-ended question might be, "What value do you believe you can bring to this project?"

Background/Experience Questions: These questions are designed to determine the extent and depth of the person's experience. For example, "Which estimating models have you used?" Then you may wish to follow up with, "Which model (or models) would you recommend for the forthcoming project, and why?"

Capability/Limitation Questions: This type of question is asked to determine any limitations that the candidate might have. For example, if the position requires flexibility regarding the work schedule or possible travel, you might ask: "This assignment requires occasional second shift assignment and short-notice travel to three out-of-state locations. Would that be a problem for you?"

Sample Questions   The following is a series of questions used by a project manager to interview technical and business people (all internal transfers). In preparation for the interviews, the project manager supplied a copy of the Project Charter to each candidate. As with any list, some of the questions may need to be changed to meet your specific project and recruitment needs.

- In your opinion, what satisfaction will this particular position provide that your current position does not?
- What are some specific motivational factors for you?
- What criteria do you typically use to define success?
- What criteria would you suggest that we use to define the success of this specific assignment?
- What work-related goals have you defined for yourself?
- How will this assignment help fulfill your goals?
- Have you ever missed a deadline? How did that impact the project?
- What strengths will you bring to this position?
- What specific working conditions did you not find enjoyable during the past twelve to eighteen months?
- What specific traits would you not like to see in your next project manager?
- A number of our customers are very aggressive and have a history of wanting to increase scope after the Project Charter has been approved. How do you suggest we approach the situation?
- Can you think of two or three specific suggestions you made to your current/last manager to improve specific operations or functions?
- What specific metrics would you suggest we use to assess project status on the upcoming project? Why?

There are a number of questions one should *not* ask. Most of these have to do with the policies and procedures established by your organization regarding personal information that is outside the information needs of the organization. The best policy is to check with your human resources department and ask for formal orientation on the subject. Making mistakes in this area of the interview is sure to result in an awkward and embarrassing situation; it may expose you, as well as the organization, to legal procedures.

Depending on your experience in interviewing job candidates, the importance of the project, the number of people to be interviewed, and the available time, it may be highly beneficial to conduct mock interviews. Interview a selected number of your core team members or other appropriate colleagues to try out the questionnaire you plan to use to interview the real candidates. To us, mock interviews are very much like prototypes, and the practice will help you refine the questions, check out the timing, and help improve the overall orchestration of the real interviews that you plan to conduct. The extra time spent on this will assure better team member selection and help reduce mismatches between your needs and team member expectations.

An interview is not a one-way street; the candidate will also want to learn about the project, the role, its responsibilities, the sponsor, other team members, and you personally. Most of the time, the candidate is as concerned about the right fit as you are. It is important that you be fully prepared for their questions, provide forthright answers, and do not mislead the person. If the person being interviewed is from outside the company, make sure that you do not divulge any sensitive or proprietary information.

As you conduct the interview, keep in view your job skills profile and description. If you developed a Kiviat chart for the position, one of your objectives is to assess and plot the candidate's skill levels on the various spokes of the Kiviat chart. This will provide you with a clear picture of any gaps between what you need and what the person has. At this point, do not be distracted by any large gaps; focus on making sure that you are able to collect the best information possible. For a selected number of candidates, you may wish to have other members of the core team also conduct interviews so that you can benefit from a second opinion. If you choose to arrange additional interviews, make sure the interviewer receives a copy of the job description and the candidate's resume prior to the interview and is properly prepared.

Typically, project managers limit their discussions with the prospective team members to, "What skills and experiences will you bring to the job?" and "How will your skills help the cause of the project?" While this information is vital, an important area of discussion that many project managers leave out is, "What skills would you like to learn from this project to help you fulfill your career path aspirations?" This additional information will help the project manager decide which work responsibilities to assign to the different team members and will help with the development of team member education and training programs. Our experience shows that, when project managers take specific steps to learn about team members' skills development needs, and then work diligently to incorporate these into team members' work assignments and training plans, the team motivation remains high—even in the face of adverse project conditions.

Making the Selection   Once the interviews for a given position are completed, you can begin the process of making your decision about offering the position to the appropriate candidate. We recommend consulting with the core team members prior to making an offer; their input will help you make better decisions. As you assess each candidate's qualifications, keep in mind that gaps between the skill and experience levels you need and what they possess are likely to exist. As long as the gaps are not too large, you need not be discouraged by them. At times, people who have somewhat lesser experience and skills but have the desire to learn and contribute can be better team members than those who have extensive knowledge and experience. Not everyone needs to be an expert in every needed skill. If you are using Kiviat charts to profile the needed and actual skills of various candidates, we would suggest the following options in relationship to any gaps (shortage) between what is needed and what the candidate possesses:

Gap	0.5 to 1.0	OJT
Gap	1.0 to 1.5	OJT + education
Gap	1.5 to 2.0	OJT + education + mentoring
Gap	> 2.0	No primary responsibility

OJT means that the person has sufficient skills to undertake that responsibility without any measurable risk to the project and will be able to quickly learn from experience and gain the needed skill. Education means the person needs to undergo formal education on the subject. The education option is not limited only to people with a gap of 1.0 or greater; many of those who have smaller gap values will benefit from formal education programs. Mentoring means the person needs access to a SME who will advise and guide the person in a nonjudgmental manner. The SME does not conduct any performance assessment of the team member. People who have a gap of 2.0 or more do not have the skills to be given primary (sole) responsibility without the accompanying high risk of poor performance. For anyone who has a significant skill gap, the work that requires that skill needs to be delegated to someone else while the person receives the specific education and training.

Once you have made your decision to hire a given candidate, review the decision with the sponsor, and, if necessary, with your functional manager and the candidate's manager before you extend your offer. You may need to negotiate certain terms and conditions with the offer. Remember the earlier discussion regarding negotiations. Hopefully, you have been practicing and sharpening your skills; now go out there and win them over. You may need help from your sponsor, your functional manager, the candidate's functional manager, and the human resources department to resolve personnel, pay scale, and career path issues.

As you can see, even when done efficiently and effectively, it can take from days to weeks to interview, make offers, and finally assemble the team. Therefore, you need to work diligently to complete this process as quickly as possible. Having said that, we want to interject an important point of discussion: Go back to the task plan. Did you include any deliverables, tasks, and milestones for the purpose of assembling the team?

This is one of those close-ended questions requiring a "yes" or "no" response. If your answer is "no," what implications does that have on the accuracy of your final estimates and schedules to be developed using the defined task plan? We see this oversight quite often; the primary reason is that the steps to assemble a team deal with process, not product, deliverables and they are often overlooked.

Cross functional employees asked to move from their routine jobs into project teams, full- or part-time, usually have the need to discuss the following:

- Will my pay structure change?
- Who will assess my performance regarding pay increases?
- Who will be responsible for my career path and promotion?

- How experienced is the project manager in conducting performance assessments? (This can become a source of concern if the project manager is at a lower grade level than the team member.)
- How will my performance be reported to my functional manager?
- How will I be able to keep up with the changes and developments in my primary profession while I am assigned to the project?
- At the end of the project, what assurance do I have of a position in my primary department?

These are valid questions and we suggest the following:

1. The organization, as a whole, needs to address these questions, and provide clear policies and guidelines to all employees asked to work on project teams. This job is best tackled by the human resources department, who can study the overall situation, look at the industry trends, and propose equitable policies and guidelines.
2. In the absence of corporate level policies/guidelines regarding these issues, the appropriate functional managers and the sponsor must meet and develop responses to the questions. They should review their responses with the human resources department to make sure any corporate policies and procedures are not being breached.

Once they have been developed, management must communicate the appropriate responses to the project manager and various team members.

SMEs

These people, by their very definition, are senior, experienced, and highly knowledgeable people who are called upon by the sponsor, project manager, or the team members to provide information and guidance. Most organizations have processes, rules, regulations, and procedures that either are not fully documented or are open to interpretation. SMEs can help provide pertinent information, offer a second opinion, or facilitate timely resolution of many questions. It is important to note that SMEs are not considered "team members" because they do not have specific responsibility for completing any deliverables—they simply advise. There are a couple of important caveats regarding SMEs:

1. Because of their expertise, many people depend on their knowledge and advice. Consequently, they are always busy. Therefore, if you think you will need the services of certain SMEs, please contact them early. Take a number and get in the line.
2. Introduce yourself and your project, and clearly communicate the type of help you may need and the approximate time window(s). Inquire about the best manner and time to contact them and the amount of time they can spare for your project. Doing this will let them know that you are not going to waste their time. Be sure to thank them in advance for their offer to help.

When you do contact an SME for advice, make sure you have done your homework, prepared your inquiry well, and composed your question in a succinct fashion. Without this prep work, you are unlikely to have your question answered to your satisfaction and you may have to get back in line. Make sure that you educate your team members about the protocol for contact with SMEs.

In the project organization model in Figure 5.7, notice the dotted line relationship of SMEs to the project manager. Because SMEs, by definition of their responsibilities, do not produce any deliverables and do not report to project manager, they are not accountable to the project manager. Therein lies the problem: very little, if any, of their performance assessment is based on input from project managers. Project managers may complain about the quality of help they receive from a given SME, and they may choose not to use a given SME, but in the end it really does not matter to the SME. Between the project manager and the SMEs, it is the project manager who is in need of the services of the SMEs and who needs to establish good rapport with them. Don't forget to invite them to any of your project celebrations and make sure to thank them for their help and advice.

The Already-Assembled Team: What Should You Do?

At this point, we must discuss a situation in which the team has already been hired (assembled) before the project manager is assigned. What should be the actions of the project manager, when it comes to properly utilizing the skills of the team members to fit the skill needs of the project? This situation is sensitive and needs to be handled with care and consideration. We know of a situation where the new project manager "fired" all of the team members a week after he joined the team, then informed them that each would need to reapply for the job. The project manager had recently attended a seminar where the instructor preached the gospel of taking control and demonstrating aggressive leadership. The result was rebellion by the team; every one of them refused to reapply. The project manager then announced the new openings on the company bulletin board and, to his surprise, not a single person contacted him; the word had gotten around. Eventually, five of the "fired" team members filed an official grievance with the human resources department, and two of them were considering filing some type of lawsuit. This is a great example of a person with absolutely no common sense.

Let us get back to the situation and see what would be the right action for the newly hired project manager. We suggest the following steps:

1. Find out whether any job descriptions have been developed. If so, review them and (if necessary) bring them up-to-date to accurately reflect the skill needs of the project.
2. Is there any documentation of the skill profiles of various team members? How current is it?
3. Make a list of key skill needs for each team member.
4. Hold one-on-one meetings with various team members and ascertain if any of them is significantly under-skilled. It is important for you to be sensitive to team members' perception of these meetings. Don't frame the meetings as job interviews; present them as a way to learn more about team members' skills and their education and training needs.
5. At this point, open a 3 to 6 month look-ahead window on the project to see whether the skill level of any team member will have a negative impact on the project. If so, does the solution to the problem lie within your capabilities and authority? For example, decide if the problem can be solved through mentoring, on-the-job training, or formal training which are things you can put into place without having to get approval from higher-ups. If so, work with the individual team members and put a plan in action.
6. If the solution to the skill gap problem is outside your direct control, the next step is to approach the sponsor and clearly communicate the impact of your findings, keeping the project's intraproject priorities in focus—schedule, functionality, budget, and quality. Be prepared to propose solutions to the sponsor, such as education and training plans, help from SMEs, or additional, higher-skilled team members.

At this point, we will assume that you have assembled all of the needed people, and you are ready to put them to work. However, it may be a bit too early for that. What you have at this point is more of a crowd than a team, and if left to their own devices, the crowd could easily turn into a mob. On the other hand, if well directed, you have the makings of a robust, productive, and effective team.

Teamwork

The project manager needs to work diligently to focus her energies to coalesce the group of diverse people into a synergistic and productive team. One of the most commonly referenced models for team building incorporates the following stages of transformation: forming, storming, norming, and performing.[8]

The objective of a project manager is to get the team from the forming stage to the performing stage as quickly and as effectively as possible—without causing any harm to individual team members. Let us review each of these stages.

Forming   The group has just been assembled. They know the overall objectives of the project, but they know very little regarding their specific assignments and responsibilities. Many of them may not know other individuals—their work styles, work background, and aspirations. Overall, there is

---

[8]B.W. Tuckman, "Developmental Sequence in Small Groups," *Psychological Bulletin*, 63: (1965).

a sense of uncertainty because they are also unfamiliar with your leadership style. The behavior of the people in the forming stage can be summarized as:

Apprehensive	Distant
Eager	Excited
Guarded	Quiet
Unsure	Waiting

You will want to capture the eagerness and excitement factor while you work toward moving the group forward. That work involves welcoming the people to the project, discussing the value-to-business of the finished product, describing the contribution of the project to appropriate corporate strategy, and discussing each individual's contribution to the success of the project. Resist any inclination to dwell on the negative. Your job is to establish a comfort level within the group, build a sense of belonging, and quickly work through their doubts and apprehensions. The project manager must be visible, approachable, and responsive to individual queries. Do not ignore the people you just worked so hard to recruit for your project. Some steps that will help the team during this stage are:

1. Make it a point to personally welcome each new team member, introduce the person all around, and help make the individual's transition to the team comfortable.
2. Take the time to clearly define roles and responsibilities to each team member.
3. Make sure that each team member has a copy of the Project Charter, and let them know that you are available to discuss any question or points of interest to them.

Storming   Although the word can have a negative connotation, some of the applicable synonyms are: "venture," "maneuver," "foray," and "to make inroads." The job of the project manager is to help the group work through their issues and uncertainties and move them to the next stage as quickly as possible. The storming stage is critical in the group's journey toward becoming a productive team. The project manager must use the necessary leadership skills to prevent the following factors from taking over the group:

Conflict	Doubt
Polarization	Turf tussles
Finger pointing	

The process of storming may last from a few days to a few weeks. Make sure that, during this time, individuals are encouraged and given guidance; any assessment of their performance must not be in the forefront. When people make mistakes or ask for clarification, patience, not a critique, is required. If not managed well, some team members may wish to opt out, if not physically, then mentally (which actually is the worst of the two options). Few, if any, team members will be at their optimal performance. Many may miss their milestones and/or have difficulty achieving the desired quality levels. Make the team aware of this expected phenomenon and have them work jointly to minimize the problems. Make sure to communicate to them that, while the team could later make up for the lost time, letting low quality work proceed is going to result in major problems at later points in the project. Experienced and judicious project managers keep the nature of team transformation stages in mind as they develop the project task plans, estimates, and schedules. A key lesson is that when developing estimates and schedules, do not assume that the team will be in optimal performing condition toward the start of the project. Doing so will result in inaccurate schedules and unachievable management expectations.

Norming   This is the transition stage; the disparate group of individuals is beginning to morph into a collaborative and synergistic group—a productive team. Various team members are beginning to take charge of their assignments, are beginning to trust and help each other, are able to resolve most of the issues among themselves, and are exhibiting more agreements than disagreements—all signs of a productive team. Although the journey to this stage does not happen overnight, it should not consume weeks and weeks. Keep in mind that without the positive behaviors associated with this stage, the team is not going to make any major strides. Therefore, the project manager may need advice and assistance from appropriate functional managers and the sponsor to help the team become productive more quickly. Some actions helpful when working toward this goal are:

1. Open communications
2. Positive reinforcement
3. Collaborative work environment
4. Private and public acknowledgment of team member accomplishments

Performing   This stage is the preferred stage for all teams, the point at which the individuals have changed their viewpoint from "them and me" to "we and us." Various team members not only have bought into the goals and objectives of the project, but have also adopted them as their personal goals. The individual team members show appropriate professional and personal respect for each other and are able to resolve most of the conflicts, disagreements, and disputes among themselves. Once a team reaches this stage, it does not mean they will stay there for the duration of the project. A team, or some of the team members, can and will fall back into any of the other stages due to any number of reasons:

1. Arrival of new team members
2. Departure of well-liked and highly-skilled team members
3. Change of the project manager
4. Drastic changes in the project scope, budget, and/or schedule
5. General organizational malaise
6. Lack of customer buy-in
7. Uninvolved sponsor

Project managers must be diligent in monitoring their teams' disposition throughout the life of the project, and must take appropriate and timely action to keep the team in top performing shape.

Cross-Cultural Teams

In the case of cross-cultural (international) teams, communications—explicit and implied—need to be monitored carefully. Words, phrases, postures, and gestures all can communicate a different message than the sender intended. Project managers dealing with such situations will need to learn about the different nationalities and cultures represented on the team. Some of the key items to focus on are:

1. What are absolute "no-nos"?
2. What faux pas should be avoided?
3. How should group meetings be run?
4. What social etiquettes should be observed?
5. What physical gestures should be avoided, and what do they mean?

Another important area to become familiar with are holiday schedules, vacation schedules, and similar policies and procedures. Ignoring these key areas when developing schedules can lead to major problems and put the project in jeopardy. The best approach to become familiar with cross-cultural behaviors is to investigate the following options:

1. If your organization has a project office, see what help they can provide.
2. Find out if any other project managers have experience in the areas of your interest and solicit advice and guidance from them.
3. Try to find out if there are any people in your department who have origins related to the cultures/geography of interest to you and seek advice from them. Keep in mind that they may be able to give you information on social and cultural items, but not in the areas of project management—running meetings, checking on project status, feedback, and actions in the case of nonperformance.
4. Look in the phone book and see if there is a cultural society related to the geography/culture of your interest and request their help in understanding the social and work intricacies of their culture.
5. There is always the Internet. However, be careful. The person on the other side may have a weird sense of humor and may lead you into embarrassing situations.

In spite of how it sounds so far, you need not walk on eggshells. However, you will have to make the effort to learn about the different environments and take the time to prepare yourself for improved communications. Even after all your careful preparation, you may still find yourself in an embarrassing social situation. Don't get flustered. Be polite and take it in stride; enjoy yourself. You will at least have a good story to tell.

The Importance of Trust

Three key synonyms for the word "trust" are "faith," "confidence," and "hope." The underlying context is a positive outlook or outcome. Therefore, having trust in someone or something implies that one has a high degree of confidence that the person will act in a professional and constructive manner and for the common good. For a team to work effectively and efficiently, team members must have trust in each other's capabilities, performance, and interactions. Our advice is for the project manager to get the team together early in the project life cycle, soon after the project staging step, and jointly discuss the subject of trust. Discuss what it means to the team, how people can develop a level of comfort with each other, what could lead to a breach of trust, and what steps to take when a team member feels that trust has been broken. For a project that lasts longer than 3 to 4 months, or has a high political component, this discussion will need to be held more than once.

Recommended Team Behaviors

The mark of a good project manager is the degree to which he prepares the team members to take charge and not be dependent on the project manager for every decision. If such autonomy is not successfully established, team members become reactive and soon every little problem stops project progress. This type of behavior wastes time, energy, and countless opportunities for the team members to learn and grow. It is important that project managers work hard to help the team members become self-sufficient. We came across the following well thought out list of activities and behaviors that are certain to help both the project managers and team members:

- *Solicit employees' ideas and encourage participation in important discussions.*
- *Learn to speak after others have given their thoughts. The boss's (your) words can stifle input from others.*
- *Never disparage what went before, even if you disagree with it. Try to build on others' ideas rather than knock them down. Fear of embarrassment is a powerful demotivator.*
- *Provide positive feedback and recognition to those who demonstrate leadership.*
- *Let others lead. Show the way by restraining your own drive to lead and by being a supportive follower.*
- *Use failures to teach. Experience is the best teacher and failure the consummate coach. Without support from above and the ability to learn from mistakes, people will avoid risk-taking.*

Patricia Wallington, "Leadership from Below," *CIO Magazine*
(October 15, 2002).

Given below is a list of team behaviors developed by a project team at the office of one of the Center's clients at the start of a zone I project. We suggest that you review the list and consider creating one for your project.

- A robust, repeatable project management process is in place; sponsor and functional managers support the process and the team uses the process.
- Project manager and the team members are well versed with the project management process.
- Functional managers are involved throughout the project and do their best to provide agreed upon resources in a timely manner.
- Customers' time, cost, scope, and quality expectations are well managed; customer satisfaction is increased.
- Project manager and team members are not forced to estimate-to-please.
- Project manager is given the authority to manage project scope.

- Team members monitor the project vital signs and promptly and forthrightly report any abnormal variations to the project manager.
- Project manager reports project status with candor to the sponsor. Project sponsor takes an active role in championing the project, the project manager, and the team.
- Project team members become knowledgeable about the project as a whole. Sponsor takes specific steps to delegate authority to the project manager.

■ RESOLVING CONFLICTS

Now that you have the team assembled, conflicts are sure to arise. A conflict is the result of a clash of incompatible ideas or interests between two or more people. Conflicts bring disharmony, and disharmony means discord among people, resulting in reduced productivity and lower quality. To keep your team working at optimal performance, you must identify conflicts as early as possible and resolve them promptly. The project manager does not need to get involved in every conflict resolution; however, it is important that you educate the team on the fundamentals of negotiation skills and encourage them to resolve their conflicts amiably and in a timely manner. Occasionally, the team members will not be able to resolve certain conflicts and the project manager will need to step in. On a proactive basis, it is important for the project manager to keep an eye on the list of unresolved issues as many of these, if left unresolved, will become a source of conflict. Read between the lines of reports, memos, and e-mails by different team members. Paying attention to any altered behavior of a team member can help uncover conflicts simmering under the surface. Once you decide to attend to a conflict situation, we recommend the following steps:

Define the Conflict

Have each person involved in the conflict define the underlying problem in a succinct manner. Let the group know that they need to focus on the facts. No hearsay, no arguments, and no rolling of eyes and uttering deep sighs. Maintain a positive outlook as others speak. During this portion of the session, make sure you are even handed and that you give all parties equal time to convey their point of view. Here are some helpful hints:

1. Be an active listener
2. Demonstrate a positive outlook
3. Focus on the facts
4. Maintain an open attitude
5. Reflect before responding

Assess the Conflict

Once team members have had their say and the problem statements have been documented, ask each person whether they are satisfied with their statement of the problem and whether they understand the other person's point of view. Here you are not seeking an agreement; you are trying to make sure that conflicts have been clearly defined. During this portion of the session, do not allow arguments to emerge, and make sure people stay civil. Now that the problems have been defined, ask the participants if they see solutions to any of the conflicts/problems on their own. Encourage group discussion and facilitate resolutions by helping them focus on points of mutual agreements. In many situations, the group may decide to resolve the conflicts on their own once they have greater clarity of the facts. If certain items are still unresolved, continue with the following steps.

Brainstorm

The next step is to try to resolve the conflict through brainstorming. In a typical brainstorming session, participants begin to suggest their best ideas to resolve the problem at hand. As each person puts forth a suggestion, the facilitator of the session records it on a flip chart. Ask the group to be creative and think of new and innovative ways of solving the problems at hand. As the ideas are being elucidated, allow absolutely *no* discussion of the merit of any idea—only clarification. If you have not already had the experience, you will quickly discover that the restriction of not allowing any discussion regarding any given idea in a brainstorming session is not easily enforced. From our experience with scores of sessions, we have found that there is always at least one person who just cannot wait to comment on someone else's idea. Often, when you try to interrupt these people to remind them of the rules of the session, they retort with, "but, but . . ."

The process of putting forth ideas continues until no new ideas are offered by any of the participants. The next step is to discuss the most viable ideas, and determine whether resolution to the outstanding conflicts is feasible. The job of the project manager is to act as a facilitator and help the participants come to agreements. If certain conflicts are still unresolved, continue to the next step.

Decision Time

At this point, the project manager should step in and take charge of the conflict. The project manager has heard all of the arguments, both pro and con, understands the views of the various participants, and has made a list of their best suggestions to solve the problem. With all of this in mind, the next step is to make a decision. Not everyone in the group is going to be happy with the outcome, but there comes a time when the project manager will need to make an "executive decision." It is not necessary that each conflict be resolved completely by the end of the session. At times, the project manager may need to take certain items under advisement (this is not a sign of indecisiveness, unless the project manager does so routinely). Inform the group of the probable time of your decision and then make sure the decision is clearly communicated to all concerned in a timely manner. Successful project managers learn to set specific milestones to monitor the results of their decisions and then take proper actions if the results do not match expectations.

What we have discussed is a model for collaborative decision making with the final responsibility residing with the project manager. Project managers may be reluctant to take charge and make a decision for fear of being wrong. They choose to procrastinate, hoping the problem will go away. Although it is possible, the odds of this happening are quite low. When conflicts are not managed in a timely manner, the end result is heightened tension. If one is wrong, one will have at least gained from the process of learning. We are reminded of the following relevant observation:

> *You always pass failure on the way to success.*
> Mickey Rooney (http://www.quotationspage.com/subjects/failure/11.html).

■ TEAM MOTIVATION

The term "motivation" can be defined as certain emotional or physiological needs that act as stimulation to action. Of course, the fundamental desire for basic survival (to have the assurance of a job), is a powerful motivator for doing one's work. However, consistent project success and high quality work is not a result of meeting peoples' basic survival needs. We all come across people in our personal and business lives who are slower than a sloth and could not care less. We also meet people who are thrilled to do their jobs and consistently go out of their way to help the other person. What motivates one person over the other? Next time you meet a highly motivated person, ask her. You may learn some very useful information. One of the most often quoted research studies on motivational factors was conducted by Fredrick Herzberg,[9] a management consultant who theorized that there are two dimensions to job satisfaction: hygiene and motivators. We consider the former to be a systemic issue primarily under the control of organizational management and the latter to be a tactical issue where project managers can play a strong role. According to Herzberg, hygiene issues do not specifically motivate employees, but if handled appropriately, can help minimize job dissatisfaction. Hygiene issues, related to the organization's environment, include company policies, salary, supervision, interpersonal relations, and working conditions.

Of the five items, a project manager can have a considerable amount of influence on the last three items: supervision, interpersonal relationships, and working conditions. The quality of supervision is

---

[9]Fredrick Herzberg, "One More Time: How Do You Motivate Employees?" *Harvard Business Review* (February 1968).

dependent on the degree of leadership skills of the project manager. Therefore, do your best to lead the team to success by assessing your leadership skills and then proactively seeking help where necessary. Keep in mind that a considerable part of the satisfaction of a job is the quality of one's social environment at work. Therefore, it behooves a project manager to work diligently to develop a working environment of mutual respect, camaraderie, and teamwork. Various team members should feel comfortable and should develop a sense of belonging. Inappropriate and disruptive behaviors are always major demotivators. Similarly, a project manager needs to do his best to ensure high quality working conditions because the work environment can have considerable effect on the staff's level of self worth and their performance. We strongly advise that the project manager meet with the people responsible for facilities and supplies quite early in the project life cycle and work hard to create the best possible work environment.

Motivators, on the other hand, create satisfaction by fulfilling individuals' needs for personal growth. Herzberg defined these as work, responsibility, achievement, recognition, and advancement. A project manager can have a much greater influence on these drivers for employee motivation.

Work

This is what people do day in and day out. For them to be motivated, it is important that they find satisfaction and accomplishment in the work they do. Now that they are assigned to your project, you must make sure that you have conveyed to them the importance of the project and the contribution it is designed to have toward the corporate strategy and the ultimate well-being of the organization. Another approach to help motivate team members is to involve them, as much as possible, when detailed work plans are developed. Team members take their cues from the project manager and the sponsor. Their motivation will be directly proportional to the degree of excitement you and the sponsor have about the project. If they primarily hear disparaging comments about the project from you and/or the sponsor, their motivation will suffer dramatically. This does not mean that a project has to be easy and at the top of everybody's list. What you do have to emphasize to team members is the value of the project to the business and, ultimately, to their own careers. It is important for the project manager and the sponsor to set a good example by their personal actions—champion the project, speak well of the customers, and maintain a positive attitude.

> *Three people were at work on a construction site. All were doing the same job, but when each was asked what his job was, the answers varied. 'Breaking rocks,' the first replied. 'Earning my living,' said the second. 'Helping to build a cathedral,' said the third.*
> Peter Shultz, *Executive's Book of Quotations*, Oxford University Press.

Responsibility

Earlier, we discussed the subject of the sponsor empowering the project manager—giving the project manager sufficient freedom and power to do her job without being micromanaged. The individual team members need the same sense of empowerment. Team members will be more motivated to do high quality work if they have ownership of their work. This means you must treat team members as adults who can be trusted with their assignments rather than as children who require constant supervision. Ownership can be easily achieved by involving the team in planning the work and equipping them to monitor their own performance through the use of well-defined vital signs and milestones. Earlier in this chapter, we discussed the importance of delegation as a core competency of a project manager. To skillfully motivate your team, delegate as much responsibility as possible to your people, along with the authority to carry out that work. Once in a while, a team member will take the wrong turn and cause problems. Remember that it happens to the best of us.

Achievement

In his work, Herzberg made a strong point that most individuals sincerely want to do a good job, and the actions of a project manager can go a long way in encouraging people to perform well. The first and foremost action toward this goal is to make sure that each team member is positioned for success and not set up for failure. Make sure you do your best to match people's assignments to their talents and provide them with sufficient challenges. Goals set too low can demotivate people and unachievable goals usually result in frustrations. Keep in mind that what would be frustrating to one team member might be a challenge to someone else. Because motivating people is very much a one-on-one process, the project manager needs to know the needs and desires of each team member and then do his best to develop the most appropriate motivators for each. To help people become high achievers, set clear, achievable goals and define uniform standards for assessing performance. Make sure that each team member clearly understands these goals and standards. After the work is assigned and as progress continues, make sure that each team member receives timely feedback on performance.

Recognition

When was the last time you went over to a team member and thanked the person for work well done? If it has been longer than a month, then either they are not doing their jobs well or you have been too busy. Most probably, it is the latter. Individuals at all levels in the project will be highly motivated to go the extra step if you take the time to recognize their contribution, both privately and in public. When thinking about the people to thank, don't forget the customers, key stakeholders, various functional managers, and the sponsor. A particular contribution does not have to be on a grand scale to deserve recognition. Sometimes it is the little things people have taken the time to do that can make a big difference between project success and failure. To be effective, the act of recognition needs to be immediate and *sincere*. Do not patronize people in the name of recognition; they will figure it out and it will backfire. Remember the goody bag we talked about in Chapter 1; dispense some favors to people to recognize their contributions. Where applicable and possible, work with the appropriate functional managers and the project sponsor to arrange for an official recognition—a raise in salary, a bonus, or even a promotion. Remember to ask yourself, "Will my current team members volunteer to work on another project with me?" The answer will tell you how well you are doing your job.

> *If you want your merit to be known, acknowledge that of other people.*
> Oriental Proverb (http://www.refdesk.com/nov00td.html).

Advancement

Project managers, by the nature of their roles and authority, may not be able to provide this motivational stimulus. However, they can play a strong role in helping team members advance to better and higher positions. The first step is to make sure that team members receive sufficient and timely education and training to help them perform their current duties and prepare them for their long-term career aspirations as well. One of the points we routinely discuss with project managers is the degree to which they have incorporated the team's education and training plan into the project task plan. Often, this area is overlooked because tight schedules and limited resources do not allow for education and training. Another excuse is lack of funds. Finally, the most inane reason of all is: "If we train them, they will leave."

Now that we have discussed the fundamentals of team member motivation, let us ponder the proverbial question, "What is the best approach for a project manager to motivate the various team members?" In answer to the question, we state the adage, "Motivation is in the mind of the beholder." What motivates one team member may not be what the next one needs. Different people are driven by different needs, based on their personality and individual short- and long-term needs. Therefore, the best approach is to simply ask the team members what motivates them. The inquiry process can be both public, in a meeting, and in private, where the project manager meets with each individual to discuss the subject in more detail. The following process works well:

1. Brief the team on the fundamentals of motivation. Then, give them a day or two to think about personal motivation drivers during their tenure on the project. Make sure they understand that the follow-up discussions must be realistic, pragmatic, and not an opportunity to vent against the organization and general management. Don't encourage distractions and diversions from your goal.

2. Hold a follow-up meeting and, using the brainstorming approach, facilitate the development of a clearly-stated list of pragmatic motivational drivers. At this meeting, do not try to attach names of individuals to specific motivational drivers. Another helpful list to generate is that of current situations that team members consider to be key demotivators. Be careful, as you approach this part of the meeting, that participants don't get "carried away."

3. The next step is to have the team focus on the list of motivators and demotivators and select those that are under the influence and control of the sponsor and the project manager. Once the two lists have been sorted out, ask each team member to think through the items and provide you with their top five items in each list. This could be done during the meeting or in the privacy of team members' offices shortly after the meeting.

4. Another step that can lead to individual team member motivation is to ask each person to provide you with a list of one to three skills they possess but do not have any bearing on their current responsibilities. Ask them to list the skills they have that can help another team member. Taking the time to learn about these skills and then doing one's best to provide opportunities for individuals to practice their special skills can be a great motivator. One important caveat here is to make sure that the extra time needed to help others does not interfere with the team member's primary responsibilities.

At this point, you have very useful information from your team members and can develop plans for meeting their motivational needs. You have now set certain expectations. The ball is in your court. We advise that you seriously review each list, see what is within your abilities and where the sponsor's help may be needed, and then work diligently to do your best to meet individual team member needs. Success in this area does not always mean that you are able to fulfill each need to its fullest; however, your sincere effort is sure to be highly appreciated by the team. Motivating the team is a continuous effort and you must make sure that your peoples' needs are a part of your day-to-day work and your overall management style.

I Can't Hear You, It's Too Dark In Here

This is an old vaudeville joke that features a maintenance team gathered around an open manhole cover. The crew supervisor, standing by the side of the opening, is trying to yell instructions to a worker far below. The person below yells back, "I can't hear you, it's too dark in here." How does that translate to a project team? We have all experienced instances where a project manager believed that she communicated instructions very clearly to one or more team members, but what actually happened as a result was completely different. On learning about the disconnect, the project manager asks, "Didn't you hear what I was trying to say?" Usually, the situation continues to deteriorate. Of course, the person heard, but the person did not understand; the message received was quite different than the message delivered. The eventual outcome then ranges from minor distractions and delays to major disasters. Therefore, it is imperative that project managers and team members develop their listening skills to make sure all communications are clearly understood. It is a well-documented fact that, due to the normal ongoing distractions, most people retain less than half of what they hear. Retention falls drastically after 48 hours unless the person has made specific effort to make strong mental notes or jot down the message. What leads to this type of behavior? One key reason for imperfect retention is that when most people are listening to someone, especially at work, they are *already* preparing their response. The listener may be physically responding with gestures to convey that he comprehends the message (eye contact and up and down movement of the head), but limited mental engagement occurs. This phenomenon escalates when the two parties are dealing with performance issues. Ironically, just when the need for clear communications is highest, the parties do not communicate well at all. The project manager must be aware of these behaviors and work diligently to improve communication skills, especially the skill of active listening. From our personal experiences and observations of both poor and good listeners, we have delineated a number of qualities and traits that separate the two. They include the following:

Focus   Good listeners focus on the incoming message with the intent of learning as much as possible from the other person. They keep the focus on the other person's message rather than starting to think of holes in the message or objections that could be raised. Early in the conversation, the idea is to understand and process the meaning behind, and the purpose of, the other person's communications. Focus also means that you minimize all distractions and pay attention to the person, both mentally and physically. Turn to face the person, unfold your arms, and maintain steady eye contact; don't allow your attention to roam between the person, your computer screen, the view outside, and the pictures on your walls. If the conversation is crucial, turn off the telephone. Management guru Peter F. Drucker wrote about a senior executive who never got any calls during important meetings. When queried, the executive stated, "My secretary has strict instructions not to put anyone through except the President of the United States and my wife. The President rarely calls—and my wife knows better."[10] It is indeed a shame that project managers no longer have executive assistants.

Open Your Mental Door At the start of any discourse, make sure you convey to the other person your strong willingness to hear the message. Your facial and body gestures convey more than you would like to think. Having your arms folded, looking away or at the ceiling, tapping your fingers, doodling, and general listlessness all convey a message of disinterest and apathy.

Patience A good listener has patience. Occasionally, the other person has not prepared the message well or is not able to communicate clearly. A good listener works to put the other person at ease by engaging her in a conversation and by asking message-related questions. These questions should be open-ended and should require discourse rather than simple "yes" or "no" answers. Showing one's patience and interest in what the other person is trying to convey is the mark of a great listener.

Don't Step on Their Lines We all have known people who, during any conversation, just can't hold back. They have to put forth their views and points right away. They want to be the first to show that they thought of it, whatever it is. Untimely interruptions make others lose their train of thought and are also terribly rude. Your job is to listen; you should give the stage totally to the other person. Soon, you will have sufficient time to respond.

Keep Your Eyes Open Not all communication is verbal; much of it is through facial and body language. Don't get so involved in note taking and focusing on the verbiage that you overlook the vehicles of the message—voice inflections, facial expressions, body gestures, and the overall demeanor. The verbal message does not always match nonverbal clues. Stay alert and be a good listener. Remember the words of Yogi Berra: "You can observe a lot by watching."

Hold Your Horses We all know that some conversations can get heated, emotional, and can turn into an argument. The other person may be upset about a glitch in a process, an issue with a deliverable, an unreturned phone call, or even something they have done wrong but would rather not be held accountable for. You may even find out that the person is really annoyed with someone else and you just happened to be a convenient target. Resist the urge to strike back, even when you are right (especially when you are right).

> *Be swift to hear, slow to speak, slow to wrath.*
>
> James 1:19.

> *The habit of common and continuous speech is a symptom of mental deficiency.*
> Walter Bagehot (http://www.quotationspage.com/
> quotes.php3?author=Walter+Bagehot).

Ask yourself the question, "If someone else gave me the same message, how would I react?" Open-ended questions are appropriate in this situation; trying to pinpoint the person early in the conversation through closed-ended questions may lead to even greater outbursts. The other person may perceive strong emotion on your part as an attack. The second important point is to keep your cool. Feel free to show your surprise at the situation or express your dislike of the current state of affairs, but do so with a calm voice and controlled posture—don't flail about the room expressing your annoyance and frustration. Histrionics may work for coaches of professional sports teams, but it is

---

[10]Peter F. Drucker, *The Effective Executive* (New York: Harper Business 1993).

not recommended for project managers. In almost every situation, the person who maintains emotional control and retains a calm disposition is seen by colleagues as the more professional and mature individual. The next step is to communicate to the person that you acknowledge, not accept, their anger with the situation and that you are ready to do your best to resolve it. Make sure you do not communicate that the problem will be resolved in their favor. Let them know that a decision will be made only after you learn all the facts. If the person is right, and you have the power, the correct thing to do is to take action in their favor and offer a sincere apology. Whatever you do, do not overstep your bounds and promise action that it is not in your power to deliver.

Pencil to the Paper   During any given workday, a project manager will communicate with dozens of people and receive scores of verbal messages. A sharp listener makes a habit of recording the point of each (important) message promptly and then takes the extra step to reiterate it to the other person to make sure that the communication was as intended. This action not only confirms that the message has been received and understood, it assures the sender that the intended message got through. In case of any misunderstandings, both parties can refocus and correct any problems in a timely fashion. The next step is to follow through and send a record of the agreement to the person.

The discussion and advice on listening skills is not meant for project managers alone; it applies to every team member. We strongly suggest that you discuss the subject with your team members, have them assess their communication skills, and then develop a plan to help improve the skills where necessary. Sloppy communication styles lead to misunderstandings, ill feelings, and an overall unsatisfactory work environment.

Healthy Competition

One of the most difficult areas of team development is the process of inculcating "healthy competition." The word "competition" brings to mind such behaviors as rivalry, antagonism, and contention, to name a few. Healthy competition means that team members have a desire to surpass each other, but not at the cost of those on the losing end. This concept is difficult to put into practice because society in general, and sports teams in particular, value individual performance over team accomplishments. The following practices and principles of team management will help you move the team into a healthy competitive environment:

- Recruit people for your team who have an expressed desire, and proven record, for personal contribution combined with a strong desire for the team's success.
- Avoid rewards, remunerations, and recognitions that highlight individual accomplishments through competition over team members.
- Do not bestow preferential treatment on individuals who have succeeded by stepping over their colleagues.
- Do your best to remove those people from the team who display gross self-interest over the welfare of their colleagues and success of the project.

There is a fine line between healthy competition and destructive competition; you must be diligent in ensuring that the team clearly understands your views on the subject and *consistently* practices what you preach.[11]

Trouble in Paradise

As a project manager, you hope that all team members will remain highly motivated throughout the life cycle of the project, they will perform to their optimal capacity, they will get along marvelously with other team members, and they will develop a deep liking for all of the project's customers. We all know that a time will come when one or more of the team members will not perform to expectations and that people's actions will have a negative impact on the disposition of the team. What

---

[11]One of the best treatments of the subject of internal competition appears in chapter 6 of *The Knowing Doing Gap* by Jeffrey Pfeffer and Robert I. Sutton.

options does the project manager have? Complex problem, simple answer: be prepared. Toward the start of a project, the project manager must do sufficient research to learn about the policies, procedures, and guidelines defined by the human resources department. Learning and understanding these corporate processes will provide the foundation for actions that can be taken to deal with team member nonperformance. Within the broader spectrum of the subject, we will address two primary subtopics:

1. Actions to be taken when a team member breaks a *rule* of behavior.
2. Actions to be taken when a team member fails to perform his roles and responsibilities.

In the case of the breaking of a rule, the project manager should first confirm the problem and then promptly discuss the subject with her direct boss, provide specific information (no hearsay), and seek advice. It may also be necessary to contact the direct superior of the person in question. If the transgression is serious, the project manager should make a formal entry of the incident in a personal log. This entry should include the details of the problem and names of the people who the project manager contacted to report the incident. At this point, the project manager will need to seek guidance from the sponsor regarding the status of the person's assignment to the project. Because these types of incidents can have a lasting and dramatic effect on people's careers, the project manager should avoid discussing the matter with other team members and must never spread any rumors. Over the years, we have known of many project managers who invited a representative from the human resources department to brief their newly formed teams regarding corporate policies, procedures, and guidelines to make sure that the team is fully aware of the necessary information.

Now we come to the question of performance problems—a team member falling behind in the schedule and/or quality of work. The steps required to deal with such problems are:

1. Carefully document the problem and then hold a one-on-one meeting with the person to discuss the specifics of the problem and how the person's behavior is impacting the project and, if applicable, other team members. Make sure to focus on the facts that you have gathered (rather than hearsay) and do not take an accusatory or threatening tone. Try to learn about the real reasons behind the problem and discuss whether these issues could be addressed and solved through your joint actions. If this is the case, make a note of an agreed upon action plan, track the person's performance, and compare it to the agreed-upon plan.
2. If the team member takes the plan of action to heart and subsequently improves his performance, make sure to compliment the individual for the effort. If, on the other hand, the problem persists, you will need to start a "problem instance" log and document the incidents of nonperformance diligently. At this point, it may be necessary to consult with your immediate boss and the immediate boss of the person in question. Of course, throughout this process you should be working directly with the individual to produce a mutually agreeable solution. Keep a sharp eye on the project's intra-project priorities (schedule, scope, budget, and quality), and if you determine that any of these are being impacted beyond their thresholds, you need to escalate the problem to the sponsor promptly.

Depending on the reactions of the person in question, and if the problem continues to escalate, it may be time to remove the person from the project team. Although this is an unpleasant task, project managers must face it and take appropriate action. The troublesome actions of just one person can have considerable negative impact on other members of the team and the project. At this point the sponsor, perhaps in consultation with the individual's manager, and the human resources department will need to approve the removal order. A decision to remove the person from the team does not necessarily mean that the person will be fired from the company. Although we recognize that the task can be very unpleasant, we believe that the project manager must be the one to communicate the decision to the individual. Keep in mind, you are the leader of the team and it is your responsibility to manage the team. It may be prudent to arrange for someone from the human resources department to be present when the message is finally delivered.

Once this action has been carried out, you need to meet with the team and brief them on the reasons for the action. During this briefing, make sure to focus solely on the facts of the situation, the impact of the situation, and the need to move forward as a team. Not all the team members will take the news well; some may be upset because they sympathize with the person who was disciplined.

However, being a project manager is not a popularity contest; you will likely be required to take actions that will not generate "warm fuzzies" for some of the team members. However, as long as you decide fairly, and act professionally, most will understand your position and your decision.

A Safe Project Environment

A short while back, during a group meeting at a client site, a most intriguing announcement came over the company intercom. The person said, "My name is _____, I'm in cubicle _____, I believe I just deleted an important customer file, I don't think there is a backup, I need help and I need it now." The candidness of the message was most surprising as it was announced to the entire building. The interruption caused a short lull in the meeting; a few participants murmured good luck to the individual and the meeting continued. Later in the day, I requested a meeting with the individual and had the opportunity to ask her a few questions regarding the candidness of her message and how was she able to muster the courage to announce it over the intercom. She did acknowledge that it was not easy, but she had been with the company only a few days, was in the midst of learning the intricate file access and management system, and had executed a wrong command by mistake. She could not reach her immediate supervisor or any of the team members who could help her. As a part of her orientation and training program, she had been repeatedly instructed on the need for not hiding mistakes that could result in bigger problems. She specifically remembered her immediate supervisor telling her that mistakes will be made, but trying to sweep them under the rug, point fingers, or place blame would not be acceptable. She knew that it would not be comfortable to be associated with the mistake she made, but she was more concerned about the harm to the company if the problem was not resolved correctly and promptly. It is important that you work hard to build a trustworthy environment where team members feel safe to ask for help when needed, especially in the face of a mistake. If team members feel that you will yell and scream and heads will roll whenever problems occur, they will do their best to mask their mistakes and hide them or blame others. Whenever a mistake does happen, instead of trying to pin the mistake on an individual, first look into the underlying communications, process, education, and training related to the problem. If an individual does not learn from his mistakes, the next step is to escalate the problem to the appropriate functional manager and/or the sponsor.

If you are new to the position of project management, you may have some difficulty making the transition from your recent role and responsibilities to the role of a project manager. As a team member, your role was more task-oriented—getting your hands dirty doing the work—while as a project manager you are responsible for having work done through others. The process of delegating the tasks you are accustomed to doing (until recently) to team members can be fraught with uncertainties and accompanied by a feeling of loss of control. The problem really becomes acute in situations where a team member falls behind and the project manager has the desire to step in to finish the task because she is an expert at it. This rescue attempt will not help either the project manager or the team member. The team member still does not know how to perform to his responsibility, and the project manager is spending time doing, rather than managing and leading. The act of stepping in and finishing a team member's work is actually a way to avoid managing the team member, which is obviously a more difficult task. Therefore, don't let the urge to step in and finish a job get in the way of your real job of managing and leading the team.

> *Tech people are notorious for feeling more comfortable in front of a computer instead of dealing with people.*
> Christian Buckley, *San Francisco Chronicle* (August 29, 2003, p. E1).

■ COMMUNICATIONS PLAN—PPA STEP 23

As you moved through the Idea, Pre-Launch, and Launch stages, you probably developed an appreciation for the need for clear and well-focused communications. The need for effective communications will increase as the project moves to the Execute stage. Effective project managers, as well as team members, aggressively communicate with their stakeholders, management, sponsors, customers, vendors, and among themselves. In selected projects, communications with the external world (public agencies, the press, and shareholders), are key to the success of a project. Communications can take many forms—formal or informal, written e-mail or voice mail, urgent or routine—but in all cases, communications must be accurate, forthright, timely, and properly distributed to be effective. Well-designed and timely communications are key to the management of expectations, whether in a formal briefing for management or in an informal conversation with a fellow team member. As you contemplate any communication, think of the following key attributes: the recipient, the mechanism, the message, and the frequency.

Recipient

Within the structure of a project, the two best sources you can use to identify the recipients of your communications include the Stakeholder Analysis undertaken in the Pre-Launch stage (Chapter 4) and the project organization structure designed earlier in this chapter. To ensure that the communication channels are all inclusive, partition your audience into key groups (steering group, sponsor, functional managers, other project managers, team members, project office, portfolio manager, consultants, and vendors). In the days of rotary telephones, it took some effort for a person to dial a number and make a call. Then came touchtone phones, followed by redial and speed dial facilities, and then e-mail. Now, with the touch of a single button, one individual can send the same message to countless recipients.

> *U.S. workers send and receive an average of 204 messages per day via voice mail, cell phone, e-mail, fax, pager, interoffice mail, postal mail and handwritten notes.*
> *Computerworld* (August 28, 2000, p. 56).

Even with an average response time of only 30 seconds per message, one spends at least 1½ hours per day communicating in some fashion. Consider the resulting increase in wasted time, rise in irritation, and drop in productivity. Our advice to project managers is to carefully review their mailing lists and those of the various team members and make sure that the distribution lists contain only essential personnel. Similarly, project managers should be assertive in informing people to remove their names, and the names of the team members, from any superfluous message distribution lists.

Mechanism

Communications can be oral or written and formal or informal. Information can be communicated through hard copy (internal mail, external mail, fax), telephone (personal or voicemail), e-mail, one-on-one meetings, group meetings, a project website, or an emissary. Each type has its own benefit and each one is suitable for specific situations. For example, individual team member status reports could be communicated through any of the channels listed; however, project status is best reported in a face-to-face group meeting. Occasional conference calls involving the team may work, but will not produce the camaraderie and cohesion necessary for a synergistic team environment. Similarly, the first set of meetings with key stakeholders should be face-to-face rather than through telephone calls or e-mail. Typically, communications during the early stages of a project, during high stress situations, and toward the end of the project should be face-to-face. Once the project is well underway, and various individuals have developed a level of comfort with each other, other forms of communication become more efficient. Effectiveness of all communications must still be managed diligently.

> *E-mail traffic has doubled, and employees can simply pass problems on, batting them off into cyberspace instead of taking care of them, . . . There is a need for accountability. . . . The idea is not about establishing an e-mail police but rather to get people to think before they send e-mails, . . . People are exchanging e-mails with coworkers who sit only six feet away.*
> Daniel J. Horgan, "You've Got Conversation," *CIO Magazine*
> (October 15, 2002).

Following is a summary of an interesting study regarding the communications mismatch between IT professionals and their key stakeholders:

Non-IT executives prefer human-to-human, experience-rich interactions over any other form of information exchange. But the data from the study revealed the following distribution of communication modes by IT leaders:

- *E-mail 33%*
- *Meetings 33%*
- *Telephone 20%*
- *Face to face 10%*
- *Other 4%*

IT professionals do not spend enough time involved in high-impact, person-to-person conversations.

Thornton May, "Tell the Truth Effectively," *Computerworld* (February 3, 2003).

Where do you fit in? How much face time do you get with the sponsor, key stakeholders, and the team? Do you rely too much on passive (e-mail and telephone) communication? Look up, make eye contact, and communicate with passion and verve.

Messages

Most often, the higher the level of the recipient, the less detailed the information needs to be. For example, a project sponsor does not need the same level of detail about the project as a functional manager. It is important that team members provide the project manager with detailed information regarding the status of their assignments. However, the sponsor only needs to review the summary status (the status of the vital signs). To make the communication process efficient and effective, the project manager must work with the key stakeholders to define their respective communication needs and then establish a system for follow through. Sound engineers spend inordinate amounts of time trying to filter out noise and amplify the signal of communication. The project manager must work very hard to do the same and take the time to train the team as well.

IT managers can't make any sense of the IT director's plan to reorganize the department—each one has a different understanding of what the boss means in the meeting when it was announced. The pilot fish asks the director for clarification, eliciting the helpful response, "I was intentionally vague so that no one would get the wrong idea."

Computerworld (July 17, 2000, p. 90).

Many people who have a technological background have a proclivity for "techno talk" or "geek speak"—rattling off the jargon and acronyms associated with technology—which leaves most business customers confused and irritated. It is important that project managers and team members learn to read their audience and adjust their communications to match the specific situations. For example, for IT professionals, the acronym "CRM" means "customer relationship management," but there are a few honest reasons for confusion:

- In a photography shop, it means "camera ready material."
- In a hospital setting, it means "cardiac rhythm management."
- In an airline back office, it means "crew resource management."

Project professionals must learn to use the correct vocabulary when communicating with their customers and other stakeholders. Doing otherwise means they will generate a lot of noise, but very little signal.

The space between business and IT is a 'cataclysmic gulf.' . . . Within this continental divide, budget overruns are born, serious errors in judgment are made, [and] organizations pay millions of dollars only to experience catastrophic failure. . . . One of the factors that helped transform my career was my ability to alter my geek speak. . . .

Somewhere along the road, I stopped alienating those around me. I started talking like a real businessman instead of a geek.

Deryck G. Jones, in "Failure to Communicate," Kathleen Melymuka, *Computerworld* (August 26, 2002, p. 44).

Another important point regarding project communication is the clarity with which the message is composed. The project manager, in consultation with the project office (if one exists), should devise a standard template for all outgoing communications. For example:

Project ID and name
Subject
Message
Action required
Sender's contact information

With the advent of the Internet, many people have decided that normal grammar and composition rules should not apply to e-mail messages. It is quite common to receive messages composed of all lower case letters, full of abbreviations, and with absolutely no punctuation. The message the sender is trying to convey is, "I'm so busy, there is no time to hold the shift key, and the use of punctuation slows (important) me down." Using proper grammar is rarely a choice. Many people don't even bother to review their compositions before they hit the Send button. Sloppy work that would garner an F grade in an English composition class is now routine in many communications. It should be obvious how we feel about this attitude. Demonstrating respect for the quality of one's work is a matter of pride. We believe that those who are consistently careless in their communications will lean toward carelessness in their other work, which is a very undesirable trait.

Telephone Messages   A primary tool for communications, used by project managers and team members, is the telephone, with which they leave messages for each other and key stakeholders. It is important that everyone on the team practices sound telephone protocol and ensures that all communications are effective and efficient. Given below are a number of suggestions designed to help you and the team improve telephone communications, especially when you need to leave a message:

1. Plan your thoughts and specific points of discussion before you dial the phone number. Don't think out loud as you record the message; it conveys disorganization and incompetence.
2. Limit your message to a maximum of four specific points; any more than this will make your message difficult for the listener to keep track of and the individual may have to replay your message, which is an annoying step.
3. Do not use slang, acronyms, and abbreviations unless these are a routine part of the day-to-day vocabulary of the recipient.
4. People seem to speed up as they proceed through their message, with the last few seconds at the speed of an auctioneer. By the time they state their phone number, they are speaking at the speed of light. The recipient may be forced to play the *entire* message a number of times just to retrieve the phone number. It is best to identify yourself and give out your phone number at the start of the message and then slowly repeat your phone number at the end of the message.
5. If you are calling across time zones, consider identifying your location and the time of the call.
6. Clearly state the next step. Do you expect a call back? By what time? Statements like ASAP (as soon as possible) and at your convenience can be confusing. Your ASAP may be very different than that of the other person.
7. Do not be abusive, threatening, condescending, or "smart" in your message. Keep in mind that the person may play the message on the telephone speaker and people may be present or in the near vicinity. Therefore, if you are frustrated or angry, take a deep breath, compose your thoughts and keep in mind your objective for your message—having the other person do something for you. Focus on how well your message will accomplish that.

Frequency

Frequency of communications is inversely proportionate to the recipient's level in the project organization. While team members may report to their project managers on a daily or weekly basis, the project manager's report to the sponsor may be biweekly or monthly. Similarly, the project status report to the steering group may be bimonthly or quarterly. It is usually a good idea for the project manager to meet with her boss, various functional managers, key stakeholders, and the sponsor and discuss the optimum frequency of various communications. In this way, the project manager can meet their expectations to the best of her ability. Similarly, the project manager and the team need to jointly decide on the frequency of the team's communications with the project manager. For example, a project manager may decide that an inexperienced (or a new) team member needs to report on the start and finish of each task, more experienced members of the team may be asked to report weekly, and the most senior team members may be asked to report at the start and finish of deliverables. All team members should understand the expected frequency of their communications.

This discussion is not intended to imply that all communication is very formal and has predetermined frequency. In any project, a large portion of significant information is exchanged in an informal and unplanned manner—by the coffee and snack machines, standing in the lunch line, passing by in the hallways, and in elevators.

We have yet to discuss a very important component of communication skills—speaking. Every project manager must excel at this skill because most communications are through one-on-one or public speaking. Discussing, in detail, the skills necessary for speech communications is outside the scope of this book, but we will list the key components of good speech:

Eye contact	Facial expression
Gestures	Pace
Posture	Voice projection
Voice tone and modulation	

Project managers must understand the importance of effective public speaking and must acknowledge the fact that it does not come easily to most people. Interestingly, in the U.S., the fear of public speaking is more acute than the fear of snakes, spiders, heights, darkness, and even death. It is difficult to imagine that most people, if given the choice, would choose death over public speaking. However, standing up and talking to a group of people upsets the average stomach at the very least. If you are apprehensive about public speaking, find out if your organization offers training on the subject. If so, register at your earliest opportunity and work diligently to improve your skills. If your organization does not offer any training, you should investigate joining a chapter of Toastmasters International, a nonprofit organization dedicated to helping individuals overcome the fear of public speaking.

■ PROJECT NOTEBOOK—PPA STEP 24

A Project Notebook is a very important contributor to the successful organization and management of a project. It provides a standard framework for project documentation and acts a repository for essential documents and working papers developed during the project. Imagine a meeting midway through a project. A new sponsor, a number of functional managers (some of whom are also new), and the project manager have gathered to discuss the status of the project. The sponsor and some of the functional managers then raise the following questions:

1. What was the primary reason for the start of the project?
2. Has there been any increase in the scope? If so, how much?
3. What are the critical success factors of the project?
4. What is the current status of the schedule and cost?
5. Is there a gap in the planned resources and resources currently assigned to the project?
6. How many deliverables were planned, how many have been completed, and how many are in progress?
7. Are the shutdown conditions being monitored routinely?

How many of these questions can a typical project manager answer on the spot, with sufficient documentation at hand to support the responses? Without a well organized Project Notebook, not many. Our advice to all project managers is to inquire whether the organization has a recommended structure and outline for project notebooks. If not, talk with other project managers and find out what they use. If no structured format exists, be a pioneer and create one. It will place you in good favor throughout the project life cycle. For projects driven by contracts with vendors, mandated statutes, and/or mandated processes, meet with the legal department and decide what documentation needs to be maintained, in what format, and for how long. Make sure that you educate the team on the resulting policies and procedures and convey to them the risk of breaching the defined policies and procedures. Meet with the sponsor and explore the need for using representatives from the internal audit department (or appropriate project office SMEs) for a periodic audit to ensure compliance. To the uninitiated, this may all sound like too much bureaucracy, but in case any disputes (or lawsuits) develop, you will be glad that you have the necessary documentation to support your side of the story. Following is a list of headings for a comprehensive Project Notebook:

> Appendices/miscellaneous
> Change history
> Correspondence
> Deliverables list
> Facilities
> Glossary and reference information
> Hardware and software configuration
> Meeting minutes
> Outstanding issues
> Policies, standards, and procedures
> Project authorization and budget(s)
> Project Charter
> Project manager's log
> Project organization
> Project plan, estimates, and schedules
> Project security plan
> Status reports (vital signs reports)
> Vendors, consultants, and contractors

We did not include headings for documentation, such as requirements, design, code, and test data. To us, these are system/product life cycle documents and need to be maintained separately, as they can become quite bulky. As with all other lists, it will be necessary to tailor the nomenclature and the number of individual items to meet specific organizational needs. Once finalized, the list must then be further customized to meet individual project size and scope needs. The following steps will help you create and maintain a comprehensive Project Notebook:

1. Select the medium for the notebook (preferably an electronic form). The preferred choice is to maintain it on a server that can be shared (through appropriate security protocols).
2. Working with the project office (if one exists), fellow project managers, and/or core team members, finalize the topics, standards, and procedures for the notebook.
3. Design the notebook structure (the logical order of various notebook components).
4. Identify a primary, as well as a backup person, responsible for maintaining the notebook.
5. Provide the sponsor, team members, and appropriate customers with access to the notebook (you may need to use different levels of access authorization protocols).

A Project Notebook is going to be useful only if it is kept up-to-date. Make sure that the individuals responsible for notebook maintenance perform their responsibilities in a disciplined and timely manner. Incomplete and out-of-date Project Notebooks are of little value.

■ CHARACTERISTICS OF A SOUND PROJECT PLAN

Let us review what we have accomplished to this point. At the start of the Launch stage, we started with an approved Project Charter and then developed a variety of plans to lay out the project in detail. Before we continue to the next important step, developing detailed task-based estimates, it is always a good idea to look back to assess the quality of the planning process. If the project plan is not sound, the resulting estimates and schedules will be of questionable value. We judge the soundness of any project plan by the following five attributes:

Comprehensiveness

The scope of a sound project plan covers all aspects of the project, including those that are the responsibility of support organizations. Every significant task in the project is identified and its logical sequence and relationship to other tasks is explicitly stated.

Uniqueness

It is the only approved overall plan for the project. Subplans for lower level managers can be useful and necessary in certain situations. However, independent plans (plans that are developed and executed independently of the official project plan), are a common cause of schedule slippage and other difficulties that result from poor communication and coordination.

Unambiguousness

Each task is assigned to one and only one individual. The deliverables are clearly defined so that progress can be assessed realistically. In the absence of clearly defined deliverables, fuzzy claims of completion are often used to imply progress when, in fact, little real progress has been made.

Authoritativeness

It has been approved by the sponsor and endorsed by the functional managers from each organizational unit participating in the project. Time estimates, as a result, represent commitments by those responsible for completing individual tasks.

Keeping Current

It is reviewed, updated, and revised on a regular and disciplined basis so that it represents a true picture of the project at all times.

The planning portion of the Launch stage culminates in a comprehensive and robust project plan. The team can now move to the next step of developing detailed estimates. Because it is quite a rigorous subject, we will devote Chapter 6 to estimating.

As we discussed in Chapter 1, the PPA can be scaled to fit the size and complexity of a given project. Complex projects will require more of the steps as well as more rigor, while simpler projects will do well with fewer steps and less rigor. Please refer to Figure 1.12 for the steps recommended for simple, average, complex, and very complex projects.

■ SUMMARY

We have focused on the process of assuring that a committed sponsor is in place, who in turn assures the assignment of a skilled project manager. The project manager, working with the key team members, stages the project and develops a task plan consisting of a comprehensive WBS and an accurate task network—keeping in mind any constraints. This work is followed by the development of an organizational change management plan, a prototyping plan, a design of the project organization structure, a staffing and training plan, a communication plan, and the start of the Project Notebook.

Following is a list of the key subject areas covered in this chapter. We invite you to review the list and assess your level of comprehension of each topic. The best approach is to take a separate sheet of paper and write a short narrative to explain your knowledge of the topic and then go back and compare your summaries with the material covered in the chapter. Another approach is to find a colleague who is also interested in these topics, discuss your understanding of the topics with her, then jointly review the chapter materials to assess your degree of understanding.

- Launch stage of the PPA
- Project kickoff (staging) meeting
- Project organization models
- Team size
- Project task plan
- Prototyping plan
- Organization change management plan
- Scope management plan
- The Velcro suit
- Change control board
- Staffing plan
- Sponsor's roles and responsibilities
- Intelligent disobedience
- The Forty questions
- The Kiviat chart
- Roles and responsibilities of the project manager's supervisor
- Roles and responsibilities of functional managers
- Project manager's roles and responsibilities
- Project manager's skills and competencies
- Dumb mistakes and good traits
- Team selection and teamwork
- Cross-functional teams
- Conflict management and team motivation
- Active listening
- Communications Plan
- Project Notebook
- Characteristics of a sound project plan

■ QUESTIONS AND DISCUSSION POINTS

1. What is the key purpose of the Launch stage of the PPA?
2. How many steps does the Launch stage contain? Can you name each step (don't worry about the order)?
3. Who has the primary responsibility for completing the various steps of the Launch stage?
4. What process group of PMBOK does the Launch stage relate to?
5. Why complete the work defined in the Project Staging step of the Launch stage?
6. In what ways can the project kickoff meeting help the project manager?
7. Who should attend the project kickoff meeting?
8. Think of a specific project and comment on the importance and value of the following items, as they relate to that project:
   a. Project website
   b. Team name, slogan, and logo
   c. Monthly newsletter
   d. Periodic (monthly) lunch sessions
   e. Family outings
   f. Individual and group recognition programs
   g. Project completion celebration
9. Keeping in mind the discussion of the dysfunctional project organization in this chapter (Figure 5.2), have you had any similar experiences? Have any of your colleagues?
10. What are the different types of project organization structures and what are their relative benefits?
11. What is the most commonly used project organization structure in your work environment? Is this structure well suited to the needs of the projects?
12. Draw a diagram of the Center's recommended project organization structure. What are its key benefits? Do you believe this structure will serve your organization well?
13. What are the key differences between project management and general (functional) management responsibilities?
14. Why is it important to keep team size to a small number of full-time team members?

15. What are the numbers of possible communication lines in a team of five, six, and seven people?

16. What is the role of a system/product development methodology when developing a WBS and a task plan?

17. What is the importance of developing the current system retirement plan this early in the project life cycle?

18. What role does prototyping play in the development of a project plan? Have you had experience in the use of prototypes? If so, please expand on your response.

19. Focusing on three recently completed projects, what was the level of quality of their end products?

20. How would you define the overall quality of the end products of your organization's projects? If improvements in quality were needed, what actions would you suggest?

21. Why should a project manager take on the responsibilities for organizational change needed as a result of the proposed project? Some people believe, "If the people who requested the project don't want to change, then it's their problem and it's no skin off the project manager's nose." How would you respond to this thought process?

22. How is the scope management plan different from the organizational change management plan? Does a project need both? Why?

23. Do you agree with the phenomenon of the Velcro suit (contributing to scope growth) as discussed in this chapter? Have you observed this phenomenon among your colleagues? Has it happened to you? How did you react?

24. What are the key reasons for scope growth? What can a project manager do to manage (control) scope growth?

25. Why not simply freeze the scope statement at the end of the Pre-Launch stage and be done with it?

26. What impact can scope growth have on project infrastructure design?

27. What is the benefit of formulating a change control board to manage the scope growth of a project?

28. Can you recall some of the sponsor's roles and responsibilities? Make a list, briefly describe each, and compare your list with the list in the chapter.

29. Describe the intelligent disobedience trait that sponsors and project managers should encourage. Do sponsors in your organization encourage intelligent disobedience? If so, can you recall an example (of your own or from any of your colleagues' experience)?

30. The chapter includes a list of questions the sponsor should ask of a project manager (*The Forty Questions*); do you know if sponsors in your organization are familiar with this list? Randomly pick one question from each of the subsections and see how you would fare in response to the selected questions. What would be the benefits of the sponsor making a point of asking the project manager these questions?

31. Review the list of the project manager's roles and responsibilities, pick eight items, and develop a Kiviat chart to plot your skills map. How skilled are you? What actions, if any, do you need to take to improve your skills?

32. How would you rate the overall skills of the project managers in your organization?

33. How well versed are you in the business of your organization?

34. In this chapter, we listed seven dumb mistakes a project manager might make; can you recall any? Do you know of any project managers who are prone to these mistakes?

35. What are the differences between closed-ended and an open-ended questions? Can you think of examples of each?

36. We listed the four stages of team development: forming, storming, norming, and performing. Can you describe each? Think of four project team members (your team or any other team) and describe which stage are they in.

37. What are some of the traits of an active listener? How well do you map to these traits? Use a Kiviat chart to plot your "active listener" skill profile. What are your next steps?

38. What are the key benefits of creating and maintaining a Project Notebook?

39. Can you recall any of the quotations used in this chapter? If so, why this quotation?

6 Launch Stage: Developing Detailed Estimates

OBJECTIVES

In this chapter, you will learn about the following project management elements:

- Task-based estimates
- Range values
- Estimate review points
- Estimating responsibility
- Baseline effort
- Effort variance factor
- Defining team member skill profile
- Impact of skill profile
- Profiling the unknown team
- Computing the task effort and duration estimates
- Computing the project duration estimate
- Computing sponsor, management, and project management effort
- Computing reserves
- Time losses often overlooked
- Computing cost estimates
- Compress the critical path
- PERT estimating method
- Words to avoid
- Developing a historical baseline database
- Steps to reduce estimates
- Obtaining budget approval
- Stage gate review

T his chapter covers the last two steps of the Launch stage: developing a detailed task-based effort, cost, and duration estimate for the proposed project and then obtaining budget approval from the project sponsor. The task-based estimating method presented in this chapter was developed at the Center for use by a number of our clients. Most project management books simply direct the reader to develop "accurate" estimates without providing sufficient guidance on the detailed steps needed to come up with viable results. The estimating methodology covered in this chapter deals, in detail, with all aspects that lead to accurate estimates—skill level, work interruptions, multiple project assignment, and productivity environment. The often-overlooked estimates for sponsor and management effort are discussed, and the need for incorporating rework and scope growth reserves is described. A detailed discussion of reducing the computed estimates to map to the constraints of the project is included. We address the reality that there will be push-backs from project managers who state, "Why bother with all of the work needed to come up with realistic estimates when management is going to cut them by half or more regardless?" Such actions often take place because project managers have not gone through the necessary steps to develop accurate estimates, and they have little to show as proof when management questions their estimates.

■ DETAILED ESTIMATES—PPA STEP 25

An estimate is based on a set of tasks, a group of people who will do the tasks, and a number of environmental variables that can impact the estimate, for example, the size and complexity of the project, the skill levels of the project team, the percent availability of each team member, work interruptions, and the quality of the work environment. All these factors will impact the estimated values. If project managers do not incorporate the appropriate factors into their estimating algorithms, the resulting estimates will not reflect reality and will not be accurate. A good estimating method should not only incorporate these variables, it should also include tools necessary for "what if" analysis. The ability to change the team size and/or the team skill levels easily, and to recompute the estimates quickly, will certainly enhance the project manager's credibility.

> *It is very difficult to make a vigorous, plausible, and job-risking defense of an estimate that is derived by no quantitative method, supported with little data . . .*
>
> Brooks, 1995, p. 21.

Task-based estimates include estimates of effort, cost, and duration based on detailed WBSs, network diagrams, and resources profiled for their respective skills. Two key terms to keep in mind while developing task-based estimates are *effort* and *duration*.

> *Effort:* the number of *hours* it will take a person who has specific skills to complete a given task.
> *Duration:* is defined as the *elapsed time,* usually in days, needed to complete a given task.

Often there is not a one-to-one relationship between the number of hours (effort) and the number of days (duration). The estimated duration is dependent on a number of variables: the prime one is the percent of time the person assigned to a task can actually devote to the task. Consider, the task of developing a Project Description. The estimated effort for the task might be 6 hours, and as a result, a logical assumption is that the estimated duration would be 1 day (there are at least 6 productive hours in most people's workday). However, a further analysis of work assignments for the individual responsible for developing the Project Description reveals that this person is already assigned to two other projects. As a result, this individual can devote a maximum of 2 hours each day to this task. Consequently, the 6-hour effort will translate to 3 days of duration.

Range Values

Because of the nonspecific nature of IT/Business projects, a range value should be acceptable for task-based estimates (we first discussed this subject in Chapter 4). From our experience and research, we recommend a range value of up to 15 percent for task-based estimates. Make sure that both your managers and customers clearly understand the degree of uncertainty accompanying the task-based estimates. It is important to emphasize that, unlike size estimates, task-based estimates *can* be used to generate the project schedule. Likewise, only task-based estimates provide the type of front-end information that is needed by scheduling and tracking tools. Keep in mind that range values are not used for individual task estimates, only for the final project estimates.

Estimate Review Points

Most project managers face an endemic problem: their estimates, once communicated to management and customers, become etched in stone. Combine this with the common belief that estimates are done only once, at the start of a project, and it spells big trouble for the team. It is important that the project manager identify and communicate to the customer the key points at which the estimates will be reviewed and, if necessary, adjusted. For example:

- When the critical path, budget, or scope is breached by more than 15 percent
- When there is resource turnover of greater than 15 percent
- Points where planned contingencies become realities
- Major changes in stated assumptions
- End of each project phase or every quarter

Review of an estimate does not necessarily mean that the team will be able to revise the remaining estimates automatically. Each review has the following benefits:

- Early warnings of possible future variances based on to-date experience
- Opportunity to negotiate with management and customers
- Knowing, at an early date, the extent of underestimating and the resulting need for overtime work by all concerned
- Opportunity to compress future estimates

We rarely see estimate review points included specifically in project plans and schedules. With specific inclusion of estimate review points, the message to management and customers is that the current estimates will need to be reviewed, and perhaps revised, during the life of the project.

Estimating Responsibility

In most cases, the following steps outline the manner in which the majority of estimates are developed:

1. The project manager develops the estimates, keeping in mind the team's skill, work interruptions, and appropriate productivity-influencing factors.
2. The project manager asks team members to develop estimates for their portion of the project work and then assembles a final estimate for the project.
3. The project manager gathers appropriate SMEs and they collectively develop the estimates.
4. The project manager uses historical data to create project estimates.

The various methods are not mutually exclusive. In any given project, two or more methods may be used to develop the final estimates.

We must reiterate an important point: project plans are seldom static; they often change as the project progresses. The more complex the project is, the higher the possibility that the plans will change. An inevitable outcome of changing plans is a change in estimates. Too often, however, customers hold the belief that once it is presented, an estimate is an immutable promise and nothing shall change. This type of thinking has been a key contributor to mismatched expectations between project managers and their customers.

In this chapter we do not plan to discuss the impact of holidays, vacations, sick leave, time taken for training, travel time, and similar other time elements. According to our methodology, any time-related information is taken into account when the estimated task duration values are plotted on team/organization calendars to produce a schedule, which is discussed in Chapter 7.

Computing Accurate Estimates: The Concept

How does a project manager create accurate and realistic estimates for work to be done in the future, without knowing who will actually be assigned to the project and the conditions under which the team will perform its work? The following unknowns further complicate the process of developing estimates for future work: the skill/experience levels of the team members and the productivity environment of the project. This concern applies especially to projects that are based on emerging technologies and/or projects in unstable condition because of mergers, major reorganizations, and volatile financial conditions.

To address these problems, and to make sure that estimates accurately reflect the different variables, we developed a three-step estimating process:

1. Define a standard estimated effort value for each task. This standard estimate is called the *baseline effort.*[1]
2. Define an adjustment factor, considering variables such as team members' skills and work conditions. This adjustment factor is called the *effort variance factor (EVF).*
3. Compute the estimated effort for various tasks by *adjusting* their baseline effort values using the appropriate EVF of the assigned resources.

This process results in effort estimates that are not only accurate, but can be easily explained to management and customers. A summary view of the process is depicted in Figure 6.1.

FIGURE 6.1
Converting Baseline Effort
to Task Effort Estimate

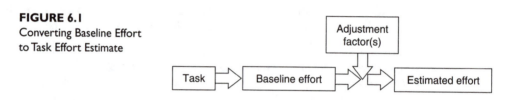

Task Types

Project tasks can be classified into two primary categories: effort-driven tasks and duration-driven tasks.

Effort Driven Task   Extra resources can help reduce the duration of effort-driven tasks. For example, the task of conducting twelve different interviews, each requiring 1 hour of effort, will take one person almost 2 full workdays (if the interviewer has no other tasks to perform). However, two interviewers assigned to the task could finish the interviews in 1 workday (if neither interviewer has any other tasks to perform).

Duration Driven Task   For these tasks, extra effort typically will not reduce the duration of the task. For example, the task of driving a vehicle from one location to another, which requires a 1-day duration, cannot be shortened by using two drivers. Another example of a duration-driven task is a group meeting scheduled for 1 hour. As you add more people, the net effort goes up but the duration does not change. In fact, with the addition of extra people, the duration of the meeting is more likely to increase, unless the meeting facilitator is highly skilled. The following discussion relates to *effort-driven* tasks. We will assume that any duration-driven task will not be appreciably impacted by the various influencing attributes referred to in the discussion.

■ BASELINE EFFORT: DEFINED

Baseline effort is defined as the effort hours it will take a person to complete a given task under the following assumptions:

- A high level of business knowledge (no application learning curve)
- A high level of technical proficiency (no technology learning curve)
- Full-time assignment to the task

---

[1]The term "baseline effort" is not to be confused with the terms "cost baseline" and "schedule baseline" used to describe the originally approved budget and schedule of a project. Also, over the years, other terms have been used to describe the baseline effort: "prime effort," "standard effort," and "best effort." Interestingly, the legal department of one company advised against use of the term "best effort." We did not try to find the reasons behind the advice.

- A high-productivity environment
- *No* interruptions

A typical reaction by many project managers at this point is quick and specific: "There is nobody in my group who has the profile outlined in the list." Most go on to add, "There is no way a highly skilled person can work without interruptions." They are *exactly right*. At this point, we refer the person to the diagram in Figure 6.1, with a reminder that the baseline effort values are *always adjusted* to reflect the *skill profile* of the person assigned to the task, and the *working conditions* in which the work will be completed.

A commonly asked question regarding baseline effort data is: "What is the source of baseline effort values?" Typical sources for baseline effort data are corporate history, project managers, SMEs, team members, and industry data.

Most professionals (construction, engineering, manufacturing, automotive, and medical) base their estimates on historically collected and periodically updated effort databases. Using this approach, you would consult the database for baseline effort values for tasks in a given project plan, and then adjust them according to the team's skill profile and project conditions.

Creating a Baseline Effort Database

In the last chapter, we discussed the subject of creating a master task list that project managers could reference to develop their individual project task plans. One place to record individual task baseline effort estimates is that master task list. Find out if one exists in your organization; if so, ascertain whether it has any baseline effort values recorded. The project office, if one exists, may also be able to provide you with a master task list and associated baseline effort values. In the last chapter we discussed the steps necessary to form a team of volunteer project managers to develop a master task list. Find out whether anyone has done that and if their knowledge base included baseline effort values. If you do not have access to an existing master task list, another way to obtain baseline effort values is to convene a small group composed of a couple of senior team members from your project and two or three project managers. Then, ask them to populate the master task list with baseline effort estimates. If you decide to take this approach, use the same steps as listed in Chapter 5 for creating a master task list (see *Developing a Master Task List*). An important point to keep in mind is that a baseline effort value represents the amount of effort a *proficient* team member, assigned *full-time, without* any interruption, will need to complete a given task. This is a mythical person, but as you know, baseline values will be adjusted to reflect the skills and work environment of the actual people on the team. Figure 6.2 shows a short task list with respective baseline effort values. We will discuss the steps needed to convert team members' actual effort data into baseline effort values later in this chapter (see *Developing Historical Baseline Effort Database*).

■ EFFORT VARIANCE FACTOR (EVF)

When multiple team members are working on a project, their rate of performance (the speed at which they complete their tasks) can vary considerably. In fact, the productivity of the same person can vary widely depending on the quality of the work environment. This variance in the rate of different team members' productivity can have dramatic results for the effort and time needed to complete a project. You must account for these variances while computing project estimates.

> *These studies have revealed large individual differences between high and low performers, often by an order of magnitude.*
> Sackman, Ericson, and Grant, in Brooks, 1995, p. 29.

The reasons are many—team members' skill and experience level, work interruptions, motivation, performance objectives, and the very nature of the work by IT/Business teams. Before realistic estimates can be computed, you must profile various team members for their respective proficiency

FIGURE 6.2
Example of Baseline
Effort Values

No.	Tasks	Baseline effort hours
1	Prepare initial plan	4
2	Build project organization	14
3	Identify customer/business opportunity/need	2
4	Establish project binder	4
5	Prepare and submit RFI	12
6	Evaluate the project progess	8
7	Prepare phase end document	40
8	Approve phase end document	4 + lag
9	Develop planning-level data model	8
10	Measure risk	12
11	Prepare feasibility study	24
12	Prepare implementation order	40
13	Assemble business case	24
14	Approve business case	32 + lag
15	Perform phase end review	8
16	Prepare and distribute RFP	60 + lag
17	Evaluate RFP	80
18	Select vendor	20
19	Obtain vendor approval	20 + lag
20	Develop user-level context diagram	16

levels and derive a specific effort variance factor (EVF). The EVF is a composite of the following productivity influencing factors:

- skill factor (SF)
- work interruption factor (WIF)
- multiple project factor (MPF)
- project productivity influencing factor (PPIF)

The EVF for a particular team member is computed as follows:

$$EVF = SF \times WIF \times MPF \times PPIF$$

Skill Factor (SF)

Of the four productivity-influencing factors, the skill factor has the biggest influence on the time needed to finish a given task. The computation of a team member's skill factor is a two-step process:

1. Assess the individual's skill level (SL) and assign a numeric value
2. Compute the individual's skill factor

Assess SL   In this step, the project manager reviews the information regarding the individual's experience and skill and assigns a numeric skill level value ranging from 1 to 4. For example:

- Skill level 1 denotes a *novice* (trainee) resource. This person has a decent understanding of the subject matter but has not worked independently on similar tasks. Typically, novice resources are *not* given primary responsibility for tasks. They may assist someone until a sufficient level of experience has been gained.
- Skill level 2 denotes an individual who has an *average skill* in this or related tasks. This person has perhaps assisted someone engaged in similar tasks or has a theoretical understanding of the task.

- Skill level 3 denotes an individual who has *above average skill* in the task and has a good understanding of the subject matter.
- Skill level 4 denotes a *highly skilled* resource (an SME).

A resource's skill level could be assessed at a level between the four listed. For example: 1.5, 1.75, 2.25, and 2.5. Increment levels other than 0.25 are not recommended because they imply a degree of precision that is difficult to discern when assessing skill levels. A person can move from level 1 to level 2 very quickly, depending on her drive, learning ability, and desire to excel. Moving from level 2 to 3 will take at least a few months or longer. Arriving at level 4 requires extensive experience, good discipline, and the ability to solve problems. Figure 6.3 depicts the skill grading (novice to expert) and associated *skill level* values. Notice that while the novice and the learner categories have three levels each, the competent and proficient categories have only two levels of grading.

FIGURE 6.3

Skill Descriptions and Associated Skill Levels

Skill level	Description
Proficient Level 2 4.0	Fully experienced, SME
Proficient Level 1 3.75	Fully experienced, extensive subject matter knowledge
Competent Level 2 3.5	Competent in all task-related skills, solid knowledge of subject, good experience
Competent Level 1 3.25	Competent at similar tasks, solid subject knowledge, some learning curve required
Learner Level 3 3.0	Possesses basic competencies for the task, some subject knowledge, little experience
Learner Level 2 2.75	Possesses most of the basic competencies for the task, some subject knowledge, little experience
Learner Level 1 2.5	Possesses less than half of the basic competencies for the task, some subject knowledge, little experience
Novice Level 3 2.0	Some knowledge of subject matter, extensive training required in basic task competencies, good work habits
Novice Level 2 1.5	Little knowledge of subject matter, complete training required in basic task competencies, good work habits
Novice Level 1 1.0	No knowledge of subject matter, complete training required in basic task competencies, little or no work experience

Project managers who are new to the process of skill level assessment often have difficulty in assessing various team members (especially their colleagues) for their representative skill levels. At times, you might hesitate to rate a person at a medium or low level of proficiency because of personal and/or political reasons. In addition, you might not know enough about the person, or the skill itself to accurately evaluate the various skill levels. Whenever possible, skill evaluations should be handled in consultation with the team member being profiled. Another good source is the individual's functional manager. Our advice is to keep the resulting skill level ratings confidential. In any event, it is essential that the assessment be factual and pragmatic.

Compute SF   Once an individual's skill level has been determined, the next step is to compute the individual's *SF,* which will reflect the *rate* at which the person will do his work. The *lower* the skill level, the *longer* the time that will be needed to finish a given task. For example, for a person who has a skill level of 4 (an expert), the SF would be 1. Similarly, for a person who has a skill level of 1 (a novice), the SF would be 4. Figure 6.4 shows precomputed SF values defined and used by one of the Center's clients.

FIGURE 6.4
SF Values

Skill level	Description	Skill factor
Proficient Level 2 4.0	Fully experienced, SME	1.0
Proficient Level 1 3.75	Fully experienced, extensive subject matter knowledge	1.25
Competent Level 2 3.5	Competent in all task-related skills, solid knowledge of subject, good experience	1.5
Competent Level 1 3.25	Competent at similar tasks, solid subject knowledge, some learning curve required	1.75
Learner Level 3 3.0	Possesses basic competencies for the task, some subject knowledge, little experience	2.0
Learner Level 2 2.75	Possesses most of the basic competencies for the task, some subject knowledge, little experience	2.25
Learner Level 1 2.5	Possesses less than half of the basic competencies for the task, some subject knowledge, little experience	2.5
Novice Level 3 2.0	Some knowledge of subject matter, extensive training required in basic task competencies, good work habits	3.0
Novice Level 2 1.5	Little knowledge of subject matter, complete training required in basic task competencies, good work habits	3.5
Novice Level 1 1.0	No knowledge of subject matter, complete training required in basic task competencies, little or no work experience	4.0

Work Interruption Factor (WIF)

The WIF is the measure of the loss of productivity as a result of nonproject activities and unplanned interruptions *during* the work day. For example, ad-hoc meetings, being volunteered by one's manager, conversations with colleagues, departmental social gatherings, personal errands, reading and responding to voice messages and e-mail, and unavailability of computer resources (virus, crashes, maintenance).

We are sure you can think of many others. A natural result of any interruption is the accompanying loss of productivity, mostly because of the time needed to refocus and restart. This is true of airplane travel (nonstop *v.* multiple stops), trains and elevators (express *v.* local), and automobiles (city *v.* highway driving). Work interruptions represent a person's nonproject activities and should not be automatically viewed as "goofing off." Often, the interruptions are the result of an uncontrolled work environment. For example, a person who supports ongoing production systems and is also part of a project team will have numerous *unscheduled* interruptions to help solve production problems and otherwise engage in customer support activities. In another situation, a team might have a number of novices or new members who need assistance with getting up to speed. Therefore, they may continuously interrupt a senior person. Other work interruptions might include unscheduled departmental meetings, informal conversations with colleagues, and personal/family business. These types of interruptions are inevitable and often necessary. However, interruptions *must* be accounted for when developing estimates.

When a team member is interrupted, the net time lost is *much greater* than the actual interruption time. The reason for the additional loss is that the person has to refocus on what she was doing. For a typical team member, each interruption can easily translate into a resulting loss of about 10 minutes or more. With 10 minutes of lost time per interruption, a total of 8 interruptions in a day would result in a net loss of 80 minutes. How many senior team members do you know who are interrupted less than 8 times in a day? Some SMEs may spend their entire day responding to inquiries from colleagues and customers.

You should never allocate more than 80 percent availability of a person to do project work, even when that person is fully dedicated to only one project.
> Jim Lewis, *Successful Project Management*, Vienna, Va.,
> Management Concepts, Inc., June 2001, 3:3, p. 1.

If every day was a Saturday, we could finish the project sooner.
> A sign on a project manager's desk.

Computing the WIF   An important question is: what is the relationship between work interruptions and the time it takes to complete a given task? The answer is: it is *not* linear. If a person is interrupted 25 percent of the time, the net increase in the time needed to complete a task will be *more* than 25 percent. The reason for the increase is that once a person is interrupted, concentration is broken and *additional time* is needed to ramp up. The formula to compute the WIF for a team member is:

$$\text{WIF} = (100 \div (100 - \text{Percentage of time lost due to work interruption}))$$

Therefore, if a person were interrupted 25 percent of the time, the WIF for that person would be:

$$\text{WIF} = (100 \div (100 - 25)) = 100 \div 75 = 1.33$$

The formula shows that if a person requires 10 hours of effort to complete a task *without* any interruptions, the same person will require 13.3 hours of effort to complete the same task if *interrupted* 25 percent of the time. Most estimating algorithms *do not* treat the impact of interruptions in this manner. The common approach is to simply add a *direct equivalent* of the interrupted time. This failure to account for the extra time is one of the reasons that most estimates are incorrect. Figure 6.5 depicts the WIF values for up to 75 percent work interruptions. Notice that a 50 percent work interruption results in a WIF of 2.0. Now let us increase this person's interruptions to the 75 percent level. The WIF will be 4.0 and the 10-hour task will therefore take 40 hours of effort to complete.

Over the years, we have known a number of managers who did not want the project manager to account for any interruptions. These managers have the desire to show 100 percent utilization for all team members (with absolutely no time accounted for interruptions) because anything less than a 100 percent utilization rate will make their department look bad in the eyes of senior management and customers. No wonder Dilbert is so popular.

> *Basing timetables on 100 percent resource utilization—in other words, all the allotted staff working at 100 percent productivity all of the time—simply doesn't work. People get sick or take vacations, and plans need modification.*
> Gary Sutula in Slater, Derek, "Faster, Cheaper, Under Control,"
> *CIO Magazine* (August 1, 2000, p. 111).

FIGURE 6.5
WIF Values

Percentage of time lost due to interruptions	WIF
10 %	1.11
15 %	1.18
20 %	1.25
25 %	1.33
30 %	1.43
35 %	1.54
40 %	1.67
45 %	1.82
50 %	2.00
55 %	2.22
60 %	2.50
65 %	2.86
70 %	3.33
75 %	4.00

An important point to note here is that, if a person is assigned 50 percent (half time) to a project, this does not translate directly into 50 percent work interruptions. The work interruption value represents the percentage of time lost due to interruptions while at work. Additionally, WIF *does not* include time off for items such as holidays, vacations, and sick leave. WIF is the time lost to interruptions *while* one is at work. Time off for holidays, vacations, and sick leave is brought into play when estimates are converted into schedules.

Losses Due to Multiproject Assignment

Theoretically, the best approach to achieving maximum productivity by team members is to assign them full-time to one project, assuring full attention to the work at hand. When a person is assigned to more than one project in the same time period, switching back and forth among multiple projects will inevitably lead to a loss of focus and a loss of productivity. The extent of this type of time loss is highly dependent on the *working style* of the individual team members. Some team members can handle multiproject assignments without much loss, while others may have great difficulty with frequent back-and-forth switching. It is important to remember that this loss in productivity is in *addition* to the loss of time due to work interruptions. The recommended values are as follows:

One project	0%
Two projects	Up to 10%
Three projects	Up to 15%
Four projects	Up to 20%

Computing the Multiple Project Factor (MPF)   The formula used to compute MPF is similar to the formula used to compute the WIF. It is expressed as follows:

MPF = (100 ÷ (100 − Percentage of time lost due to switching between projects))

Therefore, for an individual who is assigned to two projects simultaneously, the MPF value is computed as follows:

MPF = (100 ÷ (100 − 10)) = 100 ÷ 90 = 1.11

Figure 6.6 illustrates the computed values for the MPF for one person who has up to a four-project assignment.

FIGURE 6.6
MPF Values

Number of projects	Percentage of time lost	MPF
One	0%	1.00
Two	Up to 10%	1.11
Three	Up to 15%	1.18
Four	Up to 20%	1.25

The Project Productivity Influencing Factor (PPIF)

A number of additional factors can also have significant impact on the productivity of team members. Listed below are the most common productivity influencing factors and their respective influencing values:

Number of nemeses	1.0 to 1.5
Team locations	1.0 to 1.5
Customer locations	1.0 to 1.5
Team size	1.0 to 1.5
Team synergy	1.0 to 1.5
Team-customer synergy	1.0 to 1.5
Tool stability	1.0 to 1.5

Turnover rate (staff)	1.0 to 1.5
Vendor support	1.0 to 1.5
Project manager's skill	1.0 to 2.0

In the list, the value of 1 indicates efficient working conditions, and a value of greater than 1 indicates the existence of *constraints and obstacles* that result in extended effort needed to complete the assigned work.

Number of Nemesis Stakeholders: Use the value 1 for up to three nemesis stakeholders, with the belief that any astute project manager should be able to manage this level of problem. For more than three nemesis stakeholders, use a value higher than 1.

Team Locations: The value for this attribute is 1 if the team is limited to one location. Use a value of greater than one for more than one location due to travel, telephone tag, time zone differences, and other similar and time-consuming problems.

Customer Locations: The values for this are similar to those for team location.

Team Size: The value of 1 is used for teams of seven or fewer individuals. In the case of a larger team size, use a value greater than 1.

Team Synergy: It is common knowledge that a well formed team that has clear objectives, strong leadership, and high motivation will get much more work done in a shorter period of time. Conversely, a team that has no clear leadership and conflicting objectives will take longer to finish its assigned work. Therefore, you must keep this factor in mind when developing estimates. The value of 1 is used for a team that works well together. A value of 1.5 for this factor would mean that the team is in a chaotic mode—members do not work well together and have lost their focus and drive.

Team-Customer Synergy: This attribute is quite similar to the team synergy attribute. We know that some customers can be difficult to work with. For the purpose of estimating, you must account for the quality of team-to-customer relationship; the reasons for adverse relations are immaterial. A weak relationship with the customer would garner a value greater than 1.

Tool Stability: The value is 1 when a tool has been in stable and consistent use by the team for at least 3 months. A tool in place for less than 3 months or that is still unstable will invariably require additional effort. Remember the last update of the operating system, the new version of the database, or that new copying machine? After the update, did it cause any hitches or did everything go as smoothly as the vendor representative assured you? A value greater than 1 means that the tool is getting in the way of the team.

Turnover Rate (Staff): We consider a staff turnover rate of 10 percent normal. Any turnover greater than 10 percent can result in lost productivity by the team and would mean a value of greater than 1. A value of 1.5 would mean a turnover rate of 30 percent or more. What if the staff turnover rate exceeds 30 percent? This level of turnover indicates intrinsic, deep-rooted problems with the organization, and any estimates you develop are going to be inaccurate because of a high inflow and outflow of people.

Vendor Support: The value for this factor is 1 when the vendor provides a quick (less than 4-hour turnaround) response by a knowledgeable person who can actually *solve* the problem or *resolve* the issue. Poor vendor service and support would mean a value greater than 1. A value of 1.5 would mean that your organization is in, or about to engage in, litigation with this vendor.

Project Manager's Skill: We assign a value range of 1.0 to 2.0 to this factor because we believe it is the *most* influential factor in the list. The value of 1 means a highly skilled project manager and the value of 2 means a novice. We all know that a highly skilled and astute project manager can make a project move quickly. Conversely, a project manager who lacks the necessary skills can drag a project down and extend the time taken to complete even the simplest tasks. It is important not to overlook this factor.

The list of items, though comprehensive, is not meant to be complete. There can be a number of additional factors that will impact the team's productivity, and you are encouraged to include those in your list. In the same manner, not every factor needs to be used in every project. Assume that the productivity factor values for a given project are:

Number of nemeses	5	Value: 1.25
Team locations	4	Value: 1.20
Customer locations	4	Value: 1.20
Project manager's skill	Average	Value: 1.50

To compute the PPIF value for the project, add each of the individual values together and divide the sum by the number of assessed factors. Therefore, the PPIF value would be:

$$PPIF = (1.25 + 1.20 + 1.20 + 1.50) \div 4 = (5.15 \div 4) = 1.3 \text{ (rounded)}$$

EVF Computed

Now that we have discussed the four primary attributes (SF, WIF, MPF, and PPIF) that impact a team member's productivity, we need to compute an EVF, which can be used to *adjust* the baseline effort estimate values. The formula for computing the EVF is a serial multiplication of the SF, the WIF, the MPF, and the PPIF as follows:

$$EVF = SF \times WIF \times MPF \times PPIF$$

To illustrate, let us assume that a specific team member has the following factors:

- Competent
  - Skill factor of 1.5
- 25 percent interruptions
  - $WIF = (100 \div (100 - 25)) = 1.33$
- Full-time assignment
  - $MPF = (100 \div (100 - 0)) = 1.0$
- Productivity environment
  - $PPIF = 1.2$

From these values, we can compute the EVF for this person as follows:

$$EVF = SF \times WIF \times MPF \times PPIF$$
$$EVF = 1.5 \times 1.33 \times 1.0 \times 1.2$$
$$EVF = 2.39 = 2.4 \text{ rounded}$$

From the computation, we see that the EVF for this resource is 2.4. Therefore, a task with a baseline effort of 10 hours will require 24 hours of effort by this person. According to the formula, the *higher* the EVF is, the *greater the effort* that will be required for that person to complete the task.

■ IMPACT OF SKILL LEVEL

The following two examples illustrate the impact of a team member's skill level on the time required to complete a task. In the two examples depicted in Figure 6.7, the *only* attribute that changes is the SL (hence the SF). All other factors remain the same. Resulting EVF values have been rounded up to one decimal place.

FIGURE 6.7
Impact of SL

Team member	SL	SF	WIF	MPF	PPIF	EVF
Resource A	4.0	1.0	1.18	1.0	1.2	**1.4**
Resource B	2.0	3.0	1.18	1.0	1.2	**4.2**

According to the computed EVF values for the two resources in Figure 6.7, if the baseline effort for a given task were 10 hours, resource A would need 14 hours to complete that task and resource B would need 42 hours. As you can see, the skill level of the person has a *big* influence on the time needed to complete the work.

We strongly believe that developing accurate resource profiles based on skill levels, work interruptions, multiple project assignments, and various productivity influencing factors becomes even more important under the following, all-too-common circumstances:

1. You don't know who will actually be working on the project at the time you develop your estimates.
2. There is a high probability of high turnover in the team during the project life cycle.
3. The productivity environment of the project might change appreciably during the project life cycle.

In each of these circumstances, you can develop your estimates by documenting the currently assumed resource profiles. Then, when the team is actually assembled and the project work begins, develop profiles of the various team members. You should then compare these profiles with the assumed (documented) profiles and note any differences. Assess the impact of the differences on the computed estimates and if the results are unfavorable, discuss the findings first with your manager and then with the sponsor.

EVF values for individual team members may change during the course of a project. For example, after working several months with a new programming language, tool, or environment, team member may show considerable improvement in several important areas. Conversely, if the productivity environment or development tools change mid-project, the team member may suddenly have a higher effort variance factor, resulting in longer effort and duration values.

■ PROFILING THE UNKNOWN TEAM

A considerable gap between project estimation and the project start date is common. As a result, you may have no way of knowing which individuals will be assigned to the project. In these instances, you need to develop estimates based on a clearly defined set of assumptions—the *expected* skill profiles and the resulting EVFs of the unknown team members. Once the project is under way, the project manager will need to ensure that there are no significant variances between the assumed skill profiles and the specific skills of the assigned team members. In the case of significant skill profile variances, the project manager will need to *reevaluate* the estimates based on the skill levels of the actual resources assigned to the project.

■ COMPUTING TASK EFFORT

The estimated effort for a task is computed by multiplying the task's baseline effort by the EVF of the person responsible for the task. Assume that the baseline effort for a given task is 18 hours and the EVF of the team member assigned to this task is 2.0. Therefore, the computation for estimated effort for this task is:

$$\text{Estimated effort} = \text{Baseline effort} \times \text{EVF}$$
$$\text{Estimated effort} = 18 \text{ hours} \times 2.0 = 36 \text{ hours}$$

Our experience shows that, at times, project managers have great difficulty assessing their colleagues at a below-average skill level. Project managers end up assessing most team members as above average or even at the proficient level. Despite these pressures, we strongly believe that without the use of the adjustment factors that make up the EVF, estimates are going to remain where they are now—on a collision course with disaster.

By now, you have realized that the concept of baseline effort and EVF is composed of discrete, measurable, defensible components (SF, WIF, MPF, PPIF), and a consistent "repeatable" formula. Your managers, customers, and colleagues may not like your estimates, but you can explain, defend, and negotiate each component with more confidence.

■ COMPUTING TASK DURATION

To compute the estimated duration for a task, we must divide the estimated effort value of the task by the number of hours spent (per day) by the person responsible for completing the task. Figure 6.8 depicts the steps to compute the estimated duration of a given task.

FIGURE 6.8
Task Duration Estimate

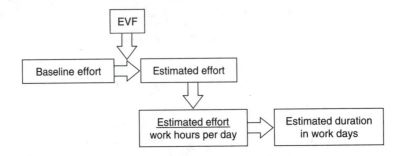

Assume that a task has a baseline effort of 20 hours, the person responsible for the task has an EVF of 2.0 and a *work day* of 8 hours, and that the person will be working *full-time* on this task. To compute the estimated duration for the task, we will use the following steps:

Estimated effort = Baseline effort × EVF = 20 × 2 = 40 hours

Estimated duration = Estimated effort ÷ Work hours/day

40 ÷ 8 = 5 Work days

Notice the use of the value of 8 for work hours to convert the estimated effort into estimated duration. Eight hours represents the length of the person's workday (we have already accounted for interruptions and other lost time in the EVF computation). Often, this expenditure of time is called the "burn rate"—the rate at which the estimated effort hours are being "consumed." Figure 6.9 lists the steps to compute the estimated effort and duration of a given task.

The steps in Figure 6.9 are summarized as follows:

1. Describe the task.
2. Obtain/specify the baseline effort for the task.

FIGURE 6.9
Steps to Compute Task Effort
and Duration Estimates

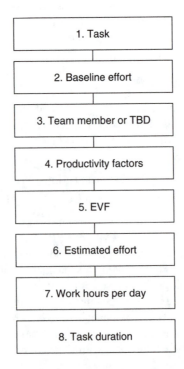

3. Specify the team member responsible for the task. If a specific team member name is not known at this point, enter notations such as TBD (to be decided).
4. Specify the various productivity factors (SF, WIF, MPF, PPIF) that influence the speed at which the team member can complete the given task. For team members noted as TBD, enter the *expected* SF, WIF, MPF, and PPIF values.
5. Compute the EVF for the team member.
6. Compute the estimated effort hours for the task by multiplying its baseline effort hours by the value of the EVF.
7. Specify the number of work hours per day (for this task) for the team member.
8. Compute the estimated duration (work days) of the task by dividing the estimated effort hours by the number of work hours.

■ COMPUTING PROJECT DURATION

Now that the various tasks in a project's WBS have been estimated, the next step is to compute the expected project duration (the total workdays needed to complete the project). The correct way is to create an accurate task network based on the logical sequence of various tasks and any constraints, as discussed in Chapter 2. Once you have built a *constrained* task network and developed the estimated durations for various tasks, the critical path through the network will give you the estimated project duration in *work days*. It is extremely important that we state the following warning: The estimated duration of the project will be greatly impacted by the skill profiles of the resources you assume will be available and their skill profiles. Be very careful that the numbers you use are realistic rather than what you hope you will get when the project goes into the Execute stage. Keep in mind that most sponsors and customers will only remember your estimates, especially the duration estimates, and will totally forget any assumptions you used as a foundation for your calculations.

Analysis of a large number of project duration estimates and the associated task networks has shown us that, too often, project managers forget to include all of the lag values in their networks, resulting in inaccurate (low) estimated duration values. It is important that you review the task network carefully to ensure that appropriate lag values are properly documented and accounted for.

■ SPONSOR EFFORT

In Chapter 4, Figure 4.44 depicts the recommended values for the sponsor's time. It is important that the project manager clearly and specifically convey to the sponsor the time demands created by the project. Too often, this communication does not happen and the sponsor does not actually set aside the time needed to "oversee" the project. Our recommendation is that the project manager and sponsor jointly define the roles and responsibility of the sponsor and then use the values depicted in Figure 4.44 as a guide to decide on the time commitments for a given project.

■ MANAGEMENT EFFORT

The task-based estimating method consists of three different approaches to computing the management effort estimate:

1. Review the roles and responsibilities of the functional managers and customers, and then define the necessary deliverables and tasks to fulfill their roles and responsibilities. These deliverables and tasks are then included in the task network of the project. This approach allows the project manager to develop the effort and duration estimates for these tasks and communicate the same to their respective owners. Our experience shows that this tactic results in more accurate estimates because many of these tasks could appear on the project's critical path. Project managers who used this approach have occasionally been surprised by the negative reactions from managers and customers who objected to being told what to do. They considered the list of deliverables and tasks given to them by project managers as an intrusion, and some even accused the project managers of being "control freaks."

2. The second approach is to use the percentage values suggested in Figure 4.45. The benefit is that computations take only a few minutes, but the drawback is that someone still has to define the actual work (deliverables and tasks) that various managers and customers need to do as a part of their responsibilities. It has been our experience that whenever a project manager has conveyed these estimates to managers and customers, they just cannot see why so much of their time is required. Typically, most of them expect to go to a few meetings and answer a few questions.

3. The third approach is a hybrid of the first two approaches. In this case, the project manager uses the appropriate percent values (Figure 4.45) to compute management effort estimates and then limits the planning process to the development of a list of deliverables and milestones for each manager. That way, they know the extent of time that is expected of them and they also know about the deliverables they are responsible for and the milestones they will need to meet. Then it is up to them to develop their own task lists.

We would prefer the first approach described above and would settle for the third if anyone objects. As in the case of any disagreement, first try to resolve the issue directly with the party involved, and if there is no resolution, escalate the problem to the sponsor along with your preferred approach.

Project Management Effort

Our experience shows that the best approach is to use the percent computation described in Chapter 4. Based on project complexity, the statistical range for the project management effort can vary from a low of 8 percent to a high of 20 percent of the total estimated project development effort. At times, the computed project management effort per month may be higher than the available time per month. For example, consider a project that has the following estimates:

- Seven FTE team
- 8,000 hours
- 162 work days—9 work months (18 productive days/month)

Further assume that the project lies in the middle of zone I of the complexity chart. The project manager used the 18 percent figure to compute the project management effort.

$$PM \text{ effort} = 8,000 \times .18 = 1,440 \text{ hours}$$

Now, with an estimated duration of 9 work months, this computes to 160 hours per month. Using 18 productive days per month and 7 productive hours per day, the project manager has only 126 hours per month for this project. There is a shortfall of 34 hours per month ($160 - 126 = 34$). In these cases, the project manager has the following options:

1. Delegate some project management responsibilities to experienced team members.
2. Delegate some responsibilities to the project management office (if one exists).
3. Become more efficient in managing personal time and overall delegation of work to team members.[2]
4. Work extra time, on the average 2 hours per day for the duration of the project.

Although working overtime has become the routine for most project managers, too much overtime will eventually put both the project manager and the project in jeopardy.

■ REWORK RESERVE

You must not overlook the need for rework, especially with high-complexity projects. The subject of rework was discussed in Chapter 4 (see *Need for Rework*) with specific rework suggestions given in Figure 4.55. Based on the project's complexity, make sure that an appropriate amount of rework reserve is included in the project estimate; otherwise, the rework will extend the estimated project

---

[2]For one of the best articles on the subject, see "Management Time: Who's Got the Monkey?" by William Oncken Jr. and Donald L. Wass, in the *Harvard Business Review* (Nov.–Dec., 1974).

duration and cost. As already stated, the project lies toward the middle of zone I of the complexity chart (high complexity). Using the recommended 12 percent for rework, the rework reserve for this project would be:

$$\text{Rework reserve: } 162 \times .12 = 19 \text{ Work days}$$

Some people will object to this much reserve time being set aside for the team to redo its work. Remind them that this is a high complexity project that has a large number of unknowns. A project that has a seven FTE team and an estimated duration of 9 months can expect about 2 days of rework for every month of work. We don't believe that is an above normal rework reserve. Our experience shows that most of the rework effort directly affects the critical path of the project. Therefore, it is *added* to the estimated project duration.

■ SCOPE GROWTH RESERVE

As discussed in Chapter 4, Figure 4.56 (*Scope Growth*), high-complexity projects can have scope growth of up to 15 percent, after the Project Charter has been approved and signed off on by the sponsor. Therefore, make sure that your estimate accounts for the inevitable scope growth. Computing this reserve involves the following steps:

- Because the project at hand is located toward the middle of Zone I, the project manager used a 12 percent scope growth rate, and computed the scope growth reserve as follows:

$$8,000 \times .12 = 960 \text{ Effort hours}$$

This means that the project manager is setting aside 960 hours of time for scope additions once the team starts the development work on the project. During the Execute stage, the project manager will need to keep a separate record of the time being taken up by the added scope and will also need to monitor the reserves. The problem is that at this point in the Launch stage, it is difficult to know how the time spent on incorporating the added scope will impact the project's critical path (its duration). Because of this unknown factor, the project manager will need to decide whether to convert the estimated scope growth effort hours into estimated duration days and add these to the project's estimated duration. We prefer not to convert the estimated hours to duration. We keep a record of the estimated scope growth reserve hours and manage these during the Execute stage as new scope is added.

Accounting for Reserves

At this point, the project manager has three sets of figures for the project's estimates:

Preliminary estimate:	162 work days
Rework reserve:	19 work days
Scope growth reserve:	960 effort hours

If the same project were in the lower complexity area, the rework and scope growth reserves would be much less. The project manager presented the following estimates to the sponsor:

- $162 + 19 = 181$ (estimated preliminary duration)
- $181 + 18 = 199$ work days (10 percent error range)
- $199 \div 18 = 11$ work months (rounded)
- 960 effort hours of scope growth reserve

The number 18 in the third bullet represents the assumed number of productive days per month. At this point, two important questions are:

1. Should the project manager show the sponsor the original 162 day (9 work months) estimate?
   No, because that is an *interim* number and cannot be treated as the final "estimate."
2. Should the project manager inform the sponsor of the reserves for rework and scope growth?
   Obviously, these two values are used to arrive at more realistic and accurate estimates and do not

need to be spelled out to the sponsor, especially if the sponsor has not been briefed on the processes used to compute estimates. An "unenlightened" sponsor may not understand the need for the reserves for rework and scope growth and could interpret these as "padding" the estimate.

Our recommendation is that the project managers take steps to educate the sponsor on the principles and practices of developing realistic and accurate estimates. This tutorial should result in educated and *enlightened* sponsors, who should welcome the opportunity to discuss the various reserves with the project managers. However, such enlightenment will not preclude any negotiations that may be necessary to match the sponsors' expectations. The discussion regarding project rework and reserves reminds us of a sign we created some time ago, which read: Projects are bigger than they appear.

■ TIME LOSSES OFTEN OVERLOOKED

In our assessment of a large number of projects where deadlines were missed, we found a pattern of overlooked items:

1. Multiple sequential approval steps
2. Moving and remodeling interruptions
3. Hardware, network, and software upgrades
4. Project administration activities
5. Meetings
6. Organizing and mobilizing large teams
7. Travel
8. Global/Dispersed team
9. Different time zones
10. Long distance communications
11. Languages
12. External dependencies
13. Hardware and software vendors
14. Various contractors
15. Staff turnover

Let us focus on the last item: staff turnover. Most of the estimating algorithms used to compute estimates for IT/Business projects treat people as if they were easily replaceable, without any noticeable loss of productivity. This misconception is a stubborn carryover from the estimating practices of the engineering (construction) profession. In the case of an engineering project, if four plumbers, six wallpaper hangers, and two masons leave a job, the contractor can often replace these resources within a day or two and can continue the project without much delay. However, what happens when an IT/Business project loses four analysts, six programmers, and two business unit representatives? Good-bye project deadline. It might be weeks before replacements can be found, and in many cases, it can be months before some of the new hires become fully productive. You can see how important it is for you to review the turnover history (information should be available from the human resources department) and incorporate appropriate contingencies in project estimates.

> *If one of my programmers leaves, it would probably take a year to bring someone in and get them trained.*
>
> Lloyd Ellis, "Research: Are Your Older Systems Slowing You Down?"
> *CIO Insight* (December, 2002): p. 73.

It would be educational for you to look back 6 months to see which of the items resulted in specific time losses. The next step would be to look ahead 6 months to determine which of the time losses are most likely to hit your current project. To complete this exercise, use the list of items shown in Figure 6.10. Feel free to add any of your items in the blank rows provided in the diagram. In the column titled "Next 6 months," the value of 1 implies a low probability of occurrence and the value of 5 implies a high probability of occurrence.

FIGURE 6.10
Overlooked Time Losses

Overlooked time losses	Past six months		Next six months
1. Multiple sequential approval steps	Yes	No	1 2 3 4 5
2. Moving and remodeling interruptions	Yes	No	1 2 3 4 5
3. Hardware, network, software upgrade	Yes	No	1 2 3 4 5
4. Project administration activities	Yes	No	1 2 3 4 5
5. Travel	Yes	No	1 2 3 4 5
6. Global/dispersed team	Yes	No	1 2 3 4 5
7. External dependencies	Yes	No	1 2 3 4 5
8. Staff turnover	Yes	No	1 2 3 4 5
	Yes	No	1 2 3 4 5
	Yes	No	1 2 3 4 5
	Yes	No	1 2 3 4 5
	Yes	No	1 2 3 4 5
	Yes	No	1 2 3 4 5

■ COST ESTIMATES

Project cost estimates should include labor (employees, contractors, consultants), hardware, software, supplies, telecommunications, and travel expenses. The first step towards developing an accurate cost estimate for a project is to define the relevant expense categories that need to be captured for a given project. Typical cost categories often include the following (don't overlook the last two items):

Administration	Software licensing
Consultants	Software purchase
Contractors	Supplies
Equipment	Support services
Help desk	Telecommunications
Labor	Training
Legal	Travel
Marketing	"Goodies" for the team
Materials	The closing ceremony and party
Office space	

While building the cost categories list, it is necessary to find out whether the time spent by customers in activities such as requirements definition, prototyping, training sessions, test case development, and system testing is to be accounted for. Similar decisions must be made regarding the time spent by executives and managers. Figure 6.11 shows an example of a cost worksheet.

Some of our customers have simplified the costing process by developing a "burdened" billing rate for various categories of project team members. A burdened (fully loaded) billing rate typically means taking a person's yearly salary; adding the cost of payroll benefits, office space, equipment, telephone, and administrative support; and then dividing the total dollar amount by the number of productive hours per year. For example, one customer uses a $95-per-hour rate for most corporate IT resources and a different rate for contract employees.

Task-Based Estimating

The next few pages contain an example of a task-based estimate. The project is to create and manage a worldwide distribution of 1,000 copies of a policy document. The basic assumptions for this project are that the document will be approximately 30 pages long and will be distributed in three-ring binders with tabs. The resource assumptions are:

1. One senior technical writer
2. One senior customer representative (the SME) needed for consultation and advice
3. Three reviewers—two from the customer department and one technical editor

FIGURE 6.11
Cost Worksheet

Task	Effort estimate	×	Burdened rate	=	Labor cost	+	Additional expense	=	Total cost
		×		=		+		=	
		×		=		+		=	
		×		=		+		=	
		×		=		+		=	
		×		=		+		=	
		×		=		+		=	
		×		=		+		=	
		×		=		+		=	
		×		=		+		=	

Subtotal

Appropriate range value +_____%

Estimated project cost

The project is routine and therefore is rated as a zone IV project. Because this is a small project (less than a 3-month duration[3]), the WBS (shown in the following list) for the project includes deliverables and tasks only.

Deliverables List   The deliverables for the project are:

Approved outline
Approved binder design
First draft
Approved final copy
Address labels
Assembled policy document

Task List   The following tasks, with associated effort and duration estimates, are *not* listed in any particular order.

Task	*Effort*	*Duration*
T1. Define readership/audience and content	30 hours	5 days
T2. Decide production issues	4 hours	2 days
T3. Outline document	6 hours	2 days
T4. Approve outline	2 hours	1 day
T5. Write the first draft	60 hours	14 days
T6. Review the draft		
T6.1 Reviewer 1	8 hours	8 days
T6.2 Reviewer 2	8 hours	5 days
T6.3 Reviewer 3	8 hours	4 days
T7. Write the final copy	15 hours	5 days
T8. Approve the final copy	3 hours	1 day (lag)
T9. Format the copy (for printing)	6 hours	2 days
T10. Proof and approve the final copy	4 hours	1 day

---

[3]The project manager had previously developed a deliverable-based size estimate to determine the size of the project.

T11. Print the policy document	5 hours	2 days
T12. Assemble and package the policy binders	15 hours	5 days
T13. Ship the policy binders	4 hours	2 days
T14. Contact print shop(s)	1 hour	1 day
T15. Design binders and tabs	6 hours	3 days
T16. Order binders and tabs	2 hours	1 day (lag)
T17. Obtain and validate address list	3 hours	1 day
T18. Print address labels	4 hours	1 day

Lag Values   The following affect lag:

Binders and tabs (after task T16)	25 days
Approval of the final copy (after task T8)	4 days

Issues List   While creating the task list, the project manager raised the following issues:

1. Is there a need to make language translations?
2. What will be the primary mode of distribution (post office, shipping carrier, etc.)?
3. Is an up-to-date address list available?
4. Is there a need to develop a glossary?

The issues were resolved as follows:

1. No language translation for the first release.
2. The corporate shipping department will decide on the shipping mode.
3. The project manager will need to make sure that the latest address list is used for printing the address labels.
4. There is no need for a glossary (at least for the first release of the policy document).

Figure 6.12 shows a network diagram for this project. The numbers in the various boxes (T1, T2, T3 . . .) represent the tasks listed. Each box also contains the estimated duration for the task. The critical path (the estimated project duration) spans 52 *workdays*.

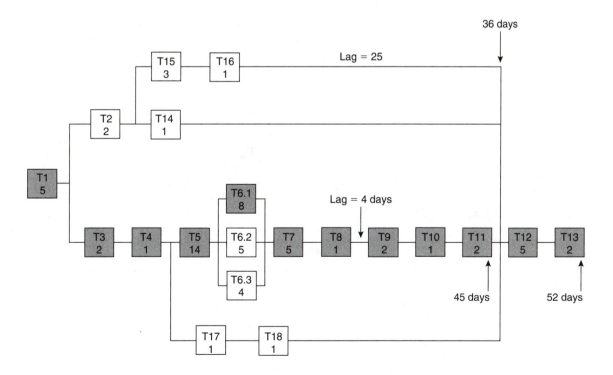

Critical Path = T1 + T3 + T4 + T5 + T6.1 + T7 + T8 + Lag + T9 + T10 + T11 + T12 + T13 = 52 to 57 work days

FIGURE 6.12
Task Network

The project manager summarizes the estimates as follows:

- Estimated team effort: 194 hours
- Sponsor effort:

    3 months $\times$ 4 hours/month   12 hours

- Management effort:

    194 $\times$ .05   10 hours

- Customer effort:

    194 $\times$ .15   29 hours

- Project management (PM) effort:

    Total effort = (194 + 12 + 10 + 29)   245 hours

    PM effort = 235 $\times$ .15   37 hours

- Estimated billable effort (team + PM)

    Team + PM = (194 + 37)   231 hours

- Estimated labor cost

    231 $\times$ \$100 = \$23,100

- Materials cost

    \$ 2,000

- Shipping: To be determined
- Estimated cost (Labor + Materials)

    \$23,100 + \$2,000 = \$25,100

    \$25,100 to \$27,600 plus the shipping cost

For the estimated cost, the project manager used the rate of \$100 per hour for all billable effort. The range values for the final cost and duration estimates are +10 percent. Because the project is a zone IV project (low complexity), the project manager did not incorporate any reserves for rework or scope growth. The project manager estimated the project duration as follows:

Estimated project duration: 52 to 57 workdays (+10 % range), i.e., approximately 3 months (52 workdays $\div$ 17.5 workdays/month). Keep in mind that this is *not* a schedule.

The process of first computing the effort/cost of the lowest level of the WBS and then summing them to arrive at the total estimates is also known as bottom-up estimating.

■ COMPRESS THE CRITICAL PATH

A common question asked of most project managers is, "Can you reduce the duration of this project?" Not only that, the customer may even offer to eliminate certain deliverables and their respective tasks in exchange for reduced project duration. A word of caution: all deliverables and tasks are not created equal when it comes to reducing the estimated project duration. In Figure 6.12, the estimated project duration is 52 workdays. The customer objects that this duration is too long and offers the following suggestions to the project manager:

- Reduce the binder and tab lag time from 25 days to 15 days (this is possible by offering the company responsible for supplying the binders and tabs an incentive of \$250 for earlier delivery). The customer believes this will cut 10 days from the project duration.
- Do only two reviews, shown in tasks T6.2 and T6.3, and drop the review shown in task T6.1, which is expected to take 8 days. The thinking behind this suggestion is that three reviews are not necessary and this will save 8 days—the duration of task T6.1.

Obvious questions are: "Are these good options? Will they reduce the estimated duration sufficiently? If not, what other options are there?" Before we can answer these questions, we need to focus on the critical path tasks, the tasks that contribute to the project duration. In Figure 6.12, we can see that the binders will be ready on the 36th day, as computed in the following equation (d indicates days):

$$T1\,(5\,d) \,+\, T2\,(2\,d) \,+\, T15\,(3\,d) \,+\, T16\,(1\,d) \,+\, (25\,d)\,Lag \,=\, 36\,d$$

Analysis of the critical path tasks shows that Task T12, Assemble and package the policy binders, is planned to start on the 46th day (9 days *after* the binders and tabs arrives). Therefore, reducing the delivery time for binders and tabs is *not* going to help reduce the project duration—these two items are *not* on the critical path. In fact, completely *eliminating* both the binder and tab activities will *not reduce* the critical path at all. Of course, eliminating the binders and tabs will certainly save money.

The next question revolves around *not* doing the review, T6.1, thereby saving 8 days of work. This modification will certainly reduce the project duration, but *not* by 8 days. Once task T6.1 is eliminated from the network, task T6.2, with a duration of 5 days, will come on the critical path. Therefore, removing task T6.1 from the plan will reduce the project duration by only 3 days $(8 - 5 = 3)$.

The steps to reduce the duration (the critical path) of the project should focus on analyzing tasks T1, T5, T6.1, and T7 to see if the duration of any of these tasks[4] can be reduced by adding resources, or by reducing the scope of the policy document. Another target for reduction is the lag of 4 days between tasks T8 and T9. For additional discussion on the steps to help reduce project duration, see *Steps to Reduce Estimates* later in this chapter.

■ TASK-BASED ESTIMATING EXAMPLE—LESSONS LEARNED

A project manager at one of the Center's client organizations was given the responsibility to design a website for one of the departments. The project manager assessed the complexity of the project and determined that it was a mid-zone III project. His resource assumptions were as follows:

Analyst   Secondary developer
Primary developer   Web artist

Figure 6.13 depicts the project task list along with the estimated effort hours for various tasks. Figure 6.14 shows the task network, estimated duration for various tasks, and the critical path (boxes with bold letters).

Tasks 4, 6, and 9 are group meetings, and the secondary developer assisted the primary developer in tasks 3, 5, and 7. The project manager did not compute the cost of sponsor, management, and customer time in the project cost estimate (company policy). The following is a summary of the estimates for the project:

- Analysis effort: 106 hours
- Design effort: 154 hours
- Artist effort: 68 hours
- Estimated team effort:

$$106 \,+\, 154 \,+\, 68 \,=\, 328 \text{ hours}$$

- Sponsor effort: 8 hours
- Management effort:

$$328 \times .15 \hspace{4cm} 50 \text{ hours}$$

- Customer effort:

$$328 \times .15 \hspace{4cm} 50 \text{ hours}$$

---

[4]We chose these tasks because of their "longer" duration values.

FIGURE 6.13
Project Task List and
Estimated Effort Values

Tasks	Analysis effort hours	Design (developer) effort hours	Artist effort hours
1. Discovery			
Interview customer	12		4
Assess complexity and risk	4		
Review infrastructure	4		
Review data requirements	4	6	
2. Analysis			
Review business environment	12		
Define business object relationships	4	8	
Research technology requirements	4	8	
3. Design			
Create storyboard for client review	6	12	8
Design the GUI	6	8	4
Model database relationships	4	6	
Design site navigation plan	6	6	8
4. Review navigation plan with the customer	4	4	4
5. Construction			
Develop web page	4	18	8
Develop on-line help	2	8	6
Implement search function	2	6	
Configure security protocol	2	8	
Build security code		6	
Develop customer training document	4	8	12
6. Review the Web page with the customer	4	4	4
7. Test			
Develop test plan	4	8	
Validate interactive forms & hyperlinks		4	
Verify reports	4	4	
Test local site		8	
Test internet interface		4	4
8. Customer review: 2 days lag			
9. Test with customer	6	6	6
10. Review and resolve test results	4	4	
Total hours:	106	154	68

- PM effort:

$$(328 + 8 + 50 + 50) \times .15 = 65 \text{ hours}$$

- Estimated billable effort (Team + PM)

$$(328 + 65) = 393 \text{ hours}$$

- Estimated cost $= 393 \times \$120 = \$47,160$ to $\$54,234$
- Estimated project duration: 24 to 28 days (From Figure 6.14)

For the estimated cost, the project manager used the rate of $120 per hour for all billable effort. The range values for the final cost and time estimated are +15 percent. Because the project was of relatively short duration, the project manager did not believe that he needed to incorporate any reserves for rework or scope growth.

We contacted the project manager 2 months after he had given us this estimate and learned that, during the Execution stage, the schedule had grown by more than 15 days (an approximately 60 percent increase from the original estimate). Here is a summary of our discussion:

- He underestimated the complexity of the project, especially the business complexity. The increased complexity became apparent when, during the requirements definition phase, he learned that this was the first web-based project the customer had ever requested. Because of a lack of experience and history, the customer had not adequately thought through what was needed.
- This being a short duration project, 24 to 28 days, the project manager did not foresee much scope growth or rework.

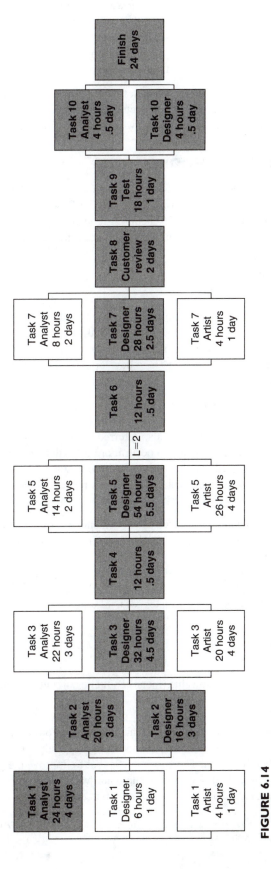

FIGURE 6.14
Web Project Task Network

343

- The primary designer/developer was not as experienced as the project manager had assumed, and this resulted in added effort and duration due to quality problems and the need for rework. The secondary designer/developer was able to make up for some of the lost time.
- No prototypes were used to validate customer requirements. Even though steps 4 and 6 in (Figure 6.13) show reviews with the customer, these were not true prototypes. Finally, during customer review (after step 7), the customer worked with the Web page and came back with a number of suggestions and new requirements.

The project manager made a remark that he had learned his lesson and plans not to skip the Idea and Pre-Launch stages in the future, even for what appear to be small projects. Additionally, he plans to use reserves for scope creep and rework in all his future estimates.

■ PERT ESTIMATING METHODS

In 1958, the U.S. Navy, the consulting firm Booz Allen & Hamilton, and Lockheed Aircraft Corporation developed PERT (Program Evaluation Research Task, later to be called Project Evaluation and Review Technique) for scheduling and managing the Polaris weapons systems project. All PERT estimates are based on three estimates for each task:

1. Optimistic
2. Most likely
3. Pessimistic

Probability-based simulations are then used to compute the probability of the project completion prior to, on, or after a specific date. In the following discussion, we present a *simplified* version of the PERT technique,[5] which focuses on developing effort estimates for individual tasks. In the PERT technique, the first step is to develop three estimate values for each task under consideration. These three values are:

1. $T_o =$ Optimistic estimate: This number represents the estimate that would be bettered only one time in twenty if the activity were to be performed repeatedly and under similar circumstances.
2. $T_m =$ Probable estimate (also referred to as the *most likely estimate*): This number represents the estimate that is likely to occur more often than any other value if the activity were to be performed repeatedly and under similar circumstances.
3. $T_P =$ Pessimistic estimate: This number represents the estimate that would be exceeded only one time in twenty if the activity were to be performed repeatedly and under similar circumstances.

Once the three estimates have been stated for a given task, the next step is to arrive at the expected time estimate (T_e), using the following formula, which results in a weighted average of the three estimates:

$$T_e = (T_o + 4T_m + T_p) \div 6$$

Assume that three time estimates for a task are:

Optimistic:	4 hours
Most likely:	8 hours
Pessimistic:	18 hours

The expected estimate value (mean) could be computed as follows:

$$T_e = (4 + (4 \times 8) + 18) \div 6 = 54 \div 6 = 9 \text{ hours}$$

Figure 6.15 depicts the probability distribution of the PERT calculation. From the data presented in this figure, we can conclude that the T_e value (in this case, 9 hours) represents the 50 percent probability point. The curve shows that to improve the probability to 68 percent, we will need to add one standard deviation to the mean value. The probability rises to 95 percent for estimates with two standard deviations, and to 99 percent with three standard deviations.

---

[5]For detailed coverage of the subject, refer to: *Project Management with CPM, PERT and Precedence Diagramming*, 3rd ed., by Joseph J. Moder, Cecil R. Phillips, and Edward W. Davis.

FIGURE 6.15
Probability Distribution
Curve

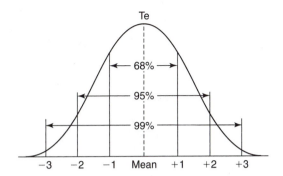

The formula to compute one standard deviation (S_t) for a task is:

$$S_t = (T_p - T_o) \div 6 = (18 - 4) \div 6 = 2.3 \text{ hours}$$

Therefore, if you would like to create an estimate with varying degrees of probabilities, the values would be:

- $9 + 2.3 = 11.3$ hours, probability of the actual effort matching this estimate is 68 percent
- $9 + 2.3 + 2.3 = 13.6$ hours, probability of the actual effort matching this estimate is 95 percent
- $9 + 2.3 + 2.3 + 2.3 = 15.9$ hours, probability of the actual effort matching this estimate is 99 percent

There is no use of negative values in the computations. We discussed the subject in Chapter 1 under the heading *Range Values*. Figure 6.16 depicts PERT estimate computations for five tasks. The estimated values in the rightmost columns were the decisions of the project manager and were based on her experience.

We do not advise the use of the PERT technique for estimating every task in a large project. Not only can the resulting computation become overwhelming, the process of three estimates for each task is too time consuming. Additionally, the need to use this technique on every task means that there are too many uncertainties regarding the project and the resulting final estimates would be of questionable value. We typically use the three-estimate technique for tasks that have a *high level of uncertainty* or when team members are reluctant to commit to estimates for their tasks. Asking them to think about three estimates (optimistic, most likely, and pessimistic) assures them that uncertainties are not being overlooked.

There is always the question: "What assumptions are being made about the person associated with these three estimates?" To keep things in line with our discussions, we always estimate the *baseline* effort estimate values, in other words, the time taken by a proficient person, assigned full-time, with no interruptions, working in a high-quality environment. Once the PERT technique is used to create these estimates, the values can be adjusted to reflect the actual team member skills and work environment.

Task	Optimistic estimate hours T_o	Probable estimate hours T_m	Pessimistic estimate hours T_p	Expected estimate hours T_e	Standard deviation hours S_t	Estimate (1 std. dev.)	Estimate (2 std. dev.)	Estimate (3 std. dev.)	Estimate value hours
Task A	10	15	20	15	1.7	16.7	18.4	20.1	19
Task B	25	30	40	31	2.5	33.5	36	38.5	36
Task C	8	12	16	12	1.3	13.3	14.6	15.9	15
Task D	15	20	25	20	1.7	21.7	23.4	25.1	24
Task E	4	15	30	16	4.3	20.3	24.6	28.9	27

FIGURE 6.16
Examples of PERT Estimates

■ WORDS TO AVOID

Find your hammer and chisel to etch in stone the words you *must never use* as a project manager:

1. *Guess:* Professional project managers do not guess. They develop size estimates or task-based estimates.
2. *Guesstimate:* This is an aberration. It is neither a guess nor an estimate and it must be avoided.
3. *Pad* or *fudge factor:* Do not pad your estimates. Do not add fudge[6] factors either. Both imply that you are inflating your estimates, which is certainly not the action of a professional project manager. Use appropriate range values to match the overall accuracy of your size and task-based estimates. Inform the customer up front of the range values and the reasons behind them. If your projects routinely finish much earlier or later than your estimates, improve your estimating process or use narrower ranges.
4. *Rehash:* The word "recompute" is much more appropriate than "rehash." Recompute implies that you are going to revisit your numbers. The word "hash" implies confusion, hodgepodge, and mess.

■ TASK-BASED ESTIMATING: A SUMMARY

1. Develop a comprehensive WBS (phases, deliverables, and tasks) for the project.
2. Obtain or develop the baseline effort value for each task. This value can be obtained from historical data, specified by the project manager, or through PERT (three estimate) computations.
3. Specify the project resources (people).
4. Compute the EVF for each resource.
5. Adjust the baseline effort value for each task using appropriate EVF values to compute the estimated effort (hours).
6. Convert the estimated effort for each task into estimated duration (days).
7. Organize the tasks into a network chart.
8. Specify any lag values.
9. Compute any project reserves (rework and scope growth).
10. Compute contingency estimates.
11. Compute the estimated project duration using the CPM.
12. Compute sponsor, management, and customer effort estimates.
13. Compute the project management effort estimate.
14. Compute the project cost estimate.
15. Specify an estimate expiration date.

From the previous list, it is clear that accurate task-based estimating begins with a comprehensive WBS. A comprehensive WBS, resulting in a detailed task list, is the foundation for an accurate estimate. Post-implementation assessment of a large number of projects by the Center's consultants has shown us that the discovery of new tasks during project execution is a major factor in cost and time overruns. Therefore, we recommend that you take extra care to develop a comprehensive WBS before developing any estimates. Next, you would specify the team, keeping in mind the skills needed to complete the various tasks in the project. Each team member is profiled in terms of knowledge, skills, individual work interruptions, and the project's productivity environment. Where necessary (or applicable), steps 2 through 5 can be replaced by directly estimating the task effort values. Wait times for management and customer approvals must be included in the estimate, and do not overlook the needed reserves for rework and scope growth (especially for high-complexity projects). Make sure to use the appropriate range value for the final estimates and specify an expiration date. Finally, a few points regarding management:

- Educate sponsors, managers, and customers about the estimating process. The more they understand, the easier it will be to negotiate with them.

---

[6]Some of the definitions of the word "fudge" are: to make or put together dishonestly or carelessly, to fake, to be dishonest, to cheat. Pretty dismal picture, isn't it?

- Always communicate the effort and cost of developing an estimate; too many people overlook this important component of the process.
- Keep in mind that the first estimate a sponsor, manager, or customer dictates to you is their first *bid*—they must start somewhere. You need to bid back; just make sure that you have good information to support your response.

Once the work on a given project begins, team members must keep records of their work, and you will need to compare their actual effort values to the original estimates at regular intervals. The resulting data is used to analyze the reasons behind any marked differences between the original estimates and the actual effort and duration values. If the estimated and actual values do not converge, the next step is to review and improve the estimating process. A word of caution: if the actual values are greater than the estimates, it does not automatically mean that the estimates were incorrect. These variances can be due to a number of reasons, such as an incomplete task plan (resulting in the discovery of new tasks as the work progresses), incorrect task dependencies, inaccurately profiled resources, and overlooking the impact of complexity.

At this point in the project life cycle, you are ready to submit your estimates to the sponsor for the final step in the Launch stage—Project Charter Review and Budget Approval. However, as discussed toward the end of Chapter 4, it is always a good idea to assess the quality of work done to produce the estimates you are about to submit to the sponsor. The best approach for this assessment is to start with the template depicted in Figure 6.17.

In the first column is a list of the steps leading to accurate effort and duration estimates. To use this assessment tool, you have two choices:

1. Indicate which of the thirteen steps you used by circling either *Yes* or *No* for each selected step, or
2. List only those steps that you used for the project at hand and delete the second column from the chart.

The next step is to assess the quality of work done to complete each of the selected steps by using the scale values between 1 and 5, where 1 indicates a poor quality of work and 5 indicates a high quality of work. For this assessment to have any value, you need to be forthright in your responses. A good way to arrive at accurate values is to ask one or two of your key team members to independently

FIGURE 6.17
Estimating Process Assessment

Estimating step	Applicable		Level of confidence	Action plan
1. Comprehensive WBS	Yes	No	1 2 3 4 5	
2. Use of baseline effort values	Yes	No	1 2 3 4 5	
3. Resource skill/productivity profiles—EVF	Yes	No	1 2 3 4 5	
4. Task duration estimates based on realistic percent assignment to the project	Yes	No	1 2 3 4 5	
5. Accurate task network based on realistic number of resources	Yes	No	1 2 3 4 5	
6. Lag values incorporated	Yes	No	1 2 3 4 5	
7. Sponsor effort computed and incorporated	Yes	No	1 2 3 4 5	
8. Management effort computed and incorporated	Yes	No	1 2 3 4 5	
9. Customer effort computed and incorporated	Yes	No	1 2 3 4 5	
10. Project manager's effort computed and incorporated	Yes	No	1 2 3 4 5	
11. Rework reserves computed and incorporated	Yes	No	1 2 3 4 5	
12. Scope growth reserves computed and incorporated	Yes	No	1 2 3 4 5	
13. Contingency reserves computed and incorporated	Yes	No	1 2 3 4 5	

develop their assessment, then you can compare the different assessed values and arrive at a consensus. If any of the individual items is rated below 3.0, we suggest a review of the work done to complete that item and see what needs to be done to improve the quality rating to 3.0 or above.

Task-based estimates are the only estimates suitable for developing the project schedule. Therefore, these estimates must be accurate and realistic. It is imperative that project managers become experts in the process of developing accurate and realistic task-based estimates.

■ DEVELOPING A HISTORICAL BASELINE EFFORT DATABASE

Collection of historical information regarding estimates is essential for developing accurate future estimates. Begin to collect historical baseline effort data *now*. Compiling a solid database is a vital step toward developing a standard approach for establishing a measurable, efficient, and disciplined estimating process. The availability of a standardized historical effort database can lead to greatly improved estimates and schedules. A number of our clients have been collecting baseline effort data from a wide variety of projects for over a decade. Figure 6.18 depicts a suggested template for the process.

The baseline effort collection template contains the following fields:

Task Name: A descriptive task name.
Key Words: Selected words that would help in a future search of the database.
Actual Effort Hours: A record of the *total* "actual" hours spent to complete this task, including any unreported overtime. It is important that this record be factual and accurate. The person responsible for completing the task should enter this information directly.
Effort Variance Factor (EVF): The EVF value of the person who completed this task.
Baseline Effort: This is computed by dividing the actual effort hours by the EVF value.
Remarks: Any remarks or comments that will help a future project manager develop accurate effort estimates.

Notice that the template does not include the name of the person supplying the data. The reason for this omission is that we wish to encourage those who supply the actual effort data to be more forthright in their reporting by keeping them anonymous. In discussions with a number of team members, we observed that when names were required, the value of the actual effort was close to what was expected of them rather than the actual time spent completing those tasks.

It is necessary to separate the recording of actual project effort for historical purposes from payroll time recording. This distinction must be made because the payroll time recording system may have a policy limiting the number of hours that can be recorded during a given week, for instance, 35 or 40 maximum hours for salaried employees. Under these circumstances, team members stop recording their time once the predefined weekly limit is reached. As a result, an accurate database of the actual historical effort data cannot be constructed. We have also known of a few instances where project team members were asked to match their actual effort values to the number of hours originally estimated. This was an attempt to prove that the original estimates were correct; however, the historical effort database is now of little value for future use. These differences, between the time spent and the time actually recorded, can make the payroll data useless for computing the baseline effort values. Our advice is not to use the payroll data for building a historical effort database unless the recorded data includes *all the hours* actually spent by *all* team members.

FIGURE 6.18
Baseline Effort Collection
Template

Task name	Key words	Actual effort hours	EVF value	Baseline effort hours *	Remarks

*Baseline effort hours = Actual effort hours ÷ EVF

When a project team decides to record historical effort data for creating a baseline effort database, it is not necessary to collect data on every task in a given project. The key reason is that not every task in a given project is a repeatable task—a task that a future project manager can use. Certain tasks are specific to a project and will rarely be repeated in future projects. In addition, it takes time and effort to record the actual effort, compute the EVF, and then create the baseline effort value. Most project teams do not have the extra time needed to do justice to data collection. The best approach is for the project manager to review the completed WBS for the project and decide which tasks are prime candidates for data collection.

For the historical baseline data to be useful for future estimates, it is necessary to use a uniform task naming (nomenclature) process. In the absence of uniform nomenclature, future project managers will have difficulty using the historical information. Make the data collection a separate step from the reporting of official project time. By doing so, people will be more forthright, and the resulting data will be more accurate. Eventually, disciplined historical effort data collection—baseline effort database creation and updates—should become an integral part of the organization's project management metrics collection program.

◼ STEPS TO REDUCE ESTIMATES

At this point, you have developed detailed task-based resource, cost, and duration estimates for your project and you need to compare them to the size estimates submitted as a part of the Project Charter (Chapter 4). Under the best of conditions, your task-based estimates would fall within the range values of the size estimates. If that is not the case, you must try some "what if" analysis to see if there are any ways of reducing the estimates to match the previously set expectations. The following steps can help reduce the effort, resource, cost, and/or duration estimates of your project.

An important point regarding the reduction of the project duration estimate: focus your work on the tasks that lie on the critical path, and near-critical path, of the project.

Review Constraints and Obstacles

We discussed constraints and obstacles in Chapter 2 (see *Network Constraints*) and Chapter 4 (see *Constraints and Obstacles*). Many of these constraints will impact the critical path of the project. We suggest that you ascertain which constraints have a direct influence on the critical path and then determine how they can be negotiated in your favor.

Reduce Scope

Most project requirements include deliverables and features that, while nice to have, are not absolutely necessary. Eliminating the tasks associated with these deliverables and features from the project's plans will certainly reduce cost and may reduce the project duration. As we discussed earlier (see *Compress the Critical Path*), many deliverables and features when removed from the project, do not necessarily reduce the project duration because the tasks to accomplish them do not lie on the critical path. Therefore, when looking at the option to reduce project duration, focus on the deliverables and features that lie on the project's critical path. Additionally, when dropping deliverables and features, be mindful of dependencies. Keep in mind that removing certain deliverables and features may make it impossible to deliver some other planned items or may have an adverse impact on the quality of the end product. Reducing scope can help reduce effort, resources, cost, and duration estimates.

Split/Overlap Tasks

Make a list of the tasks that compose the critical path, and see if any of the long duration tasks can be split into subtasks. Overall duration can be reduced if some of these subtasks are started earlier or if extra resources can be assigned to the smaller (parallel) tasks. When tasks are too large, the team might miss the opportunity to do things in parallel by failing to know about the multiple, independent tasks.

Validate Task Dependencies

Dependencies represent the specific order in which various tasks must be completed. These dependencies have a direct impact on the resulting duration (critical path) of the project. For example, consider the following two situations:

1. Three tasks (A, B, and C), each of 2 days duration are specified as linear—A precedes B and B precedes C. In this case, the net duration through these three tasks will be 6 days.
2. Tasks A, B, and C are parallel—there is no dependency between these three tasks because all of them can be executed at the same time. In this case, using three different resources, the net duration of these tasks will be 2 days, a difference of 4 days from the previous situation. Of course, three resources are needed to achieve this result.

Linear dependencies invariably add to the project duration. It is important to add a step in the planning process to double-check dependencies to make sure they are specified correctly. At the same time, be aware that converting linear dependencies into parallel dependencies incorrectly will produce shorter estimated duration values, but the problem caused by the error will rear its ugly head during the Execute stage when the team members discover the miscalculation and are unable to execute the tasks in the order specified.

Aggressively Manage Lag

Lags that lie on the critical path add to the duration of an estimate. Carefully evaluate all lag values in the project and work with the appropriate entities to reduce the lags that contribute to the critical path. For example, the impact of a long lag between ordering equipment and its delivery can be reduced either by ordering the equipment at an earlier date or by working closely with the supplier to reduce the lag—this may involve a financial incentive for early delivery. This step will help reduce the duration estimate but may increase the cost estimate.

Improve Team Skills

Improving team skills can be accomplished in several ways. One technique is to request higher proficiency team members, particularly for critical path tasks. A team's skills can also be improved through the education and training of selected team members. This step will help reduce the effort and duration estimates but may increase the cost estimate. However, the best benefit will be the improved team morale.

Use Overtime

Requiring team members to work overtime can be a viable choice, but is one that should not be used to the extent that they begin to resent the work, resulting in a lower-quality product. *Be sure to direct the overtime effort to critical path tasks.* Keep in mind that although the overtime effort may reduce the project duration, it is sure to increase the project cost and may even hurt the product quality because of team burnout.

Add Team Members

Adding team members will help only if the project's task network indicates that the additional team members can work on more tasks concurrently. For example, having more than one person available for the network depicted in Figure 6.19 is not going to reduce the project duration unless the tasks can be broken into independent, parallel, subtasks with no cross-task dependencies. A key point to consider is the loss of productivity as new resources are brought on board. Unless supported by good analysis and good planning, this step may not have the desired result.

FIGURE 6.19
Network with Linear Tasks

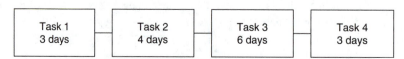

Improve the Work Environment

Earlier in this chapter, we discussed the impact of the work environment on productivity; see *Effort Variance Factor (EVF)*. It is always a good idea to take a serious look at the net EVF of the project team and then work to improve any of the factors that result in a low productivity environment. This step will help reduce the effort and duration estimates and it may increase the cost estimate.

Transfer Risk Responsibility

Transfer selected risk(s) to the customer—the customer agrees to live with the consequences if and when the risk happens. If the customer accepts the responsibility, you can drop selected contingency plans from your project. Transferring risk will reduce the duration estimates but, if and when a contingency does occur the team may have to work extra hours to keep the project on track.

If these steps do not help reduce the estimates to the desired level, then you need to consider the following two steps:

1. *Short term:* Review your size estimates to determine why they were considerably smaller than the task-based estimates. Hopefully, you will have sufficient information to help you plan for your negotiations session with the sponsor because you will need to ask for added budget, resources, and/or time.

2. *Long term:* Carefully review the processes used for developing size estimates and see if any of the size estimating models need to be recalibrated.

■ PROJECT CHARTER REVIEW AND BUDGET APPROVAL—PPA STEP 26

At this point, you are ready to meet with the sponsor for a final review of the Project Charter, task plan, and detailed estimates to make sure that the work done in the Launch stage can help achieve the stated objectives, that risks are reasonable, and that the estimates are in line with management and customer expectations. If all seems well, and the sponsor is satisfied with the quality of the team's work, it is time to approve the project's budget and proceed to the next stage: to execute the project.

■ STAGE GATE NO. 3

As you know, the purpose of a stage gate is to ensure that the quality of the project management process is in concert with the complexity and the inherent risk of the project, and that the project can safely proceed to the next stage. The template in Figure 6.20 depicts a suggested list of attributes for the stage gate review at the end of the Launch stage. Keep in mind that this is a suggested list, and you will need to tailor it (delete and/or add items) to meet the needs of your project.

We will reiterate the stage gate review process here:

1. The project manager and the core team meet to assess the degree to which each of the attributes has been accomplished. To make the assessment useful, we suggest that the team members, under the facilitation of the project manager, collectively review their work products and decide on the quality of each item. In Figure 6.20, in the column titled *Confidence level*, the value of 1 implies poor quality or incomplete work and the value of 5 implies high quality and comprehensive work. Any item with an assessed value lower than 3 means low quality work which, if not corrected, will result in problems during future project stages.

2. Next, the project manager meets with the sponsor to review the assessment. The sponsor then decides whether to open the stage gate no. 3 to let the team proceed to the Execute stage, or directs the team to do the rework needed to improve any of the low quality work products. Occasionally, the sponsor may open the stage gate even if some of the work is not up to par. This conditional approval implies that the team will remedy the situation to the sponsor's satisfaction in the near future.

3. Another possibility is to move the project to the suspend portfolio or the canceled Project portfolio (refer to Chapter 10).

FIGURE 6.20
Stage Gate No. 3—
Launch Stage

Stage gate no. 3: attributes	Confidence level	Action plan
1. Strategy alignment	1 2 3 4 5	
2. Value-to-business	1 2 3 4 5	
3. Ownership	1 2 3 4 5	
4. Project kickoff meeting	1 2 3 4 5	
5. Project organization structure	1 2 3 4 5	
6. Sponsor	1 2 3 4 5	
7. Project manager	1 2 3 4 5	
8. Project team	1 2 3 4 5	
9. Customer buy-In	1 2 3 4 5	
10. Project duplication/overlap	1 2 3 4 5	
11. Change management plan	1 2 3 4 5	
12. Task plan	1 2 3 4 5	
13. Scope management plan	1 2 3 4 5	
14. Communications plan	1 2 3 4 5	
15. Team education/training plan	1 2 3 4 5	
16. Estimates	1 2 3 4 5	
17. Up-to-date project notebook	1 2 3 4 5	
18. Budget	1 2 3 4 5	

■ ORDER OF PPA STEPS

At this point, let us address the question raised at the start of Chapter 5: Is there a specific sequence in which the various steps of the Launch stage need to be executed?

Figure 6.21 depicts our recommendation.

Begin with step 16, Project Staging, followed by steps 17 and 18:

- Step 17: Project Organization
- Step 18: Task Plan

After the task plan has been completed, steps 19 through 23 can be initiated:

- Step 19: Prototyping Plan
- Step 20: Organization Change Management Plan
- Step 21: Scope Management Plan
- Step 22: Staffing Plan
- Step 23: Communications Plan

At this point steps 25 and 26 can be executed:

- Step 25: Detailed Estimates
- Step 26: Project Charter Review and Budget Approval

Notice that these two steps have a finish-to-start relationship, because step 26 needs the output of step 25. Step 24, Project Notebook, can start soon after Project Staging (step 16) has been completed. Although it is not shown in Figure 6.21, step 11: Issues Management, from the PreLaunch stage will continue through this stage and then through the remaining project stages.

It is not necessary to *completely* finish a step before starting the next step. For example, it is not necessary that the entire project be planned (step 18) before starting one or more of the steps that follow. This is specifically true in the case of large projects, where task planning may be done progressively. In such cases, when a sufficient amount of project planning has been completed, a sub-team could begin to review the list of deliverables for prototyping (step 19). Similarly, once the WBS

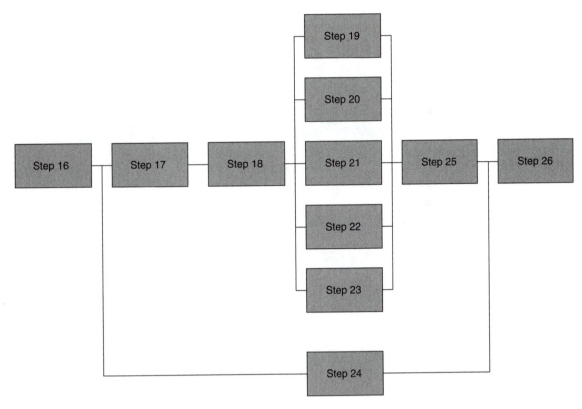

FIGURE 6.21
Suggested Execution Order of Launch Stage Steps

portion of step 18 has been completed, a subteam could begin to develop effort estimates (step 25). The suggested order of steps in Figure 6.21 is to provide you with a plan that will keep you from starting too many steps concurrently, which can become unwieldy.

As we discussed in Chapter 1, the PPA can be scaled to fit the size and complexity of a given project. Complex projects will require more of the steps as well as more rigor, while simpler projects will do well with fewer steps and less rigor. Please refer to Figure 1.12 for the steps recommended for simple, average, complex, and very complex projects.

■ SUMMARY

In this chapter, we continued with the last two steps of the launch stage of the PPA (Estimating and Project Charter Review and Budget Approval). We discussed the steps necessary to develop detailed task-based estimates. These estimates are compared to the size estimates developed in the Pre-Launch stage and the value-to-business computations are also revisited. The next important step involves the approval of the project budget, a go-ahead for the project manager to proceed with the project. The final milestone is the tollgate review by the sponsor. If approved, the project moves to the next stage; if not, the project may be sent to the suspended or canceled portfolio.

Following is a list of the key subject areas covered in this chapter. We invite you to review the list and assess your level of comprehension of each topic. The best approach is to take a separate sheet of paper and write a short narrative to explain your knowledge of the topic and then go back and compare your summaries with the material covered in the chapter. Another approach is to find a colleague who is also interested in these topics and discuss your understanding of the topics with her and then jointly review the chapter materials to assess your degree of understanding.

- Task-based estimates
- Range values
- Estimate review points

- Estimating responsibility
- Baseline effort
- Effort variance factor
- Defining team member skill profile
- Impact of skill profile
- Profiling the unknown team
- Computing the task effort and duration estimates
- Computing the project duration estimate
- Computing sponsor, management, and project management effort
- Computing reserves
- Time losses often overlooked
- Computing cost estimates
- Compress the critical path
- PERT estimating method
- Words to avoid
- Developing a historical baseline database
- Steps to reduce estimates
- Obtaining budget approval
- Stage gate review

■ QUESTIONS AND DISCUSSION POINTS

1. What are the key differences between the size estimates developed earlier and the detailed (task-based) estimates?
2. Why develop detailed (task-based) estimates?
3. Why do detailed (task-based) estimates need range values?
4. What is the primary difference between effort-driven and duration-driven tasks?
5. As it pertains to estimates, what is the definition of a baseline effort?
6. What are the possible sources of baseline effort data?
7. What is EVF, and why use it?
8. What is the correlation between skill level and skill factor?
9. What is the correlation between interruptions and productivity level?
10. Does working on multiple projects simultaneously have any negative impact on productivity? Why?
11. The chapter lists a number of project productivity influencing factors. How many can you recall? Describe each factor that you are able to recall.
12. What are the four components of the EVF of an individual team member?
13. Of the four factors of EVF, which one seems to have the highest impact on a team member's productivity level?
14. Can the EVF of a team member change during the life cycle of a project? What can cause the change? What impact would the change in EVF have on the project?
15. Is it necessary to compute sponsor, management, and project management effort when developing detailed task-based estimates, or is it a moot point?

16. Is it necessary to compute rework and scope growth reserves when computing detailed task-based estimates? Why?
17. In this chapter, we presented a long list of time losses often overlooked when developing an estimate. Can you recall five items from the list? What do you think is the frequency of oversight regarding these items? Have any such omissions impacted your projects? In what way?
18. Other than the cost of the team's time, what are some of the other items that need to be included when estimating the cost of a project?
19. What are the key characteristics of computing task estimates using the PERT method? Would you recommend the use of the PERT method to compute estimates for all project tasks? Explain your response.
20. We listed a few words to avoid. Can you recall any?
21. What is the value of developing a historical baseline effort database? Does your organization have one? Do you believe that you and your colleagues would benefit from the use of a historical baseline effort database? How?
22. In this chapter, we listed ten steps to reduce estimates. Can you recall any? Briefly describe the ones you can recall.
23. Why is it important to review the Project Charter after developing the detailed task-based estimates?
24. What is the purpose and benefit of the stage gate at the end of the Launch stage?
25. Can you recall any of the quotations used in this chapter? If so, why this quotation?

7
EXECUTE STAGE: SCHEDULE, TRACK, AND CONTROL THE PROJECT

OBJECTIVES

In this chapter, you will learn about the following project management elements:

- Execute stage of the PPA
- Project management software
- Build project schedule
- Account for risks
- Account for rework and scope growth reserves
- Validate the schedule
- Schedule compression
- Budget compression
- Task and resource Gantt charts
- Scope change management
- Progress review and control
- Tracking team members' progress
- Project vital signs
- Project health report
- Look-ahead window
- Project fuel report
- Short- and long-term forecasts
- Earned value management system
- Analytical tools
- Reporting project progress
- Project status reports
- Dealing with deadlines
- Troubled project assessment
- Troubled project cancellation
- Stage gate review

This chapter covers the Execute stage of the PPA. Although this stage has only two steps, between 60 and 70 percent of the project team's time will be spent in this area because of the extent of the work to be accomplished: a project schedule is developed, the team begins to work to produce project deliverables, and the project manager oversees the team's progress to the planned end of the project. The chapter starts with the processes needed to develop a viable project schedule by loading the detailed estimates developed in the last chapter into a calendar that incorporates both the team and organization nonwork days. Schedule and budget compression, both inevitable realities of a project manager's life are discussed, as are the steps to manage any changes to the project scope. The chapter includes a detailed discussion on the process and steps used to monitor, manage, and control project progress. The use of vital signs as opposed to percent complete to monitor the team's progress and the use of the look-ahead window as a periscope to what lies ahead are discussed. We introduce the concept of the earned value management system, as well as a variety of analytical tools, as an addition to the project manager's toolbelt. The chapter includes an extremely important, but seldomly discussed, process of identifying and dealing with troubled projects and concludes with a few words for the wise project manager—a summary of action items that have served us well.

■ THE EXECUTE STAGE

Congratulations for arriving at the Execute stage in the project life cycle; it's time to engage. You will now schedule the project, the team will begin to execute the task plan, and you will begin to track their progress and do your best to deliver a successful project. Let us review the steps taken to arrive at this point in the project life cycle.

The foundation for effective tracking and control was built during the last three stages—Idea, Pre-Launch, and Launch. During the Idea and Pre-Launch stages (Chapters 3 and 4), you clearly defined the customer's needs, reviewed priorities and stakeholders, assessed the complexity of the project, identified and evaluated risks, made a preliminary determination of scope, and developed size estimates of effort, cost, and duration. You then documented your findings in a comprehensive Project Charter and obtained a go-ahead from your sponsor to move forward with the project.

During the Launch stage (Chapters 5 and 6), you drew up detailed plans for the project. Those plans included a WBS, which is a detailed list of the deliverables and tasks you believed the team must complete to deliver the project successfully. You arrayed those tasks in a network diagram to show the order in which they must be performed. You also planned how you would organize and staff the project and how you would communicate vital information to the various stakeholders. Finally, you prepared detailed estimates of the project effort, duration, and cost. You documented your work in a Project Notebook and presented a summary of your plans and estimates to your sponsor. The sponsor reviewed the team's work and opened stage gate no. 3, giving you a go-ahead to proceed to the Execute stage. Figure 7.1 depicts the steps that compose the Execute stage.

As you can see, the Execute stage consists of only two steps, but as we mentioned earlier, between 60 and 70 percent of the project team's time is spent in this stage because of the extent of the work to be accomplished. During the Execute stage, a project schedule is developed, the team begins to work to produce project deliverables, and the project manager oversees the team's progress to the planned end of the project.

FIGURE 7.1
The Execute Stage

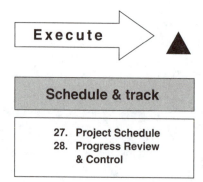

At this point, you are ready to schedule the project and have the team begin their task execution. Too often, project managers begin to schedule their projects long before the project plan and estimate have been approved. They do so, despite the obvious drawbacks, because scheduling is an action-oriented process and has more of a sense of finality than planning and estimating. Most of these schedules are based on wishful thinking rather than on well-thought-out plans, estimates, and team member availability. Invariably, the results are attractive schedules that please the sponsor, but the team eventually runs out of time and the inevitable "behind schedule" monster raises its ugly head.

More software projects have gone awry for lack of calendar time than for all other causes combined.

Brooks, 1995, p. 14.

Ironically, of the four intra-project priorities—schedule, scope, budget, and quality—schedule is the one to which most customers pay attention. The main reason for customer interest is that, of the four, it is the most measurable attribute. Therefore, our advice to project managers is to be very careful when developing a schedule because once it is announced, customers will hold you to it, regardless of how unrealistic it turns out to be. Schedule delays, in addition to breached expectations, inevitably drive up net project cost in one or more of the following ways:

- Delaying the realization of project benefits
- Driving up the labor content of the project
- Delaying the reassignment of key personnel to subsequent projects
- Disrupting the orderly management of any dependent projects
- Increasing exposure to unfavorable developments outside the project manager's control
- When time runs out, quality suffers!

■ PROJECT MANAGEMENT SOFTWARE

Before we delve into the discussion of the steps needed to develop a project schedule, we must visit the question of project management software. For any project that lasts more than a few weeks and uses more than a few team members, the use of a software tool can be of great help—not only in developing the initial schedule, but also in recording and tracking project progress. A software tool can also help minimize the time needed to change, update, and publish a new schedule as project parameters change. The myriad project management software packages available are quite similar in their final outputs, although they each have specific ways to input and display project data. We have opted not to engage in any tool-based discussion in this chapter because management of the tool's functionality can get in the way of the message. Also, most software tools remain in a high state of flux, and their functionality and interface protocol continues to change with successive releases, making many screen printouts obsolete. At this point, we will assume that you are adequately familiar with whichever project management software tool you plan to use and are able to understand any tool-related discussion in this chapter.

■ PROJECT SCHEDULE—PPA STEP 27

Scheduling is the process of assigning specific resources to tasks in relation to a specific calendar and consists of the following steps:

1. Schedule the work
2. Validate the schedule
3. Establish a baseline schedule and budget

Schedule the Work

To develop a schedule, plot the resource-based estimates (developed in the last chapter) on a calendar. The steps to create a viable schedule follow, along with brief discussions.

Define Cross-Project Dependencies   Before building the project schedule, you must have a clear understanding of the cross-project dependencies that exist for your project. Your team may be dependent on timely completion of certain deliverables by other project teams. Similarly, other teams may be dependent on completion of certain deliverables by your team. It is important to identify all such dependencies and incorporate the same into your project schedule. Figure 7.2 depicts a template to identify and document cross-project dependencies.

FIGURE 7.2

Cross-Project Dependencies

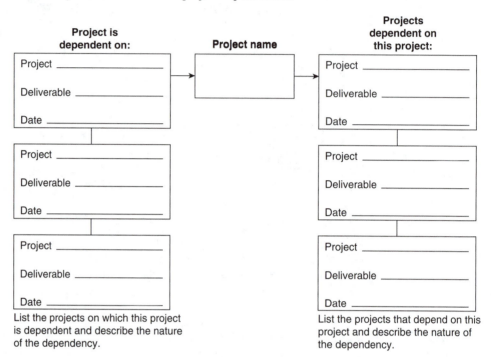

Figure 7.2 clearly shows that completing this step will require research. Start with the project impact information that has been gathered (as discussed in Chapter 3) and the cross-project dependencies that were identified (as discussed in Chapter 4). The next step is to consult with the project office (if one exists) to find out whether the organization has a centralized project portfolio database. If not, talk to other project managers and see what you can learn about other project activity (it may entail some footwork, but it is necessary). Once you have completed the information in Figure 7.2, you will need to work with the various project managers to coordinate and manage cross-project dependencies, as delays in their project schedules will impact your project's schedule.

Build Organization Calendar   This calendar defines the working and nonworking dates and times at the organization level. When setting up the organizational calendar for your project, be sure to indicate such information as: official holidays, weekends, preplanned business events, and default working hours. For a project that spans national boundaries, you will need to build customized calendars for each country, as the official holidays, weekends, and default working hours may differ. Make sure that the functional managers are integral parts of developing the organizational calendar to ensure that project work does not disrupt the key business cycles to the point of causing major financial risk to the organization. Pay attention to geography. Many project managers forget that when it's morning in California, it's night in India. Display a "project map" with team locations noted along with clocks showing the local times of your satellite locations. Consider posting pictures of your key offsite staff, with captions indicating appropriate title and responsibility, next to the project map. Just recently, a project manager at a client site in Chicago, with remote sites in multiple time zones, had four clocks on his office wall set to each time zone. Posted below each clock were the pictures of the satellite team members with their phone numbers. With all this at his fingertips, he was the admiral of his far-flung project fleet.

Specify Team Member Information   During the Launch stage, you designed a team structure, identified the team members, and defined their skill and competency profiles. Now you are ready to schedule their work assignments. At this point, it may be beneficial to see how well each team member performs to the success equation we introduced in Chapter 1. We suggest that you use the following six success factors to assess each individual team member's readiness to be a productive member of the team.

- *Process:* How well is the project management process defined and how well does the individual team member understand the process used to accomplish his assignments?

- *Skill:* What level of proficiency does the team member possess (as it relates to the complexity of the project and assigned deliverables and tasks)?

- *Techniques:* How proficient and effective is the individual in applying specific techniques (individual expressions of excellence) to accomplish high-quality results?

- *Tools:* Are the required tools stable, appropriate, and easy to access and use? What is the degree of proficiency of the team member in using the tools?

- *Accountability:* How well does the team member understand her responsibilities, and how committed is the individual to achieving the project objectives?

- *Discipline:* Can you and other team members count on this person to act in a professional manner without extensive oversight?

An example of a template used to analyze team member performance is shown in Figure 7.3.

FIGURE 7.3
Team Member Performance

Team member	Process	Skill	Technique	Tools	Accountability	Discipline
Bill	☑ High ☐ Medium ☐ Low	☐ High ☐ Medium ☑ Low	☐ High ☐ Medium ☑ Low	☑ High ☐ Medium ☐ Low	☐ High ☑ Medium ☐ Low	☐ High ☑ Medium ☐ Low
Joe	☑ High ☐ Medium ☐ Low	☑ High ☐ Medium ☐ Low	☑ High ☐ Medium ☐ Low	☑ High ☐ Medium ☐ Low	☐ High ☑ Medium ☐ Low	☐ High ☐ Medium ☑ Low
John	☐ High ☑ Medium ☐ Low	☐ High ☑ Medium ☐ Low	☐ High ☑ Medium ☐ Low	☐ High ☐ Medium ☑ Low	☑ High ☐ Medium ☐ Low	☑ High ☐ Medium ☐ Low

From the assessment in Figure 7.3, we can conclude:

- *Bill:* Skill/technique deficient; will benefit from training and mentoring

- *Joe:* Medium level of accountability and low level of discipline; these are behavior related issues and require a deeper look into the underlying reasons before a solution can be developed

- *John:* Poor tool quality; if this begins to impact John's performance, look into providing expert level help and/or alternate tools

This type of analysis provides the project manager with valuable insight into the underlying causes of any performance issues. The project manager can then use this information to develop individual action plans to alleviate any problems. All such assessments must be done in a confidential and professional manner and must be based on firsthand knowledge of the performance issues rather than hearsay or cursory views. The optimum time to use this tool is in advance of developing the project schedule. Early assessment can help pinpoint any problems that, if left unattended, can result in unviable schedules. Many project managers use this assessment tool on a quarterly basis as part of their ongoing team quality management program.

If you are using a project management software package, you can specify the name and billing (labor) rate of each of the project team members. Two important points to keep in mind are:

1. Whenever a team member is assigned to more than one project, it is important that the person's name be spelled exactly the same for each project. If this precaution is not taken, when the resources from different projects are rolled up into one report, the individual will appear as two different people. We see this problem all the time; individual names are spelled differently by

different project managers, and when someone tries to roll up the information from various projects, the total number of resources adds up to more than the true number of people employed by the department.

2. Make sure that the actual skill profiles of team members entered in the system match the EVF assumed while computing resource estimates (in Chapter 6). Remember, a team member's EVF is a function of four specific attributes: skill factor, work interruption factor, multiple project factor, and project productivity influencing factor. If any of these factors vary by more than 10 percent, you should recompute the estimates for the tasks to be assigned to that particular team member. In fact, this type of rework will be necessary whenever the underlying assumptions used to develop any estimates change.

Before you begin to develop the project schedule, you must account for the time the team may need to move through the four steps to high efficiency: forming, storming, norming, and performing (as discussed in Chapter 5). Keep in mind that during the first few weeks of the project, a team's productivity level may not be as high as you assumed when developing estimates. Because the time from forming to performing depends on the team's skills, the perceived value of the project, the work environment, and the leadership of the sponsor and the project manager, you may need to adjust the schedule to account for the maturing process. You have a few options:

1. Account for the need for extra time while you develop your schedule. One way to do this is to use a lower value for the default working hours (in the software package). The moment you do this, the length of the schedule will increase, and you will likely experience some pushback. Be sure to change (increase) the default working hours once the team is performing at a higher level of efficiency.

2. Require the team to work overtime to compensate for their inefficiency. Unfortunately, this approach rarely helps, as the team may stay stuck in the storming stage as a protest to the mandated overtime.

3. Use your leadership skills to move the team to full proficiency quickly.

Specify Team Member Calendars   The calendar for individual team members mimics the same format and structure as the organizational calendar. It is modified for each team member to account for such nonwork periods as vacations, sick leave, off-site training, travel, and their working hours per day. Most software packages use 8–12 and 1–5 as the default; you may need to adjust the default time for different team members. Although the organization's calendar stays fairly stable throughout the year, individual calendars for IT/Business professionals are seldom stable for more than 3 months at a time. This assumption is especially true for people who are assigned less than full-time to the project. Therefore, it is important that both the individual team members and the project manager keep a close eye on these calendars.

Build a Task List   At this point, you need to enter the detailed task list (phases, deliverables, and tasks) and their dependencies (predecessor and successor relationships) into the software. Remember that the task network developed using the sticky notes to plan the project in Chapter 5 (see *Task Network*) is the source of the dependencies for various tasks. Entering task dependency relationships into software can be time consuming and tedious work because the project often entails a long list of tasks. Most project management software typically employs more than one method to specify task dependency relationships. Because this step is quite prone to error, make sure that you understand the intricacies of the different methods and use them correctly. Asking someone to verify the assigned dependencies is important because any errors in the dependency relationship will produce an erroneous schedule.

To compensate for the less than useful pert/network diagrams developed by most project management software, we recommend that you retain the sticky note version of the plan for the duration of the project (you may need to tape the various notes with clear adhesive tape to hold them in place). The sticky note plan is very useful for the following reasons:

1. The project team was actively involved in creating the plan; they now own it, and can revisit the plan anytime as the work on the project progresses.

2. As a team member completes a task (and the team agrees that it's done), place a colored dot on the task, usually green, indicating its completion. This visual cue enables the team, executives, and any visitors to watch the project team move forward through the project. A certain pride shows among team members when they walk up to the sticky note plan and affix their own dots.

Having the sticky note version of the network, along with the colored dots, is a great tool for identifying which tasks must be revisited if the team discovers new tasks later in the project. Newly discovered tasks that fall in the midst of already completed tasks act as a signal for the team to determine whether the new tasks will impact any of the already completed work. In addition, when change requests are being analyzed for approval, having the sticky note plan provides the team with timely information regarding the amount of rework needed to accommodate the change. You can readily show the customer why certain "small" changes will require proportionately extensive effort.

Specify Task Assignments, Effort, and Duration   This step involves assigning individual team members to the various tasks in the project plan as well as specifying the effort and duration of each task (these are the estimates you developed earlier). Any given software package may offer more than one method of entering the task effort and duration information. Make sure that everyone on the team understands the various methods and their implications and uses them correctly.

Specify Lags   When tasks are entered into software, the *default* dependency between any two tasks is finish-to-start with no lag. We discussed the concept of dependencies and lags in Chapters 2 and 6. Specifying a lag involves entering a specific dependency relationship as well as the duration of the lag. Some examples of lags are:

- Consider two consecutive tasks: 1) order workstations and 2) install workstations. Typically, a certain amount of lag exists between the task of ordering and the task of installing—the wait time for the hardware to arrive. Let's assume 5 days. This wait time will typically be added as a finish-to-start dependency with a lag value of 5 days.
- Consider a situation where a specific team member is needed to complete certain work—Internet security testing. The project manager discovers that the software development group will be finished by March 15, but the individual needed to conduct security testing will not be available for 7 more days (after March 15). This delay in availability needs to be entered as a lag.

In most software, the two methods to enter lag are:

1. Position the cursor on a given task, activate the *Task Dependency* feature, select the appropriate dependency from the list of possible dependencies, and specify the lag value.
2. The second method involves specifying the lag within the WBS of the project (the lag is specified as a "dummy task" with duration, but with no effort. This method actually adds a new item to the task list, which is physically visible as a task on the screen and any printouts.

The perennial question is, "Which is preferred?" and the answer is, "It depends on who you talk to." We find that most theorists prefer the first method because it does not create a new "dummy" item in the WBS. We prefer the second method because it very clearly shows the lag amount. Our advice to project managers is to be consistent rather than switching between these two approaches—especially not within the same project.

Specify Floating Risk Contingencies   In Chapter 5, we discussed two types of risks: time dependent and floating. At this point, one would assume that any time-dependent risks have been accounted for in the schedule already built. Now we need to attend to any floating risks and related contingency plans, estimates, and schedules. Because it is not known when a floating risk may actually materialize, the best approach is to add each risk's task schedule at the end of the task list built in the previous steps. Using this approach, each floating risk is accounted for. Then, if and when any of these risks materializes, you will need to move the set of deliverables and tasks to the appropriate point in the project schedule. Many project managers shy away from including the floating risks in the project schedule because it extends the end date of the project. To us, overcoming such reluctance is a problem of communications and expectations management and needs to be addressed accordingly.

Keep in mind that, during the Execute stage, if a known risk does not materialize (its trigger date has passed) you will need to *remove* the deliverables and tasks associated with the risk from the project schedule and inform the respective stakeholders of the good news. Similarly, if a given floating risk became a nonitem (its window has passed), you would *delete* the associated deliverables and tasks from the end of the project schedule.

Risk management is an ongoing process, so *new* risks need to be monitored, assessed, and managed throughout the project life cycle. As any new risks materialize, they will have an impact on the currently baselined budget and schedule. Therefore, at some point, the sponsor and key stakeholders may need to assess the viability of the project. It is always a good idea to assign the responsibility for risk monitoring to a senior team member and have that person take special note of any emerging risks, especially when the team discusses the look-ahead window during team update meetings (discussed later).

As the project execution work continues and as risks materialize, the risk reserve will continue to diminish. Keep track of the reserve because once it is depleted, any additional risks will breach the currently baselined budget and/or schedule. When that happens, you will need to have the sponsor approve additional budget and/or schedule unless you can address the problem through schedule compression.

Specify Reserves   Remember in Chapters 4 and 6 we discussed the different types of reserves: rework reserve, scope growth reserve, and error range. Even though these reserves are computed during the estimating process, project managers often overlook the steps to incorporate them into the project's schedule. One of the main reasons for the oversight is that, to our knowledge, none of the software packages have built-in functionality to enter these reserves. Therefore, you will need to jerry-rig the software to accommodate any such reserves. We typically add each of these reserves as a "deliverable" at the very end of the task list for the project and assign an estimated duration (equal to the estimated reserve) to each of these deliverables. The final reserve deals with the *error range* value for the schedule. We suggest a range equal to 10 percent of the critical path duration (we talked about this reserve in Chapters 4 and 6).

When you incorporate these three reserves into your schedule for the first time, practically everyone you talk to will question your decision because the resulting finish date of the project may be far beyond what they would like, or expected, it to be. To most people, the very concept of these reserves goes against all they have come to believe about scheduling, especially those who believe that any estimates and schedules submitted by the project manager should be cut at least in half. Many will accuse you of padding your schedule, being too risk averse, and only thinking of what can go wrong. Our response to these pronouncements is to first make sure that the reserves you use are realistic and are based on well-documented complexity and risk assessment. With that in mind, you need to focus on explaining to them the rationale for your conclusions with all the calm you can muster.

Build Project Schedule   You have now entered the basic information needed for the project management software to build the project schedule. You can initiate the schedule build in two different ways:

Specify Project Start Date: At this point, you specify the planned start date of your project. It is extremely important to make sure that the planned start date of the project is realistic, i.e., the appropriate resources *will* start work on their assigned tasks. At times, we have seen project managers specify start dates with only the hope that the team members will be ready to start their work. This supposition will invariably result in erroneous schedules, and the project delivery date will be compromised. Once you have entered the project start date, the system will compute the critical path of your project and show you the scheduled finish date.

Specify Project End Date: Most project management software packages have a feature that allows you to specify the desired finish date of the project after loading the detailed task list, dependencies, and estimated durations. At this point, the system performs backward scheduling and computes the *start date* of the project; this is often referred to as backward scheduling. If the computed start date is in the future, it marks the latest date you must start the project in order to finish it by the desired end date. If the computed date is in the past, the project is already behind schedule. The variance between the software computed start date and your planned start date is the number of days you will need to compress in order to finish the project by the desired end date.

Once the system has constructed the project schedule, you may notice that the computed project duration is longer than the estimated duration developed in Chapter 6. The reason for the difference may be that, while building the schedule, you specified a considerable number of nonwork days (weekends, holidays, vacations, travel, and training).

Must-Do Dates   Any project, in addition to the client-specified project delivery date, is likely to include a number of important interim "must do" dates. For example:

• Ordering equipment
• Approval of vendor contracts
• Renewal of real estate rental/lease contracts
• Regulatory requirements
• Corporate policy requirements
• Specific customer training dates due to their availability

A frequently asked question at this point in schedule development is, "Should one specify the must-do dates before building the schedule (the step above) or after?" Many project managers prefer to specify the must-do dates, for example, no earlier than, no later than, and on a specific date, *prior* to building the schedule with their software. Most software packages do not have sufficiently "smart" logic to deal with the complex constraints set by the must-do dates and, as a consequence, results can vary from strange to mind boggling. Our preference is to first build the schedule, and then verify the respective must-do dates and see if there are any breaches (delays). If so, you will need to delve into the steps for critical path compression to adjust the project schedule to match the must-do dates. Any dates that cannot be matched represent a risk to the project; you will need to put your risk management process into action.

Validate the Schedule

An important point to keep in mind is the need to review the results from step 10 of the PPA (*Stability Assessment*, Chapter 4) before finalizing the project schedule. Remember that, during the Stability Assessment step, you looked into the future of the project and forecasted the events that might have significant impact on the project. You and the team must review the findings and adjust the project schedule accordingly. The next step is to make sure that the schedule is viable. To this end, we suggest the following checklist:

The resource assignments are realistic and dependable.
The organization and team member calendars are current and accurate.
Task dependencies are accurately recorded.
All of the lag values are properly defined.
Cross-project dependencies are accounted for.
Appropriate reserves and risk contingencies are accounted for.
Must-do dates are verified.

For a project that has a "must not miss" deadline, always plan to finish the project at least *2 full weeks* prior to the deadline. The reasons for this precaution are:

1. If your project is delayed somewhat, you still have the planned cushion (approximately 2 weeks) to cover the delay.
2. Any IT/Business project often requires a certain amount of last-minute fine-tuning in the human-to-computer interfaces; the early finish gives you the time needed to smooth out any of these problems.
3. Customers are known to either miss the planned training or to pay minimal attention during a training session. They often need last-minute instruction.

Business Cycles: Conflict Assessment

Now that you have a schedule for the project, it is time to review the information you collected regarding key business cycles (see *Business Cycles* in Chapter 4). It is important to make sure that the demands on the business units (ranging from business people needed for requirements definitions, prototype assessment, testing, and final project implementation) do not adversely impact key business cycles. If there are periods of time in the planned project schedule that do interfere with key business cycles, you will need to work closely with business stakeholders, business unit functional managers, and key end-users to minimize the adverse impact on the business and to the project. Any important business cycles that cannot be circumvented become risk events and must be managed as such through disciplined risk assessment and mitigation.

Window of Opportunity Assessment

At this point, it is important to look back (see *Window of Opportunity* in Chapter 3) and see whether there is a specific window for the project and is it still viable. If you find the project completion date past the window of opportunity, work diligently to compress the project schedule (as described) and see if the compressed schedule meets project needs. If the schedule is still a problem, you need to have a group meeting with the sponsor and key stakeholders to assess your alternatives.

Schedule Compression

If, at this point, you find the project finish date exceeds the customer specified date, you will have to either compress the appropriate components or negotiate a later delivery date. We discussed the subject of project duration compression in Chapter 6. As a refresher, review the summary of the necessary steps:

1. Reduce scope
2. Split/overlap tasks
3. Validate task dependencies
4. Aggressively manage lag
5. Improve team skills
6. Use overtime
7. Add team members
8. Improve the work environment
9. Transfer risk responsibility

For a detailed discussion of these items, see *Compress the Critical Path* and *Steps to Reduce Estimates* in Chapter 6. Let's discuss two additional approaches to reduce project schedule:

Crashing   Crashing is the process of analyzing schedule and cost tradeoffs with the objective of achieving the greatest amount of schedule reduction for the least amount of incremental cost. Crashing the schedule typically involves applying additional resources to selected tasks on the critical path. Consider a situation where a task is scheduled to be completed in 8 days using one team member. A closer look at the task shows that it could be broken into two independent subtasks and two people could now finish it in 4 days. This approach is unlikely to increase cost because twice as many resources are being applied for half the time. This scenario would be considered a "good" crash. However, if the two people need 5 days each, due to cross task coordination, then the schedule reduction has been achieved at an *incremental* cost of 2 workdays (a total of 10 days *v.* the original 8 days). Keep in mind that, unlike construction engineering (labor-based) work, adding more people to knowledge-based work rarely produces a proportionate reduction in the elapsed time needed to finish the work. For example, in the case of plumbing, wall papering, laying of carpet, and painting walls, adding more resources will reduce the time needed to finish the work. However, the task of writing a report that is expected to take 35 hours over 5 days of one person's time will be very difficult to finish in 1 day, even if five people are assigned to it. Three reasons for this difficulty are:

- It will take time to parse the report into five separate independent components and then assign each to the right person.
- The five people will need to communicate and coordinate with each other a number of times regarding the knowledge that is not expressly documented—most of it resides in the brain of the primary person.
- It will take time to assemble the five different report components developed by the five team members, check for duplications and gaps, and make sure that the different styles of writing (vocabulary, terminology, and punctuation) do not clash with each other and are cohesive.

Providing the primary person with an assistant who could take over some of the responsibilities for research and coordination will help to reduce the effort and duration necessary to complete the deliverable.

Another example of schedule crashing is when a contractor requires a certain amount of lead time for delivery of hardware or equipment, and this lead time is on the project's critical path. In some instances, if the contractor were given a financial incentive for early delivery, the materials could be delivered earlier. The simplest example is that of 1-day laundry service or the classic 1-hour film processing. In both cases, you get the work done faster by paying extra for the deliverable. Crashing becomes important when the project's intra-project priorities place the schedule as the number one priority, and the actual project schedule computes to a date past the customer's desired delivery date.

Fast Tracking   Fast tracking offers another way to reduce the project's critical path. In this approach, certain tasks on the critical path that are shown as linear (FS) are started partially or totally in parallel; they are assigned an SS dependency or a lead time (as discussed in Chapter 2); for example, starting the product design before requirements are complete or starting the product build before its design is complete. The fundamental belief behind fast tracking is that a sufficient amount of work has been completed on the precedent task or tasks, and a very low probability of anything unexpected happening exists. Although fast tracking can reduce the project schedule, we know of countless examples where the assumptions made while completing the fast track work did not hold true and the team had to scrap what they had built. This misfire happens often in the construction of factories and processing plants. Due to fast tracking, the actual build of machinery starts long before the structure to house the equipment has been fully designed and built. Not surprisingly, Murphy wakes up, and the machinery is either too large to fit in the building or too heavy for the foundation. As a result the project experiences massive delays as the structures are dismantled, redesigned, and rebuilt. The cost goes through the roof. Another common example of fast tracking occurs in manufacturing where the shipping and display boxes are designed and produced in parallel with the design and build of the product itself. Often, during the product design and build, changes occur that make the boxes useless (the product becomes too large or too heavy for the box). With this in mind, fast tracking needs to be managed through tightly coupled communications between the two groups, and they need to inform each other of any changes in the underlying assumptions in real time.

A final note regarding schedule compression: with any options you use, make sure that your actions focus on deliverables and tasks that lie on the critical path of the project. Reducing duration of tasks on any path shorter than the critical path will not result in schedule compression.

Budget Compression

A project's budget is a function of its scope, effort hours spent by the team, their billing rates, cost of materials, infrastructure, and certain other support functions. The best approach to reduce the budget is to parse the various cost categories to determine which ones are open to cost reduction. For example:

- Reduce scope. Review the deliverables and tasks yet to be completed and (working with the appropriate customer representative(s)) determine which deliverables and tasks could be eliminated and/or cut in size without adversely impacting the project's critical success factors.

- Improve team efficiency by reducing work interruptions, reducing the number of concurrent project assignments, and improving the team's work environment.
- Try the resource leveling process—have fewer team members complete the work by taking advantage of available slack. Keep in mind that the resource leveling process may actually extend the project schedule.
- Review the billing rate of various resources and see which rates could be negotiated down and/or replaced by resources who have lower billing rates without adversely impacting the project's critical success factors.
- Review the goods and services acquisition plan and see which goods and services could be acquired at a lower rate and/or eliminated altogether.
- Request that the team members work unpaid overtime hours (we do not recommend this as a primary budget reduction mechanism).

Some of the items can have certain drawbacks. For example, reducing scope beyond a certain point may make the end product less useful. Lower paid employees typically have fewer skills that may negatively impact both the schedule and the product quality. Similarly, lower cost goods may be of lesser quality. The use of unpaid overtime means a hit on the team's disposition. Therefore, you must evaluate both the pluses and minuses of your cost reduction plan. Then the skill lies in obtaining the maximum benefit with minimum negative impact.

Establish Baseline Schedule and Budget

Baseline schedule and budget are defined as the *first* sponsor-approved schedule and budget of the project. As the project progresses, the actual project performance will be continually compared to these two baseline values. In the case of significant overruns, the sponsor will need to decide on the fate of the project. If, at any given point during the execute stage, the projected finish date and/or the projected final costs exceed the baselined values, the sponsor may agree to extend the breached schedule and/or budget. In such cases, you will *rebaseline* the appropriate item, which will establish a new end date and/or budget for the project. In cases where the sponsor is unwilling to extend the breached baseline, you have two options:

1. Look at the steps to compress the schedule and/or the budget and see if you can bring the project within the baselined values.
2. See whether the project is a candidate for cancellation (refer to *Dealing With Troubled Projects* later in this chapter).

Baseline Version Control System

As previously discussed, during the execution of the project, it may become necessary to renegotiate the baselined schedule and/or budget. Therefore, it is a good idea to create a version control system. This system must not only track the baseline versions that have been set, but also must establish the number of baseline versions that will trigger a full review of the project. In our experience, a project that has had the baseline reset more than three times could, in reality, be a runaway project. Runaway projects are not likely to produce the expected ROI and therefore must be reviewed prior to further investment. In light of this discussion, we suggest the following steps:

1. Discuss the concept of baseline and rebaseline with your sponsor, and define the point at which the schedule and/or budget will be rebaselined. This will help avoid setting new baselines due to minor fluctuations.
2. Have the sponsor define the baseline version that will trigger a "runaway project" condition and require an in-depth assessment of the project's viability.

Having this discussion and defining the trigger points will alleviate constant worry about schedule and/or budget fluctuations and will define specific points of Go/No Go decisions.

At this point, the project is scheduled and the team is in place and eager to proceed. You must communicate the work assignments to individual team members so they can then begin the work to accomplish their assignments. When using a software package, two reports that will easily help accomplish this are a task Gantt chart and a resource Gantt chart.

Task Gantt Chart   A task Gantt, a time-scaled bar chart, is used to show the chronological flow of the project by showing individual tasks with their start and finish dates. Figure 7.4 is an example of a task Gantt. It shows seven different tasks that have been assigned to four different team members.

Resource Gantt Chart   A resource Gantt is designed to depict the various tasks assigned to a given resource (team member). Figure 7.5 depicts a resource Gantt for Nancy, one of four team members.

FIGURE 7.4
Task Gantt Example

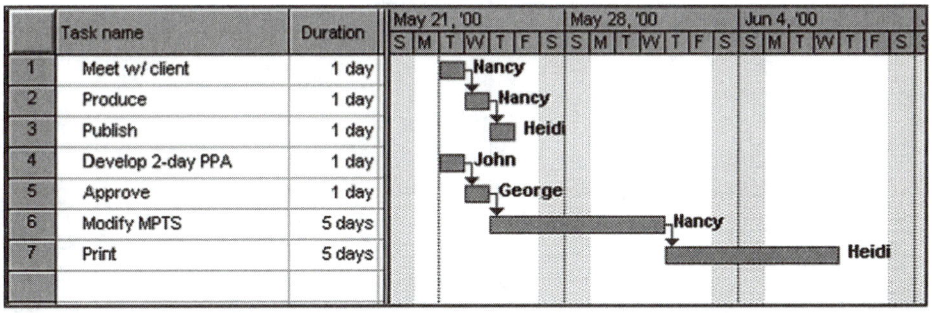

FIGURE 7.5
Resource Gantt Example

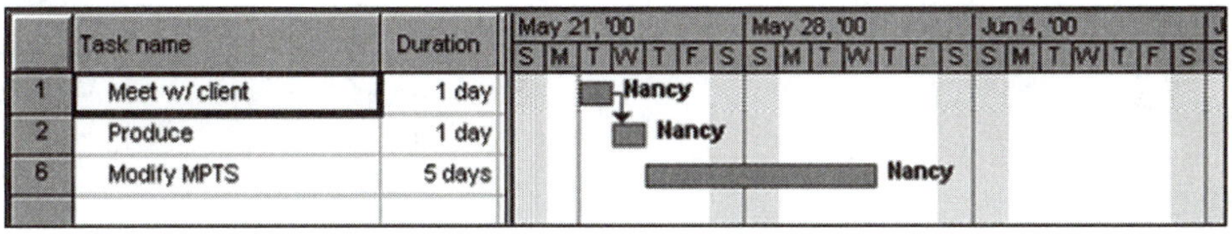

Figures 7.4 and 7.5 show that the task Gantt chart is a good tool to use to look at the overall picture of the project, while the resource Gantt chart helps the project manager and team members focus on individual work assignments. Once you have entered the task information in your project management software (to build a project schedule), you can easily produce the two types of Gantt charts shown.

Most project managers, as they gain experience, develop a set of favorite reports to help them manage their projects. We predict that you will also. We have found the following three reports very helpful:

1. List of deliverables
2. List of deliverable owners
3. List of milestones

List of Deliverables

This list contains the various project deliverables, sorted in alphabetic order, as depicted in Figure 7.6. This report is designed to provide the project manager with a list of deliverables, along with their current status. In this report, if a given deliverable did not start on its planned date, and this delay has an impact on the project's critical path, the information will be so noted in the second column from the right, titled *Impact of variance*. This information provides the project manager and the deliverable owner with an early warning of the impact of the late start and gives them sufficient time to take the necessary steps to make up for the delayed start.

Similarly, in Figure 7.7, if the actual finish date of a deliverable is beyond the planned finish date, and the delay has an impact on the project's critical path, the project manager will need to analyze the net impact of this delay and devise plans to recover the lost time. If a deliverable finishes earlier than its planned finish date, the project has developed a reserve that can be used either for any future delays or for early completion of the project.

FIGURE 7.6
List of Deliverables:
Focus on Delayed Start

Deliverable	Owner	Start date		Variance	Impact of variance	Action required
		Planned	Actual			
					❑ Schedule ❑ Scope ❑ Budget ❑ Quality	
					❑ Schedule ❑ Scope ❑ Budget ❑ Quality	
					❑ Schedule ❑ Scope ❑ Budget ❑ Quality	
					❑ Schedule ❑ Scope ❑ Budget ❑ Quality	
					❑ Schedule ❑ Scope ❑ Budget ❑ Quality	

FIGURE 7.7
List of Deliverables:
Focus on Delayed Finish

Deliverable	Owner	Finish date		Variance	Impact of variance	Action required
		Planned	Actual			
					❑ Schedule ❑ Scope ❑ Budget ❑ Quality	
					❑ Schedule ❑ Scope ❑ Budget ❑ Quality	
					❑ Schedule ❑ Scope ❑ Budget ❑ Quality	
					❑ Schedule ❑ Scope ❑ Budget ❑ Quality	
					❑ Schedule ❑ Scope ❑ Budget ❑ Quality	

FIGURE 7.8
List of Deliverable Owners

Owner	Deliverables	Planned start date	Actual start date	Critical path variance	Planned finish date	Actual start date	Critical path variance

An alternative approach is to combine the two reports into a single report for a more comprehensive look at deliverables.

List of Deliverable Owners

Another one of our favorite reports is a list of alphabetically sorted team members that depicts their respective deliverables, as shown in Figure 7.8. This report helps the project manager see the net assignment for each team member and the status of their deliverables.

List of Milestones

Figure 7.9 depicts a report that lists the various milestones and their status. In this report, milestones are listed in date order—from start to finish of the project. This report helps the project manager track the status of the various milestones and provides a quick view of their performance history.

Scope Change Management

Yes, the bane of all project managers! We hope that you have taken off your Velcro suit (we talked about this in Chapter 5) and made sure that none of the other team members have put it on. In Chapter 5, we discussed the process to manage scope (see *Scope Management Process* and *Change Control Board*) and in Chapter 6 we discussed the process to estimate and specify effort and time for possible scope growth as the team proceeds through the Execute stage (see *Scope Growth Reserve*). Make sure that you have activated the change control board and reminded them of the importance of managing scope changes with discipline and a professional approach. They should clearly understand that if the scope changes end up exhausting the scope growth reserve, the project budget and/or schedule will be breached and the sponsor will have to agree to additional budget and/or time (a delay in the project completion).

All through the Execute stage, whenever a change is requested, make sure that the requesting individual completes the change request template (Figure 5.17) and then ensure that the request goes through the steps outlined in the scope management process. For each change that is approved, you should keep a specific record of the impact of the change on the reserves. This discipline will help you monitor the status of the reserves and will help provide an early warning on

Milestone	Owner	Date		Variance	Impact on the critical path	Action required
		Planned	**Actual**			

FIGURE 7.9
List of Milestones

excessive depletions. We suggest that you create a spreadsheet-based form to keep track of change requests. Here is a suggested structure:

- Change ID
- Requestor's name
- Request date
- Brief description
- Approval date
- Change impact
  - Effort hours (the actual hours it took the team to implement the change)
  - Cost (the net cost of implementing the change)
  - Duration (days) (the period of time it took to implement the change)
- Critical path impact
  - No
  - Yes (If so, specify the number of days the critical path was impacted. Not every change will impact the critical path. At other times, only a portion of the time taken to make the change will impact the critical path.)
- Scope reserve status (net amounts)
  - Effort hours (the number of available reserve hours, computed by subtracting the actual effort hours required to make each change from the current scope reserve)
  - Budget (the available reserve budget, computed by subtracting the actual dollars required to make each change from the current scope reserve)
- Status indicator
  - Effort hours (green, yellow, or red)
  - Budget (green, yellow, or red)

The status indicator is similar to the fuel gauge in an automobile and is designed to warn the project manager of the "low reserve" conditions. Typically, this indicator turns to yellow status when 70 percent of the reserve has been consumed and remains yellow until 90 percent is depleted; at that time, the indicator turns red.

If you decide to use this type of scope management report, we advise that you take a copy of the report to progress review meetings with the team, functional managers, and the sponsor. Having quick access to the data in this report will help you manage expectations and project scope in a professional and disciplined manner.

An important point to keep in mind is that if at any given time the scope reserves are depleted, any additional changes will breach the currently baselined project budget and/or schedule. At that time, you must have the sponsor approve additional budget and/or schedule unless you can address the problem with schedule compression techniques.

Project Scope Management: Summary

Project scope is defined as the total sum of deliverables and features (the total functionality) delivered to the project customer at the completion of the proposed project. Consequently, it must be managed diligently. We have already discussed the subject in detail in this and previous chapters, so we will just summarize the key components of the scope management process. It consists of the following key steps:

1. *Scope initiation:* The point at which the project is originally proposed (the Idea stage). The customer envisions a need and it is formulated in terms of who will use it, strategy alignment, and value-to-business.
2. *Scope planning:* One of key activities in the Pre-Launch stage of the project. At this point, the preliminary project scope is defined and approved by key customers and the project sponsor. Approval of the Project Charter results in the first baselined scope statement.
3. *Scope definition:* In the Launch stage, the project manager, core team members, and key customer representatives work together to create a comprehensive WBS (the deliverables and tasks) which is needed to create the scope defined in the Project Charter.
4. *Scope verification:* This involves the formal review and acceptance of the project scope by the sponsor and the key customers. The first verification should take place when the WBS for the project has been completed (Task Plan, step 18 of the PPA), the next verification needs to be done as a part of Project Charter Review & Budget Approval (Step 26 of the PPA), and then verification continues throughout the Execute stage as various deliverables are completed. The final scope verification needs to take place in the Implement stage after the project has been deployed.
5. *Scope change control:* A well defined scope change management plan is put into action at the start of the Execute stage to ensure that scope creep problems don't waylay the project team.

A point of caution: It is important to formally close the scope change process once the project enters the testing phase of your system/product development life cycle. This is also known as freezing the requirements. The reason for doing so is that any changes to the requirements this late in the life cycle are sure to result in poor quality of the end product. The policy of freezing requirements at the start of the testing phase should be clearly and broadly communicated to the customer group very early in the project.

■ PROGRESS REVIEW AND CONTROL—PPA STEP 28

We have lift off! At this point, the team has started to execute their assigned tasks, and they can begin to record and report the actual effort (hours) spent on tasks assigned to them, along with the status of their milestones and deliverables. The project manager's responsibility is to analyze whether the project is on track and, if not, where and why it has gone off track. You do this by comparing the baselines to the actuals that you record as the project progresses. The difference between the *planned* and *actual* values is the *variance*. Use of project management software can simplify the detection of variances. It automatically calculates the variances between the team members' actual performance and the baseline data. It will tell you, for instance, if a particular task is exceeding the estimated effort, if a deliverable is likely to cost more than planned, or if the project completion itself is likely to be delayed beyond the currently baselined finish date.

Progress reviews are meaningful only if they are based on a sound and comprehensive project schedule that progress can be compared to. Therefore, schedules must be systematically reviewed and revised to ensure that they do not become obsolete and lose their credibility as a yardstick for measuring progress. Finally, the review process and the tools that support it should be straightforward and easy to use so that project status reports are consistently realistic, accurate, and timely. Before we take a look at the best practices for assessing project progress, we must proclaim nine important rules of scheduling:

1. Team members own their schedules and are responsible for them.
2. All problems and delays are reported to the project manager promptly and forthrightly. No surprises down the road!
3. Deliverable completions should be crisp and clean.
4. Revise schedules when necessary, but do so formally and distribute the results broadly.
5. Avoid lengthy recitations of past work.
6. Resolve issues promptly and publish their resolution.
7. Meet on a regularly scheduled basis.
8. Work hard to build and maintain a spirit of teamwork.
9. Deal privately with matters of unsatisfactory individual performance.

Project managers are responsible for knowing, at all times, where they are relative to where they are supposed to be. Their job is to use their wits, team, and tools to close the gap between where they are and where they are supposed to be, if necessary.

Tracking Team Members' Progress

Keeping tabs on the team members may turn out to be one of the more difficult parts of your project management experience. As we discussed in Chapter 1 (see *Accounting for Effort*), IT/Business professionals (especially business professionals) are not accustomed to recording their time on a day-to-day basis. Most people come to work, attend to their responsibilities, and leave when they believe they have accomplished most/all of what they are expected to do. Because many IT/Business people do more than one type of work during any period of time, they are not accustomed to recording specific information regarding the time spent on daily activities. Then they get assigned to a project that consists of a series of specific tasks, each has a specific amount of estimated effort and duration, and many of them have a specific finish date. The nature of determining the status of project progress requires that different team members report their effort, and more importantly their *progress*, to the project manager on a routine basis. Progress reporting is an example of a process *change* that is not always easy to institute among IT/Business team members. Additionally, the act of reporting one's time usage is a specific manifestation of a project manager's authority over team members. This requirement is somewhat in conflict with the fundamental structure of IT/Business project organization structures because few, if any, of the team members are under the authority of the project manager. The reality is that the project manager rarely has salary, hiring/firing, or career path promotion powers.

Another factor that contributes to the problem is that progress reporting by a team member typically involves three key components:

1. Estimated effort and time to complete the assignment
2. Actual effort and time spent on the assignment
3. Remaining effort and time to complete the assignment

The first and the third items in this list are based on the ability to accurately compute estimates. How many IT/Business team members do you know who have been educated and trained in estimating? We discussed the subject of task-based estimating in Chapter 6, and it will help your team provide you with more accurate information if you take the time to educate and train your team in this important skill.

The next important contributing factor is the nature of the project manager's reaction to the team member's status report. The test is how you react when a team member is forthright, but the news is not good. Obviously, flying off the handle is not the wise thing to do. It is important that the project manager deals with any nonperformance in a professional manner by focusing on the underlying reasons and staying away from the blame game. A simple, yet very useful, way to get status information from team members is to ask them to supply the following data for each of their tasks:

- Task name
- To date effort hours and time (days) spent on the task
- Status—complete or incomplete [if incomplete, estimated remaining effort hours and time (days) to complete the task]
- Any task-related issues

We believe that it is important for a project manager to work hard to ensure that team members are forthright, accurate, and timely in reporting the progress of their work. This consistency is necessary because the sum of the team members' status information is the backbone of all other project status reports.

Project Status

In order to accurately assess the status of a project, the project manager must focus on two important sets of information:

1. The current status (where are they now)
2. The future (a look ahead into the near future to see whether the team will be able to progress as currently planned)

Ironically, most teams and project managers spend relatively little time and effort on the two actions. Instead, they spend most of their status reporting time looking back and talking ad nauseam about the past—what they have been doing and what difficulties they encountered while doing it. The end result is a wealth of information about the past, but little information about the true status of the project. Worse yet, they leave most progress report meetings with an insufficient view of the future. Knowing *where you have been* is of interest only if you want to return to where you came from. Knowing where you are relative to where you are supposed to be is a tougher question to answer, but is essential when assessing how to proceed. Yet, progress reviews often focus on what people *have* been busy doing instead of focusing on where they are, and what *remains* to be done. Project managers *must* look ahead if they expect to avoid obstacles in their paths. Looking ahead is the essence of successful project progress assessment and control. We suggest a combination of two different methods: the first designed to assess the current state of a project and the second to look into the future and plan for it:

1. Project vital signs (Current status)
2. Look-ahead window (Forecast)

Project Vital Signs   Everybody reads vital signs—doctors, auto mechanics, and pilots. When a baby is born, the doctor monitors the infant's pulse, reflexes, temperature, and general disposition. During a medical examination, the physician checks the patient's vital signs—temperature, weight, blood pressure, and reflex. Auto mechanics monitor a car's performance during a service, and airline traffic managers study the airplane's takeoff and landing performance. Every industry has its methods of checks and balances to assure efficient performance and to secure the safety and health of its customers. Every industry, that is, except for IT. Ironically, the profession whose fundamental tenet is to produce precise information lacks the most basic information about its own projects. This observation is quite clear from the survey results depicted in Figure 1.6.

Often, by the time sponsors realize that their projects are in trouble, it is too late to take corrective actions. Project managers must monitor the vital signs of their projects, enabling prompt interventions and midcourse corrections. Project vital signs are aggregate indicators of the overall health of the project, very much like a hospital's nursing station monitors patients' heart and respiration

FIGURE 7.10
Project Vital Signs

Project vital signs
1. Strategy alignment
2. Sponsorship
3. Customer buy-in
4. Technology viability
5. Value-to-business
6. Vendor viability
7. Status of the critical path
8. Milestone hit rate
9. Deliverable hit rate
10. Unresolved issues
11. Cost-to-date
12. Actual resources v. planned resources
13. High probability, high impact risks
14. Overtime utilization
15. Team disposition (effectiveness)

rates. To aid project managers and sponsors in this arena, we recommend a 15-point plan for monitoring the vital signs of an IT/Business project. Our recommended list of vital signs is depicted in Figure 7.10.

The various vital signs listed in Figure 7.10 can be grouped into three key categories:

1. *Strategic:* vital signs 1–6. These vital signs focus on why we are doing the project and whether it is the right project. Abnormal variance in any of these vital signs should cause a serious reevaluation of the project.

2. *Tactical:* vital signs 7–13. These vital signs focus on how well we are accomplishing the goals of the project. Although abnormal variances in this area can also have a high degree of negative impact on the project, it is much easier to recover from the resulting problems.

3. *Environmental:* vital signs 14–15. These vital signs relate to the work environment. These factors are difficult to institute and measure because they relate to the management style of a particular organization, but they are nevertheless important to everyone involved.

In the same way that a physician monitors the vital signs of a patient, the vital signs just presented form a comprehensive method for monitoring, reporting, and taking timely actions to correct problems during an IT/Business project. Failure to do so will bring emergency teams in to perform crisis management on projects that may already be comatose. Based on the complexity of the project, the sponsor and the project manager develop a tailored list of appropriate vital signs and prescribe the acceptable thresholds (variances from the norm) for each selected vital sign. The project manager then monitors the selected vital signs, each of which can have the following status:

• Green—all is well
• Yellow—caution, trouble ahead
• Red—danger, measurable negative impact on the project

Green: For a given vital sign, a green flag means the variance between planned and actual, if any, is within an acceptable range. For example, in the case of the critical path, a variance (delay) of up to 10 percent may be defined as being normal and acceptable, as the team members have the ability to close the gap between planned and actual.

Yellow: For a given vital sign, a yellow flag indicates the point at which a breach in the performance of that vital sign will begin to negatively impact the project progress; it is usually beyond the team's own ability to recover from the problem. For example, in the case of the critical path of a project, a variance (delay) between 10 to 20 percent should be defined as a yellow condition. If a vital sign reaches this state, the project manager needs to meet with the appropriate team members, and at times with their functional managers, and put a plan into action to bring the vital sign back to the green status.

Red: For a given vital sign, a red flag indicates the point at which a breach in the performance of that vital sign is beyond the project manager's ability to recover from the problem and the project's success is in jeopardy. For example, in the case of the critical path, a variance (delay) of greater than 20 percent should be defined as a red condition. Once a given vital sign reaches the red condition, the project manager needs to meet with the functional managers of the appropriate team members and devise a plan of recovery.

In addition to monitoring the individual vital signs described, the project manager also needs to keep an eye on the collective impact of the various vital signs selected for a given project. We will discuss this topic later in this chapter, under the heading *Project Health Report*. The following is a detailed discussion regarding each of the vital signs listed in Figure 7.10.

Strategy Alignment: Determine whether the project continues to fit with the currently stated organizational strategy. At times, a project begins with a good strategic fit, but due to changes in overall strategy, the project may no longer be a compelling investment. For example, at the time of project approval, the strategy was growth and market share, but due to changes in the economy and the organization's direction, the new strategy is cost savings, profit, and efficiency. If the project at hand deals primarily with increasing the organization's market share without much (or any) focus on cost savings, profit, and efficiency, the sponsor must take a serious look at the project and decide whether it should be allowed to continue. It is important that the project manager and the sponsor *specifically* discuss the subject of their project's alignment with the current organizational strategy during their monthly project update meeting. The status of this vital sign can be interpreted as follows:

Fully aligned:	Green
Somewhat aligned:	Yellow
No alignment:	Red

Sponsorship: A sponsor's performance is not only one of the most important vital signs to monitor, but it is probably the most difficult. It is important because without a committed sponsor who meets her responsibilities and time commitments, any project is doomed to failure. It is difficult because in the case of sponsor nonperformance, the project manager is unlikely to feel confident enough to inform the sponsor about his shortcomings. Only a project manager who has great fortitude would take on such responsibility. Therefore, the responsibility for monitoring this vital sign rests squarely on the shoulders of the sponsor. In Figure 4.44, we defined the sponsor's time per month to fulfill her sponsorship duties. About half of this time is dedicated to one-on-one meetings with the project manager (and occasionally the project team) and the rest of the time is required to fulfill the various sponsorship responsibilities. The following questions are designed to help sponsors assess their personal commitment to their projects:

1. Is the sponsor aware of her specific responsibilities? Has the sponsor discussed these with the project manager?
2. Has the sponsor set aside the appropriate time needed to be a committed sponsor?
3. Does the project manager have quick and easy access to the sponsor for resolution of important issues?
4. Does the sponsor routinely meet with the project manager to assess the status of various vital signs and project progress?

As mentioned, this vital sign is difficult to assess because it involves the sponsor, and most project managers are reluctant to follow through with an assessment for obvious reasons. However, a positive trend seems to be emerging where more sponsors are beginning to see the impact of their supportive behavior and have implemented the assessment of this important vital sign. Figure 7.11 depicts a sponsor performance checklist used by one of the Center's client organizations to assess this vital sign. If you decide to use this list, discuss the subject first with your functional manager and then with the sponsor. If the sponsor is agreeable to its use, review the sponsor's roles and responsibilities list in Chapter 5 and then, working with the sponsor, develop a customized list for your project. In addition, discuss with the sponsor the process to be used to assess sponsor's performance

FIGURE 7.11
Sponsor Performance
Checklist

Sponsor performance checklist		Rating			
Rating: 1 = Rarely 2 = Sometimes 3 = Most of the time		4 = Always			
1.	Champions the project.	1	2	3	4
2.	Timely approval of the project charter, plan, schedule and budget.	1	2	3	4
3.	Ensures sustained buy-in at key stakeholder level.	1	2	3	4
4.	Champions the project and the project team.	1	2	3	4
5.	Helps ensure timely availability of human resources when needed.	1	2	3	4
6.	Helps resolve major policy and/or political issues.	1	2	3	4
7.	Formally manages (oversees) the project scope.	1	2	3	4
8.	Values the stage gate review process.	1	2	3	4
9.	Remains informed about the status of the project.	1	2	3	4
10.	Provides regular feedback to the project manager and team on performance.	1	2	3	4

and the implications of recording negative news—nonperformance on the part of the sponsor. When completing the data in Figure 7.11, make sure that the person providing the information does not use it as an opportunity to vent against management.

When using the list in Figure 7.11, the status of this vital sign can be interpreted as follows:

All items rated 3 or above:	Green
One to two items rated <3:	Yellow
Three or more items rated <3:	Red

Customer Buy-In: This vital sign is designed to assess the degree of *ongoing* buy-in to the project by key implementation-level stakeholders. It is not uncommon for a team to continue working on a project while there is widespread dissatisfaction among the key customers. Buy-in, like the other strategic vital signs, is difficult to measure because it is a qualitative assessment. This vital sign is best assessed through discussion and observation. The status of this vital sign can be interpreted as follows:

High degree of buy-in:	Green
Medium degree of buy-in:	Yellow
Low degree of buy-in:	Red

Technology Viability: This vital sign is designed to ascertain the viability of the technology infrastructure being used to develop and deploy the project. Key questions to ask are:

1. Is the enabling technology available and viable for project development?
2. In Chapter 5 (*Scope Growth—The Limit*), we discussed the need to monitor scope growth because it invariably results in putting additional pressure on the performance capabilities of the system. A key purpose of this vital sign is to make sure that the technology remains viable as any new scope is incorporated into the system.
3. Will the technology escalate easily to meet the project's operational requirements?
4. Can it be supported by the IT organization?
5. Will the customers be able to adopt it?

The status of this vital sign can be interpreted as follows:

High degree of viability:	Green
Medium degree of viability:	Yellow
Low degree of viability:	Red

Value-to-Business: A reasonable assumption is that the Project Charter for any given project is approved only if it shows sufficient value to the organization. However, as a project progresses along its life cycle, certain assumptions and realities can change and the project's value can be compromised. The purpose of this vital sign is to make sure that projects with low value potential are identified and brought to the attention of the sponsor, who then must make the decision on the continuation and/or redirection of the project. The necessary information regarding this vital sign must be collected and provided by the appropriate *business* representative(s). When the requisite information is collected and developed by any of the IT team members, we view that as a risk in itself. The status of this vital sign can be interpreted as follows:

High value-to-business:	Green
Medium value-to-business:	Yellow
Low value-to-business:	Red

Vendor Viability: For projects that are outsourced or have a considerable number of vendor-supplied consultants/contractors on the project team, this vital sign is particularly important. As in the case of the previous vital sign, the capabilities and capacities of a vendor can change drastically and for the worse. The results can vary from a vendor who has over committed to customers and is not able to meet obligations to a bankrupt vendor. The project manager collects the background information for this vital sign with help from the sponsor, senior team members, procurement (purchasing) department, and other project managers. The status of this vital sign can be interpreted as follows:

High viability:	Green
Medium viability:	Yellow
Poor viability:	Red

Status of the Critical Path: This vital sign is used to track the progress of the project along its critical path and to answer the question, "Is the project on schedule?" The status of the critical path is a specific metric, and it clearly communicates to the sponsor whether the project is on schedule, ahead of schedule, or behind schedule.

In medical terms, a less than 10 percent negative deviation from the norm means that the patient is suffering from minor ailments, so the doctor prescribes a routine of exercise, improved nutrition, and vitamin supplements. In the case of a 10 percent to 20 percent deviation from the norm, the doctor runs a few tests, prescribes medication, and schedules a return appointment to assess the patient's progress. In the case of a greater than 20 percent deviation from the norm, a visit with a specialist is arranged for in-depth assessment and possible surgical or medical intervention. However, if a patient is deemed extremely fit, has a strong heart rate, healthy cholesterol levels, and normal blood pressure, although the doctor may congratulate the patient, she does not prescribe a period of heavy drinking, excessive eating, and no exercise. Similarly, a project that is ahead of schedule is indeed worthy of praise and recognition. Being ahead of schedule is not, however, a green light for a time-out, because all gains should be capitalized in anticipation of delays. The status of the critical path vital sign can be interpreted as follows:

Breach of <10%:	Green
Breach of 10% to 20%:	Yellow
Breach of >20%:	Red

A breach of less than 10 percent indicates a fairly standard fluctuation from the norm. Though it is of concern, such delays can usually be recovered with strong guidance from the project manager and focused work by the team. A breach of 10 percent to 20 percent means that the problems leading up to the breach are beyond the control of the project manager, and he may need the help of certain functional managers or the sponsor to put the project back on its schedule. A breach of greater than 20 percent means that it would be extremely difficult to recover from such delays without compromising the other three key components of the project—scope (functionality), budget, and quality. The project manager will need to work with the project sponsor to institute a recovery plan, and the two of them will also need to assess the project management process to ascertain the reasons for such a large breach of the critical path. Unless the underlying problems are corrected, the project will continue on its downward slide.

To calculate percentage of variance of the critical path, compare the currently projected critical path duration to the baselined schedule. This comparison will show you how far off, as a percentage, the actual performance is from the baselined schedule. The formulas for calculating the percent variance are:

$$\text{Variance} = \text{Current} - \text{Baseline}$$

$$\text{Percent variance} = (\text{Variance} \div \text{Baseline}) \times 100$$

Consider, for example, the following data:

Vital sign	Baseline	Current	Variance	% Variance	Status
Critical path	150 days	172 days	22 days	+14.7%	Delay

$$\text{Critical path variance} = 172\,\text{days} - 150\,\text{days} = 22\,\text{days}$$
$$\text{Percent variance} = (22\,\text{days} \div 150\,\text{days}) \times 100$$
$$= (0.146) \times 100$$
$$= 14.6\%$$

The critical path variance in this example is between 10 percent and 20 percent and merits yellow status.

We have discussed the implications of underperformance (being late). What if a project is completed early? Is that good news? Only if it is handled properly. For example, a project that is completed significantly early could cause scheduling problems because the customer may not be ready to accept the final product. Also, in the case of early completion, the project team could find itself without assignments, as other project managers may not be ready to absorb them into their respective teams. This development does not mean that if a project is progressing faster than planned, the project manager should slow the team down. It is important that the project manager communicate to the affected stakeholders the possibilities of early completion in a timely manner, so that they are able to make arrangements for the acceptance of the project. *Unannounced* early completion can actually be perceived as an irritant rather than an accomplishment.

Milestone Hit Rate: A milestone is a point of *considerable progress* in the project. We define the completion of each deliverable, as well as the start and/or end of selected tasks, as milestones. On average, for each team member on the project (working full- or part-time), a milestone should appear every 10 days, or sooner. Milestones are used to monitor the speed and direction of the project team as it travels towards its goal of timely completion. The milestone hit-rate indicates the number of milestones the team was planning to hit and the number of milestones they actually hit during a specific reporting period. We recommend two separate monitoring cycles:

1. To-date performance: The total number of milestones planned to be hit *v.* the total number of milestones actually hit.
2. A shorter monitoring cycle—every 2 weeks: The total number of milestones planned to be hit *v.* the total number of milestones actually hit.

These measures will deliver important information about the performance of the team. The to-date hit rate tells the project manager of the overall speed and progress of the team, and the shorter monitoring cycle indicates the team's recent progress. The status of this vital sign can be interpreted as follows:

Breach of $<10\%$:	Green
Breach of 10% to 20%:	Yellow
Breach of $>20\%$:	Red

A breach of less than 10 percent means a fairly standard fluctuation from the norm. Although of concern, such delays can usually be recovered with strong guidance from the project manager and focused work by the team. A gap of 10 percent to 20 percent means it has not yet become a catastrophe, but the team is beginning to fall behind and the critical path will soon be breached. Obviously, some issues are not being resolved in a timely fashion, or the team is being interrupted with unplanned work. The yellow flag is a signal for the project manager to meet with the team, bring it back on track, and refocus its work without delay. Additionally, the sponsor and the project manager must review the situation, devise a plan for recovery, and work with the team members to ensure that they begin to increase the milestone hit rate. A gap of greater than 20 percent means there is little progress on the project, the team is barely crawling, and the project has lost focus and momentum. This type of slow down will result in considerable delay in the currently promised delivery date of the project. With such a serious delay, problems must be brought to the attention of the sponsor immediately.

In our assessment of a large number of projects, we encountered many project managers who routinely run their projects at more than 20 percent below the planned milestone hit rate and do not raise any warning flags. Many managers accept such slowdowns as an unpleasant fact and believe that they will soon catch up. Experience points to a different reality; preventative or corrective measures are not put into action until it is far too late. Our project "doctors" are so lax at monitoring the health of their patients that by the time they take action, the patient is in a coma. Such is the fate of many failed IT/Business projects.

Consider a vital signs check made near the midpoint of a 4-month project. According to the project plan, 24 milestones were to be met within the first 8 weeks of the project. The project manager determined that 20 of the 24 milestones were met on time. The formulas for calculating the percent variance are:

$$\text{Variance} = \text{Milestones planned} - \text{Milestones achieved}$$
$$= 24 - 20$$
$$= 4 \text{ Milestones}$$
$$\text{Percent variance} = (\text{Variance} \div \text{Milestones planned}) \times 100$$
$$= (4 \div 24) \times 100$$
$$= 16.7\%$$

The milestone hit rate variance in this example is between 10 percent and 20 percent and merits the yellow status.

Deliverable Hit Rate: Whereas milestones measure the speed at which the team is moving toward its goal, the deliverables tell us about the team's *accomplishments*. It is important that the project manager and the sponsor monitor the team's accomplishments in terms of deliverables planned for completion *v.* the number of deliverables actually completed. The failure of the team to maintain a consistent deliverable hit rate suggests that there are deep-rooted issues that need to be resolved.

An important rule regarding deliverables is to define deliverables so that each one involves no more than 20 days of elapsed time. By chunking the workload in this way, delayed deliverables are noted at a time when the effort required to catch up is manageable. In the cases where the deliverables take more than 20 days to complete, often the warning flags are not raised until it is too late and the effort to catch up becomes a daunting prospect.

When assessing deliverables, the use of *percent complete* is insidious. For example, what does 90 percent testing completed imply? Does it mean the programmer was looking for ten bugs, has found nine, and has one to go? To us, a deliverable is either complete or incomplete; we do not recognize partial states of completion. It is important for the project manager to frame the inquiry regarding the state of any deliverable clearly and specifically. For example:

- Was the camera ready copy of the report delivered to the print shop?
- Was a successful regression test completed using the version 4 regression database?

Lacking such a specific deliverable completion inquiry, the project manager may not get a completely candid answer. Take for example, the following situation:

> *In one case, user testing failed even after an elaborate system check had been conducted by the offshore IT staff.[1] When the IT director turned to the vendor and said, "I thought you told me you tested it," the vendor responded that he had. But he added that the IT director had never asked him whether the test had been successful.*
>
> Julia King, "Benefits Can Be Elusive, Costs Are Deceptive," *Computerworld* (May 18, 1998, p. 16, http://www.computerworld.com/news/1998/story/ 0,11280,30960,00.html).

This response is the equivalent of a nurse taking the pulse of a patient at a doctor's request, telling the doctor that she had completed her task, but failing to relate that the patient has no pulse. Such problems may be local or systemic, but they require attention immediately. Once the team falls behind, if the underlying problems are ignored, the effort required to catch up to the planned deliverables hit rate may be too great. Even if the problem is solved, the stress placed on the team is extremely high because team members will be required to deal with their present day workload as well as backlogged deliverables. For deliverables, we recommend two separate monitoring cycles:

1. To-date performance: The total number of deliverables planned to be completed to-date v. the total number of deliverables actually completed
2. A shorter monitoring cycle—every 4 weeks: The total number of deliverables planned to be completed v. the total number of deliverables actually completed

The to-date completion rate of deliverables tells the project manager about the rate of the "build" of the project, and the shorter monitoring cycle indicates the ongoing progress. The status of this vital sign can be interpreted as follows:

Breach of <10%:	Green
Breach of 10% to 20%:	Yellow
Breach of >20%:	Red

A gap of less than 10 percent means a fairly standard fluctuation from the norm. Although it is of concern, such delays can usually be recovered with strong guidance from the project manager and focused work by the team. A gap of 10 percent to 20 percent indicates that some of the team members are encountering obstacles that are keeping them from *finishing* their deliverables. The yellow flag is a signal for the project manager to meet with the appropriate team members and help them refocus on their work. The situation has not yet become a catastrophe, but the critical path will soon be breached. The sponsor and the project manager must review the situation, devise a plan for recovery, and work with the team to ensure that work begins to speed up. A gap of greater than 20 percent means that too many deliverables remain incomplete or have not yet been started. The incomplete deliverables could be due to problems such as shortage of resources, lack of appropriate skills, poor specifications, an ad hoc change management process (that allows too many changes), or discovery of new functionality. It is important that the project manager develop a quick and comprehensive analysis of the underlying problem and work with the sponsor to remove the obstacles and refocus the team onto the right track.

We suggest that, in order to determine the level of risk imposed on the project by a poor deliverable hit rate, the sponsor should request a "steep hill" report from the project manager. The concept of such a report is best illustrated by an example:

---

[1]The fact that this was an offshore contractor is incidental to this story. We see such communication problems in all types of organizations.

- Suppose the team was planning to complete eight deliverables, but completed only five; they are now behind by three deliverables.
- At the next assessment cycle, the team was supposed to complete eleven additional deliverables but finished only seven and are short by four deliverables.

Now they are behind by a *total* of *seven* deliverables. An important question to pose here is, "What is the total number of incomplete deliverables that can be tolerated before the project's schedule and functionality are put at high risk?" The steep hill report is designed to delineate the point (time) at which the backlog of incomplete deliverables is almost insurmountable. Should such a report indicate that the incline is about to become too steep to climb, and the project is about to collapse, the sponsor and project manager together need to outline the specific steps to level out the course. Initially, problems, issues, and distractions should be resolved or removed. The project may then need to be rescued and the less vital deliverables may need to be moved to a future version of the product. Barring this, a new project delivery date will need to be established.

The process and formulas for computing the deliverable hit rate are the same as discussed in the *Milestone hit rate* section. For example, consider a vital signs check made near the midpoint of a 4-month project. According to the project plan, twelve deliverables were planned for completion within the first 8 weeks of the project. The project manager determined that eleven of the twelve deliverables were completed on time. The formulas for calculating the percent variance are:

$$\text{Variance} = \text{Deliverables planned} - \text{Deliverables completed}$$
$$= 12 - 11$$
$$= 1 \text{ Deliverable}$$
$$\text{Percent variance} = (\text{Variance} \div \text{Deliverables planned}) \times 100$$
$$= (1 \div 12) \times 100$$
$$= 8.3\%$$

The deliverable hit rate variance in this example is less than 10 percent and merits the green status.

If we were to compare the milestone hit rate variance of 16.7 percent (yellow status) to the deliverables hit rate variance of 8.3 percent (green status), we might wonder why there is a difference. Two possible reasons are:

1. Because the milestone hit rate is a measure of the "speed" of the project, we would conclude that the project is apt to fall even farther behind because the team is not able to "complete" their tasks.
2. There are many more milestones than the deliverables, implying that a number of nondeliverables related milestones have not been met.

Whenever this vital sign reaches a yellow or red flag status, the project manager must look into the reasons for the poor milestone hit rate performance and solve any underlying problems.

Unresolved Issues: An issue can be anything from an unanswered question to a difference of opinion. Unresolved issues are like potholes; if left open, they will grow and impact the performance of the team and the quality of the end product. In most cases, an issue remains unresolved because of inadequate communication and direction or because the team is not a unified body. The project manager has the responsibility to discover why an acknowledged issue remains unresolved and to apply all necessary skills to make the team of one mind. In some cases, the sponsor, or a SME, may need to direct the team members to put their differences aside and agree to disagree. Unresolved issues have one of three effects on the team members:

1. Some retreat, and because they are unable to do productive work, they occupy themselves with irrelevant work.
2. Others go underground and continue to work on what they believe is the right thing to do, regardless of the direction of the rest of the group. Just like a football team whose coach fails to call the play, the team will go onto the field and try to work something out, even though each member may be working on a different maneuver. Either way, nothing valuable is achieved.

3. Some individuals quit the team, not wanting to be a part of a project they believe is unworthy of their time.

In an effort to monitor the resolution of issues in an orderly manner, the project manager should assign a specific date by which an issue must be resolved, and the sponsor should review the aging history of unresolved issues. Any issue that has not been resolved within 5 days of its resolution date raises a yellow flag, and a delay of 7 days or more raises a red flag. Although stipulating a date by which each issue must be resolved may seem somewhat arbitrary, the alternatives are all dire.

As a rule, any project that has more unresolved issues than the number of outstanding deliverables is in serious trouble. In such a case, the team does not have a comprehensive plan; it has a plan full of holes. Another important warning: make sure that there is only one issues list for the project, and that it is under the full control of the project manager. The status of this vital sign can be interpreted as follows:

No unresolved issues:	Green
Unresolved issues < outstanding deliverables:	Yellow
Unresolved issues > outstanding deliverables:	Red

A project rarely has zero outstanding issues. Therefore, make sure that the value is zero, because there really are *no* outstanding issues. The zero value could be a sign that issues are not being recorded, which in itself is a high risk situation.

Cost-to-Date: Historically, with IT/Business projects, cost has been a difficult vital sign to monitor because project managers fail to hone their estimating skills. The typical project manager is not skilled in developing accurate cost estimates, and the typical project management software is not good at capturing the actual effort and cost data. Combine this with an inconsistent and incomplete time recording discipline, and the cost-to-date data is almost always suspect. However, if your project has been justified by a specific ROI, or is under a fixed-price contract, it is extremely important to develop accurate cost estimates and then to diligently capture comprehensive and accurate cost-to-date data. As the project proceeds down its development path, it is imperative that the actual cost-to-date data be compared to the estimated cost-to-date, and that the project manager carefully monitor any breach (overspending). The status of this vital sign can be interpreted as follows:

Breach of <10%:	Green
Breach of 10% to 20%:	Yellow
Breach of >20%:	Red

Fluctuation of less than 10 percent is fairly normal. Although it is a concern, such cost overruns can usually be recovered with strong guidance from the project manager and focused work by the team. If the actual cost-to-date is 10 percent to 20 percent higher than the estimated cost-to-date, the degree of strain on the budget will adversely affect the ROI. This type of deviation can be due to a number of events. It could be that the original estimates were too optimistic, or that the team members are discovering complexities they had not forecast at the start of the project. Another key reason could be that the work environment is not very productive and too much time is being lost due to interruptions. The overrun could also be due to scope creep. It is important for the project manager to ascertain the reason(s) behind the cost overrun and take the necessary steps to address any problem areas. If left unaddressed, the benefit to the bottom line will be considerably less than what was originally promised to the client.

If the actual cost overrun is more than 20 percent of the estimated cost, the project's cost is running at a rate that may fail to return *any* financial benefits at all, and the currently approved budget may be outstripped before the end of the project. Apart from the bottom line implications, high actual costs may encourage unprofessional behavior by the team. For fear of being admonished or having the project canceled, the project manager and team members may try to hide overspending by transferring cost overruns to other projects in progress or may try to skimp on documentation, quality assurance, and testing. The team may even begin to use unrecorded overtime to make the numbers look better. Excessive overtime leads to low productivity, low quality of the end product, and team burnout. None of these tactics ever work and the dollar chasm grows wider and wider.

An instructive example is the case of the California DMV, where a major project was launched in 1987 to revitalize the driver's license and registration application process. In 1993, 6 years and $45 million later, the project was abandoned. One of the key reasons given for the project's failure was the *lack* of diligent cost tracking, which allowed team members to continue on a course of massive overspending without comprehending the actual financial status of the project. It is shocking, but not atypical, that the sponsor did not notice or sense disaster early. By the time they did become alarmed, it was $45 million too late. This calamity is not an isolated example, and the problem is not limited to public agencies. Extensive cost overruns are prevalent in the IT/Business departments of private companies as well.

As an example of assessing this vital sign, consider the following data:

- Currently baselined cost-to-date estimate: $175,000
- Actual cost-to-date: $220,000

With these figures, we can compute the cost variance as:

$$\text{Cost variance} = \$220\text{K} - \$175\text{K} = \$45\text{K}$$
$$\text{Percent cost variance} = (\$45\text{K} \div \$175\text{K days}) \times 100$$
$$= (0.257) \times 100 = 25.7\% \text{ (Overrun)}$$

The actual *v.* estimated cost variance is greater than 20 percent and merits red status.

A final note: Team members working on multiple projects may charge their time (cost) to the wrong project by mistake (or occasionally, on purpose). In fact, in an actual situation at a client site, three different project managers charged over $1 million dollars to a project (not their own) without the knowledge of the project manager. Because the project accounting system was quite cumbersome and he failed to exercise disciplined oversight, by the time the project manager discovered the ruse, the project was out of funds.

For organizations that do not monitor the *total cost* (effort, materials, and technology) of their projects, we suggest capturing and monitoring the estimated effort-to-date *v.* actual effort-to-date data. The effort (hours of work) on a project can be divided into the following three categories:

1. Team effort: The effort (hours) expended to complete various tasks and deliverables in the project. This can be further divided into the effort by the IT team members, end user (customer) team members, and contractors.
2. Project management effort: The effort expended by the project manager to complete various project management activities.
3. Management's effort: The effort expended by various managers to fulfill management duties of the project.

It is important to first decide which of these effort categories is to be monitored and compared to its corresponding estimated values. Although it would behoove any team to capture actual values for all three categories, our experience shows that the effort data for end users and management is rarely estimated and captured. Most IT/Business project organizations that do collect effort data limit their collection to the time spent by the members of the IT department and contractors. This narrow view, of course, skews the figures for the eventual effort (and cost) put into a given project. We urge project managers and team members to diligently and accurately record their *actual* hours spent in completing various tasks and deliverables and carefully monitor any deviations from the corresponding estimated values.

Actual Resources v. Planned Resources: The resources we refer to in this vital sign are the bodies and the brains of the team members—the fuel of the project. For each individual on the team, the project manager must specify not only the amount of time (hours per day) she will be spending on the project, but also her individual skill profile. This vital sign has three measurements:

1. The gap between the number of FTE team members actually working on the project *v.* the number of FTE initially planned

2. The gap between the skill levels of people actually assigned to the team *v.* the skill levels used to develop the project estimates
3. The amount of unplanned turnover—the number of team members that have left the team unexpectedly

For example, if the actual FTE is less than what was originally planned, the project's schedule, scope, and/or quality will be compromised. Therefore, the project manager must carefully monitor the FTE numbers. The second measurement relates to the planned *v.* actual skill levels. In Chapter 6, while developing various estimates, the project manager specified the skill levels of the expected team. It is important to make sure that the actual team's skills match (or preferably exceed) those assumptions. The third measurement of resources is that of *unplanned* staff turnover. Bearing in mind that it can take from several weeks to many months to advertize, interview, hire and then initiate a new individual into the project, the resignation of a core team member can seriously delay the completion of a project.

The status of this vital sign can be interpreted as follows:

Breach of <10%:	Green
Breach of 10% to 20%:	Yellow
Breach of >20%:	Red

A gap of less than 10 percent, if short term, usually does not result in any appreciable hit on the schedule, functionality, or quality of the end product. If the project is underresourced by 10 percent to 20 percent, a serious hit on the quality of the end product is guaranteed because there will be a little less testing, a little less documentation, and a little less prototyping than planned. Also, this level of gap usually means that the remaining team members are called upon to work overtime to make up for the loss. To us, a resource gap of greater than 20 percent means red status. In addition to a hit on the quality of the product, there will be a hit on the scope of the project. Clearly, the client will not receive what was promised. A special note of caution: a resource gap of over 20 percent means SOS. The schedule, scope, and quality of the project are all in jeopardy.

Judging by our experience, the impact of unplanned turnover is as follows:

• Unplanned turnover of a core team member can cause the critical path to slip behind schedule by 4 to 6 weeks
• Unplanned turnover of a project manager can delay a project by 6 to 9 weeks
• The change of a sponsor can jeopardize the entire project, as a new sponsor often wants to reapprove the project's mission, budget, and schedule

> *It is not best to swap horses while crossing the river.*
>
> Abraham Lincoln (Bartleby.com).

In many organizations, IT/Business projects are routinely launched with fewer resources than were originally planned. Often, many of the available resources have lower skill levels than what was expected. The lack of resources may exist either because other projects are running over schedule and cannot spare the personnel or they are over budget and the sponsor is looking for new avenues of economy. Whatever the reason, a project bears a high risk if it is underresourced by 10 percent or more of the original plan.

High Probability, High Impact Risks: Although it is a fairly logical vital sign, many project managers routinely fail to monitor it. Most projects carry risks, and astute project managers quickly alert their sponsors to *high-risk* items. It is imperative that the project manager clearly delineates the potential impact of each high-risk item on the project's schedule, scope, budget, and quality along with a feasible mitigation plan. In turn, the sponsor must ensure that diligent risk monitoring is in place and appropriate mitigation plans are in concert with the severity of the risk. In this way, each risk is managed effectively and efficiently, and the stress on the project manager and the team is reduced when the project suffers a setback. The status of this vital sign can be interpreted as follows:

One to 3 risks:	Green
4 to 5 risks:	Yellow
6 to 7 risks:	Red

For one to three high-level risks, we recommend the green flag because most projects have a few risks and an astute project manager should be able to handle these risks without jeopardizing the project. If the project carries four or five high-level risks, we recommend the yellow status because, if left unattended, so many risks will begin to cause problems for the team—which means the project could be in jeopardy soon. When six or seven high-level risks are identified, we recommend the red status because it means that the project is in great jeopardy and needs the attention and intervention of the sponsor. Why impose a top limit of seven risks? A project with more than seven risks has so many problems that the process of monitoring the vital signs becomes futile.

Overtime Utilization: Overtime is not an easy item to include in the list of suggested vitals signs because it is a handy tool for most managers. Many project managers, functional managers, and sponsors we talked to held the belief that (unpaid) overtime was a natural component of the world of fast approaching deadlines. We often heard statements such as, "If you sign on my project team, expect to work overtime."[2] We also came across a sizeable number of situations where there was extensive pressure on project managers and teams to use unpaid overtime to reduce project budgets. The problem is further complicated when the project team involves contractors and/or unionized team members. Obviously, these team members get paid for overtime while "regular" employees don't. We understand that occasional overtime is a routine part of work life, but we also hold a strong view that consistent overtime is a symptom of deep, systemic problems caused by poor project management practices. The status of this vital sign can be interpreted as follows:

Overtime <15%:   Green
Overtime of 15%–25%:   Yellow
Overtime >25%:   Red

An inverse correlation exists between the amount of overtime and the quality of the end product. Sustained overtime leads to reduced quality, which then requires more overtime for improvement. A vicious cycle develops. Additionally, excessive overtime results in a negative impact on the quality of life of the team members. The overtime is in addition to the daily commute time. People who work 25 percent overtime (2 hours per day) and commute 1 hour have an 11-hour day. This grind takes a toll on family and personal life. If overtime is greater than 25 percent, make sure the corporate mission statement does not have wording promoting "family values."

Team Disposition: The disposition of the project team is often the most neglected vital sign. From the discussion of overtime, it is obvious that most of the vital signs are *quantitative*, comparing planned performance to actual performance and stating the difference as percentages. However, this vital sign is a *qualitative* evaluation. Therefore it is far more difficult to monitor. The general disposition of the team is a reflection of the personal time and interest of the sponsor and the leadership skills of the project manager; it is akin to the "bedside manner" of a doctor. A team that is overworked, feels unappreciated, and has little support from the sponsor, project manager, or key stakeholders will not perform to the best of its ability and the project will definitely suffer.

Monitoring the general disposition of the team requires a skilled and experienced individual to perform the assessment. Ideally a perceptive project manager will make his observations by walking around the floor, chatting informally with team members, and keeping the lines of communication open. At times, the project manager may deem it necessary to exercise some preventative therapy to safeguard the well being of the team—occasional team lunches, group outings (preferably with families), and one-on-one meetings with team members to discuss their project related issues and general professional needs and aspirations. These overtures, and similar small expenditures of time and money, go a long way to keep morale high and keep the team enthusiastic about its work. Figure 7.12 depicts a tool designed to assess team disposition. You may need to tailor both the wording and the number of items presented in the table.

---

[2]Our advice to project managers faced with having to force their teams to put in extensive overtime is to discuss the subject with the sponsor *as well as* the human resources department. We know of many instances where extensive use of overtime, even by officially exempt employees, resulted in messy situations—complaints to the state labor department and even lawsuits.

FIGURE 7.12
Team Disposition
(Effectiveness) Assessment

Team disposition (effectiveness) survey	Rating			
1. Goals: Clearly communicated to the team; shared by all; all care about the goals, and feel involved	1	2	3	4
2. Participation: All are involved; all are listened to	1	2	3	4
3. Problem solving: When problems surface, the project manager involves the team to help diagnose the root causes before proposing actions; remedies attack basic causes	1	2	3	4
4. Decision making: Consensus sought and tested; various points of view appreciated and used to improve decisions; decisions (when made) are fully supported	1	2	3	4
5. Trust: Members trust one another; they reveal to group what they would be reluctant to expose to others; they respect and use the responses they get; they can freely express negative reactions without fearing reprisal	1	2	3	4
6. Creativity and growth: Team members are flexible, seek new and better ways	1	2	3	4
7. Leadership: Project manager is well equipped to manage the team and does it professionally	1	2	3	4
8. Professional growth: There are ample opportunities for individual growth—both through work experience and education and training programs offered by the organization	1	2	3	4

Rating: 1 = rarely, 2 = sometimes, 3 = most of the time, and 4 = always

When using the list in Figure 7.12, the status of this vital sign can be interpreted as follows:

All items rated 3 or above:	Green
One to two items rated <3:	Yellow
Three or more items rated <3:	Red

Project Health Report

The discussion of the various vital signs clearly indicates that all are not created equal—some have a greater weight than others. For example, any of the first six vital signs (the strategic grouping) has more weight in decision making than any of the remaining items. To help us interpret the meaning of the various vital signs, we need to take a look at how an insurance company might interpret the results of "health tests" of an individual applying for insurance. The overall test results can be grouped into three main categories:

1. Drug (illegal) use and certain life threatening viruses
2. Lipids (cholesterol, triglycerides)
3. Weight, smoking, profession (high risk), hobbies (high risk)

A positive reading in the first set automatically raises a red flag. Because the second set of vital signs has acceptable ranges, deviations from the norm can raise a yellow or red flag, depending on the readings. The third set of items is more open to interpretation. The same pattern applies to the various project vital signs. We offer the following suggestions: The strategic vital signs (the first six) are looked at individually, and if any one is off the mark, the project is in jeopardy and the situation needs to be discussed with the sponsor without delay. The tactical vital signs are looked at as a group and are assessed against predefined individual and collective threshold values.

The sponsor and the project manager jointly decide which signs to use and specify the respective thresholds. The best approach to track and report a project's health using the vital signs is a three-step process:

FIGURE 7.13
Project Health—Example 1

Project health report—tactics

Project name: _____ Date: _____

Project vital sign	Variance	Value	Assessed value
1. Status of the critical path (breach)	<10% 10% to 20% >20%	0 1 2	
2. Milestone hit rate (breach)	<10% 10% to 20% >20%	0 1 2	
3. Deliverable-hit rate (breach)	<10% 10% to 20% >20%	0 2 4	
4. Unresolved issues	No issues Issues < Deliverables Issues > Deliverables	0 1 2	
5. Cost-to-date (breach)	<10% 10% to 20% >20%	0 1 2	
6. Actual resources *v.* planned resources (breach)	10% 10% to 20% >20%	0 2 4	
7. High-probability, high-impact risks	1–3 risks 4–5 risks 6–7 risks	1 3 4	
		Total	

Total value: 0–5 = green, 6–10 = yellow, greater than 10 = red

1. Define the thresholds for green, yellow, and red conditions for each vital sign
2. Assign a numeric (weight) value to the green, yellow, and red conditions of each vital sign
3. Define the threshold values for green, yellow, and red status for the project as a whole

Let's take a look at a health report, Figure 7.13, supplied to us by a project manager. From Figure 7.13, we see that this project manager has selected seven vital signs. Notice that each vital sign variance threshold has a specific numeric value attached to it. To ascertain the health of the project at any given time, identify the deviation from the norm, if any. Then enter the appropriate number in the rightmost (assessed value) column and compute the sum of the various values. In the case of this particular project, the project manager used the following thresholds:

- Total value between 0 through 5: green; the project is OK. The project's performance is on track; continue the project, monitoring key variances and vital signs
- Total value between 6 through 10: yellow; this is a warning sign. The project's performance has deteriorated beyond the project manager's ability to improve it. It is now at risk of becoming a runaway project. The project manager informs the sponsor of the situation and then begins to work with appropriate functional managers to devise a plan to fix the problem(s). The best approach is to employ root cause analysis, problem solving, and action planning steps. The project manager will need to evaluate the four key attributes of the project, schedule, scope, budget, and quality, and then decide (with the sponsor's approval) on the necessary adjustments in one or more of these attributes to put the project on the path to recovery.
- Total value greater than 10: red; this is a danger sign. The project has breached its runaway status and is approaching the shutdown condition. At this point, the sponsor must take a serious look at the project's viability and help the project manager and the team develop a recovery plan to put the project back on track. For cross-functional and mission critical projects, the sponsor must escalate the problem to the project steering committee and jointly devise a plan to recover from the problem. If recovery efforts do not achieve the desired improvements, the project becomes a candidate for shut down (refer to *Dealing With Troubled Projects* later in this chapter).

FIGURE 7.14
Project Health Report—
Example 2

Project health report—tactics

Project name: _____ Date: _____

Project vital sign	Variance	Value	Assessed value
1. Status of the critical path (breach)	<10% 10% to 20% >20%	0 1 2	
2. Milestone hit rate (breach)	<10% 10% to 20% >20%	0 1 2	
3. Deliverable hit rate (breach)	<10% 10% to 20% >20%	0 2 4	
4. Unresolved issues	No issues Issues < Deliverables Issues > Deliverables	0 1 2	
5. Cost-to-date (breach)	<5% 5% to 10% >10%	0 2 4	
6. Actual resources *v.* planned resources (breach)	10% 10% to 20% >20%	0 2 4	
7. High probability, high impact risks	1–3 risks 4–5 risks 6–7 risks	1 3 4	
		Total	

Total value: 0–5 = green, 6–10 = yellow, greater than 10 = red

Now let's look at the health report for another project, as depicted in Figure 7.14. This project has a fixed price contract and the project manager customized the health report so the variance thresholds for the cost-to-date vital sign are lower than the values in Figure 7.13. At the same time, the weight values in the value column are higher. The sponsor wanted close monitoring of any cost variances.

Figure 7.15 is an example of a health report, and the project manager selected all of the tactical vital signs. This example comes from a project in zone I of the complexity chart. The sponsor wanted all of the vital signs monitored to allow close monitoring of the project performance.

An important point to note in Figures 7.13, 7.14, and 7.15 is that although the number of vital signs, their thresholds, and the associated weight values are different the interpretation values shown towards the end of each health report are the same (0–5 = green, 6–10 = yellow, greater than 10 = red). The next natural question put forth by many project managers is: When a larger number of the tactical signs are included, the project can go into the yellow and red conditions earlier. Is that acceptable? Of course. The reason for the selection of the larger number of vital signs is to monitor the project closely because of its complexity and because of the negative consequences of nonperformance. Therefore, monitoring a larger set of vital signs will provide an early warning of any problems.

> *In a project, you get what you inspect, not what you expect. You monitor the metrics and make sure you stay on track.*
>
> Jerry McElhatton, in Marc L. Songini, "How They Learned To Lead," *Computerworld* (January 6, 2003, http://www.computerworld.com/ networkingtopics/networking/management/story/0,10801,53014,00.html).

Lines of Command and Frequency of Reporting

The monitoring of the vital signs of a project begins at the grassroots level, and the first line of responsibility lies with each and every team member. In the same way that new parents leave the hospital with their baby and a copy of the most recent book on child rearing tucked safely in their arms, the ongoing checks and counterchecks prevent team members from having to raise emergency

FIGURE 7.15
Project Health Report—
Example 3

Project health report—tactics

Project name: _____ Date: _____

Project vital sign	Variance	Value	Assessed value
1. Status of the critical path (breach)	<10% 10% to 20% >20%	0 1 2	
2. Milestone hit rate (breach)	<10% 10% to 20% >20%	0 1 2	
3. Deliverable hit rate (breach)	<10% 10% to 20% >20%	0 2 4	
4. Unresolved issues	No issues Issues < Deliverables Issues > Deliverables	0 1 2	
5. Cost-to-date (breach)	<10% 10% to 20% >20%	0 1 2	
6. Actual resources *v.* planned resources (breach)	10% 10% to 20% >20%	0 2 4	
7. High probability, high impact risks	1–3 risks 4–5 risks 6–7 risks	1 3 4	
8. Overtime utilization (breach)	<15% 15% to 25% >25%	0 1 2	
9. Team disposition (effectiveness)	Highly motivated Somewhat motivated Low level motivation	0 2 4	
		Total	

Total value: 0–5 = green, 6–10 = yellow, greater than 10 = red

flags every time there is a minor problem. The information gathered by the team members on a daily basis will continually feed the project manager with the data he needs to compare the *actual* progress with the *planned* progress. Formal reporting from the project manager to the sponsor should take place *every 2 weeks* if all is going according to plan. Without these direct and formal lines of communication, unnecessary panic attacks will occur and many serious problems may slip by unnoticed, which would put the project in crisis mode.

Because the aim is to provide timely warnings to the sponsor and avoid any surprises, project managers and team members must learn to monitor the various vital signs of their project. They need to recognize acceptable fluctuations as well as the onset of any serious problems. By monitoring the vital signs of the project at regular intervals, teams will be able to deliver a greater number of healthy projects—projects that are on schedule, within budget, and meet customer expectations. To make all of this possible, the project manager must feel confident to report to the sponsor any deviations from the norm with *candor* and without fear of blame or punishment.

During the years of consulting with a large number of project managers, we have often been asked, "At what point of variance in the selected vital signs should one report upwards?" The idea behind the question is the need to minimize unnecessary communications. Because of the different management styles, especially the varying degrees of authority delegation from the sponsor to the project manager and the team, it is difficult to provide a universally applicable answer to this important question. However, we offer the following suggestions:

• *Variance of up to 10 percent:* The individual team member is responsible for analyzing the reasons for the variance and its impact on the project, and then for initiating an action plan of recovery. The team member may need help from a senior colleague, an SME, or the project management office (if one exists). The team member can wait until the next scheduled team update meeting to report this level of variance to the project manager. The purpose of this demarcation is to shift the authority and responsibility for minor variance management to individual team members and to reduce the amount of communications between the team and the project manager. If, at any given point, the variance breaches the 10 percent mark, the team member needs to inform the project manager promptly (not wait until the next scheduled team update meeting).

- *Variance of 11 percent to 15 percent:* At this point, the project manager takes control of the situation and works with appropriate team members (and their functional managers, where applicable) to analyze the reasons for the variance and its impact on the project. Then, they develop an action plan for recovery.

- *Variance of 16 percent to 20 percent:* We assume that the project manager's intervention did not enable the project's health to recover from the variance and, in fact, the problem has grown while the recovery efforts were in place. At this point the project manager must escalate the problem to her functional manager and they must work together to analyze the reasons for the variance and its impact on the project, then develop an action plan for recovery.

- *Variance of 21 percent to 25 percent:* Obviously, the action plans put into place did not bear fruit and the project's health is deteriorating even further. At this level of variance, the project manager must escalate the problem to the sponsor (not wait for the next scheduled sponsor update meeting). In addition, the project managers and the sponsor must work together to analyze the reasons for the variance and its impact on the project, then develop an action plan for recovery.

- *Variance above 25 percent:* A variance of this level means that, for whatever reason, the recovery efforts have not resulted in any improvements and the project is approaching the danger zone—it is out of control. At this stage, the sponsor should convene a meeting of the executive steering committee (if one has been formulated for the project), who will then decide on the fate of the project. If a steering committee does not exist, either the sponsor personally makes the next set of decisions, or consults with other key stakeholders. At this point, the options are as follows:
  - Visit the project's intra-project priorities and restructure one or more of the key components— schedule, scope, budget, and quality. With the appropriate decision in place, the project manager will need to revise the plans, estimates, and schedule for the remaining project.
  - Move the project to the suspended project portfolio (see Chapter 10).
  - Make a decision to scuttle the project and have the project manager start the necessary steps for an orderly project closure (refer to *Dealing With Troubled Projects* later in this chapter).

As a closing thought on the escalation process, work with your sponsor, key functional managers, and the team to define the various suggested variance thresholds. In some cases, they may need to be adjusted to match the management styles of people involved and the risk factors of the project.

Despite your best efforts, you may find that your project is in trouble; the vital signs have breached the runaway conditions and are fast approaching the project's shutdown conditions. Reasons for the breach might include a change in corporate strategy, loss of key personnel, fundamental changes in customer needs, significant changes in the market, or substantial problems within the project team. This state of affairs should prompt the question: "Should the project continue?" Allowing a highly challenged project to continue will result in unnecessary expenses and damaged relationships with customers and key stakeholders, and will take a heavy toll on project personnel. As difficult as such a decision is going to be, it is necessary to face the facts and *formally* assess the project's fate: continue or shut down. Unfortunately, few organizations have a well defined process in place to do just that; usually, the process is no better than a hit and miss affair with less than desirable results—challenged projects are allowed to continue until they become black holes and suck in scarce organizational resources. Our advice is to switch to the process for *Dealing With Troubled Projects*, described later in this chapter.

Look-Ahead Window

Now that we have discussed the process of assessing the current status of the project, the next important action to take is to look into the project's future and forecast the team's ability to continue its work as planned. This prognostication is accomplished through the use of a look-ahead window that allows the team to focus on upcoming deliverables, milestones, tasks, risks, and issues. The look-ahead window can be short-term, only a few weeks, as well as long-term (looking toward the end of the project).

Short-Term Forecast The purpose of the short-term window is to look anywhere between 2 and 8 weeks into the future and to forecast:

- Timely availability of resources
- Timely initiation and completion of tasks with special attention to critical and near-critical path tasks
- Timely completion of deliverables
- The possibility of identified risks becoming a reality
- Emergence of new risks
- Changes to project scope

Figure 7.16 depicts a graphic representation of a 4-week look-ahead window.

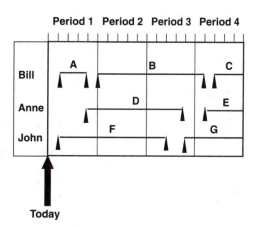

FIGURE 7.16
Look-Ahead Window—
Cycle 1

The left-most column lists the names of the team members who are currently scheduled to work on the project. The four columns to the right depict the tasks and/or deliverables and milestones associated with each team member for a period of the next 4 weeks. To visualize the use of the look-ahead window, imagine the following scenario:

1. The project manager has decided to use a 4-week window.
2. With the help of the project manager software housing the project schedule, the project manager has identified and printed the look-ahead window information and forwarded a copy to all of the team members.
3. Team members have taken the time to review their planned assignments and have validated the underlying assumptions (their percent assignment, personal calendars, work interruptions, and any cross-team dependencies).

The project manager now conducts a project status review meeting and goes through the following steps:

4. Asks Bill whether he will be able to start and finish Task A as depicted in the look-ahead window. At this point, Bill can respond with one of the following statements:
   a. "Yes"
   b. "No," along with a *brief* explanation
   c. "I don't know," along with a *brief* explanation

At this point, there is no discussion of why and there are no long explanations by Bill. Limiting the discussion is easier said than done, especially when a team member answers "No" or "I don't know." The desire to offer and hear explanations is powerful. However, it is extremely important for the project manager to hold people to succinct accounts. The project manager then follows the same routine of inquiry for Tasks B and C for Bill. Next, the project manager moves to Anne and then to John with inquiries regarding their assignments. For Tasks C, E, and G, the discussion will focus only on the team member's ability to start the appropriate tasks because the end of these tasks is not within the look-ahead window. In summary, the focus of the discussion is:

1. Will it (task or deliverable) start on time?
2. Will it (task or deliverable) finish on time?
3. Are there any obstacles?

As a result of this "round robin" process, the project manager, as well as the team, should develop a solid picture of the next 4 weeks—especially any obstacles in the planned path. At this point, the team as a whole should also focus on any external dependencies during the look-ahead window.

The benefit of a look-ahead window is that within a very short time (15 to 20 minutes) the project manager can find out the near future outlook for the project. Then the project manager, in concert with the team, can begin to analyze the underlying reasons for any problems and jointly develop solutions and workarounds. We suggest the following process: Have the individual team members propose any solutions that they can see for their own problems. If certain problem areas are still unresolved, open the discussion of solution development to the team. You, as the project manager, may need to facilitate the discussion and solution development. If the team is not able to suggest a solution or arrive at a consensus, then the final responsibility for solving the problem will rest on your shoulders (we will discuss this subject in more detail later in this chapter, see *Solving Problems*).

Let us now look at the next cycle of look-ahead window review. Figure 7.17 depicts the same look-ahead window shown in Figure 7.16, but shows a 5th week.

FIGURE 7.17
Look-Ahead Window—
Cycle 2

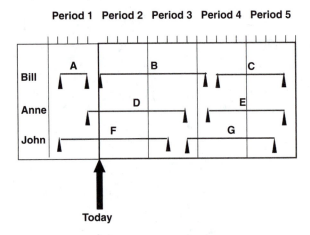

Notice that the "Today" label has moved forward by 1 week and the team will view the next 4 weeks. The discussion will go like this:

1. Project manager asks Bill if Task A is complete. Bill's response is one of two options:
   a. Yes (skip to number two) or
   b. No. If this is the case, Bill should be prepared to provide the next finish date, the impact of the delay on the critical path (if any) and a *brief* explanation.
2. Now the project manager will continue with Bill regarding Task B and Task C (the finish date of Task C is now within the look-ahead window).

Discussions with Anne and John regarding the start and finish of their tasks will follow. As in the last cycle, the project manager and the team work together to focus on any problems and their solutions.

One of the key benefits of the look-ahead window is that it forces the team to look at their upcoming work and think through any obstacles. This preview provides them with ample early warnings of problems, in turn reducing the number of surprises that can cause unexpected delays. Before we close the discussion on the use of this method for short-term forecasting, here are a few important points to keep in mind:

- We recommend a span of 4 to 6 weeks for the look-ahead window.
- It is important for each team member to take the time to review his individual look-ahead window prior to attending the review session. Computer-based tools are especially helpful in facilitating

the use of look-ahead windows because they allow tasks to be selected, sorted, and printed in a variety of ways.

- All of the team members whose work falls within the selected window span must attend the review session. If anyone is not able to attend, his proxy should be given to the project manager and not another team member. When the absentee team member uses another team member as a stand-in, opportunities for miscommunications arise.
- In situations where team members have not been able to complete their work as planned, or see obstacles in their path, make sure they don't start narrating "dark and stormy night" stories or give lengthy recitations of past accomplishments. Focus on the facts.
- Don't start solving individual team member problems until after the last team member has discussed her look-ahead window.

We have often asked team members the question, "In the absence of a well-defined look-ahead window, how do you know what to do next?" Invariably the answer is, "We hold a lot of meetings and try to find out who is supposed to do what next." Other answers are: "I wait for the project manager to tell me, or I bring up the project schedule and try to figure out what is next (but often it is not up to date)." Occasionally, the response is: "I try to look busy until the project manager tells me my next assignment." This muddle reminds us of one of our favorite sayings: If you don't know where you're headed, speeding up is not the best move.

Long-Term Forecast   Long-term forecasting is used to assess how the trends that are developing in the project will ultimately impact the project. Long-term forecasting is also used to assess how adjustments that are made to schedule, scope, budget, and quality expectations will ultimately impact the project. When presenting forecasts to the sponsor and customers, it is essential to use range values rather than precise numbers. The size of the range should represent the level of confidence in the forecast. The broader the range, the lower the confidence level will be. Long-term forecasts should be done on the:

- Estimate-at-completion
- Resource availability
- Finish date of the project

Estimate-at-Completion: To control the project budget, it is necessary to forecast spending at several points during the project life cycle, especially for projects where budget is the number one priority, as in fixed price projects. A simple method to forecast the budget of a project is to compute what is known as the burn rate—the rate at which money is being spent—and use the burn rate figure to forecast the final cost of the project, known as the estimate-at-completion (EAC). If the EAC matches the allocated budget, no adjustment would be necessary. However, if money is being spent at a rate that would exhaust the budget before the project is completed, steps need to be taken to curtail the spending or renegotiate the budget. The steps to compute the EAC of a project are as follows:

$$\text{Burn rate} = \text{Cost-to-date}/\text{Elapsed duration}$$
$$\text{Remaining cost-of-effort} = \text{Burn rate} \times \text{Remaining duration}$$
$$\text{EAC} = \$ \text{ Effort to date} + \text{Remaining cost-of-effort} + \text{Fixed cost}$$
$$\% \text{ Variance} = ((\text{EAC} - \text{Estimated project cost})/\text{Estimated project cost}) \times 100$$

Figure 7.18 shows that, if the burn rate were to remain constant and if the fixed costs occur as shown, the project will be 19 percent over budget.

An important question to ask at this point is, "Would the customer have approved this project if the original cost estimate was $1,977,000?" If the answer is no, then the next question is, "Is the customer willing to invest $1,152,000 to have the team finish this project?" Keep in mind that the increased cost is sure to have a negative impact on the project's value to the business. Timely use of this metric can help the sponsor ward off the massive cost overruns so prevalent in IT/Business projects. Of course, the sample forecast shown above would raise the following questions:

1. Will the burn rate be consistent throughout the project?
2. Will the fixed cost expenditures occur as planned?

Estimated Project Cost	Cost-To-Date	Elapsed Duration	Burn Rate	Remaining Duration	Remaining Cost	Fixed Costs	Estimate-At-Completion	Variance
$1,660K	$575K	4 months	$144K	8 months	$1,152K	$250K	$1,977K	(+19%)*

* It is customary to show over spending within brackets.

FIGURE 7.18
Budget Forecast

The burn rate of a project is rarely consistent throughout the entire project. It may be necessary to calculate the burn rate for different parts of the project if the spending rate will be radically different. However, analyzing the spending rate and forecasting the overall project cost early and often provides the opportunity to spot variances and develop recovery plans as early as possible.

In the case of a simple project, it may be adequate to check project spending at the mid-point of the project and forecast the EAC. For large and complex projects, we recommended the following triggers for EAC forecasting:

- At the end of each month
- At the end of each phase
- When new scope is introduced
- When high risk events become reality
- When resources are reallocated

A number of project managers we know have added EAC to their vital signs list. As with all other vital signs, the project manager and the sponsor must decide on appropriate threshold values for the green, yellow, and red conditions.

Resource Availability: It is critical for both budget and schedule control to keep informed as to the availability of resources during the life cycle of the project. Remember that the term "resource" includes far more than team members. Listed below is the variety of resources that the project manager needs to track to assure agreed upon scope, budget, schedule and quality performance:

- *Team members:* Their availability may be hampered by their primary job responsibilities and other project assignments, personal needs/crises, and unplanned turnover. It is important for the project manager to consistently look ahead to ensure that planned availability is not jeopardized.
- *Tools:* IT/Business projects are often at the mercy of the technology supplied by vendors, and promises often don't match the performance. This is especially true with software tools. Worse, many tools arrive in their "alpha and beta" states and require consistent and extensive staff training. A look-ahead window in this area is very important.
- *Budget:* Projects often come to a standstill because of delays in budget approvals by the right level of management, or because the project manager did not follow certain budgeting and financial procedures. This financial holdup can become a real problem in projects that cross the annual budgeting cycle or are funded by multiple entities. It is important for the project manager to become knowledgeable about the budgeting process and avoid approval problems.
- *SMEs:* Project progress often slows to a crawl because IT/Business SMEs are not available as expected. The team has to either wait for their availability or make decisions on their own. Neither course of action is desirable because the end result is a choice between delayed delivery and poor quality. Therefore, the project manager must have an extended look-ahead window open to verify and assure SME availability.

Finish Date of the Project: Project managers are constantly asked the question, "Are we there yet?" Most project managers find it difficult to respond with any certainty because schedules for IT/Business projects are highly indeterminate. However, not providing the sponsor and the customers with timely warning of any delays, or for that matter even an early finish, often leads to dissatisfied and unhappy customers. Therefore, project managers must muster all of their skills, tools, and techniques to forecast the project completion schedule. The underlying areas that help in managing project schedules are:

1. Resource management
   a. Timely availability
   b. Appropriately skilled
   c. Disposition
2. Risk management
   a. Planned risks
   b. Impending risks
3. Scope management
   a. New discoveries
   b. Adherence to scope change process
4. Cross-project dependencies
   a. Competing projects
   b. Timely performance
5. Organizational stability
   a. Reorganizations
   b. Mergers
   c. Moves

At a given point in the project life cycle, the project manager must look at the to-date history of these key areas, assess their current status, forecast the future, and identify those factors that are likely to affect the project schedule. A project manager's next step is to develop recovery procedures and try to mitigate the negative impacts of any potential delays on the currently baselined schedule. If you find that the news is not good, don't hide it. Promptly inform the sponsor and then the key stakeholders of the possible delays—nobody likes to be surprised, especially about schedules.

Project Fuel Report: No responsible race car driver would consider leaving the start line without first checking the amount of fuel in the fuel tank. The discovery of low fuel during the race will require an unscheduled stop, a most risky detour. Similarly, project managers must be certain that they have sufficient fuel (the sum total of the effort hours available from all team members) before starting a project. In far too many cases, project managers do not assess their fuel needs and fuel availability; they simply assume that sufficient fuel will be available through the life cycle of the project. Often they get stuck with an empty tank, trying to hitchhike to their next milestone. To help managers forestall any such problems, we would like to introduce you to one of our favorite metrics, the fuel report. This report works very well if you use the look-ahead window consistently. In this context, project fuel consists of the number of work hours available from the team. We believe that keeping an eye on the fuel level of a project, like the gasoline in an automobile tank, is a good idea. Therefore, as a part of the look-ahead window review process, we recommend that you ask team members to document the time (effort hours) they will have available to work on the project (the *available hours*). Make sure that the team members are *realistic* in their forecasts and take into account any holidays, vacations, sick leave, travel, training, jury duty, and time committed to other projects and/or routine work. Next, you compute the sum of the estimated effort hours of all the tasks in the look-ahead window (the *needed hours*). If the available hours are less than the needed hours, you are short on fuel. At this point, the important questions to consider are:

1. Is the gap sufficiently large to be a concern?
2. Will you be able to get more fuel (additional time by team members) down the road?
3. Could there be further drain on the current fuel (the available hours)? For example, a key team member has just received the summons to serve jury duty, has received a National Guard activation notice, or may have been asked to do some volunteer work by a senior manager.

The project fuel report is a reliable early indicator of any upcoming shortages and the teams' ability to complete the work as scheduled. If you are consistently running low on fuel, it should come as no surprise that your project may soon be stranded on the project highway. While we are on the subject of "project fuel," let us also look at three additional important points:

1. *Fuel leakage:* It is important that you ensure that team members do not use your project time to work on other projects. This problem can easily occur when team members are assigned to multiple projects. Either by mistake or by design, some of them may work on other projects while billing the time to your project.

2. *Fuel redirection:* The functional managers of some of the team members may direct their people to spend "emergency" time on other work, with a promise that they will make up for it at a later time. In most instances, the fuel (team member's time) is gone forever unless the team member works overtime.

3. *Fuel contamination:* Team members begin to be interrupted much more than the assumed work interruptions (see *Work Interruption Factor*, Chapter 6) and their productivity begins to decrease without the project manager having any knowledge of the problem.

Therefore, it behooves a diligent project manager to closely monitor the project fuel—the team members' time on the project.

Earned Value Management System

The Earned Value Management System (EVMS) is designed to track project progress. EVMS is used to:

- Determine the dollar value of work completed to date
- Measure progress by comparing the dollar value of work completed to the dollars that you had planned to spend and the dollars that you have actually spent

The earned value approach has roots that date back to early production-line practices. Progress was often assessed by counting the units that rolled off a manufacturing line, adding up their dollar value, and comparing that dollar value to planned and actual expenditures. That basic earned value concept was captured in a series of management approaches that have evolved within the U.S. Department of Defense (DoD) since the early 1960s. By the mid-to-late 1990s, the approach took on its present form. Before we delve into the subject, it is important to point out that some terminology related to various components of EVMS has gone through revisions. In Figure 7.19, the first column lists the more recently revised terms and the column to the right lists the terms used in the original EV literature.

Earned Value Basics   Three values provide the starting point for EV calculations. Each is determined at the project status date, which is the reference date for project progress assessment.

1. PV: The sum of all budgets for work scheduled, up to the project status date.
2. EV: The sum of all budgets for work actually performed, up to the project status date
3. AC: The amount of money actually spent, up to the project status date

Consider a project to produce ten different items; each budgeted for $100,000 (a total budget of $1,000,000) and estimated to last just over 6 months. At the end of the 2nd month, the project manager reports the following data:

- Two of the three items have been completed
- Actual cost to complete the two items was $400,000

The basics of the earned value approach are illustrated in Figure 7.20.

The PV, EV, and AC projections for this project are depicted in the chart in Figure 7.21. In the chart, we can see that the AC is higher than the planned cost resulting in a lower earned value. From this data, one would conclude that the project is not earning value, or completing scheduled work, at the planned rate.

From the data in Figure 7.21, one could conclude that after 2 months, one third of the way into the project, only one fifth of the deliverables (2 out of 10) have been completed but two fifths of the

FIGURE 7.19
EV Terminology

EVMS term	Original earned value term	Definition
Planned value (PV)	Budgeted cost of work scheduled (BCWS)	The sum of the authorized budgets for all planned work scheduled to be accomplished within a specific time period (from project start to the status date)
Earned value (EV)	Budgeted cost of work performed (BCWP)	The sum of the authorized budgets for work actually performed within a specific time period (from project start to the status date)
Actual costs (AC)	Actual cost of work performed (ACWP)	The costs actually incurred, up to the project status date
Budget at completion (BAC)	Budget at completion (BAC)	The sum of all authorized budgets for the project
Cost variance (CV)	Cost variance (CV)	Any difference between the budgeted cost of an activity and the AC of that activity $CV = EV - AC$
Schedule variance (SV)	Schedule variance (SV)	The numerical difference between the EV and the PV $SV = EV - PV$
Cost performance index (CPI)	Cost performance index (CPI)	The cost efficiency ratio of EV to AC $CPI = EV/AC$
Schedule performance index (SPI)	Schedule performance index (SPI)	The schedule efficiency index of EV accomplished against the PV $SPI = EV/PV$

budget has been spent. Things are not looking good. As we will see in the following discussion, project progress can be computed based on the assessments of PV, EV, and AC. These indicators can be useful in *forecasting* future project costs and schedules.

FIGURE 7.20
EV Basics

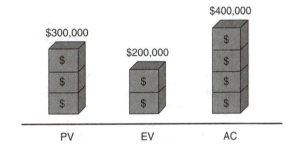

Cost Variance (CV)   CV is the difference between estimated costs and actual costs, determined at the project status date. In mathematical terms:

$$CV = EV - AC$$

To continue our example, the EV at the status date was $200,000 and the AC was $400,000. CV is as follows:

$$CV = \$200,000 - \$400,000 = -\$200,000$$

A negative value indicates that costs were greater than planned. In the example, the work completed is over budget by $200,000.

FIGURE 7.21
Project Projections

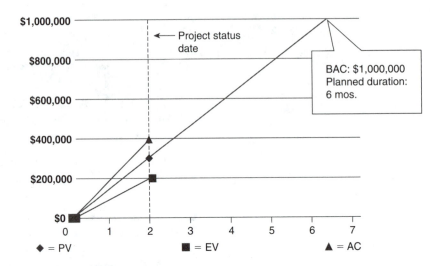

Schedule Variance (SV) SV is defined as the difference between EV and PV. While it is challenging to think about schedule in dollar terms, schedule variance can provide a useful indicator of whether the project is ahead of or behind schedule. In mathematical terms:

$$SV = EV - PV$$

In this example, the EV at the status date was $200,000 and the planned costs were $300,000. SV is as follows:

$$SV = \$200,000 - \$300,000 = -\$100,000$$

A negative value indicates that the project is behind schedule. In the example, only $200,000 of value was produced by the status date (two items were produced), when the plan called for the completion of three items at a cost of $300,000.

Cost Performance Index (CPI) The CPI provides a measure of the burn rate of money in the project, measured at the project status date. In mathematical terms:

$$CPI = EV \div AC$$

In this example, at the status date the EV was $200,000 and AC was $400,000. The resulting CPI is computed as follows:

$$CPI = \$200,000 \div \$400,000 = 0.5$$

The CPI of 0.5 indicates that the project is gaining only fifty cents of value for every dollar spent. As of the status date, the project has cost twice as much as it has earned. A CPI equal to one indicates that the project costs are equal to those planned; less than one indicates that the costs are greater than planned; and more than one indicates that the costs are less than planned.

Schedule Performance Index (SPI) The SPI provides a measure of the rate at which work is accomplished, measured at the project status date. In mathematical terms:

$$SPI = EV \div PV$$

In this example, EV was $200,000 and PV was $300,000. The resulting SPI is:

$$SPI = \$200,000 \div \$300,000 = 0.67$$

The SPI of 0.67 indicates that, at the status date, the project is gaining only 67 cents of value for every dollar of PV. This means that the project is completing work at only two-thirds of the planned rate. Therefore, all other things being equal, it would take 1.5 times as long to complete the project as originally scheduled. A SPI equal to one indicates that the project is on schedule; less than one indicates behind schedule; greater than one indicates ahead of schedule.

Project Cost Forecasting

The CPI and SPI can be used to estimate both a "low-end" and "high-end" value for the total cost of the project. In earned value terminology, the predicted total cost of the project is known as the estimate-at-completion (EAC).

Low-End Forecast   Two equivalent formulas for a low-end EAC are:

$$EAC = AC + ((BAC - EV) \div CPI)$$

or

$$EAC = BAC \div CPI$$

Examining the longer version of the formula, we start with AC (what we have spent so far). We then add to that an estimate of what we think it will cost to complete the work that remains. The result is often referred to as the estimate-to-complete (ETC). In mathematical terms:

$$EAC = AC + ETC$$

To calculate the ETC, we need to estimate the value of the remaining work. We determine this by subtracting EV at the status date from the total PV of the project, the BAC. We then divide the value of remaining work by the CPI. This operation adjusts the cost of remaining work to account for the rate at which we are creating value. Let's refer to the earlier example:

$$AC = \$400,000$$
$$BAC = \$1,000,000$$
$$EV = \$200,000$$
$$CPI = 0.5$$

Using the formula for computing EAC:

$$EAC = \$400,000 + ((\$1,000,000 - \$200,000) \div 0.5) = \$2,000,000$$

In the equation, you can see that the EAC is the sum of the \$400,000 we have already spent and twice the value of the remaining work.

High-End Forecast   The low-end forecast is based on the assumption that project work will be performed at the originally planned rate. However, as we saw earlier, work may move more slowly than planned and the project may take longer than expected to complete.[3] The high-end EAC is based on the longer project duration, as indicated by the SPI. The high-end EAC is calculated as follows:

$$EAC = AC + ((BAC - EV) \div (CPI \times SPI))$$

Therefore, the high-end EAC is calculated as follows:

$$EAC = \$400,000 + ((\$1,000,000 - \$200,000) \div (0.5 \times 0.67)) = \$2,788,060$$

Based on CPI alone, we calculated the low-end EAC of \$2,000,000. However, when we factor in the slower rate of accomplished work, the estimate of the cost of the remaining work is increased considerably. In summary, a realistic EAC for the project is \$2,000,000 to \$3,000,000 (rounded).

Rate of the Remaining Work

The EVMS can also be used to determine the rate at which the remaining work on a project must be performed to meet the original budget. That index is called the target cost performance index (TCPI). The TCPI can be calculated using one of two following formulas:

$$TCPI = (\text{Remaining work } \$ \div \text{Funds remaining})$$

or

$$TCPI = (BAC - EV) \div (BAC - AC)$$

---

[3]This formula also applies to a case where the project is moving faster than planned. In this case, the SPI would be greater than one and the high-end EAC would actually be less than the low-end estimate.

Continuing with our example, let's compute the TCPI for this project:

BAC = $1,000,000
EV = $200,000
AC = $400,000
TCPI = ($1,000,000 − $200,000) ÷ ($1,000,000 − $400,000) = 1.33

The TCPI of 1.33 means that, from this point to the end of the project, we must gain $1.33 in earned value for every dollar spent to complete the project at the planned cost. The TCPI calculation leads us to one of two actions:

1. If there is only a minor difference between the CPI and TCPI, it may be possible to complete the project within the original budget by making adjustments to the scope and quality expectations where appropriate.
2. If there is a significant difference between the CPI and TCPI, it may not be possible to complete the work within the original budget, thereby triggering a reevaluation of the project budget, scope, schedule, and quality requirements.

Project Schedule Forecasting

EVMS offers another way to estimate a project schedule. The estimates obtained using the EV approach can be used to reinforce the forecasts made using the CPM. An example of the EVMS schedule forecasting approach is shown in Figure 7.22.

In Figure 7.22 we see that the project attained an EV of $200,000 at the 2-month status date. The PV line shows that an EV of $200,000 should have been achieved at approximately 1.33 months into the project. This variance indicates that the project is roughly two-thirds of 1 month behind schedule. Additionally, if no corrective action is taken, the project schedule will *continue* to fall behind by two thirds of a month every 2 months.

EV of a Partially Completed Task

Within EVMS, no single method exists for estimating the EV of a task that has been started but not completed prior to, or at the time of, the status date. In the example in Figure 7.23, Task C was started prior to the status date (shown as a dotted line), but has not yet been completed. Some of the methods used to assign an EV to a partially completed task are:

• Credit a certain percentage of the PV of the task as soon as it is started, then credit the balance when complete (25 percent at start, the other 75 percent at finish).
• Credit 50 percent at the start and the other 50 percent on completion.

FIGURE 7.22
Schedule Forecasting

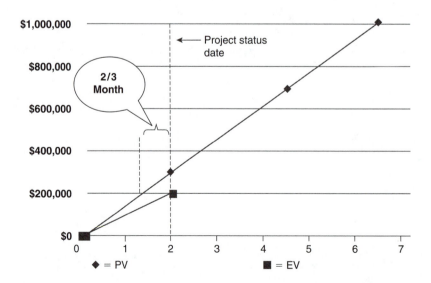

FIGURE 7.23
Partially Completed Task—EV

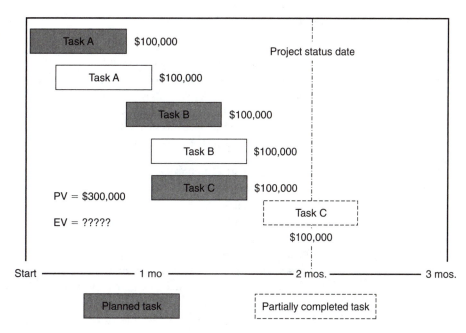

- Credit 0 percent at the start and 100 percent only when completed.
- Determine milestones within the task and assign a predetermined EV when each milestone is attained.
- Estimate the percentage complete and assign this percentage of the PV as the EV not recommended.

You can see that none of these methods are that simple, and trying to have an agreement on one common approach to be used by different project managers is not going to be easy. Keep in mind that we do not attach any value to a partially completed task or deliverable; therefore, the discussion is presented only to portray what many EVMS practitioners try to do.

EV—The Bottom Line

The EV approach is cost-centered, as all computations are based on the dollar value of work planned, the dollar value of work completed, and the actual dollars spent completing the work. Therefore, your organization must invest in a highly *accurate* system for capturing the *actual* dollars spent on projects. We have found this to be a problem in far too many IT/Business projects because many team members don't record their time using a detailed WBS. Therefore, if your organization decides to use EVMS to track project progress, make sure that the policies and procedures for cost estimating and actual cost recording are in full alignment. Some important considerations for using EVMS are:

- It can be a useful for tracking and predicting project cost.
- The EV schedule variance is an indicator of whether you're ahead of schedule or behind; it is not a useful tool to forecast the project completion date. The CPM is still needed for the effective tracking and control of a project's schedule.

What we have presented is an introduction to the basic elements of EVMS. For those who would like to pursue this topic in more detail, both books[4] and web resources[5] are available.

---

[4]Koppelman, Joel M. and Fleming, Quentin W., *Earned Value Project Management*, 2nd Ed., Newton Square, Pennsylvania: Project Management Institute.
[5]The Department of Defense Earned Value site is a good starting point for information on the Web: http://www.acq.osd.mil/pm/.

Analytical Tools

We have discussed in detail a variety of methods to assess any variance between what was planned and the actual performance. The next step is to put an action plan in process and implement appropriate solutions to put the project back on track. However, before a solution can be developed, it is important to delve into the root cause of the problem that caused the variance. A number of tools are available to help you determine root causes of a variance. Many of these tools are used in quality management processes, now embedded in IT/Business project management practices. We would like to provide you with a refresher about four such tools:

Fishbone Diagram   This technique is designed to help analyze problems that may have many interrelated causes. The basic structure of the fishbone diagram, also referred to as the cause and effect (C&E) diagram, is shown in Figure 7.24. Popularized by Professor Kaoru Ishikawa in 1943, it was then known as the Ishikawa diagram. To start analyzing a problem, draw a horizontal arrow in the middle of a page and write down the problem, in a box, at the head of the arrow; this is also referred to as the *effect*. The next step is to identify potential *causes* leading to the problem; each major problem is depicted as an arrow (fishbone) pointed at the horizontal arrow (the backbone of the fish). This work can be done by an individual or in a group, using the brainstorming process (see *Brainstorm,* Chapter 5).

Consider the following example of how the fishbone diagram can be used to probe for the root cause.

1. A project is under way to prepare a student manual for a project management course. The project manager, Susan, has divided the manual into twelve chapters and has assigned them to three different writers.
2. Susan discovers that one of the writers, Jack, who is responsible for six chapters, has been significantly late in completing the first three chapters. After examining the critical path, Susan determines that Jack's late chapter deliveries are leading to a delay of the overall project.
3. Susan decided to use a fishbone diagram to organize her thinking about the root causes for the variance in Jack's performance. As shown in Figure 7.25, in a discussion with Jack, she elected to use four major cause bones:
   a. Policies and procedures
   b. The person performing the task
   c. Equipment (including IT networking)
   d. Work environment

It should be obvious that the proper selection of cause bones is very important because these make up the foundation of the root cause analysis.

Once you have selected the major causes, your deeper investigation begins. The best approach is to brainstorm the next level of causes. For instance, Jack may not fully understand the subject matter; he may be constantly interrupted to work on things not related to chapter writing; he may have an unreliable network connection to the company server; or he might be following a document layout procedure that doesn't fit well with the content of his chapters. Figure 7.26 depicts the next level of causes on the fishbone diagram. Of course, one could discover many more than the four causes shown

FIGURE 7.24
Fishbone Diagram—
Structure

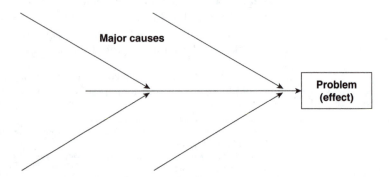

FIGURE 7.25

Fishbone Diagram—Level 1

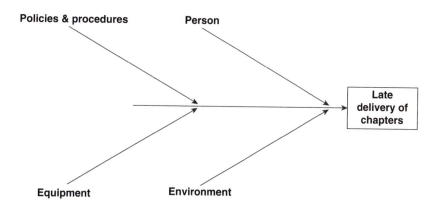

in Figure 7.26, but Jack and Susan deemed these to be the primary contributors to Jack's late completions.

Having identified a second level of causes, probe deeper. Ask why a number of additional times. Add more arrows (or bones in the fish) to indicate their relationship to the major causes. In this case, Susan and Jack eliminated polices and procedures, equipment, and environment and focused on the person (fishbone). Their next level assessment is depicted in Figure 7.27. Notice the deeper analysis of the bone: "Unable to consult reference material."

Probing the causes further, they delineated the following as *the* root causes for the late deliveries:

1. Jack was unable to access the reference material (on the company server where most of the reference materials and the other writers' work is stored).

   Further analysis of the fishbone pointed to two key problems:

2. Lack of training in accessing the company server
3. Problems accessing company server (performance problems), slow modem, slow line, curtailed avaialability

The project manager arranged for a training session for Jack and also worked with the technology group to provide Jack with improved server access.

We have found the use of the fishbone diagrams very useful. They help an individual, or a group, focus on the key causes of a problem, encourage brainstorming, and provide a visual image of the problem solving process. Typically, it is a good idea to limit the level of detail to three; any more details get in the way of focusing on the solution.

Affinity Diagram With this tool, the first step is to state the problem succinctly. A common practice is to state the problem as a single-sentence question. For example: "What is leading to Jack's delays?"

The next step is to identify the probable causes using the brainstorming approach—everyone involved states their ideas, each of which is recorded on a sticky note and pasted onto a flip chart. Remember, there is no discussion regarding any of the ideas during idea generation. Once the brainstorming is complete, ask the team to silently move the sticky notes into "affinity" groups, groups in

FIGURE 7.26

Fishbone Diagram—Level 2

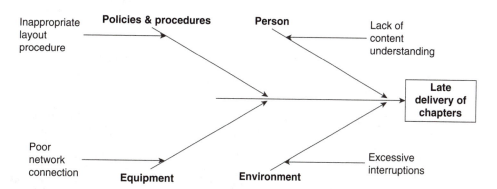

FIGURE 7.27
Fishbone Diagram—Level 3

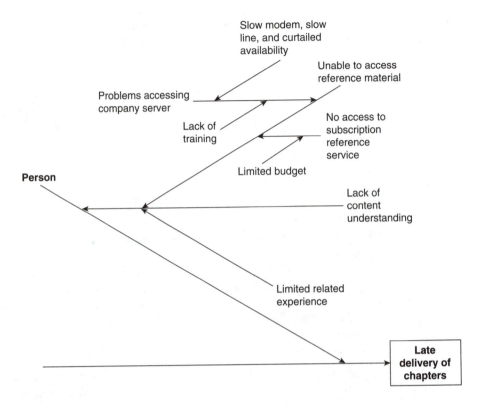

which some similar characteristics link the solutions on the notes. As the process unfolds, team members are likely to move the notes back and forth from one group to another before the groups become stable. This vacillation is normal. The next step is to write a "header card" that best describes the "solution" represented by the grouped sticky notes. Take care with this very important step because each header card describes a possible solution to the problem. The next step, if there are too many solutions, is to rank order the solutions to focus on the top one or two items. Figure 7.28 depicts a graphic representation of the process.

FIGURE 7.28
Affinity Diagram

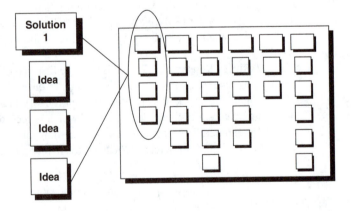

Nominal Group Technique (NGT)   This approach is often used when you are faced with a number of closely ranked solutions to a problem and you need to rank order their value. The NGT primarily consists of two steps:

1. Create a table where the rows list the various possible solutions to the problem (the order of their listing does not imply any relative value) and each column represents a team member asked to participate (see Figure 7.29).
2. Ask each of the team members to rank the solutions from 1 to N, where N is the number of solutions. N is the highest ranking and 1 is the lowest ranking. Add the rankings for each solution. The highest score is the top ranked solution.

FIGURE 7.29
NGT

	Fred	Sally	Ashok	Mario	Sue	Total
Solution 1	3	4	2	1	2	12
Solution 2	2	1	1	3	3	10
Solution 3	1	2	3	5	1	12
Solution 4	5	3	4	2	5	19
Solution 5	4	5	5	4	4	**22**

In Figure 7.29, each team member rank ordered the five proposed solutions from 1 (low) to 5 (high). Solution 5 was ranked highest overall, receiving the greatest number of points. Solution 4 was not far behind.

Matrix Display   Many forms of matrices can be used, from very simple ones to very complex ones. An example of a simple matrix is shown in Figure 7.30. Each solution is rated according to a set of decision criteria you define. More complex matrices often use weighted, numeric ratings to distinguish between solutions. In the example, the team decided that the most important decision-making criteria were the cost of the solution, the need for additional resources, and the impact on project quality. A "high" rating means that the solution strongly meets the criteria, a "medium" rating means that the solution meets the criteria fairly well, and a "low" rating means that the solution only weakly meets the criteria. Solution 5 fared well in this analysis.

FIGURE 7.30
Matrix Display

	Acceptable cost	Acceptable HR impact	Acceptable quality impact
Solution 1	Medium	High	Low
Solution 2	Low	High	Medium
Solution 3	Medium	Low	Medium
Solution 4	Low	High	Medium
Solution 5	High	Medium	High

At this point, you have identified the variance, determined the key causes, and selected one or more possible solutions to the problem. In selecting the best alternative, be sure you stay focused on project objectives and the Intra-Project Priorities—schedule, scope, budget, and quality. The best solution is one that corrects the problem but does not inhibit your ability to achieve what you set out to do. Your next step is to implement your best selection. Often, you can do this on your own without having to obtain any specific approvals, but certain solutions may need to be reviewed and approved by the sponsor and/or certain key stakeholders.

When presenting possible solutions to the sponsor or a key stakeholder, choose the method wisely. Be sure that the method of presentation is effective for the particular individual. Check with the sponsor/client if you are unsure which method is most appropriate, and be sure to speak the language of the sponsor/client. Speak finance to a finance person, technical terms to a technical person, and business language to a business person. An effective presentation depends on materials that are well prepared and include well-thought-out conclusions along with the data to support those conclusions. If necessary, rehearse the presentation. It will help you develop confidence, which is very powerful when attempting to influence others. Be prepared to negotiate. It is not unusual that the eventual solution will be one that is developed through one or more give-and-take sessions with the sponsor/client. Effective negotiation is a core skill for successful project management.

If your presentation is going to be given to a group of people, it is always a good idea to pre-sell your solutions to those who hold the most influence, prior to the formal presentation and approval process. Build your case through informal communications with people who share your point of view. Keep in mind that staying aware of those who exhibit nemesis behavior is as important as knowing the champions of the cause—in many cases, even more so.

Make sure that you obtain formal written approval from the sponsor for any changes made to project schedule, scope, budget, or quality. Depending on the situation, formal approval could be as simple as a signature on a form, or as complicated as a multitiered approval process with full documentation.

FIGURE 7.31
Plan-Do-Check-Act Cycle

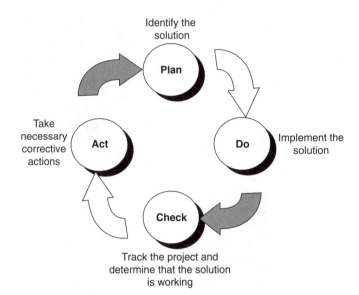

The problem solving processes and tools are grounded in the quality management Plan-Do-Check-Act (PDCA) cycle, defined by Dr. W. Edward Deming, which consists of the following four steps:

1. Identify the solution (plan)
2. Implement the solution (do)
3. Use your project tracking measures to check that the solution effectively addresses the problem (check)
4. Take corrective actions (act)

Figure 7.31 is a pictorial representation of the PDCA process. We highly recommend that you discuss the process, as well as the various problem-solving techniques, with your team and help them learn this well-tested approach to problem identification and solution implementation. Making this process a part of day-to-day problem solving is sure to produce high-quality results.

Reporting Project Progress

Now that we have discussed a variety of ways to monitor the project's progress, we need to discuss the methods of reporting project progress starting with the team members to the project manager and then from the project manager to the various people interested in the project status: project manager's manager, sponsor, key stakeholders, and the executive steering committee.

Team Members to Project Manager   The most frequent reporting cycle, team members reporting to the project manager, can be timed to one or more of the following events:

- *Start and end of tasks:* We advise this frequency of reporting toward the start of a project, when the need to get everyone up to speed fast and to make sure that unattended tasks don't result in big delays, is vital. This type of reporting is one-to-one, i.e., from the team member to the project manager as the team member starts and finishes the assigned tasks. Usually, the team member reports via e-mail messages. Another situation that may merit this frequency of reporting is when a person joins an ongoing project, and the project manager has not worked with the individual on any recent project—there is no history of performance between the two. Typically, this higher frequency of reporting will last only for a few weeks at the most, and then the team members progress to one of the following cycles.

- *Milestones:* This is the most typical cycle of reporting from team members to their project managers. Because most milestones are set at a maximum 10-day interval, using this basis for reporting means that the team members are diligently keeping the project manager informed of their work progress.

- *Deliverable completion:* We find these to be very important points of progress, and therefore we highly recommend that team members report the completion of their deliverables promptly to the project manager.

- *Breach of a vital sign:* Each team member should clearly understand the specific vital signs she needs to monitor and the threshold at which the project manager needs to be informed. Typically, these include such tactical vital signs as the critical path, cost-to-date, unresolved issues, risks and any of the strategic vital signs such as customer buy-in, technology viability, or vendor viability. This is an important point to keep in mind—the team members have the responsibility to monitor the vital signs and report variances beyond acceptable thresholds to the project manager.

From the information in the points above, it should be clear that the reporting from team members to project managers is *proactive*—team members take the initiative when a predefined reporting event takes shape. With this system, the project manager is kept informed of the current state of the project at any given time. We will discuss the team's group meeting shortly. In any reporting from a team member to the project manager, we recommend a very structured communication style:

- Punch line
- Current status
- Next steps
- Explanation

In journalism, this approach is known as the inverted pyramid style. The writer begins with the conclusion, usually expressed in a single sentence. The conclusion is followed by the most important facts and figures, and the details are then expounded in the rest of the text. This style is in contrast to typical academic writing (research papers and dissertations), where the writer opens with a problem statement, then elaborates on the background, discusses influencing factors, and *finally* states the conclusions. Unfortunately, most people are fast asleep by the time the punch line appears. The experience is just short of that of a torture chamber. That is precisely why we start with the punch line.

- *Punch line:* State the facts succinctly, no adjectives, adverbs, or modifiers. For example "Milestone 4 was not hit on time, and I did not start Task 8 as planned." If the punch line news is positive, the team member makes that statement and completes his report. For example "Received charter approval as planned."

- *Current status:* The key impact the punch line statement has on the project. For example "Because of the miss on milestone 4, the critical path has been breached by 5 days (delay)."

- *Next steps:* The solution the team member has in mind to address the problem, if any. For example "I will be able to make up 3 days during the next 2 weeks, but will still be behind by 2 days. In the case of any delays, it is important for the team member to report the remaining effort, remaining duration, and any issues that may negatively impact the planned completion."

- *Explanation:* The reason behind the punch line statement. For example "Two of the 5 days delay is due to late discovery of a hardware interface problem, and the remaining 3 days delay is due to being called to help the customer support staff for a production problem."

Notice the almost reverse order of these points, as compared to the common reporting style, in which the team member starts with a long explanation of why things went wrong. Using the four steps described above, the project manager learns about the most important information first, followed by support information to help complete the story. Over the years of consulting with project managers and their teams, we have found that, once they become accustomed to this recommended order of steps, they truly enjoy the clarity of the message and the short time it takes to get the point across. However, for many people, the point of first stating the punch line can be a bit disconcerting. Our advice: Try it; you'll like it.

It is important that you, as a project manager, learn to assess the veracity of the information provided to you by team members. You need to become adapt at separating the chaff from the wheat and reading between the lines for the real message. This word of caution is in no way meant to convey that your team members will lie to you. However, keep in mind that in times of stress when they have not accomplished what was expected, they might be tempted to give the truth a slight twist. Here are five signs that will help you ascertain how forthright the individual is in her communications:

Denial and Half Truths: The individual redirects your attention by emphatic denial while not owning up to the truth. For example, President Richard Nixon's statement, "I am not a crook" did not proclaim that he was honest and trustworthy, only that he was not a criminal. Here is another example:

> *In one case, user testing failed even after an elaborate system check had been conducted . . . When a Sprint IT director turned to the vendor and said, 'I thought you told me you tested it,' the vendor responded that he had. But he added that the IT director had never asked him whether the test had been successful.*
> Julia King, "Benefits Can be Elusive; Costs are Deceptive," *Computerworld*
> (May 18, 1998).

Distance: These individuals put a greater distance, both physical and psychological, between you and them. For example, they will sit or stand far away from you at the meeting. Another manifestation of distance is the lack of eye contact and the tendency to look away or stare at notes or other documents. To avoid contact, they will leave a phone message when they know that the recipient is away from the office. More often, they will choose to communicate through e-mail when a personal contact is the preferable choice. They also have the tendency to use the terms "they and them" rather than "I and we" when referring to their team.

Disclaimers: They tend to use disclaimers to explain the situation rather than affirming the truth. For example, "Honestly speaking . . ." "I'm not going to lie to you . . ." "You won't believe what happened to me on the way to this meeting . . ." and "It's not my fault that . . ."

Roundabout: This tactic involves long-winded explanations with many digressions—beating about the bush and providing plenty of details but no specific conclusions. The individual does not clearly end the story, leaving it open for multiple interpretations and possible retractions.

Smokescreens: Responses that add confusion through the use of word play, such as diverting attention from the subject at hand by nitpicking at your inquiries. Examples include President Clinton's now famous (or infamous) rejoinder, "That depends on what the meaning of 'is' is."

The best approach to ensure that your team members do not engage in this type of behavior is to hold a meeting soon after the project kickoff meeting (see Project Staging, Step 16), and discuss the items in an open forum. Convey to the group that you expect forthright communications not only from them to you, but among all team members. Reinforce the "inverted pyramid" style, where the punch line comes first. Keep in mind that you must practice what you preach.

Once you have the information from your team members, you can't just sit back and take it at face value. You must go out and validate what you have learned. This is not an issue of trust—it is the issue of making sure that their understanding of progress is in line with that of yours. We believe it is a great quality assurance step if at least 30 percent of the completed deliverables were reviewed for completeness and quality. The selection of these deliverables can be a random pick from the work being completed. The most equitable way to do this is by "lottery." Jot down the names of completed deliverables on pieces of paper, drop them in a bowl, and have the team members pick out about 30 percent for review by colleagues.

Percent Measurements: You may have noticed that we did not use the percent complete measurement when assessing task and deliverable completion in IT/Business projects. The omission is deliberate. We find percent compete to be a useless measurement for a majority of IT/Business project tasks and deliverables. A highly experienced consultant and esteemed colleague, George Glaser, has developed an equation he uses to discuss percent complete:

$$\text{Percent complete} = \text{Fantasy} \div \text{Fantasy}$$

In this equation, both the numerator (the original estimate) and the denominator (the current status) represent pure fantasy. We will go a step further and redefine the equation as:

$$\text{Percent complete} = \text{Fantasy} \div \text{Lie}$$

In our opinion, anyone who offers percent complete as a measurement of progress in IT/ Business projects is not disclosing the true status of the project; hence the lie. Often we see team members and project managers enter a percent complete value into the software package based on how much effort *has been* spent. For example, if a task was estimated for 30 hours and the person responsible has already spent 15 hours, she enters 50 percent complete. This reckoning is similar to a pilot deciding that the journey is 50 percent complete because the fuel gauge shows that half of the fuel has been consumed. Not smart. If you enter the percentage of completion, the program will cal- culate how much effort is remaining. This practice is very dangerous because the remaining effort number computed by the system may or may not be realistic and, therefore, will be of little value. It is important to realize that in the case of IT/Business projects, the relationship between effort and progress is rarely linear—if a deliverable is estimated for 30 hours and the first 15 hours resulted in 50 percent completion, it does not necessarily mean that the remaining 15 hours of work *will* result in 100 percent completion. Figure 7.32 shows a number of progress scenarios for IT/Business work.

FIGURE 7.32
Effort *v.* Progressive
Scenarios

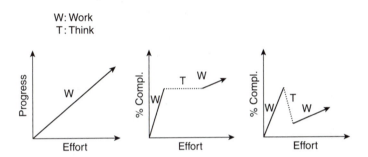

The first graph implies a linear relationship between effort and progress, and the percent com- plete measurement is based on this relationship. The second chart shows that during the first few hours, the individual working on this task made rapid progress and then he went into thinking (prob- lem solving) mode and progress on the task stopped. After a few hours, the individual began to make headway but at a much slower rate. The last chart shows that after initial progress, additional effort actually resulted in a reversal (negative progress) and then after a short period of time began to make headway again. In the last two examples, the simple percent complete calculation will have pro- duced erroneous measurements. For this reason, we highly recommend posting the sign shown in Figure 7.33.

The only situation in which percent complete might be acceptable is where the percent com- plete value is computed by using the following numbers:

1. Original effort (estimate)
2. Effort-to-date
3. Remaining effort to complete the task/deliverable

FIGURE 7.33
No Percent Complete

In reference to the task example, if the person responsible has already spent 15 hours and then reports that the current estimate to complete the task is 15 hours, then percent complete will give a more accurate picture. Because now the percent complete is computed by dividing the effort-to-date by the sum of the original effort and the remaining effort. However, we don't believe that totaling up the percent complete of the various tasks associated with a deliverable provides an accurate completion status of the deliverable and never for the project.

On a recent segment of Paul Harvey's "Rest of the Story" radio show, he spoke of a health inspector who visited a restaurant and noticed a four-egg quiche on the menu. The inspector instructed the restaurant owner to change the menu to a three-egg quiche. The owner wondered whether that was due to the high cholesterol content of the four-egg quiche. The inspector responded that on the average, one in four eggs could carry the salmonella infection. Hence, a three-egg quiche would be safer. Such is the mindset of people who believe in using percentages and averages for metrics.[6]

Task Behind Schedule: The first step is to find out whether the task in question is on the critical path. If so, we suggest a two-step process:

1. Talk to the team member responsible for the task and see if any of the following actions will help finish the task without any further delay: issues resolution, fewer interruptions, additional help, and/or overtime work.
2. Open a look-ahead window and see whether any future critical path tasks can help make up for the lost time. Once you have identified the task or tasks that can be completed within a shorter duration than currently planned, discuss your options with the core team, review their input, and put a plan into action. Trying to reduce the estimated duration of noncritical tasks is not going to help.

If the delayed task is not on the critical path, indicating that the current delay is not impacting the project schedule, make sure that the responsible team member has a plan in place to finish the delayed task before it comes on the critical path. This plan will involve the same steps.

Rework Reserve: If you incorporated the rework reserve into your project schedule, then you need to track and manage the rework being done by different team members. Rework, as we defined it in Chapters 4 and 6, means the effort spent correcting omissions and errors primarily due to inadequate skills, poor quality tools, technology upgrades, design redefinition, latent defects, and steep learning curves. Some degree of rework is difficult to avoid, especially in IT/Business projects. However, extensive rework points to systemic problems that if not addressed will result in challenged (if not failed) projects. Over the years, we have noticed that few project managers actually track the rework, even when they have added rework reserve to the project schedule. Two primary reasons for this behavior are:

1. It is not always easy to differentiate between regular work and rework.
2. Team members feel that the recording of this data will reflect on their skills and competencies, and they are afraid of being singled out as not being knowledgeable and efficient.

Both of these are valid concerns and need to be discussed and addressed before beginning to collect this metric. Consider an example of a restaurant. Rework would involve such situations as: underchilled champagne delivered to the customer, undercooked or overcooked meat, sautéed vegetables when the customer asked for steamed vegetables, or dirty cutlery or china at the table. Now, should the restaurant owner be informed about all these mishaps or should the manager, chef, wait staff, and the dishwasher keep it to themselves? Occasional missteps by an employee are to be expected, and accidents do happen, but *persistent* problems will impact the bottom line

---

[6]Reminds one of the individual who was diagnosed with a rare brain tumor. After much research, he found a neurosurgeon who specialized in his type of tumor, and to his delight assured him of a 100 percent safe operation and full recovery. Just to be on the safe side, the patient did extensive research on the Internet, and to his great disappointment learned that on the average, nine out of ten people (90 percent) who undergo the operation die. He brought this fact to the attention of the surgeon, who responded, "That is true. The last nine people I performed that surgery on did die, you are the tenth and therefore get the 100 percent guarantee."

of the business. The same is true for a project. The project manager must know the extent of the rework so that appropriate steps can be taken to assess the problems and to devise a plan of recovery.

Team Updates: In any project, it is important for the entire team to come together as a group and not only report individual project progress but learn about the status of the whole project—the status of key vital signs—as well as what lies ahead. Because the project consists of a number of intertwined tasks, milestones, and deliverables, the various team members must know how individual performance is impacting the team's performance. In addition, the project manager needs to bring the entire team up-to-date regarding the project as a whole—the information he has gathered from the various key stakeholders, the sponsor, and the customers at large.

Team update meetings are best held on a fixed schedule, at a fixed time, and for a fixed duration. The advantage of this routine is that team members understand their time commitments and can set the time aside to participate. We also recommend that you inform the respective functional managers, key stakeholders, and the sponsor of the meeting schedule so they don't plan conflicting meetings. If some of your team members are on multiple assignments, you will need to consult their project managers to make sure that any conflicts are avoided. If you discover that any of the team members are not able to attend the update meetings because of recurring last minute demands on their time by other managers, consider it a good indication of the erosion of your authority and ability to manage your team—it is time to visit the sponsor and discuss the responsibility *v.* authority issue. You should make it clear to the sponsor that, if you don't have the authority, your ability to manage the project to success will erode. The following is a list of a few important caveats for ensuring productive and efficient team update meetings:

1. Select the span of the look-ahead window and include everyone whose work appears in the look-ahead window in the meeting. We recommend a 4-week look-ahead.
2. Hold the team update meetings on a weekly basis with occasional bi-weekly intervals (based on team member availability or other unavoidable scheduling conflicts).
3. We suggest a 60 minute session (with a limit of 90 minutes). Consistently try to reduce the length of your meetings; team members will appreciate that greatly and more will attend.
4. A team meeting can be a double-edged sword. Being together with their colleagues can impose peer pressure on individual team members to finish their work on time, but such pressure may intimidate others and interfere with forthright reporting.
5. It is important for the project manager to work hard to ensure that team members report their progress with full candor. One effective way to encourage such candor is to not "shoot the messenger," and to deal with any individual performance problems at another time.
6. Create the list of look-ahead window deliverables, tasks, milestones, and issues and distribute prior to the team update meeting (e-mail works well).
7. After you have conducted a few of these meetings, you will be able to develop a sense of timing for the various components of the session. Make sure the team members become aware of the need to mind the clock.
8. Allow only one speaker at a time, respect all viewpoints, do not tolerate personal attacks, and allow no finger pointing.
9. Create a "parking lot" for all issues and record meeting minutes.
10. Many project managers we know lock the door to the meeting room 5 minutes after the start of the meeting. Anyone arriving late has to wait until the person speaking finishes before being admitted. A little embarrassment goes a long way.
11. About every 3 months, set aside some time at the end of a meeting to assess the quality of the meetings—assess effectiveness and efficiency. Take complete and clear notes and work with the team to make the necessary improvements.

For team update meetings, we suggest a standard format composed of the following three components:

1. Look back   Typically lasting a total of 15 minutes, the project manager asks each team member to state the status of her work since the last team update. This must be done following the

four steps described above—punch line, current status, next steps, and explanation. Make sure that they keep their explanations *short*. At the end of this look-back, the project manager and the team should have a clear knowledge of what has and has not been accomplished. Two additional areas to focus upon are:

   a. Work planned but not completed
   b. Work done that was not planned

2. Current status   Current status involves a group discussion, usually lasting 15 minutes or less, to collectively ascertain the status of the project and pinpoint any vital sign variances beyond acceptable thresholds, along with any unresolved issues that may impact the project progress in the near future. At this point, you should have clear and up-to-date status of each applicable vital sign.

3. Look ahead   Using the steps described earlier (see *Look-Ahead Window*), the project manager asks each team member to describe his ability to complete the work as planned. This process should not take much time, as each team member should have prepared for discussing the look-ahead window prior to the group meeting. Again, if any team member begins to narrate a fable full of pathos and intrigue, please stop the individual and remind him of the need to be succinct. Remember, people come to the meeting to report on a deliverable, not do them.

Once the last team member has finished the look-ahead window reporting, the team and the project manager should have a good understanding of the project status. At this point, we suggest that the team ask itself the following questions:

1. What went well?
2. What did not go well?
3. Who could use some help?
4. Can I be of help to any of the team members (each team member asks herself/himself this question)?

We recommend that the project manager act as the facilitator and help the team answer these four questions. Use of flip charts to record and post the responses helps the team focus on the challenges, leverage their positive experiences, and learn to support each other.

Then the project manager, in consultation with the team, needs to review the look back, current status, the period covered by the look-ahead window, any unresolved issues, and update the project plan and schedule. The project manager and the team may use a variety of tools (Fishbone diagram, Affinity diagram, NGT, or a Matrix display (see *Analytical Tools*)) to focus on the underlying reasons for any problems and their possible solutions.

At this point, we reiterate our strong belief that problem solving should take place off-line, i.e., after the four questions previously outlined have been answered. Too often, we see teams go to problem solving mode soon after the first team member states a problem. This approach distracts the team from reporting the project status and, in the end, few of the problems ever get solved. In fact, once the status review portion of the meeting is over, a number of people could actually leave the meeting and have the project manager and the core team work together to address the findings and develop solutions to any problems. The end product is an updated project scope statement and an updated schedule (if any changes have taken place). The next step is to communicate the updated scope and schedule to all team members and the key stakeholders; some may only need summary information. A few important caveats are:

- Be prompt. Implement corrective action as designed. Failure to act promptly could result in further variances.
- Be thorough. Make sure that the recovery procedure is implemented properly so that the project stays on course.
- Measure results. As soon as possible, verify that the recovery procedures are working.
- Report results promptly to the sponsor and affected stakeholders.

A good point to consider is: Should the status of the various vital signs of a project be made public—made visible to people not on the project team? We believe that projects do not belong to project managers, they belong to the organization and, as such, their vital signs should be a public (departmental) record. Many project managers we know have adopted posting their project's vital signs in their office. Some of them paste a sheet of paper that displays the vital signs on the inside of their hallway windows, and some have even designed the project vital signs list into a screen saver. The underlying idea is that if any vital signs indicate trouble, their colleagues should know. Often, people who are not even on the team offer to help when they learn of the problems being faced by a project team. The process actually helps build camaraderie among people. Many project managers we work with confide that when their project is in trouble, most people find out about it anyway and, therefore, the posting of project vital sign status is not a problem for them. We wholeheartedly endorse the practice.

Team Nonperformance: Despite your best efforts to select the right team members, there will be times when people will not perform well. As a skilled project manager, you will need to deal with the problem in a mature manner. Let us explore the key reasons for a team member's failure to perform as expected:

- People make mistakes
- They didn't know any different
- People do bad things, sometimes by intent or with what they believe to be reasonable cause
- Accidents happen

Regarding the first item, *mistakes* happen to best of us. The ideal approach is to catch them early, work with the person individually to determine the root cause (try using the Fishbone diagram), and help the person recover. It is important to convey to the individual the importance of diligence in the future to minimize any repetitions. The second item in the list, points to either miscommunication or lack of attention to detail. It may also be that the person places a low priority on the work product, which allows carelessness to develop. The problem here is commitment and accountability. You will need to spend a little extra time with the individual to make sure that roles and responsibilities are clearly communicated, that the individual understands the importance of quality output, and what the consequences of any future nonperformance are. The third item, is more serious. The individual in question is lacking in accountability, discipline, and presumably ethics. From the first time this happens, you need to take a firm (private) stand with the individual. Clearly convey your disappointment in the behavior and the manner in which the individual's actions have impacted the project. Communicate strongly to the individual that you do not expect the behavior to repeat and that the next time it happens you will escalate the problem to her functional manager and the project sponsor. Nipping the problem in the bud promptly is the best approach. The last item has to be addressed at face value—an unpleasant outcome due to unpredictable external influences. Of course, if the accidents happen too often, carelessness may be the cause, or it may indicate that the individual does not have the appropriate skills to carry out the assignment. Education, training, and mentoring will certainly help prepare the individual to be less accident prone. All of the items listed have to do with "soft" skills and require a professional and considered approach to problem solving and the ability to negotiate and motivate, as well as strong leadership skills.

Let's summarize the purpose of team updates:

1. To ensure that task owners assess the status of their assigned tasks on a routine, scheduled basis
2. To ensure that task owners anticipate problems and develop ways to avoid them before they occur
3. To ensure that the project manager is informed of task status
4. To ensure that the project manager is given the factual information needed to update project plans, estimates, and schedules
5. To inform all team members of the status of tasks owned by others and of problems requiring resolution by the team as a whole
6. To inform all team members of changes to plans, estimates, and schedules
7. To foster communications and cooperation among team members
8. To provide a platform for reorganizing outstanding accomplishments by team members
9. To identify any problems to be escalated to any functional managers and the project sponsor

Project Manager to Functional Managers   The best approach for this type of reporting is for the project manager to discuss the subject with the various functional managers and jointly decide on the information to be reported and the frequency of reporting. Reporting typically focuses on the performance of various team members on the project team to their respective managers. Reporting can be on a biweekly or monthly cycle. Often, we see this type of reporting resorted to only when there are problems and issues with certain team members. We believe this is an unfortunate decision because the project manager will communicate only bad news—certainly not a pleasant relationship from the functional manager's point of view. Therefore, a monthly meeting is strongly recommended. The project manager can discuss the overall status of the project, report the performance of various team members, discuss any open issues, and keep the key functional managers informed about the project's health.

Project Manager to Her Manager This reporting is necessary when the project sponsor and the project manager's boss is not the same person. In this situation, it is important that the project manager keep her manager informed about the project's overall status—progress, issues, and risks. The overall reporting process is the same as described in the previous paragraph. To make sure that the manager's expectations are met, the project manager should work with her manager to define the reporting frequency, vital sign thresholds, and the format and structure of reporting information. This reporting does not replace the reporting the project manager must still do one-on-one to the project sponsor. If this happens, and the sponsor now gets his information from the project manager's manager, the end result is a new level of bureaucratic hierarchy that will likely put a spin on the information reported to the sponsor. We strongly suggest that the project manager report directly to the sponsor.

Project Manager to Sponsor The project manager and the sponsor should meet formally to review the project status, issues, and risks every month (preferably, biweekly). During these meetings, the two of them review the selected vital signs for the project and open a look-ahead window to map the future of the project. At this level, we suggest a 3-month window, allowing them to see any upcoming obstacles in the project path. In Chapter 5, we discussed in detail the importance of an actively involved sponsor toward the success of a project and will reiterate the point. One specific sign of sponsor commitment is the regularity of project manager and sponsor meetings and the degree to which the sponsor is interested in reviewing and tracking the selected vital signs. Even though a project manager cannot force a sponsor to live up to the agreed upon review sessions, successive postponement and/or cancellation of these review sessions is a vital sign to monitor. The weaker the sponsor involvement is, the greater the risk of a challenged or failed project.

One of the key responsibilities of a project manager is to continually "market" the project to the primary stakeholders and assess their ongoing buy-in. However, there may come a point, where despite the best efforts of the project manager, key stakeholders begin to lose interest in the project. If this happens, become more alert to the variance in the vital signs, and if they begin to approach their runaway conditions, we strongly advise the project manager to develop a cause and effect report and discuss the findings personally with the sponsor. Make sure that you put forth specific recommendations, and then ask the sponsor for specific actions. If the sponsor shows a lack of interest, or is overly distracted by other problems, the next step is to begin to move toward the *Troubled Project Assessment* discussed later in this chapter. Because of the inherent lack of overarching authority over the people whose behavior leads to the problem, we strongly believe that there comes a time when the responsibility for stakeholder involvement and buy-in needs to be transferred to the sponsor.

Steering Committee Update If a steering committee has been established for your project, they will need periodic updates on project status and may be called upon to solve certain high-level policy issues. This reporting is typically the responsibility of the sponsor who summarizes the project status information supplied by the project manager. The frequency of steering committee update meetings vary anywhere from ad hoc sessions at the request of the sponsor to regularly scheduled bimonthly or quarterly sessions. We strongly believe that if the project complexity, risks, and importance were high enough to merit the formation of a steering committee, then the members should meet regularly to review the project status and health. We recommend a regularly scheduled, bimonthly meeting. A common question is, "Should the project manager be present in such meetings?" To us, this question points to a certain apprehension of having the project manager present at a meeting where corporate-level strategy issues may be discussed, and the executive committee does not want the project manager to be present during those conversations. We believe this is a valid concern, which can be addressed by using the following approach:

- Break the steering group meeting into two separate parts. The first part deals primarily with the project's current status, its overall health (vital signs), escalated issues, and a 3- to 4-month look-ahead window. During this part, the project manager is present in a support role to the sponsor (to answer any questions that require detailed knowledge of the project).
- At the end of the first segment, the project manager leaves the meeting. Now the sponsor and the steering group are free to discuss any policy-level issues.

The project manager's presence in the steering group meetings sends a clear message to all of the stakeholders and the team that the project manager is held in high esteem by the management group, that he has access to the right people, and that the project manager is privy to the strategic thinking of senior managers, as it relates to the project. This inclusion goes a long way in demonstrating management's trust in the professional capabilities of the project manager.

Project Status Reports

In this and previous chapters, we have defined and described a variety of standardized reports, including:

- Issues List, Figure 4.27
- Risk Management, Figure 4.28
- List of Deliverables—Focus on Delayed Start, Figure 7.6
- List of Deliverables—Focus on Delayed Finish, Figure 7.7
- List of Deliverable Owners, Figure 7.8
- List of Milestones, Figure 7.9
- Sponsor Performance Checklist, Figure 7.11
- Team Disposition (Effectiveness) Assessment, Figure 7.12
- Project Health Report, Figure 7.13
- Budget Forecast, Figure 7.18
- Project Projections, Figure 7.21

A number of other reports are available from any project management software package (for EV, resource loading, and cash flow, etc.). We advise you to talk to your sponsor and jointly define the set of reports most suitable for your own management needs and those of any other people you report to. You can then meet the information requirements of all concerned.

Exception Reporting

Within the project status assessment and reporting process, we strongly recommend the use of the exception report. This type of report is produced whenever the variation of a vital sign *exceeds* its predefined tolerance level. The benefit of an exception report is that it focuses on variations from the norm, thereby drawing specific attention to key problem areas. To be effective, such reports must be specific, to the point, and brief. We suggest the following structure:

1. *Description of the variation:* Using the punch line first style, identify the vital sign in question and describe the specific deviation.
2. *Cause of the variation:* Describe the underlying reason/source for the variation.
3. *Impact of the variance:* Describe the impact of the variance on the project's Intra-Project Priorities (schedule, scope, budget, and quality), any critical success factors, and key stakeholders.
4. *Recommendations:* Generate a succinct list of alternatives and their respective impacts on the project's Intra-Project Priorities (schedule, scope, budget, and quality), any critical success factors, and key stakeholders.
5. *Comments/explanations:* Provide any additional information that may be helpful to the report recipient in understanding the problem and making a decision.

Progress Review Principles

Your project reporting mechanism must ensure realistic, accurate, consistent, and timely reporting of project status at all levels. Towards this goal, we present the following important points:

- Review frequently and in detail
  - What gets measured, gets done
  - What you don't know *will* hurt you
- Don't confuse effort with progress
  - Percent complete is insidious
  - Use objective measures; we recommend vital signs
  - Know what was planned and what was accomplished
- Look ahead, not backward
  - Determine what remains to be done
  - How long will it take to do it?
  - Are there any obstacles in the way?
- Focus on critical tasks
  - Start and complete critical tasks at the earliest possible time
  - People who habitually start late will finish late
  - Schedule overrun and cost overrun go hand-in-hand
- Know the current outlook at all times
  - Strategy alignment
  - Sponsor commitment
  - Customer buy-in
  - Team disposition
  - Project health
- Problem solving should not be a part of the review meeting
  - Solve problems after the review process is complete
  - Use as few people as possible to solve problems
  - Communicate problem resolution broadly
- Don't shoot the messenger
  - Learn to take bad news in stride
  - Encourage forthright communications

> *'Show those numbers to the [expletive] auditors and I'll throw you out the [expletive] window.'* WorldCom accounting executive Buford Yates, to an underling who questioned the company's books, according to investigators.
>
> *Newsweek* (June 23, 2003): p. 27.

Dealing With Deadlines

We discussed the steps to manage critical path compression in Chapters 2 and 6 as well as earlier in this chapter. We are sure you have kept a sharp eye on the project schedule. However, a time comes in every project manager's life when, despite all of the rigor, discipline, hard work, and leadership, the schedule slips and you discover that the currently computed finish date falls far beyond the currently specified finish date. Now what? Let's propose a method that has worked very well for us. The underlying principle for the proposed solution is based on risk management. In this case, the risk is in terms of a number of specific days (delay) and it needs to be mitigated. Figure 7.34 depicts the risk to the schedule. As you can see, on a given date, the project manager discovers that the difference between the deadline and the currently projected finish date is 28 days, which imposes a risk or stress on the project.

FIGURE 7.34
The Dreaded Deadline

To deal with this stress situation, we will use the classic engineering method of distributing the total stress across different components of structure, making sure that no individual component is unduly stressed. Consider the following example: You are in the midst of changing a tire on your car and you accidentally step on the rim of the hubcap, sending the nuts flying off into the drainage ditch. Adding to your frustration, you discover that the grate over the drain is bolted down, you can't retrieve the nuts, and you forgot to bring your cell phone. One solution is to take a nut from each of the other wheels, use them to secure the tire you are changing, and then drive slowly and carefully to the nearest repair shop. You have parsed and distributed the problem into different components, without overly stressing any single one. We propose a similar solution to the dilemma of the new deadline depicted in Figure 7.34. To solve our problem, we go back to the project equation we first introduced in Chapter 4, which is depicted in Figure 7.35, along with a two-level parsing of each of the four components.

FIGURE 7.35
Project Equations—
Parsed to Two Levels

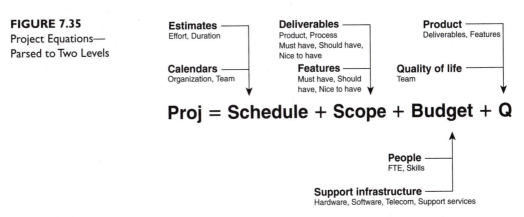

Let's review the components of Figure 7.35, where we have parsed each of the four key project attributes into subcomponents:

- Schedule
  - Estimates
    - Effort
    - Duration
  - Calendars
    - Organization calendar
    - Team member calendars
- Scope
  - Deliverables (product, process)
    - Must have
    - Should have
    - Nice to have
  - Features
    - Must have
    - Should have
    - Nice to have
- Budget
  - People
    - FTE
    - Skills
  - Support infrastructure
    - Hardware
    - Software
    - Telecommunications
    - Facilities
    - Support services

- Quality
  - Product quality
    - Deliverables
    - Features
  - Quality of life
    - Team members

Once the parsing is complete, you can focus on each component and see to what extent you can reduce the project duration by manipulating these attributes. This mission is going to be an exercise in negotiations because you are going to need to convince the people responsible for the different areas to make some adjustments. So, put your negotiations face on and let's go.

Schedule Review   Because the project schedule is "owned" by the functional managers, the project manager, and the team members, you will need to bring together the core team and the people who control team members' assignments. Here you have two options:

- Ask the team to focus on the estimates of various tasks on the critical- and near-critical paths and see whether the respective team members can reduce the estimated durations of these tasks by taking one or more of the following actions: reduce the work interruption factor, reduce the number of concurrent project assignments, and/or improve the productivity environment of the team. Figure 7.36 shows that the team was able to reduce the critical path by 5 days.
- Ask the team whether the people who are assigned to the critical- and near-critical path tasks can volunteer to work overtime (longer shifts and fewer days off—week ends, holidays, and vacations) to help reduce the critical path of the project. In Figure 7.36, we can see that the team was able to reduce the critical path by an additional 3 days; now you have 20 days to go.

Scope Review   Because project scope is "owned" by the customers, you will need to bring together the customer representatives who are authorized to negotiate the project scope. Because of the 20 day expected delay in project completion, the customer needs to decide which of the deliverables and features can be either delayed until the next version of the product or deleted from the requirements list. You and the team should have already analyzed the list of deliverables and features and developed a best candidates list. Now, through discussions with the customer representatives, develop a list of items that can be removed from the current "to do" list and determine what impact that has on the project schedule. Figure 7.36 shows that the group deleted certain deliverables and features; this action reduced the critical path by 10 additional days. At this point, the group has shaved off a total of 18 days, with 10 days still to go.

Budget Review   The project budget is "owned" by the customers and management. It consists of the salaries and expenses of the team members and the support infrastructure—hardware, software, telecommunications, facilities, and support services. You will need to negotiate with management regarding any additional budget that could help to reduce the critical path by adding additional team members, providing training and mentoring to existing team members, and/or improving the

FIGURE 7.36
Dealing with Project
Deadline

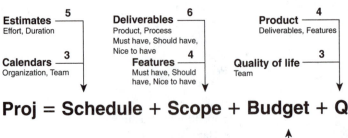

$$Proj = Schedule + Scope + Budget + Q$$

infrastructure. As you can see in Figure 7.36, additional budget for people helped reduce the critical path by 2 days; however, no such options were available through infrastructure improvements. This effort has reduced the critical path by a total of 20 days, with 8 days still to go.

Quality Review The project quality is "owned" by management and customers and consists of the quality of the end product and the quality of life of the team. At this point, you need to ask the owners of the product quality what compromises they will be agreeable to in order to deliver the product at the earlier schedule. Again, you and the team should have investigated this avenue beforehand and developed a number of suggestions for discussion. Referring back to the number of attributes related to product quality that we described in Chapter 4 (see *Quality Definition*), you need to work with the customers to see which ones could be compromised to what (safe) degree to help reduce the project schedule. The first and most common reaction from many project management professionals as well as customers is: "There is no way to compromise product quality; it has to be the best." Ask them if they ever eat at fast food restaurants, buy anything other than the safest cars, and travel only in first and business class. The idea here is to review the quality requirements of the project and offer a trade-off in this area as an option. The option of delaying the project delivery is always available. As you can see from Figure 7.36, the project manager was able to negotiate a reduction of 4 days from the customer group, resulting in shaving a total of 24 days from the critical path of the project.

The *last* item to review is the quality of life of the team, which typically means longer work hours and fewer days off (weekends, holidays, vacations, and sick leaves). Unfortunately, far too many project managers (and their bosses) rely exclusively on this option to reduce a project schedule. We strongly believe this choice to be ill-advised, because in the long run the product quality suffers in proportion to the decrease in the quality of life for the team. Figure 7.36 shows that the project manager has asked certain team members to work overtime to gain 3 additional days. This action results in the reduction of a total of 27 days, leaving the project manager still with a 1-day delay. At this point, you have two options:

1. Suggest a delay of 1 day in the project completion, or
2. Go back to the project equation and see where the day could be gained

We strongly suggest you do not start with overtime for the team. Rather, that should be your last option. We are certain that some macho project managers will object to this statement because they believe that, when push comes to shove, the team should be the first to sacrifice. (Long live Dilbert.) Also, remember the car tire example; removing too many nuts[7] from any one wheel will cause major problems.

As you look at Figure 7.36, we do not mean to imply that you will be able to reduce a certain number of days from most of the parsed attributes. On occasion, you will deliberately choose not to include a given attribute in the process of duration reduction. For example, if Quality was ranked first as a part of the intra-project priority definition (see Chapter 4), then you would not include the quality attribute in this process. Similarly, in the case of a fixed price project, the budget attribute will be excluded because any additional costs will impact the final cost of the project.

From the discussion above, you could conclude that each group needs to be contacted separately to discuss their possible contribution to schedule reduction. While that is an option, the best approach is to invite the appropriate representative(s) of each group to a joint meeting. Make sure that the people attending the meeting have the authority to make decisions promptly and that their management will support their actions. As in all negotiations, make sure that people know what the objectives are and what is expected of them. Participants should also have prepared for the session by holding appropriate premeeting discussions with their groups.

Worst Case Scenario

In Chapter 4, we discussed the need to define the worst case scenario for the project. It is important that you monitor the defined thresholds throughout the Execute stage.

---

[7]This by no means refers to team members, and certainly not the customer.

■ DEALING WITH TROUBLED PROJECTS

The news is in and it is not good. Close to 30 percent of IT/Business projects are delivered extensively over budget and/or behind schedule, and an additional 40 percent fail or are abandoned before completion. Even worse, the majority of troubled projects are abandoned long *after* millions of dollars have been wasted on hapless development. Nationally, it adds up to hundreds of billions of dollars down the giant IT drain. Perhaps the saddest example of the problems caused by a troubled project not being canceled in a timely manner is that of Tri Valley Growers. A 100-year old California company, Tri Valley Growers filed for bankruptcy in July of 2000 due in part to a failed IT/Business project. Why do so many sponsors and project managers refuse, or fail, to recognize the coming disaster, and why don't project sponsors abandon the proverbial sinking ship?

> There's a natural tendency to get overly committed to something, especially when there are no clear signals telling you you are off course,' said Mark Keil, an associate professor at Georgia State University in Atlanta.
>
> Kim Nash, "Companies Don't Learn From Previous IT Snafus,"
> *Computerworld* (October 30, 2000).

The primary reason stems from an attitude born of such empty pronouncements as:

- Failure is not an option
- Just do it
- No project cancellations on my watch
- We did not see it coming

As we saw in Figure 4.4 (Chapter 4), 70 percent of the respondents indicated that they *do not* specify the conditions under which the continuation of their projects should be critically evaluated—the "shutdown conditions" for their projects. Our experience shows that most project managers are afraid of being labeled as quitters or failures. As a result, the majority of troubled projects are canceled too late in their life cycles, often after millions of dollars have been spent. In light of the *late* abandonment rate of troubled projects, it is imperative that project organizations institute a robust process to identify and cancel failed projects before irreparable damage is done.

> Shortly after World War II, the British, in order to relieve a shortage of cooking oil, embarked on a gigantic plan to grow groundnuts (peanuts) in East Africa. The plan came to grief after eight years of fighting hostile soil and adverse climate conditions. Eighty million dollars were lost. The project was abandoned when someone finally remembered that it was West Africa, *not* East Africa, *where peanuts thrive.*
>
> John Gall, *Systemantics* (Ann Arbor, MI:
> The General Systemantics Press, 1986): p. 90.

The two key questions that need to be asked regarding any project in progress are:

1. Are we doing the right project?
2. Are we doing the project right?

Our advice to all of our IT/Business clients is to institute a continuous process of reviewing all projects in progress with one specific objective: Should we continue with this project or institute cancellation procedures?

■ TROUBLED PROJECT ASSESSMENT

What follows is a process to help project managers and sponsors determine the health of a project in progress. The key objective is to help project sponsors make *timely* project shutdown decisions for troubled projects. Figure 7.37 depicts a high level view of the process.

In Figure 7.37, we see that the process involves three key steps: analysis, decision, and action.

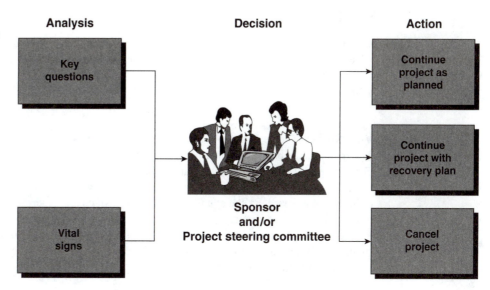

FIGURE 7.37
Troubled Project Assessment

Analysis

The project manager must ask a set of questions regarding the project and must assess the status of the project vital signs. The information gained through this analysis will help the project manager to develop a good picture of the project's health.

Key Questions The questions that follow are designed to assess the strategic health of the project—is this project appropriate for the organization?

- *Is this an approved project?* Determine whether the project received specific approval by an authorized person. Is the person still with the organization? If the answer to the last question is "No," confirm that the current sponsor is fully committed to the project.

- *Is this a unique project?* Determine whether any similar projects are underway and whether unwarranted duplication exists. Answering this question may require significant effort unless a mature project portfolio management process is in place.

- *Is there a fit with business strategy?* Determine whether the project has a well-defined fit with the currently-stated organizational strategy. At times, a project begins with a good strategic fit, but due to changes in overall strategy the project may no longer be a compelling investment. For example, when the project was approved the strategy was growth, but due to changes in the economy and the organization's direction the new strategy is cost savings.

- *Is the technology viable?* Is the enabling technology available and viable? Can it be supported by the IT organization? Will the customers be able to adopt it?

- *Is there an appropriate sponsor?* Determine whether the project has a clearly-identified and actively-involved sponsor. Does the sponsor understand the project's business and technical complexity? Is the sponsor committed to the project? Does the sponsor have the appropriate authority, including the authority to shut it down?

- *Is there customer buy-in?* Assess the degree of buy-in by customers toward the project. It is not uncommon for a team to continue working on a project even though key customers express widespread dissatisfaction with the project.

- *Is the project dependent on another project?* If the successful deployment of the project at hand is dependent on another project, the possibility that the dependent project is in jeopardy is a cause for concern.

- *Is the defect rate acceptable?* Is the number of defects in the product/process within the acceptable range?

The responses to the questions are interpreted as follows:

- Positive answers to all of the questions means a green flag (things are OK).
- Negative answers to one or more questions, but a solution is in sight, means a yellow flag (a warning about a runaway condition).
- Negative answers to one or more questions, but no solution is in sight, means a red flag (danger, you are approaching a shutdown condition).

Vital Signs The next step is to assess the status of the various project vital signs. As we discussed earlier in this chapter, all projects need to be tracked using a set of specifically defined vital signs. For example, status of the critical path (schedule), cost-to-date, scope, risks, and customer buy-in. Vital sign thresholds are used to define project runaway and shutdown conditions. For this step, the project manager reviews the status of various vital signs and determines if any have breached their thresholds and by how much. This information will help ascertain how well the project is progressing. Next, the project manager, working with the core team and appropriate SMEs, analyzes the findings from the steps and develops a set of recommendations for the sponsor. Figure 7.38 depicts the structure of the decision process.

FIGURE 7.38
Weighing the Facts

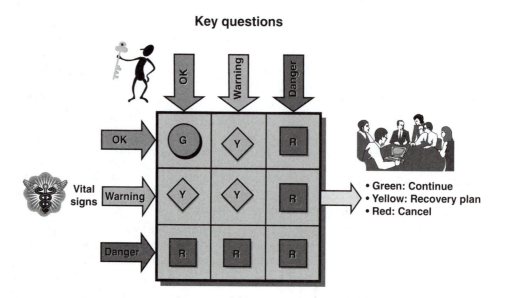

Decision

The sponsor and/or the steering committee reviews the analysis submitted by the project manager and then they decide on the fate of the troubled project—continue the project with an appropriate recovery plan or cancel the project. In one commonly used method, each steering group member casts a vote with a value between 1 and 5. A value of 1 means the project has a low significance and a value of 5 indicates a project of high significance. With most of our clients, only projects receiving an average value of 4 or greater are deemed worth saving. Figure 7.39 depicts the structure of the decision process by the sponsor and/or the steering committee.

Action

At this point, there are two options:

1. Deploy a project recovery plan and continue the project
2. Develop a cancellation plan and cancel the project

Deploy Recovery Plan If the steering committee votes in favor of saving the project, the project sponsor is directed to develop and deploy an *aggressive* project recovery plan. The objective of the recovery plan is to bring the project's strategic and tactical vital signs within the acceptable limit

FIGURE 7.39

Decision-Making and
Action Steps

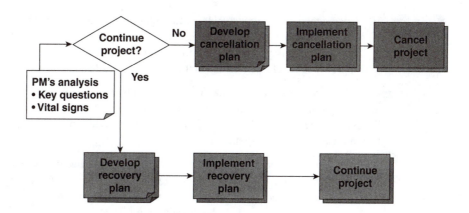

of variances—as close to the green status as possible—and then continue work on the project. Any such project will warrant close monitoring to assure that its health does not take a turn for the worse. Once the recovery plan is put into action, the sponsor must oversee project recovery closely and report the project's progress to the steering committee on a routine basis (often weekly).

Deploy Cancellation Plan   Doing this is likely to be very difficult because a large number of people, especially the team, are going to be impacted by this decision. It is imperative that the sponsor and the project manager develop a sound plan to cancel the project efficiently while, at the same time, ensuring that the people involved with the project incur only minimal damage. To this end, we suggest the following steps:

1. *Review with HR:* Because any canceled project means reassignment of team members, it is important to bring the HR department into the loop to ensure that any career related issues are addressed properly and in a timely manner.

2. *Review with legal:* If the project to be canceled involves vendors or contractors, review the cancellation plan with the legal department.

3. *Official decision to cancel the project:* Once the steering committee has voted to terminate the project, and the decision has been reviewed both by the HR and legal groups, the project sponsor makes the final decision to cancel the project.

4. *Develop cancellation plan:* At this point, the sponsor and the project manager work together to develop a well-defined plan, with specific responsibilities, to cancel the project. This deliberation ensures that minimal "damage" occurs to the end customer, the key stakeholders, and the project team.

5. *Communicate to all stakeholders:* The sponsor communicates the reasons for and the benefits of the decision to cancel the project to all key stakeholders. We strongly advise that any announcements (e-mails or memos) be preceded by personal telephone calls by the sponsor. At times, a brief meeting of the key stakeholders, where the sponsor personally announces the termination decision, is the best avenue.

6. *Cancel project:* After notifying stakeholders, put the project cancellation plan into action.

7. *Project component salvage plan:* In any project, there are always certain components—requirements, design, code, and test data—that can be salvaged for use in other projects. Develop a plan to salvage any or all such components.

8. *Capture lessons learned:* Every failed endeavor yields important lessons that can help improve future project work. The sponsor should direct the project manager to draft a set of "lessons learned." The project manager can best capture this information through interviews with key team members (including customers) in combination with a review of the project history.

9. *Reassign project team:* With any canceled project, the project team must not become the "fall guy." It is important that no blame be attached to the team because it is rarely the team's fault that a project goes awry and is canceled. If team members are made to bear the brunt of a canceled project, morale will plummet, and they may not be forthright with their assessment of the vital signs in the future.

10. *Open access to the sponsor:* It is important that the sponsor of a canceled project be available to answer questions regarding the reasons for and benefits of the decision to cancel the project. One key caution to the sponsor is not to begin to second-guess the decision or to lay blame. The best approach is to refer any critics to the Cancellation Plan and the Lessons Learned document.

A process titled ProjectHALT™ designed by the Center to identify and cancel troubled projects was published as a Whiteboard in the September 1, 2001 issue of *CIO Insight* magazine.[8] We believe that the success of any new process depends greatly on the existence of a positive and proactive mindset within the organization.

> *. . . do the team awards and lessons learned. . . . You need to recognize that there's a grief period and help the team through it—and still have the ending celebrations to say, "We took our best shot.' This is important for team morale.*
> Karen White in Minda Zetlin, "When The Plug Gets Pulled,"
> *Computerworld* (January 13, 2002).

The key points to achieve success in identifying and canceling troubled projects are as follows:

- A change in thinking that canceled projects carry a stigma
- Carefully defined performance thresholds—runaway and shut down conditions
- A systematic process for identifying problems early in a project's life cycle
- A systematic process for canceling projects
- A process for capturing key lessons from the cancellation process and improving future performance

Our experience shows that in organizations where canceling a project is viewed as a failure, few projects will ever get canceled. Conversely, if the corporate culture can see something positive in *timely* project shut down, more project managers and sponsors might be willing to jettison troubled projects. However, if IT and business management do not put a well-defined *process* to identify and cancel troubled projects into practice, project teams will drag around comatose projects mercilessly. In the U.S. alone, over 100 billion dollars are lost annually in failed IT/Business projects because few have the foresight to yell, "Abandon ship!"

> *Survival Tip: Don't let a doomed project run on—or die a quiet death. Admit it's failed and announce the failure.*
> Tom Field, "To Hell and Back," *CIO Magazine* (December 1, 1998).

Our study of the project portfolios of a large number of private and public organizations shows that most would benefit greatly by instituting an ongoing process to identify troubled projects. This type of proactive thinking will help them single out projects that, if allowed to proceed uninterrupted, are sure to result in massive disruptions and losses.

> *Jeff Chasney, CIO at CKE Restaurants, confirms that a project manager who volunteers to cancel a project that's in trouble can gain respect from top managers. "It's real career enhancement when someone can forecast out and see that a project won't work."*
> Zetlin, 2003.

> *People have an aversion to stopping projects, but the majority of projects I cancel are done because there's a change in company strategy—a change in priority or direction. . . You can't complete projects just because you started them.*
> Jeff Chasney in Todd Datz "Portfolio Management How to Do It Right,"
> *CIO Magazine* (May 1, 2003).

Figure 7.40 depicts a summary of the project scheduling and tracking process. The figure is divided into three key areas as follows:

1. *Left:* The key inputs to this area are the detailed plans, estimates (on the top), and actual team performance data (toward the bottom). The project schedule is created and actual team performance data is recorded as the project progresses.

---

[8]http://www.cioinsight.com/article2/0,3959,16486,00.asp

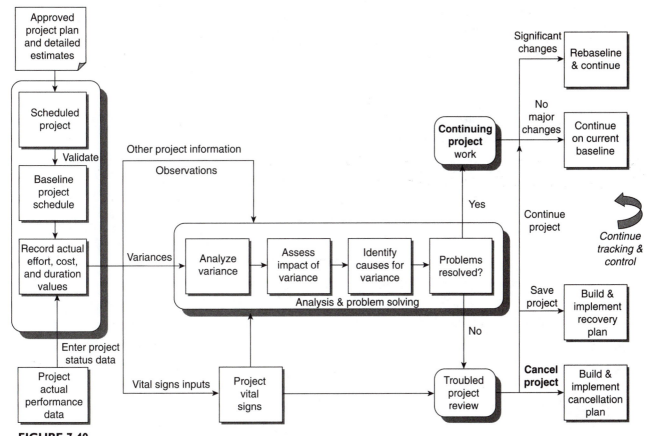

FIGURE 7.40
Project Scheduling and Tracking Process

2. *Middle:* Inputs to this process are the vital sign data, any variances from planned to actuals, and general observations regarding the project progress. The objective here is to analyze the project progress information and resolve any problems.

3. *Right:* This area has two key components: 1) continue the project execution work after making any necessary adjustments to the project schedule or, 2) if problems persist, assess whether the project is a candidate for cancellation.

■ WORDS FOR THE WISE PROJECT MANAGER

Keep in mind that being a project manager is a position of leadership and team members do take their cues and direction from their project manager's explicit and implicit actions. Also, keep in mind that there are few, if any, private conversations. In fact, the fastest way to propagate a pronouncement is to tell the listener that it is off the record and just for his ears. By a few hours later, everyone is sure to hear the message (with considerable twists and turns thrown in). Not that you have to walk on eggshells, but be mindful of what you express and what you convey in an implicit manner. This is especially true in stressful situations, when what you meant as an innocuous remark shows up as a point of great concern by many team members and stakeholders. Listen to the grapevine and don't ignore any damaging rumors.

■ STAGE GATE NO. 4

As you know, the purpose of a stage gate is to ensure that the quality of the project management process matches the complexity and inherent risk of the project, and that the project can safely proceed to the next stage. The template in Figure 7.41 depicts a suggested list of attributes for the stage

FIGURE 7.41
Stage Gate No. 4—
Execute Stage

Stage gate no. 4: attributes	Confidence level					Action plan
1. Strategy alignment	1	2	3	4	5	
2. Value-to-business	1	2	3	4	5	
3. Ownership	1	2	3	4	5	
4. Customer buy-in	1	2	3	4	5	
5. Sponsor	1	2	3	4	5	
6. Project manager	1	2	3	4	5	
7. Project team	1	2	3	4	5	
8. Change management plan	1	2	3	4	5	
9. Customer readiness	1	2	3	4	5	
10. Quality assurance	1	2	3	4	5	
11. Communications plan	1	2	3	4	5	
12. Project health (vital signs)	1	2	3	4	5	
13. Customer training plan	1	2	3	4	5	
14. Current system retirement plan	1	2	3	4	5	
15. Up-to-date project notebook	1	2	3	4	5	
16. Budget	1	2	3	4	5	

gate review at the end of the Execute stage. Keep in mind that this is a suggested list, and you will need to tailor it to your specific project.

We will reiterate the stage gate review process here:

1. The project manager and the core team meet to assess the degree to which each of the attributes has been accomplished. To make the assessment useful, we suggest that the team members, under the facilitation of the project manager, collectively review their work products and decide on the quality of each item. In Figure 7.41, in the column titled *Confidence level*, the value of 1 implies poor quality or incomplete work and the value of 5 implies high quality and comprehensive work. Any item with an assessed value lower than 3 means low quality work and, if not corrected, will result in problems during the future project stages.

2. Once the team has finished the assessment, the project manager meets with the sponsor to review the assessment, and the sponsor then decides whether to open stage gate no. 4 to let the team proceed to the Implement stage, or to direct the team to do rework to improve any of the low quality work products. Occasionally, the sponsor may open the stage gate even if some of the work is not up to par. This conditional approval implies that the team will remedy the situation to the sponsor's satisfaction in the near future.

Another possibility is to move the project to the suspend portfolio or the canceled project portfolio (refer to Chapter 10).

As we discussed in Chapter 1, the PPA can be scaled to fit the size and complexity of a given project. Complex projects will require more of the steps as well as more rigor, while simpler projects will do well with fewer steps and less rigor. Please refer to Figure 1.12 for the steps recommended for simple, average, complex, and very complex projects.

■ SUMMARY

In this chapter, we discussed the steps to generate a resource-based schedule, after which the team members begin to execute their assigned work, and the project manager starts to monitor the vital signs (the health) of the project. A green condition means that all is well with the project, yellow means that a number of vital signs are showing "negative" values, and red means that most of the vital signs have breached their threshold levels and the project is in major jeopardy. We also discussed the problem of troubled projects continuing without cancellation because sponsors and project managers are afraid of being labeled as quitters or failures. We outlined the importance of IT/Business organizations establishing a well-defined process that sends a clear message to sponsors and project managers that problem projects should be jettisoned rather than toughed out before irreparable damage is done. We then introduced a methodology that can be used to determine the health of a project and, if necessary, the point at which to shut it down, along with a set of well-planned shutdown steps.

It is essential that the project sponsor fulfills her responsibilities and provides the project team with the right level of support and guidance. Committed sponsorship means investment of personal "political" capital and personal time. Projects from the Execute portfolio move to the implement portfolio when they meet their previously defined completion criteria (critical success factors and vital signs' thresholds). Projects that breach the completion criteria are moved either to the suspended or canceled portfolio.

Following is a list of the key subject areas covered in this chapter. We invite you to review the list and assess your level of comprehension of each topic. The best approach is to take a separate sheet of paper and write a short narrative to explain your knowledge of the topic and then go back and compare your summaries with the material covered in the chapter. Another approach is to find a colleague who is also interested in these topics and discuss your understanding of the topics with him, and then jointly review the chapter materials to assess your degree of understanding.

- Execute stage of the PPA
- Project management software
- Build project schedule
- Account for risks
- Account for rework and scope growth reserves
- Validate the schedule
- Schedule compression
- Budget compression
- Task and resource Gantt charts
- Scope change management
- Progress review and control
- Tracking team members' progress
- Project vital signs
- Project health report
- Look-ahead window
- Project fuel report
- Short- and long-term forecasts
- Earned value management system
- Analytical tools
- Reporting project progress
- Project status reports
- Dealing with deadlines
- Troubled project assessment
- Troubled project cancellation
- Stage gate review

■ QUESTIONS AND DISCUSSION POINTS

1. What is the key purpose of the Execute stage of the PPA?
2. How many steps does the Execute stage contain, and can you name each step (don't worry about the order)?
3. Who has the primary responsibility for completing the various steps of the Execute stage?
4. What process group of PMBOK does the Execute stage relate to?
5. What are the key inputs to preparing a project schedule?
6. How can cross-project dependencies impact a project's schedule?
7. What is a Gantt chart?
8. What is a PERT chart?
9. What are the key differences between a Gantt chart and a PERT chart?
10. What is the best way to account for rework and scope growth reserves in a schedule?
11. Do project schedules typically include rework and scope growth reserves? If your answer is "No," what are the implications?

12. What does "crashing" mean and when should it be used?

13. What does "fast tracking" mean and when should it be used?

14. What are some of the ways to reduce the budget of a project?

15. In this chapter, we discussed a number of vital signs to keep track of the status of a project; how many can you recall? Briefly describe each one that you recall.

16. What is the underlying concept behind the use of the look-ahead window? How can it help a project manager manage the project progress?

17. What is the underlying concept behind the use of the project fuel report? How can it help a project manager manage the project progress?

18. What are the main reasons for not using the percent complete value to specify project status (progress report)?

19. We propose a highly structured team update meeting consisting of look back, current status, and look ahead reports. Please describe the three components in detail and comment on the benefits of this structure.

20. What are the key differences between a team update, a sponsor update, and a steering committee update meeting?

21. Why is it important to institute a process to identify and stop troubled projects? Do you believe such a process is in place in your organization? If not, what response do you expect from your colleagues, key customers, and sponsors to the idea of instituting such a process as a part of your project management methodology?

22. What is the purpose of the stage gate review at the end of the Execute stage?

23. Can you recall any of the quotations used in this chapter? If so, why this quotation?

8 IMPLEMENT STAGE

OBJECTIVES

In this chapter, you will learn about the following project management elements:

- Implement stage of the PPA
- Project implementation and closure
- Preparing the operations group and the customers
- Site assessment and preparation
- Security infrastructure
- Project implementation office
- Rolling wave implementation
- The celebration
- Process Assessment
- Project closure
- Stage gate review

This chapter deals with the process necessary for a smooth transition from the project development stages (Chapters 3 through 7) to the Implement stage of the PPA. If not done well, the hard work put forth to finish the project can easily dissipate into a series of missteps as most of the development team begins to look for new assignments while the customers and the operations group struggle to put the project into production. The chapter details the steps to diligently and properly prepare the customers and the operations group to take over the project from the development team, as well as the orderly shutting down of the project development team. The chapter ends with the important step of collecting and recording the lessons learned (by the team) by reviewing the process used to develop the project. Finally the chapter reminds the project manager of the importance of celebrating project completion.

■ PROJECT IMPLEMENTATION AND CLOSURE—PPA STEP 29

Figure 8.1 depicts the key steps of the Implement stage of the PPA. During this stage, you and the team will turn over the end product of the project to the customer and the operations group and then initiate project closure procedures.

Here you are at last. You and the team have worked hard and are hoping for a smooth finish. We wish you success. How many times have you been in an airplane when the pilot announces, with pride, that the flight is early? Unfortunately, after the plane lands, it sits on the runway for a while and the *copilot* comes on the intercom to announce, "I'm sorry to inform you that our gate is still occupied (or there is no ground crew at the gate to receive us), and we need to wait a while, thank you for flying . . ." The same problem occurs with countless IT/Business project deployments, where the customers and the operations group are not ready to receive the project and collective apathy meets the elation of the team.

As the project moves from development into the Implement stage and then to the Operation stage, the ability to handle logistics efficiently becomes paramount. Therefore, if the project manager is not thoroughly experienced with managing project logistics, it is extremely important to assign a logistics SME to the team. Logistics management means paying attention to minute details and interactions, which is not an innate capability.

> *A little neglect may breed mischief: for want of a nail the shoe was lost; for want of a shoe the horse was lost; and for want of a horse the rider was lost.*
> Benjamin Franklin (http://www.ushistory.org/franklin/quotable/quote69.htm).

Keep in mind that you and the team have been working on the project for months, but the customer often receives only a few days notice. The preparation for a smooth deployment is a two-step process:

1. Prepare the operations group
2. Prepare the customer

Typically, the work starts with the operations group and then with a short lag, the customer preparation needs to begin. These two steps have a start-to-start relationship with a few days of lag.

FIGURE 8.1
Implement Stage

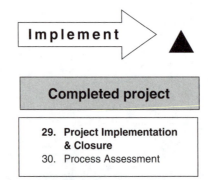

Prepare the Operations Group

The project team needs to define the procedures to be followed by the operations group for day-to-day operation of the project's end product. Most often, the steps for putting a project into operation are quite repeatable, but they still need to be defined, reviewed, approved, and put into place. Project managers typically need to use SMEs from the operations group to help them through these steps because most project managers do not have in-depth knowledge of the myriad procedures needed to put even a small project into operation. This is not a comment on project managers' deficiency; it is a fact of life. However, many project managers wait too long to contact the operations group, at times just a few days before they are ready to put the project into operation. Being treated as an afterthought invariably upsets the operations group and tension builds. The first step to a successful transition is to identify the key stakeholders related to project implementation and its continuing operation. Review the following list of possible stakeholders and then create one that meets the needs of your project.

Data center operations	Quality assurance
Database administration and support	Security
Hardware and software	Technical support
Help desk	Telecommunications (voice) support
Network and desktop support	Vendor support groups
Production control	

The following list includes typical deliverables/steps that need to be considered as you prepare to move your project from the development mode into implementation and then to operations.

1. Change management policies and procedures
2. Database performance monitoring, tuning, and data archiving plan
3. Desktop management team policies and procedures
4. Desktop management team training plan and schedule
5. Disaster backup/recovery policies and procedures
6. Disaster backup/recovery testing plan and schedule
7. Disk/storage monitoring and management plan
8. Downtime and preventative maintenance plan
9. Hardware/software vendor and license management plan
10. Help desk policies and procedures
11. Help desk team training plan and schedule
12. Network monitoring, management, and performance tuning plan
13. Network management team training plan and schedule
14. Parallel test plan and schedule
15. Production readiness certification
16. Production rollout communication plan
17. Production rollout schedule
18. Production turnover documents
19. Security policies and procedures
20. Security team training plan and schedule
21. System technical support plan, policies and procedures
22. System/data audit policies, procedures and schedule

As you can see, the list is long and you must work closely with the operations group to develop a plan to fit the needs of your project. As we have suggested before, the optimum time to talk to the operations group is while you are still in the Execute stage, in order to plan the work long before the project is ready for deployment. Figures 8.2 and 8.3 are examples of checklists that will help you prepare for a smooth and orderly transition.

Prepare the Customer

We hope that you have carried out the following steps:

1. During the planning portion of the Launch stage (Chapter 5), when you developed the project task plan, you *included* the necessary deliverables, tasks, milestones, and

FIGURE 8.2

Implementation Readiness
Checklist—Production
Control

Item	Needed	Date needed	Owner	Action required
Document list	❏ Yes ❏ No			
Turnover procedures	❏ Yes ❏ No			
Parallel processing procedures	❏ Yes ❏ No			
Naming standards	❏ Yes ❏ No			
Current system shutdown procedures	❏ Yes ❏ No			
Operations walkthroughs	❏ Yes ❏ No			
Security requirements	❏ Yes ❏ No			
Safety requirements	❏ Yes ❏ No			
Disaster recovery plan	❏ Yes ❏ No			
Downtime requirements	❏ Yes ❏ No			
Downtime procedures	❏ Yes ❏ No			
Capacity management plan	❏ Yes ❏ No			
Operational schedule	❏ Yes ❏ No			
Service level agreements	❏ Yes ❏ No			
Output distribution policies	❏ Yes ❏ No			
Output distribution procedures	❏ Yes ❏ No			

resources to prepare the customers for organizational change management and project implementation.

2. During the estimating portion of the Launch stage (Chapter 6), you *estimated* the resources, budget, and time needed to prepare the customers for organizational change management and project implementation.

3. During the Execute stage (Chapter 7), you *scheduled* and then actually *began* to carry out the steps to prepare the customers for organizational change management and project implementation. Keep in mind that most of the preparation should have been done *prior* to the start of the Implement stage.

If, by chance, you have missed these steps, we'll see you at the mocking post. It is amazing how poorly so many project managers prepare for the implementation phase of their projects. The stubborn belief is that the team has done its job, and now it's the responsibility of the customers to step up and do the right thing; unfortunately, the results of this approach leave much to be desired.

> *Much of the employee resistance could be traced to a mistake that dated back to the project's inception: None of the groups that were going to be directly affected by the new processes and systems were represented on the key stakeholders team . . . We were always surprising [the heads of sales and the divisions] . . . By the beginning of 2000, the rollout had collapsed into chaos. Not only did workers not understand how to use the new system, they didn't even understand the new processes. And the divisional*

FIGURE 8.3

Implementation Readiness
Checklist—Help Desk

Item	Needed	Date needed	Owner	Action required
Technical support standards	❏ Yes ❏ No			
Technical support procedures	❏ Yes ❏ No			
Technical support documents	❏ Yes ❏ No			
Technical support/help desk training	❏ Yes ❏ No			
Support requirements	❏ Yes ❏ No			
Customer call escalation procedures	❏ Yes ❏ No			
Vendor support procedures	❏ Yes ❏ No			
Support agreements	❏ Yes ❏ No			

executives, who were just as confused as their employees—and even angrier—didn't go out of their way to help.

Ben Worthen, "Nestlé's ERP Odyssey," *CIO Magazine* (May 15, 2002, http://www.cio.com/archive/051502/nestle.html).

The preceding quote affirms the fact that many developers have a pervasive habit of overlooking the resistance to change by implementation-level stakeholders. The belief seems to be, "If we build it, they will come." Well, not exactly. The Implement stage is one area in which the development team needs extensive support and involvement from management, especially the policy level stakeholders. We believe that the project manager should work hard to ensure that the sponsor's involvement rises to a high degree and stays that way all through the Implementation stage. In the case of any challenged or failed implementation, we hold the sponsor equally responsible with the project manager, even more so. Over the years, we have seen a direct cause and effect relationship between sponsor involvement and project implementation success and failure.

Recently, in a meeting of policy level and implementation level stakeholders of a zone I project with deployment in four countries and seven locations, the sponsor (international chief financial officer) made some very important points:

We had a good idea and now we have a good product with enormous capability. We spent a huge amount of effort, money, and political capital on the project. The journey to this point, though rough at times has been very successful. However, it is important that everyone realizes that the expected ROI will only happen if the rank and file begins to use the new system consistently, efficiently, and soon. The development team has done its job, and now it is up to us to make sure that our people step up to the plate and make the new system operational, the real effort is about to begin. This is going to require changes in processes and behaviors that our people have been using for years. As they switch over, they will make mistakes, the system will malfunction, and service to our customers will be disrupted. The next thing we know, most will revert to their old habits—spreadsheets, faxes, and workarounds. Pretty soon, we will have two *dysfunctional systems running in parallel—the out of date current system and partially deployed new system. The company can't afford it, I can't afford it, and I am sure you can't afford it. We must make two things happen:*

- *A well orchestrated new system deployment plan*
- *A well orchestrated current system retirement plan*

If the rank and file believes that they can behave as they have in many similar situations in the past, this expensive project will implode and take many of us with it. I do not want to be on that train. I want you to know that I have assured my boss that each of you is going to take on the sponsorship role at your division, and will make the deployment of this project you top priority.

Our highest kudos to this sponsor.

The implementation process, which may last from a few days to a few weeks, needs to be managed efficiently and effectively. Over the years, we have learned a number of important lessons regarding project implementation:

1. Make sure that the customer training materials are actually tested by appropriately selected customer representatives before rolling out the customer training program.
2. Do not implement a project just before major holidays (year end or the month of August in many European countries). If your project spans multiple countries, consult with your local project coordinators to learn about *inopportune* deployment windows.
3. Do not plan to deploy a project just before peak transaction periods. For example, do not deploy an ERP system for a U.S. candy company just prior to Halloween or an automobile shipping and tracking system just before the release of next year's models.
4. Make sure that there is a well-defined and broadly communicated fall-back plan in case something goes terribly wrong.
5. Do not let your senior team members, especially from business units, be reassigned to other projects or responsibilities. The deployment team needs all the experience you can muster.

6. Make sure the implementation team includes the right number of people from the operations, support, and help desk groups.

Not following all of these points would be a very unwise move. Yet, project teams often violate each of these items and then some, resulting in massive disruptions in operations, millions of dollars in lost orders, and hundreds of thousands of finished goods stacked in warehouses and shipping docks. The cost in lost customers, damaged reputations, and all around ill will is practically incalculable.

A key document to review at this point is the work done to assess the level of stress the proposed project might cause the customer. We discussed this subject in Chapter 5 (see *Project Stress Analysis*) and used the following five attributes to ascertain the extent of the stress:

1. Time away from primary responsibility
2. Degree of change (technology, process, culture)
3. Willingness to absorb the change
4. Ability to absorb the change
5. Timing of the change

Make sure that the implementation team is well aware of the assessment and keeps the findings in view as it executes the project deployment steps. One of the key results of any deployment, even under the best of circumstances, is the fact that customers end up with more work—their routine assignments along with the additional effort needed to deploy the new project. Remember that during deployment it is the customers who will find most of the errors/bugs/defects in the product, and it is their work that will be interrupted. Occasionally, the customers will get upset and wish the deployment team would go away. It is extremely important that you (and the team) not resort to blaming the customers for the defects they detect, which is tantamount to shooting the messenger for the bad news. Rather, you should acknowledge the problem and thank the individual for finding it. Many project managers we know actually create a prize for the person who finds the most defects, usually dispensed at the end of each week. This attitude conveys to the customers that you appreciate their participation and are sensitive to their discomfort.

Figure 8.4 depicts a list of suggested items to help you prepare the customer to take on the responsibility for project deployment.

FIGURE 8.4
Implementation Readiness
Checklist—Customer
Preparation

Item	Needed	Date needed	Owner	Action required
Change documentation log	☐ Yes ☐ No			
End-user training requirements	☐ Yes ☐ No			
Implementation success factors	☐ Yes ☐ No			
Communication standards	☐ Yes ☐ No			
System availability expectations	☐ Yes ☐ No			
Service level agreements	☐ Yes ☐ No			
Data migration procedures	☐ Yes ☐ No			
Old system retirement procedures	☐ Yes ☐ No			
Archival procedures	☐ Yes ☐ No			
Parallel processing requirements	☐ Yes ☐ No			
Production ready criteria	☐ Yes ☐ No			

Site Assessment

A crucial step in planning the implementation is to assess each of the sites where the application or system will be installed. The purpose of this assessment is to:

1. Inventory the existing hardware/software to understand what may need to be purchased or installed prior to implementation.

2. Identify the business flow so that appropriate installation timing can be established.
3. Identify the skill level of the on-site personnel and determine the impact of that skill level on the implementation.

Site Preparation

Once you have competed the site assessment, the next step is to develop a site preparation plan. No two sites are going to be exactly alike, so it is important to understand the nuances of the sites in which the system or application will be implemented. The site preparation plan should contain the following components:

1. The name of the site
2. The name of the site owner
3. The name of the site inventory owner
4. A description of the process to manage the inventory so that the implementation team can be kept informed of any inventory changes
5. The date by which the site needs to be prepared
6. The date on which the site will be prepared
7. The owner of the site preparation
8. Issues regarding the site preparation

This very important step will require cooperation of the staff at each site. Most new deployments require shuffling of schedules and resources, and invariably end up in overtime work by the local staff. Therefore, it is imperative that you become familiar with their limitations and be sensitive to their concerns.

Security Infrastructure

Security is one of the most important components of efficient and effective project deployment, yet it continues to be a surprise to many project managers. Often, they think of security late in the deployment cycle and, as a result, things either come to a halt or continue with major security exposure. It is not uncommon for members of the project team to show up at an implementation site without having obtained the necessary security clearances (especially for any contractors). Then they must wait in the office lobby while everyone scrambles to get the team members cleared for access. Here are two important steps:

1. Determine whether project team members require specific security clearances in order to be granted access to customer sites, data centers, or data processing environments.
2. Determine whether the team members will need passwords, specific types of IDs, key cards, or any specific equipment to access local and network systems.

At times, the security clearance process may require background checks and key information verification. All of this, if not planned properly, can add days (if not weeks) to the deployment process. Figure 8.5 is a suggested template to help you define the security clearance plan for various team members.

Project Implementation Office

An important step toward smooth implementation is to establish a project implementation office, which is usually set up in a room or a large cubicle in the midst of the customer space. You and the core implementation team need to be visible and available to the customers. Make sure that the implementation team is composed of at least 50 percent customers. One of the most successful steps to help create a customer-centered deployment environment is to assign each team member up to seven key customers. The team member is now personally responsible for their "deployment" well being. Each of the team members routinely meets with the assigned customers to keep them informed of the upcoming activities, any possible problem areas and associated contingency plans,

FIGURE 8.5
Team Member Security
Clearance Checklist

Team member name:

Security item	Needed	Date required	Owner	Action required
Background check	❑ Yes ❑ No			
Security clearance	❑ Yes ❑ No			
Drug test	❑ Yes ❑ No			
User ID	❑ Yes ❑ No			
Password	❑ Yes ❑ No			
System rights	❑ Yes ❑ No			
Building access rights	❑ Yes ❑ No			
Entrance keys/cards	❑ Yes ❑ No			
Others:	❑ Yes ❑ No			
	❑ Yes ❑ No			
	❑ Yes ❑ No			
	❑ Yes ❑ No			

and to answer any questions. At the same time, the customers must clearly understand the importance of their cooperation in ensuring on-time deployment because the promised benefits cannot begin to be reaped until then. The opening of a project implementation office is a good time to broadly reiterate the reasons why the project was initiated and review its contribution to the corporate success strategy.

We have found that many customers, especially any nemeses, often have the belief that they can continue using the old processes and procedures and don't need to switch over to the new system. This dogged resistance is exactly the reason for including a specific step (PPA Step 33, see Chapter 9) that will start an orderly retirement of the current system. Make sure that customers know about the plan, broadcast it widely, and discuss it often. We strongly advise that you post the current system retirement plan prominently in your office and the project deployment office. These activities convey a strong message to people that those who refuse to come on board will not have much to fall back on.

We have known project managers who went out of their way to make the implementation process less painful by incorporating such activities as:

- Customer of the week/month
  - The individual who contributed the most toward smooth deployment
  - The individual who found the most bugs. They get a helium-filled balloon for each bug (the size of the balloon matches the seriousness of the bug)
  - The individual whose system crashed most often (they get the first pick of any refreshments). We have known project managers who have arranged for massage therapists to give in-chair massages to help these people cope with the resulting stress—a very considerate gesture
- Team member of the week/month
  - Usually voted by customers
- A quick celebration at key milestones
- Daily briefings
  - The project manager and/or a key team member is available at predefined time slots to answer questions and provide guidance
- Key stakeholder briefings by the sponsor, typically once a week

What do these actions accomplish? They show the customer that you care, that you recognize the difficulties inherent in project implementation, and that the team will be available for last minute problem resolution and help. Keep in mind that you and the team are the experts, and the customers are just starting to learn about the new processes, new technology, new screens, and new reports. We realize that all of this may sound trivial to people who have literally lived with the technology. Consider these real life examples of customer and tech support exchanges we received recently via e-mail:

> *Tech Support: Ok Bob, press the control and escape keys at the same time. Now type the letter P to bring up the Program Manager.*
> *Customer: I don't have a P.*
> *Tech Support: On your keyboard, Bob.*
> *Customer: What do you mean?*
> *Tech Support: P on your keyboard, Bob.*
> *Customer: I'm not going to do that!*

> *Tech Support: Sir, are you running it under Windows?*
> *Customer: No, my desk is next to the door. But that's a good point. The lady in the cubicle next to me is under a window, and her system is working fine.*

> *Customer: I'd like a mouse pad, please.*
> *Tech Support: Certainly sir, we've got a large variety.*
> *Customer: Do you have one that's compatible with my mouse?*

Our best advice is to be kind to your customers and wait until you hang up the phone before laughing.

Implementation Plan Basics

As you plan and prepare the customers to take over the project, here are a few important areas of information you need to document:

1. Describe what support the client can expect from the project team during deployment.
2. Describe the roles and responsibilities of the client to facilitate smooth deployment.
3. Describe what long-term support, if any, the client can expect from the development team.
4. Describe the problem-reporting process that will be used, including the specific points of contacts.
5. Describe the process for escalating the problems. When the team is not able to respond (or help), what is the next level of resolution?
6. Prepare a contact information document that should include the following information:
   a. Contact person's name(s)
   b. Title
   c. Contact hours
   d. Phone number
   e. Pager number
   f. E-mail address
7. Indicate the cost of seeking and receiving support (hourly charges, per incident charges, charge-back, annual maintenance fee) if applicable. This information is necessary when the support services are to be provided by contract/vendor personnel.
8. If your project is replacing an existing system/product, describe the length of time the old system/product will be in parallel operation with the new.
9. Implementation contingency plan. It should be obvious that the implementation process itself can be a high-risk item; therefore, you must have a well-defined and easy-to-follow fallback plan if the system deployment does not proceed as planned.

Rolling Wave Implementation

Occasionally, an IT/Business project needs to be deployed at multiple geographically distant locations. Let us look at an example of a system that needs to be deployed at ten locations. Management often exerts pressure to hurry so that the new systems are operational within a few short weeks—if not days. We have known many project managers who would succumb to such pressure and would schedule the deployment in two rollouts of five locations each. Invariably, the end result would be chaos—incomplete deployments, unsupported customers, overworked teams, and unhappy management. A better approach would be to plan three (if not four) cycles. The steps for each cycle are:

1. Select one or two locations where the local management and customers have acted as champions, and the implementation-level stakeholders have been supportive.
2. Establish a central project implementation office for rollout at the development (home) location to support the deployment effort.
3. Establish a local project implementation office in each of the deployment locations.
4. Make sure that each location has a detailed deployment plan, that the team members clearly understand the plan, and that the assignments are clearly communicated.
5. Make sure that each local project implementation office is a pleasant place for the deployment team as well as the local customers. We have seen teams decorate the deployment office with posters, balloons, ribbons, placards, and bowls filled with candies, fruits, and other light snacks.
6. Plan occasional success announcements, quick celebrations, and group "high fives."
7. Have a team member take notes on all the things that went really well and those that caused glitches or problems.

After the first deployment cycle is over, take a few days to review the lessons learned and plan the next implementation cycle. We would suggest that you choose three to four locations, followed by another deployment for the remaining locations. This strategy may seem to take longer than deploying at all locations in one fell swoop, but the shotgun approach does not bring significant success.

Scope Verification

This is an opportune point to review the latest baselined scope statement (the deliverables and features that comprise the scope) and make sure that the completed project incorporates the scope promised to the customer. Keep in mind that the statistics show that IT projects don't usually deliver what was promised to them.

> . . . studies have shown that most system development projects are delivered with less than the contracted scope.
>
> Harvey A. Levine (http://www.myplanview.com/expert25.asp).

Therefore, it behooves a professional project manager to diligently review the scope statement (promised scope) in conjunction with the delivered scope, and note any shortcomings. It is important to discuss the shortcoming(s) with the sponsor and key customers and provide them with your best and most plausible reasons for the shortfall. This list of missing functionality (deliverables and features) must be communicated to the group responsible for ongoing maintenance and support of the system because they may need to build emergency workarounds for any key missing functionality. In certain cases, the sponsor may not sign off on the delivered system and may require that certain important functionally be completed before she is willing to sign off (accept) the project. We would advise the same type of verification for quality and budget.

Fine Tuning

Most project end products require a certain amount of fine tuning as the customers go through the deployment process. These adjustments are often necessary because the testing done prior to the deployment step is rarely to the same breadth and depth as is required for this stage. Therefore, it is important for the project manager to make sure that a sufficient number of resources (team members, technology, budget) are available to tweak the end product to meet customer needs. Because this work needs to be done quickly and to a high quality, it is necessary to retain a number of senior team members through this stage. Another highly important point to keep in mind is that a complete freeze on scope changes is imperative during the Deployment stage. The introduction of scope changes at this point in the project will put a high degree of stress on the team, which can result in an end product of disappointing quality.

Customer Support

As you move through the implementation process, it is important to begin to put in place the infrastructure for providing customer support (a help desk) on a long-term basis. Even though the ongoing operation of the customer support facility may not be a part of the project plan, it is important to make sure that plans are underway to deploy a well-trained and adequately staffed customer support facility. We know of many sponsors who will not sign off on the deployment of their projects unless they have well-documented proof that fully functional customer support services will be in place as the project moves to the operation stage.

The Celebration

We first discussed this subject in Chapter 1 (see *Celebrating Project Success*), then in Chapter 4 (see *The Signing Ceremony*), and Chapter 6 (see *Cost Estimates*). We know you did not forget. Take a lesson from the restaurant profession (the grand opening), construction business (open house), entertainment industry (the cast party), and sales profession (the big deal closure party) and plan a celebration to thank all concerned for their hard work, contributions, and commitment to the cause. Make sure you don't have the team do all the work; they have done enough. You should definitely try to outsource this deliverable. Welcome the team's input in the planning and organization of the arrangements. They surely have many talents that will make the party enjoyable and successful. Take some time to prepare for your role as the master of ceremonies. Any astute project manager would have taken sufficient notes throughout the many months of project development to have possibly collected interesting anecdotes, stories, pictures, memos, and e-mails. Go through your notes and files, talk to team members and the sponsor, and then develop a script for your presentation. Make sure the focus is on celebrating people's effort and contributions, keeping in mind that the line between good and bad taste can be very thin. When in doubt, don't do it. The only person you should make fun of is yourself.

■ PROCESS ASSESSMENT—PPA STEP 30

In Chapter 7, we introduced the PDCA concept (see Figure 7.31). It can be used here to check and improve the processes and plans you used to get to this point in the project. The objective is to look back, purely from the process point of view, and see what improvements need to be made the next time around. This review will require effort and time on the part of selected team members, and needs to be budgeted into the project's original plan, estimate, and schedule. The key objectives of the assessment are as follows:

- To determine the best practices utilized in the project
- To identify areas of improvement
- To learn from the mistakes and the successes
- To determine whether client expectations were met
- To determine whether existing standards, procedures, and guidelines were followed
- To determine how well each process step aided or hindered the successful completion of the project objectives
- To identify opportunities for improvement in system development processes, products, and procedures

Ground Rules

A post-implementation review assumes that everyone wants to give and receive feedback, and that everyone wants to improve. In order for this type of session to be effective, apply the following ground rules:

1. Feedback must be honest, clear, and contain suggestions for improvement
2. Attack problems, not individuals
3. Listen and show respect for the ideas of others

4. Participate actively during the meeting
5. Take note of all the good experiences and apply these to future projects
6. Capture information—good and bad—as accurately as possible

Benefits

The Process Assessment helps future projects to:

1. Avoid pitfalls encountered by other projects
2. Apply the processes that were successful
3. Provide a feedback mechanism to improve processes and products
4. Serve to further educate personnel on project and product development processes

Key Players

The key players include the following:

1. Project sponsor
2. Project manager
3. Key project team members
4. Major stakeholders

Support Players

The projects key support players include the:

1. Facilitator
2. Scribe (someone who can record the key information promptly and accurately)

Agenda

The agenda for the Project Assessment is as follows:

1. Introduction
   a. Project manager to set the stage for the Process Assessment. Remind people that this is a review of the principles, practices, tools, and techniques, and is *not* a forum for assessing people's performance.
2. Schedule review
   a. Did we meet the deadline?
   b. If not, what were the reasons for the variance? Did the variance result in any problems?
   c. What part of the scheduling process worked well?
   d. What could we do differently next time?
3. Scope review
   a. Did we accomplish all the project objectives?
   b. If not, which objectives did we fail to meet? What were the reasons we failed to meet the objectives?
   c. How well did we manage the scope?
   d. What part of the scope management worked well?
   e. What might we do differently next time?
4. Budget review
   a. Was the budget for the project met?
   b. If not, what were the reasons for the variance?
   c. What part of the budgeting process worked well?
   d. What should we do differently next time?
5. Quality review
   a. Did the project meet the quality expectations of the sponsor, customer, and end user?
   b. If not, what are the reasons that quality expectations were not met?
   c. What part of the quality management process worked well?
   d. What would we do differently next time?

6. Identify client issues
   a. What went right?
   b. What went wrong?
7. Root cause and identification and discussion
   a. Why, where, and how did the problem occur?
8. What needs to be improved?
   a. Identify improvement opportunities
   b. Prioritize problems/issues
   c. Identify processes and standards to be created or revised
   d. Assign action items and milestone dates
9. Recommendations
   a. Based on the findings from the participants, what recommendations would you make regarding the overall project management process?

From the list, it should be obvious that this assessment requires the well-focused participation of key people whose time is valuable and difficult to obtain. Therefore, we recommend that Process Assessments do not need to be done after every project. We have found that, if the assessment is well-planned and professionally conducted, only 30 percent of medium and large projects need to be assessed. The information collected from a core group of projects usually is a dependable representation of the overall project management practices of the organization.

Lessons Learned Database

An important benefit of the Process Assessment step is the development of a historical lessons learned (what to do and what not to do) database to be used by project managers in the future. The information collected by the group should be entered into a well-structured database that is easy to search through the use of key words. Once the database is populated adequately, project managers and teams should be required to review the historical information as they start work on new project proposals, and at the start of different project stages.

Project Closure

Now is the time to put into action the tasks required to close up the project shop. These tasks include:

1. Documents are turned over to the support and maintenance team
2. Documents are turned over to the operations team
3. Documents are turned over to the project office (if one exists)
4. Documents are deleted/discarded (keep in mind any security and regulatory policies)
5. Deactivation of access codes and passwords
6. Return of property (hardware, software, equipment)
7. Closure of any contracts with vendors and contractors
8. Turn off the lights (in the project implementation office)

Keep in mind that some of the project closure steps might continue into the Operation stage.

■ STAGE GATE NO. 5

As you know, the purpose of a stage gate is to ensure that the quality of the project management process matches the complexity and inherent risk of the project, and that the project can safely proceed to the next stage. The template in Figure 8.6 depicts a suggested list of attributes for the stage gate review at the end of the Implement stage. Keep in mind that this list contains our suggestions, and you will need to tailor it to your specific project.

We will reiterate the stage gate review process here:

1. The project manager and the core team meet to assess the degree to which each of the attributes has been accomplished. To make the assessment useful, we suggest that the team members, under the facilitation of the project manager, collectively review their work products and decide on the quality of each item. In Figure 8.6, in the column titled *Confidence level,* the value of 1

FIGURE 8.6

Stage Gate No. 5—Implement Stage

Stage gate no. 5: attributes	Confidence level					Action plan
1. Strategy alignment	1	2	3	4	5	
2. Value-to-business	1	2	3	4	5	
3. Ownership	1	2	3	4	5	
4. Customer buy-in	1	2	3	4	5	
5. Sponsor	1	2	3	4	5	
6. Project manager	1	2	3	4	5	
7. Project team	1	2	3	4	5	
8. Change management plan	1	2	3	4	5	
9. Customer readiness	1	2	3	4	5	
10. Quality assurance	1	2	3	4	5	
11. Communications plan	1	2	3	4	5	
12. Project health (vital signs)	1	2	3	4	5	
13. Operations group training plan	1	2	3	4	5	
14. Current system retirement plan	1	2	3	4	5	
15. Up-to-date project notebook	1	2	3	4	5	
16. Budget	1	2	3	4	5	

implies poor quality or incomplete work, and the value of 5 implies high quality and comprehensive work. Any item with an assessed value lower than 3 means low quality work and, if not corrected, will result in problems during the future project stages.

2. Once the team has finished the assessment, the project manager meets with the sponsor to review the assessment, and the sponsor then decides whether to open stage gate no. 5 to let the team proceed to the Implement stage, or to direct the team to do the rework necessary to improve any of the low quality work products. Occasionally, the sponsor may open the stage gate even if some of the work is not up to par. This conditional approval implies that the team will remedy the situation to the sponsor's satisfaction in the near future.

Another possibility is to move the project to the suspend portfolio or the canceled project portfolio (refer to Chapter 10).

As we discussed in Chapter 1, the PPA can be scaled to fit the size and complexity of a given project. Complex projects will require more of the steps as well as more rigor, while simpler projects will do well with fewer steps and less rigor. Please refer to Figure 1.12 for the steps recommended for simple, average, complex, and very complex projects.

■ SUMMARY

In this chapter, we discussed the steps to turn over the project from the development team to its customers. We discussed the importance of the hands-on involvement of the core team, customer support, computer operations, organizational change management specialists, and project customers (end-users). The project manager must make sure that customers are being trained in the use of the new system and are receiving sufficient support from the project team, and that issues and operational problems are being addressed in an effective and efficient manner. This is also the point at which the "proof of the pudding" is being assessed—the new system is performing to the promised objectives, functionality, quality, and security needs. Any nonperformance must be noted and corrected. Whenever nonperformance beyond the agreed-upon thresholds continues, the project becomes a candidate for the suspended or canceled portfolio (based on the degree of nonperformance).

The following is a list of the key subject areas covered in this chapter. We invite you to review the list and assess your level of comprehension of each topic. The best approach is to take a separate sheet of paper and write a short narrative to explain your knowledge of the topic, and then go back and compare your summaries with the material covered in the chapter. Another approach is to find a colleague who is also interested in these topics and discuss your understanding of the topics with him. Then, jointly review the chapter materials to assess your degree of understanding.

- Implement stage of the PPA
- Project implementation and closure
- Preparing the operations group and the customers
- Site assessment and preparation
- Security infrastructure
- Project implementation office
- Rolling wave implementation
- The celebration
- Process assessment
- Project closure
- Stage gate review

■ QUESTIONS AND DISCUSSION POINTS

1. What is the key purpose of the Implement stage of the PPA?
2. How many steps does the Implement stage contain? Can you name each step (don't worry about the order)?
3. Who has the primary responsibility for completing the various steps of the Implement stage?
4. What process group of PMBOK does the Implement stage relate to?
5. What are some of the inopportune time periods for project implementation?
6. What is the purpose and value of a project implementation office?
7. Explain the concept of rolling wave implementation and its benefits.
8. What are some of the key activities of project closure?
9. Why is it important to look back and assess the process used to develop a project? What benefits can it provide the current team and future project managers?
10. What is the purpose of the stage gate at the end of the Implement stage?
11. Can you recall any of the quotations used in this chapter? If so, why this quotation?

9 OPERATION STAGE

OBJECTIVES

In this chapter, you will learn about the following project management elements:

- Operation stage of the PPA
- Preparing for project operations
- Operations documentation
- Value-to-Business Assessment
- Operations Metrics
- Current System Retirement

This chapter presents introductory material regarding the ongoing operation of the project. In the strictest definition, the project comes to an end at the finish of the steps outlined in Chapter 8, when the end product of the project is handed over to the customer and the operations group. However, we believe it is extremely important for project managers to understand the fundamentals of ongoing operation, the process that actually begins to produce the value promised by the project. This chapter focuses on three important steps: the steps to begin to collect and report the value-to-business metrics, collection and analysis of operations metrics, and the very important step of initiating current system retirement.

■ THE OPERATION STAGE

It is important to point out that computer (system) operations is a subprofession within the IT department. The operations professionals are responsible for the systematic execution of various application systems and operating systems for timely data processing and to keep the technology functioning without interruptions to business activities. In most companies, computer operations is a $24 \times 7 \times 365$ process that requires multiple daily shifts staffed by skilled professionals. The purpose of this chapter is to familiarize you with the overarching functionality of the operations department and to focus on the importance of orderly transition from application development and implementation to routine operations. It is outside the scope of this book to discuss in detail the myriad of deliverables, tasks, milestones, resources, and skills needed to run the operations department.

Figure 9.1 depicts the key steps of the Operation stage of the PPA. This stage marks the final part of the deployment process started in the Implementation stage of the project. From this point on, the operations group, in association with the customer support group, will be responsible to run the deployed system. Notice that we indicate this stage as a dotted line in Figure 9.1 because the ongoing operations are the responsibilities of a group other than the project team. However, it is the project manager's responsibility to make sure that the handoff to the operations group is smooth, efficient, and effective. The project manager, as well as one or two senior team members, must stay available to the operations group for timely consulting and problem solving for at least two run cycles (typically just over 2 months).

■ PREPARING FOR PROJECT OPERATIONS

Before we discuss the three steps listed in Figure 9.1, let's iterate some of the key points necessary for the smooth and efficient transfer of responsibilities from the Implement stage to the Operation stage:

1. The operations team must make sure that the development team has produced the required production/operations documentation necessary to assure successful operations. We certainly hope that appropriate representatives from the operations group were involved in creating the WBS components (deliverables, tasks, and milestones) when you planned, estimated, and

FIGURE 9.1
Operation Stage

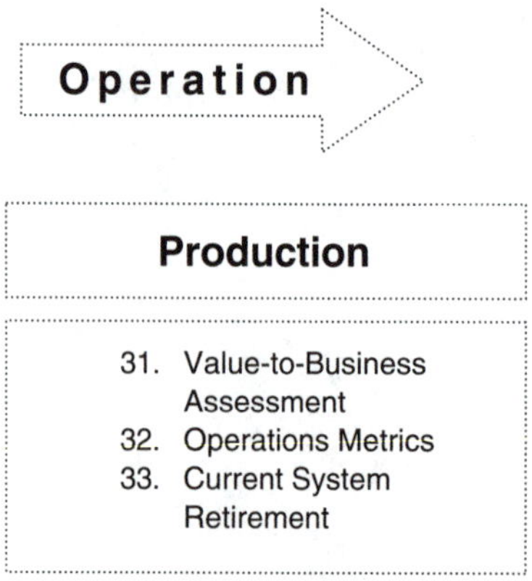

Operation

Production

31. Value-to-Business Assessment
32. Operations Metrics
33. Current System Retirement

scheduled the operations related component of the project. A suggested list of deliverables/tasks was presented in Chapter 8 (see *Prepare the Operations Group*).

2. Our experience shows that a majority of project managers are not fully familiar with the intricacies of operations and, if left on their own, tend to underplan the operations component of their projects, hoping that the operations group will have to step in to fill any voids—wrong. Astute project managers make a point to include SMEs from the operations group during the planning process to specifically define what is expected/required for a smooth handoff.

3. The documentation must be reviewed, approved, and *accepted* by the operations team prior to the transition from the Implementation stage to the Operations stage.

In the case of large projects, the transition from implementation to operations can become a project in itself, requiring a large number of deliverables, tasks, milestones, and resources for planning, estimating, scheduling, and execution of system operations. Listed below are the deliverables typically needed to support the operations phase of software projects:

- Change management policies and procedures
- Current process/system end-of-life plan and schedule
- Database management team training policies, procedures, plans, and schedule
- Database performance monitoring, tuning, and data archiving plan
- Desktop management team training, policies, procedures, plans, and schedule
- Disaster backup/recovery policies, procedures, testing plans, and schedule
- Disk/storage monitoring and management plan
- Hardware/software vendor and license management plan
- Help desk training policies, procedures, plans, and schedule
- Network management team training policies, procedures, plans, and schedule
- Network monitoring, management, and performance tuning plan
- Operations training policies, procedures, plans, and schedule
- Parallel test plan and schedule
- Production readiness certification
- Production rollout communication plan
- Production rollout schedule
- Production turnover documents
- Scheduled availability, downtime, and preventative maintenance plan
- Security policies and procedures
- Security team training policies, procedures, plan, and schedule
- System/data audit policies, procedures, and schedule
- System/process dependency matrix
- System end-user support plan, policies, and procedures
- System operations policies and procedures
- System technical support plan, policies, and procedures

Often, this part of the project gets a short shrift because many project managers hold the belief that their job is complete when they finish the project development activities and that the remainder of the project is the responsibility of the operations department. The operations department, on the other hand, retains the belief that the project manager and the core team will surely stay long enough to see the project progress into full operation. Surprise. This is one reason for the point we made in Chapter 5 (see *Operations Tasks*) that the operations group should be fully represented when the detailed task list for the project is being assembled.

> *Solid handoff of a project from the development team to the implementation, and then to the operations team, is extremely important. In American football, a clean snap of the ball puts the team in motion following a well-defined plan, the play. On the other hand, a fumble (a loose ball in play), creates a mad scramble to recover the ball. The important question here is, "When your team transitions from the Execute stage to Implement stage, will it 'make the play' or will it be forced to scramble for survival?*
>
> Wayne Schmidt.

■ OPERATIONS DOCUMENTATION

A key component of the documentation needed by the operations staff is a well-defined production schedule, which typically comprises the following items:

1. Backup/archiving procedures
2. Daily processes
3. Error recovery and restart procedures
4. Month end processes
5. Nightly processes
6. Quarter end processes
7. The order the jobs need to be run in
8. Week end processes
9. Year end processes

As you can see, the list is long and it includes the many specific steps and documents that need to be clearly defined and executed. We often see teams move to the operation stage without sufficient planning, then they find themselves overwhelmed by last minute work when operations people demand the requisite documentation and support information.

■ VALUE-TO-BUSINESS ASSESSMENT—PPA STEP 31

In Chapter 2, we discussed the various attributes that comprise the value the business is expecting to draw from the project. Some examples of typical value attributes are:

Additional revenues	Higher ROI
Competitive advantage	Increase in capacity
Cost savings	Regulatory compliance
Customer service	Market share
Efficiency of operations	Revenue generation

The actual performance of the value attributes selected by the key stakeholders will need to be measured and reported to the appropriate management. You must identify the person(s) responsible for gathering the information, the process used to collect the information, and the managers who are slated to receive the information. We often find that project managers have overlooked this step and little, if any, of this important information ever is collected or reported. Figure 9.2 shows a template for collecting and reporting value-to-business metrics.

FIGURE 9.2
Value-to-Business Metrics

Value-to-business metrics	Assessment			Action
1.	BE	ME	EE	
2.	BE	ME	EE	
3.	BE	ME	EE	
4.	BE	ME	EE	
5.	BE	ME	EE	
n.	BE	ME	EE	

BE: below expectations; ME: meets expectations;
EE: exceeds expectations

■ OPERATIONS METRICS—PPA STEP 32

Operations metrics deal with hardware and software performance, i.e., the overall efficiency of system operations. Although the responsibility for gathering and reporting this performance data usually lies with the operations group, you are still responsible for making sure that system performance metrics have been planned for and will be assessed. Be sure to include assessment methodology, the person(s) responsible for performing the assessments, the timing of the assessments, and to whom, and in what format, the results will be reported. Operations metric collection typically starts a few weeks after the deployment is finished and routine operations begin.

■ CURRENT SYSTEM RETIREMENT—PPA STEP 33

The proverbial "last but not least" important step in the project life cycle is to begin to retire the current system in an orderly manner. Interestingly, this step is rarely mentioned in IT/Business project management literature. One key reason that this step is often overlooked is that most IT/Business project management life cycles are based on the classic engineering (construction) process; engineers rarely encounter such a requirement. Most engineering projects are either new (greenfield) projects or brownfield projects, when engineers are expected to retire the old system at the start of the project—demolishing the old structure before building the new. However, that is rarely the situation for IT/Business projects. Unless the project is for a new organization, or is a completely new initiative, most IT/Business projects are upgrades and/or replacements of existing systems. Therefore, when the new project is deployed, the organization now has two "live" systems, and the old system must be retired in an orderly manner. Unless such retirement is specifically planned and executed, the following missteps are very likely to occur:

1. Many customers, especially the nemesis and comatose, will continue using the old system, which will result in duplicate and erroneous data and outputs.
2. The purchasing group may renew vendor licenses and contracts for software and hardware that is no longer needed.
3. The real estate management group may renew leases for space that is no longer needed.

This list represents only a few of the unnecessary expenses that can continue for unknown periods of time because the development team did not specifically plan for retiring the current system. We know of countless projects that did not include the steps to retire the old system. In some of these cases, the cost of running the "duplicate" system approached millions of dollars, thereby totally negating any financial benefits of the new systems. Many sponsors we know require that a fully defined retirement plan be in place before they will allow a project to pass through stage gate no. 4 (at the end of the Execute stage), followed by further preparations in the Implementation stage. We salute this wise practice, as it assures that current systems will be retired systematically.

As we discussed in Chapter 1, tailoring the PPA, the PPA can be scaled to fit the size and complexity of a given project. Complex projects will require more of the steps as well as more rigor, while simpler projects will do well with fewer steps and less rigor. Please refer to Figure 1.12 for the steps recommended for simple, average, complex, and very complex projects.

■ SUMMARY

In this chapter, we discussed the steps to transfer the project from the development team to the operations group. Once a project has been successfully implemented—the operations group is willing and able to take it over because the project no longer needs day-to-day fine tuning by the development group—the project manager formally hands over the project control to the operations staff and the customer support group. At this point, the operations and value-to-business metrics begin to be collected and analyzed to continuously monitor the performance of the project. During the ongoing operations of the project, any nonperformance issues must be noted and corrected. If nonperformance breaches the agreed upon thresholds, the project becomes a candidate for the suspended or canceled portfolio (based on the degree of nonperformance).

The following is a list of the key subject areas covered in this chapter. We invite you to review the list and assess your level of comprehension of each topic. The best approach is to take a separate sheet of paper and write a short narrative to explain your knowledge of the topic and then go back and compare your summaries with the material covered in the chapter. Another approach is to find a colleague who is also interested in these topics and discuss your understanding of the topics with him/her, and then jointly review the chapter materials to assess your degree of understanding.

- Operation stage of the PPA
- Preparing for project operations
- Operations documentation
- Value-to-Business Assessment
- Operations Metrics
- Current System Retirement

■ QUESTIONS AND DISCUSSION POINTS

1. What is the key purpose of the Operation stage of the PPA?
2. How many steps does the Operation stage contain? Can you name each step (don't worry about the order)?
3. Who has the primary responsibility for completing the various steps of the Operation stage?
4. What process group of PMBOK does the Operation stage relate to?
5. Typically, the project team is responsible for completing (developing) the project and delivering it to the operations group. Why should the project manager be concerned about the Operation stage?
6. One of the steps in the Operation stage relates to the retirement of the current system. At times, such retirement may take months to accomplish. Does that mean that the project manager needs to stay with the project until the current system retirement is complete? Please expand on your answer.
7. Briefly describe the six stages of the PPA.
8. For each stage of the PPA, how many steps can you recall (don't be concerned about the order)?
9. Can you recall any of the quotations used in this chapter? If so, why this quotation?

10 PROJECT PORTFOLIO MANAGEMENT

OBJECTIVES

In this chapter, you will learn about the following project management elements:

- Project portfolio—the concept
- Portfolio views
- Portfolio alerts—early warning signals
- Strategy fulfillment
- Stage gate reviews
- Portfolio manager
- Portfolio management software
- Lessons learned
- Benefits

This chapter outlines a process developed by the Center to help its clients manage the portfolio of their projects. Although this process is the responsibility of either the project office (if one exists) or a management steering group, it is important that project managers are aware of the methods and procedures that can help organizations define, develop, and manage a robust project portfolio. The chapter focuses on the dashboard view of the portfolio management process, without going into the detailed discussion of day-to-day management of the portfolio. The chapter includes a comprehensive set of often-asked questions (and their answers) regarding portfolio management.

■ THE IMPORTANCE OF THE PROJECT PORTFOLIO

As we discussed in Chapter 1, not formulating a comprehensive project portfolio is the last of the Seven Deadly Sins and is consequently a befitting topic for the last chapter of the book. Defining, populating, and managing a comprehensive portfolio is the responsibility of the corporate executive management group, with support from the IT department, in the form of providing the technology and tools for its efficient and effective management. The purpose of this chapter is to introduce the *basic structure* of a portfolio management process developed by the Center for its clients, the highlight of which is a comprehensive *dashboard* view of the various stages of a project as it travels from its inception, the Idea stage to its destination, the Operation stage. As a project manager, your ability to comprehend and promote the importance of a well-managed project portfolio will greatly benefit your professional standing. The key components of this knowledge are the underlying physical design of a dashboard to display the portfolio, the most frequently asked questions about setting up a portfolio, and the lessons other organizations have learned from their portfolio management successes and failures. We have purposely left the detailed principles, practices, and procedures needed to manage a portfolio out of the scope of this book.

■ PROJECT PORTFOLIO—THE CONCEPT

Imagine this: You arrive at the airport to take a flight. As you wait in the lounge you hear an announcement, "Attention passengers, all flights are delayed today, and some will be canceled. We are experiencing technical difficulties. We do not have the right staff to service the planes and our computers are down. There is no one in air traffic control tower, and we cannot give you any gate, arrival, or departure information. We apologize for any inconvenience this may cause." It sounds like a Monty Python skit, but in fact, many IT professionals and their customers participate in a similar scene daily. Major trade journals continually lament the deficiency of methods, procedures, and leadership in the management of the multitude of IT/Business projects. The result is thousands of failed or late projects, costing the country billions of dollars every year and wasting scarce resources. In the same way the pilot and crew of a specific flight cannot function in isolation from other flights, project teams flounder when they work without specific and up-to-date knowledge of all other projects in progress.

The three most often stated concerns by a number of our client CEOs regarding their IT departments have been:

- I don't know how many projects are in progress
- I don't know the true status of the mission-critical projects
- I don't know whether IT's capacity is well matched to the demand placed on it by the business community

Enter portfolio management—the principles, practices, and tools for evaluating, selecting, planning, executing, and monitoring projects for four specific goals:

1. Strategy alignment
2. Value-to-business *v.* project complexity (probability of success) balance
3. Maximize investment value
4. Project load *v.* capacity balance

FIGURE 10.1
Project Capacity *v.* Project Demand

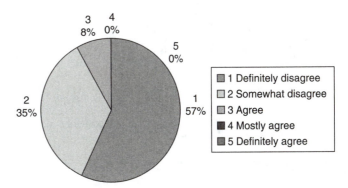

The Demand on Our IT Department is Well Balanced with the Supply It can Produce?

3 8%   4 0%   5 0%   2 35%   1 57%

1 Definitely disagree
2 Somewhat disagree
3 Agree
4 Mostly agree
5 Definitely agree

Absence of a well-balanced portfolio invariably results in duplication of effort, unnecessary delay of mission-critical projects, and internal conflict. As you know, not formulating a comprehensive project portfolio is one of the Seven Deadly Sins (as discussed in Chapter 1). Figure 1.8 shows that only 20 percent of the surveyed organizations had a well-designed project portfolio management process in place. Figure 10.1 gives further insight into the problem of project capacity versus the demands for new projects.

From the data in Figures 1.8 and 10.1, it is obvious that in many cases management is working blind, has over committed resources, has a lack of resource prediction capability, and has a piecemeal menu of information about projects. Without the necessary data, management is incapable of making informed decisions to approve the "right" new projects and to shut down projects with no hope for success. A well-designed portfolio management system tracks a project from the Idea stage through its final implementation. It provides management with answers to these important questions:

1. Do our projects map to the corporate strategy?
2. Do our projects meet the test of value-to-business and risk balance?
3. Is there a fair balance between IT's capacity and the demand placed on it by various business units?
4. Is there full visibility of the status of projects using uniform enterprise-wide metrics?
5. Do project sponsors receive timely information to stop projects that no longer meet business needs?

The project portfolio process establishes a clear path from the germination of an idea through successful project completion. A well-managed portfolio helps ensure that organizational resources are well managed, conflicts are avoided, and duplication of effort between projects is minimized. The Center's portfolio management process is designed to track a given project from the Idea stage to its implementation.

■ PROJECT PORTFOLIO STRUCTURE

The project portfolio consists of the following eight components:

1. Ideas portfolio
2. Pre-Launch (charters) portfolio
3. Launch (plans and estimates) portfolio
4. Execute (development) portfolio
5. Implement (deployment) portfolio
6. Operations portfolio
7. Suspended project portfolio
8. Canceled project portfolio

Figure 10.2 depicts the portfolio structure graphically.

Because there is no specific software package on the market (at the time of this writing) to track and display the project portfolio as depicted in Figure 10.2, individual organizations using this

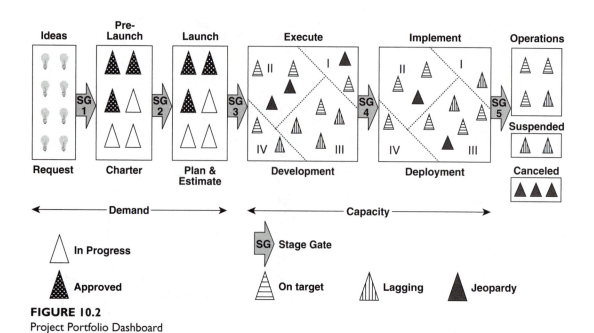

FIGURE 10.2
Project Portfolio Dashboard

approach to portfolio management have developed their own automated processes to document, record, and display the portfolio information. These methods can be as simple as a collection of spreadsheets or as custom developed front-ends to commercial project management software packages.

Ideas Portfolio

This component of the portfolio provides information about the Idea Statements that are in the process of initial due diligence and those that have progressed to completed Project Requests. The primary purpose of this portfolio is to record all of the Idea Statements and Project Requests so that management and customers can see what is being investigated and can assess the instance of duplicate/overlapping ideas, requests, and projects. For each idea/request in this portfolio, we recommend the following items of information as documentation (in a database format):

Idea ID	Key stakeholders
Critical success factors	Ownership
Customer's deadline	Requestor's name
Date of request	Security requirements
Description	Stage gate no. 1 assessment
Funding source	Status: in progress or approved request
Idea expiration date	Strategy alignment
Key assumptions	Value-to-business
Key search words	

This portfolio contains the data to provide management with such important information as:

1. Total number of ideas under review
2. Total number of approved requests
3. Overlapping and/or duplicated project ideas

Additionally, this portfolio provides the information regarding the degree to which the specific corporate strategies are being fulfilled by various project proposals. Keep in mind that ideas and requests that do not meet the test of stage gate no.1 will move to either the suspended or canceled project portfolio. Approved ideas and requests, if not moved to the Pre-Launch stage by their expiration date, become candidates for the suspended or canceled portfolio.

Pre-Launch (Charters) Portfolio

The Pre-Launch component of the portfolio provides management with information about those Project Requests that are in the process of due diligence or have progressed to an approved Project Charter. For each Project Charter in this portfolio, we recommend the following *additional* items of information as documentation:

- Charter ID
- Charter approval date
- Charter expiration date
- Complexity zone
- Cost of charter development
- Intra-Project priorities
- Proposed project manager
- Proposed sponsor
- Shutdown conditions
- Size estimate
  - Budget
  - FTE resources
  - Duration
- Stage gate no. 2 assessment
- Status: in progress or approved charter
- Top 5 risk items

In addition to this information for individual charters, this portfolio can also supply the following portfolio summary information to management:

- Total number of approved charters
- Total number of charters in progress
- Total approved budget amount (this is the demand on the project organization)
- Projects by complexity zones: I, II, III, and IV
- Total cost for developing Charters

The individual project icons (triangles) as depicted in the Pre-Launch portfolio in Figure 10.2 can be color coded to further facilitate visual reference. For example:

1. An empty triangle indicates that the charter is under development.
2. A solid green triangle represents a charter that has been approved and is waiting to be moved to the next (Launch) portfolio.
3. A solid yellow triangle means that an approved charter is approaching its expiration date.

Launch (Plans and Estimates) Portfolio

The Launch portfolio provides management with information about those charters that have been approved and are now in the process of detailed planning and estimating, or have progressed to the approved project status. For each project in this portfolio, we recommend the following *additional* items of information as documentation:

- Project ID
- Detailed estimate
  - Budget
  - FTE resources
  - Duration
- Detailed estimate *v.* size estimate variance
- Project manager
- Project organization
- Prototyping plan
- Sponsor
- Stage gate no. 3 assessment

In addition to this information for individual projects, this portfolio can also supply the following portfolio summary information to management:

- Total number of approved projects
- Total numbers of plans and estimates in progress
- Total approved budget amount (this is the demand on the project organization)
- Projects by complexity zones: I, II, III, and IV
- Total cost for developing plans and estimates

The individual project icons (triangles) as depicted in the Launch portfolio in Figure 10.2 can be color coded to further facilitate visual reference. For example:

1. An empty triangle indicates that the plans and estimates for the project are under development.
2. A solid green triangle represents a project that has been approved and is waiting to be moved to the next (Execute) portfolio.
3. A solid yellow triangle means that the approved project plan and estimates are approaching expiration date.

Execute (Development) Portfolio

The Execute component of the portfolio depicts each project that is being executed. A study of this portfolio provides management with an opus of data on active projects, including the total number of projects, the status of each project, and the differential between the client-specified time line and the project manager's currently estimated schedule. For each project in this portfolio, we recommend the following *additional* items of information as documentation:

- Actual start date
- Baseline version number
- Estimated schedule
- Milestones
- Project status
  - Schedule: green, yellow, red
  - Cost: green, yellow, red
- Stage gate no. 4 assessment
- Vital signs

In addition to the information outlined above for individual projects, this portfolio can also supply the following portfolio summary information to management:

- Total number of projects in execution
- Projects by complexity zones: I, II, III, and IV
- Status of individual projects

The individual project icons (triangles) as depicted in the Execute portfolio in Figure 10.2 can be color coded to further facilitate visual reference. For example:

1. A green triangle indicates that the project's vital signs are on target (any variances are within the acceptable thresholds).
2. A yellow triangle indicates that the project is off target (its vital signs are beginning to breach the acceptable thresholds).
3. A red triangle means that the project is in jeopardy (its vital signs have breached their thresholds).

For projects with yellow or red status, the next step may be a move to the suspend or canceled project portfolio. The number of projects in zones I, II, III and IV will vary depending on the organizational capacity (available budget, sponsors, project managers, and development resources). However, this portfolio furnishes management with information necessary to attain the correct balance of projects to achieve both the strategic and tactical corporate goals.

1. Too many red and yellow projects may indicate that the organization is failing to filter half baked ideas at an early stage, or that the project management process is flawed.

2. Too many projects in zone II may represent a leadership position in technology, but less than adequate high profile business projects.
3. Too many projects in zone III suggest that the company is moving forward in business initiatives but may be failing to leverage new technologies.

Implement (Deployment) Portfolio

The Implement component of the portfolio depicts each project that is being deployed—being transitioned from the development team to the appropriate customer site(s). Keep in mind that a given project may be deployed at multiple (different) client locations and each of these implementations will show up as a different item in this portfolio. For each project in the Implement portfolio, we recommend the following *additional* items of information as documentation:

- Customer readiness assessment
- Deployment date
- Deployment status
- Operations readiness assessment
- Stage gate no. 5 assessment

In addition to this information for individual projects, this portfolio can also supply the following portfolio summary information to management:

- Total number of projects in deployment
- Projects by complexity zones: I, II, III, and IV
- Status of individual projects

The individual project icons (triangles) as depicted in the Implement portfolio in Figure 10.2 can be color coded to further facilitate visual reference. For example:

1. A green triangle indicates that the project's vital signs are on target (any variances are within the acceptable thresholds).
2. A yellow triangle indicates that the project is off target (its vital signs are beginning to breach the acceptable thresholds).
3. A red triangle means that the project is in jeopardy (its vital signs have breached their thresholds).

For projects with yellow or red status, the next step may be a move to the suspend or canceled project portfolio.

Operations Portfolio

The Operations component of the portfolio depicts each project that, after successful deployment, has been moved to the operations group. Keep in mind that a given project may be deployed at multiple (different) client locations and each of these implementations will show up as a different item in this portfolio. At this point in the project, the operations group begins to collect both the operations metrics and, more importantly, the value-to-business metrics. For each project in this portfolio, we recommend the following *additional* items of information as documentation:

- Operations metrics
- Value-to-business metrics
- Customer satisfaction metrics
- Security performance metrics

The individual project icons (triangles) depicted in the Operations portfolio in Figure 10.2 can be color coded to further facilitate visual reference. For example:

1. A green triangle indicates that the project's operational vital signs and value-to-business metrics are on target (any variances are within the acceptable thresholds).
2. A yellow triangle indicates that the project is off target (its operational vital signs and/or value-to-business metrics are beginning to breach the acceptable thresholds).
3. A red triangle means that the project is in jeopardy (its operational vital signs and/or value-to-business metrics have breached their thresholds).

For projects with yellow or red status, the next step may be a move to the suspend or canceled project portfolio. By capitalizing on the positive points of successful projects that reside in the completed (Operations) portfolio, and avoiding the problems and obstacles that thwart projects, the organization is able to develop a best of class model for future project management.

Suspended Project Portfolio

An Idea Statement, Project Request, or Project Charter, or an active project, could move to the suspended project portfolio (the holding pen) for any number of reasons. For example:

1. Change in strategy
2. Change in priority
3. Lack of customer buy-in
4. Lack of appropriate level sponsorship
5. Appropriately skilled project managers not available
6. Lack of resources
7. Insufficient funding
8. Technology not yet ready
9. Breach of vital sign thresholds
10. Breach of the expiration date

For each project in this portfolio, we recommend the following *additional* items of information as documentation:

- Cost-to-date
- Date of suspension
- Reasons for suspension

Once a project reaches the suspend portfolio, the project manager is typically asked to review the "reasons for suspension" and devise a plan to "revive" the project and move it back to the appropriate portfolio. Any project that stays in this portfolio for more than 30–45 days (the number of actual days are decided for each project by the sponsor and the project manager) becomes a candidate for the canceled project portfolio.

Canceled Project Portfolio

The canceled component of the portfolio houses the ideas, requests, charters, and projects (under development, under deployment, or operational) that have been canceled. Failure is a recognized and necessary step to success. Although the textbooks wax lyrical about the benefits of learning from one's mistakes, canceled projects still carry a stigma in the corporate community. Nevertheless, any organization can learn a great deal from its canceled projects and can use this pool of data as a constructive tool. Lessons learned will provide information on everything, from the project managers' ability to accurately estimate budgets and schedules to the quality of the project management process. For each project in this portfolio, we recommend the following *additional* items of information as documentation:

- Date of cancellation
- Reason(s) for cancellation
- Salvage plan

Because revisiting canceled projects can be a politically sensitive issue, we advise that only an organization that has attained a certain degree of project management maturity and has achieved a solid foundation of completed projects should attempt to dissect the contents of this portfolio.

■ PORTFOLIO VIEWS

As you can see, a project in a given portfolio contains a comprehensive list of documentation items. It is important to point out that this information is recorded in a centralized database so that each item occurs only once and is updated as new information develops—from one portfolio to the next.

Also, it can be overwhelming to see all of the listed fields for a given project displayed (on a screen) when reviewing the status of a given project. Therefore, it is necessary to design different views of the portfolio for different levels of people in the organization. Typically, the first view of a project (often called the *executive view*) contains only a few selected items of documentation. For example:

- ID
- Name
- Description
- Strategy alignment
- Value-to-business
- Current state
  - The name of the portfolio
- Project manager
- Sponsor
- Current status
  - Green, yellow, or red

The second, more detailed view (often called the *management view*), contains a few *additional* items of documentation. For example:

- Key stakeholders
- Project complexity
- Project impact
- Project risks
- State gate review
- Vital signs status

The third, more detailed view (often called the *project manager view*), typically contains all of the items of documentation as listed in each of the portfolios.

■ PORTFOLIO ALERTS—EARLY WARNING SIGNALS

A highly versatile benefit of using the portfolio management approach is the ability to define specific alerts for selected projects. Some of the commonly used alerts are:

- Unaligned project
- Duplicate/overlapping project
- Breach of vital signs
  - Runaway conditions
  - Shutdown conditions
- Unsecured system
- High defect rate
- Supporting project/system nonperformance

Unaligned Project

During the life cycle of a project, if there is a change in the corporate strategy (from obtaining greater market share to increased profit), any project that was approved to meet the greater market share objective will be brought to the attention of the portfolio manager for further assessment.

Duplicate/Overlapping Project

The portfolio manager is charged with the responsibility of monitoring the entire portfolio for emergence of duplicate/overlapping projects. The best approach is to make this a weekly routine process, very much like the routine virus scanning process supported by most virus management software.

What I found was that the bulk of the more than 250 projects were dying an agonizing death . . . In about 150 cases the project was a duplicate . . .
Mike Anderson, "How to Be a Turnaround CIO," *CIO Magazine*
(September 15, 2000): p. 62.

Breach of Vital Signs

The sponsor and the project manager may wish to be alerted to the breach of a given set of vital signs beyond certain thresholds. In these instances, a specific alert is automatically sent out from the portfolio to inform the sponsor and the project manager of the breach.

Unsecured System

Ongoing tests show that the system is vulnerable to security violations.

High Defect Rate

The number of defects in the product/process is above the acceptable threshold.

Supporting Project/System Nonperformance

If the successful deployment and operation of the project at hand is dependent on another project/system, and the dependent project/system is in itself in jeopardy, an alert would be generated. The various portfolio alerts are similar to the continuous monitoring of a patient in a hospital and the transmission of *early* warning signals to the nurse's monitoring station. A well-designed portfolio alert system can provide the project sponsor with timely warnings so that appropriate corrective actions can be put in place.

■ STRATEGY FULFILLMENT

The most important reason for establishing a well-designed project portfolio is to ensure that the currently stated corporate strategy can be accomplished with the execution of the right projects. One way to assure this objective is to make sure that a sufficient number of projects are in the works to attain the strategy objectives. For example, assume the following strategy objectives:

1. Increase market share by 20 percent
2. Increase profit by 25 percent
3. Improve customer satisfaction by 30 points

At this point it is necessary to make sure that the planned projects will meet or exceed the stated objectives. Having a well-designed portfolio management process can help management assess reality *v.* the plans, as follows:

1. The approved project list from the Pre-Launch (charters) portfolio will tell us the degree to which the planned projects will help meet the stated objective(s). For example, the data in the strategy alignment and Value-to-Business fields of the various approved charters will provide the metrics for this assessment.
2. The same information from the Execute (development) and Implement (deployment) portfolios will tell us the degree to which the currently active projects will contribute to the stated objectives.
3. The value-to-business metrics collected from the Operations portfolio will tell management the actual degree to which a specific objective has been met.

With this information at hand, management can review the project portfolio periodically to see whether the planned projects will be able to meet the strategy objectives, and then take appropriate actions in a timely manner. For example, starting additional projects if the projects in progress will not be able to meet objectives, or in certain cases revise the objectives (downward) to map to the reality of the project portfolio. Figure 10.3 depicts an example of a strategy fulfillment report.

FIGURE 10.3
Strategy Fulfillment Report

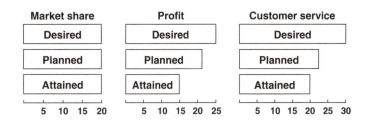

Assume a review of the portfolio by the portfolio steering committee occurred at the end of the third quarter of the fiscal year. From the data in Figure 10.3, we could draw the following conclusions:

1. The objective of increasing the market share by 20 percent has already been achieved, and the steering committee may decide not to initiate any additional projects related to this objective.
2. It is obvious that the objectives related to increased profit and customer satisfaction improvement are behind the desired mark. Unless quick action can be taken to start and complete a sufficient number of projects to meet these objectives, the portfolio will not be able to satisfy the stated objectives.

The fact that the planned projects list falls short of the desired mark should be of concern to management. This may be the case because the desired strategy objectives were too lofty and need to be revisited in a timely manner. Another reason could be that a number of active projects are far behind schedule and need special attention to assure timely completion.

■ STAGE GATE REVIEWS

Figure 10.2 depicts a total of five stage gates. At each stage gate, there is a Go/No Go decision. The decision could be Go (proceed to the next stage), or No Go (team to revisit the work done, improve the appropriate area, and seek reapproval, or the project may be canceled). At each stage gate, the sponsor diligently reviews the materials submitted by the project manager. The sponsor and the project manager then *look ahead* and ascertain whether the path to the next stage is clear of obstacles and that the necessary project *infrastructure* is in place. This preview is akin to the process used by the FAA and commercial airline pilots to allow an airplane to take off. The pilot not only has to make sure that all is well with the airplane, but that it is safe to fly through to the planned destination. During a stage gate review, the sponsor may ask the project manager for further explanations regarding certain components of the already-completed work, or may even seek a second opinion from an SME, perhaps someone from the project office. Each stage gate review is a three-step process:

- The sponsor makes a decision to open the stage gate and lets the team proceed to the next stage. Or,
- The sponsor directs the project manager and the team to rework certain deficient areas to bring them up to the needed level of quality, and when satisfied with the rework, allows the team to proceed to the next stage. Or,
- The sponsor decides to initiate project suspension or cancellation procedures:
  - After the Ideas stage, a decision may be made *not* to go ahead with the proposal because it does not live up to the necessary approval criteria, such as strategy alignment, value-to-business.
  - After the Pre-Launch (charters) stage, a Project Charter could be rejected because of high risks and low value-to-business.
  - After the Launch (Plans and estimates) stage, the project may be rejected for any number of reasons, such as no appropriate sponsor, underskilled and inexperienced project manager and/or team, lack of appropriate customer buy-in, change in organization strategy, or higher-than-expected cost estimates.
  - During the Execute (development) and/or during the Implement (deployment) stage, if a project breaches the shutdown conditions, it will become a candidate for review and then a possible Go/No Go decision.

This process of assessing a project for its ability to continue may be new to many sponsors, stakeholders, and project managers, but is vital to avoid the pervasive environment of letting massive numbers of troubled projects continue ad nauseam. In too many cases, once an idea is pronounced, it becomes a project right away and the first point at which a Go/No Go decision is looked at may be too late in the project life cycle. We believe this is a key reason for a ridiculous number of half baked ideas continuing as projects for far too long. We strongly believe that, if disciplined and progressive stage gate reviews are made routine, the number of failed and challenged projects will decrease considerably, saving IT/Business departments millions of dollars each year.

■ APPOINTING A PORTFOLIO MANAGER

Ideally, the building and loading of the corporate project portfolio should be a joint venture, undertaken by a senior business executive and the CIO. Once loaded, the *management* of the portfolio should pass to a business executive, who in close alliance with the CIO, will oversee the maintenance and evolution of the portfolio. The decisions that have to be made to efficiently manage the portfolio often carry highly political ramifications. The decision maker must be suited up with the political armor needed to meet criticism and opposition from various parts of the organization. Equally, these decisions will have a direct impact on the corporate bottom line, so the individual must have strong business acumen and knowledge of the organization's strategic and tactical needs. However, in an organization that supports scores of projects simultaneously, the executive community must also appoint a full-time and dedicated portfolio manager. While this suggestion of managing a portfolio of projects might be considered somewhat avant-garde, it is an accepted concept in the financial community. Successful investment houses train managers in the role of managing a portfolio of investments, controlling the portfolio's exposure to risk, obtaining balance, and shifting investments to maximize profit and minimize loss. The portfolio manager is also in a position to provide project managers with advice and feedback gained from a bird's eye view of the portfolio of projects.

■ PORTFOLIO MANAGEMENT SOFTWARE—THREE STRIKES AND YOU ARE OUT

Has your organization acquired portfolio management software or are you planning to do so? If the answer to either question is "Yes," please review the following questions:

1. Does your organization have a well-designed project portfolio process in place?
2. Does your project approval process require a specific and provable value-to-business justification?
3. Does the sponsorship of projects reside with appropriate level business managers?
4. Do sponsors have their skin in the game—are they held responsible for the promised project benefits?
5. Are business unit executives willing to share information about their projects with the portfolio manager?
6. Do project managers specifically know who can declare success and what measurements they will use to assess project success?
7. Does the portfolio management process have a specific course of action in place to identify and cancel troubled projects in a timely fashion?
8. Does the organization have a well-defined and well-executed project manager development program (education, training, mentoring, and certification)?

If there are three or more "No" answers, please leave the ballpark and take your portfolio management software with you. Many business executives and CIOs have not learned the obvious: technology acts only as a catalyst. For organizations that have a well-formulated project portfolio and disciplined project management process, technology acts as a *facilitator* for success. For organizations mired in chaotic project management practices, technology (at its best) *accelerates their losses.*

■ FREQUENTLY ASKED QUESTIONS—PROJECT PORTFOLIO MANAGEMENT

As a part of the Center's ongoing consulting work with a number of clients, we have compiled a list of the most frequently asked questions along with our responses. These are outlined below for your review and consideration.

1. **What is project portfolio management?**

   Project portfolio management is a best practice solution comprised of people, processes, and techniques that will enable IT/Business units to consistently, reliably, and predictably bridge the gap between business strategies and day-to-day operations. It includes the ability to:

   a. Translate corporate strategy into tangible terms (project proposal development).

   b. Align the projects with the business strategies and their respective prioritization.

   c. Align the prioritized projects with organizational capacity.

   d. Coordinate the interdependencies between the various projects.

   e. Provide management with a "control tower" view of the projects in progress.

   Project portfolio management can be summarized as an integrated multilevel approach for ensuring that an organization does the right projects, at the right time, with the right resources, using the right methods and procedures.

2. **Why implement a project portfolio management process?**

   In recent years, the demand for new projects has continued to grow well beyond organizational capacity to execute them in a timely manner, and to the requisite quality. Currently, the project demand is exceeding the project execution capacity by at least 70 percent and the demand for new projects continues to grow. Organizations need a fiscally responsible and manageable solution to select and execute only the right projects. In addition to "right-sizing" the approved project portfolio, IT/Business units must be able to deliver consistently successful projects. Simply stated, project portfolio management is the best tool available to accomplish these critical organizational objectives.

3. **What is considered a "project" for the purposes of project portfolio management?**

   For the purpose of Project Portfolio Management, "projects" are defined as activities that:

   a. Have a proposed budget, or actual cost-to-date, of $25,000[1] or more

   b. Span more than one divisional boundary

   While this definition is not intended to preclude the application of project management methods and procedures to projects that fall outside these criteria, it does require projects that fall within them to adhere to the defined project portfolio management process. For projects that fall outside the defined criteria, the respective project manager must still register these with the portfolio manager. This requirement will help ensure that duplicate/overlapping projects are identified early on and that resource and budget overallocation is less likely to occur.

4. **Who has responsibility for developing, approving, and managing the project portfolio?**

   Development and ongoing (tactical) management of the project portfolio is the responsibility of the project management office and approval of the project portfolio is the responsibility of the portfolio steering committee.

5. **Who is the portfolio steering committee and how were they selected?**

   The committee is a management-level group comprised of various business unit heads and the CIO; the COO or CFO chairs it. Most organizations rotate the chair responsibilities to a different executive each year.

6. **What are the primary responsibilities of the project management office and portfolio steering committee?**

   The project management office is responsible for the collection, review, categorization, scoring, ranking, and prioritization of all Project Charters to be considered for inclusion in the

---

[1]This is an example; your management will need to define this threshold.

approved project portfolio. The portfolio steering committee (meeting monthly) is responsible for the optimization of the project portfolio.

7. **What is the process to arrive at an approved project portfolio?**

The initial input to the project portfolio is the annual strategy and project planning process that defines ideas/projects to meet the corporate strategic objectives. Additionally, throughout the year, new ideas/projects are proposed by various business units to ensure that corporate strategic objectives are being met. Optimization of the portfolio (adding and removing projects, resequencing start dates, adjustments to scope and cost) is then undertaken to match organizational capacity. The result is the recommended project portfolio. This list is presented to the portfolio steering committee for final optimization and approval.

8. **What process is used to prioritize the project proposals (Project Charters)?**

The primary criteria used to decide the initial fate of a proposal are:

a. Strategy fulfillment
b. Financial benefits
c. Significant interruption to business
d. Regulatory or legal requirement
e. Significant safety or security concern

Project proposals that meet any of these criteria are included in the "must do" list *without* any rank order. This list is developed through the combined efforts of the respective business units and the project management office. The next step, the responsibility of the portfolio steering committee, is to rank order (prioritize) the "must do" list. The primary inputs to this process are:

a. Strategy fulfillment
b. Value-to-business
c. Project complexity
d. Budget
e. Project management capacity
f. Project staffing capacity
g. Customer deployment capacity
h. Technology (infrastructure) capacity

All project proposals are then placed in their prioritized order. It is important to note that the list of projects at this point invariably exceeds the allocated budget and project management capacity (primarily the people available to execute projects). Typically, the proposed project list is allowed to exceed the project management capacity by 25 percent, with the assumption that not all proposed projects (Project Charters) will move to the Execute portfolio.

9. **Is there a process for getting a new proposal reviewed/approved after the project portfolio has been approved?**

Primarily, the process is the same as described above with a few *added* caveats:

a. Additional budget is authorized by the portfolio steering committee specifically to include a given new project based on its contribution to the corporate strategy needs.
b. The proposing unit has the budget to fund the proposed project.
c. The portfolio is able to accommodate the proposed project because the net demand on the portfolio is less than the capacity. This may be due to cancellation of previously approved projects, early completion of projects, or additional new capacity.

Please note that the acceptance of a project into the portfolio does not automatically assure that the proposed project will actually move to the Execute (development) portfolio.

10. **What are the responsibilities of a project manager if he discovers that his project is not included in the approved project portfolio?**

Once this situation is discovered and confirmed, the project manager must inform the project sponsor of the problem and, then working with the project office, must take the necessary steps to either obtain approval for the project to continue or move the project to the suspended portfolio. Here is a summary of the needed steps:

a. Suspend all project work
b. Develop project status report

c. Document the justifications for continuing the project
d. Document the risks of project closure
e. Document the cost of project closure

At this point, the responsibility for the decision to continue with or cancel the project rests with the project sponsor and the portfolio steering committee.

■ LESSONS LEARNED

Having helped a number of clients implement the project portfolio management process, listed below are a number of important lessons culled from our experience:

1. Portfolio management entails a major cultural change in most IT/Business organizations because it requires cross-functional sharing of intimate project information.
2. Portfolio management requires sponsorship at the highest level(s) of the organization and must not be considered an IT endeavor relegated to the IT department.
3. Various business unit executives must agree to share project information with the portfolio manager. With the deployment of the project portfolio management process, project information becomes open to cross-functional view and review.
4. Initiating the portfolio management process can be highly stressful because it requires a high degree of discipline in the process of project approval and execution. The optimal time to start the project portfolio management process is 3 to 4 months ahead of the annual corporate budgeting cycle (start of the fiscal year) so that most of the portfolio management standards, procedures, and guidelines are in place by the start of the fiscal year—the point at which a majority of new projects are proposed. Also, don't try to follow every portfolio management standard, procedure, and guideline to the letter the first time around. Allow for the learning process necessary for fine tuning the portfolio management process.

■ PROJECT PORTFOLIO—BENEFITS

The primary benefits of a well-designed and well-managed project portfolio management process can be summarized as follows:

- Establishes a clear path from idea generation to project implementation
- Screens all projects uniformly
- Ensures that all projects are aligned to specific organizational strategies
- Provides strategic information to senior managers in a timely manner
- Provides tactical information to project managers in a timely manner
- Provides an early warning system of project-specific alerts
- Streamlines resource allocation
- Helps assure rational resource assignments
- Helps balance project demand with capacity
- Provides the ability to efficiently change the project mix to match any changes in strategic objectives due to changes in the economic, competitive, and regulatory environment

It is important to note that the success of a project portfolio process is highly dependent on corporate executive leadership, which in this case entails the following attributes:

1. *Knowledge:* The executive group must understand the portfolio management process and be able to elucidate it clearly.
2. *Acceptance:* The executive group must demonstrate its acceptance of the process by ensuring that projects in their departments are promptly loaded in the portfolio.
3. *Value:* The executive group must demonstrate that it values the portfolio process by providing appropriate budget and resources to manage the portfolio.

■ SUMMARY

In this chapter we discussed the problems faced by IT/Business executives who all too often don't know how many projects are in progress, what the true status is, whether they fit the company's current strategy, and if the organization has the resources to support them. To help solve the problem, we outlined the project portfolio management process to help sponsors and project managers track their projects from the Idea stage all the way to the Operation stage. The portfolio management process lets IT and business executives see both the trees and the forest. On one hand, it shows how to evaluate, select, and track individual projects as they move from the initial idea through planning, development and rollout; on the other, it offers a "control tower" view of all current projects. The process also sets forth the key questions to ask as projects move from one stage to another.

The following is a list of the key subject areas covered in this chapter. We invite you to review the list and assess your level of comprehension of each topic. The best approach is to take a separate sheet of paper and write a short narrative to explain your knowledge of the topic and then go back and compare your summaries with the material covered in the chapter. Another approach is to find a colleague who is also interested in these topics and discuss your understanding of the topics with her, and then jointly review the chapter materials to assess your degree of understanding.

- Project portfolio—the concept
- Portfolio views
- Portfolio alerts—early warning signals
- Strategy fulfillment
- Stage gate reviews
- Portfolio manager
- Portfolio management software
- Lessons learned
- Benefits

■ QUESTIONS AND DISCUSSION POINTS

1. What is portfolio management and what are its key benefits?

2. As portrayed in this chapter, what is the overall structure of the project portfolio? How many portfolios are there? Can you replicate the drawing depicting the various portfolios? Briefly define the contents of each portfolio.

3. What different types of alerts can be provided by a portfolio management system and what types of decisions can be made from these alerts?

4. What actions should a project manager take if he discovers that his project is not included in the approved project portfolio?

5. Can you recall any of the quotations used in this chapter? If so, why this quotation?

PROCUREMENT PLANNING

We believe it is important for all project managers to understand the process necessary for procuring outside services, a growing part of IT/Business project management. This appendix introduces the reader to the various steps and processes for procurement management:

- Request for information (RFI)
- Request for quote (RFQ)
- Request for proposal (RFP)
- Statement of work (SOW)
- Service level agreement (SLA)

■ PROCUREMENT PROCESS

Procurement, in terms of *project management*, means acquiring goods and services from outside sources (contractors, consultants, vendors, integrators, and service providers). Over the years, the term has developed two synonyms: *purchasing* and *outsourcing*. The term "procurement" is most commonly used in public sector organizations, "purchasing" is typically used by private sector companies (most large companies have purchasing departments), and "outsourcing" is used heavily in the IT profession. The key reasons for procurement of goods and services from an outside source can be classified as follows:

1. To focus internal resources on core business and use the external resources as needed, thereby reducing overhead costs, reducing down (unused) time, and providing more flexibility in resource management
2. To increase speed to market by leveraging available expertise without taking the time to develop internal skills and experiences
3. To identify cost-effective solutions by leveraging the economies of scale that are possible by specifically focused external sources
4. To provide access to skilled individuals on a limited basis, thereby reducing the total cost of project development

During the past decade, more and more organizations, especially IT, are depending on outsourced services to the extent that the expected outsourcing by IT departments in the U.S. alone topped $100 billion in 2003. Unfortunately, the successes desired by the organizations delving into outsourced relationships continue to be less than satisfactory. For example:

> *. . . 25 percent of all firms' functions report an outsourcing relationship failure within the past two years. "Failure" was defined as the termination by the client of a contract before its expiration date for contracts that had been in place for at least one year. The idea that one quarter of all executives experience an outsourcing failure, by this definition, is most certainly a matter of real concern.*
>
> http://www.firmbuilder.com/articles/19/48/388/

> *Half of this year's IT outsourcing projects will be tagged as losers by senior decision makers for not delivering on bottom-line promises, said research firm Gartner.*
>
> http://www.techweb.com/wire/story/TWB20030326S0006

The primary cause of this poor performance is that as the instances and size of outsourcing has grown, people responsible for managing the process have not built up their contract management (procurement) skills accordingly. Consider, for example, a group of employees in an organization given the responsibility to establish an outsourcing relationship. If you were to compare the group's degree of contract management skills with those of the vendor (contractor), in most cases, the vendor's skills will be far superior to the group's skills. Keep in mind that the vendors do it for a living but the team may have engaged in contract management only once or twice. Historically, the corporate purchasing departments provided a valuable service because procurement was limited to their unique area of expertise. However, with the proliferation of technology, outsourcing continues to become more complex, requiring not only deeper knowledge of the contracting process but a higher degree of project management skills as well. Additionally, the procurement process often results in role reversal. Under a typical project development scenario, the project team is the supplier (they build the product) and the business units are the customers. However, in the case of outsourcing, the project team becomes the customer of the outside supplier; you now have to learn how to "buy" effectively and efficiently and protect your interests. The classic procurement life cycle consists of the following seven key areas:

1. Procurement planning
2. Solicitation planning
3. Solicitation
4. Source (contractor/supplier) selection
5. Contract negotiation and approval
6. Contract administration
7. Contract closeout

Figure A1.1 depicts the seven areas of procurement management. While some overlap among various components can occur, most of the work is linear in nature and can take an extended period of time.

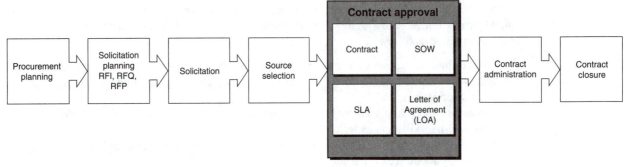

FIGURE A1.1
Procurement Management

Procurement Planning

This part of procurement management involves deciding what to procure, how to procure it, and the timing of procurement. To support procurement planning, the work carried out in the Idea stage and Pre-Launch stage still needs to be completed by the project team because the Project Charter will be the foundation of the solicitation of services. Our analysis of a large number of failed/challenged, as well as successful, outsourcing projects has shown us that failures happen when teams rush through the Idea and Pre-Launch stage work with the belief that the contractor does not need all the detailed information developed through these stages. Wrong. As a part of procurement planning, you will need to consider the type of contract that will best suit your organization. Typical contract types include:

Fixed Price Contract Also known as lump-sum contracts, these contracts establish a fixed price for the services and/or products to be delivered. These contracts carry minimum risk for the buyer. Certain conditions must exist to protect both the buyer and the vendor:

• Requirements and specifications must be clearly defined
• In-scope and out-of-scope statements must be clearly defined
• The change-request process must be clearly defined

Failure to provide clear requirements and specifications puts both the buyer and the vendor at risk. The vendor runs the risk of having to absorb the cost of the rework that results from unclear requirements, and the buyer runs the risk of not getting a product that meets the quality expectations. Fixed price contracts often include incentives for exceeding predefined performance objectives such as early delivery and reduced cost.

Cost Plus Fixed Fee Contract This type of contract involves a payment to the vendor for the costs incurred, plus a specified fee. Costs are generally divided into two categories:

- Direct costs (costs incurred for the exclusive benefit of the project) such as salaries of project staff, materials, and travel
- Indirect costs (costs allocated to the project by the vendor as the cost of doing business) such as salaries of corporate executives, facilities, and equipment

Cost plus fixed fee contracts are used with projects where requirements are vague or unknown and new technology is anticipated. Cost plus fixed fee contracts often include incentives for exceeding performance objectives such as early delivery and reduced cost.

Time and Materials Contract This type of contract is typically used when it is impossible to determine the exact requirements of the specific project work. In this contract type, the hourly rate is negotiated for each type and level of contracted resource, such as people. In some cases, budgets are established with amounts that can not be exceeded. These contracts are used because:

- They are conducive to long-term relationships
- They provide a means to add new services or modify services without starting a new contract
- They allow for substantial commitments
- They add flexibility to the project

Unit Price Contract This type of contract is typically used for the purchase of goods such as hardware, software packages, or furniture, or services such as consulting by an SME on an hourly basis. This type of contract often specifies volume discounts—the higher the volume, the lower the per unit rate.

Modular Contract A modular contract is used for highly complex projects that have been parsed into segments (phases). The contract covers the work segment by segment. Different segments may have different types of contracts, which allows for the possibility of keeping or changing vendors at the completion of each segment.

Regardless of the type, all contracts must include provisions that are realistic, clearly stated, and fair to all parties. The following list provides a number of important items to consider:

- Change management
- Expense policy
- Confidentiality
- Disaster recovery
- Exclusivity
- Knowledge transfer
- Legal obligations
- Intellectual property ownership and copyrights
- Payment terms
- Proprietary information
- SLA
- Source code escrow
- SOW
- Term of contract
- Termination
- Warranties

Over the years, we have collected a number of recommendations that have served the customers (of contractors) well. Our short list includes the following bits of wisdom:

- Hold back a portion of the total payment until after the formal acceptance (closure) of the project
- Link payments to the completion of deliverables and key milestones
- Employ shorter term contracts
- Include early termination rights
- Maintain change of vendor control
- Indicate the method that will be used to transition to a new vendor
- Include source code escrow

Our advice to all project managers is to become familiar with the fundamentals of contract law before delving into any contract negotiations. Discuss the subject with your organization's legal department to see if any such education/training is available.

Solicitation Planning

This part of procurement management is a two-step process that involves preparing the requirements definition for the service/product to be procured and the development of assessment criteria to be used to award the contract. Three common examples of solicitation documents follow.

RFI An RFI is the simplest of the three documents and is used to solicit information from one or more probable contractors regarding the services/product to be acquired and the general background of the contractor. An RFI is typically issued early in the procurement process to collect general information regarding the services/products available in the market and their overall cost structure, and to generate a list of qualified suppliers. The response information may be used to structure the final specifications of the desired service/product. A typical RFI will include the following items:

- Organization background
- Vision and background
- Scope
- Business and technical requirements
- Product/service description and needs
- Abbreviated list of contract terms and conditions

RFQ An RFQ typically is issued to seek a pricing quote (also known as a bid) and a delivery timeframe of a well-defined service (usually a product). An RFQ is most suitable when the service and/or product is well defined, acquisition is straightforward (without many adjustments and modifications), and contract negotiations are expected to be simple and direct. The structure of an RFQ typically includes the following items:

- Organization background
- Vision and background
- Scope
- Detailed business and technical requirements
- Detailed product/service description and needs
- Contract terms and conditions
- Abbreviated evaluation procedures
- Vendor instructions

RFP An RFP is used to solicit proposals and bids from perspective suppliers. An RFP should be prepared after the business (functional) and technical requirements for the proposed service/product have been completed. Keeping this in mind, the typical Project Charter does not have a sufficient level of detail and is not, by itself, suitable for creating an RFP. Invariably, the core team will need to do some work to complete the functional and technical requirements, which means some of the steps described in the Launch stage of the PPA will need to be completed. It is best to assemble a team composed of representatives from all stakeholder groups, including the procurement and legal specialists assigned to the project. The scope of an RFP may include the development of functional and technical requirements by the vendor; if so, make sure that the RFP clearly states the vendor responsibility. Typically, an RFP consists of the following elements:

- Executive summary
  - Overview of the organization
  - Overview of business needs
  - Vendor expectations
- Project background and vision
  - Statement of current situation
  - Statement of anticipated opportunity
  - Overall project fit
- Functional (business) and technical requirements
  - Product description and needs
  - Product scope
  - Detailed functional requirements
  - Knowledge transfer and training
- Vendor instructions and procedures
  - Response format
  - Response components
  - Bidders' conference
- Evaluation procedures
  - Evaluation process
  - Evaluation criteria
  - Major milestones
- Contract terms and conditions
  - Contract template
  - Competitive nondisclosure
- Glossary of terms

Most organizations (especially those that have a full-fledged procurement/purchasing office) have standard templates for preparing RFPs. We advise that you investigate the existence of such templates and use one as a foundation for creating your RFP. Keeping in mind that a copy of your RFP may be obtained by a competitor. Be careful that the RFP does not contain any proprietary information whose disclosure might compromise your organization's competitive advantage. Make sure to incorporate appropriate nondisclosure clauses. It is always a good idea to have the final draft of the RFP reviewed and approved by the legal department. You would be surprised how many project managers overlook this step, which invariably results in extensive rework after the vendor's response to the RFP has been received. Such an oversight earns the project manager a quick trip to the mocking post.

Solicitation

The purpose of this step is to seek responses to the RFP from vendors by sending out copies of the RFPs to the prospective bidders. Selecting vendors to receive an RFP is a vitally important step in the solicitation process. The very best RFP will yield poor results if sent to an inappropriate set of vendors. Solicitation includes the following steps:

- Develop a list of appropriate bidders
  - Procurement department
  - Previous and current vendors
  - IT/Business advisory services references
  - Colleagues
  - The web
- Obtain confidentiality agreement
  - Distribute confidentiality agreements
  - Receive confidentiality agreements

- Develop the solicitation schedule
  - Send RFPs to bidders
  - Bidders' conference date
  - Final date for bidders' response
  - Evaluation completed
  - Contact approval date
  - Contract award date
  - Start work (by the selected bidder)
- Develop the selection criteria
  - Evaluation team
  - Evaluation scorecard (criteria)
- Define response date from bidders
  - Usually 3 weeks
  - Specify a closing date for responses

Keep in mind that the potential bidders will need considerable time to prepare a high quality response to your RFP. It is important that you allow sufficient time; the usual recommended time is a minimum of 3 weeks. A common complaint by many bidders is that they do not get the time needed for response development and have to require their staff to work overtime to meet the response deadline. We recognize that this is a significant problem and recommend that you treat the RFP process as a project and be disciplined about gauging the viability of all schedules (the bidders' and yours). Most RFPs require that you hold a bidders' conference, a group meeting set aside for the bidders to seek clarifications regarding the bid from the buyer. A bidders' conference notice should be sent out to all prospective bidders with due lead time for them to make arrangements to attend the meeting (keep in mind that some may have to travel a long distance). Make every effort to answer each of the bidders' inquiries during the meeting; if any follow-ups are necessary, appoint a single point of contact. Any responses made after the bidders' conference should be put in writing by a single contact person. Doing otherwise is certain to cause confusion.

Source (Contractor/Supplier) Selection

During this step, you and your team will review the various proposals, make a list of the top three or four bidders (the short list), conduct in-depth assessment of the bids on the short list, and make your recommendations to the sponsor. The sponsor is then responsible to make the final decision on the bidder of choice. Once in a while, you may discover that none of the proposals fulfills the basic objectives of the RFP and you may have to start the solicitation process all over again.

As you and the team begin to review the bidders' responses, you need to keep a number of key points in focus:

- Make sure that each bidder clearly understands what the RFP is requesting and why it is important to the company. They must either provide substantive proof that they can deliver the desired product and/or services or demonstrate the capability to build it in a timely manner.
- They must clearly identify the full costs of the product/service. In addition, the vendor must explain the costs to be born by your organization (the cost of staffing, licensing, and any other costs your organization will be expected to absorb).
- They must elucidate how they are going to manage the project, which includes a comprehensive explanation of their project management process. We strongly advise that you and the team pay as much attention to their project management capabilities as you do to their technical and business capabilities. Remember the prevalent high rate of failed and challenged projects; if the project management process is weak, the project will have a low success rate.
- They must demonstrate that they have the financial strength to carry out the project.

As you can see from the list above, the challenge of evaluating the RFPs is not going to be a "walk in the park;" the process requires specific skills, time, and commitment. The following is a list of the key steps needed to review, assess, and make the final decision. The order of the listed items does not imply the order of execution. Some of the steps may be executed simultaneously while others may have some lag.

- *Receive the Proposals:* Log, with an appropriate date stamp, all proposals as they are received. If any proposals are received after the specified date, it is the prerogative of the sponsor to accept or reject the proposal (this may not be an option if you work for a government agency).
- *Prepare the Evaluation Team:* Assemble a core team of senior level people to help you review and assess the various RFPs; junior level people may provide support services but should not be responsible for RFP review and assessment. The team's first assignment will be to produce an RFP evaluation scorecard, a tool designed to help assess individual RFPs and to help compare them for their relative value. Typically, a scorecard consists of a list of key assessment attributes and each attribute is assigned a weight point. The relative weights of various attributes are driven by their importance to the final decision making process. The following is a sample list of attributes:
  - Vendor profile
  - Vendor's approach and solution
  - Proposed development plan
  - Proposed implementation plan
  - Project management plan
  - Proposed schedule
  - Proposed cost
  - Validation of functionality
  - Training and knowledge transfer plan
- *Rule on Contract Terms and Conditions:* Review each proposal to see whether it meets the minimum terms and conditions set forth in the RFP. The proposals that significantly breach the terms and conditions are typically rejected. For those that reflect a minimal breach, you may wish to inform the bidder of the nonconformance and see whether they are willing to resubmit that portion of the proposal.
- *Assess Each RFP:* The rubber meets the road at this point—the team must review each RPF and rate it for its worthiness. The best approach is to first build an electronic spreadsheet using the scorecard entries as the rows and various RFP bidders as columns. Then, you and the team must assess each of the scorecard criteria for a given RFP and enter the values in the spreadsheet. Different people are going to disagree about the assessment values. Here, you may need the help of SMEs to break any deadlocks; be prepared to call the final shots when necessary. Figure A1.2 depicts an example of an evaluation scorecard.
- *Choose Top Three Bidders:* We assume that you had more than three qualified bidders. A small group of senior team members will review the assessments carried out in the last step and then select the three most qualified bids. At this point, you may wish to contact one or more of the bidders for clarification and explanation of certain key components of their responses. Also, the team members need to begin to check the reference information provided by the bidders and have the legal department review the contract portion of the bid in more detail.
- *Schedule Bidder Demonstration and/or Office Visits:* At this point, the team should ask each bidder to schedule a demonstration of their product. Occasionally, it may be necessary to arrange a

FIGURE A1.2
Sample RFP Evaluation Scorecard

RFP assessment attribute	Available points	Vendor A	Vendor B	Vendor C
1. Vendor profile	10	7	6	8
2. Vendor's approach and solution	20	12	10	10
3. Proposed development plan	10	7	7	8
4. Proposed implementation plan	15	11	10	12
5. Project management plan	10	7	6	8
6. Proposed schedule	5	5	4	4
7. Proposed cost	10	6	8	8
8. Validation of functionality	10	7	7	8
9. Training & knowledge transfer plan	10	4	4	6
Total	100	66	62	72

visit to the bidder's office/plant where the proposed product will be developed. This visit gives the team the opportunity to observe, firsthand, the facilities and services of each bidder and to gather information that will be helpful when making the final selection. As a final check on the various responses, it is important that the selection team has kept the following key points in mind:

- Does the vendor have proven *successful* experience in the proposed products and solutions? Have they seen a demonstration of the real product, and not just a hyped-up prototype?
- Does the vendor have partnerships or contracting relationships with other vendors (third parties) that your organization does not want to do business with?
- Are you confident that the vendor has fully disclosed all relevant information regarding its products?

- *Make Recommendation:* Once the assessment team has gathered the necessary information, reviewed the pertinent documentation, checked the references, and taken the time to observe product demonstrations, they are then asked to prepare their recommendation to management. If more than one bidder must be considered, you should rank order the recommendations.

Contract Negotiation and Approval

The next step in the process of acquiring the services of the selected vendor involves defining, negotiating, and agreeing on the terms of a legal contract. Earlier in this appendix, we discussed the different types of contracts; you will need to work with the legal department and SMEs knowledgeable about different contract structures to define an appropriate contract structure for the RFP.

Based on the dollar amount and the length of the project, the negotiations between the bidder and your company (legal) representatives may take from a few days to many weeks. This can impact the start of the project and delay the final delivery of the service/product. This anticipated delay is one reason to start the contract review process early and in parallel with some of the earlier steps.

Any contract, whether it is for a product or a service, will benefit from a well-defined change management plan. Managing change is one of the most challenging aspects of contract management. It is essential that the contract stipulates a process by which changes to the agreed-upon scope are initiated, evaluated, and either accepted or rejected. During the course of the contract, changes may be driven by the vendor as well as by the buyer. Well-defined criteria for evaluating the relationship between the cost of the change and the benefit of the change are a vital component to effective contract management. The goal is to be agile and responsive to business needs. Once requested changes have been agreed to and approved, the contract targets are often reset.

At times, when a proposed project is strategically important and needs to start at the earliest possible date, but the few final steps are expected to take considerable time, the final (selected) bidder is asked to start work through an LOA. An LOA is usually accepted after the solicitation process has been completed (including issuing an RFP, receiving qualified responses, and selecting a vendor). Because the LOA is issued *before* the contract negotiations are finalized, it carries some risk for both parties. Therefore, here are a few caveats to keep in mind:

- The LOA needs to be signed by both the company and the vendor. It binds both parties until the final contract is signed.
- The vendor agrees to undertake a defined set of tasks and the company commits to pay for those services.
- Often the payment arrangement is on a time-and-material basis, even when the final contract may use some other payment consideration.
- Because the vendor has already begun work, it could bias the contract negotiation process.
- If the contract cannot be negotiated successfully, the company might want to move to a different vendor; the money and time spent on the initial tasks might be wasted if another vendor is selected to complete the project.
- The main advantage of an LOA is that it can be prepared easily and quickly. It covers a short period between vendor selection and contract execution. In an ideal world, a vendor would undertake no project work until all the terms and conditions of the formal contract were negotiated and signed. In the real world, the time-to-market may demand that work on the project commence

before the contract is executed. Once both parties sign the LOA, it is legally binding. If the contracting process is protracted, much of the project work may be done under the LOA (without all of the terms and conditions of the final contract, which represents a major risk to the buyer).

Once the final contract is signed, it is important to notify the rest of the bidders regarding the closure of the solicitation process, which is typically accomplished by issuing a letter signed by the sponsor or the procurement department representative. Keep in mind that some of the unsuccessful bidders may inquire about the shortcomings of their RFP responses. You should discuss the subject with the sponsor, the procurement office, and the legal department and work with them to decide on the manner of your response. Once a decision is made, make sure to stick to the "official" explanation, as doing otherwise will only cause confusion.

Contract Administration

While the work by the approved vendor continues, specific individuals must be in charge of ensuring that the work is progressing according to the terms of the contract. You would be surprised at the number of instances where the people put in charge of overseeing the work of the contractor have not *read* the contract, and if they have, how little they understand the meaning of the various terms and conditions. Just to prove the point, there is a term within the contract law—*constructive change order*—which states that during the contract life span, *oral* or written acts or omissions by someone of *apparent* authority have the same effect as a written and authorized change order. The two key words are: "oral" and "apparent." These two simple words can get you in very hot water when disagreements arise between the two parties. Therefore, to save yourself a ton of grief, take the time to read and understand the terms of the contract; have someone from the contract and legal groups assist you. Also, take the time to explore whether your organization provides any education regarding contract law. If so, take advantage of the opportunity and educate yourself.

Keep it clearly in your mind that managing the contractor is your organization's responsibility. We suggest that you review Chapters 7 and 8 of this book and prepare yourself for diligent monitoring of the progress by the contractor's team. Do not overlook the importance of vital signs reporting and regularly scheduled status reports. Through the contract, you are outsourcing the product development activities; however, you still own the responsibility for successful project completion.

Contract Closeout

The final step in contract management is the formal closeout of the contract. During this step, you will need to verify that all of the work outlined in the contract has been completed according to the terms and conditions of the project. This step, like other work in the project, will take time and effort and should have been planned as a part of the contract administration. Occasionally, certain variations from the contract terms and conditions will occur. If not serious, these disparities can be noted and the contractor must agree to complete the needed work in a timely manner. Take this opportunity to contact your contracting/legal department and to review the documents and materials that need to be archived for future needs. Now, you can officially close the project and notify the contractor of the project closure through an official letter. Within the overall terminology of contract management, two additional items need to be discussed.

SOW Many RFPs have an inherent problem. Unfortunately, they don't include the detailed work to be done by the vendor as a part of the original contract because the buyer is not planning to undertake the detailed work and the vendor has not had the time to create a comprehensive (deliverable level) product description. The SOW fills that gap and is typically created by the approved vendor after the contract has been signed. The SOW includes the specific requirements, deliverables, performance measures, and assumptions that the vendor will be expected to meet. Typically, the vendor prepares a draft of the SOW, which may include changes to the scope specified in the contract. These modifications, if agreed to by the buyer, become the basis for the SOW. The job of the procurement team is critical in negotiating a comprehensive and accurate SOW for the project work. Consider the SOW to be an extension of the original contract; it must be handled with the same care as a contract.

It is common for the SOW to be modified during the life cycle of a project; therefore, a well structured and disciplined change management process is imperative (remember the discussion regarding constructive change order). Given below is a sample list of components of an SOW:

- *Project Scope Statement:* Comprehensive statement of the project scope using a deliverables level WBS.
- *Deliverable Schedule:* This describes the schedule for deliverable completion by the vendor and acceptance by the buyer. Be very clear on this component of the SOW, as it is the foundation of what you will eventually receive. Keep in view any nonwork periods such as company holidays, plant closures, and any other nonwork periods.
- *Work Location:* Specify the location of the offices and buildings (both the buyer and the vendor) where the work will be performed. This can have considerable impact on travel-related expenses.
- *Performance Period:* The start, progressive finishes, and the final finish of the project.
- *Standards Compliance:* List any specific company, industry, and/or regulatory standards or certifications applicable to the project. Keep in mind any insurance and security compliance needs.
- *Acceptance Criteria:* Clearly delineate the acceptance criteria for deliverables, key milestones, and the final product closure.
- *Hardware and Software Specifications:* Outline any specific hardware and software (makers and versions) requirements pertinent to the execution of the work.

Ideally, the SOW should be a more detailed elucidation of the contents of the RFP. Otherwise, the primary contract will be subject to extensive upward revisions and will eventually end up costing more budget and time.

SLA The SLA, sometimes referred to as the service quality agreement (SQA), is an agreement that supplements a contract. It outlines the service, describes the essential elements of that service, and articulates the minimum level of service (operational performance) to be provided by the vendor. For example, the SLA with a telecommunications company regarding the performance of T-1 access between two offices may specify a penalty if the line drops below 570 kbps. It becomes the responsibility of the buyer to monitor performance and communicate any breaches to the vendor. When specifying any service levels, it is important to understand the industry standards and to define acceptable levels for each service you are acquiring. SLAs typically include the following types of information:

- Specific measurable performance criteria directly drawn from the business and technical requirements of the contract and/or the SOW, for example, the network or application availability, response time, security, recovery, and monitoring
- Identification of who will measure performance and how it will be done, preferably, measurements should be the responsibility of the buyer
- A statement of consequences if the vendor fails to deliver as committed
- A statement of consequences if the buyer fails to deliver
- A description of how the SLA can be modified

Figure A1.3 depicts an example of an SLA.

■ PERFORMANCE IS IN THE MIND OF THE BEHOLDER

Consider the well-known adage that "statistics lie." This can wreak havoc when it comes to the question of whether the vendor is performing to the agreed-upon SLA metrics. In the case of a disagreement, the meaning of the word "perform" will need to be parsed and evaluated. In all of our experience in dealing with such disputes, the crux of the problem, and the solution, lies in how well the SLA has defined the measurement process and assessment responsibilities. Let us take a look at item number 3 in Figure A1.3: Connectivity. The SLA states 99.9 percent. The question is: "By whose measure?" Consider the following:

- The telecom company might respond that the wire is always connected to your building; therefore, you have 100 percent uptime.

FIGURE A1.3
Example of an SLA

Performance attribute	Metric	Consequence
1. Application operations		
▪ Help desk incidents	< 3 per 1,000	
▪ Availability	99 percent	
2. Hosting		
▪ Simultaneous users	1,000 users	
▪ Trouble ticket resolution	< 6 hours	
▪ Refresh rates	0.01 seconds	
3. Connectivity		
▪ Uptime	99.99 percent	
▪ Bandwidth minimum	570 kbps	
▪ Availability	1.5 mbps	
4. Network		
▪ Mean-time response to service call	< 2 hours	

- The ISP might respond that their servers are up 100 percent of the time, but your telecom company keeps dropping the connection between your facility and ours.

These contentions are just two among many others. Therefore, it is important that you take the time to think through each item in the SLA and attach a descriptive explanation of the measure for each metric. For example:

- *Uptime:* 99.99 percent as measured by the connectivity and availability report and the server availability report produced by the client's network administration group.

This requirement, of course, implies that the client has the processes, tools, procedures, and *skills* in place to gather the metrics and report on them in a reliable and consistent manner. Without these processes/tools, the metrics are basically useless because they can be interpreted any number of ways depending upon who is doing the measuring. Our advice is to always include not only the metric but also a clear definition of how it will be measured and what baseline value will be used for comparison purposes (along with how that baseline value was established).

Another important area of consideration is the worst-case scenario. While most SLAs include performance measurements for best-case scenarios, such as 85 percent of external customer calls must be answered within 25 seconds, they may not provide any performance metrics for the remaining 15 percent of the calls. What if these calls go unanswered for many minutes? Also, once a call has been answered, what is the maximum amount of hold time during the call?

■ PROCUREMENT WORDS OF WISDOM

Before we close our discussion on the principles and practices of procurement, it is important to focus on a number of important points culled from our experience with both successful and not-so-successful procurement projects:

- Be very rigorous in evaluating the proposed vendors/suppliers on your final short list because once the contract is signed, there is no going back (if you try, you will face an uphill battle).
- Check out the vendor's references with focus and zeal, plan one or more field visits with the vendor's recent and current customers (without the vendor representative tagging along) and

ask hard questions, and read the literature regarding the vendor/supplier performance in situations similar to your proposed procurement.

- Clearly define the scope of the proposed project with as few ambiguities as possible. Supplement the contract with a well drawn out SOW and a clearly delineated SLA.
- Make sure that your RFP process is in compliance with applicable federal and state regulations—especially the laws related to dealing with minority-owned businesses.
- Negotiate the ownership, copyright, and confidentiality of resulting work as a part of the original contract. Once the horse is out of the gate, it's tough to herd it back.
- Do not make the upfront price the prime evaluator for your selection decision. A low upfront bid might mean unexpected later costs.
- Chunk the procurement into manageable chunks with an option to exit if not satisfied with vendor products and services.
- Do not pay big sums of money indiscriminately—tie payments to well-defined, measurable milestones and then stick to the process.
- Keep in mind that your responsibility covers not only the first delivery of the product or service but also extends to the ongoing support after the project is complete. Make sure that the details regarding support are included in the contract.

If it's not written down, it does not exist. Keep in mind that people will make all types of promises and statements but that the only thing that counts is what is in the contract.

2

FINANCIAL ANALYSIS

This appendix introduces the very important, though often overlooked, subject of financial analysis and justification of projects. We cover the steps necessary to compute a project's financial value (return) using the four most popular assessment methods:

- NPV
- IRR
- ROI
- Payback period

> *Eighty percent of IT managers say their staffs don't have the financial skills needed to quantify the benefits of IT investments, according to a recent survey of 130 senior IT executives by Northwestern University's School of Management and consulting firm DiamondCluster International. Half of their companies have no process to evaluate IT investments against business strategy.*
>
> Chris Murphy and Mary Hayes (http://www.informationweek.com/story/ showArticle;jhtm?articleID=8900045&pgno=1).

The quotation is the reason we decided to include this material in the book. However, before one casts all the aspersions at IT people, we have found that many business professionals (unless they have a solid background in finance) also lack the requisite knowledge of the subject. As you read the material, you will discover that there are four key components of financial analysis of any project investment:

1. Estimating the cost of the investment in the project
2. Estimating the benefits from the deployment of the project
3. Developing a financial analysis of the value of the investment
4. Making the Go/No Go decision

The first step is the responsibility of the people engaged in the development of the project, the second step is the responsibility of the appropriate business unit proposing the project, the third step needs to be completed by the business people with appropriate support from the IT staff, and the final step is the responsibility of the sponsor and key business area stakeholders. Unfortunately, too often we see the first three steps fall into the laps of IT professionals. Then IT management, usually the CIO, takes on the responsibility for the Go/No Go decision. Because of the minimal business involvement in the analysis, the results are often less than satisfactory, which is the prime reason for the inordinately high number of failed and challenged IT/Business projects.

■ WHOSE PROJECT IS IT ANYWAY?

We believe that the IT team should be responsible for the development of the cost estimates of the project, and the business people (the proponents of the project) should be responsible for forecasting the benefits (returns) of the project, followed by the project's financial justification. If the business people refuse to take on this responsibility, or try to delegate it to the IT team, it is an obvious sign of their noninvolvement. Most such projects are prime candidates for failure, no matter how attractive the financial analysis.

> *It is not the role of IT to determine which projects should be given IT resources each year. Nor should it be IT's responsibility to justify and develop the ROI on projects. I believe that all of this is the responsibility of those managing the business. It must be the user managers who determine what systems they need to get the job done.*
>
> Paul Ingevaldson, "It's Not Your IT Portfolio—It's Theirs," *CIO Magazine*: November 15, 2002 (http://www.cio.com/archive/111502/peer.html.)

This said, we strongly believe that IT professionals should be able to understand and, with full confidence, discuss the ins and outs of the financial analysis methods used by the finance community to assess and justify investments. The following material is designed to prepare the reader to understand these concepts and to be able to engage in thoughtful discussions with their business colleagues, business sponsors, and executives.

Before we begin the discussion of the various methods for financial analysis of project investment, it is necessary to define a number of terms. As you read the definitions (assuming you are not a person with an accounting background), don't fight with the meaning of words; some may appear illogical to you. Now you know how business people feel when IT professionals throw around their terminology.

The key point to keep in mind as you read this appendix is the concept of time value of money. Time value of money means that one dollar in hand today is worth more than receiving one dollar in the future. Put conversely, a dollar received in the future is worth less than one dollar received today. The reason for the difference in value is that a dollar received today can be invested and may earn interest. Thus, given that the investment is successful, a dollar will be worth more than one dollar in 1 year, 2 years, or whatever period.

Capitalization Rate: Also known as "Cap rate," this is the rate of return (benefit or earnings) a project is expected to produce. It is stated as a percentage (return/investment).

Cost of Capital: The cost (percentage rate) of borrowing the next dollar for the business.

Discounted Cash Flow: Restating future earnings (cash flow) in current dollar terms, considering the time value of money.

Hurdle Rate: The required rate of return above which an investment makes sense and below which it does not. The hurdle rate is typically set by the finance department for a given period of time. Also known as "required rate of return" and "required rate on investment."

Net Present Value (NPV): The NPV is a method for evaluating an investment or project, where both the cost or investment (all cash outflow) of the project, as well as all future (multiyear) earnings (all cash inflows), are restated in PV terms. A positive NPV suggests that the project grows earnings faster than the cost of capital and that the project should be considered for approval because the earnings exceed the costs/investment.

Opportunity Cost: The cost of passing up the next best choice when making a decision. For example, if money is used to fund Project A, the opportunity cost is the value the same investment would return if applied to the next highest yielding project.

Payback Period: The period of time, usually stated in months, in which the initial investment in a project can be recovered. Also known as the "breakeven period."

Present Value (PV): This indicates the value, in today's dollars, of future net earnings from a project or investment. It is calculated using the formula shown below. The formula discounts (normalizes) the future earnings using a specified interest rate. For example, if a project were to produce $1,000 earnings a year from now, at an interest rate of 10 percent, the present value of the future earning would be $909. That is, if the project were to cost more than $909 to develop, there would be a net loss.

$$PV = FV/(1 + i)^n$$

where:

PV: present value
FV: future value
i: interest rate (cost of capital)
n: number of compounding periods

Return on Investment (ROI): A financial measure of the success of a project. It is computed as net earnings divided by investment or cost. It is expressed as a percentage. Although the term "ROI" has a specific meaning within the realm of project financial analysis, it has also become the general term to refer to the financial benefits of a project, in the same manner as the terms "Kleenex" and "Xerox" have come to represent more than the brand. Therefore, when someone refers to the ROI of a project, they may actually mean the NVP, IRR, or payback period.

Time Value of Money: The idea that money is worth more today than at a point in time in the future, even after adjustment for inflation, because the money in hand today can earn interest or other appreciation (if invested) up to that point in the future.

■ PRINCIPLES AND PRACTICES OF FINANCIAL JUSTIFICATION FOR PROJECTS

Now that you are familiar with the underlying concepts of financial analysis, we can begin to discuss the principles and practices of financial justification for projects. The chart in Figure A2.1 shows three different projects; the question that must be answered is: "Which of the three projects is the most attractive investment?"

At first glance, an untrained financial mind may lean toward Project C. Shortly, we will look at a number of assessment methods and try to answer this question. Before we do that, we must take a look at how financial managers view the cash flow in and out of a project. Refer to the example in Figure A2.2.

The key message from Figure A2.2 is that financial managers see a project in terms of a stream of cash. Typically, during the development time, cash flows out and is depicted as bars representing monthly project expenses. Once the new system or product is in place, the product begins to result in cash inflow (either in terms of benefit or actual cash revenue). Financial managers are interested in knowing the cash flow ramifications of each proposed project because this information will be useful in the making investment decisions (from a purely financial point of view). There are a number of different ways to analyze and assess the financial ramifications of investing money into projects; in this Appendix we will introduce four such methods:

1. NPV
2. IRR
3. ROI
4. Payback period

FIGURE A2.1
Selecting Projects

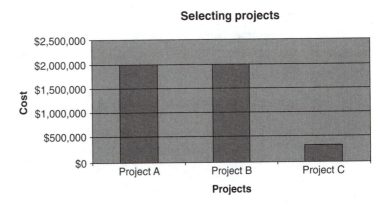

Selecting projects

FIGURE A2.2
Project Cash Flow

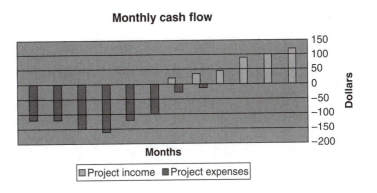

Monthly cash flow

For each of the four methods listed, we will use three project candidates:

1. *Project A:* It is proposed that the company launch a new website, which will make the company apparel available online to both customers and employees worldwide. The cost to set up the website and advertise it is estimated at $2 million. Earnings (*after* operating costs) for the first year are estimated to be $800,000. Further, market research indicates that the growth of sales and earnings will be 10 percent per year, assuming the company continues to add new and interesting items.

2. *Project B:* Redesign the accounts payable process. A prominent business process-reengineering firm has proposed a project that will cost $2 million in consulting, travel, and materials. They have projected the reduction of staff and related costs associated with the redesigned process to be $3.5 million each year, but that savings will decrease at the rate of 5 percent per year, as additions of staff will be made.

3. *Project C:* The company has been offering industry-specific safety training courses and certifications. This project would create a public website where everyone in the industry will be able to enroll in courses, track their certifications, and receive reminders about their continuing education and certification requirements. The cost of creating the website is estimated to be $350,000, and will use existing capacity of web servers, infrastructure and staff. The cost of operating this website is estimated to be $50,000 per year (technical support, mainly), and is expected to increase by 5 percent each year. The use of the site will increase goodwill for the company and also supply an up-to-date listing of all contractors and industry workers. This is seen as a side benefit for future recruiting. The estimated benefit of this approach is quantified as $100,000 with an increase of 5 percent each year. The net benefit is $50,000 ($100,000 less $50,000 in technical support costs to maintain the website).

NPV

As we mentioned above, the time value of money dictates that money (spent or received) in the future is worth less than if that money would be spent or received today. In any given project, the expenditure of project development funds occurs before the project is operational but the returns or benefits are seen in future periods. The NPV computation allows the sponsor to determine, in *today's* dollars, the cost and benefits of a particular proposed project. The NPV is the *sum* of all the present values of outflows (project expenses as negatives) and the present value of benefits for the proposed life of the new system. Therefore, if a project were expected to produce $100,000 one year from now, its PV would be:

$$PV = FV/(1 + i)^n$$
$$PV = 100,000/(1 + .10)1 = 100,000/1.1 = 90,909$$

This means that investing any more than $90,909 in this project will create a loss situation. Similarly, the future worth of money spent today on Project C can be computed by using the following formula:

$$FV = PV(1 + i)^n$$

Therefore, the FV of an investment of $100,000 today will be:

$$FV = 100,000 (1 + .10)^1 = 100,000 (1.1) = 110,000$$

For example, if one was to invest $100,000 in a project today, a year later the project must produce a cash inflow of $110,000 just to break even.

The financial profession makes use of several published tables that allow a person to calculate the PV of expenses or benefits. Microsoft Excel includes preprogrammed formulas for a number of financial calculations. Figure A2.3 shows the NPV values of the three projects. For these computations of the NVP, we used an interest rate of 5 percent.

In Figure A2.3, we see the NPV values are as follows:

- *Project A:* $2.2 million (rounded)
- *Project B:* $11.8 million (rounded)
- *Project C:* –$0.1 million (rounded)

FIGURE A2.3
NPV Computations

NPV

		Yearly payments	PV Factor @5%	PV
Project A: Year				
	1	$800,000	0.952381	$761,905
	2	$880,000	0.907029	$798,186
	3	$968,000	0.863838	$836,195
	4	$1,064,800	0.822702	$876,013
	5	$1,171,280	0.783526	$917,728
				$4,190,027
			Investment	($2,000,000)
			NPV	**$2,190,027**
Project B: Year				
	1	$3,500,000	0.952381	$3,333,334
	2	$3,325,000	0.907029	$3,015,871
	3	$3,158,750	0.863838	$2,728,648
	4	$3,000,813	0.822702	$2,468,774
	5	$2,850,772	0.783526	$2,233,654
				$13,780,282
			Investment	($2,000,000)
			NPV	**$11,780,282**
Project C: Year				
	1	$50,000	0.952381	$47,619
	2	$52,500	0.907029	$47,619
	3	$55,125	0.863838	$47,619
	4	$57,881	0.822702	$47,619
	5	$60,775	0.783526	$47,619
				$238,095
			Investment	($350,000)
			NPV	**-$111,905**

If the NPV were the most important measure in the decision for project approval, obviously you would choose not to do Project C because the expenses exceed the benefits. Between Project A and Project B, the latter is obviously more attractive because its NPV is in excess of $11 million with an initial investment of $2 million. As we will see later, NPV may not be the only measure for making the final decision.

IRR

This measure looks at the stream of cash flow (both expenses and benefits) from a project. However, instead of deriving a dollar amount, the process is to determine the percentage *growth* of money as a result of taking on the project. Another way to describe IRR is the amount of profit, stated as a percentage, that the project will produce. Many companies establish a minimum hurdle (acceptable) rate for IRR. The hurdle rate may be set aside for projects that are required for regulatory compliance. The computations for IRR can get fairly complex; however, Excel has a built in function for calculating the IRR for the stream of cash flow of a project. Figure A2.4 depicts the IRR values for the three projects.

In Figure A2.4, we see the IRR (possible profit) from the three proposed projects is as follows:

- *Project A:* 36%
- *Project B:* 169%
- *Project C:* –7%

FIGURE A2.4
IRR Computations

IRR

		Yearly payments
Project A	**Year**	−$2,000,000
	1	$800,000
	2	$880,000
	3	$968,000
	4	$1,064,800
	5	$1,171,280
		IRR 36%
Project B	**Year**	−$2,000,000
	1	$3,500,000
	2	$3,325,000
	3	$3,158,750
	4	$3,000,813
	5	$2,850,772
		IRR 169%
Project C	**Year**	−$350,000
	1	$50,000
	2	$52,500
	3	$55,125
	4	$57,881
	5	$60,775
		IRR −7%

If the IRR hurdle rate set by the finance department were 12 percent, Project B appears to be a better investment (4.5 times better) than Project A. Project C shows a net loss, and hence is not a good investment (if the final decision was based solely on financial metrics). On its face value, the use of IRR values to compare the merits of competing projects helps obscure the absolute dollar amounts of various investments. This situation can be both positive and negative: positive because the decision is made on the profit capabilities of a project and not the amount of investment, and negative because the decision maker may not realize the amount of capital being put at risk. Astute decision makers look at both numbers as the basis for project approval or disapproval.

ROI

The ROI provides a percentage return on the project cost and is computed by dividing the net income by investment, stated as a percentage. Figure A2.5 shows the ROI values for the three projects.

In Figure A2.5, we see the ROI of the three projects is as follows:

- *Project A:* 40%
- *Project B:* 175%
- *Project C:* 14%

Do you see an anomaly in the values shown above? It lies with Project C. If one is not careful, one could recommend this project because the ROI value is above the corporate IRR hurdle rate of 12 percent; however, the NPV and IRR for the project as shown in Figures A2.3 and A2.4 are both negative.

FIGURE A2.5
ROI Computations

ROI

| Project A | Return: | $800,000 | **ROI** | **40.0%** |
| | Investment | $2,000,000 | | |

| Project B | Return: | $3,500,000 | **ROI** | **175.0%** |
| | Investment | $2,000,000 | | |

| Project C | Return (See Note): | $50,000 | **ROI** | **14.3%** |
| | Investment | $350,000 | | |

Note: Return (benefit) is $100,000 less annual cost of $50,000

Payback Period (Breakeven Period)

The calculation of this measure is the straightforward summing of monthly cash inflows until the initial project investment is matched. The month in which the inflows equal the investment is the payback period or the point at which the project breaks even. Figure A2.6 depicts both the cumulative costs and cumulative income attributed to a project and shows that the payback period is the end of month 13.

Figure A2.7 (most values are rounded) depicts the payback period computations for the three projects in consideration. From the data in this figure, we see the following payback periods:

- *Project A:* 28 months
- *Project B:* 6.8 months
- *Project C:* 74 months

The longer it takes the initial investment to be recovered, the less appealing the project is. One could be more accurate if one were to use PVs shown in Figure A2.8 (just for Project A), most values are rounded. As you can see, now the payback period has extended to 31 months, or 3 months longer than the computations shown in Figure A2.7.

Now, let us take a look at all four of the financial analysis methods together. What type of information does each method convey? Figure A2.9 shows the three projects and their respective financial analysis values.

From the data presented in Figure A2.9, it is clear that Project C is not a good investment because the NPV and IRR values are both negative, the ROI is a very small number, and the payback period is very long (in fact, far beyond the expected useful project life of 5 years as put forth

FIGURE A2.6
Payback Period (Breakeven Analysis)

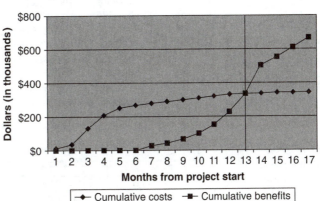

FIGURE A2.7
Payback Period Analyses

Project payback period in months

Project A Investment $2,000,000

Year	Returns	Monthly	Months	
1	$800,000	$66,667	12	$800,000
2	$880,000	$73,333	12	$880,000
3	$968,000	$80,667	4	$322,667
Total			28	$2,002,667

Payback of 28 months

Project B Investment $2,000,000

Year	Returns	Monthly	Months	
1	$3,500,000	$291,667	6.8	$1,983,333
2	$3,325,000	$277,083	0	$0
3	$3,158,750	$263,229	0	$0
Total			6.8	$1,983,333

Payback of 6.8 months

Project C Investment $350,000

Year	Returns	Monthly	Months	
1	$50,000	$4,167	12	$50,000
2	$52,500	$4,375	12	$52,500
3	$55,125	$4,594	12	$55,125
4	$57,881	$4,823	12	$57,881
5	$60,775	$5,065	12	$60,775
6	$63,814	$5,318	12	$63,814
7	$67,005	$5,584	2	$11,167
Total			74.0	$351,263

Payback of 74 months

FIGURE A2.8
Payback Period Analysis
(NPV)

**Project payback period in months
Using PVs**

Project A Investment $2,000,000

Year	Yearly net operating earnings	PV Factor @5%	PV	Monthly	Months	
1	$800,000	0.952381	$761,905	$63,492	12	$761,905
2	$880,000	0.907029	$798,186	$66,515	12	$798,186
3	$968,000	0.863838	$836,195	$69,683	7	$487,781
4	$1,064,800	0.822702	$876,013	$73,001	0	$0
5	$1,171,280	0.783526	$917,728	$76,477	0	$0
	Payback of 31 months				31	$2,047,871

FIGURE A2.9
Comparative Financial
Analysis, Four Measures of
Project Financial Return

	NPV	IRR	ROI	Payback
Project A	$2,190,027	36%	40%	31 months
Project B	$11,780,282	169%	175%	6.8 months
Project C	–$111,905	–7%	14%	74 months

earlier). If the company management were interested in maximizing future earnings, they would clearly select Project B before Project A. In addition, Project B has a relatively short payback period and that might reinforce the vote in favor of Project B rather than Project A.

■ INTANGIBLE BENEFITS

One important area of project value assessment that we have not discussed relates to the intangible benefits; these benefits are difficult to quantify in specific financial terms but can play an important role in project justification. For example, Project A and Project B are both pegged at a $2 million investment and each has its own financial justification. However, let us assume that the business unit proposing Project A raises the point that because the following benefits have not been considered, the project's financial justification is skewed against them.

- Customer satisfaction
- Brand recognition
- Competitive advantage
- New product exposure

It would be difficult to attach specific dollar values to these items, yet at the same time they must not be ignored. Both the consideration of such benefits and the degree of their contribution to decision making is the responsibility of the business units proposing the projects and the management group responsible for project approval. Our advice to project managers is to make sure that they discuss the subject of accounting for intangible benefits with their business unit colleagues, project sponsors, and the finance department; then seek guidance on the methods and procedures to be used for conducting project financial evaluations. Once such standards and procedures have been defined, remember that it is the responsibility of the business units proposing the projects to develop financial justification. Your responsibility, as a project manager, is to make sure that the estimates to *complete and maintain* the project are accurate.

■ GARBAGE IN GARBAGE OUT (GIGO)

This perhaps is one of the oldest adages from the computer age: if the input data is of questionable value, the results will certainly stink. From the discussion of each of the four financial analysis methods, it should be clear that the common denominator is the estimated amount of investment into a given project (this is the estimate of the final cost of the project over a specified period of time). Therefore, it is imperative that the estimated cost values be highly accurate. However, the history of cost overruns of IT projects shows that IT/Business projects are grossly underestimated, or when accurately estimated, unfettered scope creep balloons the final costs far above the original estimates. If at any given time during the project development phase, the estimate-to-complete value of a project exceeds the original estimate used to justify it, the project may no longer be financially viable. For example, in Figure A2.3, if the estimate at completion of Project A were to grow to $3,000,000 instead of the original $2,000,000, the breakeven period of the project will no longer be 31 months. Most likely, it would be closer to 45 months. Similarly, the ROI of Project A with an investment of $3,000,000 will compute to 27 percent, a much smaller number than the 40 percent used to justify the project. The important question then is: "If the original estimates of investment are breached considerably, is the project still worthwhile?"

Our conversations with a large number of project managers have shown us that few organizations have the process in place to validate the financial justification of projects once projects get started. This scenario is contrary to the very foundation of investment management, where the underlying precept is to continually monitor the key assumptions to make sure the investments are still financially viable. Therefore, it would behoove the project manager to discuss this important point with the sponsor and find out whether she is concerned about the project's financial viability once the project starts. If the answer is yes, then it would become necessary to monitor both the cost to date as well as the estimate at completion metrics at key milestones; we suggest monthly or bimonthly once the project goes into the Execute stage of the PPA.

■ RISK EXPOSURE AND FINANCIAL ANALYSIS

One of our clients, in addition to the measures already discussed, uses the mapping of risk *v.* financial return as a key input to the project selection process. The chart in Figure A2.10 depicts eight potential projects that management is considering.

FIGURE A2.10
Risk *v.* Return Analysis

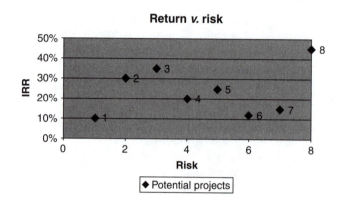

The horizontal axis represents the sum of the business and technology complexity computed in step 6 of the PPA and the vertical axis plots the IRR value. This information clearly indicates that the high risk, low return projects (projects 6 and 7) should be discarded in lieu of the low risk, high return projects (projects 2 and 3). Project 8 is a typical strategic project, which has high returns but also carries the highest risk.

Of course, the proof of the pudding will actually come *after* the project goes into operation. At this point, the business owner of the project should actively monitor the value-to-business metrics and compare them to the metrics used to justify the project. If the former fall short of the latter, then the financial justifications used to approve the project have been breached (underperformed). If such a breach happens more than occasionally, then the very process used to justify projects needs to be reassessed and improved.

73% of CIOs don't calculate ROI on projects after they're completed.

Allan E. Alter, *CIO Insight*
(http://www.cioinsight.com/article2/0,3959,940177,00.asp).

At Computerworld's Premier 100 IT Leaders Conference last month, we asked more than 150 IT executives if they measure the ROI of key projects six months after completion. "Rarely or never" said 68% of them, and 65% said they lacked the "knowledge or tools needed" to even do ROI calculations. Ouch.

Maryfran Johnson, "Dymystifying ROI," *Computerworld* (April 22, 2002): p. 28.

Accelerated Depreciation   In financial accounting, a method of depreciation that allows faster write-off than the straight line method of depreciation. Accelerated depreciation is typically used to mitigate a large tax burden (due to improved profit margins) to reduce tax obligations. Also used to write off equipment that might be replaced before its (natural) useful life due to obsolescence (typically for high technology equipment). *See* Depreciation.

Activity   Within the project management profession, a certain level of confusion exists regarding the use of the word. Some consider activities to be subsets of tasks, whereas others place tasks a level below activities. To us, task and activity are synonymous.

Activity Definition   Identifying the activities that need to be performed in order to complete various project deliverables. *See also* task plan.

Activity Float   This applies to individual tasks in a network, the total time (in days) the completion of a task can be delayed without impacting the ES of any successor tasks. Also known as "free float" or "free slack."

Activity On Arrow (AOA) Network   In this task network, tasks are shown as connecting lines or arrows between events that are shown as small circles. The length of the line has no particular significance. Typically, each task's ID and/or description is written above the line and task effort and/or duration is written below the line. *See* arrow diagramming method.

Activity On Node Network   In this task network, task descriptions appear inside of a node, a circle, square, or rectangle, and arrows or lines are used as connectors between nodes. Task durations are generally written within the node. Task responsibility is indicated by writing the resource's name or initial within the node. Nodes may also contain additional information such as start and finish dates. Also known as the "precedence diagramming method."

Actual Finish Date   The point in time when work on a task (activity), deliverable, or project was completed.

Actual Resources *v.* Planned Resources   A vital sign that tracks the following three conditions: the gap between the number of FTE team members actually working on the project *v.* the number of FTE initially planned; the gap between the skill levels of people actually assigned to the team *v.* the skill levels used in developing the project estimates and schedules; and the amount of unplanned turnover—the number of team members that have left the team unexpectedly.

Actual Start Date   The point in time when the work on a task (activity), deliverable, or project was started.

ADA Conforming   Conforming to the Americans with Disability Act, which protects the rights of people with disabilities.

Administrative Closure   The act of formally closing a project (or a contract) by ensuring that all necessary documentation has been appropriately updated, archived, and officially accepted by the appropriate group(s).

Aggressive Communication   The sender anticipates the need for communicating, takes the initiative in sending a clear, well-structured message, and follows up to ensure that it was received and understood by the addressee(s).

Analogous/Analogy Approach   An approach to developing the details for a current project (WBS, network, estimate, schedule) based on one or more previous (similar) projects.

Agile   A process for designing a system by delivering software components frequently—from every couple of weeks to every couple of months. The process welcomes changes to requirements, even late in the project life cycle.

Analogy-Based Estimating   An estimating technique that uses estimates from one or more previous (similar) projects as a basis for developing estimates for the project at hand.

Archiving Records   The process of collecting and storing project records securely for future reference and use.

Arrow Diagramming Method   In this task network, tasks are shown as connecting lines or arrows between events that are shown as small circles. The length of the line has no particular significance. Typically, each task's ID and/or description is written above the line and the task effort and/or duration is written below the line. *See* activity on arrow (AOA) network diagramming method.

As-of Date   In the project reporting process, the point in time when the project status information was obtained. The as-of date separates the historical information from the future information. *See* data date.

Assumptions   Something taken for granted or accepted as true without proof; a supposition, an opinion or belief. Assumptions often form the basis for project plans, estimates, and schedules and therefore must be realistic.

Audit   A formal examination and verification of various project components (e.g., financial records, documentation, plans, estimates, schedules, code, testing results, security).

Audit and Control Needs   The extent to which the audit or review procedures (financial, security) need to be considered.

Backward Pass   While computing the critical path through a network of tasks, the backward pass determines the latest start and finish of each task.

Balanced Matrix   A type of project team organization structure in which the authority over the team is shared equally between the project manager and the appropriate functional managers. Theoretically, it sounds workable but in reality it rarely succeeds because of inherent conflicts and power struggles.

Bar Chart   A time-scaled chart, used to show the chronological flow of the project by showing individual tasks with their start and finish dates. The tasks are listed along the left hand side of the chart and the corresponding dates are shown across the top. Individual tasks are shown as horizontal bars. *See* Gantt chart.

Baseline   The officially approved plan, budget, quality, and/or schedule of a project. The first such baselines are established at the start of the Execute stage of a project. The originally baselined plan, estimate, and schedule may change as approved by the project sponsor. It is important to assign a specific (progressive) version number to each new baseline.

Baseline Effort   Within the PPA, the effort hours it will take a person to complete a given task under the following assumptions: high-level of business knowledge—no application learning curve, high-level of technical proficiency—no technology learning curve, full-time assignment to the task, high productivity environment, and no interruptions. Armed with such data, project managers can adjust the baseline value according to their team members' actual skills to produce an accurate task effort estimate. Not to be confused with *baseline plan*, *baseline cost*, and *baseline schedule*.

Baseline Budget   The original budget plus or minus approved changes. It is important to assign a specific (progressive) version number to each new baseline budget.

Baseline Plan   The original plan plus or minus approved changes. It is important to assign a specific (progressive) version number to each new baseline plan.

Baseline Schedule   The original schedule plus or minus approved changes. It is important to assign a specific (progressive) version number to each new baseline schedule.

Base Phase   In the phase-based size estimating technique, the base phase is the phase used to compute the first (foundation) estimate of effort hours. Any phase of the system or product life cycle can be used as the base phase as long as it comprises a minimum of 15 percent of the total project/product life cycle.

Benchmarking   The process of comparing the performance of one organization (or a product/process) to the performance of another (outside) organization.

Bidders' Conference   A meeting held to answer any questions from prospective bidders regarding the bid as part of a procurement process. Make sure that appropriate SMEs are on hand to respond to bidders' inquiries. Typically, all inquiries (questions) and responses are recorded and then distributed to bidders. Make sure to archive this document appropriately.

Body of Knowledge   The purpose of a body of knowledge is to provide a standard reference for the key principles and practices of the associated profession. The typical organization of a body of knowledge document revolves around *what* needs to be done, with minimal attention given to *why* and *when*. *See* knowledge base.

Bottom-up Approach   When creating a WBS for a project, the process of starting from the lowest level of detail (defining the tasks), grouping those into deliverables, and then into phases.

Bottom-up Estimate   When creating an effort and/or cost estimate for a project, first computing the effort/cost of the lowest level of the WBS (tasks) and then summing them to arrive at the total estimates. This is also known as task-based estimating or detailed estimating.

Brainstorming   A process by which a group of people attempt to generate ideas through spontaneous and open discussion. In a typical brainstorming session, the participants begin to suggest their best ideas to resolve the problem at hand. As each person puts forth a suggestion, the facilitator of the session records it on a flip chart. As the ideas are being elucidated, it is important that absolutely no discussion, other than clarification, be allowed for any idea. Discussions regarding the merit of any individual idea should be held only after all ideas have been recorded.

Budget   The total dollar amount set aside for the completion of a task, deliverable, and/or a project.

Budget at Completion (BAC)   The estimated total cost of a task, deliverable, and/or project when it is complete.

Burdened Billing Rate   A billing rate for an individual, typically computed by taking the person's yearly salary, adding the cost of payroll benefits, office space, equipment, telephone, and administrative support, and then dividing the total dollar amount by the number of work hours per year for that person.

Burn Rate   The rate at which money (budget) is being spent on a project.

Business Cycle   Periodic times in a year where the business activity of an organization is typically very high or very low.

Cancelled Project Portfolio   The component of the project portfolio that houses projects that have been canceled.

Capability Maturity Model Integration (CMMI)   A five-level progression path for software development organizations defined by the SEI at the Carnegie Mellon University. Defines the steps needed for an organization to improve its software development processes. The five levels are initial, repeatable, defined, managed, and optimized.

Capitalization Rate (Cap Rate)   The rate of return (benefit or earnings) a project is expected to produce. It is stated as a percentage (return/investment).

Cause & Effect Diagram (Fishbone Diagram or Ishikawa Diagram)   This technique is designed to help analyze problems that may have many interrelated causes. The basic structure of the diagram resembles the backbone of a fish, hence the name. A horizontal line (the backbone of the fish) represents the problem and each fish bone is a possible cause of the problem. Popularized by Professor Kaoru Ishikawa in 1943, it was then known as the Ishikawa diagram.

Celebration Milestone   The point at which the team plans to hold a celebration of their accomplishments. Far too many project managers and their teams get too busy and neglect to take the time to celebrate key milestones. Project teams should plan a few victory celebrations to provide tangible proof of the project's importance and value to the team and key stakeholders.

Champion   An individual who sees the merits of a project and is willing to use his political capital to remove obstacles from the path of successful project completion.

Change Budget   The amount of funds set aside to accommodate the cost of incorporating changes into a project (after the original budget has been baselined).

Change Control Board (CCB)   An official group of people responsible for approving (and rejecting) change requests to the project after the initial plan, estimate, and schedule have been baselined.

Change Control System   A documented process used to manage any changes to the project after its first baseline has been established.

Chart of Accounts   A numbering system used to keep track of the cost of a project by various predefined categories.

Charter (Project Charter)   A comprehensive document assembled toward the end of the Pre-Launch stage. Serves as a proposal for the project sponsor, and once approved, becomes a business plan for the project team. An approved Charter signals the formal start of the project.

Chunking (Scope Chunking)   Chunking is a process of analyzing the project functionality and partitioning it into progressively smaller operational projects of 6 months or less.

Closed Ended Question   A question designed (worded) to elicit a yes or no response and intended to obtain specific information.

Communication   The act and process of dispensing and receiving information.

Communications Management   The subset of the project management principles, practices, and tools that focuses on the collection, analysis, dissemination, and archiving of project information. *See* project communications management.

Communications Plan (Communications Management Plan)   This is step 23 of the PPA. This step involves developing a well-thought-out plan for clear and timely communications from the project manager to all of the key stakeholders. This entails the information content, vehicle(s) for distribution, and frequency of information communication.

Communications Planning   Analyzing, defining, and documenting the processes to be used to meet the communications needs of the key project stakeholders.

Communications Vehicle   The means by which information is conveyed throughout the project. A communications vehicle could include voice mail, e-mail, one-on-one meetings, group presentations, fax, video/telephone conferences, or web-based meetings.

Complexity   Composed of two dimensions: business complexity and technical complexity. Each dimension can be characterized by a set of attributes. Typical business attributes include size, geography, and financial exposure. Typical technical attributes include level of technology integration, security needs, stability of hardware/software, and team experience.

Complexity Assessment   This is step 6 of the PPA. It is the process of ascertaining the degree of a project's complexity by assessing the weight/value of the various attributes that make up the business and technical complexity of a project.

Complexity Attributes   Both the business and technology dimensions of a project's complexity are composed of a set of elements. Typical business attributes include size, geography, and financial exposure. Typical technical attributes include system functionality, level of integration, stability of hardware and software, and team experience.

Compromising   A style of negotiation that combines an assertive stance with an attitude of cooperation to reach an agreement. This form of negotiation tactic is typically used to address medium level disagreements and to achieve short-term results as quickly as possible.

CompTIA®   A global, not-for-profit association that serves the IT industry as the world's largest developer of vendor-neutral, industry-defined IT certification exams and certifications. Its IT Project+ certification is an industry-recognized credential that

acknowledges competency and professionalism in project management.

Configuration Management   Any system or product is composed of a set of constituent components that change and evolve as the system or product is being developed. For example, computer hardware and/or software may be updated a number of times during the development life cycle of a system. Similarly, a Project Charter and a Project Schedule might undergo a number of revisions as the project progresses. The process of documenting, controlling, and managing any changes to key project components and deliverables throughout the project life cycle. Without a well-defined and rigorously followed configuration management system, various project components can easily get out of control as different people access them to review, change, and update their contents. Duplication, overlaps, and out-of-date hardware, software, and documentation are the primary results of poor configuration management.

Constrained Network   A task network created using the applicable constraints such as resource and/or date constraints.

Constraints   Restrictions and limitations that might the limit the attainment of project objectives.

Constraints & Obstacles   This is step 9 of the PPA. It involves the assessment of restrictions and limitations that typically drive up time and cost to complete a project.

Constructive Change Order   During the life span of a contract, oral or written acts or omissions by someone of apparent authority have the same effect as a written and authorized change order.

Contingency   A future emergency.

Contingency Plan   A set of deliverables, tasks, and resources to be used in case an expected risk becomes a reality.

Contingency Planning   The process of defining a set of deliverables, tasks, and resources to be used in case an expected risk becomes a reality.

Contingency Reserve   Budget or time reserves set aside to be used if and when a risk materializes.

Continuous Improvement   The ongoing and never-ending process of analyzing and enhancing (improving) a product and/or a process. Contrast this approach with the belief that "if it ain't broke, don't fix it." Continuous improvement is an integral part of the quality improvement process.

Contract   An agreement reached by two or more parties (enforceable by law). As it relates to project management, a contract is usually between an organization and a vendor (supplier), and the vendor agrees to provide a set of services and/or products for an agreed-upon sum of money. Such contracts can be classified as fixed price (lump sum contracts), cost reimbursement contracts, and unit price contracts.

Contract Administration   The ongoing process of actively managing the terms and conditions of a contract through the life of the contract.

Contract Change Control System   A specific process defined (and agreed to by all parties to the contract) to manage any changes to the contract.

Contract Closeout   The steps taken to formally complete and settle the terms of a contract, with special attention to resolving any open issues.

Control   The process of comparing the actual performance with planned performance, analyzing any variances, investigating possible courses of action, and putting in place relevant corrective actions.

Cost/Benefit Analysis   Comparing the cost of a given effort (project) to the expected benefits to be derived from the proposed effort (project).

Cost/Benefit Ratio   The value (number) produced by the formula: Benefits ÷ Cost. A value of greater than one is desirable; a value of less than one is unfavorable.

Cost Control   The process of controlling changes to the project budget.

Cost Distribution Model   A statistical template used to generate cost size estimates at a point when little is known about the project (during the Pre-Launch stage).

Cost of Capital   The cost of capital is the cost (percentage rate) of borrowing the next dollar for the business.

Cost Performance Index (CPI)   This is the ratio of the EV to AC of a project, measured at any given project status date. A CPI equal to one indicates that the project costs are equal to those planned; less than one indicates that the costs are greater than planned; and more than one indicates that the costs are less than planned. The CPI can be used to forecast the estimated cost to complete the project, as it (the CPI) is the burn rate of money being spent on the project. $CPI = EV \div AC$.

Cost Plus Fixed Fee (CPFF) Contract   A contract where the contractor is paid a fixed amount of money in addition to the cost of the work.

Cost Plus Incentive Fee (CPIF) Contract   A contract where the contractor is reimbursed for her cost to complete the project (a contractor's allowable cost is defined as a part of the contract). The contractor earns a certain amount of profit if the delivered product/service meets predefined performance criteria.

Cost-to-Date   The total money spent on a project as of the status date.

Cost Variance (CV)   The difference between estimated costs and actual costs at a given point in the project. In the case of the EVMS, it is the EV minus the AC.

Crashing   The process of analyzing schedule and cost trade-offs with the objective of achieving the greatest amount of schedule reduction for the least amount of incremental cost. Crashing the schedule typically involves applying additional resources (people and/or money) to selected tasks on the critical path.

Critical Activity   Any activity on the critical path of the project. *See* critical task.

Critical Path   The collection of tasks that represent the longest path through the project—the earliest the project can be completed.

Critical Path Method (CPM)   CPM resulted from a joint effort by the DuPont Company and Remington Rand Univac (1956–1959). Their objective was to determine how to best reduce the time required to complete a project. Key components are a network diagram of task dependencies, task duration values (one value for each task), and the critical path(s) through the task network.

Critical Task   Any task on the critical path of the project. *See* critical activity.

Cross-Project Dependency   A point in a project where the team cannot move any further because of the effort (interaction) required from a party outside the project. *See* external dependency.

Current System Retirement   This is Step 33 of the PPA. The proverbial last step in the project life cycle is to begin to retire the current system in an orderly manner. Unless the project is for a new organization, or is a completely new initiative, most IT/Business projects are upgrades and/or replacements of existing systems. Therefore, when the new project is deployed, the organization has two "live" systems. Unless the current system is systematically retired, the organization will have two systems in place, which can result in confusion, duplicate/redundant data, and cost escalations.

Current System Retirement Plan   The details (deliverables, tasks, resources, milestones, and budget) for retiring the current system after the new system is implemented. Unless this is handled skillfully, many customers will continue to use parts of the old system, resulting in duplicate work, added cost, and worst of all, duplicate and noncompatible data.

Customer   The person or group who places the order for the project; the person or group who receives the first line of benefit from the project; the person or group who will be directly impacted by the deployment of the project. Implementation level stakeholders are the customers of the project.

Customer Buy-In   A vital sign that is designed to assess the degree of ongoing buy-in to the project by key implementation-level stakeholders. Buy-in, like the other strategic vital signs, is difficult to measure because it is a qualitative assessment. This vital sign is best assessed through surveys, discussions, and observations.

Date Constraints   The limitation imposed on a specific task and/or deliverable by a specific date requirement. The variety of date constraints includes must-do dates, no earlier than, and no later than. Each of these places a specific limitation on the project.

Data Date   In a project reporting process, the point in time when the project status information was obtained. The data date separates the historical information from the future information. *See* also as-of date.

Degree of Influence   The extent and type of influence a key stakeholder wields on a project. A stakeholder's influence could span just a few people, or an entire division, and it could be classified as being a champion, neutral, and at times outright destructive.

Deliverable   The result or end product of completing a task or set of tasks that progressively give "body" to the project. Deliverables must be tangible. A deliverable must be crisply defined to avoid ambiguity and should have only one owner, although multiple team members may work to complete a deliverable.

Deliverables-Based Estimate   A high-level (size) estimate based on the effort, time, and cost required to complete project deliverables. It is typically used for projects (or phases) 4 to 6 months in duration.

Deliverables-Based Estimating Model A high-level (size) estimating technique where estimates are based on the effort, time, and cost required to complete project deliverables. It is best suited for projects (or phases) of 4 to 6 months in duration.

Delivery Mechanism The method by which the products of the project will be delivered to the client.

Delphi Technique A forecasting technique that uses estimates from experts (anonymously) until reasonable consensus occurs.

Demotivators According to the research and conclusions by Fredrick Herzberg, absence of certain "hygiene issues" such as company policies, working conditions, or salary can be employee demotivators.

Dependency The sequencing of project deliverables and/or tasks.

Depreciation The decline in the value of property due to general wear and tear and overall obsolescence. In financial accounting, depreciation is used to allocate the cost of an asset over a period of time (months or years) for tax purposes.

Detailed Estimates This is Step 25 of the PPA. This is the point where the project manager and the team develop detailed estimates (also known as task-based estimates) for the project. Task-based estimates include estimates of effort, cost, and duration based on a comprehensive task-level WBSs and resources profiled for their respective skills.

Direct Cost That portion of cost that is directly expended in developing a product or providing a service; such as the cost of labor and inventory (goods) used to create the product/service.

Disaster Recovery Plan A set of deliverables, tasks, resources, and milestones for implementing a recovery plan should a disaster take place, such as the crashing of a newly installed system, employee strike, or inclement weather.

Discounted Cash Flow The restating of future earnings (cash flow) in current dollar terms, considering the time value of money.

Discount Rate The term has three distinct meanings. In the case of project management, where project justification is to be based on the financial value (return) of a project, it means the minimum acceptable rate of ROI into the project. In this context, it is also known as the hurdle rate or the opportunity cost of the capital. Other meanings of the term are the interest deducted in advance in purchasing, selling, or lending a commercial paper, and finally the interest rate charged by a central bank on loans to its member banks.

Discretionary Constraint A type of constraint that can be changed (usually by the project manager) based on his best (educated) guess.

Discretionary Dependency A dependency between two tasks that can be altered at the discretion of the project manager, and, at times, of the individual(s) responsible for the two tasks.

Documentation The narrative and graphical description of a system. Documentation for an information system includes system documentation, technical documentation, and operating procedures.

Dummy Activity An activity with no duration and no resource used to depict a logical relationship between two activities/tasks in the arrow diagramming method.

Duration Typically, the number of workdays required to complete a task, a deliverable, a phase, or a project. The focus is the length of time. Duration can also be measured in the terms of work weeks and work months.

Early Finish (EF) Date The earliest possible time an activity can finish based on the project task network logic.

Early Start (ES) Date The earliest possible time an activity can start based on the project task network logic.

Earned Value (EV) A term used in the EVMS, that signifies the value of work actually performed up to the project status date. Also known as the *Budgeted Cost of Work Performed (BCWP)*.

Earned Value Management System (EVMS) A project progress performance method that measures progress by comparing the dollar value of work completed to the dollars that were planned to be spent and to the actual dollars that have been spent.

Effort The number of work hours required to complete a task, a deliverable, a phase, or a project. The focus here is on the amount of time (hours).

Effort Distribution Model A statistical template used to generate effort size estimates at a point when little is known about the project (during the Pre-Launch stage).

Effort Distribution Ratio A size estimating method where an estimate, expressed as a percent of total effort, is created for each phase of the project life cycle. The underlying data can be collected from in-house projects, if comprehensive and accurate time reporting systems exist, or from published industry data. This is a part of the phase-based size estimating method.

Effort Variance Factor (EVF) A factor (value) computed for a given team member based on her skills, work interruptions, any productivity loss due to less than full-time assignment, and the quality of the work environment. The resulting numeric value is used to normalize (adjust) the baseline effort values for tasks assigned to the resource. The higher the value of a team member's EVF, the longer it will take that person to complete a given task.

Elevator Speech A figure of speech for a concise and to the point statement about a subject, typically requiring 30 seconds or less. An elevator speech about the project should be in pure business terms and devoid of acronyms.

End User The person or group who uses, or will use, the end product of the project.

Estimate A tentative evaluation or rough calculation of the approximate effort, duration, and/or cost of work to be done.

Estimate at Completion (EAC) Typically, the forecasted final cost of a task, a deliverable, and/or the project. Often, the EAC includes certain adjustments to the original cost estimate based on to date performance. The formula to compute EAC = Actual to-date cost + Estimate to Complete (ETC).

Estimate Expiration Date The date after which the currently submitted estimates will expire and will need to be revalidated. It is very important to specify the expiration date for an estimate submitted to a client because without it, the recipient might assume that the estimated values are valid for an indefinite period of time.

Estimate to Complete (ETC) The expected cost needed to complete a task, a group of tasks, a deliverable, and/or the project.

Evaluation Criteria   For the purpose of qualifying a product or a contractor, the process defined to assess the viability (suitability) of the proposed product/contractor. Typically, the evaluation criteria consist of a number of items used to weigh or score the proposed product/contractor.

Exception Report   A report that contains only the major variations from the plan. Typically, the variance threshold is predefined in concert with the recipient of the report.

Execute (Development) Portfolio   The component of the project portfolio that houses the various projects being executed.

Execute Stage   The fourth stage of the PPA. In this stage of the project life cycle, the project manager develops the project schedule, the team begins to work to produce project deliverables, and the project manager oversees the team's progress to the planned end of the project. Between 60 to 70 percent of the project team's time is spent in this stage because of the extent of the work to be accomplished.

Expert Power   The power (authority/influence) that comes to an individual based on one's expertise.

External Dependency   A point in a project where the team cannot move any further because of effort (interaction) required from a party outside the project; also referred to as a cross-project dependency.

Facilities   The office space, meeting rooms, storage areas, phones, computers, and duplicating machines required by the project team to accomplish its work.

Fallback Plan   The plan to be used if the system deployment does not proceed as planned.

Fast Tracking   This is a schedule compression technique in which selected tasks on the critical path that have linear (FS) relationship are started partially or totally in parallel; they are assigned a SS dependency or a lead time. For example, starting the product design before requirements are complete or starting the product build before its design is complete.

Fault Tolerance   The degree of defects (errors) the finished process or product can have before it becomes unusable. A low fault tolerance means the system can tolerate few defects/errors.

Feasibility Study   A synonym for Project Charter.

Feature   Specific characteristics or traits of a system that are deemed useful by the customer.

Financial Analysis   The process used to analyze a project's costs and benefits in order to assess the project's economic viability.

Financial Exposure   The degree of fiscal loss that could result if the project was to be delayed and/or fail.

Finish-to-Finish (FF) Dependency   In a task network, this relationship means that the successor task is scheduled for completion a specific number of days following the predecessor task.

Finish-to-Start (FS) Dependency   In the case of the FS dependency, the successor task can, but does not have to, start as soon as the predecessor task has been finished. Another way to state this dependency is that the "from" task (predecessor) must finish before the "to" task (successor) can begin.

Fishbone Diagram (Cause & Effect or Ishikawa Diagram)   This technique is designed to help analyze problems that may have many interrelated causes. The basic structure of the diagram resembles the backbone of a fish, hence the name. A horizontal line (the backbone of the fish) represents the problem and each fish bone is a possible cause of the problem. Popularized by Professor Kaoru Ishikawa in 1943, it was then known as the Ishikawa diagram. *See* Cause & Effect diagram.

Fixed Price Contract   A type of contract where the total price (cost) of the project is set to a specific number regardless of the cost of the project to the seller (developer). Also known as the firm fixed price (FFP) contract or as the lump sum contract. *See* lump sum contract.

Float   The amount of time the ES of a task can be delayed without impacting the critical path of the project or the project finish date. *See* slack.

Forcing   An attitude and consequent behavior exhibited by a person that is based on the belief "my way or the highway."

Formal Acceptance   The official approval of a deliverable, project, and/or contract by a designated authorized individual.

Formal Power   Authority held by an individual derived from one's position (placement) within an organization (a project or a company).

Forming   The first stage in the team development model defined by B. W. Tuckman. This stage is characterized by a sense of uncertainty because the various team members are unfamiliar with each other as well as the leadership style of the project manager and the sponsor.

Forty Questions   A list of questions (developed by the author) that a sponsor should ask of a project manager.

Forward Path   While computing the critical path through a network of tasks, the forward path determines the earliest start and finish of each task.

Fixed Price Contract with Incentives for Performance (FPIP)   A contract in which the final total cost of the project is set to a specific number regardless of the cost of the project to the seller (developer), with incentives included for meeting predefined performance criteria. For example, $1,225,000 plus $10,000 for each day the project is finished early.

Free Float   This applies to individual tasks in a network. This refers to the total time (days) the completion of a task can be delayed without impacting the ES of any successor tasks. *See* activity float or free slack.

Free Slack   This applies to individual tasks in a network. This refers to the total time (days) the completion of a task can be delayed without impacting the ES of any successor tasks. *See* activity float or free float.

Fuel Report (Individual)   Given a specific look ahead window, the effort hours a team member will have available to work on the project (the available hours). Make sure that the team member is realistic in her forecast and takes into account any holidays, vacations, sick leave, travel, training, jury duty, and time committed to other projects and/or routine work.

Fuel Report (Team)   In the context of a project, fuel consists of the number of work hours available from the team. Given a specific look-ahead window, the effort hours the entire team will have available to work on the project (the available hours). Make sure that the team members are realistic in their forecasts and take into account any holidays, vacations, sick leave, travel, training, jury duty, and time committed to other projects and/or routine work.

Functional   Refers to an organization unit formed to perform a specific service or function, such as human resources, IT, marketing, manufacturing, and sales.

Functional Managers   The managers of various IT and business unit departments.

Functional Project Organization   A type of project organization structure where the project management responsibility (assignment) is given to one of the functional managers, the level of the manager is based on the level of complexity of the project, and the various team members are selected from within the function.

Gantt Chart   Henry Gantt, an engineer invented this graphic display method of tracking project tasks/deliverables in 1917. In a Gantt chart, various project tasks are listed on the left side of the chart (the Y axis) and dates are shown across the top (the X axis); also known as the task Gantt. In another version of a Gantt chart, all of the tasks for a given resource are depicted in one chart. This is known as the resource Gantt.

Geography   The areas in which the project must be managed and implemented.

Gold Plating   The process of adding functions and/or features to a product that are not asked for by the customer. Team members who believe they know more about the customers' needs than the customer typically make this decision. Gold plating is also an action taken by (unethical) contractors when the contract is not fixed price (the contractor can bill the customer for any work done on the job).

Heuristics   A problem-solving method in which the solution is developed through successive discoveries that result from investigations made by the problem solver (also known as *trial and error method*).

High Probability, High Impact Risk Events   A vital sign designed to monitor the high impact and high probability risks to the project.

Histogram   A (vertical) bar graph of a frequency distribution in which the heights of the bars are proportional to the class frequencies, such as the occurrence of the data.

Human Resources   The various people involved in completing the work on a project.

Hurdle Rate   The required rate of return above which an investment makes sense and below which it does not. Also known as *required rate of return* and *required rate on investment*.

Icon   A small, pictorial, on-screen representation of an object.

Idea   A thought or a concept. If proven viable, it may become a project.

Idea Stage   The first stage of the PPA. In this stage of a project life cycle, ideas for a proposed project go through due diligence to assess them for their viability—alignment with the corporate strategy and value to the business. The assessment results in a well-thought-out Project Request.

Ideas Portfolio   The component of the project portfolio that houses the various ideas being assessed for their viability or that have progressed into a Project Request.

Idea Statement   This is Step 1 of the PPA. The genesis of a successful project is a clearly articulated statement of the project idea by the customer.

Impact Assessment   This is Step 8 of the PPA. This is the process of identifying any systems, processes, or projects that will be impacted by the proposed project.

Implement (Deployment) Portfolio   The component of the project portfolio that houses the various projects being deployed—being turned over to the customers and the operations group.

Implement Stage   The fifth stage of the PPA. In this stage of a project life cycle, the team begins to transfer the developed product to its customers and the operations group and begins to close the project down.

Implementation-Level Stakeholders   The stakeholders who will be impacted by (shaped by) the deployment of the project.

Incentives   Inducements, enticements, and motivations incorporated into contracts to encourage the "seller" to achieve superior performance, such as financial rewards for early completion of a project.

Incremental Estimating   The process of combining size and detailed estimating methods to produce progressively more accurate estimates. This involves developing high-level phase- or deliverables-based size estimates at the start of the project and more accurate detailed task-based estimates as the project is more clearly defined.

Indirect Cost   The portion of a cost that is not directly spent in developing a product or providing a service, such as the cost of providing security at a construction site or the expenses related to the service provided by a project office to a project manager. Also known as *overhead costs*.

Infrastructure   The fundamental structure of a system or organization. The basic fundamental architecture of any system (electronic, mechanical, social, political, etc.) that determines how it functions and how flexible it is to meet future requirements. *See* technology infrastructure.

Inspection   A formal review of a deliverable (usually by one or more SMEs) to ensure that the end product meets the requisite standards, procedures, and guidelines.

Intangible Benefits   Benefits that are difficult to quantify and measure.

Interface Design   The design of the connection and interaction between hardware, software, and the user. In a given IT/Business system, users "talk" to the software, the software "talks" to the hardware and other software, and the hardware "talks" to other hardware. The mechanics of this process is part of the interface design.

Internal Policies and Procedures   Company directives selected to guide and determine present and future decisions and actions.

Internal Rate of Return (IRR)   This refers to the interest rate, or the yield, that equates the present value of expected cash flow from a project to the cost of the project.

International Organization for Standardization (ISO)   A network of the national standards institutes of 147 countries, with one member per country, with a central secretariat in Geneva, Switzerland, that coordinates the system.

International Standards Rules, methods, and processes that must be considered when managing or implementing a project across international borders (process standards, passports, work visas, intellectual property, workplace regulations, weights and measures, security, etc.).

Inter-Project Priority (Project Priority) The relative ranking given to an approved Project Request (ideas portfolio), an approved Project Charter (pre-launch or launch portfolio), and an approved project (execute portfolio). This ranking is different from the Intra-Project Priority Analysis, which is used to rank order the four key attributes of a given project: schedule, scope, budget, and quality.

Intra-Project Priority Analysis This is Step 4 of the PPA. This tool is used to establish a rank order for the four key priorities of a project—schedule, scope, budget, and quality.

Ishikawa Diagram (Fishbone or Cause & Effect Diagram) Popularized by Professor Kaoru Ishikawa in 1943, this technique is designed to help analyze problems that may have many interrelated causes. The basic structure of the diagram resembles the backbone of a fish, hence the name Fishbone Diagram. A horizontal line (the backbone of the fish) represents the problem and each fish bone is a possible cause of the problem.

ISO 9000 A quality system standard developed by the ISO that focuses on planning, controlling, and documenting quality in an organization.

Issue An unanswered question and/or a difference of opinion.

Issues Management This is Step 11 of the PPA. Issues are akin to the pot holes on a road—the more issues there are, the more difficult it becomes to navigate the project. Accordingly, issues must be managed conscientiously and in a timely manner. Once an issue has been analyzed and recorded, it is important to assign a specific person as owner of the issue resolution. The owner's responsibility is to facilitate, rather than dictate, the resolution process. Best results occur when the people who differ determine the issue resolution jointly. The project manager's negotiating skills are a vital component of issue resolution.

IT Project + Certification A project management certification offered by CompTIA, a global, not-for-profit association.

Joint Application Design (JAD) A process for designing a system that brings together the IT and the business professionals in a highly focused series of workshops.

Kickoff Meeting (Project Kickoff Meeting) The purpose of this meeting is for the sponsor to formally announce the start of the project to the policy and implementation level stakeholders, key customers, and the core team. Another important objective of the meeting is to give the sponsor the opportunity to officially introduce the project manager to the key stakeholders and to formally and publicly designate the project manager as the person charged with the responsibility for successful completion of the project.

Kiviat Chart The chart provides the ability to graphically depict the quantitative information on a set of "spokes" of a wheel. Each spoke of the Kiviat chart represents a metric and the results are plotted with reference to user-defined thresholds. The chart is named after its originator, Philip J. Kiviat.

Knowledge Base The purpose of a knowledge base is to provide a standard reference for the key principles and practices of the associated profession. The typical organization of a knowledge base document revolves around *what* needs to be done with minimal attention given to *why* and *when*. *See* a body of knowledge.

Lag Usually, within a task network, a successor task is assumed to start as soon as the one before it is completed. However, there are times when a delay is necessary between a given task and the task that follows it. This modification of dependency relationship between two tasks can be specified through the use of a lag value. Therefore, the delay between the two such tasks is referred to as lag—the wait time between two tasks.

Launch (Plans & Estimates) Portfolio The component of the project portfolio that houses the various projects being planned and estimated.

Launch Stage The third stage of the PPA. In this stage of a project life cycle, the tactics to complete the project are laid out, the project organization is designed, and communication plans are created. The detailed estimates are compared to the high-level estimates created in the Pre-Launch stage and the sponsor makes the final decisions regarding the project scope and budget.

Late Finish (LF) Date The latest date by which a task must be completed without delaying the project finish date.

Late Start (LS) Date The latest date by which a task must be started without delaying the project finish date.

Law of Diminishing Return Attributed to Thomas Malthus (1798), the law defines a point in a process where any additional resources assigned to an endeavor do not result in a proportionate increase in productivity (output).

Lead A dependency (logical) relationship used to specify the acceleration of time between two dependent tasks.

Lessons Learned The collection of examples and experiences collected typically at the end of a major project milestone (including at the end of a project) to help the future practitioners learn from past experiences.

Lessons Learned Database A compilation of summary information collected during the Process Assessment (Step 30 of the PPA) and stored in a well-structured database for quick and easy reference by project managers and team members.

Level of Integration The degree to which the project combines the activities of multiple applications or systems.

Leveling (Resource Leveling) The process of analyzing a project schedule to smooth the resource allocation peaks and valleys by rescheduling (*delaying*) tasks that have sufficient free slack.

License Compliance The requirement to meet the terms and conditions of licenses with vendors as well as meet the requirements of any licensing agency.

Life Cycle The progression through a series of stages of development of a process and/or product, such as project management life cycle, system development life cycle, product development life cycle.

Life Cycle Costing The process of computing the cost of a project/system/item over its expected life span. This approach is in contrast to the typical computations that only cover the cost of developing (or acquiring) the project/system/item. Also known as total cost of ownership (TCO).

Life Cycle Methodology   A collection of phases, deliverables, tasks, practices, procedures, and rules for developing a process or a product.

Logical Relationship   An execution dependency between one or more tasks in a task network, i.e., the order in which the tasks can be executed. There are four such relationships: FF, FS, SF, and SS. *See* precedence relationship.

Look-Ahead Window   A predetermined period of time into the future used to help the project team forecast its ability to continue its work as planned. A look-ahead window can be short term (only a few weeks), as well as long term (looking toward the end of the project).

Lump Sum Contract   A contract where the total price of the work to be performed to complete the project is set and is not supposed to be changed. *See* fixed price contract.

Management Reserve   Dollars and time included in an estimate and/or a schedule to accommodate future unpredictable situations. This typically includes rework, scope growth, and contingency reserves for potential risks.

Mandatory Dependency   Within a task network, indicates that a given task cannot begin until the preceding task has been completed.

Master Task List   A collection of "universal" tasks that can be used to develop a tailored task list for a given project.

Matrix Project Organization   A type of project organization structure where the project team is comprised of team members from a number of different functional organizations. Team members may be assigned full- or part-time to the project team and each reports to two bosses—his own functional manager as well as a project manager.

Maturity Model   This typically refers to a five-level progression path defined by the SEI at the Carnegie Mellon University. Named Capability Maturity Model Integration (CMMI), it defines the steps needed for an organization to improve its software development processes.

Methodology   A body of practices, procedures, roles, responsibilities, and rules (of a discipline). A set of working methods.

Milestone   A milestone is an indicator of significant progress in a project. It marks the beginning or completion of a key task, deliverable, phase, and/or the project.

Milestone Chart   A summary level schedule that depicts the various milestones within the project task schedule. Also known as a *milestone schedule*.

Milestone Hit Rate   A vital sign that indicates the number of milestones the team was planning to hit (achieve) and the number of milestones they actually hit during a specific reporting period.

Mitigation Plan   A set of tasks and actions, which, if taken, will help alleviate (lessen) a given risk.

Monitoring   The process of gathering, analyzing, and reporting performance metrics. This means comparing the actual performance with planned performance.

Monte Carlo Simulation   A risk assessment technique used to estimate the likely range of outcomes by simulating the process a large number of times.

Multiple Project Factor (MPF)   A metric used to designate the impact on productivity of a team member assigned to more than one project simultaneously.

Multitasking   The requirement for and ability of a team member to work on more than one task at a time.

Murphy's Law   One of the famous "natural laws" that states, "If anything can go wrong, it will." It was named after Capt. Edward A. Murphy, an engineer on the Air Force Project MX981 in 1949, which was designed to see how much sudden deceleration a person can stand in a crash.

Near-Critical Path   Any path in a task network that has a low total float (its duration is close to the duration value of the critical path through the network). We consider any path whose duration is within 20 percent of the critical path to be a near-critical path. The implication is that if the tasks on a given near-critical path take longer than estimated, it could then become the critical path.

Negotiation   The process of give and take between two or more parties to arrive at a mutually satisfying and mutually advantageous agreement.

Nemesis   An individual who does not see any merit to the project and may very well use her political capital to place obstacles in the path of successful project completion. Not all nemeses are "bad" people. Rather, it could simply be that their current perception is such that the proposed project makes no sense to them or they don't like the manner in which the project is being handled.

Net Present Value (NPV)   The NPV is a method for evaluating an investment or project where both the cost or investment (all cash outflow) of the project, as well as all future (multiyear) earnings (all cash inflows), are restated in PV terms.

Net Profit   Gross sales minus all expenses (depreciation, taxes, and other expenses). Also called *net income* or *net earnings*.

Network (Task Network)   A grouping of various tasks of a project in the order of their logical execution. A network proceeds from left to right reflecting the arrangement of tasks (deliverables and milestones) in time. Also referred to as the *PERT chart* or *PERT network*.

Network Analysis   The process of reviewing and analyzing the dependencies among various tasks of a task network in order to define the critical path.

Network Diagram   Also known as the precedence diagram and PERT chart, it depicts the interdependencies (the logical sequence and concurrence of various tasks in a project).

Node   The starting and ending point of an activity/task in the AOA diagramming method.

Noncompetitive Procurement   The process of acquiring products and/or services from a supplier without going through a competitive bidding process.

Norming   The third stage in the team development model defined by B. W. Tuckman. In this transition stage, the disparate group of individuals on a team begin to form into a collaborative and synergistic group—a productive team. Various team members are beginning to take charge of their assignments, are beginning to trust and help each other, are able to resolve most of the issues amongst themselves, and are exhibiting more agreements than disagreements—all signs of a productive team.

Objective   Something to work toward or strive for; a goal. Also, the purpose.

Obstacle   Something or someone that opposes, stands in the way of, or holds up progress in a project.

Operations   Those areas where widely accepted and repeatable processes are set up and carried out to deliver predictable results, at predicable costs, within a predictable schedule. The trait of an efficient operations group is the predictability with which it is able to complete its routine work.

Operations Portfolio   The component of the project portfolio that houses the various projects that have been successfully deployed and are in the operations stage.

Operations Metrics   This is Step 32 of the PPA. Operations metrics deal with hardware and software performance—the overall efficiency of the system operations. Although the responsibility for gathering and reporting this performance data usually lies with the operations group, the project manager is still responsible for making sure that performance metrics have been planned for and will be assessed. Be sure to specify the assessment methodology, the person(s) responsible for performing the assessments, the timing of the assessments and to whom, and in what format, the results will be reported. Operations metric collection typically starts a few weeks after the deployment is finished and routine operations begin.

Operations Schedule   The operations schedule provides information regarding system production cycles. The information for the schedule is gleaned from documents that indicate daily processes, weekend processes, job order, and back-up procedures, etc. This information is vital to facilitate a successful transition from project development to project implementation, and finally to computer operations.

Operation Stage   The sixth stage of the PPA. In this stage of a project life cycle, the project team successfully transfers the project to the operations group, and the project proceeds to its routine operations.

Opportunity Cost   The cost of passing up the next best choice when making a decision. For example, if money is used to fund project A, the opportunity cost is the value the same investment would return if applied to the next highest yielding project.

Optimal Full-Time Equivalent (OFTE)   In computing size estimates, it is the heuristics-based formula to compute the number of FTE resources that can be absorbed by any given project phase. OFTE = (Square root of the work months) + 1.

Order of Magnitude Estimate   An estimate that might have an error range of up to "times ten." We do not recommend such estimates because they do not produce useful data—management cannot make sound business decisions based on such estimates.

Organization Calendar   This calendar defines the working and nonworking dates and times at the organization level. When setting up the organizational calendar for your project, be sure to indicate such information as official holidays, weekends, preplanned business events, and default working hours. For a project that spans national boundaries, build customized calendars for each country, as the official holidays, weekends, and default working hours may differ.

Organizational Breakdown Structure   Similar to a WBS but the different levels depict the various organizational units, such as sales, marketing, and manufacturing.

Organization Change Management Plan   This is step 20 of the PPA. Any project means new ideas, which means a change to the status quo, and changes to status quo cause resistive behavior in many. Therefore, just because a project has been sold to, and approved by, highly placed executives, it does not automatically mean that there will be little resistance among the rank and file. As an integral part of successful project deployment, it is imperative that you develop a comprehensive plan to assist the project's customers/end users make the transition from the old to the new. Key steps involved in this process are: learn about the psychology of change, perform project stress analysis, develop a change management plan, and be kind to the customers/end users.

Organization Plan   During the Launch stage of a project, it is important to define the project organization structure, reporting lines, primary project responsibilities, and issue-escalation procedures.

Overallocation   The situation where a given resource is allocated for more hours/days than are actually available; also, the situation where more resources than are actually available are allocated to a project.

Overhead   The portion of cost that is not directly spent in developing a product or providing a service; such as the cost of providing security at a construction site or the expenses related to the service provided by a project office to a project manager. Also known as *indirect costs*. On occasion, some IT customers see the cost of project management as overhead; we take strong issue with this mentality because project management is an integral part of completing any project.

Overtime Utilization   A vital sign that tracks the amount of overtime by individual team members. Overtime is not an easy item to track because many project managers, functional managers, and sponsors hold the belief that (unpaid) overtime is a natural component of the world of fast approaching deadlines. Occasional overtime is a routine part of work life, but consistent overtime is a symptom of deep systemic problems caused by poor project management practices.

Parametric Estimate   An estimate developed using the statistical relationship between historical data and the object to be estimated (a deliverable and/or a project).

Parametric Estimating Model   Any estimating technique that employs a statistical relationship between historical data and the current situation to compute estimates.

Parkinson's Law   A maxim that states that the work expands to fill the time available for its completion.

Path Float   This denotes the amount of time (days) by which the completion of a task on the path in question can be delayed without impacting the critical path of the project. *See* total slack.

Path   A set of sequentially connected tasks in a project task network.

Payback Period   The period of time, usually months, in which the initial investment in a project can be recovered. Also known as the *breakeven period*.

Peer Review   The process or processes by which project deliverables are evaluated relative to the stated objectives of the project by the developer's colleagues in a nonthreatening environment. The objective is to detect errors and omissions early. The hallmark of a successful process is a mutually respectful environment where the focus is on detecting errors and omissions with minimal focus on the individual responsible (for errors and omissions). *See* walk through.

Penalty Power   The ability to punish (reprimand) an individual or a group as a result of nonperformance. Typically discussed in relation to nonperformance of a contract with a supplier/vendor.

Percent Complete   A value, expressed as a percent, used to specify the degree of completion of a task, deliverable, phase, or the project. We do not support the use of percent complete as a measure of progress.

Performance Reporting   Collection and distribution of information such as project status reports, team progress and accomplishments, and system operations.

PERT Chart   A task dependency network is also referred to as a PERT chart (although technically it is an incorrect use of the term, it has become a part of current project management vocabulary).

PERT Estimate   A weighted average of the most likely, optimistic, and pessimistic estimates, typically computed as Optimistic estimate + (Most likely estimate × 4) + Pessimistic estimate ÷ 6.

Phase   Projects are broken into a set of phases. Phases often end with checkpoints such as when management approval is sought prior to undertaking additional work.

Phase-Based Size Estimate   A high-level effort, cost, and duration estimate created by using project phases as a base.

Pilot   A portion of a product or software application that is engineered, designed, constructed, tested, and implemented as a model for the final product.

Pilot Plan   The plan for piloting the system/process in one or more locations/environments to ensure that it works properly. Piloting helps ensure that things work correctly and that the organization is equipped to handle possible error conditions with minimal impact to the business.

Plan of Record (POR)   The POR refers to the project plan after it has been completed, validated, and fully approved.

Policies, Procedures, and Standards   This is step 7 of the PPA. It involves the assessment of the policies, procedures, standards, and regulations that can significantly impact the project schedule and cost.

Policy Level Stakeholders   Stakeholders who will impact (shape) the project.

Politics   The degree of competition existing between competing interest groups or individuals for power and/or leadership.

Portfolio Alerts   A set of early warning signals indicating the need for heightened watchfulness on the project due to a breach in one or more of its vital signs. Examples of alerts are unaligned project, duplicate/overlapping project, unsecured system, high defect rate, and supporting project/system nonperformance.

Portfolio Manager   An appropriate level manager who has the authority to manage the project portfolio. The individual needs to have the political armor to meet criticism and opposition from various parts of the organization.

Potential PERT   A network diagram that depicts the logical order in which the various tasks of a project can be undertaken, assuming that there are absolutely no constraints. In such a diagram, sufficient resources are assumed to be available to start a task as soon as the preceding task is completed.

Precedence Diagramming Method (PDM)   Same as the activity on node diagramming, where task descriptions appear inside a node, a circle, square, or rectangle, and arrows or lines are used as connectors between nodes. Task durations are generally written within the node. Task responsibility is indicated by writing the resource's name or initial within the node. Nodes may also contain additional information such as start and finish dates.

Precedence Relationship   An execution dependency between one or more tasks in a task network, such as the order in which the tasks can be executed. There are four such relationships: FF, FS, SF, and SS. *See* logical relationship.

Predecessor   In a task network, the preceding task or "from" task.

Pre-Launch (Charters) Portfolio   The component of the project portfolio that houses the various Project Requests that are being assessed for their viability or that have progressed into Project Charters.

Pre-Launch Stage   The second stage of the PPA. The purpose of the Pre-Launch stage is to systematically analyze a project in order to produce a solid Project Charter. The Project Charter is the proposal for the project, which becomes the business plan for the project when approved.

Preliminary Scope Statement   This is step 13 of the PPA. The project scope defines the sum total of functions and features to be delivered to the project customer at the completion of the proposed project. At this early point in the project life cycle, although we know a lot more about the project than we did at the end of the Idea stage, it is not possible to clearly define the final scope because detailed customer requirements are not yet defined. However, as a part of the Project Charter to be submitted to management, we must provide a reasonable idea of the "size" of the proposed project so that a decision can be made whether to move forward with the project. It is important to communicate clearly to the customer and any key stakeholders that the proposed scope will need to be revisited and reapproved later in the project life cycle.

Present Value (PV)   This indicates the value, in today's dollars, of future net earnings from a project or investment.

Prevention Plan   A set of steps to inhibit or thwart a risk.

Priority Analysis   A tool used to quantify the priorities of a project. Project priorities are usually expressed in terms of schedule, scope, budget, and quality targets. Stated priorities often conflict. For example, there may be a tight deadline in the face of a low budget or large scope. The existence of such conflicts makes it essential that priorities be well-defined, rank ordered, and broadly communicated.

Probabilistic Estimate   Estimates based on using optimistic, most likely, and pessimistic estimates of a deliverable, activity, or task instead of one specific (deterministic) estimate. Probabilistic estimates are the foundation of PERT estimates.

Probability   The likelihood that a specific, given outcome (of all possible outcomes) will occur.

Probable Full-Time Equivalent (PFTE)   In size estimating, the number of team members that will most likely be available to work on a phase of the project. The number of PFTE can be *equal to*, or *less than*, the computed OFTE resources. It is important that you not succumb to the pressure of using a PFTE value higher than the computed OFTE.

Process   A particular method of doing something, which generally consists of a number of steps or operations; moving forward. A series of actions that result in a predictable outcome. The implication of a process is that the actions have been tried and tested and have consistently resulted in a desired outcome.

Process Assessment   This is step 30 of the PPA. The objective is to look back, purely from the project management process point of view, and see what improvements need to be made the next time around. Of course, this review will require effort and time on the part of selected team members and needs to be budgeted into the project's original plan, estimate, and schedule. We have found that, if the assessment is well planned and professionally conducted, only 30 percent of medium and large projects need to be assessed. The information collected from a core group of projects usually is a dependable representation of the overall project management practices of the organization.

Procurement   The act of acquiring goods and (outside) services to meet the needs of a project.

Procurement Management   A subset of the project management process with a focus on the steps to identify, assess, and select one or more qualified vendor/contractors to undertake the project. *See* project procurement management.

Procurement Management Process   The process and procedures for soliciting, selecting, and acquiring goods and services from suppliers and vendors, including contact approval, contract administration, and contract closeout.

Procurement Plan   The portion of the project plan that relates to the solicitation, selection, and acquisition of goods and services from suppliers and vendors.

Procurement Planning   The process of determining what to procure, as well as when and how to procure it.

Product Development Life Cycle Methodology   A collection of practices, procedures, roles, responsibilities, and rules for developing a product.

Profit   Revenue (gross intake) minus expenses (cost).

Profit Margin   Net profit divided by income, expressed as a percentage.

Program   In the context of project management, this means a group of interrelated projects, each to be completed in a specific order (business people often use the term "initiative" to describe a program).

Program Evolutional and Review Technique (PERT)   In 1958, the U.S. Navy; Booz, Allen, & Hamilton; and Lockheed Aircraft Corporation developed PERT (Program Evaluation Research Task, later to be called Project Evaluation and Review Technique) for scheduling and managing the Polaris weapons systems project. Three time estimates are defined for each activity or task: most likely, optimistic, and pessimistic.

Program Manager   The term "program," in the context of project management, means a group of related projects, each to be completed in a specific order (business people often use the term "initiative" to describe a program). A program manager is an individual who has the responsibility to coordinate and oversee the implementation of the group of projects.

Progress Report   A report that describes an individual (or team's) accomplishments in a given period of time.

Progress Review & Control   This is step 28 of the PPA. At this point, the team has started to execute their assigned tasks, and they can begin to record and report the actual effort (hours) and days spent on tasks assigned to them along with the status of their milestones and deliverables. The project manager's responsibility is to analyze whether the project is on track and, if not, where and why it has gone off track. The analysis consists of comparing the planned (estimates) to the actual effort and durations that are recorded as the project progresses. The difference between the planned and actual values is the variance. Progress reviews are meaningful only if they are based on a sound and comprehensive project schedule against which progress can be assessed. Therefore, schedules must be systematically reviewed and revised to ensure that they do not become obsolete and lose their credibility as a yardstick for measuring progress. Finally, the review process and the tools that support it should be straightforward and easy to use, so that project status reports are consistently realistic, accurate, and timely.

Project   A temporary endeavor to create a unique product or process. A business solution, an investment that has appropriate level ownership, and a change in the status quo.

Project Capacity   The sum total of projects that can be safely undertaken by an organization given its resources—people, budget, technology.

Project Charter   This is step 15 of the PPA. The Charter is a comprehensive document assembled toward the end of the Pre-Launch stage and serves as a proposal for the project sponsor. Once approved, it becomes a business plan for the project team. An approved Charter signals the formal start of the project.

Project Charter Review & Budget Approval   This is step 26 of the PPA. At this step, the project manager meets with the sponsor for a final review of the Project Charter, task plan, and detailed estimates to make sure that the work done in the Launch stage can help achieve the stated objectives, that risks are reasonable, and the estimates are in line with management and customer expectations. If all seems well, and the sponsor is satisfied with the quality of the team's work, it is time to approve the project's budget and proceed to the next stage—execute the project.

Project Closure   This is a part of Project Implementation & Closure, step 29 of the PPA, and involves the steps needed to close the project. Key actions include turning the appropriate documents over to the operations, support and maintenance team; deleting/discarding unneeded documentation, deactivating access codes, return of property, closure of contracts, and financial books.

Project Communications Management   A subset of project management principles, practices, and tools that focuses on the collection, analysis, dissemination, and archiving of project information. *See* communications management.

Project Coordinator   Within some organizations, used to refer to the role of the project manager. We advise against such use of the term in the context of project management because it implies little authority. The term might occasionally be used to describe an individual who has the responsibility to coordinate the order of execution of a group of related projects. In such cases, we prefer use of the term "program manager."

Project Cost Management   A subset of project management principles, practices, and tools that focuses on the collection, analysis, dissemination, and archiving of project cost data.

Project Description   This is step 3 of the PPA. The Project Description is key to developing and communicating your understanding of a project at the time a project is conceived, and it will continue to play an important role in subsequent planning steps as you refine and build on that understanding. The inputs to developing a clear Project Description are the Idea Statement and Project Request information completed in the Idea stage. The additional key components include the nature of the project, project objectives, validated assumptions, conceptual build, runaway trigger, and the project shutdown conditions.

Project Feasibility   The process of assessing the viability of a proposed project. This relates to the work carried out in the Idea and Pre-Launch stages of the PPA.

Project Forecasting   Predicting the project future by analyzing the to-date project performance.

Project Human Resource Management   A subset of project management principles, practices, and tools that focuses on the effective acquisition, deployment, and utilization of people (primarily, the project team).

Project Implementation & Closure   This is step 29 of the PPA. This is the point where the project team has finished the development work on the project and begins to deploy the project—prepare the customers and operations group to begin project operations. The preparation for smooth deployment is a two-step process: prepare the operations group and the customer. Typically, the work starts with the operations group and then with a short lag, the customer preparation needs to begin, i.e., these two steps have a SS relationship with a few days of lag. Another important component of this step is the initiation of the step for project closure.

Project Integration Management   Within the PMBOK, a subset of the project management process that ensures that various elements of a project are properly coordinated. Project integration management is one of the nine project management knowledge areas of PMBOK®.

Project Kickoff Meeting (Kickoff Meeting)   The purpose of this meeting is for the sponsor to formally announce the start of the project to the policy- and implementation-level stakeholders, key customers, and the core team. Another important objective of this meeting is to give the sponsor the opportunity to officially introduce the project manager to the key stakeholders and to formally and publicly designate the project manager as the person charged with the responsibility for successful completion of the project.

Project Life Cycle   A collection of project phases, deliverables, tasks, and milestones. PPA is an example of a project life cycle.

Project Load   The sum total of the projects being undertaken by an organization.

Project Management   Judicious use of people, knowledge, skills, techniques, and tools to transform an idea into a useful process or product in an effective and efficient manner.

Project Management Body of Knowledge (PMBOK)   The PMBOK is a project management knowledge base compiled by the PMI.

Project Management Information System   Often used to refer to both the manual and automated system(s) a company uses to track project work and status—planning, estimating, scheduling, and tracking.

Project Management Institute (PMI)   A premier international, nonprofit, professional association serving the needs of project management professionals.

Project Management Knowledge Areas (Segments)   The PMBOK of PMI consists of nine project management knowledge areas: project integration management, project scope management, project time management, project cost management, project quality management, project human resources management, project communications management, project risk management, and project procurement management.

Project Management Methodology   A collection of steps, practices, procedures, and rules for managing a project. PPA is an example of a project management methodology.

Project Management Office (PMO)   A group established within an organization with the responsibility for developing and deploying project management governance procedures and providing SMEs to project managers. *See* project office (PO).

Project Management Professional (PMP)   Certification credential provided by PMI.

Project Management Software   The class of software designed to help manage the various components of a project: planning, estimating, scheduling, and tracking.

Project Manager   An individual who has the responsibility and requisite authority to help transform an idea into a useful process or product through the judicious use of people, knowledge, skills, techniques, and tools.

Project Network Diagram   A grouping of various tasks of a project in the order of their logical execution. A network proceeds from left to right, reflecting the arrangement of tasks (deliverables and milestones) in time. Also referred to as the PERT chart or PERT network.

Project Notebook   This is step 24 of the PPA. It provides a standard framework for project documentation and acts a repository for essential documents and working papers developed during the project. Also known as *project binder*.

Project Office (PO)   A group established within an organization. Has the responsibility for developing and deploying project management governance procedures and providing SMEs to project managers. *See* project management office (PMO).

Project Organization   This is step 17 of the PPA. This is the point where the project manager, working with the sponsor, designs a project organization structure suited to the needs of the project. Many project managers do not take the step to design a specific team organization structure for their projects. Instead, they accept the existing team structure and try to make it work. This approach leads to less-than-desirable results. Our advice to project managers is to work hard to design an organization structure that is tailored to fit the project at hand and then work diligently to put it into practice. The extent to which the designed structure cannot be made practical represents the degree of added risk to the project. If the resulting risk is considerable, the next prudent step is to invoke the risk management process.

Project (or Projectized) Organization Structure   In this project organization structure, the entire team is fully dedicated to the project at hand and reports directly to the project manager. Various people on the team are either hired for the project and/or transferred from their current departmental duties and are assigned to the project full time; they do not have any responsibilities for their day-to-day jobs during the project life cycle (this is easier said than done).

Project Phase   Phases are distinct stages of product development. Projects are typically broken into a set of phases to group together similar activities, such as requirements, design, build, test, and implement (the phase names are usually based on the system/product development methodology in use in the organization). Phases often end with major checkpoints. Phase names can be verbs and/or nouns.

Project Plan   The sum total of the phases, deliverables, tasks, milestones, task dependencies, resources, and budget defined to complete a project.

Project Plan Development   The process of creating a WBS and a task network for a project.

Project Plan Execution   The process of completing the various tasks (and deliverables) and achieving the milestones planned in a task network of a project.

Project Portfolio   A process designed to track an organization's projects from idea formation to project completion. A comprehensive project portfolio includes an Ideas portfolio, a Pre-Launch (Charters) portfolio, a Launch (plans & estimates) portfolio, an Execute (development) portfolio, an Implement (deployment) portfolio, an Operations portfolio, a suspended project portfolio, and a cancelled project portfolio.

Project Portfolio Management   The principles, practices, and tools for evaluating, selecting, planning, executing, and monitoring projects for four specific goals: strategy alignment, value-to-business *v.* project complexity (probability of success), maximize investment value, and effective resource utilization.

Project Priority (Inter-Project Priority)   The relative ranking given to an approved Project Request (Ideas portfolio), an approved Project Charter (Pre-Launch or Launch portfolio), and an approved project (Execute portfolio). This ranking is different from the intra-project priority which is used to rank order the four key attributes of a given project: schedule, scope, budget, and quality.

Project Process Architecture (PPA)   A 6-stage, 33-step, project management methodology developed for IT/Business projects by the Center for Project Management.

Project Procurement Management   A subset of the project management process that focuses on the steps to identify, assess, and select one or more qualified vendor/contractors to undertake the project.

Project Productivity Influencing Factor (PPIF)   A factor derived by assigning specific values to a set of attributes that can have an impact on a team member's productivity, such as the number of nemeses, team location (central or dispersed), customer locations, team size, and team disposition.

Project Quality Management   A subset of the project management process that focuses on the steps to ensure that the project's end product will meet the defined quality criteria.

Project Request   This is step 2 of the PPA. The development of a Project Request requires additional examination of the Idea Statement. The purpose of this step is to provide enough information to the requesting customer and to the decision makers to facilitate an informed and intelligent evaluation of the proposed project. Keep in mind that not every Idea Statement would qualify to be advanced to the Project Request step.

Project Schedule   This is step 27 of the PPA. Scheduling is the process of assigning specific resources to tasks in relation to a specific calendar and consists of the following steps: schedule the work, validate the schedule, and establish a baseline schedule.

Project Schedule   The project plan with dates associated with each task and milestone. Dates depict the planned start and finish of each task.

Project Scope   The total sum of deliverables and features (the total functionality) delivered to the project customer at the completion of the proposed project.

Project Scope Management   A subset of the project management process. Focus is on the steps to ensure that the project scope is defined clearly, that the project task plan will produce the planned scope, and that any scope changes will be successfully managed.

Project Size Estimate   This is step 14 of the PPA. As a part of the Project Charter, the project manager will need to include an estimate of the proposed project's duration, resources, and cost. The dilemma at this early stage is reconciling the degree of accuracy desired by the customer with project reality. The customer would like an estimate that will be close to the eventual cost and time to complete the project. However, unless the proposed project is less than 4 months in duration, sufficient information is not available to create accurate estimates. The best that can be done at this early stage of a project is to create a high-level estimate, known as the *size estimate*. By their very nature, size estimates can have an error range of up to +35 percent.

Project Staging   This is step 16 of the PPA. Project Staging is the process of assembling the infrastructure of the project. The activities in this step can be compared to the advance work done before an important person comes into town—a politician, a celebrity, or an author on tour. The work is usually handled by a small number of experienced people, the core team, who have the wherewithal to get things done on their own. Their responsibility is to "scope the landscape" and prepare for a smooth start. A key step in staging a project is to hold the project kickoff meeting.

Project Stress Analysis   Any project means new ideas and a change to the status quo. Changes to status quo result in stress for the project's implementation level stakeholders. The purpose of project stress analysis is to assess the level of stress on each key stakeholder group and then plan accordingly.

Project Time Management   A subset of the project management process. Focus is on the steps to ensure that the project is planned, estimated, scheduled, and executed efficiently and effectively.

Projectized (Project) Organization   The entire team is fully dedicated to the project at hand and reports directly to the project manager. Various people on the team are either hired for the project and/or transferred from their current departmental duties and are assigned to the project full-time; they do not have any responsibilities for their day-to-day jobs during the project life cycle (this is easier said than done).

Prototype   A model of key deliverables, interfaces, or algorithms designed as a representation of what the final product may look like.

Prototyping   A technique for quickly building a model of a key deliverable, interface, or algorithm.

Prototyping Plan   This is step 19 of the PPA. In any given IT/Business project, a number of deliverables may need to be prototyped (mocked up prior to their actual development). The best approach to developing a prototyping plan is for the core team and key customers to come together and review the project's WBS to identify the deliverables that are good candidates for prototyping.

Purchase Order (PO)   A document used to request that a vendor/seller supply goods and/or services in return for payment.

Qualified Supplier Lists   A list of outside sellers/contractors/vendors that have been prequalified (they meet the defined standards of the organization).

Quality   An inherent or distinguishing characteristic of a product or service. A trait or characteristic used to measure the degree of excellence of a product or service. Conformance to requirements—the project produces what it was supposed to. Fitness for use (the end product satisfies user needs).

Quality Assurance   The process of determining whether the plans (deliverables, tasks, resources, and milestones) to ensure the quality of the product are appropriate and adequate. Periodic assessment of the project in progress to assure that the finished product will meet quality requirements.

Quality Assurance Plan   The task's deliverables, resources, and milestones defined to assure that the finished product will meet the quality requirements.

Quality Audit   A formal review to determine whether the quality characteristics of a product or service meet the defined quality criteria.

Quality Control   The process of monitoring a project to ascertain whether the defined quality standards are being met and identifying the steps required to remove the sources of unsatisfactory performance.

Quality Control Tools   The variety of tools and techniques used within the "quality profession" to help ascertain the quality of project deliverables. Some examples of quality tools are checklists, control charts, fishbone diagrams, inspections, Pareto charts, trend analysis, and walk-throughs.

Quality Management   The processes put into place to assure that the end product of a project (process or product) meets the defined quality thresholds.

Quality Planning   This involves defining the ranking of quality pertaining to schedule, scope, and cost; defining the quality standards (thresholds) for the end product; and defining the requisite deliverables, tasks, resources and milestones to ensure that the end product achieves the defined quality standards.

Range Values (Range Estimates)   Given the fact that an estimate is an approximate value, it is important to convey a sense of appropriate uncertainty to the customer. This is best done by using range values for estimates communicated to sponsors, customers, and key stakeholders. We recommend a range of up to +35 percent for phase-based estimates, up to +25 percent for deliverables-based estimates, up to 15 percent for task-based estimates, and up to 10 percent for schedules.

Regulations   Typically, governmental rules and procedures with which the project must comply.

Remaining Duration   At any given point, the time (usually in work days) needed to complete a task, deliverable, phase, or the project.

Remaining Effort   At any given point, the work hours needed to complete a task, deliverable, phase, or the project.

Repository   A database of information.

Request for Proposal (RFP)   A document used to solicit proposals from prospective sellers/providers of goods and services. Also known as *request for quote (RFQ)*.

Required Return on Investment (RROI)   At times, organizations establish a threshold, the minimum acceptable ROI on an investment, below which projects are not deemed financially viable. Also known as the *hurdle rate* and *required rate of return*.

Reserve   A stipulation in a project plan, estimate, and schedule to respond to future rework, scope growth, and risks.

Residual Risk   The lingering (residual) risk still outstanding after a risk response has been planned. An example of a residual risk is the deductible one has on insurance.

Resource   The various means available to complete a project, such as people, budget, facilities, technology, software, and time.

Resource Calendar   Indicates the time (days and hours) that the resource will be available to the project.

Resource Constrained Network   A task network based on the number of resources (typically team members) available for the project.

Resource Gantt   A version of a Gantt chart. All of the tasks for a given resource are depicted in one chart.

Resource Histogram   A (vertical) bar graph that depicts the allocation (hours and/or the number) of resources to a project.

Resource Leveling   This is a form of network analysis where the project manager tries to reschedule (delay tasks that have sufficient free slack to smooth out resource utilization). Resource leveling becomes necessary when there are major peaks and valleys in the number of resources assigned to a project. Be very careful when you use a project management software package to automatically level resources. Many packages will wreak havoc with your project schedule.

Resource Management   The process of defining, acquiring, and managing the various resources (people, facilities, technology, budget, and time) needed to complete a project.

Resource Planning   The process of identifying and outlining the resources (people, facilities, technology, budget, and time) needed for a project.

Responsibility   Identify the person, group, or department responsible for completing a specific task and/or deliverable.

Return on Investment (ROI)   A financial measure of the success of a project. Computed as net income divided by investment (expressed as a percentage) over a defined period of time. Although "ROI" has a specific meaning within the realm of project financial analysis, it has also become the general term to refer to the financial benefits of a project. Therefore, when someone refers to the ROI of a project, they may actually mean the NVP, IRR, or payback period.

Reuse   The manner in which all or the greater part of the same programming code or system may be used in another application.

Reward Power   The authority to award incentives to project team members, contractors, and vendors.

Rework Reserve   A stipulation in a project plan, estimate, and schedule to respond to any rework necessary in the future to improve/correct work by team members.

Risk   Exposure to perils that can adversely impact the project.

Risk Acceptance   To recognize, acknowledge, and understand that a given risk is the responsibility of the project team and needs to be managed. Once a given risk has been accepted, the next step is to devise ways to manage the risk (outline the step to monitor the risk and to limit, or restrict, its adverse impacts).

Risk Assessment   This is step 12 of PPA. Most medium- to high-complexity projects carry some degree of risk—a strong possibility that some emergencies will arise and the team members will be distracted from their planned path of action. These distractions invariably require last minute actions that add extra effort, cost, and duration to the project and drive down the quality of the end product. Such ad hoc responses often leave much to be desired in efficiency and effectiveness and they convey an impression of "loss of control" on the part of the project manager. The solution lies in foresight and preplanning, and this step is designed to help the project manager and the team to assess the risks to the project.

Risk Averse Behavior   Reluctance to take risks.

Risk Avoidance   To stay clear of, pass up, or sidestep a given risk. For example, if the technology under consideration does not meet project requirements, avoid the risk by not choosing the specific technology. Investigate alternatives instead.

Risk Event   The occasion or incident that produces a risk to the project.

Risk Identification   The process of finding (uncovering) risks.

Risk Management Planning   The process of defining the deliverables, tasks, resources, and milestones to identify, categorize, prioritize, track, and mitigate risks.

Risk Mitigation   Any action taken to reduce the probability of occurrence and/or the degree of impact associated with a specific risk.

Risk Monitoring   The process of scrutinizing the project environment to ensure that risks are appropriately tracked.

Risk Owner   The individual who has the responsibility to monitor a given risk and to put into place the risk mitigation plan (if appropriate).

Risk Quantification   Assessing the probability of the occurrence of a risk and its impact.

Risk Response Plan   The deliverables, tasks, resources, and milestones defined to respond to project risks.

Risk Response Planning   The process of defining the deliverables, tasks, resources, and milestones to respond to project risks.

Risk Response Strategies   Specific approaches to be used to respond to project risks. Typically, these include avoidance, acceptance, transfer, and mitigation.

Risk Tolerance   The degree to which the project (and the organization) can endure risk.

Risk Transfer   To shift or reassign a given risk to some other party.

Risk Trigger   An event or situation that will bring about a risk.

Rolling Wave Implementation   A project implementation plan developed in response to the need for deploying a project in multiple (geographically dispersed) locations. The plan typically involves deployment in one or two locations followed by another deployment cycle at a few more locations, then repeating the process until all locations have been deployed. This approach replaces the "big bang" deployment where the project is deployed at all (most) locations concurrently.

Rule of 40   Make sure that a task takes no longer than 40 hours of effort.

Rule of 777   Break all IT/Business projects into a maximum of 7-month chunks, keep the team to less than 7 core team members (as many full-time as possible), and keep the budget down to $700,000 (the dollar figure is a guide and does not include any capital costs and may vary due to salary fluctuations).

Runaway Project   A project whose vital signs have breached a predefined threshold indicating the runaway condition.

Runaway Trigger   A budget and/or schedule threshold above which the project would be considered a runaway and would automatically come under management scrutiny.

Sarbanes-Oxley Act   A Congressional Act passed by the United States Congress in 2002 to protect investors by improving the accuracy and reliability of corporate disclosures.

Schedule (Project Schedule)   The project plan with dates associated with each task and milestone. Dates depict the planned start and finish of each task.

Schedule Compression   Steps taken to reduce the project's critical path without negatively impacting its scope, budget, and quality. When attempting to compress project schedule, one or more of the three attributes may need to be compromised.

Schedule Development   The process of assigning resources to a task plan, using the corporate and individual resource calendars.

Scheduled Finish Date   The specific date on which a task, deliverable, phase, or the project is planned for completion.

Schedule Performance Index (SPI)   Within the EVMS, the ratio of work performed to work scheduled. $SPI = EV \div PV$. *See* earned value.

Scheduled Start Date   The specific date on which a task, deliverable, phase, or the project is planned to start.

Schedule Variance (SV)   Any difference between the scheduled completion of a task and the actual completion of that task.

Scope   The total sum of deliverables and features, i.e., the total functionality, delivered to the project customer at the completion of the proposed project.

Scope Ball   Our euphemism for the scope increase (new functionality) customers insist on adding to an ongoing project.

Scope Baseline   The originally approved scope of a project, plus or minus any approved changes.

Scope Change   Any changes to the project scope after the scope has been baselined and typically after the project requirements have been approved.

Scope Change Control   The process to control (manage) any changes to the project scope.

Scope Chunking (Chunking)   A process of analyzing the project functionality and partitioning it into progressively smaller operational projects of 6 months or less.

Scope Creep   The slow increase in the total scope of the project due to an unmanaged addition of functionality—deliverables and features.

Scope Definition   The process of identifying and describing the deliverables and features of the finished project.

Scope Growth Reserve   A stipulation in a project plan, estimate, and schedule to respond to any additional scope of the project. Scope added after the first baselined scope statement (as a part of the Project Charter).

Scope Management Plan   This is step 21 of the PPA. The objective is to develop a well-defined and widely communicated plan to manage any modifications (additions, changes, deletions) to the baselined project scope.

Scope Management Process   The process by which change to scope is evaluated and then either dropped or integrated into the project.

Scope Statement   The sum total of deliverables and features (the total functionality to be delivered to the project customer at the completion of the proposed project).

Scope Verification   The steps to make sure that the project (end product) is delivered according to the promised scope (functionality).

Security   The degree to which the project needs protection from theft, copying, or corruption.

Security Plan   The plan to assure the right degree of security for the project. Typically, a security plan focuses on three areas: team members (backgrounds, clearances, etc.); system/software access (user IDs, passwords, etc.); and building access (keys, cards, etc.).

Seven Deadly Sins (of Project Management)   The most common mistakes: mistaking half-baked ideas for projects, dictated deadlines, ineffective sponsorship, underskilled project managers, not monitoring project vital signs, failing to deploy a sound project management process, and not formulating a comprehensive project portfolio.

Seven Run Rule   As a part of statistical sampling, it states that if seven data points in a row are above the mean, below the mean, or progressively increasing or decreasing, then the underlying problems are not random (they have a specific pattern) and need to be analyzed to determine the root of the problem.

Self-Managed Project Organization   In self-managed teams, the work is assigned and accomplished through consensus. No one has any real authority over the team. Everyone is about at the same level. The project manager's role can shift to different team members. This fluid structure does not absolve various team members from individual accountability.

Shutdown Conditions   This represents the next threshold after the runaway triggers at which a project becomes a candidate for shutdown.

Signing Ceremony   We strongly believe that a Project Charter should be viewed as an actual contract. The signatories are the proposed sponsor and the key stakeholders. To us, these signatures mean that a sponsor has been assigned, she has accepted and approved the proposed project, and the key stakeholders understand and agree with the Project Charter and are committing to provide the necessary resources and support to the project team. We strongly advise that project managers hold a meeting where the sponsor, the key stakeholders, and the project manager sign the Charter as an indication of its formal approval. Once the Charter is signed, we advise the project manager to make a copy and file it away as Version 0 (if using electronic media, make Version 0 a read-only file).

Site Preparation Plan   A collection of deliverables, tasks, milestones, and resources that document the steps needed to prepare a site prior to project implementation.

Six Sigma   A rigorous and a systematic methodology that uses customer requirements, teamwork, and statistical analysis to measure and improve operational performance, practices and systems by identifying and preventing defects. The most common methodology employed in six sigma projects is known as Define-Measure-Analyze-Improve-Control (DMAIC). The goal of six sigma is to reduce variation, improve the capability of systems and processes, and reduce defects to less than 3.4 incidents per million opportunities.

Size Estimate   A high-level estimate of the proposed project in terms of overall effort, cost, and duration (work days, weeks, or months). A size estimate is usually needed during the Pre-Launch stage for such strategic concerns as project approval, portfolio assessment, and assessing resource needs.

Skill Factor (SF)   A numeric value indicating the rate at which a team member will do his work. The lower the skill level, the higher the skill factor and the longer the time needed to finish a given task.

Skill Level (SL)   A numeric value between 1 and 4 indicating the level of a team member's knowledge, experience, and skills necessary to complete the assigned work.

Skill Profile   An assessment of a team member's knowledge, experience, and skills as they relate to the work assigned to her.

Slack   The amount of time the ES of a task can be delayed without impacting the critical path of the project or the project finish date. *See* float.

SMART Criteria   An effective method to use to assess the clarity of an objective. The SMART filter consists of: S: Specific, M: Measurable, A: Achievable, R: Relevant to the strategy, and T: Time Bound.

Soft Skills   A set of skills that are more difficult to define, observe, and assess, and are also difficult to teach and learn. These skills, often called competencies, are related to social, political, and general management aptitudes. Some examples include: charisma, decisiveness, delegation, integrity, leadership, negotiation, and positive outlook.

Software Engineering Institute (SEI)   Group at Carnegie Mellon University that developed the CMM.

Solicitation   The act of sending out a call for bids/proposals from potential seller(s) of goods and services.

Solicitation Planning   The process of defining the deliverables, tasks, resources, and milestones to solicit bids/proposals from potential seller(s) of goods and services.

Source Selection   The process of selecting one or more qualified suppliers of goods and services.

Special Provisions   Specific terms and conditions created to meet the unique needs of a contract. Typically, an addendum to a master (standard) contract.

Sponsor   An individual with the right level of authority and personal commitment who will make sure that the team is able to complete the project efficiently and effectively.

Sponsorship   A vital sign that tracks a project sponsor's performance—commitment, time, and leadership. The sponsor's performance is not only one of the most important vital signs to monitor, but it is probably the most difficult to measure. Important, because without a committed sponsor who meets his responsibilities and time commitments, any project is doomed to failure; difficult, because in the case of sponsor nonperformance, the project manager is unlikely to feel confident enough to inform the sponsor about her shortcomings. Only a project manager with great fortitude would take on such responsibility. Therefore, the responsibility for monitoring this vital sign rests squarely on the shoulders of the sponsor.

Stability Assessment   This is step 10 of the PPA. The objective is to assess the steadiness of the project environment as the project progresses to its final stage. Items that are unstable will require special attention, as they will impact the project scope, schedule, and cost.

Staffing Plan   This is step 22 of the PPA. The purpose of this step is to assemble the right group of people who will collectively provide the necessary skills to complete the various project deliverables in a timely manner, and to the right quality and cost. The key components of a comprehensive staffing plan are: management team, sponsor, project manager's supervisor, functional managers, project manager, team members, and SMEs.

Stage Gate   A stage gate follows each stage of the PPA. At each stage gate, the sponsor diligently reviews the work done by the team and makes a Go/No Go decision regarding the project moving to the next stage.

Stage Gate Review   Toward the end of each project stage, the sponsor, working with the project manager, reviews the completeness and quality of the work completed by the team and then makes a Go/No Go decision about the project. The decision could be Go (proceed to the next stage), or No Go (team to revisit the work done, improve the appropriate area, and seek reapproval or the project may be suspended or cancelled).

Stakeholder   Stakeholders are those organizations or individuals who impact, or are impacted by, a project. The organizations and individuals may be internal or external to the organization executing the project; the impacts may be positive, negative, or a combination of the two. Stakeholders can be divided into two primary categories—policy level, and implementation level.

Stakeholder Analysis   This is step 5 of the PPA. It involves the analysis of the attitude and behavior of various stakeholders toward the project. Stakeholder behavior can be classified into the following categories: champion, neutral, nemesis, comatose, invisible, or ignored.

Stakeholder Management   The process of identifying the various policy and implementation level stakeholders of a project, determining their interests and expectations, and outlining the steps to meet their needs.

Standard Deviation   A statistic that indicates how much variation exists in a distribution of data.

Start Date   The specific date on which a task, deliverable, phase, or project is supposed to start. The date that the assigned resource will start executing the task, deliverable, phase, or project.

Start-to-Finish (SF) Dependency   In this type of dependency, the successor task is scheduled to be completed a specific number of days following the start of the predecessor task.

Start-to-Start (SS) Dependency   This dependency means that a successor task can begin once the work on its immediate predecessor has begun. The start-to-start dependency is typically specified when the start of the successor task is to be delayed a specific amount of time after the start of the predecessor task.

Statement Of Work (SOW)   In the case of a negotiated contract with a vendor, the SOW includes the specific requirements, deliverables, and performance measures the vendor will be expected to meet as well as the assumptions made in developing the requirements and scope statement. An SOW can also be used in noncontract situations, i.e., between a project manager and a team member, especially for remote (virtual) team members.

Status of the Critical Path   A vital sign designed to track the progress of the project along its critical path and to answer the question, "Is the project on schedule?" The status of the critical path is a specific metric and clearly communicates to the project sponsor whether the project is on schedule, ahead of schedule, or behind schedule.

Status Report   Designed to document and communicate the project progress (standing) at a given point in time.

Status Review   The process of assessing the project progress (standing) at a given point in time.

Status Review Meeting   A meeting scheduled to assess the project progress and to exchange information among the people at the meeting.

Storming   The second stage in the team development model defined by B. W. Tuckman. Even though the word can have a negative connotation, some applicable synonyms are: *venture*, *maneuver*, *foray*, and *to make inroads*. In this stage of team development, the group works through their issues and uncertainties.

Straight Line Depreciation   In financial accounting, a method of depreciation that allows an equal amount to be depreciated for each year of the expected use of the asset.

Strategy Alignment   This vital sign is designed to determine whether the project continues to fit with the currently stated organizational strategy. At times, a project begins with a good strategic fit, but due to changes in overall strategy, the project may no longer be a compelling investment. For example, at the time of project approval, the strategy was growth and market share, but due to changes in the economy and the organization's direction, the new strategy is cost savings, profit, and efficiency. As a result, the project is not aligned with the strategy and needs to be evaluated.

Strategy Fulfillment   In the case of an individual project, the degree to which the project will contribute to the strategy to which it is aligned. In the case of the project portfolio, the degree to which a given strategy is being fulfilled by the projects in the operations portfolio.

Strong Matrix Project Organization   A matrix project organization structure can vary from a weak matrix where the project manager has a low level of authority over team members, to a strong matrix where the functional managers have agreed to give the project manager substantial authority over team members.

Success Equation   Success = (((Process + Skills + Techniques + Tools) × Accountability) × Discipline)

Successor   In a task network, the following task or the "to" task.

Sunk Cost   Cost already incurred on a project, cannot be recovered regardless of any future actions.

Suspended Project Portfolio   The component of the project portfolio that houses projects that have been put into the suspend state—development work has been temporarily stopped.

System Development Life Cycle (SDLC)   A collection of practices, procedures, roles, responsibilities, and rules typically used for developing computer software.

System Impact Document   A document that articulates the impact the project will have on existing systems, manual and/or automated, internal and/or external.

Tangible Benefits   Benefits that are concrete and can be easily quantified and measured.

Task   An element of work assigned to an individual to be completed in a specified period of time, leading to the completion of a deliverable.

Task Duration   Typically, the number of workdays required to complete a task, a deliverable, a phase, or a project. The focus here is the length of time. Duration can also be measured in the terms of work weeks and work months.

Task Effort   The number of work hours required to complete a task, deliverable, phase, or project. The focus is on how much time.

Task Force Organization   A typical task force is a group of SMEs representing a variety of different functional organizations (internal and external), brought together to investigate a given subject area and produce recommendations. The members of a typical task force continue to perform their current duties in addition to the work needed on the task force.

Task Gantt   A type of Gantt chart on which various project tasks are listed on the left side of the chart (the *Y* axis) with dates shown across the top (the *X* axis).

Task Network (Network)   A grouping of the various tasks in a project in the order of their logical execution. A network proceeds from left to right, reflecting the arrangement of tasks (deliverables and milestones) in time. Also referred to as the *PERT chart* or *PERT network*.

Task Plan   This is step 18 of the PPA. A task plan represents the "how to" tactics of completing the project (phases of the project, deliverables required for each phase, tasks necessary for each deliverable, and a network depicting the logical execution order of the various tasks). Outside of the classic engineering discipline, there has been, and continues to be, a certain aversion to developing detailed task plans. Some find the process too time-consuming, others avoid planning because they know the plan might change, and others just are simply unaware of the effective and efficient steps to create a comprehensive task plan. A comprehensive and accurate task plan paves the way to project success.

Team   The group of people who do the work involved in producing the product.

Team Development   A subset of the project management process that focuses on the steps to improve team member skills and performance.

Team Disposition   A vital sign designed to assess the morale of the project team. Team disposition is often the most neglected vital sign because it is more of a qualitative evaluation rather than quantitative, and therefore is far more difficult to monitor.

Technology Infrastructure   The database, hardware, software, and telecommunications designed for system operations. *See* infrastructure.

Technology Viability   A vital sign designed to ascertain the capability of the technology infrastructure being used to develop and deploy the project.

Termination Clause   A specific wording in a contract that allows the buyer and/or the seller to terminate the contract.

Terms and Conditions   The provisions, stipulations, and requisites of a contract.

Time and Materials (T & M) Contract   A contract where the contractor is paid the cost of the time he spends on the project plus the cost of any materials used in completing the project.

Time Scale   The tightness of the development schedule for the project.

Time Value of Money   The idea that money is worth more today than at a point in time in the future, even after adjustment for inflation, because the money in hand today can earn interest or other appreciation (if invested) up to that point in the future.

Tolerance to Fault (Fault Tolerance)   The degree of defects (errors) the finished process or product can have before it becomes unusable. A low fault tolerance means the system cannot tolerate too many defects/errors.

Top-Down Approach   Creating a WBS and/or an estimate by starting with the highest level of abstraction and progressively breaking it down into smaller (finer) elements.

Total Cost of Ownership (TCO)   The process of computing the cost of a project/system/item over its expected life span. This approach is in contrast to the typical computations that only cover the cost of developing (or acquiring) the project/system/item. Also known as life cycle costing.

Total Quality Management (TQM)   An integrated system for defining, planning, and assuring quality that guides every aspect of the work in an organization through continuous process and product improvement steps in order to ensure the highest customer satisfaction.

Total Slack   This denotes the amount of time (days) by which the completion of a task on the path in question can be delayed without impacting the critical path of the project. *See* path float.

Trend Analysis   The process of examining results over a period of time to determine whether the performance is improving or deteriorating.

Transference   Within risk management, the act of transferring a given risk to another party through specific risk mitigation steps (insurance, guarantee, and warrantee).

Travel Restrictions   Weather, time zones, carriers, or entry and exit regulations that may impact the travel necessary to complete the project.

Triple Constraint   Balancing of the project scope, time, and cost objectives. In classic project management, project quality is a part of the scope statement. We find this way of thinking about a project to be too restrictive and we prefer to use four constraints: schedule, scope, cost, and quality.

Turnover   The number of team members who have left the project in a given period of time.

Unit Price Contract   A type of contract where the contractor is reimbursed for each unit of work completed.

Unresolved Issues   This vital sign is designed to track the number of unresolved issues. An issue can be anything from an unanswered question to a difference of opinion. Unresolved issues are like potholes; if left open, they will grow and impact the performance of the team and the quality of the end product. In most cases, an issue remains unresolved because of inadequate communication and direction or because the team is not a unified body.

Value-to-Business   This vital sign is designed to assess the value the business will draw from the project. The expected metrics for this vital sign are originally defined during the Idea stage and finalized during the Launch stage. Some examples are: additional revenues, competitive advantage, cost savings, customer service, efficiency of operations, and higher ROI.

Value-to-Business Assessment   This is step 31 of the PPA. Once a project moves to the Operation stage, the actual value-to-business will need to be measured and reported to the appropriate management. You need to identify the person(s) responsible for gathering the information, the process used to collect the information, and the managers who are slated to receive the information. We often find that project managers have overlooked this step and little, if any, of this important information ever gets collected or reported.

Variance   The difference between the planned (expected) and actual performance on a project.

Variance Analysis   The process of examining any differences between the planned (expected) and actual performance.

Variance At Completion (VAC)   The difference between the total budget of a task, deliverable, or project and the estimate at completion. VAC = BAC − EAC. VAC represents the amount of expected overrun or underrun.

Vendor Viability   This vital sign is designed to track the capabilities and capacities of a vendor (ability to meet contractual obligations and financial robustness).

Version Control   The management of project documentation. Version control provides a mechanism that keeps track of the revisions made to a project deliverable.

Version 0 Charter   A copy of the original Project Charter saved to compare any changes made to it during project development life cycle.

Version 0 Network   A task network created with the assumption that there are no constraints (any and all resources needed to execute the various tasks will be available as needed and there are no other limitations). This is also known as a nonconstrained network or a potential network.

Visibility   The degree to which the outcome of the project is visible to upper management, stockholders, and the general public.

Vital Signs   A set of metrics designed as indicators of the overall health of a project. We have defined a set of 15 vitals signs: strategy alignment, sponsorship, customer buy-in, technology viability, value-to-business, vendor viability, status of the critical path, milestone hit rate, unresolved issues, cost-to-date, actual resources *v.* planned resources, high probability, high impact risks, overtime utilization, and team disposition. The sponsor and the project manager jointly decide on the specific vital signs to be monitored for a given project.

Walk-Through   The process or processes by which project deliverables are evaluated relative to the stated objectives of the project by the developer's colleagues in a nonthreatening environment. The objective is to detect errors and omissions early. The hallmark of a successful walk-through process is a mutually respectful environment where the focus is on detecting errors and omissions with minimal focus on the individual responsible (for errors and omissions). *See* peer review.

Weak Matrix   In a matrix project organization, the project team is composed of team members from a number of different functional organizations. Team members may be assigned full- or part-time to the project team, and each member reports to two bosses: her own functional manager and a project manager. In a weak matrix organization structure, the project manager has a low level of authority over team members.

Workarounds   Spontaneous (unplanned last minute) responses to a risk or a defect in a product.

Work Breakdown Structure (WBS)   A process of progressive parsing (decomposing) typically used to break a project into phases, deliverables, and tasks.

Work Interruption (WI)   This represents the part of a person's workday that is lost to nonproject activities. Time is lost for a variety of reasons: ad-hoc meetings, being volunteered by one's manager, conversations with colleagues, departmental social gatherings, personal errands, reading and responding to unsolicited voice messages and e-mail, and unavailability of computer resources (virus, crashes, maintenance).

Work Interruption Factor (WIF)   The measure of the loss of productivity as a result of work interruptions—nonproject activities and unplanned interruptions during the workday.

Work Package   The classic definition of the term is, "A deliverable at the lowest level of a work breakdown structure. A work package may be divided into activities." We find this definition confusing because, to us, the lowest level of a WBS is a task, and a task does not need be further broken into activities because we recommend a high limit of 40 effort hours for any task.

Our definition of a work package is best illustrated by an example: A project manager extracts from the master schedule a specific group of deliverables, tasks, and milestones to be completed by various team members in an upcoming period of time, and assembles these into discrete work packages, one for each team member.

REFERENCES

Alcott, A. B. http://www.thebroadroom.net/fun/wit_wisdom.html (accessed April 12, 2004).

Alter, A. E. 2003. ROI: Do you have any faith in your ROI numbers? *CIO Insight*, March 17. http://www.cioinsight.com/article2/0,3959,940177,00.asp (accessed April 29, 2004).

Anderson, M. 2001. How to be a turnaround CIO. *CIO Magazine*, September 15. p. 62. http://www.cio.com/archive/091501/insights.html (accessed April 24, 2004).

Bagehot, W. http://www.brainyquote.com/quotes/quotes/w/walterbage136261.html (accessed April 29, 2004).

_____ . http://www.quotationspage.com/quotes.php3?author=Walter+Bagehot (accessed April 29, 2004).

Berinato, S. 2001. Recipes for disaster. *CIO Magazine*, July 1. http://www.cio.com/archive/070101/secret_sidebar_2.html (accessed April 29, 2004.)

_____ . 2001. The secret to software success. *CIO Magazine*, July 1. http://www.cio.com/archive/070101/secret.html (accessed April 29, 2004.)

_____ . 2002. The big fix. *CSO Magazine*, October 7. http://www.csoonline.com/read/100702/fix.html (accessed April 29, 2004).

Berra, Y. http://www.famous-quotes-and-quotations.com/yogi-berra-quotes.html (accessed April 29, 2004).

Billings, J. http://www.brainyquote.com/quotes/authors/j/joshbillin129239.html (accessed April 29, 2004).

Brooks, F. P. 1995. *The Mythical Man-Month*, Anniversary Edition. Reading, MA: Addison-Wesley.

Brown, D. 2001. U.S. Suspends Human Research at Johns Hopkins After a Death. *USA Today*, July 20.

Brown, P. B. 2002. Honeywell CEO Counsels, 'Just Do It'. *CIO Insight*, July 17. http://www.cioinsight.com/article2/0,3959,2124,00.asp (accessed April 29, 2004).

Buckley, C. 2003. *San Francisco Chronicle*. August 29. p. E1.

Buffet, W. http://www.businessweek.com/1997/21/b352856.htm (accessed April 29, 2004).

Burrows, P. 2001. The era of efficiency. *BusinessWeek*, June 18. http://www.businessweek.com/magazine/content/01_25/b3737701.htm (accessed April 29, 2004).

Business Leader Online. Do you hear what I hear? http://www.businessleader.com/bl/nov98/t3.html (accessed April 29, 2004).

Carney, D. *Quotations from Chairman David*. Software Engineering Institute, Carnegie Mellon University.

Carter, R. B. 2002. Forging Partnerships. *Computerworld*, August 26, 39.

Case, S. M. 2001. *Reader's Digest*, September, 61.

_____ . 2001. *The Mind of the C.E.O.* Basic Books/Perseus Publishing, 2001.

Chabrow, E. 2003. I.T. staffs lack financial chops for project analysis. *Information Week*, March 24. 20. http://www.informationweek.com/story/IWK20030321S0016 (accessed April 29, 2004).

The CHAOS Report. 1994. The Standish Group. http://www.pm2go.com/sample_research/chaos_1994_1.php.

Chassin, M. R. and E. C. Becher. 2002. The wrong patient. *Annals of Internal Medicine*, Volume 136, Number 11, June.

Clinton, Bill. http://www.yale.edu/ypq/articles/mar99/mar99b.html#fn7 (accessed April 12, 2004).

Collett, S. 2003. How will you connect with customers? *Computerworld*, January 6. http://www.computerworld.com/managementtopics/management/story/0,10801,76951,00.html (accessed April 29, 2004).

Computerworld. 2000. Shark tank: Talkin' trash, shark tank. July 17. p. 90. http://www.computerworld.com/softwaretopics/software/appdev/story/0,10801,47188,00.html (accessed April 12, 2004).

Computerworld. 2000. Briefs: Turnover Toll. August 28. p. 56. http://www.computerworld.com/managementtopics/ebusiness/story/0,10801,48994,00.html (accessed April 12, 2004).

Cone, E. 2002. Detroit financial system sputters after overhaul. *Baseline*, August 6. http://www.baselinemag.com/print_article/0,3668,a=29846,00.asp (accessed April 29, 2004).

Cooper, T. 2003. East Bay tech types connect through eBIG. *San Francisco Chronicle*, August 29. p. E1.

Corbett, M. F. & Associates, Ltd., Outsourcing Failures? Firmbuilder.com. http://www.firmbuilder.com/articles/19/48/388/ (accessed April 29, 2004).

Cramm, S. H. 2002. The business knows best. *CIO Magazine*, November 1. http://www.cio.com/archive/110102/hs_agenda.html (accessed April 29, 2004).

Crowley, P. 2000. NFL losers never win. *Newsweek*, U.S. Ed., December 9. http://www.keepmedia.com/ShowItemDetails.do?itemID=312222&extID=10030&oliID=226 (accessed April 29, 2004).

Datz, T. 2003. Portfolio management: How to do it right. *CIO Magazine*, May 1. http://www.cio.com/archive/050103/portfolio.html (accessed April 29, 2004).

Deming, W. E. http://www.motivatingquotes.com/survival.htm (accessed April 29, 2004).

Dilbert Newsletter 46.0, February 2003. © 2003, United Feature Syndicate, Inc., http://www.dilbert.com/comics/dilbert/dnrc/html/newsletter46.html (accessed April 29, 2004).

Dinsmore, P. C. 2003. Five ways not to pitch project management in your organization. *PM Network*, February 60.

Doran, G. T. 1981. There's a S.M.A.R.T. Way to Write Management Goals and Objectives. *Management Review*, November.

Drucker, P. F. 1993. *The Effective Executive*. Harper Business, New York. Ch 5, 585.

_____ . 1995. *Managing in a Time of Great Change*. New York: Dutton.

_____ . Quoted in a syllabus of an Operations Management Course offered by the University of St. Thomas, http://www.stthomas.edu/gradbusiness/syllabi/Courses/MBOP/mbop600_nicolay.htm (accessed April 29, 2004).

_____ . http://www.brainyquote.com/quotes/quotes/p/peterfdru129829.html (accessed April 29, 2004).

The Economist. 2000. No gain without pain, June 22, http://www.economist.com/surveys/displayStory.cfm?Story_id=80764 (accessed April 13, 2004.)

The Economist, June 24, 2000, http://www.mcnees.org/mainpages/misc/security/sec_subpages/GovnetEconJun24.htm (accessed April 29, 2004).

Edison, T. A. www.phnet.fi/public/mamaa1/edison.html (accessed April 29, 2004).

Eisenhower, D. D. http://www.eisenhowerinstitute.org/programs/livinghistory/solarium.htm (accessed April 29, 2004).

Ellis, L. 2002. Research: Are your older systems slowing you down? *CIO Insight*, December: 73.

Federal Times. 2002. System Upgrade Delivers Little to Veterans. November 11. 3.

Field, A. 2001. Project management 2001. *CIO Insight*, September 1. http://www.cioinsight.com/article2/0,3959,2333,00.asp (accessed April 29, 2004).

Field, T. 1998. To hell and back. *CIO Magazine*, December 1. http://www.cio.com/archive/120198/turk.html (accessed April 29, 2004).

Franklin, B. http://www.ushistory.org/franklin/quotable/quote69.htm (accessed April 29, 2004).

Gall, J. 1990. *Systemantics: The underground text of system lore, how systems really work and how they fail.* Ann Arbor, MI: General Systemantics Press, 1990. 21, 77, 90.

Gaudin, S. 1998. "System migration? Don't forget to consider users." *Computerworld*, October 26. http://www.computerworld.com/news/1998/story/0,11280,33136,00.html (accessed April 29, 2004).

Gilmer's Motto for Political Leadership. http://membres.lycos.fr/TheWalrus/g.html (accessed April 29, 2004).

Glaser, G. Projects: Orphans at birth. *Meridian Report*. 2. Winter 1993: 3.

Glaser, R. and C. Glaser. 1996. Negotiating style profile. Organization Design and Development, Inc.

Guide Dogs for the Blind, Inc., San Rafael, CA, http://www.guidedogs.com (accessed April 29, 2004).

Hayes, F. 1999. Frankly speaking. *Computerworld*, September 27, p. 106.

Heraclitus of Ephesus. http://www.brainyquote.com/quotes/quotes/h/heraclitus152640.html (accessed April 29, 2004).

Herzberg, F. 1868. One more time: How do you motivate employees? *Harvard Business Review*, February.

Hoffman, T. 2003. "How will you prove IT value?" *Computerworld*, January 6. http://www.computerworld.com/managementtopics/management/story/0,10801,77166,00.html (accessed April 29, 2004).

_____ . 2003. "IT departments face a lack of project management know-how." *Computerworld*, August 11, p. 16.

Hooker, R. http://www.bartleby.com/66/28/28828.html (accessed April 29, 2004).

Horgan, D. J. 2002. You've got conversation. *CIO Magazine*, October 15.

Ingevaldson, P. 2002. It's not your IT portfolio—It's theirs. *CIO Magazine*, November 15. http://www.cio.com/archive/111502/peer.html (accessed April 29, 2004).

Jardine, B. 2001. The secret to software success. *CIO magazine*, July 1.

Johnson, M. 2002. Demystifying ROI. *Computerworld*, April 22. 28, http://www.computerworld.com/managementtopics/roi/story/0,10801,70323,00.html (accessed May 4, 2004).

Kawasaki, G. 2000. *Rules for Revolutionaries: The Capitalist Manifesto for Creating and Marketing New Products and Services.* New York: Harper Collins.

Kearns, David from *Executive Book of Quotations*, Oxford University Press, 1994.

Keizer, G. 2003. Gartner says half of outsourcing projects doomed to failure. *TechWeb News*. March 26. http://www.techweb.com/wire/story/TWB20030326S0006 (accessed May 4, 2004).

King, J. 1998. Benefits can be elusive; costs are deceptive. *Computerworld*, May 18. 16. http://www.computerworld.com/news/1998/story/0,11280,30960,00.html (accessed April 29, 2004).

_____ . 2000. Parts maker pins profits dip on IT. *Computerworld*, February 21. http://www.computerworld.com/news/2000/story/0,11280,41403,00.html (accessed April 29, 2004).

_____ . 2002. Back to basics. *Computerworld*, April 22. 36. http://www.computerworld.com/managementtopics/roi/story/0,10801,70253,00.html (accessed April 29, 2004).

_____ . 2003. Identify, Kill Nonessential Projects, CIO Recommends. *Computerworld*, March 3. http://www.computerworld.com/managementtopics/management/story/0,10801,78940,00.html (accessed April 29, 2004).

Koppelman, J. M. and Q. W. Fleming. 2000. *Earned Value Project Management*, 2nd ed. Newton Square, PA: Project Management Institute.

Lambert, L. R. 2002. Leading the charge. *PM Network*. September.

Lee, L. 2001. "Gap: Missing that ol' Mickey magic." *BusinessWeek*, October 29. 84A4. http://www.businessweek.com/magazine/content/01_44/b3755100.htm (accessed April 29, 2004).

Lehman, D. 2000. Software snafu could put bank merger in jeopardy. *Computerworld*, March 13. http://www.computerworld.com/news/2000/story/0,11280,41804,00.html (accessed May 4, 2004).

Levenson, S. http://www.creativequotations.com/one/2009.htm (accessed April 29, 2004).

Levine, H. A. http://www.myplanview.com/expert25.asp (accessed April 29, 2004).

Lewis, J. 2001. *Successful Project Management*, June. Management Concepts, Inc., Vienna, VA. p. 1.

Lincoln, A. Reply to the National Union League, June 9, 1864. http://www.bartleby.com/100/448.11.html (accessed April 29, 2004).

Lucovsky, M. 2000. Microsoft manager, Windows 2000 development team quoted in *Computerworld*, February 21, 82.

Machiavelli, N. 1961. *The Prince*. New York: Penguin Classics.

May, T. A. 2003. Tell the truth effectively. *Computerworld*, February 03. http://www.computerworld.com/managementtopics/management/story/0,10801,78046,00.html (accessed April 29, 2004).

Melymuka, K. 2001. Building new IT culture. *Computerworld*, October 1. 25.

_____ . 2002. Failure to Communicate. *Computerworld*, August 26. 44.

Moder, J. J., C. R. Philips, and E. W. Davis. 1983. *Project Management with CPM, PERT and Precedence Diagramming*, 3rd ed. New York: Van Nostrand Reinhold.

Murphy, C. and M. Hayes. 2003. The changing IT workplace. April 14. http://www.napusa.org/napwp/public_html/article.php?story=20030503063155149 (accessed April 29, 2004).

Murr, A. 2000. "Final answer: It crashed." *Newsweek*, April 10. p. 46.

Nash, K. S. 2000. Companies don't learn from previous IT snafus *Computerworld*, October 30. http://www.computerworld.com/networkingtopics/networking/management/story/0,10801,53014,00.html (accessed April 29, 2004).

_____ . 2000. Merged railroads still plagued by IT snafus *Computerworld*, January 17. http://www.computerworld.com/news/2000/story/0,11280,40721,00.html (accessed April 29, 2004).

_____ . 2000. Top 10 corporate information technology failures, *Computerworld*, October 30. http://www.computerworld.com/networkingtopics/networking/management/story/0,11280,40721,00.html.

Newman, M. 2003. Software errors cost U.S. economy $59.5 billion annually. National Institute of Standards and Technology. June 28. http://www.nist.gov/public_affairs/releases/n02-10.htm (accessed April 29, 2004).

Newsweek. 2003. Perspective. June 23, p. 27.

Oncken, W. and D. L. Wass. 1974. Management time: Who's got the monkey? *Harvard Business Review* Nov.–Dec.

Oriental Proverb. http://www.refdesk.com/nov00td.html (accessed April 12, 2004).

Panchak, P. 1998. The future manufacturing. *Industry Week*, September 21. http://www.findarticles.com/cf_dls/m1121/1998_Sept_21/53049110/p1/article.jhtml (accessed April 29, 2004).

Pearson, D. 1998. To hell and back. *CIO Magazine*, December 1. http://www.cio.com/archive/120198/turk.html (accessed April 29, 2004).

Pfeffer, J. and R. I. Sutton. 2000. *The Knowing-Doing Gap*. Harvard Business School Press.

PMI: Project Management Institute, PMBOK: Project Management Body of Knowledge.

Prahalad, C. K., M. K. Krishnana, and S. Mithas. 2002. The technology/customer disconnect. *Optimize*, December 14, 3. http://www.optimizemag.com/issue/014/customer.htm (accessed April 29, 2004).

Publilius Syrus, http://www.brainyquote.com/quotes/authors/p/publiliuss130896.html (accessed May 5, 2004).

Roetzheim, W. Improving our track record. *SD Times*, http://www.costxpert.com/resource_center/sdtimes.html (accessed April 29, 2004).

Rooney, M. http://www.quotationspage.com/subjects/failure/11.html (accessed April 29, 2004).

Samuelson, J. B. http://www.cyber-nation.com/victory/quotations/authors/quotes_samuelson_joanbenoit.html.

Scheier, R. 2001. Central Intelligence. *CIO Insight*, December. 66. http://www.cioinsight.com/article2/0,3959,5138,00.asp (accessed April 29, 2004).

Schneider, P. 2000. Another trip to hell. *CIO Magazine*, February 15. http://www.cio.com/archive/021500/hell.html (accessed April 29, 2004).

Schweitzer, Albert from *Executive's Book of Quotations*, Oxford University Press, 162.

Shultz, Peter from *Executive's Book of Quotations*. 1994. Oxford University Press, 198.

Side Effect. Dictionary.com. http://dictionary.reference.com/search?q=side%20effect (accessed May 5, 2004).

Simmons, C. *The New Dictionary of Thought: A Cyclopedia of Quotations*. Standard Book Company, p. 300.

Slater, D. 2000. Faster, cheaper, and under control. *CIO Magazine* August: 111.

Soat, J. and S. Stahl. 2003. Procter & Gamble uses IT to nurture new product ideas. *InformationWeek*, February 24. http://www.informationweek.com/story/IWK20030221S0003 (accessed April 29, 2004).

Songini, M. L. 2003. How they learned to lead. *Computerworld*, January 6. http://www.computerworld.com/managementtopics/management/story/0,10801,77198,00.html (accessed April 29, 2004).

Stepanek, M. 2002. Management matters. *CIO Insight*, December 21. http://www.cioinsight.com/print_article/0,3668,a=34988,00.asp (accessed April 29, 2004).

Sutton, R. I. The creativity dilemma. *CIO Insight*, October 1. http://www.cioinsight.com/article2/0,1397,38146,00.asp (accessed May 5, 2004).

Thayer, H. B. AT&T archives. http://mikescottandassociates.com/quote.php (accessed April 13, 2004).

Thibodeau, P. 2002. Study: Buggy software costs users, vendors nearly $60B annually. *Computerworld*, June 25. http://www.computerworld.com/managementtopics/management/itspending/story/0,10801,72245,00.html (accessed April 30, 2004).

Tuckman, B. W. 1965. Developmental Sequence in Small Groups, *Psychological Bulletin*, vol. 63.

Twain, M. http://www.brainyquote.com/quotes/quotes/m/marktwain141774.html (accessed April 30, 2004).

Varon, E. 2003. Ambassdors of IT. *CIO Magazine*, April 1. http://www.cio.com/archive/040103/practices_ambassador.html (accessed April 30, 2004).

Wallington, P. Leadership from below. *CIO Magazine*, October 15.

Webster's Revised Unabridged Dictionary, 1996, 1998 MICRA, Inc. http://dictionary.reference.com/search?q=project (accessed April 30, 2004).

Worthen, B. 2002. Nestlé's ERP odyssey. *CIO Magazine*, May 15, 64. http://www.cio.com/archive/051502/nestle.html (accessed April 30, 2004).

Wysocki, B. 1998. Companies let down by computers opt to 'de-engineer' after clashes. *Wall Street Journal*, April 30, p. A1.

————. 1998. Pulling the plug. *Wall Street Journal*. April 30.

Zetlin, M. 2002. When the plug gets pulled. *Computerworld*, January 13. http://www.computerworld.com/managementtopics/management/project/story/0,10801,77453,00.html (accessed April 30, 2004).

————. 2003. Cancellation as a career plus. *Computerworld*, January 13.

INDEX